GW00671960

Published by Brabourne Church Publishing
St Mary's Church, The Street, East Brabourne,
Ashford, Kent, TN25 5LR

© St Mary's Church, Brabourne

Copies of this book are available from
brabournechurchpublishing@gmail.com

First published 2013

Also from Brabourne Church Publishing:
*Brabourne in History*
by John Talbot, produced by Derek Gurr

# Archives & Anecdotes

Reflections on English Village Life from Brabourne in Kent

Kathleen Embleton-Smith & Christine Gurr

This book is sold to raise funds for St Mary's Church, Brabourne

The Production Team


Text researched and assembled by
Kathleen Embleton-Smith & Christine Gurr


Editor
Sam Thackray


Layout and Cover Design
Peter Embleton-Smith & Derek Gurr


Produced by Biddles Ltd,
King's Lynn

# Foreword

by the Reverend Richard Le Rossignol

I am delighted that this fascinating book has finally been published as it has been a long term project for Kathy, Christine and their helpers. For almost eight years I have had the privilege of serving the church in Brabourne and surrounding area and have got to know many of the characters described and featured here. It has been good to have played a small part in the life of Brabourne, but I realise that its story continues and that a work such as this can never be fully completed. The people and the places change and move on, but it is good to have a record of what came before.

Richard Le Rossignol
Priest-in-Charge of the
parishes of Brabourne, Smeeth,
Monks Horton, Stowting,
Mersham and Sellindge

# Contents

## DISCLAIMER

The purpose of this book is to raise funds for Brabourne Church. Based largely on the memories of over 170 people dating back decades, we are unable to guarantee the accuracy of the information presented. We apologise in advance for any errors. It has not been our intention to misrepresent situations or offend in any way.

# Introduction & Acknowledgements

Writing a book is a bit like setting out on a long journey. It's a little unnerving at first because there is such a long way to go, with so many unknowns, but at the same time the anticipation of adventure can make it exhilarating. Once the exploration phase begins the authors never know in which direction they will be drawn, but by the time the book is complete one thing is certain: the privilege of sharing others' new information and experiences, demanding new levels of understanding from different points of view, will have changed their lives for ever. Many of these shared experiences may be entertaining and uplifting, but others can prove much more challenging for the writer.

Our original aim was to produce a book to raise funds for Brabourne Church. There was no need for a history book as we already have one, Brabourne in History. Elegantly written by John Talbot and beautifully produced by Derek Gurr, it tells of the distant past of the church. But what of its more recent past? We felt that there was a gap in our knowledge on this and yet, within our villages, there are many unacknowledged "specialists", with abundant memories of the church, dating back to the early years of the 20th century. Such recent history is in danger of vanishing, so we thought that it would be worthwhile and enjoyable to record people's tales of village life in East Brabourne, at the heart of which is St Mary's parish church.

Within days of starting our interviews, our plans changed. Memories relating to the church took us deep into the realms of local lives and livelihoods, linking us with farming, with other economic and social activities and with the communities of Brabourne Lees, Smeeth and West Brabourne. Our horizons expanded and, rather than maintaining our initially narrow focus on the church in East Brabourne, we talked with people from the

1

wider community, encouraging them to range widely in their recollections. We even spoke with some who had left the area but who still felt very much part of it. The result is a book that documents the history of different aspects of life in East Brabourne, Brabourne Lees, West Brabourne and Smeeth, with occasional sorties into Stowting, Monks Horton and Sellindge. The parish and civil boundaries are precisely drawn, but in terms of daily life such boundaries have always been porous and they still are, and so, too, our book has focused on including the memories of local people, rather than excluding them because of their location. We would remind you that memory is not necessarily "fact" and that two people recalling the same incident rarely agree on the details of the event. Nevertheless, there is sufficient common ground from all the material collected from over 170 contributors to suggest that this book does represent a fairly true picture of life in these villages over the past century or so.

You will notice frequent references to "the village", "the villages" and "our villages" – these are terms with different meanings in different contexts and left for you, the reader, to interpret as you will. In spite of our wider focus, we begin with the ancient history of St Mary's Church, Brabourne, just to remind us that this church was the starting point and inspiration for this book.

The experience of collecting pieces of living history has been pure pleasure for us because people have shared their lives so generously. People whom we have known very slightly at the start of a meeting have become veritable friends by the end of an afternoon in which a wealth of recollections, happy and hilarious, have been recounted alongside memories of sad and tragic events. The task of assembling the book has been equally pleasurable, but we are well aware that first-hand experiences and personal memories can rarely be written and retold with the same vivacity, warmth, humour and accuracy with which they were recounted by the "owners". We have thus chosen to vary the ways in which accounts have been recorded and presented in order to both sustain the energy of the book and to provide a rich patchwork of effects for the reader.

We have tried to check and crosscheck the manuscript, but there are still bound to be numerous errors and omissions. If you see any with regard to points of fact, please do let us know so that we can correct the basic text. You never know, we might be fortunate enough to have a second edition.

Promoted by St Mary's Brabourne, this book has been produced to raise money for the fabric of Brabourne Church and we are truly grateful to all who have participated: to those with the abundant memories; to those with knowledge of more distant history; to those who have written sections of this book; to those who have taken photographs, drawn maps and shared precious historical photographs and literature with us; to those who have researched factual material, identified people and places in photographs, sketched, filled in details on maps, photocopied, scanned photographs, designed, checked points of detail, edited and printed for us; to those who have helped with publicity and marketing; and to those, including the children of Brabourne School, who provided modern perceptions to contrast with those who were children just a few years ago.

Our special thanks go to several long-time residents of the villages who have kindly read, and in some cases re-read, the manuscript, paying attention to detail and correcting and enriching the text. Listed in alphabetical order, these are Pauline Anderson, Eric Ball, Ron and Jenny Cooper, Karl Engels, Anthony and Jackie Finn, John and Audrey Hammon, Rosemary Hendry, John and Pam Jamieson, Ted and Margaret Pile, Philip and Sheila Stone, Oliver Trowell and John and Vi Varrier. We are most grateful to John Jamieson and Jean Bates who painstakingly proofread the text, and to Vincent Chan, the Head Teacher of Brabourne School, and Audrey MacCormack, School Secretary, who have been more than generous in photocopying drafts for our readers. Without your assistance we would have struggled. Thank you also to a more recent resident of the village, Emma Lenthall, who has kindly read the manuscript, suggesting amendments to give us peace of mind.

Our sincere thanks are due to those who have generously funded the printing and publishing costs of this book. In alphabetical order, they are Jean Bates, Anthony and Jackie Finn, George and Vicki Jessel, Michael Marshall, The Monday Club and the following trusts: The Roger De Haan Charitable Trust, The Sir Charles Jessel Charitable Trust and The HR Pratt Boorman Family Foundation. We have also been very grateful for the assurance of a top-up (if needed) from the Vicar and Churchwardens' fund of Brabourne Church. This was kindly agreed in 2012 by the Reverend Richard Le Rossignol and churchwardens Don Palmer and Charles Sinden. Without such generous support from all our donors we would never have been able to complete this book.

Finally, an enormous thank you to members of our production team: to Sam Thackray for her skill in editing and for her persistent good humour while working on acres of text; to Derek Gurr who, over many years, meticulously collected pictorial material about Brabourne, much of which is now incorporated in this book; to Phil Anthony for helping to provide essential software; and to Peter Embleton-Smith for adding to our archive of pictures and for bringing together so much text and so many images so effectively. Tragically, our printer, John Claydon of Crown Print, Wye, who had become a good friend to us, died before printing this book. Nigel Mitchell at Biddles Ltd. came to our rescue and we are most grateful to him for taking on the task of printing. Our thanks, too, to Dominic Thackray for introducing us to Biddles.

We are truly grateful for the support of everyone involved, our apologies if we have left anyone out, and we thank you all for your generous and warm-hearted contributions.

Kathleen Embleton-Smith and Christine Gurr
(former churchwardens, St Mary's Brabourne)

# 1

# ST MARY'S, AN ANCIENT PLACE OF WORSHIP

John Varrier outlines St Mary's distant history:

Situated at the foot of the North Downs, the parish of Brabourne includes within its boundaries the villages of East Brabourne, West Brabourne and Brabourne Lees. The latter has grown significantly over the past century, while West and East Brabourne have changed remarkably little, being partly within a Conservation Area, and partly within an Area of Outstanding Natural Beauty. Tucked away at the end of The Street in East Brabourne is the parish church of St Mary the Blessed Virgin, which dates back, over 800 years, to Norman times. A Grade I-listed building, St Mary's contains many architectural treasures, and the site on which it stands may well have been a place of worship since the late Stone Age.

## PAGAN SETTLEMENT IN THE LATE STONE AGE

Significant finds of flint arrowheads and scrapers, some in the immediate vicinity of the church, indicate clearly that there has been a settlement in East Brabourne since the late Stone Age. Oliver Trowell, whose home adjoins the churchyard, has found several in his garden, though these pale into insignificance when compared with a find in the field to the south of the church, just beyond the graveyard. The late James Hamilton, a previous owner of Parsonage Farm of which the field was part, was ploughing there when he turned up what was later to be described by the British Museum as one of the finest examples of a polished flint axe head that has ever been found in this country. It was an object of beauty, with a cutting edge quite undamaged and a polished flint still shining as new. How such a valuable item came to be "lost" can only be a matter of conjecture. Perhaps it was a pointer to things yet to come since it was found on the probable site of the original Scott's Hall which is thought to have been near Brabourne Church.

An added feature of pagan times would undoubtedly have been the large yew tree found in Brabourne churchyard, which, in 1698, was described as "the Great Yew of Brabourne" by John Evelyn, a contemporary of Samuel Pepys. Evelyn spent some time measuring its girth and described it as having a circumference of 59ft. This must have been a great tree indeed, and perhaps had stood there for more than 1,000 years and possibly as long as 3,000 years[1]. Yews were thought to have had mystical properties by the pagans and this particular example may have formed the centre of their rites of worship. It was destroyed in one of the two great storms that struck the church in 1698 and 1700 and opinion suggests that it probably stood to the southeast of the present tower. (Igglesden suggests that it was still there in 1861.)

Though not as large as the Great Yew described by either Evelyn or Igglesden, the circumference of Brabourne's largest yew is currently 16ft 4ins, the measurement being taken by Charles Sinden and Ray Lucas on 14th April, 2013. It is estimated that this tree dates from about 1728 +/- decades. We are grateful to Dr Philip Wilson for his help with estimating the age of the tree.

---

1  Igglesden, Charles (1913) A saunter through Kent with pen and pencil. Ashford: Kentish Express, pp14-15. (The page number varies in different editions).

## ARRIVAL OF THE SAXONS IN BRABOURNE

The next significant era that should be considered was the arrival of the Saxons, from whom the name Brabourne is believed to have evolved. Some history books list deBradeburn as a local princess, and therefore a possible source for the name, while Bradde Burne is also thought to have meant a broad stream, although the hamlet itself, Bredeburna, was mentioned in a Charter as early as AD846[2].

The Saxons occupied the area of East Brabourne and built what must have been a typical wooden Anglo-Saxon church on the site of the present church. There is considerable evidence of this Anglo-Saxon settlement: in recent times the arrival of a badger sett in a strip of trees to the south of Pilgrims' Way turned up human remains, which caused some excitement until forensic tests showed that these were ancient bones. Having obtained suitable permission, a small excavation was carried out there, which uncovered the iron haft and guard of a sword, as well as the boss of a typical Anglo-Saxon shield. Participating in the excavation, Jean Bates also discovered part of what was thought to be an Anglo-Saxon belt. Later still, in 1995, when Mr Priestly, who owns the lower field to the west of Canterbury hill, was having the steep driveway up to his land widened, just above Iden Corner, the digger driver struck something unusual and stopped his machine. I accompanied John Hammon, a local archaeologist, to have a first quick look at what turned out to be a complete and apparently as-yet-undisturbed Anglo-Saxon grave. Once again, investigations were necessary and a coroner's inquest was held. All this suggests that Brabourne may have been a quite extensive settlement. Further Anglo-Saxon graves were later found among the trees just off the road to Wye after foxes uncovered more human bones.

## THE ESTABLISHMENT OF A NORMAN CHURCH

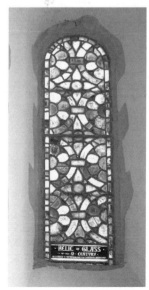

The Anglo-Saxon era lasted until the arrival of William the Conqueror in 1066, who, as is widely known, caused the destruction of Anglo-Saxon life, the churches in particular. Aspects of Anglo-Saxon life did continue post-conquest during an overlap period (until c1120), but gradually, churches were replaced, Norman churches being constructed on their sites. This, of course, is what happened at East Brabourne. The original Norman church comprised a typical nave, chancel and western tower and this arrangement remained in place until the arrival of John Balliol and the Scott family in the 13th or early 14th century, during which time it is suggested that a north aisle may have been added contemporaneously with the existing south aisle (more on this later).

2        Brabourne Parish (www.saxonshore-kent.gov.uk/aboutbrabourne.html; accessed 19/01/12).

The church is well known for its extensive range of Anglo-Norman features, and perhaps most importantly for the small stained-glass window, which is said to be the only complete Norman stained-glass window still in its original setting (pictured on the previous page. Another feature is the wooden stairway in the bell tower. This was constructed from a single oak tree, with quartered oak treads all pinned with wooden pegs to the risers, and has recently been dated to c1320 by archaeologists from Queen's University Belfast. Oliver Trowell has pointed out that many of the treads had to be replaced in 1936, due to the ravages of the deathwatch beetle.

*A report about the staircase, which is thought to have appeared in the local press (exact source unknown) in 1935, and which the Reverend C.R.L. McDowall – then priest at Brabourne – pasted into his Parish Notes states:*

*"To preserve this most useful piece of mediaeval carpentry from Death-watch Beetle and decay it is estimated that at least £50 is required, towards which the Diocesan Board of Finance is prepared to make a grant of £15. The architects in charge of the work are Messrs. Caröe and Passmore.*

*Donations may be sent to the Vicar."*
Source: possibly Kent Messenger (KM) Group

Don Palmer takes up the story of the staircase:

In the early years of the 21st century, a team of archaeologists and dendrochronologists

Don Palmer

from Queen's University Belfast asked the Reverend William Cooper, then priest in charge at Brabourne, whether they could date the wooden staircase in the vestry of Brabourne Church. They explained that the staircase was unique in that few "normal" wooden objects have survived from the high Middle Ages (c AD1000-1300). They wanted to take small core samples from the staircase to determine its age, and the PCC willingly gave their permission. Unfortunately, no sapwood was present in the samples taken, so establishing an exact date using this technique was not possible. However, carbon dating by Oxford University provided a calibrated date that, when taken in conjunction with the dendrochronological results obtained by the Belfast team, provided a felling date for the timber of between AD1345 and AD1380. This was unexpected and slightly disappointing to church members, as it had been thought that the staircase was as old as the tower, which had previously been dated to about AD1180. The reason for this assumption was that "the east end of the base-plate of the stairs was located in a slot in the stonework of the tower arch evidently made for that purpose"[3]. However, this scientific evidence revealed that the staircase was a later addition that had presumably been slotted into the stonework of the tower, probably replacing an earlier staircase.

Clockwise: Brabourne's 14th century staircase; the wooden pegs holding the treads in place; John Varrier, Oliver Trowell and Vi Varrier

---

3      Gardiner M, Brown D and Murray E.(2006) Timber Fittings and Fixtures in Churches and Secular Vernacular Buildings: Mid Fourteenth Century Timber Stairs at Brabourne Church, Kent. The Journal of the Society for Church Archaeology. Vol. 7/8/9 pp45-50. Quotation from p46.

## THE BALLIOLS AND THE SCOTTS

The arrival of John Balliol (sometimes referred to as John de Baliol) and his family following his defeat in the early 13th century by Robert Bruce (grandfather of Robert the Bruce), in Scotland, led to the next developments at the church. What brought the Scott family to this district is a matter of conjecture. One possible explanation is that they were supporters of the Cluniac order, as the adjoining parish, now known as Monks Horton, had Horton Priory at that time, which was occupied by members of the Cluniac order. The Scotts went on to build the Lady Chapel in the 15th century, now known as the Scott Chapel, and the history of the family and their chapel is well documented. They may also have been responsible for the building of the suspected north aisle in the late 13th century, as discussed below by Justin Ball. Many members of the Scott family occupied high offices of state and are listed on the brass plaque on the north wall of the church. In addition to this, there are four beautiful monumental brasses in the Scott Chapel which were moved from the chancel and restored in 1970. These depict two William Scotts, Isabel, the wife of one of them, and Dame Elizabeth Powynges (pictured on page 19).

Memorial to the Scotts on the north wall of St Mary's

## THE MEMORIAL TO THE SCOTTS READS AS FOLLOWS:

### To perpetuate the memory of

**Monseigneur William Balliol Le Scot,** VIIth Crusade, Cousin of John Balliol King of Scotland. d. 1313

**Sir William Scot,** Lord Chief Justice and Knight Marshal of England. d. 1350.

**Sir John Scot,** Lieut. of Dover Castle. d. 1413.

**Sir William Scotte,** Sherif of Kent, Knight of the Shire, Sword bearer to King Henry V. Battle of Agincourt. Built the Scott Chapel and restored this Church, d. 1433

**Sir Robert Scotte,** Lieut. of the Tower of London. d. 1424.

**Sir John Scotte,** High Sherif of Kent, Knight of the Shire, Member of the Privy Council, Lord Warden of the Cinque Ports, Governor of Dover Castle, Marshal of Calais Ambassador to the Duke of Burgundy and Bretagne, Comptroller of the Household of Edward IV d. 1485.

**Sir William Scott,** High Sherif of Kent, Lord Warden of the Cinque Ports, Constable of Dover Castle, builder of Eden Church, Sussex. d. 1524.

**Thomas Scott,** Cardinal Archbishop of York (Rotherham). Member of the Privy Council, Lord Keeper of the Privy Seal, Lord Chancellor of England, Chancellor of the university of Cambridge, Master of Pembroke, Rebuilt and Re-endowed Lincoln College. d. 1500

**Sir John Scott,** Sherif of Kent, Knight of the King's Bodyguard, served in Guelders. d. circa 1530.

**Sir Reginald Scott,** Captain of Calais and Sangatte, High Sherif of Kent. d.1544.

**Sir Thomas Scott,** Sherif of Kent, Knight of the Shire, Commissioner for Dover Harbour and Romney Marsh, Colonel Commandant of the Kentish Forces, Spanish Armada. d. 1594.

**Reginald Scot,** Author of 'The Discoverie of Witchcraft'. d. 1599.

**Sir Edward Scott,** K.B., Sherif of Kent, Knight of the Shire. d. 1643.

**Sir John Scott,** Knight of the Shire, served in Spain and Flanders. d. 1616.

**Sir William Scott,** Ambassador to Turkey, Florence and Venice. d. 1612.

And all other members of the family of Scott of Scotts Hall whose memorials have perished and many of whom are buried in this Church.

Historical fact and legend from this era are considerable and well worth pursuing on a visit to Brabourne Church. On Balliol's death (1268/9), church legend has it that his heart was interred in the little heart shrine adjoining the present-day altar rail. Such a shrine is relatively rare nowadays. It is said that, initially, his wife, Devorguilla, had his heart embalmed in a gold and ivory locket that she wore for the rest of her life. She, herself, was buried at Sweetheart Abbey, Dumfries. Another version of events was that the embalmed heart was secured in an ivory casket that would be placed before Devorguilla at meal times. Each day she would give her husband's share of every dish to the poor[4]. It has also been said that, after her death, the heart was re-interred in the church's heart shrine. We have no real knowledge as to when the heart was finally removed, but what is certain is that the shrine is now empty.

John de Balliol of Scotland
b.1190-1236, d.1268/9

Lady Devorguilla
of Galloway 1234-90

Balliol is believed to have been the founder of Balliol College, the oldest at Oxford University, but here, too, there is uncertainty as to how he was linked to the college. One explanation is that, in an act of great charity in the mid-13th-century, he rented rooms in Oxford and helped to support a group of poor students, which could have been the start of the college. An alternative explanation was that, after his death, Devorguilla endowed a college at Oxford University with her husband's name. However Balliol came to be linked with Balliol College, the college archive is scathing, to say the least, about Brabourne's connection with their founder and their website states: "The Parish [of Brabourne] has vague associations with the Balliol / Scott family, and there is a persistent false tradition that the heart shrine in St Mary's Church is John Balliol's"[5]. Whatever the truth, this tale, linked with the legendary love of John Balliol and Devorguilla is now part of the history of our parish church and so we feel wholly justified in including it in our book of anecdotes.

4      Summary history of the early Baliol (Bailleul) family (earthfriendarts.tripod.com/Baliol.htm; accessed 19/01/12).

5      Balliol College Archives and Manuscripts (archives.balliol.ox.ac.uk/History/gazetteer.asp; accessed 19/01/12).

Image of John da Balliol of Scotland accessed from en.wikipedia.org, 12/03/13.

Image of Devorguilla of Galloway accessed from www.guide2womenleaders.com 12/03/13.

Balliol Shrine

We acknowledge the variety of spellings of the names that persists – Balliol/Baliol/le Baliol, and similarly Scotte/Scott/Scot/Le Scot. These are not errors but variations that have arisen over time.

REGINALD SCOT (1538-1599) AND THE DISCOVERIE OF WITCHCRAFT
The stone altar tomb, which is thought to date from the late 16th century (see Brabourne in History, 2003), somehow survived the Cromwellian period. It is also a monument to the Scott (Scot) family and bears the coats of arms of the Scotts and those families to which they became related. In the early 1970s the altar tomb was restored by Oliver Trowell, whose restoration process has been described thus: "The text, being then barely decipherable, Oliver wrote down all the lettering he could detect and the Reverend Ray Sheekey, then vicar of Brabourne, discovered the "missing links" in the Geneva Bible of 1567. The spelling is quaint, to say the least, but the ghosts of the original lettering were just visible enough to detect once it was known what to look for. The task was not made easier by having to paint the dark background up to the lettering, which of course had to be painted first. The colour

Oliver Trowell restoring the lettering on the altar
tomb. Kentish Express, 7th June, 1974

The altar tomb, at Brabourne Church

on the shields was also much perished but enough remained to restore them to their original appearance. Oliver left one tablet untouched, at the north end of the altar, to show the perished state of the paintwork. The whole project took about 300 hours to complete."

The altar tomb itself is believed to contain the remains of Reginald Scot, possibly a black sheep of the family, but remembered for his writings. He published a treatise on hop growing, an account of the rebuilding of Dover Harbour and a book for which he is best known: The Discoverie of Witchcraft (1584). In this he exposed the dreadful practices that led to the deaths of so many innocent people, particularly old women, during the infamous witch hunts.

Not only was Reginald's book the first one to be written in English on the subject of witchcraft, but it was also the first to deny it truly existed. It was a manual of contemporary belief and practice and, in it, Reginald argued strongly that faith in witchcraft could be rejected by reason and religion. It was not popular with the establishment at that time as it exposed the ways in which belief in witchcraft was being used by the unscrupulous, and it clearly implicated many in the position of power and authority. The substance of the book, therefore, certainly merits a few moments' digression.

Around the time Reginald wrote his book it was possible for a person who bore a grudge, or perhaps even genuinely suspected that he was under the influence of a spell placed upon him by a neighbour, to accuse others of witchcraft as a means of retribution. For example, if a man's sheep died and that man bore a grudge against a neighbour, he could accuse that neighbour of using witchcraft to cause the sheep's death. The accused would then be seized and taken before a local court that engaged the services of a witch-finder to determine whether or not the accused was a witch.

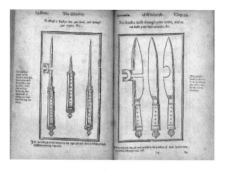

Instruments for witch testing

The tests for this included such things as a strip-search of the accused for moles or birthmarks anywhere on their body. The witch-finder would test these marks using a pointed tool that was cunningly mounted on a spring within the handle – when pushed onto a surface, this point would retract into the handle in a way that could not be seen by onlookers. The test was to see whether the bodkin would draw blood. If it did, the victim was considered innocent; if it did not, however, the witch-finder would claim that "the Devil looked after his own" and the accused was, therefore, guilty of witchcraft and put to death by one of a number of gruesome methods, such as burning at the stake. It is a matter of shame that some members of the magistracy, the witch-finders themselves and even members of the church were in on these wicked practices, and benefited financially from them. In a recent TV programme Stephen Fry remarked that the number of women put to death as witches was no greater than 500. To us, this seems an enormous number of women who suffered and died unjustly and needlessly, and a shameful part of England's history.

Though Reginald exposed the falsehoods of witchcraft and simultaneously attacked the cruelty and injustice of witch trials, he did look more positively, if in

less depth, on "the magical art of legerdemain [sleight of hand]", which he considered a source of harmless entertainment. It is probably his distancing of sleight of hand from witchcraft that has so endeared Reginald to the Magic Circle, which remembers him annually even now, sending a member to Brabourne Church to leave a single red rose on the altar on 9th October each year, the anniversary of his death. Indeed, Reginald is looked upon as the founding father of modern magic as the means of public entertainment as we know it today.

Reginald Scott

Not surprisingly, Reginald's exposure of the wicked practices of witchcraft was not universally welcomed and it is suggested that the King himself – James I of

England (VI of Scotland) – was displeased at its publication. (It is worth noting that Reginald is the only Scott listed on the Memorial Tablet (shown on page 10) who does not have a title.) The book was banned from further publication and any existing copies were allegedly burnt in public. In the normal course of events, things could have turned out very badly for Reginald, but perhaps he was fortunate in having an uncle of the same name who was a knight of the realm and Captain General of the ports of Sangatte and Calais, and therefore a man of distinction and, no doubt, in a position to offer his nephew some degree of protection. Despite the rejection of the book by many in authority, there was widespread feeling that Reginald was speaking the truth and the book was reprinted in 1651, 1654 and 1655. The first modern edition was published in 1886, with several more appearing in the 20th century. Through his book, Reginald was influential in changing and abolishing the laws relating to witchcraft.

## OTHER SCOTTS REMEMBERED

Returning to the church, the helmets hanging in the chancel are also from the Scott family. Superficially, the most attractive helmet is a funeral helm and would probably have been made by the village blacksmith to be carried on the bier of a knight at his funeral. The other, also pictured here, which is much less conspicuous and is sadly missing its visor, is a jousting helm, and may well have been worn in battle, perhaps even by the elder Sir William Scott (d.1433), who was sword bearer to Henry V at Agincourt, and who is depicted on one of the memorial brasses in the Scott chapel.

Jousting helm

Funeral helm

## AGINCOURT ... BRIEFLY

Deviating from the brasses for a moment, we turn to the battle of Agincourt, in northern France (approximately 320 miles from Calais), which took place on 25th October, 1415, and must have been one of the greatest defeats inflicted on a French army, where the victors were some 9,000 sick and exhausted English soldiers, many of whom were longbow men. Most of these soldiers were said to be suffering from dysentery and had cut the seats out of their trousers, so dire was their condition. In this debilitated state they faced and defeated the flower of French chivalry, an army of some 12,000[6] cavalry and foot soldiers, a victory largely due to two factors: first, the absurd pride among the French that every knight had to be at the forefront of the battle; and second, since the battle took place on a somewhat-narrow strip of land bounded by woodland and the village of Agincourt, there was insufficient space for the knights to manoeuvre, enabling the English archers to shoot them down in droves. For those who travel to Calais, it is worth making a detour to the modern-day village of Agincourt where, rather surprisingly, the French have created an excellent museum showing the course of the battle and their own humiliating defeat.

## MONUMENTAL BRASSES AND OTHER DETAILS

Returning to the brasses now in the Scott Chapel, the wife of the elder Sir William Scott, Isabel (later Lady Clifton) was apparently also of sufficient importance to be commemorated in a monumental brass. An unusual feature is that she is not wearing any form of headdress other than a circlet, and there is no clear reason why this should be so. (All well-bred ladies at that time would usually have worn a wimple.) More typically, on the last brass, the wife of Sir Edward Poynings of Ostenhangar (the daughter of Sir John Scott (d.1485), whose tomb is across the chancel) is wearing the traditional headdress. She died in 1528. One of the two male figures depicted in the brasses on the floor of the Scott chapel is that of the younger Sir William Scott (d.1524) who, it is believed, was with King Henry VIII on the field of the Cloth of Gold.

In brief, the Field of the Cloth of Gold was the location for an ostentatious meeting in 1520 between Francis I of France and Henry VIII, just outside Calais, between the villages of Ardres and Guines. Henry had been persuaded to forge a political alliance with France but he and Francis were rivals, each priding himself on the magnificence of his own court. The meeting was thus a major opportunity to impress. The castles in both the villages were considered in too bad a state for the guests, so Henry and Francis camped, setting up the most elaborate of tents and pavilions. During the meeting, which lasted from 7th-24th June, the kings tried to outdo each other with

---

6        Source: Curry, A. (2010) Agincourt: A New History, Stroud: The History Press, p233. Post victory it seems that English chroniclers exaggerated French superiority in numbers to make Henry V's victory seem more amazing.

Sir William Scott, sword bearer to
Henry V at Agincourt (d 1433)

Isabel wife of Sir
William Scott (left)

Dame Elizabeth Powynges wife
of Sir Edward Poynings
of Ostenhangar

Sir William Scott, thought to have
been at the Field of the Cloth of
Gold with Henry VIII (d 1524)

their lavish hospitality, feasts, jousting tournaments, military sports and balls, among other events. It was this display of ostentation, power and strength and the wealth of gold cloth in evidence that gave the event its name. If the younger Sir William Scott was present, Brabourne was clearly well connected.

## THE SCOTT CHAPEL

Built in the early fifteenth century and known originally as The Chapel of the Holy Trinity, the Scott Chapel was both a place of worship and a place for memorials to the Scotts. A few years ago, the Reverend Ray Sheekey drew our attention to a plaque in the Scott Chapel in memory of Douglas Scott. Margaret Balliol Scott, a relative, and one of the last surviving members of the Scott family living in the area, wanted to put it up in his memory and engaged an undertaker to prepare a draft. The Diocese

The Scott Chapel

objected to the Roman-style lettering and proposed an alternative that was thought quite unsuitable. In an attempt to resolve the problem, Oliver Trowell "tidied up" the Roman lettering and the Diocese finally accepted the plaque. Oliver Trowell added that, "Margaret Balliol Scott lived at Burgate in Mersham, where she lived from 1923, until she married for the first time at the age of 83. Two of her cousins, Katie and Augusta Scott, lived at St Cyriac, near the church in East Brabourne, from the mid-1920s to 1944." Other memorials to the Scotts are to be found on the walls of the church, making it evident that this family long provided distinguished servants of the Crown. They have contributed to the nation not only in battle but also as members of the judiciary and as holders of other high offices of state.

*"The Rev. C.E. Owtram, now Rector of Woodchurch [possibly curate at Brabourne in the 1890s], sends us the following reminiscence: 'Between 1889 and 1892, I think, the lead roof of the Scott Chapel in Brabourne Church was taken off, and an immense block or slab of honey-comb, some 4ft by 3ft, was carried into the Vicarage.'"*

A published extract, exact source unknown, pasted into the Parish Notes of the Reverend C.R.L. McDowall, priest at Brabourne in the 1930s.
Possible source: KM Group

## THE SCOTT CHAPEL, RESTORED AS A PLACE OF WORSHIP

Though built as a place of worship, the Chapel was not used for this purpose for many years during the 20th century, and instead was used as a vestry. In 1957 it was restored as a place of worship as the following extract from the church archive explains:

Also known as the Chapel of the Holy Trinity, the Scott Chapel in Brabourne Church was, for many years, used as a vestry. It also housed the organ. Extracts from a request for a Faculty (June 1956, probably written by the Reverend Thompson-Evans) to reinstate an altar and move the organ tells us:

"This Chapel was built in the 15th Century, probably circa 1420-1430, by Sir William Scott of Scot's Hall, nearby. The family had just previously contributed with other Kentish families to the building of Christchurch Gate, Canterbury Cathedral.

"For very many years the Chapel has ceased to be a place of worship, for which purpose it was originally built and dedicated, and has been used as a vestry.

"It also houses the organ, the seat of which is placed over one of the memorial tombs in the chancel-chapel wall. Latterly the Vicar, the Rev. O.W. Thompson- Evans ... and the PCC have plastered the interior of the Belfry Tower and have fitted an oak screen in the arch; this accommodation is now being utilised as a vestry.

"The sole obstacle which now prevents this gem of 15th Century architecture, The Chapel of the Holy Trinity, from being re-established as a dignified place of worship is the presence of the organ, which obstructs nearly half the Chapel. It is therefore desired to remove the organ from the Chapel to a new site in the South aisle.

"A formal appeal to the Scott family resulted in their helping with the costs of refurbishment of the chapel. Since 1957, or thereabouts, the chapel has been known as the Scott Chapel [and the organ has had its home in the South aisle]".

Source: Brabourne Church archives

## EXPLORING QUESTION MARKS OVER LINEAGE LINKS

The Scott family associated with Brabourne are those believed to have a direct line of descent from John Balliol, not to be confused with Scotts, whose name derives from the practice of referring to someone as, for example, Robert the Scot. This, with the passage of time, was foreshortened to Robert Scot – nothing to do with John Balliol. To be true Scotts of Scott's Hall, it is important to show descent from Balliol, so if this applies to you, please let us know…

The debate over whether or not the Balliol and Scott lines merge involves some contention. On one side is the view commonly subscribed to in Brabourne: William le Scot, who died in 1350 and who was reputedly the founder of the Kentish family who lived at Scott's Hall, was a descendant of John Balliol, King of Scotland, and Alexander de Balliol, Lord of Chilham, Kent. He was thought to have been Knight Marshall and Chief Justice of England and was buried at Brabourne Church. Others, including the website of The Genealogist deny the link between the Balliols and the Scotts, as does the website of Balliol College Oxford. Exploring the history of the saints in the beautiful east, stained-glass window in Brabourne Church, it emerged that St Catherine of Alexandria was the patron saint of the Scott family, hence the Catherine wheels on their coats of arms[7]. Catherine of Alexandria is also the patron saint of Balliol College Oxford. There is a stained glass window in the chapel showing the fellows bowing before St. Catherine, and a Catherine wheel in stained glass appears in a window in Hall at the college[8]. Furthermore, St Catherine with sword and wheel are depicted on an ancient college seal[9]. Perhaps this link between the Scotts and Balliol College is just coincidence – or perhaps it does go deeper. We believe there is room for further research into the relationship between the Scotts and the Balliols.

St Catherine of Alexandria

So does a link between the two families matter for our purposes? Not a jot. It merely emphasises how flimsy the "facts" of history are and how much more intrigue and entertainment is to be derived from anecdote and yarn. It also gives strength

---

7       Catherine wheels are plentiful in Brabourne Church and children at Third Sunday Xtra, the Sunday School at Brabourne Church, recently counted 86 Catherine wheels throughout the church.

8       http://www.balliol.ox.ac.uk/about-balliol/buildings-and-stained-glass  Balliol College University of Oxford, buildings and stained glass. Accessed 03/05/2013.

9       http://archives.balliol.ox.ac.uk/Exhibitions/exhib05.asp  Balliol College archives and manuscripts. Accessed 03/05/2013.

to our cause, which is to document history within living memory. Whether or not one believes there is a genetic link between Balliols and Scotts, what is evident is the strength of the Scott presence in Brabourne. This is clearly borne out in the Scott Chapel of Brabourne Church, which, with its rich array of memorials, brasses and other Scott relics, is well worth a visit. Evidence also suggests that there may have been a north aisle at Brabourne Church during the Scott era...

## A NORTH AISLE FOR BRABOURNE IN THE LATE 13TH CENTURY?
Justin Ball (a local buildings conservationist) considers the case:

Justin Ball

"During a long life and in response to changing pressures, the original form or function of buildings can, and do, alter and adapt. Physical changes to built fabric can still be visible after many centuries – a blocked doorway or window; the "scar" on a wall marking the position of earlier building; a straight vertical join in stone, brick or timber, indicating alterations and rebuilding. Such evidence helps to develop theories about historic changes to a building, which can often be tested through archaeological investigation.

"Within the English landscape parish churches generally appear as the most enduring of all early buildings, even though the course of history has physically shaped and altered them and, in most cases, handed them down to us an in altered form from that originally planned and executed.

"Relying solely on the visible evidence of alteration to the building fabric of the parish church of St Mary the Virgin, Brabourne, we put forward the case here for the existence of a north aisle, erected with its existing counterpart to the south, sometime in the late 13th century. We seek only to propose the existence of such a structure and not to speculate on the reasons for its removal, perhaps as early as the late 14th century. It is, at this time, only an hypothesis and has not been tested by archaeological field investigation.

"The Anglo-Norman church of Brabourne we see today, altered and enlarged during the course of almost a millennium, dates to the mid- to late 12th century, and probably occupies the site of an earlier, pre-Conquest church. It was originally constructed as a two-cell building of chancel and nave with a west tower. During the later 13th century a south aisle of three bays was added [possibly at the beginning of the Scott era in Brabourne, or even earlier]. The erection of an arcade of three arches with clerestory over at this time would have necessitated the removal of the entire south nave wall. The arches of this arcade rest on circular pillars of freestone with moulded capitals and bases of Bethersden marble, a reasonably locally occurring fossiliferous limestone.

South aisle arcade

"The east end of the aisle leads through a similar arch into a mid 14th century chapel [now known as the Scott Chapel]. The responds, or half piers, that carry this arch (the arch itself and the Bethersden marble bases) are identical to the piers and arches forming the arcade of the south aisle. The erection of this arch cuts through the jamb of an east window [visible from within the Scott Chapel], suggesting that, prior to its insertion, there existed an east wall with window to the south aisle. Unless an earlier chapel was built at the same time as the aisle, which seems unlikely given the evidence of a blocked window, the conclusion must be that this arch was originally located elsewhere and subsequently re-used in the 14th century when the chapel was built, the arch serving to connect the aisle and chapel.

" The hypothesis for the re-use of the arch can be examined in more detail by looking at the arch itself (pictured on next page):

Looking towards the Scott Chapel from south aisle

i.      The upper parts of the arch show damage that may be consistent with it having been taken down. Such damage to the face of the stones is absent on the three arches forming the aisle arcade.

ii.      The stones at the point of the arch have been badly inserted, are uneven and repaired. This is at variance with the triple arcade.

iii.      The responds, capitals and bases all exhibit signs of weathering and/or damage, which is less obvious on the arcade.

The bases of chapel arch (left) have been set lower than
those of the south aisle arcade (right)

iv.       The bases of this arch are set into the floor at a significantly lower level than those of its south-aisle counterparts. Why should this be if the arch was erected contemporaneously with the south aisle?

v.        The arch has been inserted asymmetrically, which may suggest that the builders had difficulty centering it when using stones of an earlier, much larger arch that had to be adapted to fit a more restricted space than that originally intended when it formed part of an arcade of a north aisle.

The available evidence strongly points to the re-use of earlier arch material. Since the component parts of the south-aisle arcade and the eastern arch are in all respects identical, it is highly improbable that the single arch is later than the south-aisle arcade. If it is contemporary with the arcade, as appears likely, then it must have originally been erected elsewhere because of the evidence of its having cut through a now-blocked east window in the exterior east wall of the aisle.

The logical place for the original location of this arch would seem to be somewhere on the north side of the nave, since the chancel and tower both contain enough 12th-century material to make it impossible for their having been structurally altered.

My proposition is that a north aisle was built in the late 13th century with the south aisle. Externally, it extended from the northeastern corner of the church tower to a position on the north nave wall, approximately 1.7 metres in from the chancel. It would have been slightly shorter than the south aisle.

Externally, the north nave wall shows a distinct interruption of the building fabric (pictured on the next page). The original late-12th-century flint work of the west tower and chancel is constructed of well-coursed, rubble flint with Caen stone quoins and jambs. This work continues west from the chancel into the nave for approximately 1.7 metres, after which, almost aligned with a downpipe, there appears a clear vertical interruption in the fabric of the building.

The mix of stonework used in the space between this point and the junction with the west tower changes from predominantly well-coursed flint work to a pattern of more irregularly spaced flint with irregularly spaced sandstone and ragstone blocks from plinth level. This more randomly mixed material is distinct from the earlier work, suggesting a breech in the north wall between these two points.

Today we see a late-14th- or early-15th-century Perpendicular window in the north wall of the nave. Clearly, by this date, a north aisle would have been removed. Some

Clear vertical interruption to the fabric shown just left of the downpipe

recent authors have cited the resetting of the stones of the late-13th-century north doorway in the north nave wall, after the removal of an aisle, and hacked-off jambs in the north nave wall as further evidence for the existence of a north aisle[10].

A recent study makes no mention of this evidence. The authors accept the fabric of the north nave wall as of late-12th-century work. They show on plan the position of what they consider to be a blocked 12th-century window above the west slope of the porch roof [11]. However, the evidence against this being an early window is compelling for the following reasons:

i.        The authors "reconstruct" the 12th-century north elevation to show the position of the window as being aligned with the existing 12th-century chancel windows. The "scar" of this former "window" is below that alignment, which is uncharacteristic of this time.

---

10        Gardiner M, Brown D and Murray E. (2006) Timber Fittings and Fixtures in Churches and Secular Vernacular Buildings: Mid Fourteenth Century Timber Stairs at Brabourne Church, Kent. The journal of the Society for Church Archaeology. Vol. 7/8/9 pp45-50.
11        Berg, M. and Jones H. (2009) Norman Churches in the Canterbury Diocese, The History Press, pp69-72.

Looking towards the northeast corner of the tower.
Whilst there is a clear difference both in materials used and coursing of materials below the ridge of the porch, the flint work above the porch, though seemingly similar to that of the church tower, is in reality more random and less well-coursed

ii.      A more convincing argument against the existence of a window at this point is provided by an architect's ground plan of 1874-1879 of the church. This shows repairs to the church at that time. It includes a working drawing of a new lancet window to be inserted into the nave wall at the position of the scar. The drawing is annotated thus: "Sketch Shewing new window at F.F. Omitted as finding no trace of the original window"[12].

It seems likely that the external scar does not mark the position of an earlier window, but "opening up" works in the 1870s to establish the existence of a former window. In discovering the absence of such evidence the wall would have been "made good", resulting in the scar we see today.

In conclusion, the evidence appears to support the existence for the building of a north aisle sometime in the late 13th century simultaneously with the erection of one in the south. However, as stated earlier, this hypothesis has not been tested using archaeological intervention. Confirmation of this must therefore await a time when such intervention can be undertaken, when hopefully the puzzle of the single arch can be conclusively resolved and, in so doing, another page may be added to the history of St Mary's.

12      Colpoys, A.A.G. (Architect) for a ground plan (afterwork) IC35 file 07719. www.churchplansonline. org Brabourne, St. Mary the Virgin (1874-1879).

THE 17TH AND 18TH CENTURIES IN THE HISTORY OF ST MARY'S
John Varrier continues:

---

*The following is the agreement with reference to the work to be to be done on the tower of the church 230 years ago, signed by the builders:*

*"Aprell ye 2 day 1700 then it is agred by the Chorch-wardenes and overseares of the parresh of Braborn for the said Thomas Marlow and Thomas Werrell and John Thornby Breck-Layeres it tis Agred By the three partes that they have Agreed for to bild up the botteres and Lickwis Round the steple after ye Reat of thre peres a foot Lowen the said partes ten shilling In To the hool matter we the said parrishoneres at to fin all materrales. Witness hear unto we have set our hands.*

 *THO. MORLEY*
 *THOMAS WHERRELL*

 *JOHN* **T** *THORNBY (his mark)*

---

One of the most important events of the 17th century was when a great storm destroyed the spire and the top storey of the church tower in 1698. The churchwardens of that time arranged for the repair, which must have cost a great deal of money, and the extent of this repair is still visible in the changing pattern of stonework towards the top of the tower. Unfortunately, in 1700, another great storm caused

serious damage again to the tower and the southwest corner collapsed. The churchwardens during that period, whose initials were TW and TT (to be seen on the plaque inside the church, made of lead from the roof), by some means managed to secure funds yet again to repair the tower and also to construct the great buttresses that now support it on the south side. However, the upper storey of the tower and the spire were never replaced, hence the rather squat, and even ugly, appearance of the tower as we see it today. There is a difference of opinion with regard to the upper storey of the tower, as Oliver Trowell disputes that there ever was one.

One of two lead panels bearing the initials of Thomas Webb and Thomas Thompson, churchwardens in 1700

A newspaper extract (exact source unknown) pasted by the Reverend C.R.L. McDowall into his Parish Notes, possibly 1930/31, records that the total amount collected in 1700, 1701 for work on the tower was £208-11-2.

It is worth noting that John Thornby, who signed his name with the mark "T", is none other than Pat Thornby's great (x9)-grandfather, also similarly related to many other Thornbys. According to Pat (who writes in chapter 8), the original John Thornby is probably related to every Thornby in the southeast today and to Thornbys in the West Country, the Midlands and the north (with whom he has yet to establish a link); also to those who have gone on to Australia and the USA.

Reading the stones on the church tower, Justin Ball argues that: "The southwest corner of the tower is supported by a massive diagonal five-stage buttress of squared ragstone. At the time of its construction the entire upper level of the tower was rebuilt in squared ragstone. Additional repairs in rag were made to a substantial area of the south face, with a more limited rebuild to the west face. A smaller, set-back buttress has been built to the centre of the south face of the tower. This smaller buttress, constructed of flint with limestone dressings, is constructionally different from its larger neighbour and more closely resembles the buttresses supporting the south wall of the aisle. It may therefore be earlier in date. In confirmation of this, the damage to the south face of the tower appears to have been limited to an area west of this buttress, suggesting that it may have already been in place at the time of the building of the diagonal five-stage corner buttress. My view is that the major repairs to the tower, using the evidence of the corner buttress and the paired label-headed belfry openings to each face in the upper stage, date to the 15th century and not to the late 17th/early 18th centuries.

"Was there an upper storey? Almost certainly. Such a squat tower is atypical during the Anglo-Norman period within what is now the Canterbury diocese, although Leeds has such a tower, as does St Margaret-at-Cliffe.

"The late-17th-century works are recorded in the churchwardens' accounts. These show accounts for the building of a new spire (suggesting the existence of an earlier one) between 1699 and 1701 at a cost of £200 11s 6d. A final account is rendered in 1701 and this presumably relates to the completion of the works in 1700. I have found no evidence in these accounts or other church records to show that the tower collapsed in the early 18th century or that the corner buttress or ragstone repairs to the tower were undertaken at that time. Given the evidence of the accounts it seems reasonable to assume that the churchwardens TW and TT oversaw the erection of a new spire and perhaps some remedial works occasioned by the removal/loss of an earlier one."

## MOVING ON TO THE 19TH AND 20TH CENTURIES
John Varrier continues:

John Varrier

"By 1806, the threat of a Napoleonic invasion had resulted in the building of an army camp, hospital, prison and mortuary at Brabourne Lees, which, it is believed, accommodated as many as 2,000 people, comprising soldiers and civilian employees, the latter probably being included on the army payroll. In addition, there would have been vast numbers of camp followers, which would have included wives and children of the soldiers, prostitutes, harlots, washerwomen – virtually anyone. The camp would also have attracted many workmen, such as builders, carpenters, iron workers and less-skilled labourers. With such numbers, Brabourne Lees would have been a larger settlement than it is today." The effects of the camp would have been felt beyond Brabourne Lees as according to the reflections of Sid Ashdown, captured in a recording in the late 1990s, not long before he died, Primrose Cottages in Bulltown Lane were housing for officers. Apparently, the horses were kept in stables on the ground floor of these cottages while the officers slept above them. The men were in the barracks on the Lees.

Jeremy Secker adds that possible invasion from France meant that Kent was a frontline county and the purpose of the military in Brabourne was to provide reinforcements for the coastal defences, the Martello towers and the military canal, all of which were under construction by 1804. Though some seven miles from the coast, Brabourne was well placed for the camp, as the turnpike road that linked London (via Ashford) with the coast at Hythe passed through the village. Extracts from the deeds of The Towers, kindly lent by the Bragge family, show that in 1823 the turnpike passed the end of the land on which The Towers stands, now part of Plain Road. In 1834, well after the Napoleonic wars, the turnpike was re-routed between Mersham and

Sellindge to more or less the present route of the A20. This new route was flatter and avoided the hills between Brabourne and Sellindge. It thus made travel easier, particularly in wetter months, when unmade roads on slopes such as Plain Hill and Stone Hill would have made travel difficult.

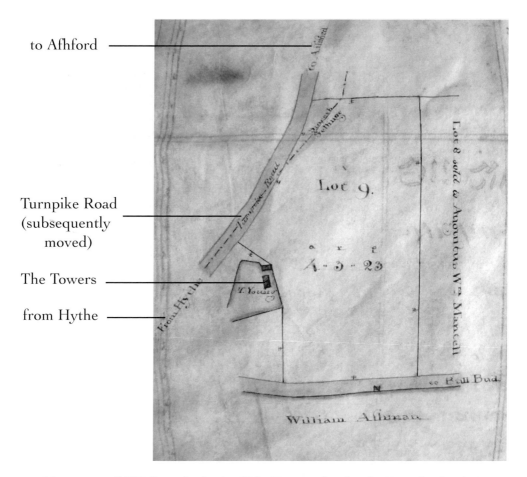

to Afhford

Turnpike Road
(subsequently
moved)

The Towers

from Hythe

Map extract (1823) from the deeds of The Towers, showing the Turnpike Road passing along the boundary of part of this property. This part of the Turnpike Road is now part of Plain Road

Jeremy explains that Brabourne was a suitable choice for the army camp because much of the area that is now Brabourne Lees was covered by a large common, probably similar to that at Stelling Minnis. The map below shows the extent of the common at Brabourne (marked with tussocks) and the barracks within it, the position of landmark buildings, as well as the older and larger houses and farms situated around it. These included Bog Farm, Lodge House, Lily Vale Farm, Washington, Granary Court Farm, Pound House, Pemsey Farm and Court Farm, not all of which can be seen here. The map (scale not given) suggests that the common may have been over a mile long and three-quarters of a mile at its widest. Part of the common was requisitioned by the military for the barracks, which were situated in that part of the Lees now bounded by Bridge Road, Plain Road and Canterbury Road. According to

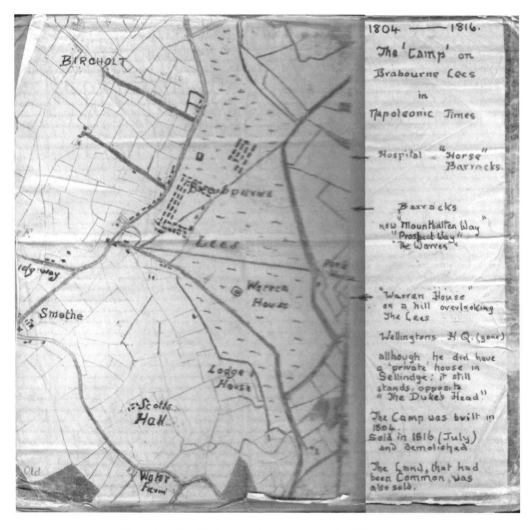

Map showing Brabourne Lees in the early 19th century
(source: Don Skeer's archive)

Jeremy, the army were at first encamped in tents but with time, more durable buildings were constructed. The map suggests that the barracks would have been built where the houses of Mountbatten Way and Prospect Way now stand, and extended down to the Baptist Church and to Canterbury Road. The military are also believed to have constructed a two-storey hospital that had nine wards. This was thought to have been located in Hospital Field, to the north east of Mountbatten Way. Igglesden claims that the hospital was built for victims of the Crimean War (1853-1856) but Don Skeer's map suggests that the hospital was linked to the army camp in Brabourne Lees, half a century earlier[13].

Jeremy Secker

The reference to "horse barracks" on the map opposite is interesting. It is possible that these were stables and may have been along Canterbury Road. Karl Engels who has ploughed the field adjacent to Canterbury Road explained to us that the soil in the field along Canterbury Road was different from the rest of the field. It contained bits of metal, mule shoes and plenty of rubble, all pointing to the existence of buildings there in an earlier period. Relating this field evidence to the map of the camp, we would tentatively hypothesize that the horses may have been stabled along Canterbury Road.

And what of the Duke of Wellington? Did he stay at Warren House as suggested by the ancient map? Being a military strategist, it seems quite feasible that he would have been in the area and moved around to keep morale high and to ensure that England's defences were as strong as possible. He may well have visited Hythe to keep an eye on the building of the military canal and other defences along the coast. He may also have visited the Small Arms School at Hythe where his soldiers were billeted and trained. There is evidence to suggest that he lodged at the Abbot's Fireside (public house) in Elham, and he was at one time warden of Walmer Castle. With such strong links with Kent, Colonel Wellesley (as he was in 1806) may well have stayed at Warren House, or at very least visited the army camp at Brabourne Lees where troops were being mustered and kept ready to move swiftly to the coast at Hythe in the event of an invasion by Napoleon from across the Channel. We would add that this paragraph is no more than conjecture as we have not researched the movements of the Duke, this being beyond the scope of this book.

---

13      Igglesden, Charles (1913) A Saunter Through Kent with Pen and Pencil. Ashford: Kentish Express, p13. (Page numbers vary slightly in different editions).

## BRABOURNE LEES BECOMES AN IMPORTANT CENTRE

The military encampment must have had a major impact on Brabourne Lees and the thinly populated villages nearby. The presence of 2,000+ people must have been a considerable stimulus for social and economic activity, and it may well have been at this time that East Brabourne, which with its church had been the centre of Brabourne, lost its importance to Brabourne Lees. Almost certainly, cottages, shops, alehouses and a host of other services would have emerged in response to the needs of such a large population. Robin Marsh told us that remnants of ancient buildings thought to have dated from Napoleonic times had been unearthed along Canterbury Road when George Brooks's house, Providence, and others nearby were being built. These would probably have been built of wood. According to Margaret Pile (Ward), research by Mr Hewitt of Bog Farm in 1953 revealed that Rock Cottages in Bridge Road, Brabourne Lees, were built for the officers of this camp. Vi Sprawling told us that the old Handy Stores, now converted to dwellings, was constructed during Napoleonic times, and a little further away and towards East Brabourne, Park Corner Cottages on Canterbury Road, not far from the top of Manor Pound, were also believed to have been the dwellings of soldiers. Doubtless there are other buildings in Brabourne Lees that date from this era, too.

John Varrier's research has shown that, with so many additional people in the locality, a larger graveyard was needed, and in the early 1800s the one to the south of Brabourne Church was virtually doubled to its current size. The ancient register of burials at Brabourne shows that many military graves were dug between 1804 and 1808: burials for 1801 and 1802 were seven and three respectively, while for 1804 and 1808 they were 59 and 68 respectively. However, we have no records or reliable knowledge of who was buried, or where the graves were located, as they would have been marked, at best, with a small wooden cross that would have quickly rotted away. Jeremy Secker found the situation to be very similar at Smeeth Church, where there was a marked increase in births, and hence baptisms, but also, tragically, an equally marked increase in child and infant mortality. Under the floor of the chancel in Smeeth Church is the grave of an infant son of the colonel of the camp's troops.

John notes that, in many cases, the registry entries at Brabourne are very moving, and say no more than, for example, "a follower of the Xth regiment, and her infant child", or "a soldier of the Yth regiment". Very few were actually named. Sometimes, a whole page of burials covered a period of very few days. This was probably due to epidemics breaking out in a large camp that had inadequate water supplies and little in the way of sanitation. Having said that, there is evidence that a brick-lined barrel drain, "sufficiently large for a child to stand in", according to Karl Engels, crossed Mountbatten Way, where it was discovered when the foundations for the houses were

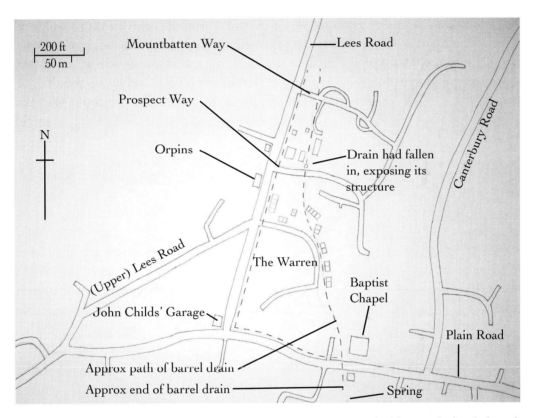

200 ft
50 m

N

Mountbatten Way

Lees Road

Prospect Way

Orpins

Drain had fallen
in, exposing its
structure

Canterbury Road

(Upper) Lees Road

The Warren

Baptist
Chapel

John Childs' Garage

Plain Road

Approx path of barrel drain

Approx end of barrel drain

Spring

Sketch map showing the approximate path of the barrel drain (pecked line), which is believed
to date from the days of the Napoleonic army camp in Brabourne
(1804-1816)

being constructed. David Sawyer, who worked on the construction of Mountbatten Way, confirmed that a large drain was indeed unearthed beneath one of the houses near the end of the first cul-de-sac on the right after entering Mountbatten Way from Lees Road. The drain, he recalled, had to be filled with concrete to ensure that the foundations of the house would be secure. The drain then crossed the land where the farm buildings for Prospect Farm stood, went across what is now Prospect Way and across the Warren, emerging near the spring, the waters of which came to the surface behind Vincer's Cottage, on the opposite side of Plain Road from the Baptist Church, and which were used for generations for domestic purposes – with no recorded ill effects. We have no details as to when the drain was built, but those who have seen it say that it is not a drain of the modern era. The brickwork is thought to be old and

it is assumed locally that the existence of the drain is related to the existence of the army camp and that they both dated from the same period. Further research, however, is needed to confirm this.

A sketch map (page 37) constructed with the help of Robin Marsh, John Hammon and Karl Engels shows the approximate location of the main drain, which, from its size, and together with the map from 1803-1816, suggests that it would almost certainly have been designed to serve the barracks. There is as yet no evidence as to where the drain started. If it had been the drain for the hospital in Hospital Field, and if the hospital was where the map suggests, then any drainage

John Hammon

installed would surely have been directed towards Bircholt, or Canterbury Road, where there was an ancient culvert for superficial drainage. But if, as is claimed, the hospital was two storeys high and had nine wards, it would have been large for its time. And if, as we believe, the barrel drain crossing Mountbatten Way, Prospect Way and the Warren was installed in Napoleonic times, wouldn't such a major engineering project have been positioned so that it was usable by both the hospital and the barracks? Again, this is no more than guesswork, which has been prompted by Karl. But perhaps such reasoning suggests too much planning and forethought, as few would have expected the Napoleonic Wars to continue for so long, nor the army camp to be based in Brabourne for so long. If this were true then buildings and drainage may not have been planned as

Robin Marsh

Karl Engels

suggested above, but the drain may have been built after the barracks were in place, and the sizeable hospital, which had already been constructed in a different place, may have used a different drainage system. Whatever the situation, the significant size of the drain suggests that when it was blocked it could have been cleared manually.

A second, smaller, brick barrel drain of similar construction to the larger one is known to have run along past The Plough, Ames' Stores, Caroline's, Orpins and in front of Hawkins' butcher's shop (as was) and John Childs' Garage, before turning down Woolpack Hill to join the other drain near the spring (see sketch map on page 37). Several of our contributors remember this latter drain being used by those whose properties were nearest to it, including Mr Hawkins, the butcher, who reportedly added all the liquid residues from his shop and slaughterhouse to the drain, which emerged near the much-used waters of the spring. It is thought that some of the properties past which the smaller drain flowed may still be connected to it.

It seems likely that the army would have had the drains constructed in the full knowledge that some form of sewage removal was necessary both for reasons of cleanliness and to keep at bay bad smells that emanated from putrid or decaying matter in the camp. At that time, it was believed that that foul-smelling air, or miasma, was the agent by which disease was spread. It wasn't until the 1840s that the link between polluted water and illness became known. We cannot know that the installation of the drains was driven by considerations such as these but it does seem a strong possibility.

We don't know where the drain started but Karl Engels, who worked in the dairy at Prospect Farm in the late 1950s, knew exactly the route that the barrel drain took, as it passed through the buildings of Prospect Farm. At one point, the drain had fallen in, exposing its considerable size and expert construction, and at another opening among the farm buildings Karl and others used to sweep slurry into the drain – with little thought for where it went. The council discovered the slurry accumulating in an inspection chamber in the Warren, and asked Karl and his colleagues to stop doing this. Thus we have evidence from both Karl and Robin Marsh of the route taken by the drain from Mountbatten Way, through Prospect Farm buildings, Prospect Way, across the Warren and across Plain Road into what is now Calland. We would add that mains drainage was installed in the 1960s, well after the discovery of the barrel drain. According to Robin Marsh and John Hammon, when the floor of the silage barn at

Prospect Farm was dug out, remnants of the drain were revealed beneath it. Karl is confident that the drain into which he used to sweep slurry was in front of the silage barn, thus he suggests that the drain may have had branches into different parts of the army camp and possibly the local settlement that grew up while the military was based in the Lees. Karl also describes the existence of narrow paths, possibly hardened with cinders, which traversed the land on which Prospect Farm House and its buildings stood. He thus suggests that this may have been the site of several cottages, two of which were still standing in the 1950s, but one of which has now disappeared (the other later being used for the doctor's surgery).

The size of the settlement at Brabourne Lees in Napoleonic times was not to be underestimated, and as Jeremy Secker suggests, the presence of the military changed patterns of development in Brabourne Lees and the surrounding area forever.

By way of a postscript, Oliver Trowell told us that he had heard tales that a sack of French gold coins had been found stashed in the chimney at Coquet Lodge in East Brabourne, just near the church gates. These may have been hidden by French prisoners in the area who intended to return and collect them. Oliver added that this was before his time and emphasised that the chimney was taken down many years ago and there are absolutely no French gold coins at Coquet Lodge now!

## AFTER WATERLOO

Shortly after the Battle of Waterloo (1815), and the end of the war, much of the military surplus equipment was sold by auction on 22nd July, 1816; the sale, we are told, lasted six days. We're guessing, but it seems likely that, even though the army camp had left the village, some of those additional people who were by now living in Brabourne Lees probably continued to live there, and with the shops and services that had developed, the village retained its local prominence[14], eclipsing East Brabourne which was thought to have been a substantial settlement in Saxon times. Allowing our imagination to run on, one can picture a reduced population in the wake of the Napoleonic Wars but, possibly, local people would have begun re-reclaiming the common for pasture once the army camp had gone. This could not have lasted for long, however, as enclosure of the common soon followed and this would have then changed everything forever.

---

14      Samuel Bagshaw's History, Gazetteer and Directory of Kent 1847, Vol. II, published by G. Ridge, Sheffield, (p468) lists over 25 businesses in the Manor of Brabourne in 1847. Bagshaw doesn't specify exactly where these businesses were located but it seems reasonable to assume that most were in Brabourne Lees, and that the significant economic activity locally was a legacy from the days of the army camp which had been sold in 1816, some 31 years before the Directory was published. The extract from Bagshaw can be found at the end of Chapter 4.

ENCLOSURE OF THE COMMON
Jeremy Secker writes:

"By an act of parliament, The Enclosure Act of Brabourne, which received Royal Assent on 15th May, 1822, power was granted to commissioners to sell this common land in lots, which included the site of the former military encampment. The commissioners were William Murton and Francis Whitfield, both described as gentlemen. It seems that as there was so much property to be sold it took place in several stages. Simple particulars were drawn up [a hand bill copy exists in the County Records office at Maidstone].

"The auction was held at the Woolpack, Stone Hill, Smeeth (not to be confused with the Woolpack at the top of Woolpack Hill). Stone Hill was then part of the parish of Smeeth, and the Woolpack (now long gone, converted to private dwellings), which then stood at the corner of Cooper's Lane, was an important coaching inn on the main route from London to the Channel.

"The auction advertisement held at the County Records office Maidstone reads:

'Brabourne Lees Inclosure
To be sold by Auction
By Thomas Thurston
At the Woolpack Public House at Stone Hill in Smeeth on Monday 31st of March 1823 at 12 o'clock subject to such conditions as will then and there be produced About 40 Acres of Freehold Common Land in the Parish of Smeeth Bircholt and Sellindge in lots as under.'

"As an example of the auction, the land now the site of Cherry Trees, Lilyvale, Smeeth, was described as:

'Lot 10, A piece of Common Land in the Parish of Smeeth fronting the Turnpike Road near the Bridge by Stone Hill, Eastward and to an Occupation Road near the Bridge leading into the land of William Harris southward [William Harris owned the house named Washington at that time].'

"We know little about the auction, except that lot 10 was sold for £76 to a Mr John Scott, a gentleman of Ashford, probably related to the local Scott dynasty. It seems that most plots were purchased by local landowners, as few of the villagers would have had the finance to purchase land, still less to build a farmhouse or cottage. It is apparent from the enclosure map that many of the lots were bought by local nobility, including Sir Edward Knatchbull and William Deeds.

"In November 1842, the South Eastern Railway reached Ashford from London. In June 1843, the line to Folkestone was completed and a station was built in Smeeth parish, about two miles to the west of Brabourne Lees. Opening in October 1852, Smeeth Station added significantly to the economic advantage of Brabourne Lees."

THE FIRST WORLD WAR (1914-18)

The men of the village responded to Kitchener's call and went to war. Sadly, 22 men from Brabourne and Smeeth lost their lives, and are suitably commemorated by the British Legion in our local churches.

One of those from Brabourne who lost his life was George Brooks's father, also George, who died a month before the war ended, leaving behind a wife and three children, Ruth, George and Naomi (Nancy), the youngest, who was born shortly after he died. The hardship caused by losing a husband and father by such young children, and in a world where social security didn't exist, was devastating, and George never forgot the pain of it all.

Mr Birchett, a former churchwarden at Brabourne, fought in the First World War, and Dick Andrews confirmed Mr Birchett as one of those in the trenches in the picture opposite.

War memorial in Brabourne Cishurch

George and Ruth Brooks 1913

In the trenches. Mr Birchett is third from left

## RECORDING THE TREASURES IN BRABOURNE CHURCH
Jean Bates writes about Brabourne's NADFAS record:

Jean Bates

"Brabourne's ancient church holds many treasures, and details of every single object of furnishing or decoration that is of historic significance have been photographed and extensively described by recorders from the National Association of Decorative & Fine Arts Societies (NADFAS). NADFAS has branches all over the country and its Ashford members meet monthly at Aldington Village Hall to hear professional speakers give talks on all kinds of art. Many branches of NADFAS also have an affiliated Church Recording Group; Ashford's one is led by Mrs Jenny Beaugie. Brabourne Church was the second church to be 'recorded' by this group, between 1993 and 1998. The resulting NADFAS record is kept in the parish by the Brabourne Parochial Church Council (PCC). Other copies are stored with the Diocesan Records Office, the Council for the Care of Churches and the Victoria and Albert Museum Library.

"The format of the record is set by the national body so that there is uniformity between all the records throughout the country. It is a comprehensive inventory of the contents of the church and the record is arranged under the following chapters:

Memorials, Metalwork, Stonework, Woodwork, Textiles, Paintings, Library, Windows and Miscellaneous

"The record is of great value to anyone interested in the history of Brabourne Church, with its fine Norman architecture, unique belfry staircase and Norman stained-glass window still in its original setting in the chancel. The church contains many memorials to the Scott family, dating from the 13th century to the 18th century, including the Scott chapel, a heart shrine, a large memorial altar and four floor brasses. The record can be viewed on application to the PCC.

"The local Ashford NADFAS recorders were: Jenny Beaugie, Ann Finucane, Wendy Glover, Dorothy Johnstone-Hogg, Virginia Latham, Judith Moore, Piers Raymond, Moyna Snelson, Jan Talbot, Barbara Tate, Cicely Thompson; the record was typed by Jean Bates."

## CONSERVING BRABOURNE CHURCH: THE FRIENDS OF ST MARY'S CHURCH, EAST BRABOURNE
Registered with the Charity Commission for England and Wales
Registered No. 1095462 on 17th January, 2003

The Friends of Brabourne Church (The Friends) was conceived by John Varrier, of East Brabourne, in 2001, when he was still churchwarden. He envisaged this body as an independent organisation run by people who were interested in the maintenance of Brabourne Church but who were not members of the PCC and not necessarily regular church-goers.

Its creation came about as, at that time, extensive repairs to the fabric of Brabourne Church were required and members of the PCC were looking for financial help with the proposed work. Peter Clayton, who was chairman of Brabourne Parish Council at the time, suggested to John that the church should register with Entrust, so that it could apply for a grant through the government Land-Fill Tax Credit Scheme, which had been introduced by the Inland Revenue as a way of improving the image of firms that operate land-fill sites. It meant that a church could apply to be registered as an "environmental body" and then apply to a local land-fill site for a grant. The PCC duly registered and applied for a grant of £17,000 from a local firm called Cleanaway for the re-plastering and decoration of the vestry and new heaters for the church and vestry. However, it was necessary to provide Cleanaway with 10% (£1,700) of the proposed grant from a third-party donor, so John suggested to the PCC that The Friends should be established, which could then become the "third party" to facilitate the grant.

The Friends was informally established in October 2001 and Tom Bates took responsibility for drawing up a constitution and getting The Friends registered with the Charity Commission, which was finally accomplished in January 2003.

The Constitution, which was adopted on 16th June, 2002, states that:
"The Aims and Objectives of the Friends are primarily to raise funds for the maintenance, repair and restoration of the Grade I listed XII Century Norman church, its furnishings, fittings, fixtures and churchyard in order to preserve it as a place of Christian worship now, and for future generations. Secondarily, to provide occasional financial help at the request of the PCC, and at the discretion of the Friends Committee, to meet specific costs which may arise from time to time in order to maintain facilities for worship in the Parish."

Michael Marshall generously donated £2,400 to start up The Friends in memory of his late wife, Tessa, which included her bequest of £1,000.

The Inaugural General Meeting of The Friends was eventually held on 17th March, 2003, with Tom Bates as Chairman, John Talbot as Vice-Chairman, Derek Gurr as Honorary Secretary, Mark Hollis as Honorary Treasurer and John Varrier as the President. More recently Lyn Browne has been Chairman, aided by Di Castle as Honorary Secretary. An annual subscription of £10 was established from the start, supplemented by Gift Aid from taxpayers.

Tom Bates, current Chairman of The Friends of St Mary's

Extensive projects in the church have been funded by The Friends since its inauguration. These have included the installation of a loop system, major building work in and around the church and tower, roof repairs, the redecoration of the church and help with the purchase of stacking chairs. Most recently, The Friends have contributed significantly to the installation of toilet facilities and a water supply to the vestry, which, for the record, came into operation on 12th February, 2013. The Church architect, George Denny of Elmsted, designed the new loos and the construction work was carried out by Richard Kennett of Kencarp Construction Ltd.

We at Brabourne Church are very grateful to all of you who have supported The Friends so generously and we hope your support will continue.

XTRA, XTRA.....Army Camp XTRA

Richard Wood has kindly lent us an original copy of the sale catalogue for items from the army camp at Brabourne Lees. This wonderful government document, which arrived too late to be incorporated earlier in the chapter, details every item put up for sale and is clear evidence of the size of the camp. Among the many items listed for sale from the hospital which comprised seven wards, two surgeries, a wash house and a yard were deal bedsteads with sacking bottoms, fenders, pokers, tongs, bellows, pails and urine tubs, jacks with pulleys, weights, chains and lines and chamber pots.

The barracks, labelled A to O, numbered 15 in all. Among the sale items from these were berths, arm racks, rails, shelves, floor boards, weather boarding, sheet copper, lead and iron scrapers on or near buildings, roof tiles and inside laths, plaster and mortar rubbish. All items were also put up for sale from granaries, stores, black holes, stables and yards - and the sale began on Monday, 22nd of July, 1816.

2

# BRABOURNE CHURCH IN MORE RECENT TIMES

## A FEEL FOR THE PAST FROM CHURCH RECORDS

How many people have worshipped in Brabourne Church during its history of 850 years or so? We shall never know, but it must be in the thousands, even though this is a small community. The plaques and memorials in the church testify to some of these worshippers, and many more who did not "qualify" for a memorial inside the church lie in the churchyard, where a quick search reveals well-known family names alongside many that have disappeared. Too many others lie in unmarked graves, with no hint as to their identity and with so much of their history gone.

We are grateful for the records that generations past have left for us, helping us to glimpse the church's past, and their value to us must surely increase our commitment to record life in the church for generations to come. The extracts below from a variety of church records are a testimony to those who took the trouble to chronicle details of different kinds. We begin with extracts from records of the 18th and 19th centuries. These were assembled by Miss Joy Finn, who was for many years the secretary to the PCC.

## EXTRACTS FROM EARLY CHURCH REGISTERS
Joy Finn writes:

"In the days when church registers were often carelessly kept, lost or allowed to perish through damp and parasites, Brabourne Church was fortunate to have had a succession of incumbents from 1560 to the present day who kept meticulous records and registers and preserved them for our generation [and those to come]. The following are a few items of local interest and for public reading."

AD1724
[The Church] Paid for destruction of vermin. Fox 2/6. Grey Badger 2/6. Polecat 4d.'

Churchwarden's Account Book AD1729
Gave to 11 seamen ship blown with gunpowder 2.6. [probably 2/6] Gave to a man that had no tongue 1.6. Gave to a man that had no arms 1.0. Gave to 2 men that had been robbed and burnt 2.0. Paid to 20 men that had been slaves 2.0.

The Rev. Joseph Price was collated [appointed] March 2nd 1767. Vicar for 19 years. He wrote his diary in shorthand. 14 vols. Using the same system as Samuel Pepys the system of Shelton 1638. He was a shrewd man of business as can be seen in his reckoning of tythe. He estimated carefully the merits and demerits of three women in consideration of asking one of them to be his bride but finally decided against all three. Vol. 6 is extant. One book is kept in this church [no longer so] and the other in Canterbury.

AD1771
April 5th        William Gilbert
April 10th       Robert Gilbert    "Children that died of a putrid fever"
April 13th       Mary Gilbert
April 15th       John Gilbert

AD1810
Thomas Hoggins Esquire of the 85th Regt. 11th Jan. Buried. Brother of Sarah, wife of Henry 1st Marquess of Exeter. Shot in duel with John Hilton Gent. Against whom a verdict of wilful murder was returned on a Coroner's inquest.

AD1811
W.B. The population of Brabourne returned this year, including soldiers' wives and children, was: Men & Boys 328. Women & Girls 340. Total 668.

Memorial

The disparity of growing excess of numbers on the Register of the Parish of Brabourne so remarkable in this period & which with more or less effect, is visible for the eleven years next following, is to be attributed to the erection of Barracks upon the Common called Brabourne Lees, for three Regiments of Infantry & two Troops of Cavalry. In the autumn of the year 1803; & the military occupation of these barracks towards the close of the same year, the Vicar, to obviate vague and uncertain conjectures in future times on the sudden augmentation of entrances in the Registers of the Parish has thought fit here to insert the above memorial & further to state & record that in the year 1816, the said Barracks were sold by public auction, and instantly taken down & removed; & the effect of them, so far regarded the Registers of the Parish, henceforth, altogether done away with.

A Pursehouse. Vicar.

## FROM MORE RECENT CHURCH RECORDS

Records dating back over a century show that the work of the church in the parish has continued remarkably unchanged and that a stream of officers of the church – churchwardens, sidesmen, sextons and many others – have worked assiduously with their priests to sustain the spiritual life of the church and the material quality of the church building. The Brabourne Vestry Book 1872 shows that Vestry Meetings were held once a year, and the limited details provided in these are all we have of what happened in the life of the church. It wasn't until 1920 that the Parochial Church Council (PCC) was "created". This met more frequently during the year and, as a consequence, we get a better picture of how the church was being managed and the fabric of the building conserved. The annual church meeting, however, retained its old title of the Vestry Meeting.

There follow selected extracts from the Brabourne Vestry Book 1872 and Parochial Church Council, 1920 to April 1st, 1937:

## AN AMBITIOUS PLAN FOR A NEW VESTRY
At a Vestry Meeting held on Friday, 28th April, 1911, we are told...

"Before the Vestry [Meeting] opened, Members present thoroughly studied the ground through which the proposed drain from the Stokehole would be carried; and on which the proposed New Priest's and Choir Vestry is to be erected [the stokehole is underneath the new toilets]. The Vicar [the Reverend Thomas Lindsay Stack] having produced the Plan of New Vestry, and fully explained the disadvantage of the present arrangement of using (e.g.) the N. Porch as a Vestry, etc., and having read a letter [dated 22nd Dec. 1910, reproduced below] he had written to the Bishop of Dover, which Letter, he stated had been shown to the Archbishop, then put the following Proposal:-

"That a Faculty be applied for:-
(1)     To lay a proper drain, instead of Pump now in use, to drain the Water from Stokehole to the stream of S. Cyriac.
(2)     To cut a Door in roof of Stokehole, and put in a Flooring over Furnace
(a)     To serve as a Place for keeping the Bier etc. for Sexton, and
(b)     Storing Coke.
(3)     To build a New Priest's and Choir Vestry:- as per Plan [accessible through the south door, as shown on the plan later in this section].

"It was agreed on the proposition of Mr. Worrell [former headmaster at Brabourne School], seconded by Mr. Wetherell [then headmaster at Brabourne and shortly to be headmaster at Smeeth School] that the Faculty be applied for."

## LETTER TO THE BISHOP SETTING OUT THE NEED FOR A NEW VESTRY

"Brabourne Vicarage
22 Dec. 1910

"My dear Lord Bishop,

With reference to the request of the Churchwardens and myself, that permission be granted us to make the above addition to the Church of S. Mary, the Virgin; I beg, herewith, as requested by your Lordship to submit in writing the Reasons, which have led to the request being made:-

Proposed Addition of Room on South Side of S. Mary's Church, Brabourne — for the purpose of providing a Priest's Vestry, Choir Vestry, Place for Sexton to keep the Bier.

Brabourne Vicarage
22 Dec: 10

My dear Lord Bishop

With reference to the request of the Churchwardens & myself, that permission be granted us to make the above addition to the Church of S. Mary, the Virgin; I beg, herewith, as requested by your Lordship to submit in writing the Reasons, which have led to the request being made:—

The Present Vestry is not really a Vestry at all; being the Porch, in front of the N. Door, & used as the regular Entrance by the Congregation until about 30 years ago, when the then Vicar made it the Priest's Vestry, Fifteen years ago, when a Surpliced Choir was introduced, it became the Choir Vestry as well. It is very small, being only 10ft X 8'. 8". The Tower is not available, as the Ringers ring on the Ground Floor; & it would be practically impossible to use this Space, as a Vestry, while the Bells were being rung.

The N. Door is in many ways the most suitable Entrance for the Congregation, especially on dark nights, being at the end of a straight brick path, leading direct from the main road, through the Entrance Gate of the Churchyard. This Door was so long the usual mode of Entrance, that I have recently learned, that, when reserved as a Vestry, it was explained, at the time, that Funerals might still pass through this Door, if Mourners expressed a wish to do so.

A return therefore, to this Mode of Entrance would be in a very true sense a return to "Ancient Custom".

Correspondence on the proposed vestry from Brabourne Church archives

"The Present Vestry is not really a Vestry at all; being the Porch, in front of the N. Door, and used as the regular Entrance by the Congregation until about 30 years ago [c1880], when the then Vicar made it the Priest's Vestry. Fifteen years ago [c1895], when Surplice Choir was introduced, it became the Choir Vestry as well. It was very small being only 10ft x 8'8". The Tower is not available, as the Ringers ring on the Ground Floor; and it would be practically impossible to use this Space as a Vestry while the Bells were being rung.

"North Door: The N. Door is in many ways the most suitable Entrance for the Congregation, especially on dark nights, being at the end of a straight brick path, leading direct from the main road, through the Entrance Gate of the Churchyard. This Door was so long the usual mode of Entrance that I have recently learned that when reserved as a Vestry, it was explained, at the time, that Funerals might still pass through this Door if Mourners expressed a wish to do so. A return, therefore, to this Mode of Entrance would be in a very true sense a return to 'Ancient Custom'.

"No proper place is provided for the Sexton to keep the Bier etc. in. Part of the Belfry is curtained off for this purpose. The present 'Holder of the Office [of Sexton]' lives near the Church, and keeps Wheelbarrow and certain implements at his own house. In the event of a new Sexton being appointed, if his house were some distance from the Church, further accommodation would have to be found in the Belfry, as the present space is quite full now; Brushes etc. of Church Cleaners being kept here also.

"Another place being provided – The Curtain, 8ft high, drawn across whole N. Side of Belfry, could then be removed, and thus thrown open again in its entirety, the 'Ancient Old Staircase' to Belfry Loft – a very marked feature of the Church.

"I now come to the proposed New Room – Site, Exterior, Interior (page 54) South Door. The S. Door opens directly on the Churchyard. This side of the Church is practically outside all range of Vision from the road; there being no Footpath even round this side; and only fields beyond. Further, in suggesting that a Room be placed in front of this Door, in the form of a Porch; we feel we should only be doing to the S. Aisle (built in 15th Century) what was done to the N. Side of the Nave (built in 12th Century) when the present Porch was added, certainly not before the Middle of 16th Century, and probably a good deal later.

"Exterior: While an 'Oak' structure on a Stone foundation, as now at N. Door would of course be much less [spelling 'lefs'] expensive, we should greatly prefer, if

"Permission be granted to build, to erect the new Room with Stone Walls and Tiled Roof, as at N. Door; as being much more permanent and durable. Unless considered absolutely necessary, by reason of S. Aisle having 'Lead' Roof, we should much prefer not to have to put a 'Lead Roof' on proposed new Structure, as the addition to the Cost of Whole, would be considerably over £30. Personally, I do not think it would look as well and have rather more of the appearance of a 'Lean to'.

"The Proposed New Building would stand between 2 Buttresses, abutting them.
The Space in front of S. Door – between the Buttresses is flat; and so far as known, no one is likely to raise any objection.
Outside Measurements 18'10" x 17'

[Clearly the Reverend Stack had already had discussions with the Bishop as the section below speaks of an 'Alternative Plan' which appears to incorporate amendments suggested by the Bishop.]

"Interior and Exterior. I enclose herewith an 'Alternative Plan' – drawn up since I saw your Lordship – Taking away 'Lights and Door' from S. Side of Porch; which I think your Lordship rather thought altered the character of the Building. This Plan also adds considerably to the space inside:-
1.      No 'Windows' or Doors on South Side.
2.      Entrance to Sexton's Portion altered from S. Side to W. Side.
3.      Besides being much more convenient to him – This does away with the need of 3 ft. path on S. Side as in original Plan – and so permits of Building being brought out this extra 3 ft. Graves prevent going any further in this direction, so that if the Path be kept then Building would have to be that much shorter.
4.      Space now is saved on Entering Vestry from Church – passage in original Plan being done away.
5.      Folding Doors, or Movable Partition would be arranged, so that on occasion, the Priest's Vestry could be thrown into the Whole – for Meetings etc. with the exception of the 3'6" (depth of Sexton's Portion) which always been reserved.
6.      Windows for Choir Vestry on W. Side; for Priest's Vestry on E. Side.
        Trusting that I have made the above sufficiently clear; and that the Reasons will appear sufficiently cogent.

"I remain your Lordship's obedient Servant,

Thos Lindsay Stack."

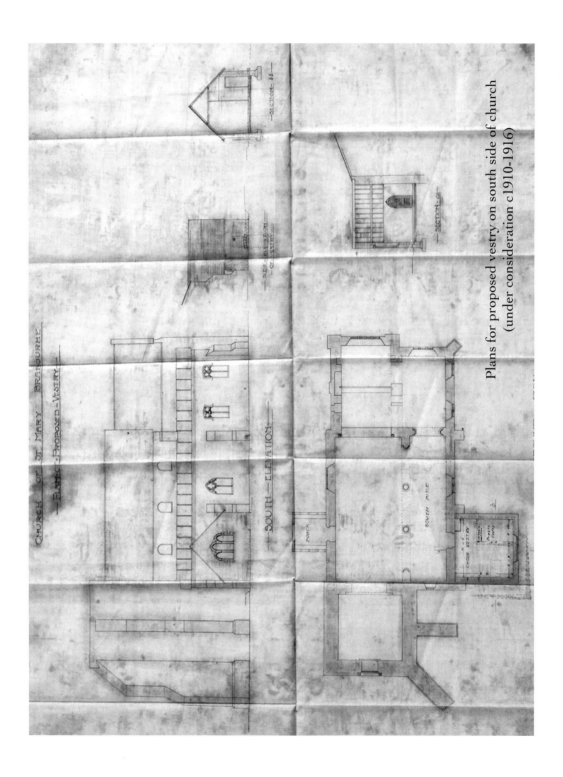

Plans for proposed vestry on south side of church
(under consideration c1910-1916)

At the next Vestry Meeting on 19th April, 1912, the following was recorded under minutes:

"As arriving out of Minutes Vicar said Stokehole drain had been laid, and proved in every way satisfactory: also that it was hoped soon to put New Flooring above Stokehole. The Vicar also produced Faculty, being a Confirmatory Faculty for New Drainage and New Flooring in Stokehole, and New Vestry."

Having accommodated the bishop's proposed amendments to his plan, and having obtained a Faculty and raised over half the money needed for the project (below), the Reverend Stack was clearly committed to getting the vestry built. However, before it was completed he moved to Newchurch and, reading between the lines of his letter to the next incumbent, the Reverend Lockyear, it does seem that the Reverend Stack wasn't entirely convinced that the new priest at Brabourne would see the vestry project through... but this is just our interpretation.

> "Newchurch Rectory
> Dec. 29th  1916

"Dear Lockyear,

"Since writing [to] you on the Matter of the New Vestry, and enclosing a Statement, I have been rather troubled as to whether I had made certain matters sufficiently clear. I determined, therefore, to draw up another, which I think makes a better Statement of all matters connecting with the Scheme, up to the present time.

"It is not a new Statement, as regards the figures. They are the same as you will see. As regards the first Statement, therefore, you may put the same in [the] Waste Paper Basket.

"Hoping to hear from you soon as regards to Induction.

> "I remain,

> Yours sincerely,

> T.L. Stack"

In his letter to the new incumbent, the Reverend Stack enclosed an estimate from the architect (A.E. Lacey, A.R.I.B.A. Architect and Surveyor, Ashford, Kent) of the costs of the work together with donations received and promised. These show that he had raised over half the cost of the project, leaving him to find a further £96/1/11. Though a significant sum for the time, the vestry was clearly within his sights.

"Estimated costs as of 25th March, 1914:

|  | "£ | s | d |
|---|---|---|---|
| Mr. Bourne's Tender | 169 | 0 | 0 |
| Faculty | 5 | 5 | 0 |
| Drainage of Stokehole | 7 | 7 | 8 |
| Architect's Fees | 10 | 10 | 0 |
| Advertisement | – | 11 | 6 |
| Cross | 3 | 0 | 0 |
| Heating | 5 | 0 | 0 |
| Surplice Rail | 2 | 0 | 0 |
|  | 202 | 14 | 2 |
| Minor additional costs | 6 | 2 | 3 |
| Total estimated cost | 208 | 16 | 5 |

Receipts:

|  |  |  |  |
|---|---|---|---|
| Captn. Perry Ayscough | £25 | 0 | 0 |
| Sale of work (1912) | 22 | 3 | 0 |
| G.B. Scott Esq. | 3 | 0 | 0 |
| Rev. T.L. Scott |  | 10 | 6 |
| Miss G.T. Scott | 1 | 1 | 0 |
| The Misses Matthew | 10 | 0 | 0 |
| Mrs. Stack | 10 | 0 | 0 |
| Rev. T.L. Stack | 5 | 5 | 0 |
| Mr. Masters |  | 5 | 0 |
| Per Rev. T.L. Stack (A Friend Name given if scheme carried out) | 25 | 0 | 0 |
|  | £102 | 4 | 6 |
| Munro Scott Esq. (promised) | 10 | 10 | 0 |
| Total raised and promised | £112 | 14 | 6 |

"The Sum now required to build the Vestry is, therefore, £96 1   11, apart from any variation in the price of Material, etc. as provided for when Mr. Bourne and others tendered.

"The above is a summary of things as they stand, and my position in the matter, if and when the Vestry is completed, or put in hand.

"The point that I also wish to make clear is my position, if, for any reason the Vestry Scheme is given up.

1)      Captn. Perry-Ayscough.  With his knowledge, and approval, after work was completed, £7-7-8 of his Donation was applied to the Drainage.  With regard to the remainder – we can leave the consideration of it, until there is occasion, if ever there should be.

2)      Sale Work.  It remains with who were responsible for it to settle where the Funds should be given.

3)      The Scott Family.  I hold that I am bound, if the Scheme is given up, to ask what should be done with their Donations, subscribed, or promised.

4)      All the other monies remain at my disposal, and would probably be employed elsewhere.

Thos. Lindsay Stack,

Newchurch Rectory,
Dec. 29.1916"


## WE NEVER HEAR ABOUT THE NEW VESTRY AGAIN

Why wasn't the new vestry built?  We shall probably never know.  In spite of having a Faculty and over half the necessary funds the project seems to have been abandoned with no explanation in the minutes of the Vestry Meetings.  Shortage of money during the First World War could have brought the vestry project to a halt though there is no evidence of this.  It seems more likely that the new incumbent, the Reverend Lockyear, did not share his predecessor's enthusiasm for the project and indeed, in his letter to the Rev Lockyear, the Rev Stack seemed to anticipate this.  It is also possible that other, more pressing problems relating to the fabric of the church were given priority: during a visit from the Archdeacon during 1915 he described the ivy as being "overgrown" and in need of cutting back – and this would have been a continuing cost.  We are also told that between 1917 and 1919 the fence on the north side of the churchyard was repaired, the organ received attention and the ceiling in the south aisle was removed.  The minutes of the Easter Vestry meeting on 25th April, 1919 state that, "After discussion as to the extras spent on the organ, and the removal of the ceiling in the south aisle, and the extra cost of necessaries owing to the war, the accounts [which showed a balance in hand of £1/17/6½d] were considered very satisfactory."   At this same Vestry Meeting on April 25th, 1919, it

Ivy on the tower was clearly a problem in 1907. It was a
problem in 1915, and according to the Rev Ray Sheekey (see
Son et Lumière section), ivy "festooned the tower" in 1961.

was decided to "commence on the preliminaries" for the restoration of the Tower, a
project that would eventually cost over £600 just a few years later:

"On the proposition of Mr. L. Finn [Anthony Finn's grandfather], seconded by Mr.
A.J. Moul [the local baker who lived at what is now Coquet Lodge, by the church
gates], the meeting unanimously agreed to apply for a Faculty for the following:-

(a)     Restoration of the Tower
(b)     Brass Plate in Memory of those from
        Brabourne who fell in the War.
(c)     To recast and rehang an old bell in
        the Tower
(d)     To erect a Pulpit, the gift of Miss
        Perry Ayscough
        [in memory of her mother and
        younger brother].

"The Vicar was requested by the Vestry
[Committee] to apply for the Faculty, to call
a meeting of the Parishioners on Friday,
May 2nd, 1919, to consider details as to the
proposed restoration of the Tower and to
write [to] W.D. Caroe, Esq., the Diocesan
Architect, with a view to his reporting to
the Archbishop and the Vestry the repairs
necessary and their cost."

Pulpit in memory of the Rev Perry
Ayscough's wife and son

## THE ESTABLISHMENT OF THE PAROCHIAL CHURCH COUNCIL

A Parochial Church Council was established in Brabourne in 1920 and the minutes tell us that: "The first Meeting of the Parochial Church Council was held on May 6th, 1920 in the Trinity Chapel [Scott Chapel]. On the proposition of Mr T. Thornby, seconded by Mr S. Finn, Mr F. Woollett was unanimously elected Vice-Chairman of the Council. Mrs L. Finn was elected Secretary to the Council."

PCCs succeeded Vestry Meetings. They were introduced by the Church of England Assembly (Powers) Act in 1919. The Parochial Church Council was intended as a body at parish level that would better enable the lay members of the congregation to be represented.

A Special Meeting of the Parochial Church Council was held on 18th May, 1922, in the belfry to hear the report of the diocesan architect on the condition of the tower and the repairs necessary to restore the same. The vicar at the time was the Reverend S.K. Lockyear, Mr T.W. Thornby, the vicar's warden, and Mr F. Woollett, the parish warden. Among the 16 members of the PCC and the 12 sidesmen who attended the meeting, there were many familiar family names, including Mr L. Finn, Mr S. Finn, Mrs S. Finn, Mr A.H. Hammon, Mrs A. Hammon, Mr Powell, Mrs E.T. Hammon, Mrs Thornby and Mr N.R. Weekes (after whose family Weekes Lane, West Brabourne, was named). Minutes of the meeting reveal:

"The architect (W.D. Caroe) reported that he had carefully examined the Tower, and found that the Lead Roof required recasting and relaying, roof timbers repaired and corbelled, cracks in walls keyed, walls stopped and pointed and parapet coped. The ends of several floor beams of the Bell Chamber are defective and require a girder for support and possible renewal, and the Bell framing to be bolted up and braced as necessary." Predictably, there was deep concern about funding the renovations, so a general appeal for funds, which was sanctioned by the bishop, was launched, "to supplement the sum, approximately £400, already in hand as a result of Local Efforts". The minutes of 7th August, 1923, record that, "The Archdeacon of Maidstone had very kindly used his influence in obtaining a grant of £50 for our Tower renovation from the Incorporate Church Building Society after they had declined to help us."

Estimates for the work, as shown in the minutes, were as follows:

| | |
|---|---|
| "Messrs Browning | £1,360 |
| C.I. Epps | £820 |
| Messrs Crowne and Paramour | £820 |
| Whiting Bros. | £700 |
| Messrs Corben | £668" |

With the proposal to accept Corben's estimate, the following question arose in the minutes of 14th August, 1923: "Had we enough money[?]. The vicar…read out how much we had in hand (£634.8.2) and said that £50 was promised from our Diocesan Building Society and everything was all officially in order…[W]e had, practically speaking, £700." This was sufficient to pay the bill, thanks largely to the public appeal. Following the renovation, it is said the church was re-insured for the sum of £5,000, with the exclusion of the chancel. The insurers were, of course, Ecclesiastical Insurance.

At the same PCC meeting, "Mr. Powell wished it to be recorded how extraordinary it was, that we were told we should require [about] £1,100 to restore our Tower, and yet now we had an estimate from a well known Builder to do the work for £668". (Similar questions were asked in 2006, when we received a range of estimates for work deemed necessary following the quinquennial inspection, so clearly, nothing changes. One of the main differences was that, in 2006, the bill for the work on the tower was closer to £14,000.) Mr Powell also said "how pleased we must feel that the Tower question was so happily settled and he proposed a hearty vote of thanks to the Vicar and Mrs. Lockyear for their share of the work it had occasioned" (PCC minutes, 14th August, 1923).

The names of Keith Finn and Arthur Ball
are to be found high above the organ

Inscriptions of other painters and decorators who
have worked in the church; all are transcribed below

Keith Finn and Arthur Ball, 1937
Jones, Canterbury, painter, 1875
R.A. Russell, painter, 1965
Kevin Lee and G.B. Haworth, painters, 2008

## THE LEGACY OF CONGREGATIONS PAST, STILL EVIDENT IN THE CHURCH TODAY

Although the following extracts are not strictly from church records, they do recall former members of the church, some of whom may have been known to readers and who have contributed significantly to the life of the church.

In late 1931, the following article in the Folkestone Herald, entitled "A Visit to Brabourne Church: additional notes" recalls former members of the church and the village.

"*The Sanctuary lamp* in Brabourne Church was given by Miss E. Foat in memory of her family, who lived at Church Farm.  The Misses Foat were energetic workers in the parish many years ago.

*"The Sanctuary chairs*, carved by Mr. James Weekes (father of Norman Weekes), were given in the year 1875, and the lectern carved and given by the same donor a year later.

Sanctuary chair and lectern carved by James Weekes, donated in 1875/6

"A correspondent recalls the names of by-gone residents of Brabourne, whose sons and grandsons in many instances are still living in the neighbourhood. Mr. George Finn was sidesman and a bell-ringer for many years [George Finn was the father of Leonard Finn, grandfather of Betty, Joy and Keith, and great grandfather of Anthony Finn]; Mr. George Worrell will be remembered as the village schoolmaster and as a member of the choir [George Worrell's youngest daughter, Ada, married Leonard Finn]. His grandson Master Keith Finn carries on the tradition of leading choirboy, and is also a server.

"Mr. Charles Butcher, the Sexton [who lived in the cottage that is now part of Coquet Lodge], is remembered on account of the emphasis he placed upon his time. The Vicar and Churchwardens were obliged to give way and accept the time given by Mr. Butcher, and he would stop ringing the bell or continue for just as long as he thought fit!

"Mr. Kingsland lived close to the Church and kept the post-office, general store and bakery [in the house that is now Coquet Lodge]. He was also the carrier. Mr. Daniels had the busy forge of those days, namely the early 'eighties'. [The Forge is now a bungalow.]

"Mr. Edmund Hammon, Mr. Thomas Hills, and Mr. Walter Andrews [who lived at Ivy Cottage, owned the Tile Kiln in Canterbury Road] are all names which will be recalled by old inhabitants."

As former secretary to the PCC, Joy Finn detailed in the Brabourne Church archive the various gifts donated or created specially for the church by parishioners:

The children's banner

### The children's banner
This was purchased from church funds in 1950 during the Reverend Wagstaffe's time. At that time there were many children who attended morning service. The banner was dedicated "To the Glory of God" by the children of Brabourne and Bircholt and was a token of their loving service. Betty Finn was said to be a "leading light" among the children at this time, always encouraging them. The banner also went to the cathedral once or twice, for choir festivals or children's gatherings.

### The hassocks
These were covered by parishioners in 1972, during the Reverend Sheekey's time. Mrs Clare Langworthy of Church Farm was the "queen bee" and made no fewer than 18, Miss Nellie Hills (no.2, Holly Cottages) came second with 11. In total, 89 hassocks were covered, 61 of which bear initials, as follows:

CL – Mrs Celia Langworthy (and for her husband) Commander Langworthy
NL – which Joy Finn indicates is Miss Nell Hills (should this be NH?)
DL – which Joy Finn indicates is Miss Dorothy Hills (should this be DH?)
WB – Miss W Barnes
ED – Mrs E Dryland
W – Willett (Fred Willett)
EH – Miss E Hincks
MO – Mrs M Ord
AB – Mrs A Birchett
JF – Joy Finn

Joy told us of other initials that she has not been able to put names to – AGT, E?AG, REB, SW, DIH, LML and DR – so, if anyone can identify any of these please let us know.

*The lace for the two cloths for the Scott Chapel*
This was made by Miss Bessie Jamieson of Smeeth. The lace was sent to Ireland to be mounted on linen.

*The fawn linen cover*
This is the cover to be found on the altar. It was given by the Reverend and Mrs Sheekey in about 1976, at the time of their silver wedding anniversary.

Candlesticks, oak cross and fawn linen cover on the altar

*Cushions for the pulpit*
Joy Finn made these in about 1970, when the Reverend Sheekey decided to do away with a very antique spotted brass book rest. Mowbrays came up with patterns of material to match the falls on the lectern. Joy added that the falls on the lectern "have been used all my life". Just for the record, Joy was born in 1913.

*Pair of dark oak candlesticks*
Given by Keith Finn in the spring on 1995, these stand 21½in tall on a 6in circular base. There were to replace those that had been stolen.

*Light oak cross with three steps*
This was given by Mrs J. Clifton, July 1995.

*The Royal Arms*
"Attention was called to the Royal Arms in the School by Mr. V.J.B. Torr on a visit to Brabourne, and the redecoration of the School was a good opportunity for moving them back to their proper place in the Church, where they now hang over the South door. The custom of displaying Royal Arms in the Church is an old one, but was not made compulsory till after the Restoration of Charles II, in 1660.

"Our Arms belong to the time of George II (1727-1760). The supporters of the Royal Shield are, on the left the English Lion, on the right the Unicorn, which came from the Scottish Arms with James I (James VI of Scotland) in 1603, with a rose and thistle respectively. The Arms are: first quarter, the three leopards of England and the lion rampant of Scotland; second quarter, three fleur-de-lys of France (our kings were styled King of France till 1801); third quarter, the harp of Ireland; fourth quarter (the German Arms of the Hanoverian George), three leopards (Brunswick), a lion rampant (Lunenburgh), a horse courant (Westphalia), in the centre the crown of Charlemagne."

The Royal Arms, which hang above the south door

Extract above from a published document probably during the 1930s, which provides an explanation of Brabourne's Royal Arms, which hang over the south door of the church. The extract was filed in Parish Notes collected by the Reverend C.R.L. McDowall, parish priest at Brabourne. Exact source unknown.

## THE BIRCHOLT MISSION ROOM

Bircholt is the sort of place one could miss quite easily if one did not know it was there, yet it has a significant history. According to Hasted (1799), Bircholt is mentioned in the Domesday Book, being spelled as Berisolt, Berisout, Belice, Briseode and Bilissold. It was once "part of the lands which were held by barony of Dover castle, and made up the barony called the Constabularie" (Hasted, 1799). The Hundred of Bircholt contained within its lands the parish of Bircholt, which had its own church dedicated to St Margaret, and part of the parishes of Brabourne and Hastingleigh. The church appears to have been standing in 1518, when a legacy was left for its repair, but by 1578, Hasted noted that, "the return made at the visitation [by a member of the clergy – nowadays it would probably be the archdeacon] was that there was no church standing". Bircholt also had its farms and cottages, most of which are now part of the Brabourne Estate, and from 1875 it had a Mission Room, though this has now been demolished. In 1934, the parish of Bircholt was amalgamated with the parish of Brabourne.

The Bircholt Mission Room was known affectionately by many as the place where the Sunday School was held. In the 1930s and 1940s, Betty Dryland (Lavender), together with some 12 to 14 other children, would go to Brabourne Church every Sunday morning and then to the Mission Room Sunday School on Sunday afternoons. Adults were always just as welcome there, too. Joy Finn would play the organ and the services were conducted by Mr Seekings, attended by his daughter Mildred, who lived at Birchdene for many years. After Mr Seekings retired, Mrs Coleman and her daughter Elizabeth took over from him.

After Mrs Coleman retired in the early 1970s Christine Gurr took over, helped by Sally Furneaux (Willett). Needless to say, Sally had been volunteered to help by her mother, Dorothy Willett, and although Sally enjoyed Sunday School, she reflected that it meant that she always had to get up early on Sundays and that it took up a significant part of her weekend. However, in those days, "you would never have dreamed of refusing to help". Sally loved the children who went to the Bircholt Mission, including Simon Gurr and the Trowell children, and in particular David Trowell, whom she thought looked like an angel. She remembers how they all loved getting stamps in their attendance books. Sally recalls the dilapidation of the building and its continued deterioration in the months prior to its demolition: the warped and

Map of the Hundreds of Stowting, Street and Heane,
highlighting Bircholt Barony and Franchise

The Bircholt Mission

rotten wooden floors, the damp and mouldy hymn books, and the need to pump the organ to get it going (this was no task for the feeble as it really did have to be pumped). One Sunday, after all the children had been dropped off at the Mission Room, it took ages for Sally and Christine to force the door open. Not long after this the building was closed down.

Everyone who knew the Mission Room was aware that it had been demolished, but no one was quite sure when it happened, so the minutes of Brabourne PCC were an appropriate place to start. The lead up to demolition proved to be a long, drawn-out and complex affair and though of limited interest to those who never knew the Mission Room, we have included all the extracts from Brabourne's PCC minutes that covered the slow demise of this building, because it was of interest to so many who did know it. It appears that the Mission Room was demolished sometime between 24th April and 30th May, 1978, which are the dates of two PCC meetings. The minutes from the former speak of the looming demolition of the Mission Room, and the second of the task having been completed. Diagnosis of the building's unsafe condition seems to have taken place in the summer of 1974, but actual demolition only happened four years later, so why the delay?

For readers who are not familiar with the Mission Room, it was located as follows: on the road from the village hall to the shops in Brabourne Lees there is a small turning on the right to Bircholt Court Farm. The Mission Room was to be found immediately on the left-hand corner with Lees Road. As the pictures above show, it was in a style similar to the Smeeth Institute Hut, which was also reduced to a mere memory when a tree fell on it on Monday, 28th August, 2006.

Impression of the Bircholt Mission by Michael Giles

According to Brabourne PCC minutes, the bell tolled for Bircholt Mission in 1974… 20th February, 1974: "The door was proving difficult to shut and lock, and the Secretary [Joy Finn] was asked to instruct Keith Finn to investigate."

21st May, 1974: "At present [Bircholt Mission] was used weekly but the possibility of holding the Sunday School at Smeeth School was being investigated."

9th September, 1974 (in the intervening months Keith Finn must have reported that the Bircholt Mission room was unsafe and we know that it was condemned by Ecclesiastical Insurance. However, there were no meetings between 21st May and 9th September and so there was no discussion by the PCC on the state of the Mission Room. The minutes of the PCC meeting of 9th September show, however, that the fate of Bircholt Mission was well on the way to being decided): "The Vicar reported that before demolition could be carried out the Church Commissioners required the Deeds of the property, which could not be found. As the building was erected in memory of the late Reverend Perry Ayscough (at Brabourne from 1872-1885), it was thought improbable that these documents were ever the property of the church.

"Mr Varrier proposed, Mr Nation seconded, that in view of the condition and potential danger involved in leaving the building standing, we should pursue, with some vigour, the question of the title deeds or right of ownership, with a view to demolition being carried out at the earliest possible date. Carried."

18th November, 1974: "The search to find the Deeds of the Building had continued without result as had enquiries of The Church Commissioners, The Charity Commission, the Diocese and perusal of our own records. To enable vital demolition to go ahead, the Canterbury Solicitors now suggest an alternative might be to claim that as the building has been carefully maintained over the years by the Vicars and Churchwardens it now belongs to them, and a document to this effect be prepared and signed by Mr H.S. Hammon, a long standing resident of the Parish." (Mr H.S. Hammon lived at Bircholt Farm at that time.)

10th February, 1975: "Unfortunately no progress had been made towards authorising demolition. The Solicitors had had second thoughts on the form for signature. They now wish to include the Diocesan Board of Finance as Legal Custodians together with the Vicar and Church Wardens or Trustee Managers, though the Board would have no financial interest, merely act to support the Trustee Manager who will retain control. The question of land on which the building stands is now in question, and whether any part of the surrounding plot actually belongs to the Church."

1st April, 1975: "Before demolition or disposal of the property can be dealt with the Diocesan Board of Finance insist that a document be drawn up and signed proving that they are Custodian Trustees with the Vicar and Churchwardens of Brabourne, the Managing Trustees. The Solicitors dealing with this are Lee Bolton and Lee. Mr Older queried what was to happen to the land if and when the building was demolished and who was to pay the legal expenses involved. It was decided the matter should go ahead as soon as these points were clear."

12th May, 1975: "The Diocesan Board of Finance at last having accepted responsibility for costs in drawing up the legal document, a Deed of Declaration vesting interest of themselves with the Vicar and Churchwardens, permission was granted for demolition. Mr Varrier proposed, Mr Older seconded this to be carried out."

8th September, 1975: "The demolition permission had now been received and it was thought the work could be commenced."

24th November, 1975: "At last, Deeds of this building have been received, and an appointment made for the Vicar to meet Mr K. Finn on the spot shortly, to discuss demolition."

23rd February, 1976: "Demolition cannot commence until S.E.E. [South Eastern Electricity] Board disconnect the electricity wires. Meanwhile the question of fencing the plot after clearance is subject of correspondence between the Vicar and the Solicitors, Messrs Hallett & Co."

14th September, 1976: "All but large items had been cleared from the Mission Room. Mr Moorhead's discovery of documents in the hands of Messrs Hallett & Co. Solicitors prove that the land the room stands on is the property of the Hatch Estate, and therefore the Vicar and Churchwardens with the Church Commissioners are tenants/trustees only. It was hoped very soon demolition can be ordered."

Once confident that the Mission Room was part of the Mersham Hatch Estate, the Archbishop of Canterbury asked Lord Brabourne if he would agree to the proposed demolition, Lady Brabourne recalled.

14th November, 1977: "The Vicar reported it is hoped the building will be demolished in the not too distant future."

24th April, 1978 (PCC meeting immediately after the Annual Church Meeting): "The Vicar said the demolition could be expected any day. Mr Finn estimated there might be 2000 tiles for which he would pay £65 per thousand. If this estimate was correct there should be no cost for demolition, but we would be £5 in pocket."

30th May, 1978: "[Bircholt Mission Room] had now been demolished and the ground levelled and fenced, and is the property of the Hatch Estate. More than 2000 tiles were salvaged, and of these 670 are now stored, for use on the church." That was the final entry in PCC minutes concerning the Bircholt Mission Room, a comparatively small physical structure but, as mentioned, remembered with a great deal of affection by many of our contributors. They remembered Sunday School there, attending it themselves, taking their children there, and teaching; they remembered going to the dentist there; they remembered cleaning and tidying the Mission and polishing the furniture, the harmonium and the brass. So many also remembered the funeral of four-year-old Gillian Denise, George and Joyce Hickmott's daughter, and little sister of Michael. Gilly and her brother Michael both went to Sunday School at the Mission Room and Michael still has a Bible presented to him by the Reverend Ray Sheekey for good attendance, 1961-62. The village thus has powerful memories of the long-vanished Mission Room, which seemed to occupy a linking position between Smeeth and Brabourne.

Cross from the
Bircholt Mission

A small wooden cross recently "discovered" in an old cupboard in the vestry at Brabourne Church was identified by John Varrier as having come from the Bircholt Mission Room. Having been restored by John, it now stands underneath the east window in the Scott Chapel. According to George Hickmott, the harmonium at the Mission Room never worked very well and a piano belonging to his in-laws, Frank and Marjorie Howland, was often used instead. George was keen to know what had happened to the piano in the Mission Room. He emphasised that he did not want it back, nor does his son Michael, just that the family would like to know what became of it. Michael has asked for any information on what happened to the pews, and Betty Dryland (Lavender) would like to know what became of the harmonium. She spent many hours dusting and polishing it, so if anyone has any information on any of these items, please let us know.

## SOME PAINFUL MEMORIES OF BIRCHOLT MISSION
John Varrier writes:

One of my own experiences of Bircholt Mission was rather less than happy and has stayed with me. I spent the first year of the Second World War with my grandmother at Dial House, Stowting, and attended Stowting School, where, coincidentally, I met the little girl who I was to marry some 20 years later. There came a day when Mrs Hickman, the headmistress who lived in the school house, announced that the school dentist was at the Mission Hall and that those of a certain age group, including myself, were to make our way over to Brabourne for inspection. Dutifully, I cycled over to Bircholt Mission, where a rather large nurse instructed us to await the dentist. The waiting room was the five-bar gate on the opposite side of the lane. When my turn came, I was called in to find a transportable dentist's chair set up in the middle of the little room with a treadle-operated drilling machine, the whole being overseen by what struck me as being a very elderly dentist indeed. After a quick inspection of my mouth, he turned to the nurse, said two to come out, and promptly proceeded to give me a couple of injections. I was then held down by the nurse and, without more ado, the dentist extracted two of my newly grown permanent teeth. After a cursory rinse of my mouth I was told to get back to school, so I cycled back to Stowting, spitting blood most of the way and resumed my school work. I wasn't alone in receiving such treatment. Such was dental care in 1940. There was little concern for shock to the system or for the discomfort for a 10-year-old boy.

## INFLUENCES ON ATTITUDES TO CHURCH

Interest in the church has declined over the years and in this section we consider two

John and Vi Varrier

major factors which appear to have affected attitudes to this institution: the first is enforced attendance at church, and the second, the effects of tithes. Interestingly, it was children in times past who disliked having to devote all of Sunday to church, and adults who were disgruntled by the enforcement of tithes. Thus some people across the entire age range were affected.

Everyone with whom we spoke for this book who was over the age of 70 used to go to church regularly as a child – usually more often than they would have wished. These included worshippers at the Anglican churches in Brabourne, Smeeth and the Bircholt Mission, those who attended both Anglican and Roman Catholic churches outside the village, the General Baptists, Zion Baptists in the village, and the Methodists in Sellindge. It was usual for children from all the churches to attend at least twice, if not three times on a Sunday: first, at Sunday School, which would be held in the morning, then with their parents at the morning service, be it Mattins or Holy Communion, and back again in the late afternoon for Evensong. Though many did not enjoy spending most of Sunday at church, children did as they were told (or so it would seem). Many also remained "children" for longer in those days and Vi Varrier (Kingston) recalls wearing ankle socks unquestioningly at the age of 18.

Vi recalls:

"Going to church was a major part of our lives. My parents were committed Methodists, which meant that we attended the chapel at Sellindge. While we were too young to ride bicycles, we would be squashed into Grandfather Kingston's old car along with two aunts who would complain bitterly about their clothes being crumpled through being sat upon. Once we were old enough, we cycled the three miles there and back from Bankside [on the Brabourne side of Fiddling Lane, postal address Stowting], whatever the weather, for Sunday School from 10am- 11am. This was followed immediately by the morning service from 11am-12 noon, and then, at times, we had to go back again for the evening service. My parents were very strict about what we did on a Sunday. There was certainly no playing of games, no sewing or knitting, and only religious books could be read. No farm work was done on a Sunday, no haying or even harvesting, only the bare essentials, such as milking the cows twice a day and feeding the stock. This went on until I was 18 years old, when I left home to go into nursing."

This pattern of life on Sundays was common to many. No one was allowed to do anything that counted as "enjoyment" or "work" on the Sabbath, and this, too, impinged on children. Vi recalls that her mother was allowed to cook on a Sunday, though in some families the wives did not and, in contrast to images of the traditional Sunday roast, only cold food that had been cooked the day before was eaten on the Sabbath. As Vi mentioned above, the only work permitted was tending to the needs of animals, which was essential in a farming community.

In the 1930s, some members of non-conformist churches were lay preachers, and one who was remembered by members of the Zion chapel for his good work as a Deacon there was George Hickmott's father, Ebenezer. George remembered his father preaching at the chapel and, though he can remember little of the substance of his sermons, he did remember that they were "very long". Every Sunday, George and his 11 brothers and sisters would go to Sunday School in the morning (Sheila Stone (Ashman) recalls that when the Zion Baptists didn't have a Sunday School for some reason, the children would join the Bethel Baptists at their Sunday School; she can remember George among the other children from the Zion Baptists). Following Sunday School, George and his siblings would attend a church service in the afternoon and possibly one in the evening as well. As well as looking after the children and making sure they all went to church as they were required, George remembered his mother, Ruth, cooking lunch for all the family. Ebenezer also used to take services away from home, and would travel all over Kent on his motorbike with sidecar, taking with him bibles, hymn books and other religious literature. He was at one time pastor at Forest Hill in south London, and would go up there every Saturday afternoon on his motorbike, preaching on Sunday and returning home on Monday. All these absences, George recollected, put a great strain on his mother who was left to look after their large family while her husband was away. George was the 11th of 13 children, one of whom died at birth; they were all born between 1909 and 1929. Inevitably, the older children helped to look after the younger ones, which probably did help his mother, but thinking back, George felt she must have been worn out most of the time. The effects of the chuch on George's home life certainly clouded his views, but not all his family members were affected in the same way. One of George's sisters, Kate (Grantham), who was 11 years older than him, lived in Smeeth, and was a regular at the Bethel Baptist Church for many years. Kate died in 2003.

Joyce Garlick's stepfather, Archibald Ashman, was also a Baptist preacher and like many others in the village Joyce remembers not only having to go to church three times every Sunday, but also attending services at Elmsted when her stepfather was preaching there. It all seemed such a long time for a small child.

On the theme of getting people into church, various vicars at the former vicarage in East Brabourne would invite morning churchgoers to lunch and to play tennis on the courts that were just to the south of the churchyard prior to the Second World War. Participants were also expected to attend the evening service as well, giving credence to the view that there is no such thing as a free lunch. Another ruse for parents keen to ensure that their children went to the evening service without a fuss was to invite other children to tea, after which everyone went to church.

The importance of religion and attending church on Sunday went past personal practice. John Hammon, whose parents were Baptists, recalled that when his great-grandfather had taken on a wagoner, one of the conditions of the job was that the man attended church regularly on Sundays. An extract from John's great-grandfather's farm accounts of 11th October, 1860, is perhaps significant: "Agreed with George Wilson as Wagoner's mate at Brabourne from Oct. 11th 1860 to Oct. 11th 1861, his wages to be Six Pounds, he also agrees to attend Brabourne Church every Sunday unless he has permission of his master to the contrary." Apparently, in the 19th century, this was not an unusual stipulation. According to John, church was the equivalent of TV in times past, just as it was the principal – indeed the only – form of entertainment on a Sunday. It demanded, and received, enormous respect. In John's words, "Even in my father's youth, before the First World War, it was customary for the village girls to curtsey and the boys to raise their caps to the parson and his wife and other village nobility." He also added that if a coffin were carried across a field as the shortest way to the church, then this path became a public right of way.

John recalls that the local hierarchy in church on a Sunday was clearly evident from the way people dressed: the working man had his flat cap, the farmer his bowler, and Lord Brabourne his top hat. Nowadays at Brabourne, it is only the vicar who is distinguished by dress. It was only after the First World War that such

John Hammon

stark social divisions began to erode. John observed that, "Subservient attitudes to the church and the master changed markedly after the Great War and, by the middle of the 20th century, pulling the forelock to the gaffer had disappeared, along with the obligation to attend church." In the words of Rosemary Hendry (Ward), "Life was less pressured in those days, but far more dictatorial." You had to do what was expected of you and common across all social classes was the expectation that people would attend church – often, as said, several times on a Sunday.

Memories of the formal atmosphere in all our churches and of having to spend two to three hours there each Sunday undoubtedly put many of our contributors off attending regularly once they had grown up. In the words of one of our contributors, "none of it was child-friendly". This is not to stand in judgement on those who took church services in those days, merely to observe that the church was a product of its history and some 60 years ago perceptions of children were different from now - they were much more controlled and had to do as they were told. But the question for the Christian church today is can such attitudes be reversed, and if so, how? It has to be said that there were also many happy childhood memories associated with all our churches, usually involving events such as the annual Sunday School outing, parties and singing in the choir. More on these later.

Dressed for church on a Sunday (mid-1940s): left, the Princess Sanda Cantacuzino and Lady Bomford

## THE POWER OF THE ESTABLISHED CHURCH – TITHES
The impact of tithes collected by the church was also a factor considered by the local press at the time to be "driving people from church".

John Hammon writes:

"The tithe collected by the established church started around 900AD. It was one-tenth of the produce of the land and was taken in kind to the village Tithe Barn. This was for the support of the village parson and the church. Through the years there were many protests and, after the Napoleonic Wars (1800-1815) and the 1830 Swing Riots, the farming community were barely earning a living and were finding it impossible to pay their tithes. This was a time of extreme poverty and a large difference between the ruling classes and the poor village people. Virtually everybody went to church at this time.

"In 1836, the tithe was changed from produce to a cash payment, and it was assessed on what the land would produce. This would all be recorded in the Tithe Book and on the Tithe Map kept in the church. The tithe, once given voluntarily to the church, was now enforceable by law and collected by the Church Commissioners. During the Depression of the 1930s many people did not have the money to pay their tithes and the resulting enforcement of the sale of their farm stock made them unable to feed their families or carry on with farming.

"Tithes collected by the church were always a sore point with country people throughout England. The matter came to a head in the 1930s with the tithe riots, when bailiffs were sent to farms to collect the money either by seizure of the debtor's property or holding a sale of farm animals or equipment to realise the debt. [In 1936, after the tithe riots, the government agreed to take over the tithes, which were legal under an Act of Parliament from the time of Queen Anne. These would be redeemed over the next 52 years.] These sales, with many police in attendance, were held all over Kent. The local auctioneers would not take these Tithe Sales, and the person who came to the Brabourne sale was a Mr Judge from Folkestone. It was later reported that the tyres on his car had been let down and the windows of his house in Folkestone had been covered with tar. The farmers made a mockery of these sales by bidding up on a lot for sale to many times its value, and when it was knocked down to one of them, several others would claim the bid and, when offered again because of the dispute, it would only make a fraction of its value. In this way these Distraint Sales were made a farce. The report in the Kentish Express of such a sale at Warren Farm in 1937 is shown in the extract below. Five cows of Mr Percy Nickolls were valued at over £50 but realised only £20/10/- when they were sold, which was well below their true value, but just sufficient to realise his tithe arrears of two years. Did the cows ever leave Warren Farm? Was there some form of help from benevolent locals? Having talked to people who remember the sale it appears that they could not remember any details."

Michael Hickmott has added the following information: the Tithe Act of 1936 replaced rent charges with annuities payable to the government for a period of 60 years, ending on 1st October, 1996. It also compensated tithe owners and set up a Tithe Redemption Committee. However, it proved very costly to administer and, in 1960, was transferred to the Inland Revenue. Michael, a chartered surveyor, can remember using the 1930 tithe maps when he worked on one or two cases himself in the mid-1970s. However, the whole scheme was wound up under the Finance Act of 1977 and the annuities were extinguished.

# "PUT BAILIFF UP FOR AUCTION"

CRY AT VILLAGE TITHE SALE

Five cows, the property of Mr P.E.S. Nicholls [correct spelling should be Nickolls] of Warren Farm, Brabourne, were sold at Brabourne on Tuesday for two years' tithe arrears due to Queen Anne's Bounty and amounting to £19/17/6. The sale of stock realised £20/10/0.

Mr Nicholls told a Kentish Express representative that he had lived at Warren Farm for 17 years and had always paid his tithe, which was over £12 a year.

"This time I wrote to the authorities explaining I had had a hard time with family illness, and offering 80 per cent," he said. "They would not take it and were most insulting."

Opening the bidding on one red cow seized by the Ashford County Court bailiff for £2/8/6 tithe on Warren Farm, Brabourne, Mr H. Judge, the auctioneer, said "Any bids? I will not say I will take them with pleasure, but I will take them." Mr S. Crump was the purchaser for £3/19/0.

THE COW WITH A CRUMPLED HORN

The Hythe County Court bailiff had trouble in picking out which cow of the herd was the one seized for the £3/19/10 tithe on Warren House Farm, Sellindge, and at last designated it as the "one with a crumpled horn". It was sold to Mr. Marshall for £5/10/0.

Three cows (for £13/9/10 tithe on Warren House Farm), which Mr Judge said were worth £58, went to Mr E. Mills for £15/16/0. During the bidding the auctioneer was exhorted "to put the old bailiff up to get a bid of £20". Mr Judge replied that he would rather not spoil a bargain. He also said, "I have never in my life sold three cows like these for such a price."

DRIVING PEOPLE FROM THE CHURCH

"I am very sorry that this business is still dragging on," said Mr H.V. Roseveare after the sale. "The last Act was passed so that, among other things, a commission might be set up to deal with tithe arrears, especially arrears owed by farmers who could not possibly pay. Yet the tithe owners are forcing those people to pay their arrears – they are driving the poor struggling farmer out of business.

"Those people who are so vindictive and persecute their fellow countrymen are the same people who vote for a peace policy in times of international strife. Yet with us they say, 'Fight to the finish!'

"Things like this are today embittering the people and driving them from church, which is a thousand pities. It is not only a thing for the country folk to protest against, but the townspeople too."

Sale at Warren Farm to realise tithe arrears
(source: Kentish Express, 1937, now part of KM Group)

Returning to the impacts of tithes, John Hammon writes:

"The rise in the non-conformists throughout the 1800s can be attributed partly to the anti-church feeling, with the farming community preferring chapel with no tithe, and meeting the ministers and church leaders on equal terms.

"It is difficult to guess when the first non-conformists met in the area. In the time of Queen Mary (1553-1558), a Baptist minister of Ashford was executed and, a hundred years later, Thomas Brewer, Baptist minister of Ashford, was sent to prison as a non-conformist. By the start of the 18th century, a much greater freedom of worship was allowed. It would seem that meetings were held in barns, cottages and houses across Kent. John Wesley (1703-1791) left the Church of England to form the Methodists. The Baptists met in the small barn [later garage] now converted to a room in Applegarth, on the east side of the Old Post Office in Brabourne Street, while others were using the old army bakehouse at Brabourne Lees. The present Baptist church on Plain Road was built in 1818 on land that may have been part of the army camp, and the Strict Baptist Church in Canterbury Road, in 1838. Soon after this, the Bible Christians built a chapel on the corner of Fiddling Lane and Mill Lane. This was converted to a house when the chapel moved up to the Wesleyan Chapel on Stowting Common. The house has now disappeared completely. Much of the rock footings were exposed when a doodlebug or flying bomb was shot down by a British Spitfire fighter aircraft and exploded on the site on 11th August, 1944."

And now we turn to more positive and fond memories of our churches – for a whole range of reasons.

## THE VARIED ATTRACTIONS OF GOING TO CHURCH

As we read with regularity in the national press about the decline in church attendance at Anglican services and about the increasing lack of interest in God and the Church, we can derive some minor satisfaction from those of our contributors who hinted that the devotion of former churchgoers, particularly the young, was to some extent sustained by the use of minor "incentives".

Eric Ball

The choir, for example, involved much more than just singing: in Brabourne, choristers have long received small inducements to encourage participation. Eric Ball used to receive ½d (a halfpenny) from the Reverend McDowall and his wife in the 1930s for attending church, and for singing in the choir. By the 1950s, this had risen to 6d. Former choristers clearly valued this payment and some from even this era refrained from telling their parents about it. One of these was Rob Thornby who, as late as 2007, surprised his father Norman when he mentioned that he had been paid for being a choirboy during the early 1960s. Sally Thornby, who was also in the choir as a little girl, remembered "earning" 6d in the late 1960s for singing at weddings. Choristers all seemed to enjoy the experience of being in the choir, and when asked for their favourite memories of being choristers, two in particular were mentioned: the first was dressing up in their surplices (they loved that as children), and the second was being "ticked off" by older members of the choir for talking and fidgeting. That, they found amusing.

Betty Dryland, a member of the choir during the ministry of the Reverend Thompson-Evans in the 1950s, recalls Betty Finn getting the choir to beat the dust out of the hassocks on the vicarage lawn one summer afternoon. The vicar was so pleased with their efforts that all helpers were treated to a glass of lemonade. At this time, Betty recalled that the choir received no remuneration, they were simply willing participants. Similarly, Tom Wratten recalls the Reverend Thompson-Evans getting the choir to come to the vicarage in East Brabourne (now East Brabourne House), to tidy up the garden and have a bonfire. The choristers thought this tremendous fun. Christine Peall (Friend) recalls being in the choir in the Reverend Ray Sheekey's days and remembers him shouting at them to sing louder, however loudly they sang. He

## BRABOURNE CHURCH CHOIR IN THE 1950s

From left: Michael Shorter, Thomas Wratten and
Anthony Finn

At the back, Derek Marsh; from left, Thomas Wratten (with cross),
Michael Shorter, James Andrews, Colin Wratten, David Bradley,
(behind David Bradley unknown), Anthony Finn and
Peter Bradley holding the Children's Banner

used to say that they should be able to fit four fingers together into their mouths, in a vertical column between their upper and lower jaws, and if they couldn't open their mouths wide enough to do this, then they certainly couldn't hope to sing sufficiently loudly!

Jackie Finn (Davis), while indulging in nostalgia, listed some of her contemporaries in Brabourne Church choir in the late 1950s (when the Reverend Thompson-Evans was the vicar): Anthony Finn; Derek and Pauline Marsh (now Anderson); Colin Wratten (who threw Jackie's doll on the bonfire); Christine, Malcolm and Jackie Friend; Christine, Susan, Anne and Charles Todd; Elizabeth, William and Mary Rice, who moved away to Devon, after which William was killed; and Tim Andrews. Also members of the choir in this period were Rosemary and Margaret Davis (Jackie's sisters), Danny and Robin Thornby, Nigel and Ruth Dalby, and Jean Lawes, and to this list Tom Wratten added Michael Shorter, Peter Bradley and Stanley Thornby (no relation of Norman Thornby).

Though Jackie might have considered that "most of the choir couldn't sing" and were there for little more than camaraderie and fun, considerable musical talent gradually emerged from some of these choristers. Anthony Finn, for example, is a fine organist, while Jackie learnt to play the cello with Mrs Trowell, Oliver's mother. She would practise at the Trowells every day and, on her way to their house, Coquet

Jackie Finn (Davis)

Lodge at the end of The Street, would always pick a bunch of violets (when they were in bloom) from the bank opposite the house – a gift for an appreciative and much-loved Mrs Trowell. At much the same time, Jackie's sister, Rosemary Davis, started learning to play the organ at Smeeth Church, though when she started she was too small to reach the pedals.

## THE BENEFITS OF CONFIRMATION

Sally Furneaux (Willett) writes:

"I feel my life may not have taken the same course had I not attended Brabourne Church, as on Ascension Day 1968 I was confirmed in the church and it so happened that my lovely future husband was in the congregation! My friend Carol Fortescue (now Pack, living in West Brabourne), also being confirmed on the same day, had invited her cousin (Graham Furneaux, the eldest son of Jean Fortescue) to attend. Although no 'dating' started for a couple of years or so, Graham and I were married at Brabourne Church by Raymond Sheekey on 20th April, 1974. It was such a happy day, despite the power cuts and the three-day week we were experiencing at the time.

Sally Willett and Graham Furneaux married by
the Rev Ray Sheekey at Brabourne

"My parents, Fred and Dorothy Willett, loved Brabourne Church, Daddy taking the collection and doing readings, Mummy helping with the flower rota and events staged for the church. Their closeness to the church was very apparent and, although this is a strange thing to say, their funerals in April and September 2010 were fitting finalities to their lives in the village."

## CELEBRATING MAJOR EVENTS IN THE CHURCH YEAR

Much was made of major events in the church year: on Rogation Sunday, the fifth Sunday after Easter, the congregation would process round the village, asking for God's blessing on the products of the land and on the countryside. On the day before Mothering Sunday each year, Betty Finn would take a group of children to pick primroses, which would then be taken back to Homehurst (now Raffles) in Canterbury Road, the home of Betty and Joy Finn. Here, they would be made into bunches by the children to give to their mothers at the service the next day. These were important and wonderful memories for Elsie Davis and her daughters Rosemary, Jackie and Margaret, and also for Pauline Anderson (Marsh), who remembers picking "armfuls of primroses" for Mothering Sunday.

Betty Finn

Boys were just as involved in picking flowers for their mothers, and Tom Wratten remembers picking primroses with Roy Southern for Mothering Sunday. On one occasion, the boys, then no more than 10 years old, took the flowers back to the shed behind Park Corner Cottage, Canterbury Road, where the Southerns lived and, as they did not have any string to tie the bunches, Tom unpicked the sleeve of his sweater and both he and Roy used the wool to tie up their primroses, which they kept carefully overnight in jam jars full of water in the shed. On the Saturday evening before Mothering Sunday both boys were told off by their mothers – Roy for being late and Tom for ruining his sweater. Imagine their mothers cringing the following morning when they both received bouquets tied with wool. Tom remembers the event well.

Tom Wratten

After Mothering Sunday comes Easter and, decades ago, Joy Finn created an Easter Garden in the chancel of Brabourne Church for Easter Sunday. The Easter Garden is re-created every year and, since Joy moved away from Brabourne, the tradition has been continued by Vi Varrier, assisted by her husband John. Since Easter in 2012, Liz Marsh has helped Vi with the garden. The tableau embodies two major

Joy Finn with great-niece Zoë

events of Holy Week: three crosses stand proud on a hill, representing the darkness of Good Friday, while not far away, an empty tomb made from rocks and surrounded by a landscape covered beautifully with mosses and flowers represents the risen Christ. Since Joy's time the Easter Garden has been appreciated and enjoyed by children and adults alike.

Similarly, dating back several decades, Keith Finn, Joy's brother, created an annual Christmas tableau in Brabourne Church: a peaceful manger scene with Mary, Joseph and the baby Jesus, surrounded by the animals. Above the manger shines the star. The crib is now put up each Christmas by Oliver Trowell. As the Easter Garden symbolises Jesus's suffering, resurrection and love for humanity, so the crib is a visible reminder of the love embodied in the message of Christmas. Both the Easter Garden and the Christmas crib are wonderful living legacies from the Finns.

The Easter garden created by
Vi Varrier and Liz Marsh (2013)

## FINN DYNAMISM

Several of our contributors agreed that Joy and Betty Finn must go down in Brabourne's history for all that they did to encourage young people to participate in the life of the church and to keep church attendance buoyant. A silver bowl given to Betty Finn for Christmas in 1959, which is engraved with the names of children whom she had encouraged to go to Brabourne Church, is further testimony to her contribution. (Jackie and Anthony Finn still treasure the bowl.) Although many of these former children may no longer be "church regulars", Margaret Older observed that they were, nevertheless, always very positive in their attitude towards the church.

The following letter from Betty Finn, which appeared in the Parish News, shows how touched she was by local acknowledgement of her impact and energy:

'Homehurst',
Brabourne.
January 6th, 1960.

Dear Children,

How very kind of you to think of giving me two such charming presents at Christmas! For a long time I have been wishing I had some pearls to wear for party occasions; and the sugar bowl is delightful. Very few aunts, I'm sure, are fortunate enough to have all their nephews and nieces at table for every meal! Thank you all very much indeed.

Although officially retired, yet I hope we shall, together, continue to offer to God, and to Brabourne Church, the loving service which has proved such a joy and privilege to all of us during the past years.

To the grown-up friends, "more than we can count," who helped, I would say thank you not only for the gift, which I greatly treasure, but also for their abiding support and encouragement; and, more precious still, their prayers.

May God bless you all, and through you, our Church and its life in Brabourne.

Yours very sincerely,
BETTY FINN.

One of those who went to church because of Joy and Betty was Margaret (Maggie) Wratten. The Wratten family lived at Forge Cottage, next door to Homehurst, where Joy and Betty lived, and Tom and Margaret's parents were not regular churchgoers. Nevertheless, Joy and Betty invited the children to go to church and Maggie was very excited the first time she went with them. However, during the service she was appalled to hear the vicar, the Reverend William Wagstaffe, keep using the word "Christ", which she believed was swearing. After the service (though she was no more than six years old at the time), she tackled him on his inappropriate use of language, saying, "You said Christ several times and my dad's trying to stop my mum saying this." A few days later the Wratten family received a visit from a concerned vicar.

Margaret and Tom Wratten

Tom (senior) and Ivy Wratten

Margaret, an imaginative child, was very absorbed by church and, through her initiative, the lavatory at the end of the Wratten's garden at Forge Cottage doubled as "her church". She made a wooden cross and put it above the door, and she decorated the entrance with bluebells and wild flowers. She would spend hours in there and recalls her parents yelling to her to get out as others wanted to make use of the building, though not for religious purposes.

But Betty, Joy and Keith weren't the only members of the Finn family to support Brabourne church: we mustn't forget both those who came before – and after them. Their paternal grandfather, George Finn who came to East Brabourne in the late 19th century from Egerton was, together with his wife, a strong supporter of the church. It is thus no surprise that George's sons, Leonard and Sidney, inherited their parents' interest in the church and that this commitment was, in turn, passed on to Betty, Joy and Keith and subsequently to Keith's son, Anthony.

Leonard eventually took over the undertaking, building, painting and decorating business that his father, George, had established in the Carpenter's Workshop and his skills were frequently used for maintaining the fabric of Brabourne Church. Furthermore, as Joy told us, whenever there was a social event in the village such as a whist drive or children's party, Finn's cart would go round Brabourne, collecting tables and chairs for the event which was usually held at Brabourne School. Both Leonard Finn and his brother Sidney were active members of the PCC, sang in the choir and were keen bellringers. Sidney Finn, who married Gwinnie Andrews, daughter of Walter Andrews who owned the kiln on Canterbury Road quite near Brabourne Lees, is remembered for his generosity to the church in both life and death.

Sidney died in January 1955, and in the March 1955 Parish Magazine of Brabourne, Smeeth and Bircholt, the Rev O.W. Thompson-Evans wrote warmly about Sidney Finn's contribution to Brabourne Church. From all that we have heard, he was a much-loved and respected man.

Four years after Sidney died another obituary appeared in the January 1959 instalment of the Parish Magazine. This time it was for Leonard Finn.

It is; with deep gratitude we acknowledge a bequest from the will of the late Mr. Sidney Finn of £1,000 for Brabourne Parish Church and a wish without any legal or equitable obligation, condition or trust whatever, " but wish the graves of my wife and myself shall be kept in good order and the Churchyard neat and tidy." The P.C.C. will certainly honour that wish and seek expert advice on the best way to invest this legacy for the benefit of our lovely historic church. Such bequests, rather than let us sit back and take it easy so to speak, spur us on constantly to improve this heritage that is ours and to add to it. The late Mr. Sidney Finn was an enthusiastic bell ringer and in later years was the captain and organiser of the team and kept a watchful eye upon the bells. As Vicar here I found his local knowledge of the history of the Church and Churchyard invaluable and frequently consulted him. We hope to have some permanent memorial to him who served and loved his Parish Church for so long and so faithfully.

A three-hour Memorial Peal was rung in memory of Mr. Sidney Finn on Saturday, January 29th. It was one of the finest rings heard in Brabourne for many years many of our parishioners thought.

Remembering Sidney Finn

# GENERATIONS OF FINNS

Leonard and Ada Finn
(formerly Ada Worrell)

Keith Finn (son of Leonard and Ada
Finn) with grandaughters Zoë and
Hollie

Anthony Finn, 2013
(son of Keith Finn)

Betty, Joy and Keith's maternal grandfather was George Worrell, a highly respected headmaster of Brabourne School. He too, with his wife Susanna and their seven surviving children were regular members of Brabourne Church. While George Worrell was a member of the PCC, ultimately becoming church warden in 1905, he too was also a keen bell ringer, member of the choir, and worked tirelessly on behalf of the church which, of course, was closely linked with Brabourne School.

George Worrell's youngest daughter, Ada, married Leonard Finn and so the two families were united. Ada was well known for her kindness to people in the village and instances that we heard about included taking food to the Canadian troops who were camped in the field opposite Homehurst (now Raffles) during the First World War, and walking across the fields to Monks Horton to welcome the Kingstons who had just arrived from Ireland, and to see whether they needed any help. George Brooks was one who spoke highly of Ada, referring to her on more than one occasion as "a really good woman". It appeared that she helped the Brooks family a great deal after George's father died in the First World War, leaving his mother, Ruth, with two small children, George and Ruth, and with baby Naomi about to be born.

> Mr. L. Finn passed away during the month after a long illness during which he was cared for with great devotion by his daughters. His end was peaceful at 81 years of age. He spent his long life with great devotion to the Parish Church as a member of the Choir, a Bell Ringer, and a member of the P.C.C. He always gave great interest and care for the fabric of the Church and it is due to the loyal churchmen like the late Mr. Finn that we have inherited this church building in such splendid condition and saved our generation from such grievous financial burdens that many other churches are faced with. Until the past three years when his health began to break down he was unfailing in his attendance morning and evening at the services. Our sympathy and prayers are with his family and we can be sure that this family tradition of church work will be carried on.

Remembering Leonard Finn

The Finn community spirit continued into the generation which followed Betty, Joy and Keith, with Keith's son Anthony who was a chorister (see page 81), an enthusiastic bell ringer and an excellent organist who has now retired but who always helps out when he's needed. In addition to being supporters of Brabourne Church, the Finns – that is Betty, Joy, Keith, his son Anthony, Anthony's wife, Jackie, and their children Karen and Andrew (who have now moved from the village) are all the product of Brabourne School where their forebear, George Worrell, was Headmaster.

## SUNDAY SCHOOL

In the 1950s and even earlier, perhaps the greatest attraction of churches in the parish of Brabourne was the Sunday School. Few seemed to have much recollection of what they did there other than meeting their friends, but no one seemed to mind going.

Tom Wratten remembers:

"Anthony Finn, who lived at 1 Holly Cottages, used to have a big train set, and one of the best things after Sunday School was going to Anthony's, as his dad, Keith, would get the steam train going. We weren't allowed at first because Joy and Betty Finn used to take us to church, but after some time we would go on our own."

In later years, when Tom's sister, Margaret was one of the older children, she used to help at the Sunday School, but always found it tedious and used to encourage the little ones to ask to go out of church so that she could take them to the toilet. Her guilt was fathomless when she was presented with a book to thank her for all her help.

For the majority of those of a mature age, the main memory of Sunday School was of the annual outing. This seems to have been a mammoth affair in the villages and involved each church arranging a coach trip for the children and their mothers. No one remembered fathers going and no one remembered having to pay; it was assumed that this was a treat from the church for regular attendance. Picnics would be packed, buckets and spades gathered together and all would board the coach. St Mary's Brabourne, together with the Bircholt Mission Sunday School, went to Dymchurch every year, as did the Baptists; Smeeth went to Margate. There were sufficient Sunday School members and their mothers to fill two coaches from each church – or so it seemed. Jane Barker recalls that, although she went to the Sunday School at Smeeth Church, she and her friends would sneak off to join the Chapel outing as well. This "doubling up" might explain why there were at least two full coaches from each church. But Joyce Garlick remembers that there was a downside to the outing, as on the Wednesday before the event, some of the children from the Bethel Baptist Chapel would have to stand up in the pulpit individually and recite a religious verse or two to the entire congregation. Joyce hated doing this, and the memory lingers. When asked what they did when they arrived at either Dymchurch or Margate, former participants such as Norman Thornby, Rosemary Hendry (Ward) and Joyce all recalled "running and playing all day" on the beach and "building sandcastles", while their mothers went window shopping. This was, without doubt, the biggest day in the year for local children. Rarely did people go on holiday and, if they did, it was usually to stay with relatives for a few days, seldom anything more adventurous.

A few people, both Anglicans and Bethel Baptists, also remembered winter Sunday School treats – usually a party with games for the children. At this event in the Baptist Chapel the children would present their Sunday School attendance books, and prizes were given out accordingly. As Joyce's stepfather, Archibald Ashman, was a prominent member of the Bethel Baptists, she had no option but to attend regularly, but it meant she always received "a good prize" at the winter treat. The Anglicans in Brabourne also had their Christmas party, which was usually provided by the generosity of Mrs Opperman and organised by Betty Finn. Anthony Finn recalls each child having to perform a party piece: he would play the piano, Jackie Finn (Davis) would play the cello, and others would sing or recite poetry.

A flourishing Sunday School was also run in the 1940s, by Miss Osman and Mrs Tomkins, Irene Tomkins's mother, in the old black Institute Hut, now replaced by the Oak Room. Participants recalled that, at Christmas, they gave a wonderful party, with every child receiving a prize. Nellie Norrington (Sawyer) and her sister, Margaret Baldock (Sawyer), used to go to Sunday School at the Institute Hut; Nellie also went to the Girls' Friendly Society (GFS) meetings there, too. The GFS had its roots in the Anglican Church and was a movement to help girls and women to develop their potential. At these meetings Nellie and many other girls from the village learned how to sew, knit, spin, dance and do many other enjoyable and useful things. In the era before the Second World War, and in the years shortly afterwards, people had to make their own entertainment and the church played a major role in the social life of the villages, which brings us back to John Hammon's very apt comment, "Church *was* the TV of those days." People had no money; consumerism as we now know it didn't exist and, as a consequence, young people were willing to entertain themselves by being useful within the community.

How true this was can be seen in a cutting from an edition of The Kentish Express in 1963 (opposite). "Miss Mops of Brabourne Church" shouts the headline above a picture of a group of volunteers, all about 14 years old, who had decided to keep the church clean. The volunteers consisted of Christine Peall (Friend), Jackie Kennett (Friend), Pauline Anderson (Marsh) and Susan Todd. So diligent and enthusiastic were they about their undertaking that they even polished one of the tombstones in the main aisle with black boot polish – and did it shine! How wonderful it looked and how proud of it they were… until people started walking down the aisle and were barely able to keep their feet. Christine has added since that cleaning the church gave the girls "something to do".

For many who used to attend church three times on a Sunday, this practice ceased as soon as they were adults. Perhaps it was the effects of the two wars that had left society more questioning of the church; perhaps it was due to being released from the pressure from very devout parents and grandparents to devote Sundays to the church; perhaps it was our education system, which, post-war, saw scientific

Cleaning the Church voluntarily (1963): from left Pauline Anderson (Marsh), Jackie
Kennett (Friend), Christine Peall (Friend) and Susan Todd
Source: Kentish Express, now part of KM Group

explanation beginning to contribute to the erosion of spiritual belief for many. In the
Anglican Church today, comparatively few among the laity attend church more than
once on a Sunday. Does this then mean that belief in God within our community
has declined? It's hard to say, because church attendance in itself is meaningless as
an indicator of belief. Rather than concern ourselves with this, we should celebrate
the current situation, whereby people are not pressured into worshipping, but attend
churches and other places of worship when they genuinely wish to do so, be it for
prayer in any of its forms, or merely for the enjoyment of the buildings.

## VICARS VARIOUS

The former vicars, rectors and priests in charge at Brabourne have all left their marks on our parishes in many ways. This section includes a mix of personal recollections of the clergy by members of the congregation, and of the parish by clergy past and present. We have not managed to obtain anecdotes about all the clerics listed below, but those pieces we have acquired are selective and appear in chronological order.

Vicars at Brabourne in the 'recent' past

| | | |
|---|---|---|
| Amos Hayton | 1831 - 1847 | mentioned in section on Brabourne School |
| | | |
| George Booth Perry-Ayscough (Vicar of Brabourne with Monks Horton) | 1872 - 1885 | |
| John Thomas Pearse (Vicar of Brabourne with Monks Horton) | 1885 – 1890 | |
| Walter Dunstan May (Vicar of Brabourne with Monks Horton) | 1893 – 1898 | |
| Alfred Fairbrother (Vicar of Brabourne with Monks Horton and Bircholt) | 1898 - 1903 | |
| Thomas Lindsay Stack (Vicar of Brabourne and Monks Horton and Rector of Bircholt) | 1903 – 1916 | |
| S.K. Lockyear | 1916 - 1931 | |
| Charles Robert Loraine McDowall | 1931 - 1945 | |
| Eric Southam (Canon) | 1945 - 1947 | |
| William Henry Wagstaffe* (Vicar of Brabourne and Rector of Smeeth) | 1947 - 1952 | |
| Oliver William Thompson Evans* | 1952 - 1959 | |
| Jack Shaw* | 1959 - 1960 | |
| Raymond Sheekey* | 1961 - 1978 (left in 1979) | |
| Michael Stephens* | 1979 - 1994 | |
| Peter Thackray (Priest-in-Residence, Brabourne and Smeeth. Peter was House for Duty Assistant Curate of the parishes – John Tipping was | 1995-1999 | |

* All Vicars of Brabourne and Rectors of Smeeth

Priest in Charge in addition to his
responsibilities at Mersham,
Sellindge, Hinxhill and Sevington)

William Cooper (Priest-in-Charge,      2000 - 2004
Brabourne, Smeeth, Monks Horton
and Stowting)

Richard Le Rossignol               2006 - present
(Priest-in-Charge of the six
parishes of Brabourne,
Smeeth, Monks Horton,
Stowting, Mersham and Sellindge)

...................................................................................................................

### THE REVEREND THOMAS STACK (1903-1916)

This is the earliest vicar of our parish of whom we were able to find a recollection. It comes from John Varrier, whose father used to tell this tale.

John writes:

"In the early 1900s, both my parents (children at the time) were members of Brabourne Church choir, my father having an extra job, in that he had to pump the organ for each of the hymns. At that time the organ was located in what we now know as the Scott Chapel. The vicar of Brabourne was the Reverend Tommy Stack, a tall, imposing, red-headed bachelor, who occupied the vicarage and had a staff of a cook/housekeeper, a housemaid and a gardener/ groom. He did his rounds of the parish driving a pony and trap and, on occasions, carried the younger members of the choir on the trap while the older ones had to run behind, vocally encouraged by the Reverend Stack. On one occasion he was confronted by the owner of Church Farm, Mr Pearson, with the accusation that the choirboys had been scrumping apples from his orchard. (He was quite correct in this claim and, indeed, my father had been one of the miscreants.) The vicar was highly indignant in his rebuttal of this accusation, claiming that his choirboys would do no such thing. At the next choir practice, however, the boys were lined up and told that if ever they were caught scrumping again, he would personally give them a good leathering. Thomas Stack was truly a man of great leadership, and it is no wonder that the boys thought the world of him (my father amongst them)."

REMEMBERING THE REVEREND BROWN AT SMEETH
(early 1900s)

Although this section focuses on priests from Brabourne, we
digress for a moment to include Sid Ashdown's memories of a
vicar at Smeeth at much the same time as the Reverends Stack and
Lockyear were at Brabourne. It is believed the vicar at Smeeth was
a Mr Brown, but this has not been verified. These memories were
taken from a recording made in the late 1990s of Sid talking about
his past; they show us that the vicar at Smeeth was a man of status.

According to Sid, in 1912, the vicar who lived at Church House in
Smeeth, a large white house, had many people working for him.
He had a coach and four (horses), two coachmen and a man in the
harness room. The vicar also had four girls working in the house
and two men in the garden, so he was employing nine people in all.
The vicar went to war (presumably the First World War) with his
own horse, but Sid wasn't sure that the horse he came back with
was the same one. After returning from the war the vicar used to
take the choir for outings in his coach. Sid, one of the choristers,
remembered an outing in 1924, when they went to the seaside at
Herne Bay. The journey was so long that they stopped at a pub,
changed horses, carried on to the seaside, then came back and
picked up the original horses. The vicar drove the coach himself,
though he usually had a coachman with him, a Mr Timmins.

Carol Lightfoot added to this that when the Reverend Brown was
vicar at Smeeth, his children used to come to Home Farm on the
A20 to share a governess with William Bedo Hobbs's children.

THE REVEREND S.K. LOCKYEAR (1916-1931)

The Reverend Lockyear was vicar at Brabourne and Smeeth. Direct
memories of him are few, though John Varrier recalls another tale
told him by his father:

"In 1923, a government-inspired competition for light aircraft
was held at Lympne airport, which was a well-established airport
following the First World War. Aircraft for this competition had
to be powered by an engine of no greater capacity than 750cc,
they needed to be capable of lifting a cockpit load, that is to say

a pilot, of at least 10 stone, and the wings had to be foldable so that the whole contrivance could be wheeled along by the pilot and pushed into an average-sized garage. Prizes were to be awarded for the highest altitude, the greatest distance covered on one gallon of petrol and the fastest speed over the circuit. The route went from Lympne to Capel airship shed, thence to South Hill near Hastingleigh, on to Brabourne and back to Lympne. During the competition one pilot suffered an engine failure and glided to a landing at South Hill. Being an intelligent man he deduced that

The Reverend and
Mrs S K Lockyear

the only telephones in a small village were most likely to be found at the vicarage or the squire's house and so, abandoning his aircraft, he set out to walk down to Brabourne vicarage. There he found a garden party in full swing; he was made welcome by the Reverend Lockyear and given the use of the telephone (which we are led to believe was available) to report his predicament to Lympne. Such was private aviation in 1923!"

..............................................................................................

### THE REVEREND CHARLES McDOWALL (1931-1945)

Memories of the Reverend and Mrs McDowall were most affectionate, but recollections of the unusual tended to relate more to Mrs McDowall than to her husband. Reverend McDowall was distinguished by having been Head of the King's School, Canterbury, from 1910-1916, and also having taught at Eton. He was vicar at Brabourne and rector of Monks Horton. One day in 1939, Mrs McDowall invited a small group of children to tea, one of whom was Oliver Trowell. When they arrived it was clear that Mrs McDowall had quite forgotten her invitation so, to give herself time to prepare tea, quickly sent the children out on a series of errands. Oliver recalls her saying in her very British, ex-India accent "…and Oliver will get the coal". Tea was ready some while later, by which time a whole list of chores had been completed by the young visitors.

Oliver remembers a comment from Mrs Liza Sharp, who lived at Peacehaven (the west cottage of the two that are now Orchard Cottage in The Street, East Brabourne) and who helped Mrs Moon at the Five Bells. In the freezing weather of early 1940, the Reverend McDowall agreed to conduct a Sunday service in the Five Bells in order to escape the arctic temperatures of the church and, according to Mrs Sharp, opened proceedings with the unlikely comment, "We will start the service with Roll out the Barrel!"

Norman Thornby remembered that Mrs McDowall used to drive a Standard 10 and, every Sunday, would drive from the vicarage in East Brabourne to the Bircholt Mission for Sunday School. The Reverend McDowall always followed on his bicycle. However, Mrs McDowall could not use reverse gear and so a group of small boys, including Norman, would await her arrival at the Mission and then push the car back and forth, gradually turning it, until it was facing in the right direction for her homeward journey.

The Reverend McDowall, who both Norman and Oliver considered "a good teacher", used to teach scripture at Brabourne School. On one occasion he was considering the meaning of the word pomp in relation to Belshazzar's Feast and asked the children if they knew what it meant. Up piped Stan Burt: "I know what a pomp is, it's what I use to put air in my tyres." It was a comment that made Stan a legend in the minds of all those present.

Eric Jenner, whose parents owned the Five Bells, used to work for Leonard Finn (painter, decorator, builder, wheelwright and undertaker) in the school holidays. Eric can remember painting the vicarage in the McDowalls' time with Keith Finn and Arthur Ball. They used to look longingly at the rows of cox apple trees laden with ripe apples, and frequently Eric would succumb to the temptation to scrump a few.

Eric Ball remembers that the McDowalls used to have "a proper village fête in the vicarage garden" each year. There was a weeping ash and stables at the back of the house and he recalls that the village children loved playing there. Mrs McDowall must be credited with organising a canteen at Brabourne School, which provided hot lunches for the children. These started on 26th January, 1942, and very soon were being eaten by all the children attending school at that time.

(For more details, see extracts from the minutes of the Managers' Meetings of Brabourne School, Chapter 6).

........................................................................................................

## CANON ERIC SOUTHAM (1945-1947)

Canon Southam had been a Canon of Guildford Cathedral before coming to Brabourne where, for some time, he lived at the vicarage. It is believed that he developed health problems while living at Brabourne, which caused him to give up the priesthood and move with his wife to Smeeth Hill House on the A20. Jane Barker remembered Mrs Southam organising jam-making for the war effort by turning over an entire cottage in the woods at the back of this house to the production of this and other WI goods.

........................................................................................................

## THE REVEREND WILLIAM WAGSTAFFE (1947-1952)

The Reverend Wagstaffe lived at the vicarage in East Brabourne along with his mother and dog, Biddy. Known by many as "Waggy", Jane Barker remembered him as "very tall, thin and bald and someone who articulated his words very clearly". This is borne out by Anthony Finn, whose outstanding memory of the Reverend Wagstaffe was that he used to say "possiebeeleetees" over-frequently, while the word that stuck in Jane's mind was "responseebeelitieees".

Oliver Trowell remembers the Reverend Wagstaffe pronounced his "ings" without the "g" and dropped his "h"s from the middle of words. Oliver had the use of part of the vicarage garden for growing vegetables and remembers meeting the Reverend Wagstaffe in the vicarage garden about 10 o'clock one morning. "Good mornin', Oliver," he said, "I've got some people comin' to supper tonight so I'm just battlin' with the flowers. Come along, Biddy [his dog]." On another occasion, Oliver remembers catching sight of Mrs "Duck" Varrier (who was heading for the vicarage), falling over on the ice-covered asphalt path that led across the churchyard from the entrance gates. The Reverend Wagstaffe, advancing up the path from the vicarage, called out "Come along, Mrs Varrier, that's not the way for the local in'abitants to be'ave!" Fortunately she was not badly hurt and he soon assisted her to her feet.

The Reverend Wagstaffe is also remembered for forgetting to take a funeral on a winter Wednesday owing to his passion for following the hunt.

The Reverend William Wagstaffe and Biddy the dog

Jean Holmes remembers him taking assemblies at Brabourne School and also allowing children to watch the State Opening of Parliament on his TV at the old vicarage at Brabourne. She noted that he did not mind whether you were Church of England, Baptist or any other denomination – all were welcome.

THE REVEREND OLIVER THOMPSON-EVANS (1952-1959)

The Reverend Thompson-Evans was the last vicar to live in the vicarage at Brabourne. We have found few anecdotes relating to him, though Anthony Finn remembers him as being "a truly good man" and several others have spoken well of him. A more specific anecdote comes from Tom (T.A.L.) Wratten, whose father, also Tom (T.H. Wratten), returned home to Forge Cottage in Canterbury Road, East Brabourne, one Sunday at lunchtime after a regular Sunday-morning visit to the Five Bells, and announced: "Well, that's the first time I've had a drink off a vicar." It transpired that the Reverend Thompson-Evans, who was new to the parish at the time, had come into the Five Bells and allegedly said, "Take no notice of my dog collar, it's my working uniform. Can I buy everyone a pint?" He was an army padre and instantly popular in the village. He married Tom and Jean Wratten, among many others. According to John Jamieson, this good-hearted and amiable man played occasionally for Mersham-le-Hatch Cricket Club, and his son, John, also played in his holidays from university. John was a very good batsman, just missing a university blue; his father, however, played more to make up the team.

THE REVEREND JACK SHAW (1959-1961)

John Jamieson recalled that, "The Reverend Shaw came to Brabourne and Smeeth for a two-year 'break' from his true vocation as a chaplain in mental institutions of some kind." However, he did not appear to like the country and, according to one of our contributors, always carried a stick when he went out to keep the cows away. Accounts from some parishioners suggest that he was not popular with everyone as some considered that he had been abrupt on occasions. In spite of this, his initial letter to the people of the parish, printed in the Parish Magazine of 1959, suggests that he had a warm and friendly side to him. We include an extract below:

"As many of you will know, I am coming to you from very exacting work in a great London hospital. In fact for the past ten years I have had a great deal to do with hospitals either as a part-time or a full-time Chaplain. Those years have provided a stimulating and humbling experience. I have seen how tremendously important our Christian way of life is, and how great our responsibility. I hope our Church life together will reflect this spirit in the years to come. I like to be in all the corners of parochial life, in all the communities' activities, and perhaps am a little less concerned to appear on platforms and make speeches. We like to keep open house at the Rectory, and we hope you will all feel that there is a sincere and eager welcome awaiting you whenever you like to come."

## THE REVEREND RAY SHEEKEY (1961-1978)
A personal account by the Reverend Ray Sheekey:

"In 1961, I was offered the living of Brabourne, Smeeth and Monks Horton by the Archbishop of Canterbury, the patron. It did not take

The Reverend Ray Sheekey

Barbara and me long to make up our minds to accept it and, very soon, arrangements were put in hand for the Institution on June 13th – except that, in the meantime, the Archbishop had retired, which meant that the Lord Chancellor had the right to appoint a new priest. The arrangements went ahead and we moved into Smeeth Rectory on June 1st, only to receive a letter from the Lord Chancellor saying that if I wished I could apply to be considered for the position of incumbent. I wrote to him and said that the Bishop of Dover and the Archdeacon of Maidstone had planned to conduct the Institution and that I and the family were firmly ensconced in the Rectory and had no plans to move out. The Lord Chancellor approved the appointment.

"Brabourne and Smeeth were nicely contrasted as parishes, and you couldn't necessarily do the same in one as you could in the other. During my time as a curate I had learned the importance of getting to know people and this was my first task. I established contact with several parishioners who, over the years, had become distanced from the church and this proved fruitful.

"I saw no reason initially to make great changes, as often happens with a new incumbent. Changes would come for a reason, and after preparing the ground. It was in these early years that great changes in Brabourne Lees and Smeeth were taking place, with the building of Knatchbull Way and Prospect Way, infilling in Canterbury Road and the Mountbatten estate. I found it very profitable to pursue furniture vans! Many people were moving in from far and wide and welcomed a visitor who could pass on local information about schools, doctors and health facilities, and of course, the church.

"At both churches we had midweek services and I would usually arrive at Brabourne with a car fully loaded with the elderly who otherwise would not have been able to get to church. I tried to keep in touch with the elderly and, in the great freeze of 1963, I had a daily round of visiting and trying to get their taps unfrozen, but I'm not a good plumber. The freeze was persistent and for several weeks we were unable to get to Brabourne. From Manor Pound to beyond the school, the road had disappeared under a mountain of snow as high as the hedges. The children had a long Christmas holiday that year.

"And who remembers the Bircholt Mission Room? It stood on the corner of a little lane leading to Bircholt, beyond which were the barely visible remains of the ancient parish church of St Margaret, Bircholt. Bet Finn and I cleaned up the room and we started to use it for a Sunday School, a task taken over by Mrs Coleman when Bet had to give it up. And when Mrs Coleman moved away, Christine Gurr stepped in to run the Sunday School and was assisted by Sally Furneaux [Willett]. But after one heavy winter Keith Finn advised us it was unsafe to use – it had always been a fight to get the door open – so it was decided to demolish it. The income from the Kent peg tiles was enough to pay for the demolition, and the land passed back to the Hatch estate and 'the place thereof knoweth it no more'.

"One of the great problems at Brabourne was keeping the large churchyard in some kind of order. Mr Jack, a contractor, cut the main grass, but his big machine would not go between graves, so I organised a monthly churchyard evening when people would turn up with shears and shovels and return some order of tidiness. Mrs Margaret Opperman, then in her late eighties, would come along from Clandon Cottage, but if the weather was poor or she was unwell, she would always send Avis [Thornby] along with a basket of goodies, especially for the young ones. [Avis looked after Mrs Opperman for over 30 years until she died in 1982.]

"Mrs Opperman was one of several elderly people who couldn't get to church to whom I took Communion once a month in their homes. It was a shortened service and much appreciated by its recipients, as was the cup of coffee and chat enjoyed by me after the service.

"Every week, on Tuesday mornings, I used to go into Brabourne School for half an hour, the infants one week and the juniors the next. With the infants it was usually a bible story, finishing with their

Induction of the Reverend Ray Sheekey
From left, 1.Ian Allard, 2.Mr Birchett, 3.Anthony Finn, 4.Iden Wetherell, 5.Derek Marsh, 6.Sue Todd, 7.Clergyman who helped during interregnum, 8.Christine Todd, 9.Rt Rev Lord Bishop of Dover, 10.Unknown clergyman but not robed, perhaps Rural Dean, 11.The Rev R.A. Sheekey, 12.Jacquie Friend, 13.Charles Todd, 14.Christine Friend, 15.The Venerable Archdeacon of Maidstone, 16.Local clergyman, 17.Ann Todd, 18.Danny Thornby, 19.Jackie Davis, 20.Margaret Davis, 21.Mr "Chug" Summers. Names of those present recorded by Joy Finn

own drawings about what they had heard. I'm sure their efforts were better than mine! With the juniors I covered the Catechism – a section in the Book of Common Prayer outlining the Christian faith – the Creed, the sacraments and the Ten Commandments. It sounds very old hat today but the series of lessons I used were well illustrated and interesting. We finished it up with some writing copied from the board – chalk and talk! – during which I took care to correct mistakes and spelling. George Hutchinson, the head of Brabourne School, and I became good friends and he was a great help in the Son et Lumière story.

"When I was coming to Brabourne, my former vicar told me of its royal connections but I never actually thought that one day I might meet the Queen. Just into the Advent season the phone rang and it was Lady Brabourne – as she then was – saying that the Queen had expressed a wish to come to Mattins at Brabourne. She advised me that it was a private visit and that the press should not be informed. She made a few points about correct procedure and how many seats should be reserved for the party. Though the visit was not to be publicised, I had to make sure that Her Majesty didn't come to almost-empty pews.

The Queen attends a Sunday service,
pictured at Smeeth Church (1960s)

"I met the Queen at the end of Brabourne's long brick path and escorted her into her pew. It was quite a silent walk as protocol means you wait for the Queen to speak first, and that path grew longer and longer. Mattins proceeded according to the book and

I preached my sermon fully aware of her presence. Then it was over and I was escorting her back to the car. I have always wished that I had asked the Queen if she would have liked to see the 12th-century Norman glass window, but the opportunity was lost. The Queen was on her way and I was left wondering, 'Did it really happen?' Was I nervous, I'm often asked. Strangely, I wasn't – perhaps a bit tense, but in reality I was only doing the job I had been trained to do. After all, there were two more visits to come at Smeeth.

"Sunday services were much more demanding than they are today. I inherited an 8.00am Holy Communion and an Evensong at 6.30pm, which alternated with Smeeth, and at 10.00am at Brabourne there was a sung Mattins every Sunday. This changed as time went on to a Sung Communion – echoes of Merbecke! – every other week. Then it was straight down to Smeeth for a repeat performance of, yes, Mattins at 11.15am! You can perhaps understand why I'm no longer keen on it. This arrangement ensured that each church had at least two services every Sunday and, as there was often an overlap of congregation, sometimes I would find it necessary to prepare three sermons for a Sunday.

"Looking back I can say that I enjoyed my 17 years at Brabourne and Smeeth, for they were almost entirely free of friction. To some extent I think that this was due to the impact of the Son et Lumière so early in my time in the parish. It showed what we could achieve through co-operation and with a sense of vision and determination. There can have been very few households throughout the parish who didn't become involved to some extent and this was a binding, trusting force. It worked for good and I felt my ministry was enriched by this mutual working together. I am grateful for those happy years, which still bring back many happy memories, and for providing the safe and secure environment in which my children, David and Anne, grew up."

Childhood memories from The Rectory by Anne Davies (Sheekey):
"I was just over two years old when we moved to the rectory at Smeeth and some of my earliest memories are of being taken by Daddy to visit the 'old ladies'. There must have been some gentlemen, too, but I can't remember them. Nine times out of ten

I was told 'Don't you look like your father!', which is not what you want to hear between the ages of three and eight! Presumably, taking me on these visits was to get me out of the house and keep me occupied. It was lovely if we were going to see Mrs Opperman because that meant some of her housekeeper Avis's homemade cakes or biscuits. Terrifying if we were going to see Miss Knaster on the Pilgrims' Way as her pigeons roosted in the front porch, so you had to run the gauntlet to get to the door. Get ready and duck! Other visits were okay but much depended on whether there were chocolate biscuits. Mummy was always very nifty with the sewing machine and had made me a cape out of red material that generated lots of comments of, 'Doesn't she look like Red Riding Hood?' One house I do remember was Broad Oak at West Brabourne, where an old couple lived. This, of course, was before any work had been done on it and the inside, I assume, had hardly changed for several centuries. There was even a wooden ladder to the upstairs. It was later renovated and, in the 1970s, rented to the racing driver Graham Hill.

"I was too young to stay up and see the first Son et Lumière at Brabourne but for the second one I was allowed to make the sound of the knights coming into the church to look for the silver. This involved me rattling our fish knives and forks in a metal wastepaper bin. Then, great excitement, I was allowed to stay up to see a performance.

"As the year turned towards Christmas there was always carol singing to look forward to. David, my brother, and I would accompany Daddy but rarely Mummy. Despite being a keen gardener and loving being outdoors, she didn't find the dark and the cold appealing. She hated Bonfire Night, too, which I always loved. So, on from the church and along The Street, stopping along the way to sing, until – joy! – we all went to Mrs Opperman's for Avis's mince pies. Delicious. We then sang outside the Five Bells, and two of the men went in to collect. Occasionally, you got a glimpse through the door, but this was forbidden territory in those days, probably for many of the ladies, too. Then down to Penstock, the lovely smell of the horses in the stable as we went past, followed by mince pies… maybe… I can't quite remember. Down to the end of the houses, then in cars to the school and dear old Mr Goble, who we used to pick up every Sunday for church. And after that – hooray! – cars to Park Farm for carols and sausage rolls, crisps, more mince pies and drinks. Yummy! When I was older and Mummy had passed her driving test, I think she used to come and meet us there. No wonder I enjoyed it.

"Talking of Park Farm and driving, it was the first place I drove to on my own after passing my test in Daddy's brown Audi, a car he had yearned to own for many a year. Fortunately, I never scratched it in all the times I drove it. Phew! He was very proud of all his cars and it was sacrilege to get a mark on any of them.

"The other time in the year that there was a parade around the village was, of course, Rogation Sunday. This was fun, but not the same without the refreshments along the way. I sang in the choir at Brabourne as girls weren't allowed at Smeeth. David was a chorister there for many years. Quite often it was just Daddy and me sitting in the choir at Brabourne, looking across at each other, for Evensong – he, tapping time with his finger on the pew end, with Meloids in his cassock pocket for a tickly throat. Boy, did they wake your throat up!

"There were reasonably regular phone calls to the Rectory from people wanting to see the church, and some from relatives of the Scotts. One day a couple came from America to visit and I can remember being present while they were talking to Daddy in the drive at Smeeth, maybe after they had been to the church. Before they left they gave me 5 shillings – in those days, a fortune. The next Christmas a box arrived and it was a lovely blonde-haired doll with a turquoise corduroy coat and bonnet. I had never had such a doll – money was tight and sensibly we were never lavished with presents, even if they could have afforded it. Out came the sewing machine and many more outfits were made for Diana, as I called her.

"Which reminds me… When I was about six, I was bit peaky one day and when asked what was the matter, I uttered words that went down in family history, 'I'm sickening for a miniskirt!' Off to Ashford Market again and the lovely large gentleman who ran the fabric stall had a length of brightly coloured flower-print denim, which Mummy duly turned into a skirt, with a white lampshade fringe around the bottom. I remember wearing it when presenting a bouquet to Lady Brabourne when she came to open the fête one year – at Smeeth, I think. I thought I was the bees' knees.

"Brabourne fêtes were held in Penstock barn, as were many happy events. One famous time I had a particularly good run on the bottle stall. I was stopped after a while as I was deemed embarrassingly successful, but not before I had won a bottle of whisky – the ticket bought with my own pocket money. It was a few months before I let Daddy have the bottle, his favourite tipple, normally only taken late on a Friday evening to help with sermon writing. It was only in the late 1970s, when we had started holidaying abroad, that he would bring home some duty-free. It was strictly rationed, though I'm not sure I didn't swap it for something I wanted.

"I made a few pennies out of the American and Australian visitors, as quite a few requested brass rubbings. This would have been in the 1970s, as I was a teenager by then and becoming more interested in art. Black on white paper or, much classier, gold wax crayon on matt-black paper. Then there was always the hunt to find tubes in which to send them overseas. A bit of extra pocket money, always welcome.

"Times were very happy at Smeeth and Brabourne, with what was, for all intents and purposes, an extended family. I was very privileged to ride with John and Vi Varrier and, in particular, to be allowed to go out on Saturdays on my own with their lovely horse Karby while they went hunting. I shall always be eternally grateful for that. Laughter was always in abundance at the Rectory and in the villages.

"To end, there was great hilarity – well, masked hilarity – when, one Sunday, Mummy, David and I were standing in the back pew at Brabourne, singing away. Suddenly, out of the corner of my eye I realised that David wasn't there. He had been resting his foot on the edge of the pew and lost his balance. We all dissolved, and every time we managed to stop, one of us would start giggling and set us all off again. No doubt we got told off by the vicar! Happy days!"

We would add that this particular pew was removed from the church a few years ago and now resides with David Sheekey and his family.

..................................................................................................................

## THE REVEREND MICHAEL STEPHENS (1979-1994)
Memories of Brabourne from the Reverend Stephens:

The Reverend Michael Stephens

"Coming from a somewhat-downtown Maidstone parish with an early Victorian church with a single bell, it was a considerable contrast to find myself appointed vicar of a country parish with its church dating back to Norman times, and its tower holding six bells. Having been a bell-ringer since April 1945, it was naturally a great joy to spend many Friday evenings ringing on easy-going bells, and the occasional full-length peal – on one occasion with five other clerical ringers.

"Many features of St Mary's Church will have been photographed by amateurs and professionals, but one feature that had escaped many locals' attention was the ancient stained-glass window in the north wall of the chancel, which for a time earned itself an entry in the Guinness Book of Records as the oldest Norman stained-glass window in existence still in its original setting. In 1986, I received a letter from the publishers, requesting a photo of this window. As nobody appeared to possess such a photo, my younger son Martin splashed out and bought himself a zoom lens for his camera. His photograph featured in the 1987 edition of the book, along with the caption 'taken by Martin of Smeeth'. Sadly, the result of this illustration produced a claim for a more ancient glass window elsewhere, bringing an end to Brabourne's entry.

"A third memory of St Mary's is inevitably the stone altar and the reredos in the chancel, wonderfully painted by Oliver Trowell, with its inscription, 'The memory of the just shall be blessed, but the name of the wicked shall rot'. I have often wondered what effect those words have had in the minds of generations of village folk through the centuries, as they seem to leave little place for the working out of any Christian ministry of forgiveness and reconciliation.

"From structural matters to people. One of my very clear memories is that of taking the sacrament of Holy Communion each month to Mrs Margaret Opperman, in her late nineties, living at Clandon Cottage, in The Street. After the service, her housekeeper served coffee. Then we would talk about recent events, Mrs Opperman frequently continuing the topic of conversation of the previous visit, to my utter amazement – and embarrassment at having forgotten what we had discussed. Her use of memory was seldom about long-distant happenings, but rather of the immediate past and its relevance to us in the present. The far-off past had its joys and sorrows and this part of her life was not to be denied, yet whilst life continued there were plenty of experiences to be fully savoured and appreciated, right up to her 100th birthday. She asked questions – 'Where does happiness come from? Why do I go on living – there must be some reason for it?' She shared her joy with so many others – old friends of long standing, young children, too, a middle-aged vicar, and the library-van staff – 'all sorts and conditions of men', to use a phrase from the old Prayer Book, and women, too. There was joy and, yes, generosity. I hope the tree that was planted in the village in her memory thrives, just as she did, for many a year.

"Another character in my early years in Brabourne was George Hutchinson, the head teacher at Brabourne Primary School for 17 years. During his time the school register grew threefold and, despite limited facilities – remember the Shack, that garden shed used for the staff room, medical examinations, interviews with parents, and everything else? – he ensured that every child enjoyed education in its widest sense. At his farewell event attended by a crowd of pupils from his early years, I recollect he was able to remember who they were, and when they attended the school. What a wonderful gift!

"One further memory is that of a snow-covered countryside on a first Sunday after Christmas. Driving from the 9.30am service at Smeeth to Brabourne's 11 o'clock service, I rounded the bend by the Five Bells, and as I straightened up along The Street, I found I was gradually mounting the roadside bank, and eventually toppled over. In next to no time, alert occupants from Subdown Cottages poured out to get me back on my four wheels, and another person hurried down to the church to explain why the vicar was delayed. John Varrier and others came out to see if I was fit, and able to start the service. Yes – I was. We did start a little later than the advertised time, though, and with a thinner-than-usual congregation!"

Remembering the day the vicar's car overturned, Katrina Bewick (Stone), who lived at Subdown Cottages, tied this to the late 1970s, probably 1979, shortly after Michael Stephens and his wife, Molly, had moved into Smeeth Rectory. Katrina had gone upstairs, happened to look out of the window and shouted to her father that there was a car upside down on the opposite side of the road to no.3, Subdown Cottages. Immediately, Phil Stone, Arthur and Emma Hudson from no.4, Norman Thornby from no.2, Subdown Cottages, and Anthony Finn from 1, Holly Cottages, almost next door, rushed to help. It was the Reverend Stephens on his way to morning service at Brabourne Church who had overturned, and, no, he wasn't hurt, though naturally he was of shaken. With the combined efforts of several residents from The Street, his car, a white Austin 1100, was swiftly back on four wheels on the road, and the vicar, deeply grateful for having been rescued so promptly, drank a quick cup of tea before continuing on his way to church.

People also remembered well Molly Stephens, Michael's wife, who was for many years a post lady in the village.

....................................................................................................

## THE REVEREND PETER THACKRAY (1995-1999)

In his position as Priest in Residence, Peter Thackray may be remembered for two things above many others: first, for his warmth and friendship to all. As Roger Vining once put it, "Peter transformed Brabourne Church from a group of people into a family." Second, he will be remembered for revising the Family Service at Brabourne with some reference to the likes and dislikes of his younger parishioners, including their request for five hymns in a 40-minute service, which meant that the congregation was bobbing up and down like yo-yos. Children unused to entertainment at Family Services and who were disinclined to attend were soon brought round by the greater part they were invited to play in the service, such as holding this or that, or taking the part of a Roman soldier, an angel or the Virgin Mary. There was remarkably frequent use of fire, and small boys in particular enjoyed lighting tapers and putting out flames. One

Peter Thackray with his daughter, Sam

enduring memory is when Peter's use of pyrotechnics to illustrate some point long forgotten during a service caused the chancel to become filled with smoke and the door to be left open so that "we might all breathe again". Children also enjoyed receiving Sunday School prizes from him, even though we did not have a Sunday School at the time.

Peter's version of the Family Services was continued very successfully by John Varrier, who retired at the start of 2012. They were both hard acts to follow. The addition of coffee and biscuits after the service was introduced by Emma Rees in about 2005, and has strengthened the family feel of the service even more. A Sunday School grew up and, for a time, was led very effectively by Vicki Jessel. It is now led by Alex Le Rossignol, who, on the third Sunday of every month, has introduced the Third Sunday Xtra.

Anna Anthony (Embleton-Smith) remembers:

Peter Thackray with his son, Dominic
(approx 1970)

"Peter Thackray was so much fun! When I first met him I was rather dismissive – I was only about 12 at the time and he was a vicar, and a fairly ancient one at that (to me anyway!). Unsurprisingly, these were not the characteristics I tended to look for in a friend in those days. But he did become such a good friend and, even in my youthful ignorance, I couldn't fail to realise what a clever, kind and funny person he was. Actually, funny doesn't do him justice; even at that age I loved chatting to him about my life and school and friends, and our conversations always seemed to end with us both in hysterics. He tried to teach me French at one point, although I think he soon realised I had no interest in learning it and really just liked going round for a chat and a chocolate biscuit.

Peter Thackray (2000)

Photographs kindly provided by the Thackray family

"Once, when I was about 12, I was home alone and managed to set off our house alarm. Rather than try to turn it off, as any normal person would, I decided to go outside and see how loud it was. Then, unbelievably, the door shut and locked behind me. So, there I was, locked out, with the alarm going off, but I was definitely able to confirm that it was very loud outside. I could hear 'scary' men from down the road – Will Wilson, Norman Thornby and Bruce Claridge – coming up to see what was going on, so I decided to hide in the garage. After making sure no one was breaking into the house (what very good neighbours), the men went away. A few minutes after that, Peter drove up. What luck! When I saw him, I came out from my hiding place and told him what had happened. He told me he would take me out for a Starbucks and that by the time we got back the alarm was bound to have stopped. I remember us driving off in that Skoda he used to have, laughing.

"I think Peter died when I was about 18 and, apart from my grandparents, he is the only friend I've had who has died. I still think about him and the things I would tell him about if he was still alive. I love seeing his children, Dominic, Sam and Ben, and their families as they all have that wicked Thackray sense of humour."

..................................................................................................

## THE REVEREND WILLIAM COOPER (2000-2004)

After Peter Thackray's retirement, there was a significant interregnum, with the Reverend William Cooper then taking over as Priest-in-Charge for Brabourne, Smeeth, Monks Horton and Stowting. The following anecdote about the Reverend Cooper came from Tom Wilson, then of 1, Holly Cottages, in East Brabourne. At that time Tom used to mow the grass in the churchyard:

Tom Wilson was mowing the grass in the churchyard one summer Saturday morning in preparation for the wedding of Andrew Martin and Sarah Gillies later that day when Tom saw the Reverend Cooper and a local resident come striding towards him. He heard the vicar ask the resident, 'So what's the trouble?', to which the resident replied, 'Well, he's making too much noise. I work all week and expect peace at weekends.' Now brought into the conversation, Tom explained, 'I work too, and I'm trying to get the churchyard ready for the wedding today.' The Reverend Cooper then said, 'I have been at the William Harvey Hospital this morning, tending the sick and dying. You should be thankful you are standing in this lovely churchyard.' He continued addressing the resident, 'I see you have a ride-on mower. Why don't

Tom Wilson and his partner, Becky Kingston

you help? Then it would all be done more quickly.' 'Well,' the resident replied, 'I don't think I can do that.' 'No, I don't suppose you can,' said the Reverend Cooper, 'and why have I not seen you at church?' The resident withdrew in haste, rather sheepishly, and Tom carried on mowing, thinking, 'We need more vicars like that.'

......................................

## THE REVEREND PATRICK GOODSELL, VISITING PRIEST AT BRABOURNE

For many years, the Reverend Patrick Goodsell has taken services at Brabourne Church. During the interregnum, before the arrival of the Reverend Cooper, and after his retirement from Brabourne, Patrick was there virtually every Sunday, giving us a sense of calm and continuity. He thus did a great job in helping us over this period of uncertainty, when we had no idea of who would be installed as priest in our parishes. As a consequence, we are delighted to include him as an honorary member of our list of priests at Brabourne.

Patrick writes:

"I remember the time I ministered in Brabourne with affection. I was called to celebrate the Eucharist on a regular basis, during the sickness of the incumbent and also during the interregnum that followed, for a lengthy period – some two years or so. I had a regular spot – the second Sunday in the month. I always remember the welcome as I negotiated the last ridge of the Downs before dropping down to the church. The bells would ring their summons and their welcome, and waiting at the church would be the faithful few – few by city numbers, but great in many ways. To start with, they were a greater percentage of the population of this scattered community than those of a city. Great, too, in their loyalty, and one sensed great in their love of our Lord, and of his Church.

"The memorable occasions were the great occasions. Christmas, Easter, harvest brought out the best, flowers and decorations enhancing worship, crib and Easter Garden lovingly assembled, helpful and meaningful as young children came to hear again the good news. The good, old, traditional framework of liturgy and teaching lived, as it had done over the centuries. Worship was enhanced by the organist, who would often compose a 'fanfare' to usher in the reading of the gospel.

"Memorable, too, was the time of remembrance. Remembrance Sunday was shared with Smeeth: one year the service would be at Brabourne, the next at Smeeth. Twice I was asked to preside over the Brabourne service and dedicate the garden of remembrance. A strong turnout by the British Legion bore tribute to the many who had served our King and country through two world wars. In Brabourne they are not forgotten.

"But I suppose the greatest impact the church in Brabourne had on me was its steadfastness and living witness to and with a scattered rural community in Kent."

..........................................................................................................

THE REVEREND RICHARD LE ROSSIGNOL
(2006-PRESENT)
Following lengthy interregnums and periods of uncertainty in our churches, we are now delighted and grateful that we have Richard and his wife, Alexandra (Alex), who have integrated so well into life in our villages.

Richard writes:

"Although I was licensed as Priest-in-Charge of Brabourne at the beginning of 2006, my associations with the church began some 20 years earlier, from 1985, when I was approached by the Reverend Michael Stephens to cover services during his annual holidays. In the years that followed I regularly undertook these duties and it became a familiar pattern to be telephoned in the middle of January to book cover for holidays during the first three weeks of June.

The Reverend Richard Le Rossignol

"For a couple of months during the 1990s our family survived without the luxury of a car and so the journeys from Willesborough to Smeeth and Brabourne were undertaken on my trusty bicycle. I usually had to cover services at 8.00am and 9.30am, and in the half-hour in between I was warmly invited to share breakfast with one of the parishioners. I even remember one occasion when both myself and my bike were transported to breakfast in a car.

"My association with the parishes continued when I was licensed as a non-stipendiary assistant in 1994. At both Brabourne and Smeeth – it was just a two-parish benefice then! – I was always welcomed with warm and generous hospitality, which has continued to this day.

Alex and Richard Le Rossignol

"Alex and I were overjoyed when we

were invited to serve the parishes in a leadership capacity and to live in Smeeth Rectory. It really was a dream come true."

......................................................................................

## THE REVEREND DENNIS ROBSON

Dennis is a retired Pentecostal minister who, at the time of writing, lives in East Brabourne. Together with his wife, Valerie, who plays the organ at Brabourne's Family Service, the Robsons are valued members of our church community.

Dennis writes:

"I confess that Brabourne was an area of the country that was unknown to me, although I had lived in Kent for over 40 years.

"Durham County was my home, where I served a seven-year apprenticeship as an engineer with The National Coal Board at a local colliery and cokeworks. During that

The Reverend Dennis Robson

time I felt the call of God to Christian ministry, so after studying for this in Bible College, I ministered in a church in Maidstone for 13 very happy years. Then, after two years serving our Home Missions Department, pioneering new churches, I was called to be the minister of The Evangelical Church in Chatham, where we served for 28 years, seeing the church grow until our retirement in 2004.

"A chance phone call brought us to Brabourne. Val and I love village life after the busy, noisy area where we had lived before. We have been impressed with the kindness and welcome of the folks here. We thought that it might take a long time to be accepted into village life, but this was not true. Although our background is Free Church, we have enjoyed the fellowship of God's people here in Brabourne and have been accepted as members of the local community."

## SON ET LUMIERE AT ST MARY'S

Inspired by the Reverend Ray Sheekey, the two stagings of the Son et Lumière at Brabourne Church in 1964 and 1966 raised significant funds to enable essential restoration work on the church to be carried out. If this had not been completed the church would almost certainly have been in a far worse condition than it is today. Below, the Reverend Sheekey describes how the Son et Lumière grew from an ambitious idea into reality:

Front cover of programme

"I became vicar of Brabourne in 1961 and at my first PCC I was presented with an architect's report that suggested we needed £6,000 to carry out essential repairs to the fabric. Ivy festooned the tower, the roof wanted retiling, and the bells were silent as the wooden frame was condemned with deathwatch beetle. Of course, the restoration fund stood at nil.

"It was encouraging that already efforts were being made to raise money for the repairs, but £6,000 – in today's terms at least £60,000 – was a daunting sum to work to and it was clear that it would require more than an extra jumble sale to achieve this much. Plans were in hand already to hold a Brabourne Festival week, with drama, music and history, and my wife Barbara introduced the idea of holding coffee mornings – familiar to us now, but then quite rare. They 'took off' and raised surprisingly more than we had imagined they would. What pleased me was people's commitment to face the challenge. In 1963 we held our first Flower Festival, again a rare event in those days and it attracted a large number of visitors who proved how generous they could be. Our flower arrangers showed us their talents on this and future occasions.

"In the early 1960s, a French architect had watched the chateau of Chambord (Loire valley) as a fierce thunderstorm raged around. He was fascinated as the flashes of lightning played

Brabourne's first Flower Festival (1963)

around the building, the turrets, towers and chimneys, whilst the crashing of the thunder lent drama to the whole scene. With great vision he conceived the idea of telling the story of the chateau just using the media of sound and light and, at Chambord, he realised his ambition. It was a great success and launched the concept of Son et Lumière, which soon became popular. Greenwich Palace was the first rendezvous in the country and I was fascinated to read in the paper how effectively a story could be told through these media, and it left an indelible picture in my mind. The only Son et Lumière I had seen was at Canterbury and although I was disappointed at the presentation, the S&L bug remained with me and, in my mind, I could imagine Brabourne's story unfold. There was so much to imagine: the building of the church, the Scott family, the heart shrine, witchcraft, the fall of the tower, colourful predecessors, the installation of the organ and, in the end, the plea for the restoration of the bells. It was all there. Brabourne had a story to tell.

"The summer of June 1964 was very hot with nights when sleep refused to come. I lay awake and it started: the vision of how Brabourne's Son et Lumière would come to life. One night, at round 2am I got up and went to the study, produced the typewriter and began writing; the words just flowed and very soon I had four pages of script. The next night another four pages were written, but where was it going?

"Barbara loved entertaining and we liked to invite newcomers to supper at the Rectory, and it so happened that Bernard Marks and his wife moved to West Brabourne. An evening with them divulged that he was a dedicated bell-ringer and interested in amateur dramatics, looking after the stage lighting. Never look a gift horse in the mouth! 'Bernard, would you be interested in…?' From the start we were on the same wavelength and he encouraged me to continue with the writing and to raise the matter at the next PCC meeting.

"The reaction there was puzzlement and I had to spell out exactly what a Son et Lumière was. But the PCC gave me its backing with the words, 'If you think you can do it, Vicar, we'll back you.' I think I may have suggested that we should aim to put the show on in the autumn, which was pure madness. The script was incomplete, I had no sound equipment at all, no tape recorder, only a promise that Bernard would look after the lighting side, approaching local drama societies to borrow spot lamps and floods and whatever else might be useful. I borrowed a mono tape recorder from a friend and so started rehearsing and recording what was so far written. We had no duplicators or modern-day equivalents, so all the scripts had to be typed making carbon copies, four at a time. Joy Finn [then Secretary to the PCC] was kept very busy with all this activity.

The lighting specialist: Bernard Marks

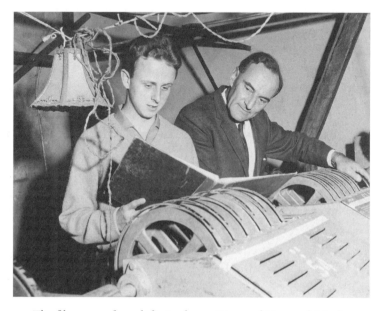

The film crew: from left, Anthony Finn and Bernard Marks

The sound engineer: the Reverend Ray Sheekey

Brabourne Church lit for the event

The interior lit for the performance

"Realising I had to come to terms with producing a good sound line, I approached Grundig to see if they were willing to help in supplying equipment in return for publicity. The approach brought me a meeting with one of their Principals, who was completely co-operative, offering me a stereo tape recorder and a mono, as many speakers as I wanted, cable for the wiring and the offer of two of their technicians to come and do the recording. We went off on holiday without a care in the world and, when we came back, Bernard assured me he had arranged all the lighting. Great! 'Strand Electric are going to provide all the equipment and do all the wiring for us! It's going to cost £140.' I nearly fell through the floor. We had no financial backing and there was no guarantee that we would sell even one ticket, presuming we got as far as an actual production.

"The script was now finished and our cast, with no lines to learn, showed remarkable dramatic talent as we worked to a final date to get it all down on tape. I had been collecting sound effects for use in the background, running water, horses, monks chanting, crashing masonry, bells and suitable music. Today you can buy discs of sound effects but back then you produced your own.

"Fixing the dates for the production was not easy. We needed the dark evenings to show the lighting to full effect, but there was a snag. The church was heated then – or warmed! – by electrical tubular heaters on a time clock. This was suspended but the supply would not allow us to use the heaters and the lighting at the same time. The presentation had to be made before the evenings got really cold, so we opted for October. The heaters were put on in the afternoon and switched off just before the performance, which meant that the church gradually got colder and colder.

"By now we had turned our attention to publicity, programmes, posters, the press and to deadlines, all of which were required for making the final audio tape. Grundig had offered to provide two technicians to do the recording and an evening was arranged when they could come and record our 'cast'. Because the technicians were coming straight from work in Croydon, Barbara laid on a really good supper for six o'clock. Time went on and on and the cast assembled in the church – no mobile phones to let them know what was not happening. After seven, they arrived, having got lost. We hurried some supper down them and briefed them while they ate, then shovelled them into the car and departed to Brabourne to the patient cast.

"It is a fact that every recorded minute of tape – audio or video – takes, at the very least, 10 times that amount to produce. Our technicians knew their stuff and, when it got too late to continue, we had recorded about three or four minutes of sound. We were recording in stereo and they produced the only true piece of stereo in which the footsteps of the Archbishop of Canterbury, coming to dedicate the new church, moved from the porch down the aisle to the altar. The Grundig folk had originally arranged to spend the next day, a Saturday, with us, but a work commitment had occurred so we were on our own.

"The script consisted of a main narration that moved the story on with dramatic interludes telling the tale. It was these interludes I needed desperately to record and here Mike Clover took over the production and I sat at the tape recorders. George Hutchinson, the Head of Brabourne School, was the narrator and it was fairly easy to get his contributions on tape and then edit them into the episodes, except that I knew nothing about editing, but George had a friend in Folkestone whose hobby was editing. I was on his doorstep with equipment at 9 o'clock the following Saturday morning and we started work and did not stop until the early evening. He sensed exactly what was needed and, when we finished, I had a tape with narration, dramatic scenes, sound effects and linking music. Exhausted, I arrived home with my precious prize, but there was no time to listen to it – it was the evening of the harvest supper in the Village Hall.

"Finally, at about 11 o'clock, Barbara and I sat down to listen to our tape, all 60 minutes of it. I was enthralled – it was just what I had imagined right from the start and now we had half of the already-publicised Son et Lumière. There was just the lighting. Bernard and I had liaised very thoroughly about what lighting effects we wanted to achieve and Strand Electric were very co-operative and able to provide all we wanted. They had arranged for two of their electricians to spend the week in Brabourne to do all the wiring. Bernard had specified that he didn't want any of the lights to be seen, and no wiring. All the equipment in those days was much heavier than it is today and the main cable, running the length of the church and about 2in in diameter, was threaded at the top of the north wall where it meets the ceiling some 40ft up. We had four dimmers to control the lighting and each one of these was a cabinet about 3ft square. Gordon Fortescue, the local builder, had erected scaffolding and a platform in the tower and the four controllers had to be hoisted up with a winch. From there Bernard and I had a complete view of the church whilst remaining out of view ourselves. Gordon gave us valuable assistance but he never charged a penny.

"By now many people had got themselves involved. Betty and Joy Finn took charge of the publicity side, sending out details to all sorts of organisations all over the county. The kitchen staff got together and planned a three-course supper after the performance in Penstock Barn – for five shillings (25p)! The flower arrangers made plans for the floral decorations, rotas were drawn up for stewards each night and contacts were made with the AA and police to direct the cars and coaches coming from far and wide. The rather special programmes, printed white on black, as were the posters, were ordered from Canterbury, together with the numbered tickets. There was to be a performance each evening, except Sunday, for a fortnight, with reserved tickets costing 7/6d (37½p).

"The lights were installed and with the sound tape all ready, Bernard and I prepared for our one and only dress rehearsal, the first time we had put everyone together in situ. I had invited the press to come and see it in the hopes of getting a good write-up in the Friday weekly papers. The harvest decorations were still left over from the Sunday, but it mattered not – we got a good press, very good indeed.

"The box office was at the Rectory and bookings for seats and supper came rolling in and, on Monday, 19th October, 1964, at 7.30pm, Brabourne's Son et Lumière got underway.

"Appropriate music set the scene as the pews began to fill, then came the opening of Beethoven's Pastoral Symphony, fading to hear George Hutchinson's arresting voice,

'Welcome, we bid you…' The show was on. Two main speakers carried the sound at the altar, with a speaker in the pulpit (narrator's), one by the porch, whilst one at the base of the tower came into use only once and briefly. One scene depicted the collapse of the tower in a fierce storm and the crashing of masonry was heard from this speaker. Those seated nearby literally jumped out of their seats!

"Within the first week we found bookings were so heavy that we had to bring in extra chairs, and Barbara, in the brief moments of conversation we could have between the telephone ringing, suggested we should go for a third week. There was no problem, for Grundig and Strand were happy to co-operate and so the show went on. I wanted to go for a fourth week, but Barbara sensed that booking demands were easing and that it was better to call a halt while on a high.

"After the last night, all those who had played any part at all joined together in Penstock Barn to celebrate. We were in euphoric mood and Bernard gave the provisional figures of the success of our endeavours. But then, for me, events took a totally unexpected turn, when Bill Deedes, the former editor of The Daily Telegraph, who had been at our final performance, presented me with a silver salver inscribed with, 'Lumière, Brabourne Kent, 1964'. I was deeply touched, as the success of our venture was due largely to the wonderful support that everyone had given me. And there was elation again on Monday morning, when the Peterborough column in The Daily Telegraph gave a glowing tribute to our venture.

"One of the unexpected aspects of our success was the great number of complimentary letters we received, and specially praising the wonderful suppers enjoyed in Penstock Barn. Our ladies, especially Joan Clifton, Margaret Older, Joy Finn, Mary Bean and many others, did a wonderful job and their culinary skills were much appreciated. At five shillings a time, they made a wonderful profit.

"As a result of the publicity, I had quite a few letters asking me how to go about producing a Son et Lumière and I set out a standard letter outlining what was required: a story to tell, how to tell it, the equipment required and a dedicated band of helpers, with a warning that success was not guaranteed. Several local churches accepted the challenge, with various degrees of success, but one lady at Milford Haven, Pembrokeshire, wrote some years later to say that they had one planned and invited Barbara and me to stay with her and see their production, something we enjoyed. It was a pleasant reminder of our own. "Even now, over 45 years later, I find it difficult to believe that the Son et Lumière was conceived, planned, produced and successfully concluded in the space of six months. I think I was mad to believe it could be done. It was a miracle – or the Holy Spirit!"

## BRABOURNE BELLS, BELL-RINGING AND ORGANISTS

It seems right that this section follows the story of the Son et Lumière as the funds generated in the 1960s from this and other events were what led to the bells being restored – and augmented. The picture below, taken from a very dark slide discovered by David Sheekey, shows the bells outside the church in the 1960s, repairs to the framework which holds them having started.

Bells outside the west door of Brabourne Church.
Although this picture is very dark we have included it because
it is the only pictorial record we have of this event

Charles Sinden writes:

"English bells and bell-ringing are unique, and the United Kingdom and some former colonies are the only countries where bells are hung for Change Ringing. This entails bells being swung through 360 degrees – the ringer pulls on the sally (the fluffy part of the rope) and lets go, the rope then winds round the wheel as the bell swings and the ringer is left holding the tail-end, which he pulls, and the rope unwinds and the ringer catches the sally again. The skill is knowing when to catch and to let go and the ringer needs a good sense of rhythm. It takes about six months to become reasonably competent.

"There are about 5,700 churches in the UK with five or more bells. Five is considered the minimum number required to ring changes, with 12 being the generally accepted maximum. When one describes a ring of bells, the number of bells is given, along with the weight of the tenor bell, the tenor being the heaviest one, the treble being the lightest. Brabourne now has a ring of eight bells, with a tenor of 11cwt 3qtr, and they are rung from the ground floor at the base of tower. Originally, the tower held a

Charles Sinden, current churchwarden and crucifer at Brabourne Church

ring of five bells, the earliest dating from 1605. At this time bells were often cast by itinerant bell-founders, who built a small furnace in the churchyard, cast the bells and chip tuned them. Chip tuning involves hitting the bell, listening to the note, and chipping at the metal to produce the right sound. The bells would be hung in a wooden frame on basic plain bearings. This often meant bells were hard work to ring, especially in hot, dry weather, when the timbers would shrink and move.

"Very little is known of the ringers of Brabourne during the early period. Ringing was very much a secular activity, with ringers congregating and usually organising themselves at the local pub, which, at Brabourne, was appropriately called the Five Bells. There have been instances of vicars having to pay ringers to ring for services. By the 1880s the relationship between ringers and the clergy had deteriorated to such a degree that things needed to change. The Reverend Knatchbull-Huggesen, the Rector of Mersham, along with the Mersham band, formed a ringing society, with certain rules concerning ringing for service: no drunkenness in the belfry, no swearing, no wearing of hats or spurs in church. This society developed into the Kent County Association of Change Ringers, which still functions today, and to which Brabourne Church is affiliated. Things at Brabourne continued very much unchanged until the First World War.

"At this time a large number of Canadian soldiers were billeted in the village and were made very welcome. They were subsequently despatched to France and fought at Vimy Ridge at the Battle of the Somme, where many were killed. However, they were so appreciative of the welcome they had received from the villagers that the survivors donated a sixth bell, which is named Canada as a memorial to their fallen colleagues. In 2011 a peal of Canada delight major was rung to commemorate these events, with a great-great-grandson of one of these Canadian soldiers ringing. Brabourne has always had a village band, with Philip Pierce the Captain for many years during the 1930s, 1940s and 1950s, and with the Finn family being great supporters of the band. At this time, outings to neighbouring towers were popular. In the 1960s the wooden frame supporting the bells became unsafe, thus making it impossible to ring the bells, and a complete re-hang was required. A concrete ring was placed in the tower to support a new, metal, eight-bell frame and the bells were tuned to modern standards.

The inscription on the bell reads

1917
"CANADA"
TO THE GLORY OF GOD, GIVEN BY
SUBSCRIPTION IN MEMORY OF THE CANADIAN
ARMY WHO FOUGHT IN THE GREAT WAR.

S.K. LOCKYEAR,    VICAR
G.J. PEARSON,   }
T. THORNBY,    }   CHURCHWARDENS

Efforts to raise the funds for the repairs were intense and culminated in two amazing Son et Lumières in the mid-1960s, inspired by the Reverend Ray Sheekey and in which Bernard Marks played a major part [see Ray's account earlier in this chapter].

"In the 1980s the Reverend Michael Stephens was appointed vicar of the parish, which proved to be very good for the band, as he was an extremely competent change ringer and was a member of the Clerical Guild of Ringers. He organised a unique peal, with the six ringers all being incumbents from churches in the Canterbury Diocese. The band continued to flourish under another long-serving Captain, Ray Lucas, achieving ringing of the highest standard. In 2002, two additional bells were donated by parishioners, thus completing the ring of eight bells. Today ringing continues under the Captaincy of Alan Bourner and, recently, the band has won a number of ringing competitions. Brabourne bells are considered one of the finest rings in the county and are popular with visiting bands and peal ringers and sound superb on a summer evening from the Downs above the church."

## BRABOURNE'S EIGHT BELLS
Ray Lucas, a former tower captain, writes:

"There is a record of four bells in the tower in 1552, and these were augmented to five in 1605, when Joseph Hatch of Ulcombe cast the present tenor. In 1656, the earlier four bells were recycled when William Hatch, a relative of Joseph, cast four bells. Between 1699 and 1702, part of the tower was pulled down and rebuilt following storm damage, and the bells were re-hung. From 1774, there were five bells in the tower and, in that same year, the third and fourth of the five bells were re-cast by Pack and Chapman.

"In 1917, the treble of the five was re-cast by local subscription in memory of parishioners of Brabourne who fought in the First World War. At the same time, a new treble, Canada, was cast and presented by the Canadian Army in memory of the members of the Canadian Army who had fought in the First World War. Many Canadian troops were still in camps in Brabourne and Smeeth at the time. The castings were carried out by Mears and Stainbank, and the bells were re-hung by them.

"In 1966, following successful fundraising by the Son et Lumière, the bells were re-tuned as the back six of an octave, with a tenor weight of 11cwt 2qtr 15lb (591kg), in the note of G. The six bells were re-hung in a steel frame for eight bells by the Whitechapel Bell Foundry, the previous wooden frame being unsafe and leaving the bells silent. The re-hanging of the bells was followed by a service of dedication in Brabourne Church. The six bells were finally augmented to eight in 2002, the two new trebles being cast by Whitechapel. One of the trebles was given in memory of Barbara Joyce Sheppard, 1943-2001, and the second new bell, for the Golden Jubilee of Queen Elizabeth II, was given in memory of June and Richard Luckhurst.

"The Whitechapel Bell Foundry has been in continuous operation for a number of centuries, although its name has changed several times. At one time, it was Pack and Chapman, and at another time, Mears and Stainbank. Thus, six out of the eight bells are from Whitechapel.

Ringers at Brabourne, 2013: from left, Judith de Leeuw, Helen Artlett, Janice Burley, Alan Bourner (Tower Captain), Marion Britton, Charles Sinden, Sylvia Lucas and Ray Lucas (former Tower Captain)

Bell hanger Peter Scott from Whitechapel Bell Foundry
with the two new trebles

Given in memory of Barbara
Joyce Sheppard, 1943-2001

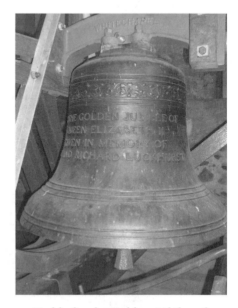

Treble for the Golden Jubilee of
Queen Elizabeth II, given in memory
of June and Richard Luckhurst

"During my time as Tower Captain, I taught bell control to Anne and David Sheekey (David is still ringing at Birchington), Anthony Braben, son of Vi Sprawling (he is still ringing and was at one time Ringing Master at Southwark Cathedral), the three eldest Trowell children, both Hamilton children, Dick Thornby, son Simon (he is still ringing from time to time and is Ringing Master at St Machar's, Aberdeen). Also, I taught Derek Gurr and Jeremy Potter, but both had to give up for medical reasons.

"In the current Brabourne band I taught Penny Walker, Helen Artlett, Mick Mugridge, Janice Burley and Marion Britten (Stowting). When I am ringing at Brabourne with these five, I confess that I feel quite smug!"

The band at Brabourne maintains hundreds of years of tradition by ringing for Sunday services and attending Friday-night practices, where different methods are attempted, some difficult, others a little easier. In the 1950s and 1960s, and probably earlier, too, it was not unusual for many local people to "have a go" at bell-ringing. Not all that many of them persisted, but several of the people with whom we spoke had tried bell-ringing, and enjoyed the camaraderie. Pauline Anderson (Marsh) can remember being confused by Bernard Marks when he shouted orders at them and was panicked by the "snaking" of the bell ropes when they were released. And everyone seemed to remember that Jean Lawes had to stand on a box to ring the bells. The Finns, however, were "regulars": Sidney Finn was a committed bell-ringer, as was his nephew, Keith Finn, and Keith's son, Anthony. According to Anthony, on Christmas mornings in the 1950s, he, his father and Derek Marsh used to climb the tower stairs at 6am and tie ropes to the clappers so that they could be swung to strike the bells by hand as there weren't sufficient ringers.

Although the picture is taken in Stowting Church, several of the ringers are from Brabourne: from left, Jack Coveney, possibly Mark Lancefield, Sidney Finn, Leonard Finn, Keith Finn and Mr Cheeseman (Source: KM Group, date unknown)

Though our congregations are small these days, we are more fortunate with the number of ringers we have and, on most Sundays, including Christmas Day, the sound of Brabourne's bells are to be heard throughout the village and beyond. New ringers are given the chance to learn more about ringing under the guidance of very experienced people. The current band comprises 12 ringers of varying standards, including a retired police officer, motor mechanic, hospital matron and retired research chemist. Some people join the band but find the process of learning to ring very challenging; others surge on to call changes and then method ringing, gaining experience over time through the practices and visits to other towers. The ringers organise an annual outing to other towers in the county and also an annual Christmas dinner, while also supporting many church social activities and events. Brabourne bells are popular with ringers from neighbouring towers who appreciate the excellent bells and skilful local ringers. Long may this continue!

George Skeer, the most decorated ringer to fall in the
First World War, and a ringer at Brabourne

## ST MARY THE VIRGIN, BRABOURNE –
## THE NEWEST EIGHT BELL TOWER IN KENT

An extract from the Brabourne and Smeeth Parish News, 2002, by Ray Lucas, Tower Captain:

Well, the two bells arrived a day ahead of schedule. They were hung by Thursday, 22nd August, and they were rung for the first time that evening. To our utter relief the sound is glorious; you would think that they had been cast as a ring of eight bells.

Jean Bates, Secretary to Brabourne P.C.C., had written to Her Majesty The Queen informing her that a bell had been cast and hung in honour of her Golden Jubilee and, in her reply, The Queen sent her best wishes for the success of the dedication on 15th September. (I know of only one other bell that was cast for the Golden Jubilee and that was for "The Queen's Restaurant" in a prestigious London hotel. Many rings of bells were augmented for the Millennium with the help of Lottery money; thus it is little surprise that Jubilee bells are rarer.)

Jean also wrote to inform Lord and Lady Brabourne of the augmentation and dedication service, and we were honoured that Countess Mountbatten of Burma attended the service. It was also a great pleasure to see Revd. Ray Sheekey and Barbara Baycock, daughter of the late Maisie and Bernard Marks, at the service. It was only through the foresight of Ray Sheekey and Bernard Marks that an eight bell frame was installed in 1966, thus making this augmentation a possibility; installation of extra framing would have caused considerable additional expense.

For the ringers in particular the dedication service, taken by our priest-in-charge, Revd. William Cooper, was a joyous occasion. The service, which was modelled closely on that used at the re-dedication of the re-tuned six bells in 1966, started with a short explanation from Revd. Ray Sheekey of the situation that was faced soon after he had accepted the incumbency. In 1963 the architect's Quinquennial Report on the fabric of Brabourne Church pointed out that the bell frame, and the tower, required extensive repairs and the estimate for these was £6000; in current values that is close to £60,000.

Money was gifted and raised also via sales, fetes, coffee mornings, etc., and via the Son et Lumière. The latter ran for three weeks, five nights per week, and, after expenses, realized £1000 (approximately £10,000 today).

The commemorative board which was blessed during the service has gold leaf lettering on a royal blue background. It records the 1917 and 2002 augmentations and the 1966 re-hang, plus the names of those who supported the present work. It is beautiful to the eye. After the service the congregation, which included many of those who had contributed to the project and ringing friends from other towers, enjoyed sherry, soft drinks and "nibbles". During this time the bells were rung to Stedman Triples, Grandsire Triples, Cambridge Surprise Major, rounds, call changes and plain hunt. All who rang enthused about the new eight."

CELEBRATING THE BELLS IN VERSE
Epitaph in Brabourne churchyard:

**In affectionate memory**
of
**PHILIP H. PIERCE**
**Feb. 4th 1952**
**Aged 86 years**
**A noted ringer in the County**
**And Captain of Brabourne Bells**
**For thirty years.**

**And of his dear wife**
**HARRIET ALICE**
**Dec 31st 1958**
**Aged 88 years.**

**UNTIL THE DAY BREAK**

Eulogy to Philip Pierce, buried in Brabourne churchyard.

CAPTAIN OF BELLS
The words now fading fast
The grave should be tidied up and the stone cleaned,
but who is there to do it, who still cares?
There are hundreds of grand old ringers
lying in country churchyards,
their stones decaying in the wind and rain and frost,
all bound for dereliction in the end.
What matter if it be this century or next?
His name can be found on some peal-boards in the district
and will remain forever in the records of the K.C.A.
Only a name on a stone, on a peal-board, in a book.
Will anyone wonder what kind of a man he was,

and attempt to find out?  Not many, if any, we may surely say!
Only someone, perhaps, keen on genealogy
who may search him out as a link in a family chain,
or a person writing a social history of the village?
The likelihood of either is not great!
Phil Pierce, smallholder and supplier of eggs and produce
to the hotels, boarding houses and greengrocers' shops
at the seaside town of Hythe, Folkestone and Dover
on the east coast, not many miles away.
His word his bond, his heart a little too soft
for business dealings, but his life richer for the weakness,
if that is what it was?
A country gentleman in all the finest senses of the word.
Not a posh ringer but a good one for the times in which he lived,
reliable, dependable and always well on time for service ringing,
after walking over a mile from Stowting,
only using his Ford van on Sundays for family reasons.
This van supplied access to the more "out of the way" towers
not on the Wanstall bus routes, the bus service owned
by Fred Wanstall, "captain of Bells" at Aldington,
another fine old gentleman.  I can't remember a "Captain of Bells"
anywhere in the district who was not!  I could name a dozen.
Along the back roads for our peal attempts,
one every now and then on a Saturday afternoon.
Always excellent ringing until the first trip or missed dodge
and then lost.  We lost most of them in that way in those days
but the ones we scored we had no doubts about.
We lost fourteen before I scored my first,
And the lesson has remained –
You don't record a peal unless it's good and true.
What point in that anyway, you may kid other people
but you can't kid yourself.
And the Great Conductor knows what's going on,
what's true, what's false!
Phil Pierce "Captain of Bells" at Brabourne fifty years ago
The headstone reminds me and I turn back the clock
to some of the hours his life touched mine, and lifted mine.
I remember with affection.  I remember with thanks.
I remember with a full heart.

(Anon. Willesborough, Kent, 1985)

BRABOURNE BELLS
Away from all I love,
Where e'er my footsteps roam
I find no joys above
The sweet delights of home.

A dear old church appears
Where memory fondly dwells,
And still my fancy hears
Those dear old Brabourne bells.

On many a marriage day
They rang their merry peals;
When all around is gay,
With hope young love reveals.

My heart is deeply stirred
With dreams of other times;
And with what joy I heard
Those dear old Brabourne chimes.

Those bells so sweet and clear
Drive sadness from my brow;
And still to memory dear
I think I hear them now.

(By a lady from Kent living in Canada)

CELEBRATING THE BELLS IN PRINT

Press cutting (possibly early 1930s) filed in Parish Notes, collected by the Reverend C.R.L. McDowall:

*"A very pleasant gathering of Change-Ringers of the Kent County Association was held at Brabourne on June 24th. Some 40 members were able to come. Tower opened at 2.30p.m. Service was held at 4.45p.m. and Mr Symonds was good enough to come and give us a most helpful and friendly address. The afternoon having cleared up we were able to have tea in the Vicarage garden, the company numbering about sixty persons. Mr Tribe of Tenterden reminded us how peace was announced during the meeting here on June 28th, 1919, and until last year an annual gathing had kept the memory of the occasion. After tea the Ringers resumed their work and the bells rang out cheerily till 9p.m. Thanks are due to Mr Pierce and Mr S. Finn and Mr A.C. Kay, the District Secretary, for arranging the meeting, which we hope will now again become an annual event. We were sorry that neither Mr Lockyear nor Mr Helmore were able to be with us."*

Exact source unknown, probably KM Group.

Press cutting dated January, 1934, filed in Parish Notes, collected by the Reverend C.R.L. McDowall:

*"St. Mary's Church*
*During the past year all the flooring north of the aisle has been taken up and the rotten joists replaced by new ones, and the wainscot repaired. New ropes have been fixed to the bells and look very well in the Belfry. Mrs Jenkin of Stowting Court has most kindly drawn out for us the list of Bells to be hung in the Tower."*

Exact source unknown, probably KM Group .

## TALES OF BRABOURNE CHURCH ORGANISTS

Music is of fundamental importance in Brabourne Church and we are fortunate to have had talented organists in our midst. In years past Joy Finn, Basil Ames and Pat Cornell (Thornby; daughter of Frank and Sis Thornby) played regularly at Brabourne and "filled in" at Smeeth when required. Anthony Finn took over from Brian Gower as one of our regular organists when Brian joined the RAF (brother of Pauline Kingston and Margaret Maple), and Ron Heap from Aldington used to help out at Brabourne from time to time. More recently, Pat Earlam, Ruth Goodsell, Eileen Harfield, Jean Pike, Val Robson and Richard Scarth have all played for Brabourne's services. Most have retired, Pat Cornell and Pat Earlam have died, but Val Robson and Richard Scarth still play regularly and have recently been joined by Steve Smith. David Kitney and John Hall, both organists from Smeeth, have also helped us when needed.

Val Robson plays regularly for our Family Service these days and Richard Scarth for Holy Communion, though both also help out at other times, playing for weddings, funerals and on church open days. We can still persuade Anthony to come out of retirement when we need him, and recently we have been delighted to add Steve Smith from Smeeth to our company of organists, as well as two younger talented players, Guy Steed, aged 14, and Tom Dewey, 18. The commitment of all our organists has been wholehearted and much appreciated by Brabourne's congregations. They all have one thing in common: they love playing our ancient church organ which was installed in 1896 and until 1957/58 was situated in the Scott Chapel. It was only in 1957/58 , when the Rev Thompson-Evans was vicar at Brabourne, that the organ was moved to its present position in the south aisle. The front and back covers of the service sheet tell us when the organ was installed and that it was the creation of Browne's of Deal, who continue to look after it. In response to our request, some of the organists have given us anecdotes related to organ playing at Brabourne.

Anthony Finn writes:
"After playing the organ for many years and retiring a total of three times (at least), one memory I have is the visit of the Queen and members of Lord and Lady Brabourne's family attending morning service at Brabourne. The Reverend Ray Sheekey telephoned me late on the Saturday afternoon to tell me that they would be attending and swore me to secrecy, emphasising that no one in the village was to be told. He asked me to switch on the heaters as early as possible next morning, adding that temporary portable paraffin heaters were being installed, as Brabourne Church can be extremely cold. Everyone in the know had clearly kept the secret, as the only people in the crowd to meet the visitors as they left the church were Jackie (my wife), and Andrew, our son, in his pram.

Anthony Finn

"On another occasion, I was playing at Morning Service, and we were just building up to the loudest part of a hymn when, suddenly, a 4ft pipe from the front of the organ descended on top of me with barely any warning. Having seen it move gave me the chance to fend it off with my right hand as it headed towards the floor. From Val Robson's contribution that follows, it seems this wasn't the only time an organ pipe came down.

"Having played for many weddings and funerals, I have found that the most memorable and moving services are always the most simple and straightforward. Hymns and prayers that are familiar to all those attending and a congregation that joins in wholeheartedly are, together, the unfailing 'recipe' for the success of a service. The atmosphere is never the same when people don't know the hymns and can't join in."

Anthony's commitment as an organist at Brabourne is well known and affectionately remembered. One of our contributors recalled seeing him running down The Street from Homehurst to play at a wedding and thus avert total disaster on one occasion. Apparently, no one had arranged for an organist and Anthony arrived with no more than a few minutes' notice and with no practice whatsoever.

Pat Cornell:
Shortly before she died, Pat wrote: "I can't think of any anecdotes, but I did enjoy playing at Brabourne and I also enjoyed being invited to the receptions of some of the weddings for which I played."

Jean Pike:
"The organ in Brabourne Church is a lovely old instrument and I have thoroughly enjoyed playing it over the years. It isn't an easy instrument to play as its performance is readily affected by changes in temperature and humidity, which can leave the organist

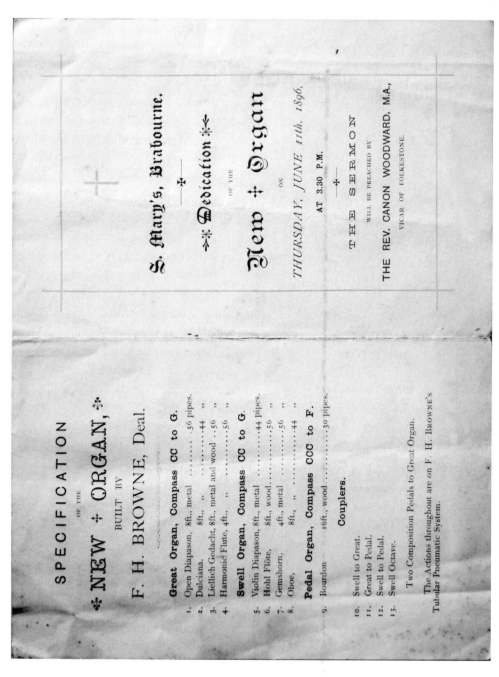

Cover of service sheet for the dedication of the new organ, 11th June, 1896, from Brabourne Church archives

Jean Pike

very 'vulnerable'. With the onset of autumn and its cold, damp days, there was one note that had a habit of 'sticking' and causing a dreadful squeal that could only be stopped by pushing in certain organ stops quickly. This was an intermittent problem that rarely occurred when the organ tuner was called in, so you could never be sure whether or not it had been 'cured'. I always hoped and prayed that it wouldn't occur during the armistice service in November and was prepared to act speedily if the noise started, but fortunately it never did.

"It isn't just the atmosphere in the church at Brabourne that affects the organ, 'wildlife' also play their part. Traditionally, churches are havens for mice, but several years ago the mice at Brabourne started taking advantage of the church's hospitality. They were everywhere – they were living in the organ, scurrying around it, leaving their droppings on the organ cover, on the seat, on the floor, and there was evidence that they were even gnawing away at the woodwork. Vi Varrier could stand it no longer and took action. She set mousetraps in the church, particularly around the organ, and caught several of them. It brought the problem more or less under control for a while and the ancient organ, which was in peril, was thus saved from further destruction – for the time being."

Eileen Harfield:
"I much enjoyed playing for Mattins (from the Prayer Book) at Brabourne. Sadly, it is now impossible to find a church anywhere near Mersham (where I live) that celebrates Choral Mattins.

"I used to enjoy coming to Brabourne to practise the music for the services. Quite often, someone who came to do a job in the church would stop for a chat, and I also enjoyed the chats with sidesmen before the services. Everyone was so pleasant and friendly. I was also very grateful for the heater that was kindly put beside me at the organ in colder weather.

"Occasionally, the organ was not on its best behaviour – the odd stop suddenly deciding to go dumb, or, the organist's nightmare, a cipher (never agreeing with the key in which one was playing!) appearing out of the blue! Another problem was, as the organ is rather far from the congregation, it could be a little difficult to synchronise the pointing in the canticles with the singing, which one couldn't always hear.

"I look back with pleasure on my days of organ-playing in the lovely church at East Brabourne and thank all those who made it such a pleasurable time."

Valerie Robson:

"When we moved to Brabourne, Dennis and I did say that we would be willing to play the organ in emergencies but, gradually, we have become more involved. I have had organ lessons since coming here and have enjoyed learning and making a contribution to the life of the church and the village. I hope that, as I play, it is not just 'mechanical' but an offering to God, part of

Dennis and Valerie Robson

my worship and thanks to Him for all that He has done for me, and means to me. I have always attended church and believed in the good news of the gospel, but it was not until I became a teenager that I realised that Jesus died for my sins and that I needed to invite Him into my life personally. Since then, He has been a real friend and daily help in my life and, in return, I want to live for Him.

"I thoroughly enjoy playing the organ at Brabourne Church, though the ancient instrument does seem to have a mind of its own. I'm not sure where to begin when it comes to anecdotes about playing the organ at Brabourne, so I shall start by telling you how the organ once tried to kill me! I came into church to practise the hymns for the Sunday Family Service, switched on the organ, opened the lid and, without any warning, one of the large lead organ pipes fell out of its place just beside me and crashed on to the pew in front of the organ. It almost got me (but not quite!).

"On another occasion I had a job to find my way out of the church after a practice session. It was a winter's afternoon and I had enjoyed playing for an hour or two without noticing how dark it had become. I locked the organ, went into the vestry and switched off the lights, only to find myself in total darkness and far from confident about how to find my way out. I learnt too late about the light switch in the porch that I should have left on."

Richard Scarth:

"I became one of the Brabourne team of organists quite by chance. My wife, Hilda, and I happened to visit the church one day to look at the Norman window. The late Pat Earlam was practising on the organ and, as she was one of Hilda's former colleagues at Ashford School, we were soon in conversation. I happened to mention that, as a retired musician, I would not mind taking a turn as organist, and soon after that, I found myself on the rota.

"Perhaps readers might be interested in some details about the organ in St Mary's. Built in 1896, it is a typical Victorian instrument, presenting challenges to the organist not encountered on more modern instruments. When the two keyboards are coupled together, the key action is heavy, especially for elderly fingers on cold mornings, but paradoxically the action also has hair-trigger properties, which make it very easy to play one note and partially sound the adjacent note. Finding the correct bass notes with the feet is not aided by the dimensions of the pedal board, which differ from the standard layout familiar to organists of today. The expression pedal (or

Richard Scarth

swell pedal) is in the form of a spring-loaded lever worked by the right foot. It locks in place with a ratchet that needs a kick to release it. This means that, when playing expressively, there is only one foot available for the bass notes. I was too rough one day and broke the ratchet, requiring a visit from the organ-maintenance people. Playing such an old instrument is like driving a traction engine compared with, say, a Ferrari. These are facts, but they sound like excuses for bad playing!

"On the other hand, we must be very grateful that this instrument has survived for over 115 years and is still going strong, which says much for the quality of the original workmanship by the builders, Brownes of Deal. As parishioners are aware, the air in the building is very cold and damp in winter, and such conditions are not helpful to the wood, metal and leather components of the organ. However, mice are the main enemy. They nibble the leather of tiny action devices that sound each pipe. These depend on air pressure, so a small hole results in a silent pipe. If such a silent note is in the middle of the keyboard, it has serious implications for the quality of the music.

"One final point about the organ. The instrument has only four speaking stops on each of its two manuals. One of those eight stops is of such a quiet and indefinite character that it is of little general use. The challenge for the organist is to use the seven remaining stops in an imaginative and useful manner.

"What is my philosophy as an organist? I consider the organist's contribution is part of worship, and my aim is to try to create a suitable ambience for a particular service, and to provide helpful accompaniments to the congregation. One of my problems when joining the Brabourne team was that I had been 'out of work' as an organist for many years. My activities in music education were slanted towards teaching and directing, and I left organ playing to younger and more brilliant student colleagues. As a result, I was out of practice and had given most of my organ music away, thinking I would not need it again. I wish I had some of those pieces now!

"There have been one or two unusual moments during my time on the organ bench. On one occasion, the celebrant walked out, having been annoyed by interruptions due to difficulties outside the church when a combine harvester attempted to pass parked cars. That service was very short. I have also been requested to play unusual pieces. At one wedding, I played Sousa's March The Liberty Bell, which was not very easy on a small village organ – it calls for a military band. In years gone by, when I was a dance-band musician, we would play that music as a Military Two Step.

"My first organ post was in a village church very similar to St Mary's Brabourne. At the age of 12, during the Second World War, when many older people were away in the forces, I became organist at St Matthew's Hutton Buscel, North Yorkshire. In fine weather, I cycled several miles there and back from my home, but travelled by bus in winter. I remember my first visit. It was a cold, dark night. My instructions were to get off the bus at a point where a minor road led uphill to the village. In the blackout, I had to rely on the bus conductor to drop me at the proper place. As I walked up the lane, I saw a wavering light coming towards me. It was one of the men, a farmer, carrying a storm lantern. I was glad to see him! He took me through the churchyard to the schoolhouse, where I stayed the night. Next day, I met the rector and the small choir of six singers – three farmers and their wives. I was very inexperienced, but one of the singers said, 'Don't worry, we shall keep going whatever you do on the organ.' So, 66 years later, the wheel has turned full circle."

# BRABOURNE, AN ACTIVE CHURCH

Celebrating Mothering Sunday, Easter and harvest

Celebrating birthdays in May and June

Social gatherings on the First Friday of every month (All welcome!)

New hymn books arrive

Organ practice

Flowers for each Sunday

Maintaining the churchyard

Striders and riders participating in the Friends of Kent Churches Sponsored Ride and Stride

Welcoming riders and striders to Brabourne Church

At the annual Easter Pilgrimage to
Canterbury Cathedral in 2011 (above)
and 2013 (below)

Celebrating pets at the Family Service

Helping to prepare materials for the Family Service

Third Sunday Xtra

One of many baptisms at Brabourne

One of many weddings at Brabourne

Fun and fundraising at The Friends' Christmas Fair

Queueing for the new loos at Brabourne Church which were
generously funded by The Friends of St Mary's

In the queue: from left, the Reverend Caroline Pinchbeck, John Varrier, Michael Mugridge,
Don Palmer (who, as churchwarden, oversaw the preparations for, and construction of, the
loos), Vi Varrier, Jean Bates, Brenda Streeter, Brian Streeter, and organist Richard Scarth
(September 2013)

3

# BRABOURNE'S BAPTIST CHURCHES

## OTHER CHURCHES IN THE VILLAGES

We have focussed mainly on the parish church of St Mary the Blessed Virgin in East Brabourne until now, but St Mary's is far from being the only local church: nearby are the Anglican churches of Smeeth, Stowting and Monks Horton, part of our Group of Six churches, the other two being Mersham and Sellindge, on the other side of the A20. We have chosen not to include much about other members of our Group of Six in this book, as our main focus is on Brabourne. There are, however, two very active Baptist churches in Brabourne Lees – the Brabourne Baptist Church on Plain Road, formerly known as the Bethel Baptists; and the Zion Baptist Church on Canterbury Road – and we have been privileged to collect information from their members for inclusion in this book.

Certain families have had very strong connections with our local churches and have done much to sustain them over the years. For example, while the Finn family is almost automatically linked with St Mary's Church in East Brabourne, the Ashman family is closely associated with the Baptist church, and the Brooks family with the Zion Baptist Chapel.

## BRABOURNE BAPTIST CHURCH, ITS GROWTH AND DEVELOPMENT

Ron Ashman has kindly provided us with background information on the Brabourne Baptist Church:

"In 1814, members of Station Road Baptist Church in Ashford began to think about 'planting' churches in the surrounding villages. The following year, an unoccupied army bakehouse in Brabourne became both a Sunday school and a place of worship, and in 1817 a plot of land was purchased and the current church building was erected. It was officially opened on 30th July, 1818; the cost had been £170. Three years later, a gallery was added for a further £20. By 1824 the church had grown sufficiently to become independent of the 'mother' church in Ashford."

Val Thorpe added that when the Sabbath School and place of worship were first opened in Brabourne in 1815, 12 children were present and about 50 people attended the afternoon service. By the end of its first year there was a school of 90 children and 11 teachers, a reflection of how the church was thriving. In 1873 a manse (minister's house) was built very close to the church but later sold, and now a new manse has been bought in Mountbatten Way.

George Ashman, grandfather of Ron Ashman and Sheila Stone (Ashman) (among others), was secretary at the church in Brabourne for 64 years. He died in 1954, so his active work with the church dated back to about 1890, if not earlier, if one presumes that he was a regular member of the church before taking on the role of secretary.

George and his wife, Alice, might be considered the pinnacle of a veritable dynasty of Ashmans, most of whom have had very close links with the Baptist church in Brabourne. George and Alice had eight children, five boys and three girls, and all except one stayed in the village. Their "middle" daughter moved away when she married, and one of the boys, Percy, was killed tragically in France in the First World War. The remaining six maintained their connections with the village, several finding employment locally, and throughout their lives sustained and strengthened the work of the Baptist church. George Ross Ashman, Ron's father, lived in the village for 94 years and was a member of the church for 78 years, working as a butcher for 66 of these. He started out working for Mr Hawkins at the age of 14, and then worked for Ron Cooper after he bought Hawkins' business (he was still doing a few hours' work each week when he was 80). The youngest of George Ashman's sons, Mark Allen, also worked at Hawkins' butchers for a while, and at Orpins Stores.

At their most numerous there were some 25 Ashmans who were regular worshippers at the Baptist church in Brabourne, and something many readers may remember is the choir there. This was formed by four of George Ashman's sons: Archibald (known as Arch), Ernest, George Ross, and Mark Allen. Succeeding generations supplemented it; not all were Ashmans, and Ron added that, on rare occasions, women were included, but in the main it was a male choir. The choir continued until 1980, when there were only three members left, all of these being Ashmans.

Brabourne Baptist Church

George and Alice Ashman

George and Alice Ashman's five sons: from left, Percival (Percy; killed in the First World War), Archibald (Archie), Ernest (Ernie), George Ross and Mark Allen.
The picture was taken in 1920s, Percy's image being added as it was after he had died

The Baptist Church Sunday School (1916).
Back row, standing, from left: Ernie, Ross, Archie and Mark Allen Ashman. Middle, standing, from left: Dorothy Ashman and Daisy Washford. The two girls in white blouses next to Dorothy are, from left, Lilly and Kitty Ashman

## MINISTRY AT THE BAPTIST CHURCH

Colonel Spillett
(photograph from
the Kent Messenger,
now KM Group)

The Baptist church has had a number of ministers since the early 1900s, some of whom were college trained, but there has also been much contribution from the laity, and inevitably, many of those who have taken services and preached there over the years have been Ashmans. According to Ron, in 1949 Colonel Spillett, a retired Salvation Army Lieutenant Colonel, and his wife were invited by the church to live in The Manse, next door to the church, and though not a Baptist he became as a pastor to the church community, taking weddings and funerals, and preaching regularly. He preached his last sermon on 1st November, 1964, and died about three months later at the age of 84, a much-loved ecumenical leader.

In December, 1966 the Reverend Ernest Monk was appointed minister at the age of 65, and stayed for 10 years. The church then had a period of internal ministry, sustained largely by lay preachers and, during

Celebrating the new organ in the Baptist Chapel:
from left, Rev H.R. Moss, Mr W.B. Pittaway,
Mrs H.R. Pratt Boorman, Mr Boorman, Colonel W. Spillett
(photograph from the Kent Messenger, 2nd March, 1951,
now part of KM Group)

this time, Ron and his wife, June, would also take services and preach. In the late 1970s discussions were held with the Willesborough Baptists to consider sharing a minister with Brabourne as both congregations were ageing and of similar size, about 30 people. In September 1979 the Reverend Alan Dinnie came from the Baptist church at Eastbourne and, for the next seven years, Brabourne and Willesborough shared a minister. During this period both churches flourished and fellowships grew. At Brabourne, the Baptist Church was altered internally: the pews and pulpit were removed, the kitchen was refurbished and usage of the building widened. Nowadays lunches are held there, as are the men's breakfasts, a playgroup, children's activities and much more – the church is full of energy. In 1986 the Reverend Dinnie became a full-time minister at Willesborough, and Brabourne subsequently called for their own. Since Alan left (and he is still pastor at Willesborough after more than 30 years), Brabourne has had five full-time ministers, the current pastor being Tim Simpson.

With increasing mobility, more recent generations of Ashmans and many other worshippers at the Baptist Church have moved away from the village, and of those families still closely tied to Church few have children living locally who are likely to continue their tradition of worship in Brabourne. Nevertheless, the village is growing and a broader mix of people is now worshipping there. Standing unobtrusively on Plain Road, the well-loved church still catches the attention of the passer-by, not least by the significant, yet often mildly humorous, posters on its notice board.

Deacons at the church (2013)
Back row: from left, Tim Simpson, David Bonnett, Clem Oliver.
Front row: from left, Corinne Herrick, Geoff Thorpe, Babs Ruck

## AN ENERGETIC BAPTIST CHURCH

Refurbishing the church, from left, Rev John Crew, former pastor,
and Geoff Thorpe

One of many social gatherings at the Baptist Church, front, from left:
Ray Ashman, Phil and Sheila Stone, John Crew (Minister);
back view, Eileen Ashman

Ladies' Day: from left, Val Thorpe, Brenda Crew
and Babs Ruck serving lunch

Children's holiday club

# THE ZION STRICT BAPTIST CHURCH

The Zion Baptist Chapel, early 20th century,
before 1915/16

The Zion Baptist Chapel (after improvements of 1915/16)

THE ZION BAPTIST CHURCH, ASPECTS OF ITS HISTORY
In Brabourne Lees, along Canterbury Road, is the Zion Strict Baptist Chapel where, amongst others, several generations and different branches of the Brooks family have worshipped.  Jim Brooks's grandfather, Daniel Brooks of Aldington, who died in 1913, was a deacon in the church. Tom Brooks, the grandfather of Jim's wife Mary, and her parents, Fred and Amelia Brooks, and her three sisters – Amelia (known as Gertrude), Miriam (Agnes) and Queenie – all worshipped there, and the girls' families have also worshipped at the chapel, too.  Fred Brooks was also a deacon at Zion. Jim Brooks, his wife Mary and her sister Miriam (Agnes; now Beadle) have all kindly

Tom and Mary Brooks in the 1920s who lived at Running
Water Farm in West Brabourne

contributed to this chapter, and for their help we are most grateful.  Other lifelong members of the chapel included George Brooks (Mary's cousin) – who as a child lived in The Street, East Brabourne – along with his mother, Ruth, and sisters, Ruth

Fred and Amelia (Millie) Brooks celebrating
their golden wedding anniversary in 1963

and Naomi (Nancy). For several years until his death in March 2012, George was the oldest member of the local church community. He was also a deacon of the church for almost 30 years.

George Brooks (in 2007),
a deacon of the church for over 30 years

The church in Brabourne goes back to 1835, or thereabouts, when a few friends used to meet for worship in Brabourne Street. Their meeting place was a small barn, later a garage and then a room in a house called Applegarth, to the left of the Five Bells in East Brabourne. The room in which the early Baptists used to meet is on the left-hand side of Applegarth, when viewed from The Street. By 1838 the congregation had grown to some 30 members, so was too large for the premises in The Street. As a consequence, the chapel on Canterbury Road was built. It is understood that Mr James Jones, who was appointed pastor in that same year, did much of the construction work on it, as well as on Chapel Cottage at the rear. The cottage has always been privately owned, usually by a deacon (the last being Mr Fred Brooks, who, with his wife, Amelia, lived there from the 1950s to the 1970s), but it no longer has any connection with the chapel.

After James Jones there were several pastors, though none stayed for any significant length of time. The last pastor was Ebenezer Hickmott, father of George Hickmott and grandfather of Michael, both of whom have contributed to this book. Reading from the minutes of former church meetings, Jim Brooks explained that Ebenezer had been preaching from 1914, if not earlier, and was appointed pastor in about 1919-20. He resigned in 1922 with no ill feeling; it was simply because the chapel could not afford to keep him. After two other pastorates he returned to Brabourne, living with his daughter, Kate Grantham, and helping at the chapel as he was able. He also took part in the centenary services in 1938, and preached his last sermon there.

Jim Brooks: a deacon in the Zion church

Reguar worshippers at the Zion Church: from left, Ruth Brooks on her
wedding day, her brother George, sister Nancy and their mother Ruth

There was a time, before 1915, when the chapel was in poor condition and services
were held at Running Water Farm for five or six weeks whilst repairs were carried out.
Extracts from Church minutes reveal the extent of the work:

"1915. This is to record the mercy of the Lord and tell it to the Generations following.
In 1915 our little chapel became very much out of repair so much so that it was
getting unsafe to worship in. A church meeting was called to consult what could be
done. It was finally agreed to Match-Board the ceiling right over which we thought
would cost about £30. Being in War time material and labour so very dear we thought
it best to collect some of the money before we commenced…[Following many, many
prayers] money kept coming in from friends both far and near so it was agreed to ask
Mr R. Weeks of Tenterden [Mr R. Weeks was pastor of Jireh, Tenterden] to come
and look at the Chapel and give us a rough estimate of how much it would cost…
In Nov 1915 he came and looked over the Chapel and found there was a lot wanted
doing but roughly estimated the cost at £93 with a new Porch. So it was agreed for
Mr Weeks to do what he thought was necessary and to put it off till the spring. So
in May 1916 Mr Weeks commenced the work. During the repairing of the Chapel it
was agreed to meet for worship at Mr T. Brooks West Brabourne which we did for
five or six Sundays. [Mr Tom Brooks was Mary Brooks's grandfather, also George
Brooks's grandfather, and grandfather to Wilfred, Rose, Mabel, Joan and Margaret
Brooks – among others.] Mr Weeks still found a lot wanted doing so that the Bill
came to £125-18s-3d Mr Weeks presenting us with the £5-18s-3d. This left us £120

The Zion Baptist Church following improvements in 2006

to pay…At the Re-opening Services we paid Mr Weeks £96-4s-0d and the following July £7-10s-0d leaving a balance of £16-6s-0d so it was again agreed to hold Special Services on Dec 8th 1916 for the purpose of clearing the remainder of the Debt and for to acknowledge the Lord's Great Goodness towards us. So the Balance was collected and paid the same day…"

More comfortable pews from Elmsted Church

Although the new porch was an improvement, the door opened on one side, presumably to reduce the effects of wind, and there were steps into the chapel. This made it very difficult to bring coffins into the building as they had to be turned, so in 2006 a new porch was constructed with the door facing the road. This is both more attractive and functional. The old bicycle shed on the side of the chapel was also demolished and a more permanent structure built consisting of a lobby and toilets. Also, the room behind the sanctuary, which had few amenities, was divided into two, giving the chapel a room with facilities for making tea and coffee and a separate minister's vestry. Another improvement made well over 40 years ago was the replacement of the original, uncomfortable, open-barred seats with pews that were being taken out of Elmsted Church.

Mary (aka Martha) Brooks

Jim Brooks

Elizabeth Beadle with George Brooks (2008). Elizabeth has worshipped at the Zion Baptist Church in Brabourne for almost 30 years. She cleans and cares for the church and also keeps the flower border on Canterbury Road bright with blooms in the spring and summer months

These were moved from Elmsted by George Brooks and George Beadle, Fred Beadle's father, on their tractors and trailers. George Brooks was certain about the year in which they did this – 1965 – as it was when they moved the pews that he realised that George Beadle was not a well man. He died in November of the same year. Though much more comfortable (as confirmed by Jim, Mary and other church members!), these pews from Elmsted turned out to be bigger than the original seats and, as a consequence, the symmetry of the sanctuary was lost, there being four seats on one side, and three on the other. Miriam (Agnes) remembers that, in spite of improvements to the building when she was a child in the 1920s, the chapel was heated by a coke boiler, which gave off fumes that made her faint during the service.

Jim and Mary have both attended services on Canterbury Road since they were infants and Jim, who used to live at Aldington as a child, can remember cycling to Brabourne on a Sunday on his fairy cycle. Mary recalls the congregation converging on the chapel on a Sunday by all kinds of means – on foot, by bike or by pony and trap. When she lived with her parents and sisters at Manor Pound they always walked there, and she can specifically remember her grandparents, Tom and Mary Brooks, driving there on a Sunday from Running Water Farm in West Brabourne in a pony and trap. But times have changed and most people arrive by car these days, though one still cycles regularly – from Ashford. In the 1940s and 1950s, when it was attended regularly by some 25-30 worshippers each week, Jim and Mary can remember having to sit outside during special services because the chapel was so full.

Like most other churches, congregations at the chapel have declined, but regular worshippers still come to Brabourne from as far afield as Ashford, and during the summer, visitors to the area frequently join in worship. During the summer of 2011, five Dutch families found their way there.

It is noteworthy that, some 50 years ago, the chapel used to be in the civil parish of Sellindge, which meant that if a registrar was needed to witness a marriage they had to come from Folkestone, not Ashford. This inevitably caused complications, but eventually the parish boundary was changed and the chapel is now within the parish of Brabourne.

Returning briefly to the issue of pastors and ministers, Zion Strict Baptist Church has, for many years, depended on itinerant ministers from various places including Eastbourne and Heathfield. However, they are now fortunate to have an experienced minister in Peter Dawson, who lives locally and, being retired, is able to help regularly with services.

# 4

# SELF-SUFFICIENT, SELF-RELIANT VILLAGES

While the fabric of St Mary's church links us with a distant past, the recollections of people within the surrounding villages and the locality bring to life a more recent history, one that has changed significantly as technology (which leapt forward after the Second World War) has come to dominate our lives. Recollections of some of our contributors date back over 90 years to the First World War, and even earlier, if one adds to their own memories the knowledge they acquired from older family members and friends. The stories they tell show that, until the 1960s, most people worked locally, the majority on the land, though many also worked for local shops, pubs, other businesses and in people's homes and gardens. The villages had a much more rural feel to them than they do today: the landscape was dominated by orchards, smaller fields, most with hedgerows and small herds of cows or flocks of sheep, often in the fields where houses now stand. Farm workers were a frequent sight in the fields, as were working horses. Much of what was produced locally was consumed locally and village communities and the individual households within them were heavily self-reliant and, to a great extent, self-sufficient.

For most people, living standards were much lower than they are today – money was in very short supply, material possessions were relatively few and families worked hard to make ends meet. People worked long hours, week in week out, with few breaks, and children were expected to play their part. Grandparents, where they were still alive, figured largely in children's lives. On more than one occasion we were told that, although grandparents were much loved, they were also treated with great respect – almost a reverence – as the repercussions could be considerable if

Brabourne Lees: view from behind the Blue Anchor. Cooper's first shop on Plain Road to the right. Houses on the left are along Bridge Road, c1912

Brabourne Lees: view along Plain Road with Baptist Church to the right
c1912

Brabourne Lees: view from Warren Bank, looking west to
Smeeth Kiln Old Forge, c1912

East Brabourne: Court Lodge & The Street. Pre-1925 as the shop and path opposite
Court Lodge were still in existence. The horse chestnuts are much bigger now

they discovered that their grandchildren had not been behaving responsibly or as was expected of them.

The nature of the hardships that had confronted people in the past were a common theme in our discussions, but rarely did people complain about them, though several did recall the misery that could be caused by alcohol. On payday, some men (and it was usually men in those days) would repair to the pub after work, and in the course of an evening spend the bulk of their week's earnings, leaving themselves and their families virtually penniless until the next payday. Perhaps this was a form of escapism from the drudgery and tedium of daily life. Services that are today taken for granted, such as household water supplies, sanitation, electricity, healthcare, transport and good roads only started to improve from the mid-to-late 1930s with the arrival of electricity and piped water. Even then, such services were not affordable for the majority. Improvements came slowly and, in the meantime, water had to be carried from wells and springs, fuel collected for fires, fires lighted for heating, stoves lit for cooking, clothes washed by hand, lavatories emptied. Travel, too, was slow, being largely by foot or bicycle. As access to better services and the road network improved, and the number of cars increased, horizons widened and village life changed significantly from the 1960s onwards, with an increasing stream of inhabitants seeking employment away from the land.

There was great economic inter-dependence within the villages, as the survival of employers of all kinds was heavily dependent on maintaining the loyalty and commitment of workers whose livelihoods were, in turn, dependent on the survival of the families or the enterprises for which they worked. Because of their close interaction, people knew each other well and, though social stratification was still pronounced prior to the end of the Second World War, employers and workers were drawn together and often became close. Closeness aside, it has to be said that the majority of workers appear to have been much closer to the poverty line than were their employers. Hardships were endured as, during that period, it was accepted that people "knew their place"; however, those employers who possessed a generosity of spirit and who treated their workers kindly are remembered with an almost reverential affection, and the wellbeing of former employers and their families was, and still is, of major concern and interest to many a former employee.

Within the villages each family and household knew the next – knew their history, their sorrows and joys. Adults worked together, children went to school and grew up together, and though not everyone may have got on well, many did. We were told time and again how people supported and helped each other, especially in times of adversity, and not just within a social class but across them, too. Such deeply intertwined economic and social ties over generations underpinned the strength of the communities within our villages. The idea of being "brought up to work" was another recurrent theme, and enjoyment of life was frequently expressed. Perhaps we do remember the best of the past, but while researching this book we were told often that, despite the hardships of life, "it was a very good past".

## CHERRY ORCHARDS AND VILLAGE CHARACTERS

In the 1920s and 1930s the villages used to look very different: essentially, orchards dominated the landscape. As everything was done by hand in those days people remembered the pace of life being much slower. Behind Prospect Farm House in Brabourne Lees and extending all the way back to Canterbury Road were cherry orchards with big, "old-fashioned" trees, the sort that you could climb. Rosemary Hendry (Ward) remembers playing with her friends every day in the summer in these cherry orchards and also in the apple orchards where Knatchbull Way now stands. Mr Nickolls of Warren Farm on Canterbury Road would let the village children make camps and play rounders in one of his fields; he would also let them collect mushrooms and blackberries on his land. There were very few houses along Canterbury Road in those days and virtually no motor vehicles; children were safe playing out of doors. There were also apple orchards at Pemsey Farm and at the top of Lily Vale, and at East Brabourne there were more cherry orchards, "all around the Finns", who lived

East Brabourne's apple orchard, from Pilgrims' Way.
The orchard was grubbed up in 2008

177

at Homehurst (now Raffles), which continued up towards the Downs and "covered the land under the hill". Joy Finn, who was born in 1913, remembered taking coffee to the Canadian troops with her mother when they were encamped in the cherry orchard opposite Homehurst during the First World War; she couldn't have been more than five years old at the time.

Joyce Garlick

Joyce Garlick (Wood) remembers "having a good laugh" while apple picking for Mr Walker at Pemsey Farm. In the morning the pickers would be given a big cup of tea, there would be soup at lunch while they ate the sandwiches they had brought with them, and tea was provided again in the afternoon. Though picking fruit was hard work, memories of the camaraderie were much cherished by former fruit pickers, who included Joyce, Norman and Basil Thornby. Joyce also remembers receiving a big box of Cox's apples from the Walkers at Christmas time.

Beyond Brabourne and on the way to Ashford along the A20, near Mersham, were the beautiful black cherry and apple orchards that belonged to Robert Hobbs of Home Farm. These extended beyond what is now the Blue and White Café on the A20. Here, too, the trees were large and, according to Jane Barker, Bert Thornby, who lived at Morley Cottage in Brabourne Lees, "used to do the ladder shifting during cherry picking". The ladders, she recalled, were "enormous great things that splayed out at the base". Cherry picking was often associated with accidents, as the pickers sometimes fell. These problems were largely overcome when plant breeders brought in dwarf stock, though the modern varieties lacked the romance of the big trees.

Several people spoke of Punch Pellet who, in the 1940s, lived in a Romany caravan in the cherry orchard belonging to Prospect Farm. According to Karl Engels, Punch's caravan was parked under a large walnut tree almost opposite The Plough, where he was a frequent visitor. Children used to enjoy playing around his caravan, jumping on and off the two steps to the door, and some earned money from him for bird scaring in the orchard, which involved periodically shaking the lines of tin cans that he had strung up between the trees. Punch seems to have been warm-hearted and generous, and is remembered affectionately. Though many people were unsure of what he did, it was thought that he was probably a contractor who bought fruit from

Plumming at Weekes' Orchard, The Limes, now The Hall,
Weekes Lane, 1929: from left, May Howland, Netta Knight,
Joyce Howland, Frank Howland and Renee Parrott

Plumming, 1929: from left, May Howland and Joyce Howland

Tom Pilcher, the owner of Prospect Farm. It should be said that, in the 1930s, the farm was extensive and included the land where Prospect Way and Mountbatten Way now stand, as well as the land down to West Brabourne. According to Phil Stone, in addition to picking fruit, Punch had a pony and trap that he would use to sell the fruit. He also had a brother in Cheriton who used to sell fruit, so may well have supplied him, too. Like many people in those days, Punch worked all summer and made enough to live on through the winter.

The children may have helped with bird scaring but no one remembers helping to harvest the fruit, possibly because this would have been too dangerous for children. No one could remember the harvest taking place either (though they were sure that this must have been done), but once harvested, the fruit would probably have been exported from the village via Smeeth Station. Records indicate that the civil parish of Brabourne has long been an important fruit-producing area that exported much of its fruit to London[1].

Why was this resident of the cherry orchard called Punch? Wishing to be generous, one of our contributors suggested that that might have been his Christian name, while several others suggested that it had been earned through his liking for alcohol. In later years Punch moved his caravan to Weekes Lane, where it was parked on land belonging to Billy and Ethel Conley. Rumour has it that Punch's partiality for The Plough would lead him there on many an evening, and on his unsteady journeys back to Weekes Lane after closing time one of the Special Constables, Wilf Harris or Frank Howland, would help him home. George Brooks recalled one evening during the Second World War, when Wilf was patrolling the village for the blackout and saw a light in Hawkins' slaughterhouse. Checking on the situation, he discovered Punch, drunk and lying fast asleep on a bundle of straw. He merely said, "Happy Christmas, Punch", put the light out and left him there. Everyone smoked in those days, especially men, and Phil Stone recalls hearing that Punch could roll a cigarette with one hand.

In addition to orchards, Phil recalls that there was much more woodland around in the 1930s. Behind Brabourne Street, for example, Jackie and Anthony Finn remember Sub-Down Wood, also known as Thornby's Wood because it belonged to old Mr Thornby, the uncle of George Barrett the blacksmith. And looking towards the Downs from opposite the village hall, woodland in the Coomb was also quite dense. Woodlands were important, not least because these were major play areas for children, but the onset of the Second World War and the need to increase food production saw woodlands being replaced by fields of arable crops. Nevertheless,

1      Lawson, Terence and Killingray, David (2004) An Historical Atlas of Kent. Chichester, Phillimore and Co. Ltd.

Phil observes that woodlands are now being restored and some of the land in the Coomb has been replanted with trees.

These images of the village that are based on childhood memories provide an idyllic picture of life in the 1920s and 1930s, and are yet again a reminder of the close association that children had with members of their community, and with their physical environment.

## WORKING AND LIVING IN THE RURAL DOMAIN

The larger farms in the area, such as Penstock in East Brabourne, Park Farm, Evegate and the Brabourne Estate, were significant employers of local people. The Brabourne Estate, which extended roughly from Hinxhill to Brabourne and Smeeth on the north side of the A20, included within it some 12 farms that supported tenants and their

Lady Brabourne

families. It was comparatively common for people to work for the same employer for many years, perhaps for their entire lives. Lady Brabourne related an example of an old Estate worker, Tom Doughty, who was about 80 years old and came out beating the first time that Prince Philip came to shoot at the Estate in 1947. He told the assembled party that the last Duke of Edinburgh for whom he had loaded on the Estate was Queen Victoria's son, Prince Philip's great-uncle, who had rented Eastwell Manor in the late 19th century, showing just how long the Estate held on to some of its workers. John Jamieson added that Tom had cut his hand off on a circular saw at the Estate wood yard at the end of The Ridgeway, to which Lady

Brabourne has added that, after the accident, Tom's daughter, Mrs Twyman, rescued him from the bus stop where he was waiting to catch a bus to hospital in Ashford, complete with arm in makeshift bandage. Clearly, his hand couldn't be saved, so from then on he wore a hook on the stump. However, Tom is remembered for always changing the hook for a gloved fist on Sundays when he sang in Smeeth Church choir.

As Lady Brabourne observed, it wasn't just individuals who had worked for the Estate, but families, often for generations. One example was the Ashdown family: Albert Ashdown had been a forester on the Brabourne Estate and Florence, Albert's wife, worked as charlady at Park Cottage, Lord and Lady Brabourne's home after they were married in 1946. She charged them the going rate for domestic work at the time, 1 shilling and 6 pence per hour (15p). Florence and Albert's son, Ernest (Ernie), worked as a footman for Lord Brabourne, the late Lord Brabourne's father, and years after Ernie retired, and until he died in 2011, aged 97, contact was maintained with the Brabourne family. Doubtless, the Brabourne link will continue with Ernie's daughter, Carole, who has been known to them since she was a child, when Ernie worked on the Estate. Several members of the Staples family also worked for the Estate for many years:

Albert and Florence Ashdown

Ernest Ashdown in footman's attire

Harry Staples was a gardener there, and his brother looked after the horses. And there were other families from whom generations of workers stayed with the Estate. Was this loyalty or simply that people did not change their jobs because opportunities were so few and they were tied to a place? Most were comparatively immobile, travelling to work (or anywhere) by foot or bicycle, so was it no

Carole Ashdown, Ernie's daughter

more than lack of opportunity that kept them with the same employer? In response to this question, our contributors maintained that finding secure employment with a good employer was greatly valued and, once they had a secure job, people were reluctant to change, especially if the employer was good. Though some remarked that the dwellings for Estate workers could have been better maintained, Millie Hodges was emphatic that the Brabournes were "lovely landlords who used to come round to their tenants to see that people were all right". Regarding the state of the dwellings, Lady Brabourne explained that the reason may have been that the then Lord Brabourne was away for six years as Governor of India from 1933, and then the war followed. It was not until after the war, when Lord and Lady Brabourne were married and came back to live on the Estate, that significant improvements were

Millie Hodges

able to be undertaken, such as the installation of bathrooms in the many farmhouses and cottages.

In the late 1940s, the tenancy for California Farm on the Brabourne Estate near Hatch Park became available, and Miriam (Agnes) (née Brooks) and Jeffrey Beadle moved in. There they brought up their three daughters: Amy (known as Esther), Elizabeth (known as Ann) and Muriel. The Beadles lived at California Farm for around 40 years, holding the longest tenancy on the Estate. They finally retired from farming in 1988. Ann Griggs (Beadle) recalled that California Farm was a small dairy

California Farm, 2010

farm where her parents also kept pigs for a short while and grew corn. In those days her father worked the land with a horse and plough. They grew strawberries, very much a speciality crop at the time, and after helping to pick the fruit she would accompany her father to Smeeth Station, from where the fruit was taken to Covent Garden. Later, the Beadles also grew swedes and potatoes, some of which were sold at a shop in Godinton Road, Ashford, which was rented by the family for several years. According to Lady Brabourne, the name California Farm is said to derive from tenants in the 1880s who left to join the Gold Rush in California, USA.

Steward Brooks (often referred to as Stuart Brooks) owned Running Water Farm in West Brabourne with his wife, Annie, and extended the area he worked by renting land from Lord Brabourne. He did a great deal of shooting on the Estate, working with the gamekeeper quite frequently, and was clearly trusted by the Brabournes. Being an "old village" person and a sergeant in the Special Constabulary, Steward was widely trusted and highly regarded. His daughter, Joan Taylor (Brooks), recalled that her parents had the greatest respect for the Brabournes, and were always treated with courtesy and kindness by them.

Tim Marsh has worked for the Brabourne family for 55 years, longer than most of the Estate workers. He was principally a tractor driver on the Brabourne Estate and initially drove a combine. Many years ago the Estate had three combines, but as machinery became larger and more powerful these were replaced by one machine. Tim regularly worked through the night, and recalls that it was a solitary existence. When he stopped working on combines, he drove other machinery, again for long hours at a time, and became involved in many aspects of Estate life, including the fencing, as well as relief milking the herd of Guernseys between 1959 and 1966, after which the herd was sold.

Like other Estate workers, Tim recalls that Lord and Lady Brabourne used to take the staff out for Christmas dinner, usually to a different local pub each year. While at dinner, Lady Brabourne would go round the table noting down how long each person had been working on the Estate. Various members of the office staff had been there five or six years, and then there was Tim with his service of 55 years which usually nearly exceeded the total number of years worked by all the other members of the Estate staff who were present.

Tim also recalled that Lord and Lady Brabourne would often go out walking on the Estate, and when they had to cross ditches between the fields Lord Brabourne would climb out of the ditch first, then push his walking stick hard into the ground so that Lady Brabourne could hang on to it and pull herself up and out of the ditch. Tim added that you always had to be extremely polite when working, as you never quite knew whom you would meet, often quite unexpectedly.

Several Estate workers, and others who had different connections with the Estate, recalled being involved in the Brabourne family's joys and sorrows, the Ashdown family being one example. In 1937 several Ashdowns, together with other workers from the Estate, were taken up to London by coach for the coronation of George VI. They were all installed in seats in the Mall very early in the day and had excellent views of the processions and all the activity.

On 26th October, 1946, at 4.30am, a coach party of workers from the Estate left for Romsey Abbey in Hampshire for the wedding of Lord and Lady Brabourne. Ernie Ashdown and his wife, Eileen, whom he had met at Smeeth School, were among those invited. Ernie's mother, Florence, who worked for Lady Brabourne, was also there; Steward was another, although he did not work on the Estate. Clearly there was a great deal of celebrating, and Ernie remembered Mrs Shorter falling into a stream later in the day. (He confirmed that she was recovered safely, though wet.) The picture below shows Ernie and his brother Sid, 50 years later, at Lord and Lady Brabourne's Golden Wedding celebrations.

Mersham Hatch Estate workers' outing in the 1940s.
Tom Doughty is third from right

Ernest Ashdown (left), aged 83, with his brother Sid Ashdown, aged 88, at Lord
and Lady Brabourne's Golden Wedding lunch, (October, 1996)

David Sawyer also remembers being invited, in the late 1960s, together with other
workers from the Estate, to celebrate the 21st birthday of Lord and Lady Brabourne's
eldest son, Norton, at Broadlands, Romsey. A coach was arranged to transport the
group, and David remembers eating freshly caught salmon for dinner.

Flyer for Sink the Bismarck!, one of
Lord Brabourne's best-known films

Ernie went to the weddings of several of Lord and Lady Brabourne's children, as
did Steward, and Steward's daughters – Joan Taylor, Mabel Oliver and Margaret Buss
– still remember their parents attending Christmas parties at Hatch House, joining
in the celebrations hosted by the Brabournes at the time of the Coronation and
seeing a special showing of Sink the Bismarck, one of the films produced by Lord
Brabourne[2].

2      Image from Google images, accessed 23/05/13.

Ernie and Steward also attended the funerals of Lady Brabourne's father, Lord Louis Mountbatten, her son, Nicholas, and Lady Doreen, her mother-in-law, who were all killed as a result of an IRA bomb attack in County Sligo in the Irish Republic in 1979. The bomb also killed a young Irish friend of the family, Paul Maxwell. Both Ernie and Steward were pallbearers at Lady Doreen's funeral, honoured to have been asked to do this, but very much saddened by events at the time. Ernie was, very sadly, too unwell to attend the funeral of the late Lord Brabourne in 2005, so his daughter Carole, together with her partner John Wenborn, attended in his place. Tim Marsh also recalled the tragedy and was proud to have helped carry Nicholas's coffin from Mersham church to the grave.

When the late Lord Brabourne was alive, he and Lady Brabourne were frequent visitors to the Ashdowns, both when they lived on the Estate and in more recent years at Calland in Brabourne Lees, where Ernie lived with Carole. Carole got on very well with Lord Brabourne, whom she had known since she was an infant. He would insist that she should call him John, not Lord Brabourne, and on one occasion, at the Scout hut, he ignored her when she referred to him as Lord Brabourne and continued to do so until she reverted to calling him John. Carole met Lord Louis Mountbatten, Lady Brabourne's father, one summer when she was about seven or eight, and remembers him asking her to teach him how to make a daisy chain.

Lord and Lady Brabourne (late 1990s)

Though the Brabourne Estate and large farms provided employment for many, so, too, did smaller farmers, and Dick Andrews worked as milkman for Percy Nickolls of Warren Farm for six years until he joined the army in 1939. Many farms also employed people at periods of peak activity in the farming calendar, harvest being one of the main times for casual work. More on farms and farming later.

## RURAL LIVING CONDITIONS

Although lasting relationships may have been forged between many employers and their employees, and there may have been mutual respect and affection between them, still the majority of rural workers lived in very basic conditions, and many who worked on the land lived in tied cottages or rented properties where maintenance was frequently poor. The incomes of rural dwellers were generally low and, where possible, people tried to grow, rear or catch their own food. Though electricity and mains water had reached the villages in the mid-1930s, many were unable to afford the connection fees and continued to depend on well or spring water, and paraffin for light. Reflecting on the state of poverty that existed, Derek Ames spoke of people being unable to afford furniture, using egg boxes instead (the wooden sort, in which trays of eggs were packed). Tea chests and other wooden crates served the same purpose.

Jean Holmes (Nickolls), who lived at Highfield in Hampton Lane with her family,

was only connected to mains water in 1954, and electricity in 1968; meanwhile, Kath and Basil Thornby, who lived in Weekes Lane, first had mains electricity in 1971.

Rats and mice were major problems for rural dwellers, regardless of the nature of their tenure, and Jean remembers that when the hay was cut rats and mice headed straight for the houses. At their home in Hampton Lane (then a chalet bungalow) the mice and rats lived under the wooden floorboards and

Jean Holmes (Nickolls)

rats lived under the wooden floorboards and frequently ventured above them to scavenge in the "scrap bucket" in the scullery. Flattened tin cans were nailed down to cover the gaps between the floor boards to keep them at bay, but Jean remembers that their determination was such that all their efforts to keep them out of the house failed.

Living conditions were little better at Orchard Cottage in The Street in East Brabourne. Originally, these were two cottages – Peace Haven and Rest Haven – which were built in the mid-19th century and were extremely damp which was far from good for the health of the tenants. George Brooks, whose

Kath Thornby (White)

Ruth Brooks, recently widowed in 1918, with her three children, George, Ruth and Naomi

family were tenants in the more easterly of the two cottages in the 1920s and 1930s, and Kath Thornby (White), who lived there in the late 1940s and 1950s, both remarked on this.

The dampness was also noted by Oliver Trowell in 1955 in his book on The Street, Rural Metamorphosis. Even when the cottages were owner-occupied in the 1950s and converted into one dwelling, dampness remained a problem right up until a much-needed damp course was installed in 1990. Though the cottages were damp, they did not have a well, and the Brooks family used to be provided with two buckets of water each day by their landlord, Albert Hammon, who lived next door in Clandon Cottage, then Albert House, and had a well between his home and the pink cottage that later belonged to the Princess Cantacuzino. If more water was needed, the Brooks family were welcome to help themselves, and as a small boy, this was always George's job. Wells were the main source of water for other houses along The Street as well.

Mention of getting water from a well prompts us to mention the spring in Brabourne Lees, which was an important source of drinking water. Before Brabourne Lees was connected to mains water in the late 1930s, there was a spring opposite the Manse and the Baptist Chapel on Plain Road. It was about 18 inches deep, very clean and with a good roof over it. Everyone would go along with a bucket, dip it in and take the water away. It cost nothing. Rosemary Hendry and Margaret Pile (both née Ward) remember being sent to the spring with buckets by their mother when they were very young, and spilling half the water on the way home. They were not alone in this; it was always assumed that children would help in the household. Rosemary recalls that before mains water arrived most people heated rainwater in coppers (copper boilers) for a bath, which was taken in front of the kitchen range. At this time homes were also lit with oil lamps. A decade or so later, in the late 1940s, Bryan Hodges remembers that when he was a lad he would sit in a tin bath in front of the kitchen fire every Saturday night listening to PC49, a programme on the radio, before going to bed. In 1938, after piped water was brought to the village, the spring was diverted and sealed - but many still remember it fondly.

Before mains water arrived many people collected their water from streams and springs, and though we have never heard of any health problems with the spring in Brabourne Lees we have heard that, in some other places, rudimentary lavatory cesspits polluted stream water which was used for drinking, thereby causing sickness. Some people even got hepatitis. There could have been problems in Brabourne Lees as the spring surfaced not far from the exit of drains believed to have been installed in the Napoleonic era and which, it is thought, are still in use today. In spite of this no one is known to have suffered adversely from drinking water from this particular spring.

Returning to The Street in East Brabourne, damp was also a problem just along from the Brooks' home, at the cottage where Wally Washford used to live. This was on the left-hand side of the pink cottage (from the front), in the days before it was owned by the Princess. According to Eric Jenner, the son of a former landlord of the Five Bells, the downstairs room in the Washfords' cottage had a stone floor that would flood from time to time in periods of wet weather, with the water simply seeping away through holes under the skirting boards.

John Varrier graphically describes aspects of the living conditions at his grandmother's house in Stowting in 1939, and doubtless into the 1940s as well:

"I spent the first year of the Second World War with my Grandmother at Dial House, Stowting. Cooking was by paraffin stoves and a cast-iron kitchen range. The toilet was a bucket in a 'wee house' – forgive the pun – in the garden, which was emptied every few days by one of my uncles. Water was pumped from a very deep well, and it was my job to pump and bring in as many as two buckets full of water, twice a day. I was then 10 years old. It was not until about three or four years after the war that electricity came to the villages, but only a few were able to afford to have it connected, and for several years we kept going on paraffin."

John Varrier

Conditions were little different at Bulltown Farm, West Brabourne, where David Orpin, whose parents ran Orpin's Stores, was dispatched during school holidays. David writes:

"Bulltown Farm, West Brabourne, was owned by my uncle, Fred Hayles. The facilities there were rudimentary compared with conditions these days – water from the pump over the sink, hot water from the cauldron and kettle on the skillet over the open-hearth fire. Lighting was by candles and oil lamps; and the toilet, a two-holer, was down the garden path. Bulltown Farm was an enjoyable place to be for a small boy, what with helping with collecting eggs and driving in the cows for milking. The highlights were when Uncle took me ferreting for rabbits some Sunday mornings. After Sunday teatime, in the light evenings, I would walk behind Uncle as he went around the hedgerows with his gun. I had the job of picking up the kill. I soon learnt to paunch and hamstring rabbits. In 1940, and throughout the war, a man came and bought them and took them away in his van. An additional perk of living in West Brabourne was that I was allowed to stay up late!"

Reflecting on access to electricity, Phil Harris recalled that his family, who lived at Vine Cottage at the A20 end of the Ridgeway, was connected to mains electricity in the early 1930s, or perhaps even slightly earlier.

Phil recalls that Mersham le Hatch, home of Lord and Lady Brabourne, was one of the first places to be connected in the area, and very soon after that power was brought to the

Phil and Betty Harris

sawmills and workshop for the Brabourne Estate, which were on the Ridgeway, not far from where Phil lived. Tom Doughty, Phil recalls, was sawman at the time. Once power was at the sawmill, electricity was made available to other nearby properties, including Vine Cottage. Consequently, those fortunate enough to live along a particular part of the Ridgeway at that time were connected to the national grid far sooner than the centre of Brabourne Lees. We are led to believe that electricity reached the Village Hall in 1935, but many houses remained unconnected then, as people could not afford the cost in those days.

While most had similar problems regarding the provision of water, sanitation, heating and lighting, one major difference was that those households with greater resources could, and did, employ people to help ease the drudgery of daily living. Thus there was demand for, and supply of, labour within the rural domain, and our contributors confirmed that there was almost always some work to be found.

Regarding tied cottages, an anecdote from Will Wilson highlights how vulnerable tenants of such properties used to be. Will's father, Bill Wilson, worked for several local farmers, but while in the employ of one of them, he lived in a tied cottage that was convenient for work on the farm, together with his wife, Nancy, and their two sons, Will and Ricky. One day, in 1961, Bill and Will were walking along the road when the farmer, who was out in his soft-topped Bentley, stopped to talk to them. He didn't get out. "I understand, Billy," he said, "that you've bought yourself a house." "Yes, Mr X," Bill replied. "Well, I've never heard of a working man owning his own house before, so you won't be wanting mine [tied cottage]. Take two weeks' notice." And that was that – Bill was out of a job. Will, who was no more than a little boy, can remember thinking, "And what do we do

Will Wilson

now?" But fortune was on their side. Tom Jeanes, another local farmer, had heard that Alan Clifton needed someone to drive the combine harvester on his farm and he took Bill on at Park Farm without delay. Some six weeks later the employer who had sacked Bill knocked on the door of Bill's new house and said, "Billy, you are going to drive my combine, aren't you?" Bill replied, "No, Mr X, I'm driving Mr Clifton's combine." That was the last time he spoke to Bill. The purpose of including this anecdote is not so much to denigrate the farmer who effectively made Bill homeless with no notice, but to reflect how vulnerable farm workers were, and how few were their rights – as little as 50 years ago. This would not have been an isolated incident in rural life at that time.

## LIMITED OPPORTUNITIES

In the late 1920s, at the age of 14, George Brooks left school and went straight out to work for Mr and Mrs Hoskins at Kite Manor in Broadstreet.

His grandfather, who used to work there two or three days a week, had got him a job as gardener. A year later he moved to Horton Park, where he worked for Colonel Wayland for several years. George used to cycle from Brabourne Street to Horton Park every day, seven days a week, including Christmas Day. He always began the day by cleaning the shoes for the household, and during the winter months would then bring in wood and coal "sufficient for the day". In addition, George looked after a mule, and in the summer mowed and tidied the lawns. George never had a holiday while he worked there. Looking back across the years, George remarked, "I have never known anything else other than work!"

A young George Brooks

Colonel Wayland kept several staff at Horton Park at that time. He had a dairy and kept a cowman, a wagoner, a dairyman, a head gardener and another gardener. There were strong links between Colonel Wayland and his brother, Sir William Wayland, who lived at Hempton Lodge, and George got to know Sir William's gardener, who did much to encourage George and stimulated his interest in vegetable gardening. This helped to prepare him for a career as a farmer (to which we will return later).

By the late 1950s and 1960s there were still comparatively few opportunities for further education, so most people went straight to work after school. Bryan Hodges, who had done several part-time jobs before he left school, was taken on as van boy for Stonegate Farmers at Wye. He used to pick up chickens from the Princess Cantacuzino's poultry farm at Court Lodge Barn in The Street at East Brabourne, as well as from other suppliers, and would sell them to local butchers. He would also take local chickens up to Smithfield Market three times a week. Bryan was 15 years old when he started work for Stonegate. At 6am each day he would cycle six miles to work, and at 5pm he would cycle the six miles home, all for £2 per week. If he went in on Saturdays to wash three or four lorries he was paid 10/- extra, but this was not as good as it sounded as he was taxed heavily, barely making this additional effort worthwhile.

## SUPPLEMENTING INCOMES

Manual workers had hard lives and, during their long years of service, often worked long hours. Money was always short, so people would take additional jobs and work even longer just to make ends meet. For much of his working life Bill Wilson was employed by some of the largest farmers in the area. During the 1960s, at the end of the day, Bill would head to Smeeth Station, where both he and his brother-in-law, Albert Stockbridge, would shovel an entire truck of coal into one hundredweight sacks for the Aldington coal merchant. Bill also worked for Norrington's agricultural contracting business, which involved him in ploughing or baling crops, and he and his colleagues would take their bikes to work, putting them on the lorry that took them to wherever they were working at the time. At the end of the day it was the accepted rule that they found their way home in their own time, and they always cycled, whatever the distance.

Pauline Anderson's father, Charlie Marsh, would come home from his day job at the Folkestone and District Water Company, where he was involved in installing water mains, and work for Keith Finn (builder and undertaker), digging graves, drains and cess pools, or any other work that Keith wanted him to do, to supplement the family income.

After the Second World War, when Jock Copland returned to Brabourne (having been billeted at the Paddocks on the A20 in 1943), he found what might now be considered a very "traditional" part-time job to supplement his income. Jock worked largely at weekends for Charlie Graves, who lived in the big house opposite Heathfield and Spicer's workshop on Church Road. At that time Charlie owned the chalkpit on Pilgrims' Way in East Brabourne. It is now disused, fenced off and heavily overgrown. Jock's work involved digging chalk for the production of quick lime, which was much in demand by farmers for improving the quality of the soil, especially clay soils. The effect of the lime was to improve the tilth and drainage of the heavy soil, and also to improve its capacity to retain both nutrients and moisture. Ron Cooper added, "Another use of quick lime was for whitewashing houses, and it was also used on the inside walls of the slaughterhouse. To make it water-repellent mutton fat was added during the slaking process, which melted and gave it this property."

Jock Copland

Jock's job, in the main, was to dig out the chalk and break it up ready for a grinder that was housed in a shed. Others, including Jack Coveney and Bert Sawyer, packed it into the kilns, which were funnel-shaped and embedded in the ground in the yard, in front of the chalkface. At the bottom was a layer of burning coal and, above, a layer of chalk. The kiln fires were kept going until the chalk had been converted to quick lime, which took days. The noxious quick lime was then loaded into trucks, taken to farms and spread on the fields.

In addition to being used as a fertiliser, quick lime was also a key ingredient in the construction of lathe and plaster walls, the use of which was already declining by the 1940s. Jock described how a "lake of sand the size of a swimming pool" would be created and filled with quick lime; the lime would then be slaked (quenched) with water. This process involved the emission of a great deal of heat and choking fumes. When the slaked lime had cooled down the residual "lime putty" would be mixed with horsehair and plastered onto walls of chestnut lathes. Jock remembers that one of the last places where this method was used was at Park Wood, Maidstone.

Rural livelihoods were thus very different from today. Not only was the type of work very different but so were the attitudes of people who were self-sufficient and self-reliant to as great a degree as possible. People with whom we spoke were undoubtedly correct in asserting that the richness of goods and services provided within our villages was considerable and this is confirmed by the page relating to Brabourne from Bagshaw's History, Gazetteer and Directory of Kent, 1847[3], which lists the enterprises, services and also the farmers in the local area. The division between East Brabourne and Brabourne Lees isn't clear – but the list confirms that there was a wealth of economic activity in the villages – enough to ensure that almost everything was available locally.

---

3 Bagshaw, Samuel (1847) History, Gazetteer and Directory of Kent, 1847. Vol. II. Sheffield, publisher G Ridge.

468     THE BIRCHOLT FRANCHISE AND BARONY.

tomb is a kind of altar-piece, ornamented with stone carved work. In the south chancel, belonging likewise to the Scott family, the brasses on the gravestones, with which the pavement is covered, are all gone. In the south aisle is a stone with the figure of a man in brass, habited in armour. The Baptists have a small chapel in the village. A fair is held for pedlery on the last day of May.

THE MANOR OF BRABOURNE was granted to the monastery of St. Augustine about the year 864; about the time of the Doomsday survey, it was held by Hugh de Montfort, and some time time after it was possessed by the Scott family, one of whom alienated it to Sir Edward Knatchbull, Bart. *Heminge, Combe,* and *Hampton,* are also manors in this parish; the latter of which was formerly held by a family who took their name from it.

CHARITIES.—*Valentine Knott,* by will 1614, left a yearly sum of 8s., which is distributed to the poor by the churchwardens. (See Bonnington.) The proportion of rent payable to this parish from the bequest of *William Fordred,* amounts £7 8s. 9½d., which is given amongst the poor by the parish officers.

POST-OFFICE, at Mr. THOS. SWAFFER'S—Letters arrive from Ashford at 9 A.M., and are despatched at 5 P.M.

Brothers Rev Jas. B.A. Vicar
Chittenden Henry, schoolmaster
Cox Rbt. tailor
Daniels Edw. blacksmith
Epps Henry baker
Epps Wm. butcher
Foord Wm. shoemaker
Foreman John, shopkeeper
Fox Wm. vict. Five Bells
Francis Geo. grcr, drpr, & gen. dealer
George Henry, blacksmith
Haycock Alfred, shopkeeper
Hayton Rev Amos, Vicarage
Hills Wm. wheelwright
Hooker Josh. baker
Kingsmill Geo. grocer

Leeds Wm. shoemaker
Lyne Fredk. National School
Lyne Louisa, National School
Moore Chas T D. tailor
Morley Godfrey, vict. Plough
Nickols Wm. bricklayer
Palmer Jas butcher
Phillpott Wm. shoemaker
Sankey Wm. shopkeeper
Sutton Samuel, shoemaker
Swaffer Thos. grocer
Venner Wm. shoemaker
Watts John, carpenter
Weekes Mr John
West Rd. corn miller
White Jas. carpenter

**Farmers.**
Andrews Onslow (and land agent)
Conley Edw. grazier
Crow Geo grazier
Gotts Philip, Coombe fm
Harvey John, grazier
Hills Thos. Parsonage

Inge Jno C. Fidling fm
Jeffrey Mich. Hampton
Lambourn Levi, Wtr fm
Marchant Thos
Morley Rd
Noble Sarah, Hemminge
Parsons Rd. grazier

Pilcher James
Purshouse, Mary
Rolfe Geo. Bull Town
Sutton Mark, Court Ldg
Thornby Thos
Vincer Jas
Weekes James, Lime hs

Our thanks to Peter Leonard for providing us with the section on Brabourne from
Bagshaw's History, Gazetteer and Directory of Kent 1847

## SKETCH MAP OF BRABOURNE LEES SHOWING SOME OF THE PLACES MENTIONED IN THE TEXT

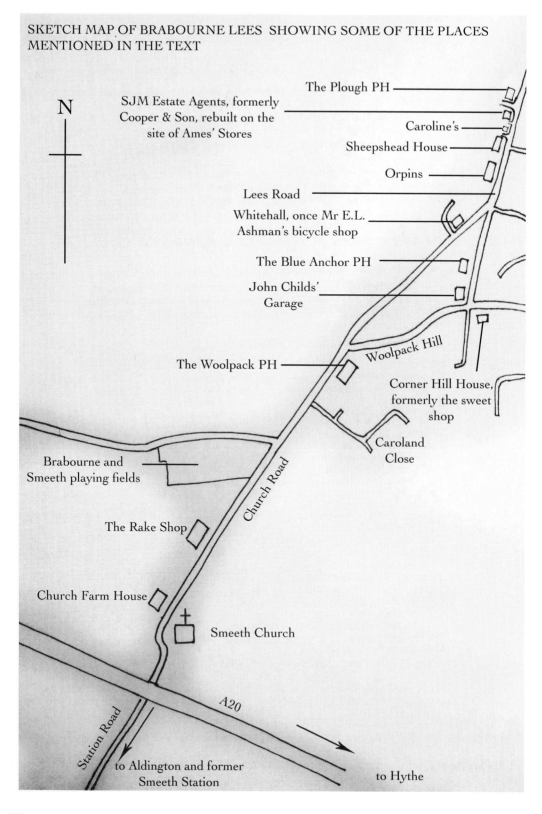

N

The Plough PH

SJM Estate Agents, formerly Cooper & Son, rebuilt on the site of Ames' Stores

Caroline's

Sheepshead House

Orpins

Lees Road

Whitehall, once Mr E.L. Ashman's bicycle shop

The Blue Anchor PH

John Childs' Garage

The Woolpack PH

Woolpack Hill

Corner Hill House, formerly the sweet shop

Caroland Close

Brabourne and Smeeth playing fields

The Rake Shop

Church Road

Church Farm House

Smeeth Church

A20

Station Road

to Aldington and former Smeeth Station

to Hythe

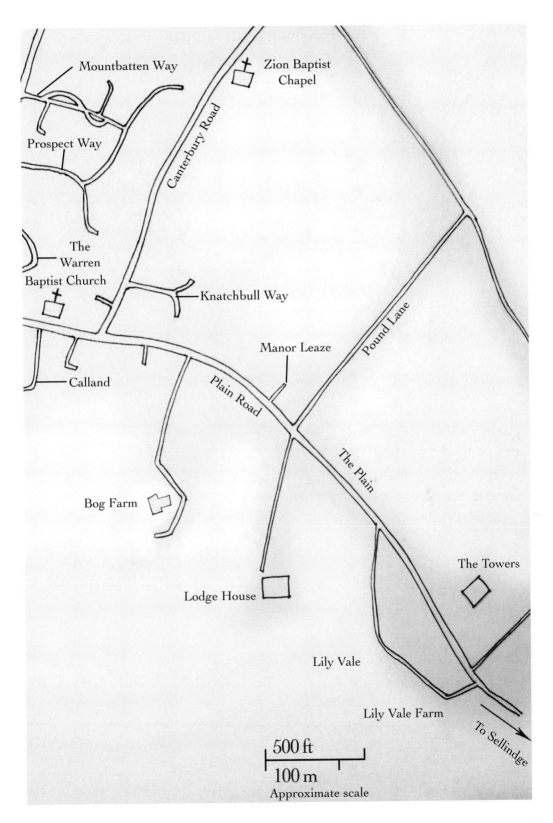

Mountbatten Way

Zion Baptist
Chapel

Canterbury Road

Prospect Way

The
Warren
Baptist Church

Knatchbull Way

Manor Leaze

Pound Lane

Calland

Plain Road

The Plain

Bog Farm

Lodge House

The Towers

Lily Vale

Lily Vale Farm

To Sellindge

500 ft

100 m

Approximate scale

# 5

# ENTERPRISE & EMPLOYMENT IN BRABOURNE LEES

We were not surprised to hear from Phil Stone  that, "there was much more going on in the village in the past than there is now".  By village, Phil was referring to Brabourne Lees, which is a focus of the three parts of Brabourne (East Brabourne, West Brabourne, Brabourne Lees) and Smeeth.  Living at Hill View as a boy, one of the bungalows opposite the Village Hall, Phil felt he was "central" to all four settlements and thus was one of many who were well qualified to tell us about life in all the villages.  In short, Brabourne Lees was a busy centre which provided essential services and also employment for those not working on the land.  Phil recalled the four pubs – the Five Bells, The Plough, The Woolpack and The Blue Anchor – as being major centres of social activity.  All are still thriving, though their individual personalities have altered with modernisation.  In addition to the pubs, which employed many local people – usually men as bar staff and many women as cleaners – there were several shops.  Orpins Stores was the largest, followed by Ames' Stores. Both were grocers and though they had much in common and competed fiercely, they were very different.  Both were significant employers, with Orpins taking on as many as 25 people in the 1950s and Ames' Stores employing a further dozen or so.

Several people worked at the local butchers, first Herbert Hawkins and later Cooper and Son, who took over the business in the late 1960s.  Many recalled Hawkins' flock of some 30 animals grazing peacefully on The Warren, outside his shop, awaiting slaughter.  This scene from the 1950s would rarely be witnessed now.  Some of this flock were bought from local farmers, some from Ashford Market, and some of the sheep were "home grown", reared by Herbert Hawkins himself.  Sheepshead

House, which is attached to Orpins Stores, stood for many years not far from the slaughterhouse just behind Hawkins' butcher's shop. It is believed that a sheep's skull was unearthed in the garden of Sheepshead House, hence its name.

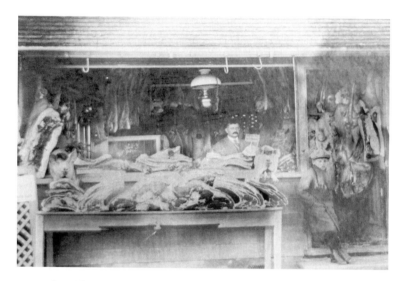

Hawkins' butcher's shop, Christmas 1933, with Herbert Hawkins
behind the counter and possibly his son, Ben, outside

Herbert Hawkins and his son, Ben, outside Hawkins' slaughterhouse

Karl Engels recalled that butchers' shops frequently attracted dogs and Mr Hawkins' shop was no different. He had a few favourite dogs, to which he gave scraps or a bone from time to time, but there were others that he clearly disliked, possibly because they were thieves and overstepped the mark in regard to his generosity. Walking towards the butcher's shop with his mother one day, Karl can remember seeing a huge meat cleaver flying out of the shop window and landing on the road, scattering several dogs that had gathered there but, almost inevitably, missing all of them. Mr Hawkins then emerged, picked up the meat cleaver, wiped the blade on his jacket sleeve and went back into the shop to continue his work.

Merrit's sweet shop, later Baxter's, then Burtenshawe's, Goreham's, Powell's and, most recently, Markham's was in the white house opposite John Childs' Garage. Here, sweets, cigarettes and even some groceries were sold. An account of working at Baxter's is given later on in this chapter by Margaret Maple (Gower), who used to work there with her sister Pauline Kingston (Gower).

Ted Ward senior (EF Ward) opened a bicycle shop behind his parents' pub, The Blue Anchor, in the years after the First World War. Later, he bought land on the corner of Bridge Road from his father, and opened Anchor Garage, which became more commonly known as Ward's Garage. In time, this was taken over by his son, also Ted Ward, and as the business grew it too provided employment for local people. It is now John Childs' Garage.

Tom Sprawling, who used to sell paraffin in the village from a small lorry, took over the shop that had belonged to Herbert Hawkins the butcher, and turned it into a hardware shop, The Handy Stores. Just along from Herbert Hawkins' shop was Mr Ernest (EL) Ashman's bicycle shop which, it is thought, moved from there to what is now Whitehall in Lees Road. We should note here that Sheila Stone (Ashman) brought it to our attention that the Mr Ashman of the bicycle shop was not a relative of the Ashman family mentioned in connection with the Baptist church (Chapter 3). Going up Lees Road there was a post office in what is now Anchor Cottage. This was run by Katy Apps, whose brothers had the corn and seed merchant that later became Orpins Stores when John Orpin bought it shortly before the First World War. According to Sid Ashdown, there was also a boot and shoemaker who, he suggested, may have made clogs, as these were often worn in the early years of the 20th century. Sid also told us that there used to be a clockmaker along Canterbury Road who used to make clocks for schools. Much was produced locally, making the villages self-reliant, and as Sid put it, "Clocks – made in Brabourne; boots and shoes – made in Brabourne; bicycles – made in Brabourne." Arguably, all this activity was a legacy of the thriving community that settled itself in Brabourne Lees when the army camp was there in the early 19th century.

Cycle shop at the junction where Bridge Road joins Lees Road, to the left
of Orpins (when viewed from the front). The signs above the window
read "E.L. Ashman, Cycle Maker" (c1910, or earlier)

We would add that we have had considerable discussion
with our contributors as to whether both, one or neither of
the properties on the opposite page was once Mr Ashman's
bicycle shop. Please let us know if you have any definite
information on this subject

Building thought to be Whitehall, which was two cottages when it was
bought by Mr E.L. Ashman in c1910.  Our contributors thought that
Ernie Ashman moved his cycle shop from round the corner in Lees Road
(pictured left), to Whitehall, shortly after he bought the property

Possibly Whitehall (1915), after it had been improved by Mr Ashman

Brabourne Lees was also well provided with services: several people worked for Claude Aldrich, a local entrepreneur who came to Brabourne in 1931, or thereabouts.

Claude originated from London, where his mother had a music school, and Sally Bulgin, his granddaughter, remembers hearing that he was "sent to the country", as were many young men in those days, to make something of himself. He had an allowance, and while living in Sussex played a great deal of tennis, which led him to meet his wife-to-be, Mildred, at Mountfield Tennis Club. They were married and came to live at Holmleigh in Brabourne Lees, where they lived all their married lives.

While in Brabourne, Claude continued to play tennis, but in the years before, during and after the Second World War he set up and ran several businesses, all of which used local labour. These included a local bus service, a haulage business and a coal-

Claude and Mildred Aldrich

delivery business. Shortly after the war he recycled the wire mesh used on the runways of local aerodromes, and delivered milk to a wide area. He also owned a couple of sandpits, one of which was on Granary Lane. Later, he was a sales "rep" for Regent Oil. Sally was a frequent visitor to her grandparents at Holmleigh when she was

Sally Bulgin, granddaughter
of Claude Aldrich

a child and remembers both Claude and Mil with great affection. She described Claude as being very family orientated, great fun – "a big person" and "larger than life". Sally and her sister and brother were clearly indulged by their grandfather, and Sally especially loved climbing into the cabin of the haulage lorries that had CPF Aldrich emblazoned on their sides; this was something she did as often as she could. She also remembers enjoying going out with Claude on his rounds for Regent

Oil and how much he loved animals as well as playing tennis – he was instrumental in setting up the RSPCA in Ashford. He enjoyed his fried breakfasts so much that, in his later years, he put on so much weight that he found it difficult to bend down to pick up tennis balls, so he used to ask others who were at the court to pick them up for him. Many people spoke of him being an excellent pianist and playing regularly at local dances and shows. Apparently, Mil loved going to these dances, but because Claude couldn't dance with her (as he was playing the piano) she had to dance with other men, which infuriated him. In the end she simply stayed at home. Claude and Mil were a strong team, though. In retrospect, Sally considers that her grandfather's creative entrepreneurial ideas were realised largely through Mil's support and driving force – she was a consistent tower of strength behind him.

Frank Howland's marquee business, which thrived from the 1950s to the 1970s, also drew on local labour to put up marquees for fêtes, weddings and parties, and for the annual point-to-point races. There were also more "traditional" businesses, such as Heathfield and Spicer, the wood turners, Frank Trice the hurdle maker, and Nelson Smith, who had a wood yard virtually opposite the Zion Baptist Chapel where he, too, made hurdles, spiles (heavy timber posts) and also erected farm fencing. On a small scale, and probably less of an employer but nonetheless a significant local business, was Ned Andrews, the cobbler.

Frank and Marjorie Howland (1960s)

We have compiled sketches of some of these businesses, including some now gone, based on the memories of people who owned them, worked for them or used them. What is important in our theme of self-reliant villages is that these and other enterprises depended on both full-time and part-time local labour. During and after the Second World War, when times were particularly hard, many families supplemented their incomes with part-time work in Brabourne Lees. These sketches also highlight how rapid advances in transport and technology since the late 1960s have contributed to the demise of some of these enterprises, and the near-demise of others. There is, however, optimism that, with the rise in fuel prices and the increased capacity to work from home, the village ethos will not disappear.

## FITTING IN PART-TIME WORK WITH A FAMILY

Betty Edenden began working at Orpins shortly after leaving school, stopping after she married and had children. Before returning to full-time employment she used to deliver meat for Herbert Hawkins; her son, Ian, just a baby at the time, would be placed in his carrycot in the back of the van and taken on her delivery round.

In the school holidays her daughters Christine and Jacqueline would be packed into the van as well, and for a treat she would stop at Stowting Post Office and buy them a packet of biscuits. Later, when Betty worked in The Plough, she depended on her mother to look after the children during the school holidays. Though Francis, her husband, was working, Betty did as many small jobs as she could, "just to make ends meet". The

Betty and Francis Edenden

Edendens were by no means unique in this regard, and most women who had children worked where and when they could to supplement the family income.

The orchard and market garden at Court Lodge in East Brabourne provided full- and part-time employment for many: Kath Spain and Elsie Davis, both of whom lived in The Street, East Brabourne, worked there part-time, along with several others.

Kath Spain

Elsie would get the children off to school each morning and then hurry off to work at the market garden, virtually across the road, until 11.30am. She would then rush home to put the potatoes on to cook and get the lunch ready for her husband, Ernie, who came home at noon. After that she would return to work from 1pm-4pm and get back again just after the children came home from school, in time to get the tea ready. In the late 1950s Elsie and Kath would each earn 2/6 for a morning's work. Ernie worked for Lady Charnwood and Miss Cochrane as gardener at the market garden for more than 40 years, another example of someone staying with the same employer for decades. Pauline Anderson (Marsh) recalls that her mother, Nancy

Ernie and Elsie Davis's daughters
from left, Rosemary, Margaret and Jackie
(mid-1950s)

Elsie Davis (mid-1990s)

Marsh, who lived at no.2, Subdown Cottages, used to do Lady Charnwood's personal washing, a useful means of supplementing the family's income from home.

The market garden was not the only such enterprise in the area. There was another one behind the Zion Baptist Chapel and Sandhurst on Canterbury Road, where a large house now stands. This market garden was run by Sid Norrington, the father of John, Tony and Tink, and a place where many local people were employed. Among these were Nellie Sawyer, who met her husband John Norrington there, and also Doris Norrington, who had been a Land Army girl who had stayed in the village and married Tony Norrington. Nellie remembers picking runner beans, apples, plums and all sorts of fruit and other produce there. Much of this harvest was loaded onto lorries destined for shops in Ashford and Folkestone, and also for the London market. Later, Tink Norrington ran the business.

Margaret Baldock (Sawyer), who used to deliver milk for Claude Aldrich, supplemented her income with part-time work at a wood yard on the Plain, near where Andrews Garage now stands. Wood from properties that had been bombed was salvaged, taken up to the wood yard, and part-time workers would help to take nails out of it so it could be recycled. Margaret met her husband, Charles, while working here; he came from Sellindge.

## TERMS OF WORK IN THE 1940s
Michael Hickmott has provided us with details from a period in his grandmother Marjorie Howland's early working life. Marjorie started work at Orpins when she was about 14, but later took up employment in Ashford. Though Marjorie's experience of work in Ashford takes us away from the village as workplace, the detail it contains is a valuable example of earnings of a woman in the 1940s:

Marjorie Howland

"In March 1943 Marjorie was offered the job of cook at the Ashford North School and Central Kitchen at a wage of £2/2/- [£2.10p], plus war addition. Two years later, on 24th September, 1945 she was offered the job of cook-in-charge at Ashford North County Modern School at a wage of £2/15/- [£2.75p] per week, plus war addition, totalling £3/8/4d [£3.42p]. She was allowed 12 working days' holiday per year, to be taken during school holidays. Midday meals and light refreshments were included. Her contract stated, 'Work in the kitchen will begin at 7.30am each school day and will end when the work is finished and when any necessary preparations for the following day are complete.' In the school holidays she was expected to '...spring clean the premises, to make jam in season and to receive and check stores for the first week of each term'. Here she learned her culinary skills, which she put to good use throughout her life."

Arguably until the 1970s and beyond, when the village shops and businesses were thriving, work was available locally, and potential employers frequently sought out those who needed work through an efficient information grapevine. Going back to the days prior to the First World War, Sid Ashdown reflected on how there was no unemployment in the villages. Everyone could get a job and few had to travel any significant distance to work. Tom (TAL) Wratten, several years Sid's junior, recalled that until the 1960s people in the villages knew what skills the residents had and they would come to you for work. On one occasion, Mr Arnold the baker approached Tom and said, "I've got a job at the bakehouse. Let's go to the Five Bells to discuss it and perhaps you can start next week." He seemed to be fully confident that Tom would be ready to accept the post.

Philip Stone explained how the family frequently influenced interests and career choices of children. Before the Second World War, many people tended to follow in their parents' footsteps when they grew up; a boy would often take up the same trade or profession as his father – Sid and Ernie Ashdown's father was a blacksmith,

Philip and Sheila Stone

and so was his father before him. A girl would do much the same as her mother. She would, perhaps, work for a while before she married and, once married with children, she would probably remain at home as a housewife or, when the children were old enough, get a part-time job locally to help pay the bills. Philip had inherited his father's interest in telecommunications and, spurred on by a teacher at his secondary school in Hythe, had chosen to work with BT's predecessors after the war. Subsequently, his sons developed similar interests, which led to their own careers in information and communication technologies. Though family influence can still be considerable, the post-war era, which brought with it major improvements in education, has seen such patterns in rural life change.

## BEYOND BRABOURNE LEES

Shops and services also existed away from the centre of Brabourne Lees. The Ridgeway Stores, kept by "Aunt Lou", predictably on the Ridgeway, was on the A20 side of the Black House, where the politician Michael Howard lived for a time. According to Ian Bull, Cyril Scott had a workshop in the late 1950s and early 1960s in one of the outhouses of the Black House, where he used to make up bikes from second-hand parts and sell them. This was a lucrative business in the days when the bicycle was still the main form of travel.

Going towards Ashford on the A20 was the Caldecott Foundation, which cared for vulnerable children and young people who had suffered extremes of abuse and neglect. Nellie Norrington (Sawyer) worked there for more than 30 years, doing "domestic work, and anything else that needed to be done" – and she loved it. She liked the people she worked with and she liked the kindly and supportive attitude of the Caldecott staff towards the children who were there. Several local people worked there, including Betty Dryland (Lavender) and Joyce Garlick (Wood).

East Brabourne had its shop and post office and, after the Second World War, the market garden and orchard. Previously, this had been Cowley Miller's chicken farm which Oliver Trowell remembers as being well established by the early 1930s. In 1952/3 the Princess Cantacuzino established a chicken farm virtually opposite in Court Lodge Barn, while other businesses in East Brabourne included Finn's builders and undertakers at what is now The Wheelwright's, where Canterbury Road meets The Street and the Five Bells pub. All these provided goods and services for the community, and also employment. Gardening was, as you will have noted, yet another source of full-time and part-time work for many. Some members of the community were self-employed, and the current Tom Wratten's grandfather (also Tom), the village chimney sweep, was one of these. He used to take his son, also Tom, to help; after his father died, Tom (the present Tom's father), who was a bricklayer and plasterer, would also sweep chimneys at weekends, so great was the need to augment the family income. However, the soot caused problems with his breathing, so he had to give this up.

## WORKING FURTHER AFIELD

Beyond the villages, some worked on the railway at Smeeth or Ashford, and after the Second World War the trickle of those who worked in Ashford increased to a stream. As transport technology improved, people found work in garages such as Hayward's (later Caffyn's), driving buses, in the rapidly advancing telephone service, as teachers, lawyers, nurses and in insurance companies.

We now look in greater detail at some of the shops and services in the villages that were the hub of the local economy for many years and some of which could see a resurgence in popularity as focus on "the local" resurfaces. Until the 1960s farming was also a major employer, of course, but we will focus on farming in Chapter 9. First, we look at Orpins.

## ORPINS STORES

"Take away the shop and you take away the life of the village," said Ivy Young, and her words have been echoed by many of our contributors who consider Orpins[1] a veritable institution in the village.

Ivy Young, one of Orpins best-known and loved members of staff

The shop dates back to the late 19th century, when it was a corn and seed merchant run by the Apps family. Shortly before World War I the store was bought by John Orpin and at this time the shop was located in the two timber-framed cottages that are now united in Sheepshead House. There was a large extension at the back of the cottages, and another smaller one at the front (which came to be known as Orpin's bakery). The original shop extended over two stories and there was a cellar where gas for lighting the shop and for bicycle lamps was manufactured for sale. Over time, the corn and seed merchant evolved into a grocer's shop that sold paraffin, a product used by everyone prior to the arrival of electricity in the mid-1930s. Orpin's also made and sold bread and confectionery and the small extension that housed the bakery was eventually taken down. The flour

Henry Apps, Mr Torr, Allen Howland outside Apps Bros Stores
(c1910/12)

---

1    Over time Orpin's has lost its apostrophe

Orpin's Stores, c1914, when it was part of the house alongside the present shop. From left, Bill Hawkes, Miss Coppins (the housekeeper), Mr Mackleden (from Lily Vale, who worked in the bakehouse), John Orpin (the proprietor), Ernest Ashman (whose residence remained only a few doors away until he died in the late 1980s), Mr Dryland, Mr Bates and Percy Ashman (who was killed in the First World War). Opinions are divided on whether the pale-coloured horse was named Gilty Pill or Golden Ball

Orpin's horse and cart, which were used to deliver groceries. Here it is loaded for water deliveries

for the bread was stored on the first floor of the shop, while the bread was made on the ground floor, behind the shop front, and baked in ovens in an extension out at the back. The extension is now gone, but the "scars" from where it was joined to Sheepshead House are still visible.

Behind the shop was a large garden with stables for the horses that drew the delivery vehicles. A pigsty with pigs provided meat for the shop. David Orpin, the son of the original owner, John Orpin, remembers, "In the 1940s, Dad had pigs. We could slaughter one and keep half, on condition that we gave up six months' bacon rations. I don't know what happened to the second half. The other pigs went to market, transported there by Aaron Shorter, the carrier."

Orpin's also had a vast vegetable garden, which was the source of much of the produce sold in the shop. Typically, everything was locally sourced in those days. In addition to delivering bread and groceries, Orpin's also used to supply milk and water, the latter being collected from the spring opposite the Baptist Chapel. The picture opposite shows the horse-drawn water cart that used to fetch water from the spring for the shop and also deliver it to customers. This was in the days before Brabourne Lees was connected to the water main, so we are talking about the first three decades of the 20th century (like electricity, the main water supply arrived in the mid-1930s). Archibald Ashman, Joyce Garlick's (Wood) stepfather, at one time worked for Orpin's and used to take deliveries to customers on the horse and cart. Sometimes he would take Joyce with him and she remembers being terrified when she was left in charge of the horse while Archibald would carry the provisions into the customers' houses. She would have been six or seven years old at the time.

Early in the 20th century the business grew and the shop moved into its present position in the cottages on the other side of Sheepshead House. The bakery, however, remained in the original shop, from where gas was piped to the new premises. These pipes are still visible in the house and it is claimed locally that the shop was the first to have lighting in the area.

Orpin's (c1925): an image of prosperity with delivery vehicle at the
front of the shop

## FIRE AND THE REBUILDING OF ORPIN'S

The shop, which was clearly a successful enterprise, acquired the name of Orpin's Stores when John Orpin bought the shop from Henry Apps before the First World War. The Orpin family had been millers at Frittenden for more than 100 years and moving to the shop represented a new type of livelihood. The shop was refurbished by John in the early 1920s, but not long afterwards, on 21st March, 1926, it burnt down, though Mr Orpin's residence and the bakery located at the north end of the premises were both saved.

An extract from a book by the Brabourne and Smeeth History Group, of which Don Skeer was chairman, describes the discovery of the fire: "Miss Smith (a maid in the employ of Mr and Mrs Orpin) was awakened by a crackling noise between 3.30am and 3.45am and gave the alarm to Mr Orpin who found flames coming through the roof of the shop. It being impossible to get to the telephone inside the premises, he hurried to a neighbouring grocer, Mr E Ames, from where a telephone message was sent to the Ashford fire station. About two minutes previously a call had been received in respect of the outbreak [of fire] at the Woolpack."

Rumour has it that the shop was set on fire by an employee who had learned that they were to be sacked, but arson was never proven. Fire damage was extensive and the whole incident is well embedded in the collective memory of the village. Joyce Garlick (Wood) remembers hearing about the fire from her mother, who had stored furniture next door, in what was then Myrtle Cottage, now Stable Lodge. All their furniture was singed and ruined. Michael Hickmott, a recent occupant of Stable Lodge, has added that evidence of fire damage to this house had recently been exposed due to refurbishment.

On the same night that Orpin's burnt down, a storage barn behind The Woolpack also went up in flames and was partially destroyed, though Don Skeer observed that the "adjoining outbuildings and the house had a very narrow escape". One of our contributors recalled hearing that "fire engines came from all around and used huge pipes to draw water from the Hatch Park Lake to quell the flames".

The cost of rebuilding and restocking Orpin's after the fire was considerable, so John Orpin went into partnership with his brother-in-law, Arthur Hubble, the owner of Hubble's stores at Headcorn. As a result, it was possible to rebuild the shop in the same location, though it needed to operate from temporary premises while this was being done. There was a large hut at the back of the old shop where newspapers were sorted that, David Orpin believes, had been bought by his father after the First World War. This was taken down and reconstructed next to The

Fire at Orpin's: total devastation on 21st March, 1926.
Myrtle Cottage, now Stable Lodge, next door to the shop was
damaged, but survived

The workforce who helped put out the fire. The corner of
Stable Lodge, next door to Orpin's, is visible on the left

Myrtle Cottage, now Stable Lodge, shortly after the fire
(1926)

Plough, and it was from here that Orpin's continued to function, albeit in limited fashion, until the shop was ready.

John Hammon confirmed that The Woolpack, much of which had escaped the fire, was also rebuilt, but only in 1937, after it was taken down possibly because it was falling down. Prior to 1937, the pub had stood on the site of the present car park, but the rebuilt Woolpack was set well back from the corner and reopened on 17th December, 1937. Gwen Matthews, who in 1945 married Les Bishopp, lived in the old Woolpack with her parents from August 1937, and moved into the new building for opening in December. We can't confirm it, but can only assume that they kept the old pub open for business until the new pub was opened.

## DAVID ORPIN'S MEMORIES OF THE SHOP

David's family started running the shop when he was a young boy, so he has some of the earliest memories of Orpin's Stores. In the 1930s, and until 1943, when Ernie Ashman took over after John Orpin died, the shop was on two floors and sold virtually everything – from the enormous range of foodstuffs, bread, milk and paraffin on the ground floor, to the wide range of other goods upstairs. Customers could get almost everything they needed. Entering the shop from the pavement, there were stairs on the left-hand side that led to a well-stocked upper storey, though in the many years

David Orpin

that Connie Franklin was in charge[2] this was only accessible to the public at Christmas time; at other times the public only had access under supervision. David recalls that pots and pans hung from hooks in the ceiling, crockery and cutlery were on shelves, all types of haberdashery were on display, bolts of fabrics were stored on shelves under long cutting tables, clothes were on racks, and that paints, paintbrushes and wallpaper, buckets, spades, garden tools and many more everyday and exotic items, even wedding dresses, were also sold there. The slogan "Orpin's for everything that's best" was adopted, and its Christmas catalogue for 1935 was entitled Orpin's for Everything. This was quite an achievement considering that the shop had been devastated barely a decade earlier. Among the many items listed in the catalogue was Electric Lung Mixture and one can only wonder what promise that potion delivered. Several of our contributors referred to Orpin's Stores as an Aladdin's cave and, if something was not in stock, it was bought in and arrived within a day or two at the most. This tradition continued well after the Orpins were no longer the owners. Foodstuffs, including elegant cakes, were sold downstairs, and David remembers a little model of a baker in the window, just to the right of the door, on whose tray were displayed cakes, buns and other produce from the bakery. Several others have remembered Orpin's cakes with affection and rather wistfully. May Fortescue recalls her husband, Gordon, talking about the big slab cakes on display that had been cut up into pieces ready for sale.

On specific days the shop workers divided up goods bought in bulk such as flour, sugar and lentils into small bags of appropriate sizes for sale to customers. When Betty Edenden started work there, one of her first tasks was to weigh the cornflour from a huge bag into 2oz packets, and the butter into 2oz packets for the weekend, cutting up cheese that came packed in hessian, and weighing out sugar. Samm Orgar, the current owner, recalls Connie Franklin describing the skill (and mess) involved in using butter pats to divide up large quantities of butter into small packets. When rationing became part of daily life Betty also had to check that customers were registered with Orpin's, so that they might be given their correct rations. She remembers that one young man used to order chocolates for the month and then leave them on the counter for her.

---

2        Connie Franklin (Ashman) was born in 1920, started work in 1934, married in 1946 and moved to Lincoln. Returned to Orpins in 1950 and retired in 1992. She died in 2000, aged 80. Thanks are due to Sheila Stone (Ashman) for this information.

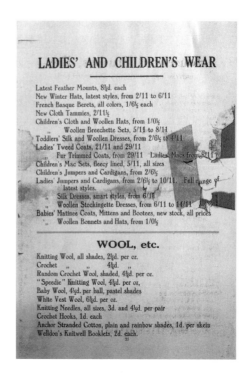

Extracts from Orpin's Christmas Catalogue, 1935

David remembers well the running of the bakery, which was still in the original shop. Flour was delivered to the upstairs of the house, now closest to Orpins Close, and this was fed into a hopper, which brought it down to the bakery on the ground floor, where the ovens were located. He recalls the deliverymen standing and talking to his father while effortlessly carrying 224lb sacks of flour. They would climb up to the first floor and set down the sacks of flour there. [This first floor doorway, now blocked, is still visible on the side of Sheepshead House overlooking Orpins Close.] The salt was also kept on the first floor to keep it dry. The ovens were fired by coal and, as we have heard, in the basement there was a gas-making plant. David describes this as "a Heath Robinson-style machine with a wind-up mechanism somewhat like clockwork". When fully wound, chemicals would combine to produce gas, which was piped through the house for the lights.

David writes:

"I clearly remember the bustle of the business, the loading of the delivery vans, the activities in the bakehouse, seeing the hot loaves coming out of the ovens and being stacked in the bread room for the van men. The bakers used to make me a little cottage loaf with a bit of spare dough. This was eaten hot, and smelled and tasted wonderful. Strictly speaking, I was in forbidden territory, and if they wanted to get rid of me they would simply say, 'Your father's coming' and I would disappear."

Oliver Trowell adds that, in the days before the Second World War, "the two bakers' roundsmen I remember coming to East Brabourne were Ernie Quested and Mr Hawkes. Arriving at his usual time, but on a Bank Holiday, my mother expressed surprise at seeing Mr Hawkes, who replied, 'All work, all work, no 'oliday – by Mi Lord Orpin's orders!'" Ernie Quested was quick to join the army at the outbreak of war in 1939, but this was possibly because he was a member of the Territorial Army and so had no choice. Oliver notes, "We bought our brown bread from Orpins and our white bread from Strudwicks, later Fred Arnold's."

Returning to David's account of the bakery:

"The dough was mixed in the evening and work started at around 4.30am to mould and bake the bread, rolls and cakes. Originally, all the mixing of the dough was done by hand, but in 1940-41 Dad got a breadmaker from a bombed-out bakery, so life became easier. The senior baker was Mr Brice, whose skill in icing cakes for weddings and Christmas was remarkable. Often he made and iced over 300 cakes at Christmas time. In the wartime he was assisted by Mr Moyle from Stowting, who was brought out of retirement. Occasionally, extra help came from 'Old Mac', who was, at times, in the workhouse at Etchinghill."

Mr Brice, the baker (left), with Ernest Ashman
(1930s)

From left, Mr Brice, Bert Sawyer, Ernest Ashman
and May Howland

Digressing briefly, David told us that, when his sister was born, the midwife remarked on Mr Brice as "the nice-looking young baker there". She later married him and they lived opposite Andrews' Garage. Digressing again, it was Mr Brice who made and iced Rose and Dick Andrews' wedding cake – a fruit cake with chocolate icing because sugar was not easily available in wartime (more details of the wedding come in the chapter on wartime).

David continues:

"After the war, Bert Sawyer and May Howland [Frank Howland's stepsister] made up the bakery staff. Bread, cakes and meat pies were baked and sold in the shop until 1958, which was when the bakery closed."

After 1958, bread was bought in from Strudwicks bakery in Stone Hill, and Samm Orgar confirms that, until 1980/82, Orpins continued to deliver bread, as Strudwicks did not have the staff to deliver to such a wide market. Margaret Baldock and Nellie Norrington (Bert Sawyer's sisters) added that Bert used to be known as "sparrow" because he would always whistle at work, not least when he started early in the morning.

## LIVING AT ORPINS IN THE 1930s AND 1940s
The Orpin family lived in the house beside the shop and David's recollections of living conditions for the family remind us that things were not always as they are now.

David writes:

"The shop, along with the rest of the village, had no electricity until 1938, when it was installed by George Edwards of Sandgate. Before this, lighting was by candles and paraffin lamps, and the shop did a good trade in paraffin oil for lamps and heaters. [Samm Orgar adds that the trade in paraffin continued until the 1980s, by which time her parents owned the shop.] Our cooking and heating was by a Kitchener in the kitchen that had an oven; in 1940 it was replaced by one that heated water. You could cook on the top hotplates and in the oven. In 1941 we got a bomb-damaged electric cooker, which still functioned in 1959. In the outhouse, called the mangle room since it housed a large mangle, was a large, three-burner oil stove with oven.

"There was no main drainage system until 1948. The toilet was a bucket under a seat that had to be hinged up in order to remove it for emptying. After my father died, emptying the toilet bucket was my Sunday job!

"The garden behind the shop was large with a tennis court and summer house at the bottom. Some of the vegetables that were grown were sold in the shop. Mr Tom Brooks was the gardener in my early years, and when he retired Mr Turner took over. He was a Boer War veteran with a large moustache and a great many tattoos on his arms, chest and back. He had had these done when he was serving in India. I liked his company and to hear his many stories. One day, he gave me a superb catapult that could fire pebbles great distances. On his birthday he used to dress up in his best suit, bowler hat, shiny shoes, and wax his moustache. Thus attired he would go to The Plough and The Anchor, often accompanied by Jack Cheeseman and Punch Pellet."

As mentioned earlier, the Orpin family also used to keep pigs in the garden and Aaron Shorter, who had a small haulage business, would take them to market. He used to wear "jam pot" glasses and it was said (rather cruelly) that he never used to stop at Smeeth crossroads because he could never see whether or not anything was coming. He was, however, skilled in manoeuvring unwilling pigs into his lorry: he would put food into a bucket and, once the pig's nose was in it, push the bucket towards the pig which, in an effort to escape, would move backwards and get directed into his lorry.

The Orpin family lived fairly comfortably but conditions changed sharply when John died.

David writes:

"My father died in March 1943; my mother became the book-keeper for the shop and we continued to live in the house, now with no maids or car! Ernie Ashman leased the business up until about 1950, then Peter Wilson of Sotheby's bought it. His partner Harry Wright [who had been his batman in the army] was nominally in charge. In 1959 we left the shop and moved to Dover to live with my sister. Mr Wilson sold the business to Mr and Mrs Sherwin; then in 1975 the business was sold to Mr and Mrs Orgar."

In 1993 it was bought by the Orgars' daughter Samm and her husband.

## WORKING AT ORPIN'S
In 1914, as briefly mentioned already, Marjorie Howland left school at the age of 14 and started working at Orpin's, serving customers from behind the counter. This was not uncommon for girls of her age. Several years later, also at the age of 14, Joyce Garlick (Wood) began working for the Orpin family, doing mainly housework and helping in the shop from time to time. Joyce would also take the dog for a walk each day, and take David and his sister to and from school. On Tuesdays, Thursdays

and Saturdays she would deliver the papers. She would start at the village hall, go round the back of Hatch Park and come out at the bottom of Hatch Hill. One day while on her paper round she was surprised and alarmed by a "flasher". She rushed back to the shop to report the incident and Mrs Orpin, thinking that he might have been a soldier, asked her if he had been wearing boots. To this, the perplexed and ruffled Joyce replied that she hadn't even thought to look at his feet! Like most other employees, Joyce worked six days a week. She would have one afternoon off during the week and also Sunday afternoons, when she would go to the Bethel Baptist Chapel with her family.

Betty Edenden recalls that nobody really thought about the hours they worked, and particularly so during the war. She would be serving in the shop, move to the bakehouse to help if they were short-handed there, would then go out and do the rounds, and once back at the shop would start serving again. The activity at Christmas time reflected the importance of the shop in the local community. When Orpin's used to deliver to customers the shop would sometimes be at work until 11pm preparing Christmas orders. In those days, a significant proportion of the population ordered Christmas cakes and everyone had a ham. The shop would order gammons and cook them in special bags in a boiler. Two were cooked at a time, and great care had to be taken not to overdo them. When ready, they were kept in a walk-in fridge that was at the back of the shop in the big hut where the newspapers were sorted. Even people with comparatively low incomes splashed out at Christmas, and Samm recalls hearing from people who had worked in the shop for decades that it was more common than one would imagine for people to buy wallpaper on Christmas Eve to redecorate their sitting rooms for Christmas. Time off work was limited and Christmas was a good time for DIY.

## DELIVERIES
Grocery and bread delivery was by Orpin's van on Mondays, Wednesdays and Fridays. The shop had four vans, plus a spare, to do the rounds to West Brabourne and Brook, Aldington and Mersham, Sellindge, Lympne and Stowting and West Hythe. Some of the earliest ones were open-topped Singers; later they were Singer saloons.

Delivery vehicles were so important to the village businesses, as until about 50 years ago people were relatively immobile, and going to the shop to buy groceries, or whatever was needed, was time-consuming and could also be hard work if the shopping bags were heavy. Thus, the number of customers visiting shops was fairly few, as orders were usually delivered. According to Betty Edenden, driving the delivery vans was "not for the faint hearted" in the early days. Her experiences date back to the 1940s, through the war and after that. Ward's Garage used to look after Orpin's vehicles and when a van "died" Mr Ward (E.F. Ward) would buy a car that was in working order, take out the engine and install it in the Orpin's van, thus getting it back on the road.

Keeping the delivery vans going was difficult in the war years and even after that as vehicles were not nearly as reliable as they are today. Betty would deliver orders to Orpin's many customers three times a week, and each time she made a delivery she would take the next order. When she left the shop on her rounds the van was filled with fuel from Orpin's own pump and loaded up with as many as five two-gallon paraffin cans roped onto the running boards. Before setting off she would have to crank the fully loaded van to get it started and then jump in quickly once the engine came to life. If the petrol started to run out while she was on her rounds, Betty would add a little paraffin from the cans to keep it going, but this was always a short-term solution as, next morning, the van would refuse to start and Mr Ward would have to drain the fuel tank and refill it with petrol. Another problem with the vans was that the lights were unreliable and frequently failed. If Betty saw someone coming the other way on dark winter afternoons and evenings, she would hop out of the van and pretend to be looking at the lights as though the problem had just occurred. Keeping the van going thus became an art. On one particularly difficult day Betty had five burst tyres on her delivery round. She phoned Mrs Orpin and said, "Please send a wheelbarrow!" To which Mrs Orpin replied, "Betty, please don't be like that!"

Orpin's deliveries took Betty to Brook, Brabourne, Stowting, Dymchurch, Aldington, Lympne and Bilsington and women did them all during the war. During one particularly snowy winter, Betty remembers, she tramped across the fields with bags of goods, only to be told by the grumpy recipients, "You're late!" A more pleasant memory from 1964 was of delivering goods to Lady Brabourne, who used to invite her in to see her newly-born twin boys.

We were reminded by some of our contributors that, in addition to deliveries from the local shops, goods were also brought round by independent travelling salesmen: there was the fish man who came on the Griggs' van and went from house to house through Brabourne Lees; men who sold household wares would bring them to the door on a motorbike with sidecar; and Mrs Moorhead recalls someone who used to cycle down the drive and sharpen knives and scissors at the house.

## TEAM ORPINS

David and others who have long associations with Orpin's recall "the old team" who were part of the institution. Ernie Ashman, Sheila Stone's father, was apprenticed to John Orpin and, as mentioned before, took over the lease on the shop when John died in 1943. Ross Ashman, Ernie's brother, worked there for a short time, as did Sheila, Ernie's daughter. Betty Edenden (whose real name was actually Violet but was always called Betty because of her attachment to the doll Betty Oxo when she was a child) started work at Orpin's when she was 14 or 15 years old, well over 65 years ago. She worked for every owner since the days of John Orpin, including Ernie Ashman, Mr Wright, the Sherwins, the Orgars and finally Samm Orgar. Connie Franklin was another member of the team who worked at Orpin's for decades, (1930s to 1990s), some of them alongside her husband, Don. David remembers Connie running the drapery section, and Samm describes her as having virtually managed the shop for many years after the war. It has been said by more than one of our contributors that Connie could find out the life history of a stranger to the village within five minutes of meeting them and, in exchange, would have given them much important local information that was relevant to them. Iris Bull, whose parents, the Jenners, ran the Five Bells, worked at the shop for a while, while Joyce Garlick, as we have said, worked mainly in the Orpin household when she was little more than a girl, and in the shop when needed. A much more recent but equally well-known member of the Orpin's team is Ivy Young, who joined the shop in the 1980s and retired in 2010. Ivy's good cheer and friendliness were remarked on by several of our contributors. And managing the post office, which moved to Orpin's when Ames' Stores closed down in the late 1960s, was Rosalind Pilcher, who cycled to work each day from her home in Stowting, whatever the weather, for over 30 years. Brenda Wright added that Rosalind was not trained for the job of postmistress but was infinitely patient with her mainly elderly customers.

When asked whether she enjoyed her working life, Betty replied without hesitation that she would not have chosen any other job. Through working at Orpin's she developed close relationships with dozens of people in the village community. Few other jobs, she observed, would have given her that opportunity. Ivy was of much the same opinion and, after working in Orpin's for around 30 years, there were still some people who would not pay for their papers unless Ivy was there to take the money from them. Like Betty, she would never have chosen to do any other form of work.

Sheila Stone (née Ashman, then Cloke) remembers:

"My dad, Ernest Ashman, left school at 14 and started work at the shop in 1914. Groceries were delivered by horse and cart in those days and hours of work were long. On most nights it was 10pm before he left the shop. He also helped out in the bakehouse with Mr Brice, May Howland and Bert Sawyer. I often heard him talk about the fire in 1926; the Miss Smith who called Mr Orpin to raise the alarm was my dad's future sister-in-law, who married Ross Ashman. Ross worked for Mr Hawkins, the butcher, while two of his other brothers worked at the shop, Arch(ibald) and Mark Allen.

"When Mr Orpin died in 1943 my dad took on the lease of the shop until the early 1950s. It was then taken over by Mr Wilson and Mr Wright, and Dad continued working there until 1959, when he took a break. He returned in 1969, to work for Mr and Mrs Sherwin. The shop was then sold to Mr and Mrs Orgar, and Dad carried on working there, part-time, until 1980, when he was 80.

Sheila Stone

"As Sheila Ashman, I left school at 14 in 1944. I then joined Dad at the shop. It was wartime, so we spent much of the time getting rationed goods ready for the customers. At the time each family was allowed 4oz butter, 4oz margarine, 4oz cheese and 4oz rashers per week. My cousin Olive Ashman worked with me for many years. We were kept very busy serving customers and getting orders ready for the roundsmen to deliver.

"My cousin Connie worked on the drapery counter, but in 1948 she married and moved to Lincoln. I then took over the drapery section, which I enjoyed very much. We sold so many things, from men's suits, shoes and boots, to ladies' frocks and cardigans, and everything you could think of was stored upstairs. Then, in 1951, Connie returned to the shop, taking on drapery again and her husband, Don, started working at the shop as well.

"In 1948 Roy Cloke from Sellindge came back from the army and joined us at the shop, working as a roundsman for West Brabourne and Mersham. I started going out with Roy, and in 1954 we were married. I didn't leave the shop until 1956, when my son was born, but only a few months after that I began helping there again, working part-time for Mr Wilson and Mr Wright. I left for good in 1961, when I had my daughter, and then another son in 1967. In 1978 I went back again to sort papers for the paperboys, starting at 6.30am. I also had to drive to Brabourne Street to take papers for a boy to deliver over there and, as I went, I delivered papers to Iden Corner and to houses along Pilgrims' Way, under the Downs, as well.

"In 1980, sadly, Roy died, but I kept working until 1990, when I met Phil Stone and we married in 1991. I really enjoyed all my working years at the shop and getting to know so many people in the village was just wonderful."

From left, Ernest Ashman, Betty Edenden
and Connie Franklin (1950s)

From left, Mr and Mrs Sherwin; group on right, from left:
Connie Franklin, Mr Michaels, Rosalind Pilcher and Betty Edenden
(1960s)

Ernest Ashman serving one of his last customers, Gertie Beadle (Brooks)
(picture Kentish Express, now part of KM Group, c1980)

From left, Peter Orgar, Kay Orgar, Bryan Orgar and
Mrs Jessica Orgar (snr), Peter and Bryan's mother
(1975)

## SAMM AND MRS ORGAR CONTINUE THE STORY OF ORPINS

When the Orgars took over Orpins in 1975 the country was in a recession, but despite this it continued to be a successful enterprise. Samm described it as "The Waitrose, or even the Fortnum & Mason, of its day. Everyone who was anyone shopped at Orpins." People bought all their needs there, not just bits and pieces, and up until the late 1980s, when the wealthier members of the community were having a shooting party or some such get-together, receiving orders totalling around £500 for the event was not that unusual. Mrs Orgar recalls that, in the 1970s, the shop was very traditional in style and very well stocked. It had an extensive cheese and a bacon counter. People queued to be served and the shop had a significant workforce.

Mrs Kay Orgar

Samm Orgar

Aware that the self-service supermarket model was becoming increasingly popular with modern shoppers, the Orgars modernised their shop accordingly. For this and many other reasons the shop has continued successfully and survived while others went under. However, when Tesco opened its Crooksfoot shop in the early 1990s, and Sainsbury's opened its store near Junction 9 of the M20 later the same year, Orpins' turnover dropped by about 30%, though it did start to recover. The next blow to the village shop came when both supermarket chains began opening on Sundays, and then introducing 24-hour opening hours. Since that time the village has lost both the butcher and The Handy Stores – Gorham's and Ames' having closed many years earlier. However, Orpins survives, a testimony to continuing local demand for its services – and it has now been refurbished and expanded.

As you have already read, Orpins has long been a major employer in the village. In addition to the staff in the shop, they had 15 paper rounds in the Orgars' time, each employing a paperboy or girl. The rounds extended from the crossroads at Iden

Corner, at East Brabourne, to The Hall in Weekes Lane, West Brabourne, to the end of the Ridgeway, to Evegate, and in the other direction to Washington on the way to Sellindge. Most of the boys in the village had their names down to do a round, and such was the demand there was a waiting list. Sally Thornby was one of the very few girls who had a round. Orpins would deliver the papers to the Thornby household in The Street, East Brabourne, and starting before 7am, Sally would deliver them from Foxburs along Pilgrims' Way to the house called Pilgrims' Way at the foot of the Gate Hill, around the orchard including The Street in East Brabourne, and then down Canterbury Road to Brabourne School. "On wet days," Sally recalls, "the postman would help and deliver the papers for me." But on many occasions when she did the full round she would miss the school bus into Ashford, which pleased her no end, as she would then have the day off school. Next morning Norman would write a note to excuse her.

During the Orgars' time, Betty Edenden was in charge of newspapers and managed the team of paperboys and girls. However, as the readership of newspapers has declined, so too have paper deliveries, and the shop now has only five paper rounds. From the age of 13, the girls in the village, and also some boys, worked in the shop on Saturday mornings (roughly from the mid 1970s). They would start off by doing two hours' work and then increase this to four hours. As a consequence, many young people in the village earned pocket money and acquired valuable experience of work before embarking on further education or careers.

Orpins, together with the other local shops, has provided a valuable service. As Samm observed, when The Handy Stores and the butcher's were open there was very little that could not be obtained in the villages. When it snowed, out would come the shovels and deliveries would be made by sledge, such was the responsibility felt by the owners of local shops towards their customers. Mention of snowy weather prompted one particular memory from Samm's mother from the winter of 1987, a historic year, as it was when we also experienced an unusually bad hurricane in the October. The snow was heavy that year and travel was not easy. Orpins was running low on supplies as delivery vans were having problems getting to Brabourne, so Mr and Mrs Orgar attached snow chains to their Volvo and canvas trailer and started off for the cash and carry at Medway, which in those days was Nurdin and Peacock (its entrance had been cleared as it was near the entrance to Rochester Airport). After reaching it safely, though not without some difficulty, and stocking up, they started heading for home. However, on reaching the motel at the Happy Eater in Lenham, they found the road blocked by Green Goddesses, placed there by Her Majesty's forces, who had decided that conditions were too perilous for cars. The Orgars explained that they needed to get supplies back to Brabourne, but an officer on duty would not allow them through. She explained again that provisions were needed by the people of Brabourne and pleaded to be allowed to continue home, but the officer was adamant and the road remained closed. Furious, the Orgars then drove to Lenham, knocked on the local policeman's door and said, "Can you help us, we have a village full of people needing supplies and we're not being allowed through." To this the PC replied, "Until they've declared Martial Law, I'm the law around here." And with that he cycled along the snowy road to the motel and persuaded the officials to let the Orgars through. Before they had got very far they encountered yet another Green Goddess across the road. This time, Mrs Orgar was so desperate when she was again told that they could not pass that she grabbed hold of the officer and made him fully aware of the purpose of their mission. Eventually, he too was persuaded to let them through. Emotionally and physically exhausted, they made it back to Brabourne and refilled the shelves of Orpins for their customers.

In response to the question about the future of Orpins in a village that has lost most of its shops, Samm was extremely positive. Since the fabric of the building, which goes back to when it was rebuilt after the fire in 1926, was in need of repair, a major renovation programme has been carried out. "The shop has been doubled in size, removing the internal staircase and the rear wall; the flat roof has been taken down and the entire shop has been refitted. A new shop front has been constructed with a much-improved door, with no step to trip up the customers. The range of goods has been extended and all white wines are refrigerated. Fresh meat, fresh bread and other fresh produce are all available and customer numbers are up. Orpins, which is now a Spar grocer, has thus come full circle as petrol prices and the capacity to work increasingly from home encourage people to depend more heavily on their local shops once more".

Picture given to Betty Edenden by her team of paperboys on her retirement from Orpins. The picture was painted for Betty by Vi Sprawling

## AMES' STORES

For a long time, Orpin's wasn't the only grocer in the village. Next door, and competing strongly, was Ames' Stores, which stood in an old timber building that Edward (Teddy) Ames bought from Sammy Parsons in 1907. The old grocery shop was pulled down in the early 1970s, several years after the Ames family had sold it, and the new building for Cooper and Son, the butcher's, built on the same site, is now occupied by Steven J Moore, Estate Agents. Peter Rigg described Ames' Stores as "from an era past, with the air of a Western movie – wooden walls, floors and wooden counters down the side". To this, others have added that it was a delightfully old-fashioned shop with paraffin stoves and a large cabinet along one wall with little wooden drawers, each containing a different spice. Memories linger of its evocative smell of fragrant spices combined with the aroma of ground coffee from Ames' famed coffee machine, the sound of the machine grinding coffee, and of old-fashioned polish. Edward ran the shop for many years; later, his son Basil took it over, with Edward appearing daily, apart from winter Wednesdays, when he always followed the East Kent Hunt. Edward was a great character and many people spoke of him fondly.

One of the earliest photographs of Ames' Stores (c1913). The person outside has not been identified; nevertheless, note the chalk board for news and the ancient lamp hanging in front of the shop

The beloved coffee grinder from Ames' Stores

There was strong competition between Ames' Stores and Orpin's, as being grocers there was an obvious overlap in the services they offered and the goods they sold. There were also notable differences: for example, Orpin's had an alcohol licence and a bakery, while Ames' had the post office. The post office moved to Ames' after the death of Miss Apps and the closing of the post office in the "top road". Orpin's is remembered as being the agent for selling newspapers, but Betty Dryland (Lavender) remembers a time when Ames' Stores were also agents for papers. Her mother-in-law started delivering them for Ames' in the late 1940s and her round covered both Brabourne and Smeeth. She would cycle in all weathers and sometimes had to return home up to three times to change her clothes because she had got so wet.

Both Orpin's and Ames' sold food, many household items including paraffin, for which there was considerable demand, and also clothes and hats, both new and second hand. Betty recalled that "the village shops were where mothers bought clothes for their children, and for the rest of the family, too"; someone remembered buying "a good coat" from Ames' for £4 in the 1960s, while someone else added, "you weren't looking for style when you bought clothes in those days, you looked for quality and something that would last". Attitudes towards buying furniture were much the same. Ames' had a thriving furniture shop next door to the main shop, in what is now Caroline's Hairdressers. Most of the furniture on sale was second hand,

and Fred Brooks was often drafted in to do essential repairs. In a rural area many people possessed shotguns and would also come to Ames' for their cartridges, which were kept in a safe. There was even a medicine "department", and Doctor Garman, who used to live opposite in Prospect Farm House, and later at Sellindge, would leave prescribed medicines at the shop for delivery to his patients – along with their groceries and other goods.

Ames' Stores, Brabourne Lees (1920-30).
The Plough (PH) in the background

The shop was a centre for news: in the 1920s Edward had a friend, a Mr Eldridge, who ran the telephone exchange in Willesborough. Both were keen sportsmen, and Mr Eldridge, who had access to news from London, would telephone the results of major sports events to the shop and Edward would chalk these up on a blackboard outside the shop for all the village to see. There was huge interest, as this arrangement meant that the results of the Grand National, the Derby, the Boat Race, the FA semifinal and final, and all cricket test matches were reported almost as soon as they were known. Rosemary Hendry (Ward) and others remember the buzz of excitement and interest at the front of the shop as the results went up on the board. Also, Miss Butcher (from Wye) used to call in each week for any village news and items of interest for the Kentish Express.

The Stores acted as informal bankers (as did several other shops and pubs), cashing a large number of cheques each week, mainly for farmers and other employers to pay wages. A taxi service was also operated from the Stores during Edward's time. In the mid-1930s he bought a car that had belonged to Edward VIII and Mrs Simpson after the king had abdicated. It was always known in the village as Mrs Simpson and became very popular – people would contact the shop and ask for Mrs Simpson to take them here and there. Ernie Thornby was employed as chauffeur and is remembered as looking very dashing in his green uniform.

In the 1950s the Stores employed about a dozen people, but even in the 1930s and 1940s, during the Depression and the war, they were significant employers, offering part-time and casual work, as well as maintaining a regular staff. Some of the people who used to work there included Fred Brooks, Mr Christmas, Cecil Cullen, Cecil Thornby, John Rigg (from Aldington, who at that time was a student and used to work in his holidays) and Denis Link. The girls in the shop were Martha (also known as Mary) Brooks and her sisters Gertie and Queenie, the daughters of Fred. There were also Rosa Finn, Pam Palmer (who used to cycle from Stowting), Lois Thornby, Margaret Pile (Ward), Peggy Down, Mrs Dryland and Mrs Gillet. Later, Rosalind Pilcher (who also cycled from Stowting) joined the shop, eventually running the post office. Tom Brooks (from Aldington), ultimately Mary Brooks's father-in-law though from a different Brooks' family, used to help in the sizeable garden, where there were two large greenhouses producing tomatoes in the summer and the most beautiful chrysanthemums for Christmas. Tom also helped to deliver the goods during snowy weather when transport was difficult. Digressing for a moment, Tom is widely remembered as one of the most pleasant and kindest of people. He was described as "always thinking about others and willing to help anyone and everyone". Christine and Derek Gurr remember waking up one snowy morning to find that Tom (then aged about 80) had cleared the snow from their drive so that Derek (then aged about 50) could get the car out of the garage to go to work.

Back to Ames': about 100 chickens produced eggs for the shop, and any that were not sold were sent to the egg-packing station. The cockerels were for the table, and went via the butcher's shop. A great village character, Charlie Thornby, used to sort the post in the furniture store before delivery.

Margaret Pile (Ward) remembers how much she enjoyed working at Ames', having started working there in the 1940s, after leaving school at 15:

"When I joined the Store it was at the start of rationing and I was just in time to be involved in counting all the coupons. Nothing was prepacked in those days, not

Margaret Pile (Ward)

even biscuits; everything came in big sacks and boxes and we weighed and packed the goods straight from these. I had to learn to tuck and twist the paper bags so that the contents couldn't escape. Sellotape didn't exist. Golden Syrup came in a large container and had to be run into jam jars by tap. It was very slow in cold weather and, on one occasion, I left it running to fill a jar and forgot to go back. What a sticky mess I had to wipe up! When Mr Ames acquired the post office I used to run the counter for him.

"Tesco now runs a similar delivery system to that of Mr Ames – and the other shops – the only difference was that we cycled to our customers to take their orders, and had to remember if they were duplicating their rations. I can remember that when they were, there was often a certain guilty look in their eyes."

Mary Brooks also enjoyed working at Ames' Stores and remembers Basil Ames's children playing in the shop. Richard used to sit on a shelf and run imaginary trains around the shop, saying "Mind the rails" to anyone who came too close. She describes Derek as a very naughty but quite lovable little boy who used to write notes to her on a regular basis when he came home at weekends from boarding school. He was then about 11 or 12 years old. Mary was known as Bill to the family and staff, or Miss Bill to the children, and in one of Derek's "letters" that Mary still

Mary Brooks, also known as Martha

has, he advises Miss Bill to "work well to please the old man" (his father, Basil). Mary observed that, although Edward Ames was a lovely person who could keep the staff entertained, he was a stickler for work and found it difficult to accept the need for staff to have coffee breaks when legislation for these was introduced. Life became more relaxed when Basil took over. Mary also remembers Stan Burt, who was a paperboy for Ames' Stores and who had a comment for everything. One day, irritated by one of his comments, Mary threw a tablet of soap at him but missed, and the soap hurtled through a pane of glass in a door. In conversation with Mary fairly recently, Stan admitted to still being amused by this incident.

Gertie Brooks (Mary's sister and Fred Beadle's mother) also worked at Ames' Stores in the 1940s and 1950s, and used to cycle round the villages collecting orders that one of the men would deliver by van a day or two later. George Brooks remarked on the miles that Gertie used to cycle "taking orders". She would go to customers in East Brabourne and work through the villages, even as far as Evegate, on the south side of the A20. May Fortescue remembers a girl from Ames' Stores (maybe it was Gertie) cycling round the village in the early 1950s, collecting orders each week. Rationing still existed in those days and "the girl" would reel off at great speed a list of available items, to which May would say "yes" or "no", and how much of the product she needed. A note was made and the delivery arrived the next day, no less efficient than shopping online, and very much more agreeable. In the 1920s, before they had vans, Ames' deliveries were done by their two horses, Grace and Tim-Tom. Margaret Older remarked on the efficiency and friendliness of Ames' Stores. When Ted (Edward) delivered her order he used to bring the groceries right into her kitchen. She described him as "a lovely man" who would probably have put the shopping away had she asked him. She remembers him saying to her when he brought her order "And you like the rind off your bacon, don't you?", indicating that he had prepared the bacon just as she liked it.

Edward Ames, left, with Leslie Elms (c1940s)

Basil Ames (late 1920s or early 1930s)

Basil Ames (late 1980s)

When the shop was busy at Christmas time the staff always stayed late preparing orders. Margaret remembers that at such times Edward and Basil would keep them well entertained with excellent stories. Both men had a great affinity for country ways and life, and had a renowned talent for storytelling. Margaret recalls that there was so much fun and laughter at the shop that nobody was in any hurry to go home, even though it was almost Christmas. Storytelling was undoubtedly linked with Edward's enjoyment of amateur dramatics and the stage: during the 1940s and 1950s he used to appear in the village concerts and plays produced by Norman Weekes, a nephew who had been a professional actor (more on entertainment in chapter 10).

The Ames family sold the shop around 1956 and moved to Westenhanger, returning to Brabourne in the early 1960s. The first supermarket had opened in Ashford, and Basil was aware that things were set to change.

The Ames family c1900, at Court Farm, near the Woolpack, Smeeth.
Back row: from left, Edward Ames of Ames' Stores, Lottie (Mrs Tritton), Harry, Kate (Mrs
Weekes), Frank, May (Mrs Kennett), Frederick of Ames' Builders, Alice (Mrs Tritton).
Front row: from left, Queenie (Mrs Hammond), Eliza Grace and Franklin (great
grandparents of Derek, Richard, Diana and several cousins), Rose (Mrs Nicholson)
and Barney the dog

## THE POST OFFICE

The Post Office is included here, along with the grocers, as it was for many years at Ames' Stores and is now at Orpins. Local historians Don Skeer and Alan Clark began researching into the history of local post offices in the Brabourne area but, sadly, never lived to complete their work. John Hammon has kindly allowed us to use some of their material and we are grateful for the privilege. Their research takes us back to Napoleonic times when post from Ashford was delivered to Brabourne Lees and collected from the army camp by a Horse Messenger. Soon after the army camp was demolished in 1816, and the Horse Messenger became redundant, Anthony Scott, the then Surveyor of the Post for this part of England, conducted a survey on the possibility of establishing a Penny Post in this area. His idea was warmly supported by the local inhabitants so Anthony Scott wrote a letter to Francis Freeling, Postmaster General, explaining that he was concerned that people in Brabourne Lees who had become accustomed to the postal delivery by messenger would lose this benefit.

On 20th December, 1816, Scott wrote, "I would wish to recommend the establishment of a Penny Post from Ashford thro' Willesborough and Mersham to the Lees. I am inclined to believe it would not pay its expenses by about Ten Pounds a year but ... we should save the allowance... of a guinea a week for the Horse Messenger ... together with £18.4.0 a year paid to the Postmaster at Ashford for Military duty." The Postmaster General endorsed Anthony Scott's idea, as his letter below reveals:

"My Lords,

I have the honour to enclose a report from the Surveyor [of the Post (Anthony Scott)], that the Allowance of One Guinea per week for the Military Post from Ashford to Brabourne Lees, and of £18..4..- per annum to the Postmaster for his additional troubles are no longer necessary and of course your Lordships will order them to be discontinued. But as the Neighbourhood has so long been served by the same means, it will not be right to leave it without any established mode of delivering and collecting letters. Mr. Scott proposed a Penny Post which, as it will be necessary to leave out the seat of Sir Edward Knatchbull, who objects, will not produce quite so much as the necessary expenses. The latter will amount to £35.8..- and the produce may be £10 less, but as £18..4..- per annum for the old Establishment will be saved, I presume your Lordships will approve it.

All which is humbly

submitted by

Francis Freeling

Postmaster General"

Francis Freeling (later Sir Francis Freeling) was Secretary of HM General Post Office. He initiated many changes to the Post Office including the introduction of local penny posts in large towns. We learn in a further letter from Anthony Scott to the Postmaster General about a year later that the Penny Post to Brabourne Lees was established on 28th December, 1816.

Update from Anthony Scott on the success of the Penny Post to Brabourne Lees just over a year after its introduction:

"Keppel Street,
7th Feb 1818

Sir,

It appearing that the Ashford Penny Post to Brabourne Lees, established 28th December 1816, has produced between the 5th January 1817 and 5th January 1818 £32.2.11 and the expense attending it being £35.8 within the same period I presume it will be thought right to make it permanent; a considerable extent of Country being served by its onset and a guinea a week for a Horse Messenger to the Barracks upon the Lees, and a Military Allowance of £18-4-0 per annum to the Postmaster of Ashford being saved. It will be seen by my Report of 20th December 1816 that I calculated upon a deficiency of £10 a year when I proposed this arrangement. It appearing also that the Penny Post from Ashford to Wye established 13th January 1817 has produced to the 5th January 1818 £33.6.0, and the expense for the year being £33.6.0 no loss has been sustained by it; and the London letters being charged with an additional Penny occasioned by their being forwarded to Ashford instead of Faversham, together with the convenience attending this establishment as detailed in my Report of 25th December 1816. I also presume it will be thought right to constitute this permanent Post    All which is submitted by

Sir, Your Obedient Servant
Anthony Scott

Francis Freeling Esq."

The Penny Post had become so popular that on 16th February, 1853 the post office at East Brabourne was sanctioned. More on this in chapter 7, on East Brabourne.

CHANGING LOCATIONS OF THE POST OFFICE IN BRABOURNE LEES
The village post office has been in Orpins Stores for many years but, before the late 1960s, it was in Ames' Stores, and before that was located in what is now Anchor Cottage in Lees Road, where at one time Katy Apps was postmistress. After passing Orpins turn right up (Upper) Lees Road or Top Road, and the post office was located in what is now the second bungalow on the left-hand side. The bungalow is much

## SKETCH MAP TO SHOW THE DIFFERENT LOCATIONS
## OF THE BRABOURNE LEES POST OFFICE SINCE 1816

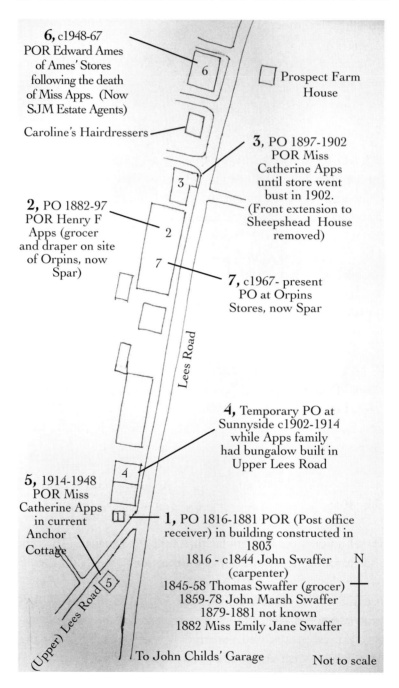

**6,** c1948-67
POR Edward Ames
of Ames' Stores
following the death
of Miss Apps. (Now
SJM Estate Agents)

Caroline's Hairdressers

Prospect Farm
House

**3,** PO 1897-1902
POR Miss
Catherine Apps
until store went
bust in 1902.
(Front extension to
Sheepshead House
removed)

**2,** PO 1882-97
POR Henry F
Apps (grocer
and draper on site
of Orpins, now
Spar)

**7,** c1967- present
PO at Orpins
Stores, now Spar

Lees Road

**4,** Temporary PO at
Sunnyside c1902-1914
while Apps family
had bungalow built in
Upper Lees Road

**5,** 1914-1948
POR Miss
Catherine Apps
in current
Anchor
Cottage

**1,** PO 1816-1881 POR (Post office
receiver) in building constructed in
1803
1816 - c1844 John Swaffer
(carpenter)
1845-58 Thomas Swaffer (grocer)
1859-78 John Marsh Swaffer
1879-1881 not known
1882 Miss Emily Jane Swaffer

(Upper) Lees Road

To John Childs' Garage

N

Not to scale

changed from when it was a post office (see picture on p252). Before the post office came to Anchor Cottage it appears to have been located in four other places in Brabourne Lees, including Apps Stores. As the post office is now in Orpins, it is more or less back where it started. Its first home in Brabourne Lees was Swaffer's Grocer's shop where, according to Bagshaw (1847)[3], "POST-OFFICE, at Mr Thos. Swaffers's – Letters arrive from Ashford at 9.0am, and are despatched at 5.pm".

The skech map (opposite), created from notes and sketches left by Don Skeer (but researched very little further), shows the different locations of the post office in Brabourne Lees.

## POST MEN AND WOMEN IN BRABOURNE LEES
From a list of auxiliary postmen – and women[4], collected by Don Skeer and Alan Clark, one set of entries in particular catches our attention:

George Marshall started 13/9/1915
Enlisted 6/11/1915
Killed 1/9/1916

L. Marshall started 1/9/1916 (Lydia Marshall, George Marshall's sister)
Resigned 29/1/1921

Margaret Pile (Ward) confirmed that Brabourne had its first postwoman during the First World War. This was her mother, then Miss Lydia Marshall and later Mrs E.F. Ward (of Ward's Garage).

Margaret writes:

"Lydia took on the job to release her brother so that he could fight in France. He left on 4th August, 1916, but was killed by 1st September, 1916. He gave Lydia a gold locket before going and my daughter has this today. Lydia lived at Rann Farm, now Warren Farm, with her parents, who were there from 1893 to 1920. My grandfather, John Marshall, was a carpenter who also delivered coal and milk at the turn of the century. He sold the business to Percy Nickolls in 1920. The name Rann Farm is interesting because it is thought to have had some connection with Old Rann and the smugglers of Romney Marsh."

---

3       Bagshaw, Samuel (1847) History, Gazetteer and Directory of Kent. Vol. II. Sheffield, publisher G Ridge. p.468.
4       Source: Don Skeer and Alan Clark's notes, taken from Ashford Post Office Archives Accounts 1860-1944, Brabourne.

Later, when the post office was at Ames' Stores, Peggy Downs was postmistress, and she was followed by Rosalind Pilcher, who moved, together with the post office, to Orpins when Ames' closed in the late 1950s.

Peg Hickmott, or "Peg the Post" as she was affectionately known, claimed to have been one of the first postwomen in the country. She was a Land Army girl during the war, billeted with the Wratten family in East Brabourne when Tom Wratten was a small boy. By coincidence, Peg ended up working with Tom and his wife Jean when the post office was located in Ames' Stores. In those days sorting would start at 5.30am in Ames' furniture shop, and everything was done by hand. The early start continued when the post office was taken over by Orpins. Jean joined the post office much later than Tom did, though she still delivered mail around the village for more than 30 years. When she eventually took on a full-time job at the post office, her round involved going down the Ridgeway then across the A20 to Water Farm and down Station Road as far as the Mill. She had to do this round twice a day, as in those days there was also a delivery in the afternoon. During one particularly cold winter she can remember pushing her bike down the A20 in heavy snow but, almost predictably, her most lingering memories of her work for the post office are of being bitten by dogs.

Jenny Cooper's father, Bob (Robert) Harvey, also worked as a postman in Brabourne in the late 1960s and 1970s. He would drive from Hastingleigh to Brabourne Lees via Weekes Lane in West Brabourne each morning, passing Kath and Basil Thornby's house, Hillside, at 6.15am. Basil preferred Bob to an alarm clock, and would get out of bed just after he heard Bob's car go past. Another who was a post lady in the village for many years was Molly Stephens.

Millie Hodges took on the role of post lady in 1982, left in 1985, became full-time in 1988, left again, and came back again in 1990. She remembers crossing Canterbury Road back and forth, delivering letters and parcels, barely troubled by a passing car. Now, however, she could not possibly risk doing that. One of Millie's outstanding memories was of delivering post in the snow. When it prevented her husband Bryan from getting to work he would pull their sledge with the post on it for Millie, and for some of the round he would pull Millie on the sledge as well.

Of course, Brabourne Lees wasn't the only post office in the area. The earliest Smeeth post office that anyone could remember stood in a lovely old building, now demolished, opposite The Paddocks (now the Caldecott Foundation) on the A20. Rosemary Hendry remembers going there when she was a girl, dating the photograph to the 1930s. Betty Harris recalls that the Post Office then moved to the bungalow on the corner where the Ridgeway joins the A20, and then to the Ridgeway Stores, though few remember using it here, probably because of the dominance of Brabourne Lees.

# BRABOURNE LEES POST OFFICE: IMAGES OVER THE PAST CENTURY

Apps' corn merchant and Brabourne Lees post office. The postbox just visible in wall on left of front face of the extension, above picket fence (c1911). This later became a bakery

Brabourne Lees post office located temporarily at Sunnyside (1913-14), on the right of the white building (PO sign below window), while the Apps family had the bungalow (Anchor Cottage) in Top Road, Lees Road, built. Also visible, on far left of weatherboard is remnant of sign for Mr E.L. Ashman's cycle shop, thought to have moved to Whitehall, Lees Road c1910

The post office at Anchor Cottage in Lees Road, c1915. From left, Mr Beech, recruiting officer who is also pictured near Five Bells, East Brabourne in Ch 7, Katy Apps (postmistress), Katy Apps's cousin, and postman, George Marshall. When Miss Apps died the post office moved to Ames' Stores (c1948)

Ernest (Ernie) Ashman (born 20th April, 1870), auxiliary rural postman. On 4th November, 1894, he received 8/- per week from Brabourne Lees post office. He later became a cycle maker; his shop was at 'Whitehall' on Lees Road (Top Road)

George Skeer, postman at Brabourne Lees,
born 19th September, 1891 (photograph taken c1911)

"Old Bill" Ashman, auxiliary postman 1915-1924, at Brabourne Lees post office. Lived
at Crusoe Hut, Lees Road, with brother Ernie (pictured opposite)

Peggy Hickmott, affectionately known as
Peg the Post. Based at Brabourne Lees
post office from the1950s to the early 1970s

Tom Wratten, postman
based at Brabourne Lees post office
1960-2000

Jean Wratten, postlady
based at Brabourne Lees post office from
late 1960s to late 1990s

Millie Hodges based at Brabourne
Lees in the 1980s and 1990s
(photograph taken in February, 1996)

Rosalind Pilcher, for many years the
postmistress, first at Ames' Stores
and then at Orpins

Samm Orgar the current postmistress at
Brabourne Lees since 1993

## POSTBOXES OUTSIDE ORPINS

Old postbox, Brabourne Lees
post office, embedded in wall at
Orpins Stores, closed Sunday
18/02/1996

(photograph 19/02/1996)

New postbox, Brabourne Lees post
office, installed outside Orpins Stores
Sunday 18/02/1996

(photograph 19/02/1996)

# BRABOURNE LEES POST OFFICE IN THE 21ST CENTURY

Postmen and woman at Brabourne Lees (2013):
from left, Ryan Kennett, Betty Clayson, Charles Sinden and Andy Johnson

Andy Johnson, postman at Brabourne Lees (June 2013).
(Bicycles were taken out of service by the post office in Oct/Nov 2013,
owing to the increase in parcels to be delivered)

Sorting office at Brabourne Lees (2013)

The modern post office at Orpins (2013). Danni Hitchin is behind the
counter, with Jock Anderson at the head of the queue

## IMAGES OF SMEETH POST OFFICE

Images of the Old Post Office, Smeeth, on A20 (c1930s). Gentleman standing
outside the post office in the picture is possibly either Mr Fagg, or Mr Spice, then
verger at Smeeth Church

Smeeth Post Office, Ridgeway Corner (c1940s)

## SKETCH MAP SHOWING DIFFERENT LOCATIONS
## OF SMEETH POST OFFICE

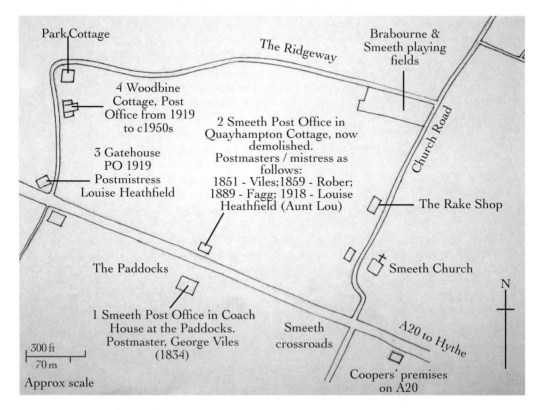

Park Cottage

The Ridgeway

Brabourne &
Smeeth playing
fields

4 Woodbine
Cottage, Post
Office from 1919
to c1950s

2 Smeeth Post Office in
Quayhampton Cottage, now
demolished.
Postmasters / mistress as
follows:
1851 - Viles;1859 - Rober;
1889 - Fagg; 1918 - Louise
Heathfield (Aunt Lou)

3 Gatehouse
PO 1919
Postmistress
Louise Heathfield

Church Road

The Rake Shop

The Paddocks

Smeeth Church

N

1 Smeeth Post Office in Coach
House at the Paddocks.
Postmaster, George Viles
(1834)

Smeeth
crossroads

A20 to Hythe

300 ft

70 m

Approx scale

Coopers' premises
on A20

Based on research carried out by Alan Clark and Don Skeer

Highlighting contradictions in the information:
some people recalled visiting Smeeth post office (PO) in its second location (in the 1930s),
but this does not correspond with the information collected by Alan Clark and Don Skeer as
the PO moved to location 3 in 1918/19 and few of our contributors were born at this time.
However, the building in which the PO was located may have been a shop that continued after
the PO had moved. Our contributors may have remembered visiting this shop (now long
demolished) which was still known locally as "the Old Post Office"

Smeeth Post Office at the shop on the Ridgeway, between
Ridgeway Corner and Brabourne Lees (possibly 1950s)

## BAXTER'S SWEET SHOP

The sweet shop was a great favourite with a great many of our contributors. Margaret and Pauline Gower (now Margaret Maple and Pauline Kingston) remember the Baxters, then the Gorehams and the Powells, at the sweet shop, which is now Corner Hill House opposite John Childs' Garage. This was always referred to as the "sweet shop", though it sold groceries as well as sweets and tobacco and, as a consequence, we have included it alongside the other village grocers.

Baxter's sweet shop; Mr Baxter behind the counter
drawn by Joan Copland.

The sweet shop was at the right hand end of what is now Corner Hill
House (from the front). Cooper's first shop was at the other end of
the building, on the left, but many years earlier. See picture (also by
Joan Copland) in the following section on Cooper and Son

Margaret keeps in touch with John Baxter, who has kindly furnished her with details for the passage below. Margaret writes:

"Mr and Mrs Baxter, their two daughters, Joan and Rosemary, and their son John moved from Albert Road, Hythe, to Fern Cottage, at the bottom of Woolpack Hill, on Plain Road. Fern Cottage had been a butcher's shop, and the iron hooks for hanging the meat were still in the outer kitchen area. In 1935 the Baxters took over the lease on the shop from a Mr Merrit. It was leased from one of the Headley family for seven years at a time, for the sum of 17/6 a year. The field opposite the shop was also owned by the Headleys, and after market day cows would be turned out in this field by the butcher, Mr Hawkins, before going to slaughter. Mr Baxter used to say that if ever the field came up for sale he would buy it, as the cows used to keep him awake at night. Apparently, he had a gentleman's agreement with the Headleys that he should have first refusal if ever they did decide to sell it. John told us that his father eventually bought the shop for £900 and the field for £100.

Margaret Maple (Gower)

"In 1958 Joan died at the age of 30 and, within two years, the Baxters moved to Whitstable, where they ran a small shop. Mr Baxter would have been happy to stay as he loved the village, but his wife wanted to move 'somewhere flatter'. According to John, the lovely old glass sweet jars that used to be on shelves in the shop window were eventually given to another sweet-shop owner in Whitstable when his parents retired.

"After the Baxters left, the shop on Plain Road was owned briefly by Mr Burtenshaw, then by Mr and Mrs Goreham, approximately 1961/62 to 1965, Mr and Mrs Powell, 1965 to 1976, and finally Mr and Mrs Markham, who then sold it as a private residence.

"As a young teenager I helped in the shop with the Gorehams and the Powells, first on Saturdays and then in the holidays. I stopped working there when the Powells left, and I still keep in touch and exchange news with their son and daughter-in-law who live in Devon."

Several people had fond memories of Baxter's: Joyce Garlick (Wood) recalled that they would always try to give you a little extra, particularly after rationing came to an end. This was a particularly difficult period, as everything was in shorter supply than it had been since before the war began. May Fortescue talked of how children loved Baxter's penny iced lollies, which were lolly sticks frozen in cubes of fruit squash, and Lady Brabourne told us that Mr Baxter's shop was a favourite destination for her children. When they were young Nanny used to push the pram down to the shop and they were allowed to spend 6d or so. Lady Brabourne recalled that Mr Baxter always wore brown overalls and a proper hat (not a cap). She said, "It was a real loss when they left the village."

Sally Furneaux (Willett) has the fondest of memories of the sweet shop when it was Goreham's. She writes:

"My favourite shop in the village – although perhaps it was officially Smeeth – was Goreham's, the sweet shop. It opened on Sunday mornings, something unheard of in the 1960s, and after church us three children were allowed to walk down there to spend our pocket money. Sherbet pips, cough candies, coconut mushrooms, sherbet fountains… Oh, yum yum!"

According to Ian Bull, Mick Markham, who was the last owner of the sweet shop before it ceased to be a business, was floor manager at the Playboy Club in London's Park Lane. His wife used to run the sweet shop.

# COOPER AND SON, BUTCHERS
## The evolution of a family business

Cooper's first shop in Brabourne, early 20th century
drawn by Joan Copland

Frank Cooper on Cooper's cart
(c1910)

Cooper's association with Brabourne and Smeeth goes back to 1900, when Ron Cooper's grandfather, Frank Willoughby Cooper, bought the butcher's business that was run by the Drylands, Joan Copland's forebears, in a wooden building at the front left-hand end of the white house at the bottom of Woolpack Hill, opposite John Childs' Garage.

The slaughterhouse (all butchers had their own in those days) was opposite, on the Warren, and is remembered by some as a black wooden and corrugated iron building. The property where the butcher's was housed was originally owned by the Brabourne Estate, but in 1920 the deaths of two Lord Brabournes within a short space of time meant it needed to be sold off to help pay the death duties. At the auction for it Frank Cooper had to drop out of the bidding; it was bought by Headley, the Ashford grocer, at £400. As a consequence, Frank, his wife Ada, sons Ronald Jack (always known as Jack) and Frank Henry (always known as Jim), and their daughters Stella and Marjorie (Madge) lost their business premises and their home. Frank's father,

Cooper's premises on the A20

who owned Fairbank on the Sellindge side of the Smeeth crossroads on the A20, had recently died and it was decided that the family should move in with Frank's mother. A butcher's shop was built here by A.J. Fortescue, who had taken over Edgar Ames' builder's business, making it the first new build of the Fortescue firm. The building still stands on the A20.

The premises at the foot of Woolpack Hill, now owned by Headley, were improved. A new shop was built at the right-hand end and the old catslide roof, under which the stables were housed, was built up to full height. The shop had the Headley trademark of rounded corners formed from brown glazed bricks, not conventional sharp right-angled corners with doors set at an angle. This is difficult to explain but may be seen elsewhere, one example being opposite Wye Church. The new premises on the right hand side of the building were leased to the Merrits, who had their sweet shop there, and later to the Baxters, who subsequently bought the property; then it was leased to Mr Burtenshaw, the Gorehams, Powells and finally the Markhams, all of whom, as we already know, sold sweets and tobacco. The old butcher's shop was used as a storeroom until the Markhams took over; it was during their time that the shop changed from a business to a residential property.

Frank's son Ronald Jack, known as Jack, was born in 1904, and became very interested in the butcher's business. When only six years old he was excused from school each Tuesday morning to go to Ashford Market and, together with another boy, walk the livestock that had been bought back to Smeeth, where the animals were slaughtered. By the time war started, in 1914, Jack had already become quite a capable butcher

A young Jack Cooper (c1914)

and slaughterman. His mentor, Clem Bean, was conscripted and sadly killed, leaving Frank to run the business more or less single-handedly. Ada helped where she could, and when Jack was 12 he was given permission to leave school to be there full-time. His sisters remained at school until they were 15 or 16, while Jim, who was born in 1914, joined the business later.

At the end of the First World War Frank got into financial difficulties and, sick with worry, declared himself bankrupt. In reality it had simply been a cash flow problem and all his debts were soon paid; however, he could no longer trade, as he didn't get his discharge from the bankruptcy courts. To circumvent this problem, Ada formed a partnership with Jack, and Cooper and Son was created. In his new role Jack made his first trip to market to buy stock at little more than 14 years old. As soon as he started to bid, the auctioneer stopped the auction and asked him if he had "the money". Jack, holding a handful of notes aloft, replied: "I've got the money guv'nor." Such responsibility for our children is unthinkable today, though during the First World War the responsibilities assumed by young people were immense.

Although the name of the business was Cooper and Son, the role of Jack's sister Stella should not be ignored. She used to help with cutting up the meat from when she was a girl, and when grown up, helped to keep the books. Jack developed into an excellent butcher. He could kill a bullock by the age of 14, and when his father thought him sufficiently competent, he gave him a knife with a curved blade for skinning cattle, a gift he treasured all his life and which his son, Ron, still keeps. Jack's skill in butchery was, indeed, considerable, and on one occasion someone bet him that he would not be able to kill and dress a bullock, sheep and pig for the shop, and run a mile, all within an hour. The mile was from Cooper's shop at Smeeth to what was Norrington's Garage, on the A20 to Ashford (now Fisher's Garage). Preparing an animal for the shop involved killing it, taking most of the skin off while it was on the floor (the curved knife would have been used for this) and hoisting the carcass off the floor so that the rest of the skin could be removed. Next, the gut would be removed, together with the heart, liver and lungs. Jack was known for being able to kill and prepare a bullock for the shop in 20 minutes, so the person making the bet was advised to think again by a friend. The bet was withdrawn, but Jack was confident that he could have won. In addition to his butchery skills, Jack was an excellent buyer: he was a good judge of quality and could gauge the carcass weight of a live animal accurately. It was his knowledge of animals and his skill and expertise as a butcher that laid the foundations for Cooper and Son's long-lasting success in the local area.

Wartime poster encouraging conservation

When the A20 shop first became operational, they had to use the slaughterhouse next to the Duke's Head in Sellindge until one was built at Smeeth. In 1933/4 the family then bought the shop and slaughterhouse at Aldington and, with this, Coopers ceased to slaughter in Smeeth. When wartime arrived, though, almost all slaughtering was required to be done centrally as part of the organisation and control of food supplies, with only a limited amount permitted on farms under licence for farmers' own consumption. Cooper's had such a licence. Ron recalls that the Horticultural Society started a pig club, the members of which would contribute scraps to feed a pig so that they could benefit from some of the meat when it was killed. Pigs could only be slaughtered when they reached a weight of 100lb, and this could only be done in the presence of an inspector, usually on a Monday. Cutting up of the carcass would follow on the Wednesday, and Ron recalls that when the owners came to collect the meat they would bring baskets lined with tea towels to absorb the blood. These were the days when packaging was at a minimum. Meat rationing finally came to an end in 1954 and local slaughtering could start again.

The Coopers bought the business at Sellindge behind the Duke's Head in 1943, but they never did use that shop as they did all their business from Smeeth. Ron's uncle always had a vision of building a shop in Sellindge and, eventually, the family bought a plot of land opposite Sellindge School. The plan was to build a shop with accommodation above it but, due to the shortage of materials in 1945/6, building controls meant that permission was granted only for the shop. Labour was much more easily available if accommodation went with the job, though providing accommodation could be a headache. Ron recalls a new butcher being taken on at Sellindge, who arrived accompanied by a wife and nine children who he had failed to mention previously. Later, Coopers bought two other cottages in Sellindge for their staff.

Jack ran the shop at Aldington until the Second World War, when he returned to Smeeth. His brother Jim went into the Air Force as a radio mechanic, and Aldington was put in the charge of Leslie Elms, Jack's brother-in-law. Leslie had been butler at the Paddocks on the A20, and Ron remembers the story of him arriving in the village to start his job there – with a linnet in a cage. The Coopers had trained Leslie as a butcher after he married Stella, but things at the Aldington shop didn't always go smoothly under his management. According to Ron, Leslie rarely managed to have sufficient meat for his customers during rationing, and his allocation had to be supplemented by the Smeeth shop. Leslie was also a great church man, and if a "man of the cloth" came in while he was serving a customer, that customer would be abandoned while Leslie engaged in conversation with the rector and attended to his order instead. (Though such behaviour would be considered unacceptable today it was commonplace in the past and Leslie wasn't alone in doing this.) Sweets were kept in the drawer beneath the scales and Leslie, known as Bertie to the boys in the shop, would eat them no matter to whom they belonged. On one occasion, after some Exlax had been left in the drawer, Leslie returned very late from lunch complaining of having had the most terrible diarrhoea; he had no idea what had brought this on. When Jim

Leslie Elms

269

came out of the Air Force in 1946 he went back to work at Smeeth but, once the new shop was completed in Sellindge in 1947, Cooper and Son at Smeeth was closed.

While the shops were important workplaces, comparatively few customers came to them until the late 1950s and early 1960s. For the most part, customers had two deliveries a week; if they gave their order on a Tuesday, for example, they would receive their delivery on the following Friday. This was the norm after the Second World War. In earlier times, deliveries were often made on a daily basis and, in some instances, ordered by post. A card posted one afternoon would arrive before 8am the next morning, meaning a delivery of meat could be made that day. Competition for customers between Cooper and Son and Hawkins was fierce and once a customer became a "regular" they tended not to change supplier. All the shops worked hard to increase their order list, but in these times, when goods were taken to the customer, the attractiveness of the shops themselves was of much less importance. As mobility improved and as more women went out to work, so people went to the shops themselves, and as a consequence home deliveries declined.

Coopers started their deliveries in a pony and trap from each of their shops; they progressed to motorbikes with panniers, then to motorbikes with sidecars, and eventually to a van. Their first was Ford's successor to the Model T; later, they ran an Austin 7. At the start of the war, in 1939, Norrington's Garage advised Coopers to buy two new vans while they were still available. Everyone was aware of the shortages that had been experienced during the First World War and had a good idea

Cooper and Son's new shop on the far side of Caroline's Hairdresser.
Jim Hendry, Caroline's father, is standing outside her shop.
Caroline's was part of Ames' Stores and was used as a furniture shop

of what might be ahead of them, so Coopers bought these vans; they did indeed see them through the difficult years. Ron recalls that Hawkins actually beat Cooper and Son to a delivery van, though the latter's popularity was such that they were able to buy Hawkins out in 1968. In 1966 Stella died suddenly, so Leslie Elms was paid for her share of the business and Ron and his brother Graham were brought into the partnership.

The premises that Cooper and Son had bought from Hawkins, including the slaughterhouse, were limited and inadequate for a modern butcher's shop. On the advice of the builder John Howland, Ron's father, Jack, bought Ames' Stores, knocked it down and built a brand new butcher's shop in its place. The new shop was built by Ted Chandler; the architect was Jim Brooks, who also kept a close eye on the work as it progressed. The shop had an innovative terrazzo floor, with marble chippings laid in cement. To the unfamiliar this might not seem significant, but it represented a major advance for those working there. Normally, floors were made of cement, which retains moisture and is extremely cold on the feet, especially in wintertime. The new floor was therefore a great improvement in this regard. All in all, the new shop with its new refrigerated serve-over counter and smart new floor was state of the art in its day. Custom at all the shops increased in the 1970s, and it was at this time that Cooper and Son employed around 25 people. The shop in Brabourne Lees always seemed to have a queue; it became a place to meet other people and chat – all that it lacked was a coffee shop!

Ron and Jenny Cooper

Ron was put in charge of the shop in Brabourne Lees and Jenny came to work there in 1971. Though most people seemed to know that Jenny and Ron were both involved with someone, nobody was aware that it was actually with each other, so this came as a surprise once the news broke. They married in 1973, widening family involvement in the business, and Ron asserts that Jenny has been indispensible to Coopers. After they were married Jenny continued to be "on call" whenever someone was on holiday or sick, or she simply "fetched and carried" at a moment's notice when her help was needed.

Butchers have never had it easy, and certainly the growth of supermarkets has made their position very difficult. Diversification has always been a means of supplementing business. During wartime the heads and feet of calves would be collected from the slaughterhouse in Ashford on a Wednesday evening and skinned at Sellindge; brawn would be made on the Thursday. Wild rabbits were also a staple during rationing, and often 100 or so would be collected from farms and skinned on Mondays. Today, taste for such products has changed and Ron observed that the comparatively new "designer" meat on sale in Tesco, such as steaks that are 21 days old, are far from a new concept. In times past meat was hung for longer before it was sold. A bullock might be killed on a Monday, for example, and it would not go into the fridge until Wednesday, where it would be hung for three weeks on the bone. Today, the freshly killed animal goes straight into the chiller, which makes the muscle tighten too quickly, which, in turn, can make the meat tough. It tastes far better if the whole process is more relaxed. Furthermore, there is far less fat on beef and lamb these days than there used to be, this being the product of selective breeding. The consequence is that meat does not last as well as it used to. An interesting observation made by Ron was that turkeys and chickens would be killed for Christmas, hung in the shop for seven days, and then eviscerated two days before Christmas Day – and they lasted. This cannot be done today, not only because health and hygiene regulations would prohibit it but also because the air temperature in butchers' shops has risen. In December they are now significantly warmer than they were in the past. In fact, prior to the 1940s, butchers' shops had removable windows and stock was exposed to the elements, so the meat lasted longer.

The greatest asset to the business created by Ron's grandfather was what many refer to as the "humble" sausage. The uncomplicated recipe, combined with the quality of the ingredients and the methods of production used by Cooper and Son, brought customers from far and wide (customers who subsequently bought other meat as well). Cooper and Son's sausages have stood the test of time, still being of great value and a major selling point when the business was sold to John Clarke in 2003. The only notable change to the recipe was the addition of preservative, not so much to extend the shelf life, as the sausages were made daily, but to keep the colour and eye appeal demanded by consumers – salt in the product turns meat grey and unappealing. In the two decades prior to the mid-1980s such was the demand that Coopers used to produce three-quarters of a ton of sausages every week. This was the peak period for the business; prices were held down by clever buying, no middleman and the sheer volume of sales, which was the envy of many in the trade.

Ron reflected that he was quite content with his life as a butcher until Health and Safety legislation intensified: sawdust on the floor was banned due to dust particles, and although Ron agrees that there is something in this, the banning of sawdust sorely vexed the trade because it used to absorb blood on the floor and also prevented butchers from slipping on fat and grease. Paperwork, Ron feels, increased markedly from the 1980s, as things that had previously been part of one's knowledge and common sense in running the business now had to be written down at every turn. The fridge temperature was recorded three times each day, as were the temperatures of all cooked meats at every stage of their production. Cleaning procedures had to be checked and recorded – the list goes on… Ron accepts that there were cases of some butchers' shops not observing good hygiene and work practice, but those who knew their trade and whose practice focused naturally on the wellbeing of customers and staff simply became frustrated with the extra paperwork.

One piece of legislation that was completely wrong in Ron's view was the banning of the traditional wooden cutting block. Wood, he argues, cannot hold bacteria, while the plastic advocated by Health and Safety can harbour bacteria in the grooves left by the knives. Artificially made surfaces do not have the resilience of wood and, furthermore, they can cause repetitive strain injury, whereas wood absorbs the impact of chopping.

Ron also recalls that, in the past, almost every part of the animal was sold: intestines were bought for sausage skins, while sheep skins and hides fetched a good price, much higher in comparison with prices today, which sees synthetic alternatives being used instead. Beef fat was made into dripping and was used for frying fish and chips – a shop in Hythe used to take 300lb a week from Coopers during summertime. Suet was sold, offal was sold, ox cheek was sold for animal feed, and hearts and lungs were sold for cat food. All the remaining waste materials were sold and used to make fertilisers. Now, due to BSE, those parts of the animal not for human consumption are incinerated.

As a population we are very remote from the meat we eat these days, and this was emphasised by Ron's description of his father driving the stock home from Ashford

Market. It was not always an easy job, but if he had trouble with a bullock lying down and refusing to move, "He simply used to pee in its ear, then it would always do what you wanted!" One cannot help but wonder how many butchers today have ever had the need to know this.

## POSTSCRIPT FROM RON COOPER

It must be remembered that a business, especially a retail business, relies heavily on a loyal and attentive staff. Over the years many people worked for the firm and a not-inconsiderable number learnt their trade there. There are far too many to recall; some stayed for a short time, others their entire working lives. These are some whom you may remember: Leslie Elms, Tom Back, Arthur Taylor, Peter Gray, Peter Bryant, Brian Wignall, Charlie Conn, Morris O'Connor, Ross Ashman and Tipper Earl (both previously with Hawkins), Simon Stickles, Colin Matthews, Maurice Croucher, Tony Excell, George Griggs, Tim Foad, Chris Dryland and Yvonne Ward. Very important, especially in the earlier times, were the book-keepers, Betty Harris (Baker), June Gray (Standen), Elsie Piddock, Jo Cleveland, Fred Beadle, Chris and Pat Fittil, Margaret Pile (Ward) and one Jenny Cooper (Harvey). Many people recall being Saturday boys, delivering and cleaning using the standard scrubbing brush, boiling water, soap, soda and "elbow grease". Sincere apologies to anyone who has been left out.

And finally: Jack Cooper was always known as "the guv'nor", even by his family. Ron can hardly ever remember him as Dad or Father after leaving school. To his grandsons he was Grantie. Jack was a tolerant man but, on one occasion, a customer whose order was always given special attention, yet who still complained on a regular basis, was told by Jack in exasperation, "The Good Lord sent the meat, but the Devil sent the Cook!"

## THE GARAGE

The first Anchor Garage, built in the 1920s by E.F. Ward.
From left, Doug Osborne (known as Harry), Ron Russell
and Mr Oyler

After serving in the First World War, Edward (E.F. Ward) Ward, also known as Ted, set up a business repairing bicycles behind his parents' pub, The Blue Anchor in Brabourne Lees. In those early days he supplemented his income by cutting hair, a skill inherited by his granddaughter Caroline Payne, who owns Caroline's Hairdressers. Later, Ted erected an ex-army hut in the field near the pub and named it Anchor Garage, after the pub.

Ted built a more permanent structure in 1939, when his 14-year-old son, also Edward, joined him in the business. Thus, as Yvonne Ward explained, "we had 'Old Ted' and 'Young Ted'". In time, Young Ted (Yvonne's husband) took over the business, though Old Ted continued to be involved in the garage until his death in 1966. After considerable soul-searching Young Ted sold the business in 1972, and the garage is now owned by John Childs.

Once Ted Ward (senior) had moved to the garage, he continued with bicycle repairs and increasingly undertook motorbike and car repairs, though there were still precious few cars around in those days. According to Oliver Trowell, "In pre-war days I recall getting bicycle-tyre punctures mended at Ward's Garage for 9d a time. Cracked beach (pebbles) on newly tarred roads inevitably caused many punctures until it was thoroughly amalgamated with the tar."

Margaret Pile (Ward), Old Ted's daughter, writes:

"Fortescue built a bungalow adjoining the garage and we moved into it on the day that war broke out. It was here that I had my first garden. Two employees had to join a munitions factory, and my sister joined the Wrens. If you enlisted voluntarily you were given a choice, otherwise you were forced to support the war effort and had little choice as to what you were given to do. It was at this time that Archie Ashdown joined the staff as a young lad and stayed through the war. Certain types of labour were exempt from joining up and among these were mechanics, who were needed to keep the tractors and farm machinery going.

Margaret Pile

"We had to be self-supporting, as cargo ships bringing supplies into Britain were being bombed. Father also transported several expectant mums to the old Willesborough Hospital by taxi, holding his breath every time for fear that a baby would be born before he arrived. In 1953 I married, and as my father was taken ill I was employed at the garage for five years as a part-time book-keeper, until I had my second child, almost the last delivered by Nurse Hills.

"Father supplied Mr Alfred Fortescue with his first car – Doctor Garman's was the first car in the village[5]. Alf's one and only driving lesson was how to hold the car on the clutch on New Barn Hill."

Returning to the subject of wartime, Yvonne echoed her sister-in-law Margaret's words: "During the war, the main work of the garage was repairing tractors and keeping the doctor's car on the road. [Young] Ted said that detonators were given to the garage to destroy the petrol tanks in the event of an invasion, but fortunately these never had to be used."

Francis Edenden, who worked for Ward's Garage from 1950 to 1963, recalls that the original wooden garage had just one petrol hand pump, and remembered with some amusement that Ames' builders always seemed to choose the wettest of days to come to the pump with their lorry stacked with two-gallon cans; it was Francis's job to fill these in the pouring rain.

---

5        Opinion was divided as to who owned the first car and it was agreed that Dr Garman's was one of the first cars in the village.

Several people have spoken of there probably being a real "treasure trove" beneath the garage and forecourt, as vast amounts of "rubbish" have been buried there over time. After the fire at Orpin's in 1926, much of the residue was buried beneath the future garage. In addition, Francis recalled that Mr Ward (senior) would buy second-hand vehicles for spare parts to maintain Orpin's delivery vans and then bury what remained of them just near the garage. Yvonne also remembered stories that her husband told of several old cars being buried to form the hard standing. We were told that when a hole was dug in the garage forecourt to install a second petrol pump a vast amount of this "rubbish" was unearthed, much of it thought to have come from Orpin's.

Yvonne Ward

In addition to petrol, the garage also sold paraffin and had other functions as well. In fact, John Childs told us that the garage "still sells paraffin from a pump, and in bulk, and that it's the only garage within a 20-mile radius to do so". Ward's also sold battery acid, refilled batteries and accumulators, one use for which was to power radios. In the 1950s Tom and Margaret Wratten were sent to Ward's regularly by Granny Wratten, who lived in one of the cottages at Park Corner, to get the accumulator for her radio recharged, and Norman Thornby and Eric Ball used to make frequent and regular trips to the garage for much the same purpose. The Ball family had a friend in Folkestone who made up the radio for them on an old gramophone base, and Eric can still remember hearing "Hitler's ravings" on it in 1938. In the same year he heard the news of Len Hutton's outstanding score of 364 runs against the Australians at The Oval. Radios were thus very highly prized.

Ward's Garage also had a telephone, one of very few in the village, and as Margaret mentioned, her father ran a taxi service from there, too. Sam Jamieson, John Jamieson's father, drove Ward's taxis for many years. Francis recalled that there were two of them, a Vauxhall and a Chrysler, and John Childs added that Young Ted had bought the Vauxhall Cresta from him while John was working for Stanhays, then the main Vauxhall/Bedford dealer in Ashford. These cars were Ted's pride and joy. Nobody was allowed to smoke in them, and they were kept immaculately clean. They took many a local bride to her wedding. One was used regularly as a school taxi for Brabourne School for children who lived some distance from the village. Sam would collect in the morning and drop off in the afternoon children who lived in West

Brabourne, Bulltown, Hampton Lane, and down the lane leading to California Farm. It must have been a challenge to keep the school taxi in as pristine a state as the other vehicles at Ward's Garage. According to George Brooks, Sam was "a good man and a most useful person" who continued to drive for Ward's for some 10 years or so. When not driving for the garage, Sam used to deliver bread for the Stone Hill bakery and was well remembered by many.

Digressing for a moment...

In 1963 Francis moved to Andrews Garage on the Plain in Smeeth, together with Doug Osborne. Francis had a Rover that he and Doug used to drive for weddings; it had first belonged to Francis's grandmother, Mrs Brice of Brook, the mother of Mr E Brice, the baker. Granny Brice had the Rover for more than 48 years and looked after it extremely carefully, taking it out only on Tuesdays, which was market day, and for church on Sundays. Its canvas body was thus in mint condition and the Edendens kept the car until recently. When Francis's wife, Betty, finally got her own car in the 1960s, a little Austin 7 called Esmeralda, she and Francis drove all the way to Monte Carlo and back in Esmeralda 'who' never broke down.

## FROM WARD'S GARAGE TO JOHN CHILDS' GARAGE
John Childs writes:

"I first met Ted – Young Ted, that is – while working for Stanhays in Ashford, when I sold him a Vauxhall Cresta that he used as a taxi. My accountant mentioned that Ted had shown an interest in selling the garage and recommended that I contact him; the rest is history.

John and Brenda Childs

"I bought the garage from 'Young' Ted in 1972, and can still remember exchanging contracts on Christmas Eve afternoon amid the parties in Halletts and Kingsford, Flower and Pain. We walked down Bank Street in Ashford to actually exchange the contracts, the urgency being that I was taking over on 1st January, 1973. The delay had been caused by Ted, who was still

John Childs' Garage, shortly after purchase
from Ted Ward in 1972

worrying about letting his family business go. I would feel the same today, having had over 40 happy years here.

"On taking over we carried on doing taxi work using a Ford Granada Estate and a Jensen Interceptor until more specialist firms grew up, making taxi work uneconomical for us.

"I installed new fuel tanks in 1973, and during the excavation work, yes, we did find many spare parts, most of which were in good condition due to having spent much of their lives in the sand. The showroom was built in 1983/84, but this time we found mainly scrap metal. We had to go down many feet with the footings because of this infill.

"We took the franchise for Yugo cars in 1984 and had this until 1992, when manufacturing of the cars ceased due to fighting in what was then Yugoslavia. As we had such a large customer base we continued to source spare parts from all over the Continent to keep the vehicles running. This turned into quite a large mail-order section of the business.

John Childs (c1987)

The new registration arrives (1988)

New fuel tanks installed in 1973

The Garage (1992) with new showroom

"In 1991 we took on the Kia franchise when it first came into the country. We continued with this until 1999, when Kia required us to move into Ashford to be more central. I was unwilling to do this, preferring a village environment, so we parted company and took on Perodua, part of the Toyota/Daihatsu family, which we have to this day. We have found this to be very successful and the vehicles to be very reliable. When I first bought the garage, the average car had 14 hours of servicing per year; these days it is in the region of 1½ hours. Although electronics now play a big part, we still find there is a need for good mechanical and welding expertise, as well as technicians competent in electrics and all the latest gadgets. We have also recently taken on the Farr franchise for Quads and UTVs, which is appropriate to our rural location, and we also carry out repair work on such vehicles."

# THE HANDY STORES

The Handy Stores (early 1990s)

Though not a family business handed down through the generations, mention of the shops in Brabourne Lees would not be complete without some reference to The Handy Stores. This was situated in what had been Hawkins' butcher's shop, one of the oldest buildings in the village – it is believed to have been constructed more than 200 years ago, during the Napoleonic threat to England.

Run by Tom Sprawling, The Handy Stores, which became part of the village only in the 1970s, has, like Orpins, been likened by some of our contributors to an Aladdin's cave, a place where virtually anything of a durable nature could be found or ordered. In Margaret Older's words, "Tom could get you anything in just a few days, from a yard of lace to a yard of concrete. How we miss him and his shop!" We have not been able to find a picture that does justice to the contents of this shop, though Vi Sprawling's picture of her husband in the shop, which she has kindly let us reproduce, goes some way towards detailing the enormous variety of its wares.

Tom Sprawling in The Handy Stores

The Handy Stores, drawn by Vi Sprawling (May, 1992)

Before coming to Brabourne in the early 1970s Tom delivered paraffin as part of a family business in Ashford. He had two rounds but realised that the Ashford ring road would constrain further expansion of his business. He also foresaw that paraffin would soon give way to other fuels. Therefore, he gave up the family business, bought the old butcher's shop in Brabourne, installed his family there and opened The Handy Stores. Initially, this was in the former shop that was the largest room downstairs, and its big window still had the old butchers' hooks in place. The upstairs was a vast open space which had been used for storage and so had no bedrooms. Tom gradually created these but in the early days he worked mainly on the downstairs so that he could get the shop going. He sealed off the front door, knocked down the old staircase behind it, took down a wall and extended the shop front across the house, moving methodically from one room to the next. Tragically, Tom's first wife, Wynne, died suddenly before the shop was complete, but he continued with his work, and in 1974/75 he blocked up the archway through to the back of the butcher's shop, and put a bay window in its place. The transformation of the shop was completed in 1979.

When he first arrived in Brabourne, Tom also put up a paraffin tank and continued selling Esso Blue for years; he received each delivery of this on a monthly basis, and always paid for it at the end of each month. One day, in the 1980s, without any warning, the deliveryman refused to fill the tank because new rules being implemented by the supplier included being paid cash on delivery. Tom, who had lived on trust all his life, was so angered by this change in procedure that he cancelled his order, ceased to sell paraffin and moved over to Calor gas. Trust was a major part of Tom's business, as it was with all other shops and tradesmen in the village. Calor gas cylinders, wire netting, peat, compost, coal and other goods were all left outside the shop door, and on occasions Tom forgot to bring them in at night. He trusted everyone and never lost anything from theft. Vi recalls that, when Mountbatten Way was built, one of the new residents came to The Handy Stores asking for wire netting with no more than a guess as to how much he needed. Tom gave him the roll, told him to help himself and let him know how much he had used. Taken aback, the man suggested that he could vanish with the lot, to which Tom replied, "Well, will you?" This produced yet another customer for life. Among Tom's many achievements was repairing the lock of the door to Brabourne Church, cutting a second key for the massive oak door, and possibly repairing the original key. (If it wasn't Tom, then someone else has done an impressive repair job on the old key).

Vi attributed the success of The Handy Stores to Tom's capacity to understand what people wanted and needed and, if he did not have what a customer wanted, he would buy it in as quickly as possible. He kept an enormous range of goods, stocked goods in both imperial and metric sizes, would sell them in small quantities, and initially used to buy from a range of tradesmen who brought their goods round in vans. Several ironmongers came from London, and electrical suppliers, haberdashers and others made regular deliveries to Brabourne. Tom was always forward-looking, and as soon as his original suppliers went out of business he changed and updated his stock to try to keep ahead of changing customer demand. For example, he went into animal food and started stocking certain garden accessories, such as bulbs, composts and gro-bags, all of which proved very successful.

Vi came to the Paddocks in 1966 with her son, Anthony Braben, who became a bell-ringer at Brabourne Church and was tower captain for a time. He moved on to become tower captain at Southwark Cathedral; now living in Snowdonia National Park, he still writes bell music. After Vi married Tom, she, too, became part of The Handy Stores. She recalls one incident when she was on her own in the shop and an old man came in and asked, "Tom all right?" She replied that, yes, he was, but the man merely repeated the question a couple more times until Vi was forced to get Tom in from his workshop. It transpired that he wanted Tomorite for his tomatoes. Fork handles come to mind…

Vi Sprawling

Stella Rigg, who worked for many years in the shop, remembers Tom's kindness to all. When a customer came in with a broken pram wheel, for example, he would put all else aside and mend the wheel, usually for nothing. Stella also recalls him saying to customers, "You know where our back door is – give us a knock if you're stuck", implying that they could always call on him, even when the shop was shut. Something else that Tom was often heard to say was, "If we haven't got what you need, it'll be in on Thursday", and Stella recalls that, usually, it was.

The Handy Stores was more than a business, it was a way of life for Tom and Vi, but they had to plan for a new future when Tom was diagnosed with cancer in 1993. In spite of his illness, they spent the next three and a half years self-building a three-bedroom house at the end of their garden. They moved in on the sale of the shop, in September 1996, to Diane and Roger Townsend, who were "reps" for the Sprawlings and so understood the unique nature of the shop and business. Tom died in early 1999. Brenda Wright recalls that, at Tom's funeral at the crematorium, the sombre atmosphere was lifted when, during the committal, the curtains made a terrible squeak, and jammed. At this most solemn of moments, someone was heard to say, "Find Tom! He'll fix it." This has been included with Vi's kind permission.

Brabourne has not been isolated from the pressures faced by small shops in rural areas and in the early part of this century The Handy Stores ceased to trade. The old building has now been converted to a series of "desirable dwellings", homes with a distinctive history and possibly a ghost or two. Vi will give you details if you ask.

Actually, if you are interested in ghosts on a wider scale, please contact Michael Hickmott, whose research has "found" several local ghosts, including the old farmer with a straw hat who roams the farm buildings at Evegate, the ghost of Hospital Field, the "Old Canteen" ghost(s) of Stable Lodge, the water carrier of Bulltown, and others.

## PUBS IN BRABOURNE LEES AND SMEETH

The Plough, Brabourne Lees (2013)

The Blue Anchor, Brabourne Lees (2013)

The Woolpack, Smeeth (2013)

The Plough (c1910)

The Blue Anchor set back in the picture, Ward's Garage at the front (1955)

## THE OLD WOOLPACK, SMEETH

c1896

c1912

c1912

c1912

## BRABOURNE'S BUILDERS

Brabourne had two builders, Ames and Fortescue. Fred Ames and his son Oswald were established builders before the Second World War, and their business continued until the 1970s, when Oswald retired. According to Frank Ames, Oswald's son, "Ames built dozens of houses in the village – at least six along Canterbury Road, some in The Ridgeway." To this, others added Caroland Villas on Church Road, Abbotsfield on Lees Road and The Crest just above Crow Corner. In addition, Ames built numerous extensions and carried out building repairs. Though Ames' Builders have not operated for almost 40 years they are still warmly remembered by many of our contributors who knew the Ames family well.

## A.J. FORTESCUE AND SON

According to Andrew and Jackie Fortescue, Alfred James Fortescue and his son Gordon became increasingly important in the village after the Second World War, though the business was well established long before this. Alfred was born in London in 1885 and, by 1901, was a carpentry apprentice in Meopham, Kent. After qualifying, he travelled to Canada, where he worked as a carpenter and builder. He returned to the UK and joined the army at the start of the First World War. He was in the Westminster Dragoons, part of the County of London Yeomanry, served at Gallipoli in 1915, and in Egypt and Palestine in 1916/17 at the rank of corporal. He then transferred to the Royal Artillery and served as a gunner in the Machine Gun Corps on the Western Front in France in 1918, when he became ill with peritonitis. He was sent home to recover and came to stay in Smeeth with his sister, Sarah Taylor, who owned The Woolpack Inn. Alfred decided to make his home in Smeeth and, at the end of the war, bought Spring Cottage, along with the joinery shop and haulage yard. After being involved for a short time in the haulage business he decided to concentrate on building and traded as A.J. Fortescue from July 1919. The company records show that in the six months from July to December

Alfred Fortescue (c1917)

1919 the business made a profit of £16/18/10.

Alfred married Eleanora Sanger in 1919 and they moved to Spring Cottage, which was renamed Fortescue House in the 1990s. Gordon was born in 1927, and Jean in 1929. They both attended Smeeth Primary School.

Alfred and Eleanora (1919)

Fortescue's built several houses in Smeeth in the 1920s and 1930s. Local knowledge suggests that their first construction in the village was Cooper and Son's shop on the A20 in 1920; this was followed by several houses on Plain Hill and Plain Road. Fortescue's carried out repairs, made alterations to houses and built extensions in Smeeth, Mersham, Aldington and Saltwood. They also carried out work at several Mackeson public houses, including The Honest Miller in Brook, The Swan in Sellindge, The Castle Inn in Saltwood, The Royal Oak at Newingreen, The Barley Mow at Newington and The Welcome Stranger at Lympne. They also carried out building work and repairs for the army during the Second World War, especially at Lympne Airport, Capel le Ferne and occasionally at Biggin Hill. Another part of the business involved quarrying sand from the sandpits on Plain Road and Granary Court Road, and selling it to the army and other local builders through the late 1940s.

Gordon Fortescue decided to follow his father into the building trade and took up an apprenticeship with Jenners in Folkestone, while also attending Canterbury Technical College. Once qualified, Gordon joined the business and A.J. Fortescue and Son Ltd was established in 1954. The company still continues to trade under this name.

Fortescue's belonged to the Building Federation and employed their own plumbers, carpenters and joiners. In the 1960s and 1970s they employed 20 to 30 staff, among whom long-term members were Fred Apps the general foreman, Phil Harris the carpenter, and Ernie Tournay the plumber, later replaced by John Hickmott. John started his working life as a farm labourer, later delivered milk, and then worked for Gordon as a plumber, having completed his training at night school (the hard way). Dick Andrews, Tony Russell, painter, Stan Burt, Brian Streeter and Peter Gray were all members of the Fortescue workforce. Of key importance to the business,

The workforce at A.J. Fortescue and Son in the late 1950s.
1 Bill Wilson, 2 Stanley Dryland, 3 Don Wynder, 4 George Clayson, 5 Les Reid, 6 John
Hickmott, 7 Albert Playford, 8 Alan Mackay, 9 Bob Clayson, 10 Tom Harris, 11 Frank
Garlick, 12 Bill Heritage, 13 P. Reed, 14 Bill Barton, 15 Mr Matthews (known as Matt),
16 Albert Kidwell, 17 Jimmy Wynder, 18 M. Driver, 19 Ernie Tournay, 20 Gordon Fortescue,
21 Alfred Fortescue 22 Fred Apps, 23 Les Bishopp, 24 Phil Harris

The workforce in the late 1980s:
1 Fred Apps, 2 Dick Andrews, 3 ?Bill Stockbridge, 4 Ernie Tournay, 5 Brian Streeter,
6 unidentified, 7 Pat Cornell, 8 John Hickmott, 9 Phil Harris, 10 Peter Gray, 11 Stan Burt,
12 Tony Russell, 13 Andrew Fortescue, 14 Alex Fortescue, 15 Gordon Fortescue

and remembered as such by many, was Pat Cornell, Gordon's secretary, who liaised very effectively between Gordon and his team. Brian remembers Pat as being both efficient and good fun. Shortly before she died in 2011, Pat wrote, "I started at Fortescue's in 1952 and worked there until 2000, or thereabouts, taking time off to produce two sons. I loved the work and enjoyed these years with the firm."

Most of those who worked for Fortescue's were local, and stayed with the firm for many years. Fred Apps worked for Gordon for more than 50 years, and for Gordon's father before him; he was well over 70 before he retired. Some of the team had thus known Gordon since he was a boy, and Dick remarked with amusement, "I can remember Gordon running around in short trousers!" Living locally, the team knew each other well, and working together for years created lasting bonds between them. The picture from the village fête in the 1950s of a float bearing the name "Forte's Follies" with Phil Harris, Les Bishopp and another, suitably attired, shows that life wasn't all work!

The beautiful yet somewhat swarthy Forte's Follies at the village fête in the 1950s.
From left, Mr Matthews (Matt), Les Bishopp, Len Smith, Phil Harris; driving, Frank Garlick

Gordon followed in his father's footsteps and became increasingly involved in civic life. He and his wife May were long-time members of the Rotary Club, the Inner Wheel (Ladies Rotary) and the Lions Club, and were thus much involved with

One of the first Colt houses being built.
From left, Phil Harris, Fred Apps and Len Smith

Brenda and Brian Streeter

charitable works. Elected to Ashford Borough Council in the 1960s, Gordon became chairman of Housing on the Borough Council and Mayor of Ashford in 1983-84. In 2007 Gordon was honoured at Buckingham Palace for his contribution to civic life and received an OBE.

After Gordon joined the firm Phil Harris recalls that, in the early 1950s, Fortescue's undertook new types of work, for example, the construction of Colt houses. These were essentially "kit" houses and a new concept in building in the post-war era. A firm at Bethersden would develop a plan with the potential occupiers, the house was then prefabricated in 4ft panels and, once the sections were on site, Phil and his colleagues would assemble them from the plan. The roof was usually covered in wooden shingles (tiles), as were the walls, though there was some variation with the latter.

Phil found the work innovative and interesting, as he did the pre-constructed wooden grain silos that Fortescue's assembled at Joe Farm, Penstock, and at many other farms. These were either square or rectangular, and the pre-cut timbers were thickest at the base and became thinner towards the top. Each would arrive ready-notched to fit in to the one above it and, periodically, the structure was secured with a metal rod or bar to ensure that it remained in the shape intended. These wooden grain stores, mellow in appearance, were later superseded by the round metal structures so clearly visible in the landscape today.

Brian Streeter worked for Gordon for many years, having previously served his apprenticeship with Jenners when they built Sandy Place. It was here, in the mid-1950s, that he learnt how to pitch a roof and hang a door, though he only worked full-time for Fortescue's some 30 years later. From the information Brian gave us it was clear that Fortescue's, and other builders such as Oswald Ames, changed the face of the village. As mentioned, in the 1920s and 1930s Fortescue's initially built several houses on Plain Hill and on The Plain; from the mid-1960s they built the two pairs of semi-detached houses at approximately the lowest point in Plain Road, the pair of detached houses on Woolpack Hill just above John Childs' Garage, and bungalows on Canterbury Road just near the entrance to Knatchbull Way (though at least one of these has been converted into a house). Fortescue's also built the first 12 houses in Knatchbull Way, though other contractors installed the roads and the services. In the late 1980s they built Bramley Close in Brabourne Lees, and a decade later, in the 1990s, they knocked down Fortescue's old joinery workshop at Spring Cottage in Smeeth, which was the original office of A.J. Fortescue and Son, and built two bungalows where the old joinery shop stood. These were called nos.3 & 4, Spring Cottages. It was at this time that Spring Cottage was renamed Fortescue

Three generations of Fortescues:
from left, Gordon, Alex and Andrew

The Fortescue family celebrating Gordon's 80th birthday,
with May and Gordon in the front

House. Fortescue's also built numerous extensions, as people became increasingly prosperous towards the latter part of the 20th century.

Fortescue's work was not confined to Brabourne and Smeeth. In the early 1980s they undertook major repairs and improvements to Plumpton Farmhouse on the road from Brabourne to Wye, and in the early 1990s they built the dairy at Ouseley, Hinxhill, which took the milk from Lord Brabourne's herd. Returning to Plumpton for a moment, there was very little left in the house when they started work there, though Brian remembers them taking down a wall on the second floor to reveal a room that had been sealed off. Despite high hopes, they were disappointed to find nothing in it, but going into the attic, Brian recalls, "was like taking a step back in time". Up here were the servants' quarters, complete with a little iron stove and walls of the original lathe and plaster, though some of this was now missing. Brian remembers the beauty of the long-neglected oak staircase and the high ceilings of the once-elegant rooms of the farmhouse. While they were working at Plumpton, all the copper pipe for the plumbing was delivered to the house just before Christmas, just when they did not want it. Martin Bower was the plumber and, together with Brian, threaded the pipe in long lengths through the upstairs windows and "buried" it under all sorts of other "rubbish" in the house. They knew the house was vulnerable to thieves and hoped they had hidden the pipe adequately. Returning immediately after Christmas they found the door to the farmhouse kicked in and all the plumbing materials gone. The thieves had also broken into the garage and taken all the lead scrap, which had been got ready for the scrap merchants. Brian phoned Gordon, who immediately telephoned the police. At the scene of the crime, the security man accused Brian and the other members of Fortescue's team of leaving the windows open, in spite of it being quite clear that the door had been kicked in. They found a few pieces of copper pipe in the field nearby, all of which had been cut up into smaller, more manageable lengths. Such vandalism and robbery were, and still are, a problem when houses are being renovated. After the great storm of 1987 the firm had a great deal of work and Brian recalls that the extensive damage saw demand for Kent peg tiles increase, and in response the thieving of tiles shot up.

Fortescue's continued for many years with Gordon at the helm, but shortly before his death his son Andrew took on the business with his wife Jacqui as manager (Jacqui and Andrew at the far right of the second and back row respectively, in family picture above). Andrew built the Oak Room for Smeeth Church, the plans for which had been passed while Gordon was still alive. Andrew has now been joined in the business by his son Alex, thus the institution of Fortescue and Son continues.

## MEMORABLE MOMENTS IN THE BUILDING TRADE

Brian recalled that working for Gordon "did have its moments". One day Brian and Stan Burt were working at a house in Romney Marsh where the drains were blocked. Though not their usual type of work, Gordon had asked the two of them to unblock them. It was a scorching day and as Stan was rodding the drains the blockage suddenly released and, fountaining upwards, instantly covered him with the unappetising contents of the pipe. The lady of the house was out and Brian quickly found a hosepipe and washed Stan down until he was clean enough to be taken home in the van. "Fortunately, it was such a hot day... " Brian remarked.

Gordon used to do a great deal of work on Smeeth Church. One memorable job came after some people had gone into the church and, for reasons known only to them, taken the hymn and prayer books up into the tower and set fire to them, scorching the wooden floor of the belfry. Fortunately, John Jamieson saw smoke coming out of the louvres in the church walls and phoned the fire brigade from Jim and Joan Berrill's cottage. They managed to stop the fire and so prevented the damage from being any more extensive. They told John that it was a good thing that he had called them, as by the time they had arrived the fire had gone well past the stage of being able to be controlled by a domestic fire extinguisher. Very soon after this Gordon's team effectively restored Smeeth Church to its former beauty.

Good health is critically important when one's work is so physical and this point was made by several people with whom we spoke. Brian suffers from Ménière's disease, a disorder of the inner ear that periodically affects his balance and "knocks him sideways" for a day or two. One day he was putting up the walls of an extension for Gordon and had been up and down the ladder to approximately ceiling height for most of the day. At around 3pm Gordon arrived and, just as Brian was about halfway down the ladder, Gordon called to him. Turning to listen, Brian's head "started to go" and he fell off the ladder into a pile of hay. He was dizzy, sick and in a terrible state. Although Gordon knew that Brian suffered from Ménière's, he had never witnessed an attack first hand and started to panic. Brian asked Gordon to fetch Brenda, his wife, who knew what to do when he suffered an attack, and though Gordon did this, he was so shaken by Brian's condition that he phoned 999, despite Brian telling him this wasn't necessary. On its way to collect Brian the ambulance got lost and so an air-ambulance helicopter was sent instead. A second ambulance had also been despatched and arrived at much the same time that the helicopter landed in Gordon and May's front garden. May had just had the house cleaned for a party; the doors were all open and, as the helicopter descended, the house filled with leaves. As Brian's condition was not life-threatening it was decided that the air ambulance should return to its base in case of a real emergency, and Brian was taken in the ambulance to the

William Harvey Hospital. He was discharged from hospital four hours later and May came to pick him up. Gordon was still very concerned and Brian can remember him saying, "Surely he can't just be left to sleep it off?"

One of the worst incidents in Brian's working life was when he fell off a ladder and fractured a vertebra in his back. Lying in the garden, he was unable to attract the house owner's attention and it was not until she took her dog out for a walk hours later that she saw him lying there. This led to Brian being in a plaster cast and flat on his back for eight weeks, and off work for eight months. He reflected that had he been doing an office job he would probably have been fit to return to work sooner, but this wasn't possible in the building trade.

## FRANK HOWLAND'S MARQUEES

Renting out marquees for events seems more appropriate to today's social climate than that of an era that extended from before the Second World War until the early 1970s, but Frank Howland was a man clearly ahead of his time. Frank had inherited the marquee business from his uncle, Alan Howland, who together with two others, James Hill and William Groacher, had run the Willesborough Marquee Company since 1898. Following the deaths of his uncle and his father before the war, Frank took over the marquee business, with his half-sister, May, as a sleeping partner. Frank's grandson, Michael Hickmott (who has kindly provided most of the information for this section), knows nothing of what happened to Alan's other two partners, but Frank set up the business on land he had inherited from his father that adjoined the stream down from the village hall. At that time there was little on the land other than several sheds that Frank used to house the marquees in and other equipment for his business. The sheds are now gone and in their place stands a house, Riverside. The marquee business proved to be a perfect second job for Frank, whose main job was as a builder for Oswald Ames. Much of the work of putting up the marquees frequently took place on Thursday or Friday evenings, ready for the weekend, so Frank did not have to choose between his marquee business and his work as a builder.

Michael writes:

"In the 1950s Frank had a creamy-yellow coloured van – a Ford? – with windows in the side Although it could seat three in the front it had no rear seating, so he made two pairs of seats from old coach seats and fixed them onto timber runners to stabilise them. These were then put into the back of the van as and when required. The unusual thing about the van was that it had a tilting front windscreen, hinged at the top, so the bottom could be swung outwards. This was great for ventilation but not so good for the insects and leaves that came through the opening.

Michael Hickmott, Frank Howland's grandson

"In the 1960s Frank bought a brand new Ford Thames 15 cwt van. This was larger than the previous van and had a better payload. There were only two seats in the front, but a makeshift seat could be made on the engine cover between the two seats as this was within the van rather than in front. The vans were Frank and his wife Marjorie's only means of transport, apart from bicycles. Frank didn't buy a car until the late 1960s, and then it was a second-hand racing green Triumph Herald 13/60.

"For the smaller 'tenting' jobs and hiring out tables and chairs the Ford van was ideal. Sometimes the workforce could travel in the van as well, but at other times they followed in one of their cars and Frank would pay for the petrol. On larger jobs Frank employed Dave Dodd of Granary Court Road, Smeeth, who ran a small haulage business with one Bedford lorry. Dave's main work was for the local farmers, taking cattle, sheep and pigs to market, so he usually had a cattle lorry body on the lorry rather than a flat-bed body. This being the case, the lorry had to be hosed out before being used for the tents. It was also loaded so that none of the tent canvas came into contact with the floor – Frank was very particular about the tents remaining as clean as possible.

Frank and Marjorie Howland

"As the marquee business was run alongside his work as a builder's foreman, Frank had to use casual labour. This enabled local men with a normal day job to earn extra money, in cash, to supplement their incomes. As a result, 'tenting' was carried out in the evenings, after work hours and at weekends. The vast majority of the work was in the summer months, so this fitted in well. The entire workforce, or preferably 'the gang', came from the village. Frank's son-in-law, George Hickmott, and George's brother John, who worked for Fortescue and Son, were regulars."

Jennifer Hooker (Hickmott), John's eldest daughter, remembers that her father "was always working on Bank Holidays and we were left at home with Mum, who used to take us to get cream soda and cherryade and crisps – a real treat – we used to love it!" Michael, who was George's son, started "tenting" when he was about seven years old and continued until Frank sold the business in the 1970s. George and John were never paid at the end of the week or the month; they accumulated their wages and Frank paid them each a lump sum, which enabled their families to go on holiday together.

Michael continues:

"In the 1950s and 1960s there was comparatively little competition from similar businesses. Dover Marquees was in existence, but there were few others, so Frank Howland's marquees were much in demand. He had a regular list of clients' events and virtually every village function would have a Howland marquee, including the local village fête, then held on the field opposite the main entrance to the village hall. Other annual events for which marquees were erected included the point-to-point races at Aldington, twice a year, and Charing, the flower shows and fêtes at Warehorne, Hamstreet and Sheldwich, and the horse trials at Linton near Maidstone. Then there were the 'one-off' jobs, principally weddings and birthday parties. These could be much more complicated, as in some instances marquees had to be erected in back gardens, sometimes over a low hedge, fountain or garden statue that couldn't be moved and would have to form part of the décor. It was also not uncommon for people to complain bitterly at the prospect of having stakes for the guy ropes hammered into their lawns.

"The regular workers all knew what to do and in what order it had to be done. Frank used to take charge of the whole team of up to 10 or 12 men, issuing orders, overseeing, advising and giving directions. He knew exactly how many stumps, ropes, poles and pegs were needed for each tent, the distance every stump had to be apart, the length of each of the guy ropes, etc.

"Frank would not tolerate any horseplay while on the job – there was work to be done, time was money and, often, time was short. Sometimes in the evenings the gang would not get back to the Tent Lodge until after dark, but it wasn't a case of 'all work and no play'. There was always a lot of ribbing of the younger or less-experienced members of the gang – those who missed hitting a stump or slipped over. More fun was had in Dave Dodd's lorry, which had a 'pen' over the cab area. This was accessed from the main body of the lorry by a sliding door. If a second floor was put in the lorry this pen could be entered from second-floor level, thus increasing the load, or it could be used for piglets, lambs or calves. Dave always ensured the pen was filled with clean straw ready for the next time it was to be used. It also provided a good riding place for some of the gang who found it preferable to sitting in the rear of the lorry on the marquee canvas. Around the sides of the lorry body and the pen were ventilation flaps. These could be fixed open to allow fresh air to enter the lorry body. One favourite thing to do, especially on the way home, was to put one's feet out through the ventilators, preferably without shoes on, to cool them down. However, on one fateful occasion, a person who shall remain nameless put his feet through the ventilators while wearing slip-on shoes – which resulted in one falling off. There was no way of getting Dave's attention, who, oblivious, carried on driving. Once we arrived back at the Tent Lodge the tale was told and the person concerned had to go home with only one shoe; the other was never retrieved.

"Our antics were fairly well known in the village, but in other areas we took advantage of our anonymity. It was possible to get one's head through the ventilators of the main lorry body and, when travelling further afield, cries of 'Help! Help!' could be heard coming from a head protruding from a cattle lorry, while contemporaries mooed and kicked the sides of the lorry from inside, imitating cattle. The looks on the faces of people as we passed by provided us with much entertainment."

More on marquees...

The larger marquees were made up in 20ft sections and the main poles were as thick as telegraph poles held up by thick guy ropes, with smaller poles round the outside (nowadays, marquees have aluminium frames that are fitted inside the tents). The marquees were made up by Amey of Canterbury, from whom Michael also remembers his grandfather buying great coils of rope. Frank would cut off required lengths of rope and skilfully make loops to be put over wooden knobs on the tops of the poles. He would bind the loops so that, as Michael explained, "they would take any amount of pulling". A major worry was rain, so getting the tension of the ropes correct was essential – if they got soaking wet they would tighten, and if they tightened too much they could snap and the marquee could collapse. Frank would therefore frequently revisit his tents once they were up, adjusting the tension of the ropes according to the weather, and if necessary, slackening them to avert disaster. He also listened regularly to the weather forecast to judge whether he needed to erect the tents a day earlier if it was going to rain. Thus the marquee business was far from trouble free.

Michael also described for us the rudimentary nature of the toilets that were supplied with the marquees. Essentially, these were dustbins painted green, with black Bakelite toilet seats. A good helping of Jeyes Fluid and a little water was poured into each to keep them as "sweet" as possible. The ladies' toilets consisted of a tent, 10ft x10ft, partitioned with canvas curtaining to give some degree of privacy. The gents' toilets were not in a tent but were surrounded by canvas curtaining. There were one or two "dustbin" toilets and a urinal built of bent galvanized steel sheet that drained into a channel and then into a pit, which was a temporary soakaway dug specially for the occasion. When the team tidied up on Sunday or Monday, the hole was simply filled in leaving everything just as it had been. Well, almost.

# RICHARD AND SUSAN PARKINSON'S POTTERY
# AT LODGE HOUSE, SMEETH

Ben Hay, Susan Parkinson's nephew, writes:

The Pottery at Lodge House operated from 1951 to 1961. It was the brainchild of Susan Parkinson (née Sanderson) and her husband Richard Parkinson. Susan had qualified as an Associate of the Royal College of Art in 1948. She had trained as a sculptress but in that year she also won the Academy's Drawing Prize. Her tutors encouraged her to enter for the Prix de Rome and study for another year. Instead she fell in love with the charismatic Richard, whom she married in 1949. Richard was practical and full of ideas and over the next year studied pottery and the technique of running a pottery business.

Susan Parkinson

In 1950 Susan's only sister's husband, Alick Hay, bought Lodge House and its surrounding land and buildings. Soon after he offered the Parkinsons the oast flat to live in and its ground floor and stables as a sculpting studio. Richard built Susan a coke-fired brick kiln in the oasthouse itself. These simple facilities allowed Susan to work on her sculpture. Gradually, orders and encouragement, increased. How were they to fulfill this promise? Could they really run a commercial business? Their answer was yes, but with months of trial and error to come.

Susan learnt to make moulds. They both learnt to slip cast, which meant devising a suitable clay mix. Not easy; there were then no proprietary mixes and those with knowledge guarded their secrets. In all it took years for the Parkinsons to perfect a porcelain mix (unfortunately hard to use and prone to process faults) and for Richard to design and build an oil-fired kiln capable of firing up to 1,400°C.

By the end of the Pottery's life, according to its last list, Susan had designed and produced a remarkable total of 157 elegant and witty pieces, large and small, usually decorated in her distinctive grey-blue and white colours. They included their first success, the Lion and Unicorn, made for the Festival of Britain and adapted for the Coronation; models of animals; decorative mugs and dishes; a set of figures of five famous actors and a fine small bust of Winston Churchill. Three of Susan's pieces are displayed in the Victoria and Albert Museum's ceramic collections under the Richard Parkinson Pottery name. Several local young people were trained by the Pottery, which in its heyday employed a staff of five. In the village it was known as The Crystal Palace, for its lights shone day and night.

As so often such high artistic achievement did not receive the reward that it merited. There was no shield against the arrows of misfortune which struck in 1960. Their keen young mould maker, Robert Hover, died tragically in a motorbike accident. Susan, already busy, had to take on his work. The business needed constant financial support. To earn more Richard took a two day a week job teaching at Hornsey School of Art in London. Susan was Hornsey's first choice, but they both judged her more vital to the daily life of the Pottery. At Hornsey Richard met and then left home for a lady who was to become his second wife. This was the final straw for the Pottery. Susan could not manage it without him and it had to cease production in 1961. Its products are now coveted by collectors.

Susan later described the essential design characteristics of her work as "enjoyment of the natural world in all its many aspects; enjoyment of discovering underlying order; and enjoyment of the absurd, principally human!" She said she felt lucky too "to have started the Pottery at a time of tremendous hope and optimism symbolised by the Festival of Britain".

If you would like to know more about The Parkinsons' Pottery, Ben Hay has kindly recommended the following book – if you can find a copy:

Susan Parkinson and the Richard Parkinson Pottery by Carol Cashmore and Tim Smith-Vincent (2004, published by Carol Cashmore and Tim Smith-Vincent, ISBN 0 9522812 4 4).

We are grateful to Ben Hay for his photographs of the different types of pottery produced by the Parkinsons, and also for the photograph of Susan Parkinson, courtesy of Keith Collie.

The lion and the unicorn

The piping ladies

Five theatrical figures (from left, Dame Margot Fonteyn, Sir Laurence Olivier, Paul Robeson, Sir John Gielgud and Vivien Leigh), made by the Pottery for Briglin Pottery, and ultimately owned by the actor Herbert Lom and his wife

Winston Churchill

# NED ANDREWS, THE COBBLER

Ned Andrews had a cobbler's workshop on Canterbury Road where Cobblers Oak now stands, and lived with his mother and brother, George, in what is now Sandhurst on Canterbury Road. Several people remember him as an excellent cobbler who worked in organised chaos. Shoes and boots were piled high in his workshop and Ned worked away at them, constantly smoking his pipe. Someone remarked that if you left your shoes there for a couple of months you would probably never find them again. Nevertheless, Rose Andrews (Smith) insisted that Ned was "a very good shoe repairer". In the shed where he worked, Ned had a machine with hard leather wheels and brushes. These were attached to a treadle which, when pressed, would cause the brushes and wheels to rotate. Children loved it and Margaret Pile (Ward) used to sit on a small chair just inside Ned's shop, hoping he would allow her to play with the machine. This was a real treat. Both Margaret and Robin Marsh recalled that Ned was "stepping out" with Daisy Washford for many years. We know from other sources that Ned was devoted to Daisy but in Margaret's words, "he left it so long that he died before they got married". Daisy lived just up the road in part of Peg Hill Cottages on Canterbury Road, which were then two dwellings, and the two of them used to go arm in arm to the Baptist Chapel on Sundays.

After the Andrews brothers died, Sandhurst was bought by Nancy and Bill Wilson. Occasionally, at 6.10pm, the back door would swing open gently and Nancy was convinced that it was Ned (or Ned's ghost) coming in. One evening, as she sat in the kitchen, the door opened as usual and she called out, "Come in, Ned." She looked up and there he stood, complete with apron. He quietly disappeared and the door never again swung open at 6.10pm. Nancy believed that he knew he was still welcome at his old home.

Robin Marsh remembered Ned and George Andrews being more or less self-sufficient. They grew almost everything they consumed, including their own tobacco, which George used to smoke. Robin's father once gave George Andrews half a pig to smoke in his chimney. This took several months but, in Robin's estimation, the ham and bacon that George produced were excellent and far, far better flavoured than the equivalent products today. Robin's father used to keep the ham and bacon in the cool cellar beneath Warren Bungalow and, to Robin's knowledge, it never went mouldy or bad.

## MILK SUPPLIERS

Percy Nickolls at Warren Farm had a milk round and Dick Andrews worked as his

roundsman for six years prior to the outbreak of the Second World War, when Dick joined the army. The milk was transported on a motorbike and sidecar, very carefully balanced. Dick would bring milk to a customer's gate with a measure in gills and pints and ladle the appropriate amount into the owner's jug. At that time Dick worked about a 50-hour week – to be precise, he worked 48 hours in the winter and 52 in the summer. He would start at 7am and deliver milk all morning. He then went back to the farm and washed up, cycled home to Stone Hill for lunch and back again to the farm in the afternoon. Milking would start at 3pm and, once that was over, he would carry out any chores that needed to be done.

Dick Andrews

Towards the end of the war, Claude Aldrich also had a milk round in partnership with Tom Jeanes, but in this enterprise milk was produced and bottled at Aldington and Claude would collect and distribute it. Many people remembered Claude's daughter Pat "coming round with the milk"; Pat Cornell (Thornby), who worked in Claude's office, would go round and collect the money from customers every Saturday afternoon. Margaret Pile (Ward) added that, towards the end of the war, "the milk rounds close to the village were delivered by horse and cart by Jean Smith and, later, Margaret Sawyer. Poor old Peg, the horse, would often wander up a bank and tip the bottles out of the cart. We loved to help but Mr Aldrich didn't approve!"

Margaret Baldock (Sawyer) started working for Claude after she left the North School and recalls that the last call on her milk round was on Woolpack Hill, to a house set above the road and reached by a flight of steps, later the home of Rose and Dick Andrews. While she went up the steps with the milk, the pony would wander off by herself and back to the Aldrich's, leaving Margaret to walk home – she seemed to know that Margaret had completed the milk round. Claude had an underground air-raid shelter just across the garden from Pat's office, which was a room in the house. If the sirens sounded on a Saturday afternoon they would all head for the shelter immediately, leaving the milk money on the table. According to Pat nobody ever touched it.

Sally Bulgin, Claude's granddaughter, who now lives just behind Holmleigh on

Canterbury Road (her grandparents' home), recalled hearing her grandfather say that, as soon as the sirens went, the dog was always the first one into the shelter. She added that the shelter is still in the garden and in good condition. Well constructed, it had electricity and even today is dry and shows no sign of damp.

Oliver Trowell recalls:

"Claude Aldrich's milk-retailing business covered East Brabourne at about the time the Smiths of Parsonage Farm sold up to Mr Hamilton. This was in 1956, bringing to an end the delivery of milk from that farm by bicycle or on foot. I recall Mrs Birchett asking Mr Aldrich what state he thought the milk would be in 'after he had swirled it round the country lanes'. Apparently it was none the worse for the swirling. Thus began the delivery of milk in milk bottles to East Brabourne. At first it was transported in a pre-war Ford 10 car, driven by Iris Jenner [daughter of the landlord of the Five Bells]."

THE MANY HATS OF CLAUDE ALDRICH
It would appear that Claude Aldrich was quite an entrepreneur, as he was mentioned by many of our contributors and, surprisingly, by people of significantly different ages. Prior to the 1930s he had a haulage business, which he sold to Gordon Fortescue's father. In the early 1930s he set up a bus service along the main road, had a coal-delivery business, had a business selling recycled wire mesh during and after the war, and had a milk-delivery business mentioned above. He also had "charas" (coaches) that he hired out.

A few weeks before she died in May 2011, Pat Cornell (Thornby) wrote:

"My father, Frank Thornby, worked for Claude Aldrich, first on his bus service along the main road, which he set up in the early 1930s. He then moved to a coal round, also for Claude. I remember this, as when it snowed it was nothing for my father to get in at 11 o'clock at night, having been stuck in snow on the hills. He would always try to deliver the coal, regardless of the weather.

"I started to work at Aldrich's when I left school aged 14, in 1943. At this time Aldrich sold big chain-link fencing all over the country. Mr Aldrich hired a lorry, would buy up all the old Anderson wire from the aerodromes and get German POWs whom he had been allocated to cut the wire up into the required lengths. They did this in a shed at the top of the Aldrich's drive. My job was to type all labels according to the orders, sort out where the netting had to go and confer with the station master at Smeeth Station so that the orders could be dispatched."

The wire mesh was much in demand by farmers for stock fencing at the time. During a conversation with Pat, she recalled that some of the German POWs were extremely pleasant people and one German at Hawkinge gave her a £5 note as a Christmas present. She saw this as "untold wealth from a very unexpected source!"

Pat continued:

"It was after the wire business came to an end that the milk business came into being. The dairy was in the building at the top of the Aldriches' drive on the left-hand side, and Barbara Sawyer washed the milk bottles and bottled the milk. Iris Jenner drove the car delivering the milk. I had to work on Saturday afternoons, checking all monies and getting them ready for the bank. When the air raids were on, Mr Aldrich was very nervous, so he would send me into Ashford on the bus with all the money and then he would telephone the bank to see if I had arrived safely!"

Will Wilson has fond memories of Claude's wife, Mil (Mildred), who in the 1960s would give him 10/- every weekend for cleaning her prized Morris 1100. This was an excellent rate compared with Will's paper round, which yielded only 7/6 a week for many hours of work.

## THE BAKERY AT STONE HILL

Mention of the bakery at Stone Hill reminded Pat Cornell (Thornby) and Margaret Pile (Ward) that they had heard that Johnnie Walker, who lived at the end of Canterbury Road, in Louvain, used to deliver bread on a donkey cart in about 1905. His oven was also used for communal baking, common in the past to reduce the risk of fire in people's homes. According to Margaret, the ovens were still in Louvain (now Hardwicke House) when Ben Hawkins moved there in the 1940s.

Margaret and Pat also remembered the time a doodlebug just missed the baker's in Southenay Lane, went down the slope and exploded. The plants were apparently so shocked by this that they came into bloom again and lilacs flowered in the autumn. This might have been the same bomb that, according to Betty Edenden, brought the ceiling down at Lady Errington's house.

# TRADITIONAL CRAFTSMEN

We must not omit the craftsmen who lived and worked locally, many of whom worked with wood. After the end of the First World War Joan Copland's father, Albert Dryland, took up fencing (Joan's grandfather was Richard). Sales of wood would take place at public houses and Albert would buy a cant, predominantly of chestnut, and take it back to his yard, which was where Katoomba now stands at the foot of Woolpack Hill. There he would cut it down and turn it into spiles, fence posts, scythe bats (handles) and broom handles. The spiles, which were foundation posts, and the fence posts were by far the most valuable products from the cant. Spiles were made by quartering a length of chestnut, perhaps 5ft long, from the base, where the pole was thickest.

Joan and Jock Copland

From further up the pole Albert was able to cut maybe four or five pointed fence posts, and still further up the pole, which grew increasingly thinner, he would cut as many scythe bats and broom handles as the length and width of the pole allowed. Thus, as much of each pole as possible was used. The cant would usually contain other types of wood as well, with ash being valuable for hay rake and broom handles. In fact, ash and hardwoods such as hornbeam were excellent for pit props, and Albert acquired the contract to supply pit props to Betteshanger, Chislet Colliery and all the coal mines in East Kent. Jock Copland, Joan's husband, noted that the pit props made were of different sizes in order to suit the varying needs of the different coal mines. Just as an aside, when the extent of the Kent Coalfield was being mapped prior to 1904, a bore was put down in Brabourne to a depth of over 2,000ft. On reaching older rocks at this depth it was decided that Brabourne was beyond the limits of the coalfield[6].

When the Second World War broke out, the government commissioned the production of poles that were to be put up in fields as a deterrent to troop-carrying gliders landing, and Albert Dryland, together with other local wood producers, capitalised on

6      Coal Mining in Kent (www.eastkent.freeuk.com/mining/index.htm; accessed 12th January, 2012).

this market. Oliver Trowell added that, "Many of these poles were willow and started sprouting leaves after a few weeks in the ground." He also recalled that, "the hourly rate paid to the men erecting the poles was higher than the current rate being paid to farm workers, causing bad feeling". Pickets were also planned for trenches that were to be dug for the war, and though many of these were produced, the trenches, mercifully, were never dug. After the war, demand for wood products continued and Albert's friend Mr Pullen, a builder who lived in Willesborough and who built houses in Hunter Avenue, Sprotlands Avenue and in other areas, gave Albert the contract to fence all these properties.

There was a considerable specialism in the uses of different types of wood. Hazel, with its flexibility, was often used to make hurdles, and Joan and Jock described how these were woven. Joan remembered Albert having a block of wood, rather like a sleeper, with holes drilled in it. He would place the uprights for the hurdle into these holes, usually four or five, each to a desired height of 3ft-5ft. Thinner lengths of hazel would then be woven through the uprights to produce the hurdle. After the hurdle was complete, the remaining twigs from the hazel branches were tied around a broom handle to make a besom broom which, Joan adds, was good for sweeping lawns. Virtually everything was used and there was little waste. All the tops of the trees were tied up and made into faggots that were used for lighting fires. Kiln owners were a significant market for faggots that consisted of residual branches of trees from the cant. These were "tied round with a wand of split hazel", according to Jock Copland, and were placed on the ground and haystacks constructed on top of them.

## FRANK TRICE, HURDLE MAKER

Described by two of our participants as "a man of the woods", Frank Trice the hurdle maker had been making hurdles since the reign of Queen Victoria . He made wattle hurdles, often known simply as "gates" in rural Kent, posts for fencing and other purposes, and a wide range of other wood products. Hurdles or gates of chestnut woven with hazel were made from wood that was cleft rather than sawn and, though there tended to be an average size for hurdles or gates, many of Frank's products were custom made. Jock Copland recalls that Frank used to make all the jumps for the point-to-point races at Aldington, usually from birch. Bryan Hodges describes the wood yard as full of fence posts and tubs of creosote, in which the posts stood. Bill Broughall, Joan Copland's half-brother, used to work for their father during the week but would work at Frank's wood yard at weekends. When Will Wilson was a young lad he too worked for Frank at weekends, "burning tops", that is, burning the tops of the chestnut branches that were not used. For a weekend's work of burning

Frank Trice, hurdle maker
(picture courtesy of Richard Filmer)

tops and doing other chores Will used to receive 3/-, barely a worthwhile wage in the late 1960s. When Will complained to his father about his derisory wages, he was told to keep quiet about it, as his father, Bill Wilson, and Keith Taylor used to transport chestnut from the woods to Frank's yard at weekends and the £5 he gave each of them for this was generous.

Will recalled that Frank[7] used to eat raw-onion sandwiches because he believed that "they kept him healthy". He always wore a cap, had allegedly smoked since he was four years old, and when they sat round the fire to eat bread and cheese he would light a roll-up and his nose would run through his ginger moustache on to the cigarette. Frank had a daughter, Miss Mabel, a large woman who died before him. His yard was just on the left as you turn into Calland – a new house stands there now.

## NELSON SMITH, ANOTHER HURDLE AND SPILE MAKER

Oliver Trowell writes:

"Nelson Smith and his father, who was known as 'Tiger' Smith, lived in the cottage east of the Zion Baptist Chapel in Canterbury Road, and for many years plied their craft of hurdle and spile making in their woodyard in the field opposite their dwelling. They also undertook the erection of farm fencing. I recall them putting up the fence surrounding Carola Cochrane's market garden at Court Lodge in East Brabourne, and also extensive fencing at Church Farm, soon after Lady Charnwood bought the farm from Horace Coleman in 1946, or thereabouts."

7    Source of image of Frank Trice, courtesy of Filmer R. (1981) Kentish Rural Crafts and Industries, Rainham: Meresborough Books.

## HEATHFIELD AND SPICER: WOOD TURNERS

Other local craftsman included the wood turners Heathfield and Spicer, whose production of rakes and scythe handles was crucial to the farming economy. As Rosemary Hendry (Ward) observed, "For many such craftsmen, their jobs were their hobbies and they would willingly put themselves out to help if someone wanted work done."

Heathfield and Spicer made hop scuppets, wooden rakes, large and small, hay sneaths (otherwise known as handles for scythes), sickles and any other wood products for which there was local demand. The firm thrived until 30 to 40 years ago, when such rural industries typical of a labour-intensive age began to dwindle.

For those too young to remember, a hop scuppet was essential in an oast house. When hops in the oast were considered to be dry, the furnace would be extinguished, and using a scuppet the hops would be removed from the kiln. The scuppet was thus a large shovel with a wooden frame and a hessian base.

This wood-turning business was started in 1875 by Albert Heathfield, one of Jane Barker's grandfathers, in the workshop not far from Smeeth Church, but on the opposite side of Church Road. Her other grandfather was John Spicer, and Jane (who was christened Janet but preferred Jane) explained how the two families came together to be united in Heathfield and Spicer.

The Spicer family came originally from Suffolk, where they worked with horses, and when eventually they moved to London Jack Spicer's father, John, took a job looking after the drays for the delivery department of Knowlman Bros, Drapers and Furnishers. Jane remembered the deep interest that John had in the horses which, when he was working in London, "won all sorts of brasses, consecutively, for about 11 years".

Jane Barker (Spicer)

Doris Heathfield, Albert's daughter, worked in the offices of Knowlman Bros department store. It was quite unusual for a young girl to go up to London to work in those days, but her mother was forward-thinking and wanted her children to experience a world beyond the village. Doris had been told about the job by Connie, a cousin who lived in London. She applied as soon as she

319

Images of Owen Heathfield (left) and Jack Spicer outside the Rake Shop
in Church Road, Smeeth

had left school, got the job, and became a boarder in the house that Jack's mother ran for girls who worked for the delivery department. Doris thus got to know Jack, but they did not marry for around 13 years and when they did, it was in Kent, as by that time Jack had grown to love life at Smeeth.

While Doris was in London she developed a patch on her lung and was sent home to Kent to recuperate. Jack went with her and, while in Kent, he also became seriously ill with peritonitis, so convalesced at the Heathfield family house in Church Road. As he recovered, he would walk up to the workshop every day, becoming ever more interested in the work done there. Jack had also worked as a toolmaker in London and he saw the possibilities for improving the workshop. He took the business over in the 1930s and, together with Owen Heathfield, his brother-in-law, ran it in partnership until the 1960s when they both retired. Thus Heathfield and Spicer became part of the fabric of the local community.

Demand for rakes and scythes was high before the 1960s, as these were the main means of cutting and clearing grass before mowers became the norm. Rakes and scythes were needed principally by the farming community, though Southern Rail was also a major customer. In the days of steam trains, fire was a hazard and all railway sidings had to be scythed and cleared with hay rakes for safety reasons. The Heathfields rented land from the Brabourne Estate for the wood-turning workshop on Church Road towards Brabourne Lees. They also rented the field beside The Chestnuts, where they bred "turkeys of good quality". Some of the turkeys were sold to local pubs such as The Woolpack, though the majority went to buyers further away

An advertisement for Heathfield Bros,
"Breeders of High-Class Turkeys"

and were sent live from Smeeth Station. Even today the field between the Ridgeway and the Chestnuts is known by many as "the turkey field".

Owen Heathfield in the Rake Shop
(picture courtesy of Richard Filmer)

The wood-turning business worked flat out over the winter, making wooden rakes of all sizes, sneaths and other goods that were needed largely in the summer. Chestnut was the main wood used, and poles cut from Hatch Wood and elsewhere were brought back to the workshop at Smeeth. Here, Jack and Owen[8] would use a draw blade along the pole to remove the bark and "knotty bits". The cleaned poles would then be steamed and straightened in a long, narrow metal container that contained a little water and beneath which was a small fire. Leverage was used in the straightening process. Jane remembers the mesmerising effect of the big round saw that ran off belts and the warmth of the workshop and boiler shed in winter. Jack and Owen used to keep a pile of bark shavings smouldering and this would keep the workers in the boiler shed warm all day. The workshop was also warm because of the constant steaming process. Labour demand was high and numerous people working on a part-time basis would come and go through the day, working for a few hours in the boiler shed or the workshop. Once the handle of a rake had been straightened, the head and the teeth had to be attached. As hundreds of rakes were produced in a year, so thousands of teeth were needed, so there was always a demand for labour to cut these teeth. Jane remembers sitting astride a seat in the boiler shed, in front of which was a cutter. A piece of wood would be hammered onto the cutter and one tooth would be made. When sufficient teeth had been accumulated, they would be cut to the same length and then hammered onto the rake. Bill Rolfe, who had been badly

8    Source of image of Owen Heathfield, Filmer R. (1981) Kentish Rural Crafts and Industries, Rainham: Meresborough Books.

injured in the Korean War (1950-53), used to be a regular worker in the boiler shed, as was Bill Jenner (retired landlord of the Five Bells at East Brabourne), who always wore a brown overall jacket. Bryan Hodges worked there after he had left school, and even Gwen Bishopp would come on her bike from Kennington to work there part-time. Winter was not the only time of intense work, though: during the summer months Jane also remembers her father and Owen starting work early, coming home for lunch, returning again for bread, cheese and tea at tea time, and then going back to the workshop until around 9pm.

A note from Jack's order book from July (no year given) confirms that business was booming:

"3rd July Plimpton & Co. (London) – 6 doz sneaths
George (London) – 5 doz 14 tooth rakes
12th – 6 doz each – 12 tooth, 15 tooth and 17 tooth rakes
21st – George (London) - 12 doz 12 tooth rakes
Dixons of Ashford 23 rakes – 15 tooth
The largest order on one day was to Plimpton & Co: 50 doz. 15 tooth and 50 doz. 17 tooth rakes. [This makes a total of 1,200 rakes]"

Heathfield and Spicer's workshop,
by Michael Giles

At the back of the workshop was a blacksmith, George Davis. He made the scythes, sickles and hoes to go on the handles produced by Spicer and Heathfield. He even shod horses, and one of the delights for children in the late 1940s and 1950s was to watch George shoeing horses, mainly hunters and the occasional pony. Jane recalled that business simply found its way to Heathfield and Spicer. They had no phone and did no advertising, but they were never short of work. When work had been completed, a cardboard sign was put up outside the workshop and, seeing this, the Southern Rail lorry would collect the rakes and other goods and take them to Ashford, from where they would be dispatched to their destination. As Jane reflected, "It was all so simple and unfussed!"

The wood-turning business was a thriving concern but, although there were seven Heathfields in Doris Spicer's generation, sadly there were no family members left to carry on the business after Owen, Doris's brother, retired. He was the last Heathfield to work in the business. There were no Heathfield sons from Owen's generation, and when Owen's only daughter died Jane lamented that "there was not a Heathfield left".

After Jack and Owen retired, the firm was bought by Trevor Austen, who had worked with them for some years. His father had come to the area as a charcoal burner for the Mersham Hatch Estate and he used to make charcoal from the pollarded branches of trees in the small area of woodland above the lake. By the time Trevor took the business over it was clear that demand was declining for traditional products such as those made by the firm. Nevertheless, Jane recalled that he did well selling his merchandise – he used to go to the Kent Show, the show at Ardingly in Sussex, and he even found markets in America. One of the items that was particularly marketable there was a small rake designed by Jack to be used with a sickle. But this recovery was short lived and the wood-turning machinery, part of local industrial heritage, remained silent for years. Trevor retired in 2009 and died early in 2011 after a long illness. The workshop became increasingly dilapidated and was demolished in 2012.

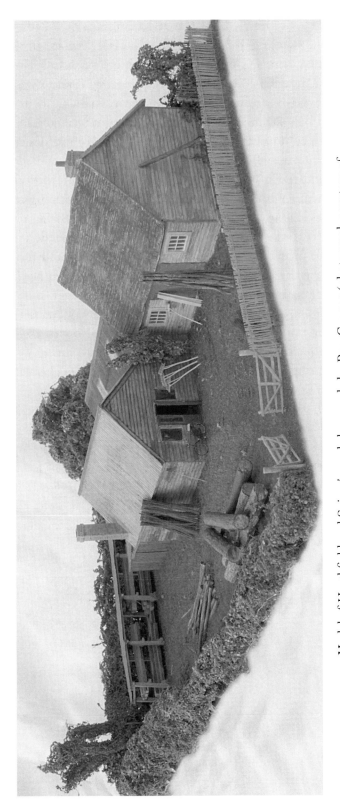

Model of Heathfield and Spicer's workshop made by Ron Cooper (photograph courtesy of Graham Cooper). This exquisite model is of particular value to village history as the workshop was demolished in 2012

## THE KILN

Leaving Brabourne Lees via Canterbury Road, we approach East Brabourne and pass the kiln, which in the 1920s and 1930s was owned by Joan Copland's grandfather, Richard Dryland, who later sold it to Walter Andrews. In Richard's days, one of the kiln workers was Tom Brooks; this was before Tom bought farmland in West Brabourne, which later developed into Running Water Farm. Clay for the kiln came from behind Mill House on Canterbury Road, and bricks and tiles individually moulded here were of high quality and much in demand throughout Kent and beyond. Joan tells of a time when her father was a young lad, probably in the first decade of the 20th century. He would load up the horse and cart with bricks and tiles to take them down to customers in Rye, or to send them further afield from Smeeth Station. Floor tiles, Kent peg tiles, tiles for the eaves of buildings, ridge tiles and more specialist tiles were all produced at the kiln and, according to Jock Copland, among these were tiles known as mathematical tiles which, when hung, fitted together somewhat like a jigsaw and looked like brick. It is thought that these may have been used on Canterbury Cathedral. In addition to running the kiln, Richard also ran a sort of village taxi service between the end of the First World War and into the 1930s. He would take people to Smeeth station in his pony and trap and also meet people off the train and take them to their destination.

The kiln on Canterbury Road
(picture courtesy of Richard Filmer)

The kiln on Canterbury Road was not the only one in the locality. According to Jock and Joan Copland, there was a second one virtually opposite what was then Fortescue's builder's yard, near the junction of Canterbury Road with Plain Road. The clay for this kiln is believed to have come from near Bog Farm. It should be added here that Kent was renowned for its tiles and bricks because of the suitability and relative abundance of Kentish clays.

The brick and tile makers at Andrews' kiln (late 19th century/early 20th century), each with brick- and tile-making tools. Tom Brooks, aka Grandfather Brooks, sits on the far right, with George Washford behind him, and possibly Stevie Washford, George's brother, second from left, front row.
(Picture courtesy of Richard Filmer)

As mentioned, the kiln on Canterbury Road was later run by Walter Andrews and continued producing tiles with the characteristic "ANDREWS" stamp on them well into the 1950s. Clay was mined locally from what is now the pond near the old kiln and, according to Karl Engels, possibly from Hospital Field among other local sites. The kiln has close links with East Brabourne, as after Walter died his daughter, Cecilia Seguin Andrews (known as Gwinnie), who married Sidney Finn, inherited it. Gwinnie and Sidney lived at Ivy Cottage beside the Five Bells in East Brabourne; thus the kiln forms part of the history of both Brabourne Lees and East Brabourne. Rosemary Hendry (Ward) remembers calling in at the kiln in the winter to warm herself on her way home from Brabourne School and to watch the men making tiles. Several other children mentioned "calling in at the kiln", including David Orpin, as he was walked home from school by Joyce Garlick (Wood), who worked for his parents. Some remember being allowed to leave a potato in the hot ashes to bake on the way to Brabourne School and eating it on their way home.

Everyone who mentioned the kiln loved going there as children. However, Keith Finn, Sidney's nephew, did not remember Gwinnie with much affection, describing her as "stuck up and disagreeable", someone who "disliked children and barred them from the premises". As Sidney was his uncle, Keith felt particularly incensed about this, but we do have to ask whether the number of children calling at the kiln might have irritated Gwinnie who, in the diaries of Cranleigh Barton (extracts from which appear later), seemed to be a perfectly affable person. Other children visiting the kiln didn't seem to remember much about Gwinnie, though their reflections on Sidney were more than generous. Several people spoke of him endearingly, and one described him as a "true gentleman".

We have come across a picture thought to be of people digging clay for brick and tile kilns. Jock Copland recalls that, after Sidney and Gwinnie Finn sold the kiln, it was bought by people in Ashford and each day workers would cycle out from the Beaver Road area of Ashford to dig clay in the Brabourne area. Even though we cannot locate the picture, the process of clay digging is in itself historically interesting.

Clay digging (1930s or early 1940s)

## PRIVATE AND PUBLIC TRANSPORT

George Brooks explained that, in the 1920s, Brabourne was almost totally isolated, except for very limited bus services to Hythe and Ashford, and Burdell's "chara" from Hythe that would come up by Horton Park gate, through Stanford, and turn off through Stowting and then go on to Brabourne Street. By the mid-1930s there were more bus trips out of the village, but the villages were still fairly cut off and, as most needs could be met locally, a trip into Ashford was still a rare event. Things started to change in the late 1960s and into the 1970s, by which time many more people worked in Ashford. Cars were becoming more numerous and, in 1978, the bus from East Brabourne to Ashford ceased to run. This change passed unnoticed by many, but was a tragedy for some, such as Mrs Spain, Nell and Dorothy Hills and the Princess Cantacuzino, none of whom owned a car and so relied on public transport.

East Kent bus (1934), known as the "little pig"

By the 1930s most people had bicycles, but very few had cars, and buses became increasingly important for getting to Hythe, Ashford or any other destination. In addition to carrying people, buses helped considerably with transporting goods. For instance, Jim Hendry, who was a local bus driver, recalled that before the war buses would take parcels left at Ward's Garage and deliver parcels from Ashford anywhere along the route. Sometimes even bicycles were taken by bus, as they would fit in the back. However, transport of goods and people was a growth area long before the war: Claude Aldrich set up a bus service in Brabourne and this was complemented by two other bus services, Wanstall's and Newman's. Claude's buses used to be kept at the garage beside the Aldriches' house, Holmleigh, on Canterbury Road; later the garage was used by Pat Browne for Brown's[9] coaches. Eventually, Claude was bought out by East Kent buses.

---

9     Coaches were all signed Brown's, with no e.

Oliver Trowell recalls that, when his family came to live in East Brabourne in 1934, "there was an excellent East Kent bus service – service 109 – between Ashford and Hythe via the Blacksmith's Arms, Mersham Turning, The Ridgeway, The Woolpack, Ward's Garage, the village hall, the Five Bells, the Anchor (now The Tiger, Stowting), Horton Corner, Stanford, Westenhanger, Newingreen, Pedlindge and down Hythe Hill to Red Lion Square,

Oliver Trowell

where the bus turned ready to return to Ashford by the same route, departing from the bus stop by Blackman's Fish Shop".

Oliver's excellent memory for detail also tells us that, "The first bus of the day from Brabourne to Ashford, having arrived at the Five Bells from Ashford bus station, left at 8.25 and arrived at the bus station in Station Road 30 minutes later." This was the bus that Vi Varrier and other children would have taken to get to school in Ashford. "Following on, there was a bus to take you from East Brabourne, either to Ashford or to Hythe, about every hour of the day until the last bus of the day arrived from Ashford at 10.20pm. This service continued right through the war years and on into the 1950s and 1960s."

Karl Engels remembers a day when the school bus crashed:

"The school bus of the East Kent Road Car Co took the secondary-school children

Karl Engels

from the Five Bells to Ashford schools at about 8.20am, and came back at about 5pm. In the 1940s, the bus was very old, heavy and tall for a single decker. As it was coming down Brabourne Lees and was about halfway between Ames' Stores and Bircholt Mission Hall, it started to run over the edge of the road and a 3ft drop into the field at this point prevented the driver from pulling it back on to the road. As it went into the field it took the hedge with it and collected the lower half of an electric pole, which snapped in the middle, the upper part remaining suspended and dangling from the wires above. This brought the bus to a stop and, as it came to rest in the field, it rolled onto its side. I was in the garden at home, at The Knoll, and think I can remember hearing the cries of the children as the bus went over. I wanted to go straight to the accident but my father forbade it and went alone. I waited at the front gate and as they started to walk past I was looking for injuries but there were no slings, splints or even sticking plaster on view. There was no relief bus for crashes in those days, no police presence, and fortunately no need [for this incident] as no children had been hurt. Very few people seem to remember this event. John Hammon is one who does but I wonder whether anyone reading this remembers the accident, or was involved in it."

Years later, in the 1960s, Michael Hickmott also used to catch the 109 bus from the village hall to Ashford Grammar School, now the Norton Knatchbull Grammar School, when there were too many school children to all go on the contract hire buses. Children from as far away as Stowting and Elmsted were collected by minibus and dropped at the Five Bells in East Brabourne to catch a contract bus. If the minibus was late and missed the connection with the contract bus, the 109 would wait until the minibus arrived and it would take the children to Ashford. Similarly, if the same children were late leaving school, they would be given a "pass" to return home on the 109, though this would only get them to the Five Bells. They would have to find their own way from there.

Katrina Bewick (Stone) also shared her own recollections of the 109 bus service. On a snowy day in the winter of 1977 Katrina, aged about 14, was at home in The Street in East Brabourne, waiting for the 109 East Kent bus, for which local school children had season tickets. Several residents of school age in The Street used to watch for the arrival of the bus from the backs of the cottages in The Street, as at that time you could see across the fields to Manor Pound, a distance of almost a mile by road. You could watch the bus reach the top of Manor Pound, turn the corner onto Canterbury Road and head towards East Brabourne. Once they knew the

Katrina Bewick

bus was approaching, school-goers would wend their way to the Five Bells, where the bus stopped. On this particular day Katrina remembers watching the bus travelling cautiously up through the snow towards the top of Manor Pound, and then... sliding off the road into the field. Inevitably, the bus never arrived at the Five Bells, so several students, including Katrina, walked to the Smeeth crossroads and caught the number

10 bus to Ashford. However, after arriving at school they were told to go home as it had been closed because of the weather. Some 30-plus years later communications have undoubtedly improved, as a recent newsletter from Brabourne School advised that in the event of the school closing due to bad weather parents would be sent a text message to let them know what was happening.

Jim Hendry was a bus driver on the service to Hythe and remembered very well the 7.15pm journey from Ashford to Hythe. The bus would leave Ashford packed, with standing room only, and on its way via the Ridgeway, Ward's Garage, East Brabourne, Stowting, Monks Horton, Stanford, Newingreen and Hythe would drop people (mainly men in those days) at the pubs along the way. The return journey, leaving Hythe at about 10pm, would collect many of the same men from the pubs and take them back to Ashford. After reaching Ashford, Jim would then cycle home to Brabourne Lees. Rosemary Hendry, his wife, recalled that he did this for five years, but then graduated to a motorbike, which he had for six years; finally, he bought a car from Caffyns.

Jim Hendry

Bryan Hodges and his friends used to go to the pictures on a Saturday in Ashford, when the cinema was where B&Q used to be, near Ashford station, and as the last bus home was at 10pm they would see the film twice, have sausage, eggs, beans and chips in Barton's fish and chip shop in Station Road, and get the last bus home. According to Bryan, "You could go out with a pound and come back with change! This was 1955-57."

At one time, Jim also used to drive one of the school buses and Bryan remembers being thrown off the bus, together with others, by Jim at the bottom of Hatch Hill on the way home from school because of bad behaviour. Jim confirmed that he would not tolerate such behaviour on the bus and when he was a conductor, before he became a driver, had no qualms about putting disobedient children off the bus. Jim also substantiated Bryan's story that, when he was the bus driver and there was bad behaviour on the bus to the North School, Jim would not let the pupils off the bus when they arrived at the school until the headmaster came out and took charge of his pupils.

## HAULIERS

Haulage was important in a rural community, providing both transport and local employment. Claude Aldrich had cattle lorries, which he used to keep in the garage beside Holmleigh. He employed Charlie Taylor and Frank Thornby to drive for him until they bought their own lorries. As we have read, Dave Dodd was yet another with a cattle lorry, who also helped Frank Howland with his marquee business. Later, Mr Jordan, a general haulier, used to employ local people to drive for him, as did Charlie Taylor when he started his own business in 1966/68. This was later taken over by his son Keith, who in turn passed the business on to his son, Kevan. This brings us up to the present, as Kevan is currently a farmer and a haulage contractor running tipper lorries and cattle lorries. Bryan Hodges recalls that the Bartons also used to have a cattle truck, as did Aaron Shorter, who is remembered for, among other things, wearing "milk-bottle glasses". However, Aaron's truck was not used solely for the transport of animals as he "moved" Millie Hodges from Newington to Mersham.

## THE CARRIERS

In the early decades of the 20th century, a carrier from Stowting named George Cheeseman would come to East Brabourne with his covered horse-drawn van to collect goods that people might want to take to Ashford, for example, a few chickens for sale at Ashford Market, WI produce to be delivered to the WI stall at the market, and so on. In this way, the transport of goods on a fairly small scale was facilitated. Years ago, Nurse Dorothy Hills and her sister Nell would talk of going to Ashford for a day in the carrier's van, and John Varrier remembers his mother, who was a friend of Nell and Dorothy's, recollecting similar journeys with the carrier. Very frequently they would be transported in one direction, usually to Ashford, and have to walk home; this would have been in the 1920s and 1930s. On one occasion, during the 1940s, George was asked to collect a calf from Ashford Market on his way home. He may have had a pint or so during the day and, on arrival back in Brabourne to deliver the calf, he realised that it was not in his van. Oliver Trowell remembers going with Mr Coleman in Mr Cowley Miller's open tourer car to Ashford Market, where they found the calf quite forlorn and all alone. With the aid of ropes they brought it safely back to Church Farm. Mr Miller then lived at Court Lodge. Oliver provides more personal detail on this incident later in the book.

Later, in the 1940s, one of the carriers was Jack Cheeseman (no relation of George), who by all accounts was quite a character. His family had a farm on the land behind Plain Road, which extended very approximately from the white house opposite John

Childs' Garage down to Bog Farm, where the Cheesemans used to keep pigs, cows and sheep. People remembered him collecting leftover food from institutions and restaurants in Ashford that he then fed to his pigs. Brenda Streeter recalled that "when Jack used to drive his animals up the road, you had to break all speed records to shut the gate to stop them getting into the garden". In those days Calland housing estate had not been built and Brenda remembers there being a small farm where you could pick your own fruit on the land where the estate now stands. Oliver Trowell recalled that Jack's normal means of transport was a pony and trap, which he drove at great speed through the lanes.

The Carrier's Van outside the Blue Anchor

The Cheesemans were thought to be fairly well-to-do, as Jack was educated at a private school in Ashford, which was quite unusual in the 1920s. As an adult he is remembered as being a socially confident man, especially with women. He often used to wear a long black coat and white silk scarf and, according to Joan Copland, always used to talk out of the corner of his mouth. He never married, though he did live for many years with Phoebe, who came to the village with a travelling funfair probably in the late 1940s or the early 1950s. They lived in one of the pair of cottages at the top of School Lane in East Brabourne, the one nearest Brabourne Lees, and as someone put it, "she kept him on the straight and narrow". Jack allegedly split up with Phoebe before he died, but he is remembered warmly as a village character who spent a great deal of his time at The Anchor and The Woolpack.

According to Jock Copland, part of the Cheesemans' land was left to charity and, ultimately, this land was used for building part of Calland.

# PROSPECT FARM AND THE DOCTOR'S HOUSE

Prospect Farm House was the home of Fred Willett and his family from 1965 until 2001 but in the second half of the 19th century, and until 1919, it was occupied by a series of doctors who both lived and practised there. Thanks to Fred's research, we have the following account of both the farm and the farmhouse:

"The 113 acres that eventually became Prospect Farm were occupied by the government in the earliest years of the 19th century. What were known officially as 'Brabourne Lees Barracks' and a nine-ward army hospital were built and, by the end of 1803, were occupied by three regiments of infantry and two regiments of cavalry.

"In 1815 Napoleon was defeated at Waterloo, and, by 1816, the barracks were closed. On 22nd July, 1816, and the succeeding five days there was a public auction on the site of 'small lots' – ranging from officers' and soldiers' barracks, storehouses, three 'blackholes' (evidently the gaol), the 'deadhouse'

Fred Willett

(mortuary), down to sentry boxes (which fetched 36 shillings each) and thousands of birch brooms. According to a letter from the vicar of Brabourne to the Archbishop at the time, the buildings were 'instantly taken down after the public auction and removed'.

"On 15th May, 1822, Royal Assent was given to, 'An ACT for inclosing lands in the parishes of Brabourne, Smeeth, Bircholt and Sellindge, certain Heaths, or Commons, and Waste Grounds, called Brabourne Lees, and Stonehill, Smeeth-hoth and Mersham-hoth, containing altogether, by Estimation, Three Hundred Acres or thereabouts;

"'And whereas Sir Edward Knatchbull, Baronet, is Lord of the several Manors of Brabourne, Evegate otherwise Theavegate, and Hall, and, as such, is entitled to the Soil of the Heaths, Commons and Waste Grounds, within the said Manors respectively;

"'And whereas the said Heaths or Commons, and Waste Grounds, yield but little Profit, and are, in their present state, incapable of any considerable Improvement, and it would be very beneficial to the several Persons interested therein, allotted to and amongst them, according to their respective Estates, Rights and Interests.'

"The Inclosure Act went on to appoint commissioners to value, divide, allot and 'inclose' the said heaths, commons and waste grounds. The 'inclose' itself took place in 1824, and from that date Sir Edward Knatchbull and his successors (Knatchbull is still the family name of the modern Lords Brabourne) had undisputed freehold to the land that eventually became Prospect Farm. The 113 acres were occupied and farmed, however, by a variety of tenants of Sire Edward and his successors until the land was put up for auction in 1919 by the fourth Baron Brabourne as a single entity, and conveyed freehold to Thomas Pilcher Jnr, who occupied the house with his family and farmed all land."

PROSPECT FARM HOUSE

Fred's research continues:

"From the second half of the 19th century until 1919, Prospect Farm House, Brabourne Lees, was occupied by a succession of doctors who served Brabourne Lees and Smeeth as the village GP and as 'District Medical Officer and Public Vaccinator'. They were all lessees of Lord Brabourne until he sold the house and surrounding land as a farm.

Prospect Farm House in 1905. Mary Smith (in the dark skirt), wife of Dr William Smith, can be seen sitting with her sister and brother, who were visiting her at Prospect. At the window downstairs on the left is Kate, the cook

Doctors known to have lived at Prospect are:

Dr Alfred Charlton (period unknown, but identified as resident in 1881 and 1882)

Dr Lionel Mason Snow (again period unknown, but identified as resident in 1891 and 1895)

Dr Hubert Stanley (1897-1902)

Dr William Smith (1902-1908)

Dr Joseph Marcus Garman (1908-1919, but after he moved to Sellindge he retained a surgery for several more years in the outbuildings at Prospect)

"In 1908 Dr Garman bought the practice from a Dr William Smith, and brought his bride, Malvina, to the house. By the time the Garmans left the house in 1919 they had seven children; after moving their home and principal surgery to Sellindge they had three more children. The sixth of the children born in Prospect Farm House, who became Father Anthony Garman, a Roman Catholic priest in Cape Town, visited Prospect on holidays in the 1970s and in 1985.

From Fred's notes: Mrs Malvina Garman, resplendent in her hat, ready in the yard at Prospect for an outing in her husband's brand-new car, which the RAC identifies as a 1909 Rover 6hp (it is the de luxe model because it has a windscreen and a hood). At the wheel is Dr Garman's chauffeur/handyman, Arthur Conley, who then lived at Southside, Lees Road

"Dr Garman owned the first car in Brabourne[10]; Father Anthony has kindly supplied a photograph of the car and his mother in 1909, in the yard outside the stable.

"Prospect House and grounds then occupied three acres, including a tennis court, on part of what became Prospect Way. Dr Garman paid Lord Brabourne an annual rent of £39 10s.

---

10      As explained earlier, that Dr Garman owned the first car in the village has been contested. He almost certainly owned one of the first cars, if not the first.

"Although Dr Garman and his family left Prospect House in 1919, he maintained his work at Brabourne and, by arrangement with Tom Pilcher Jnr, retained the use of the surgery outhouse at Prospect for a number of years. Thus, Prospect remained 'the doctor's place' until, it is believed, the late 1920s. [NB Brabourne remained an active part of the Sellindge practice. After Dr Garman retired in 1948 the entire practice was taken over by Dr Desmond Fitzgerald, who lived in retirement at Lees House, Brabourne Lees, until his death in January, 2001. The practice was then taken over by Dr Richard Morey, who after several years closed the Brabourne surgery in the late 1980s/early 1990s, then held at the Brabourne Baptist Church in Plain Road, and concentrated the practice at Sellindge.]

"Prospect House, along with 113 acres, was sold in an auction in 1918, in which the fourth Baron Brabourne sold off much of the Mersham-le-Hatch estate. The family had suffered financially as a result of the deaths in the First World War of younger Lords Brabourne. The conveyance to Tom Pilcher Jnr, however, was not until October 1919 – the gap of a year was, presumably, to allow notice to Lord Brabourne's tenants.

"It was during Mr Pilcher's occupation that mains water was first laid on to the house in 1928, although the well in the front garden, along with others in the village, was restored in 1940 by local builder Oswald Ames as a precaution against enemy action destroying the mains in the Second World War. It was also Mr Pilcher who installed the first indoor lavatory (upstairs) and the first bathroom; the doctors and their families had only a tin tub and an outside lavatory. [Fred noted that mains drainage was installed in about 1968; until then there had been a cesspit in what is now Prospect Way.]

"Prospect Farm subsequently had several owners, but it wasn't until November 1964 that, for the first time, Prospect Farm House was put up for sale separately from the farmland. The house, gardens and outbuildings (including the surgery block) – in all, about two-fifths of an acre – were legally conveyed to Frederick Ambrose Willett in February 1965, although he did occupy it from 5th January, 1965."

In 1986, a little over 20 years later, the Willetts purchased a small strip of land when the retirement bungalows were being built next door to Prospect Farm House. In 2000 the block of outbuildings made up of the former surgery, tack room and stable, by then derelict, were demolished to make way for the building of a new dwelling, Yard House. Fred and his wife Dorothy moved into Yard House in 2001 and Prospect Farm House was sold to John Browning, a builder, and his family.

The Willett family at Prospect Farm House:
back row, from left, Fred, Dorothy, Daniel, Sally and Toby;
front row, from left, Polly (Sally's daughter), Leon (Toby's son) and
Roland (Sally's son)

Sally Furneaux (Willett), Fred's daughter, remembers moving from the comfort of a modern centrally heated house in Horsham, Sussex, to the ancient, cold Prospect Farm House, where dependence on the Aga for all sources of heat was a new experience for the entire family. She frequently wondered why her parents had chosen to move there but, on reflection some time after they had died, it did seem that the name may have had something to do with it, as Fred met Dorothy at the Prospect of Whitby pub in the East End of London when he was a journalist and she a nurse. Sally recalls that, when they moved to Prospect, they inherited numerous farm cats. Charlie Wratten, who lived next to The Plough, used to feed the chickens at the farm and, on more than one occasion, announced to the family that one of the cats had had a litter of kittens. The following day he would simply say that he had drowned them all. Though perfectly practical, this is one of Sally's most powerful memories of their earliest days at Prospect, and she can still remember seeing the amazement and horror on her brother's face each time Charlie made this announcement.

## AN ERA OF CHANGE

Brabourne Lees and Smeeth have seen considerable change within living memory, as indeed have all the villages. Improved technology and transport have reduced rural isolation and brought the rural and urban domains closer together. New residents in the villages "are breathing new life into them", in the words of one of our contributors. Though communities may not be as close-knit as in the past, newcomers (i.e. those who have arrived within the past 50 years!) are not necessarily any less committed to village life. For many, however, particularly younger people, links outside the village are now as numerous, if not more so, than those within the village, so the ties within the village community could be perceived as being weaker than they were a century ago. Should we lament this change? In many ways definitely not, for without the population of Knatchbull Way, Prospect Way, Mountbatten Way and other new developments the remaining shops and services could not survive. In other ways some of the changes are lamentable, as the nature of the attachment of today's rural dwellers to the countryside is very different from that of their predecessors. Few under the age of 60 in Brabourne can claim a knowledge and understanding of the environment equal to that of people such as George Brooks, Norman Thornby, Oliver Trowell and others of similar vintage. Not only did they work on the land, but their childhood years bound them closely to the countryside. It is indeed regrettable that skills and knowledge relating to the environment have been lost over time but perhaps there are compensations: life was physically hard for much of the population in the past, even half a century ago, and few people had the opportunities available to our children today, though we have often heard that there were other advantages to living in days past. One of the main changes brought to our attention time and again has been that children now have much less liberty, in the physical sense, than children did some 50, or even 30, years ago, and many of our contributors considered the loss of this liberty to be one of the very worst features of modern life.

# BRABOURNE CHURCH OF ENGLAND PRIMARY SCHOOL

## A SCHOOL FOR BRABOURNE

Shortly after entering the village marked as Brabourne, but more commonly referred to as East Brabourne, we turn down School Lane, which is not marked as such. Here, just on the outskirts of the village, is Brabourne Church of England Primary School, a thriving school with just over 100 pupils. In its beautiful setting the appearance of the school building immediately reflects its associations with the past, but at the same time more modern extensions suggest that it has been updated for education in the 21st century. In 1845 land for the school was donated by Sir Edward Knatchbull to the then vicar of Brabourne, the Reverend Amos Hayton, and the churchwardens James Weekes and Philip Gotts, "to be applied for a Site for a School for poor persons of and in the said Parish of Brabourne". The "ownership" of this land was to be passed on to their successors in Brabourne Church. The school was located where it could be reached fairly easily from East and West Brabourne, Brabourne Lees and Smeeth, and was also within walking distance of Monks Horton and Stowting. It was built in 1846 and Lady Brabourne still has a silver trowel that was used for laying the foundation stone. The school's first headmaster was Frederick Lyne, and he and his wife, Louisa, are listed as living at the school. Pupils were being enrolled by 1850.

In the 19th century, the Anglican Church played a leading role in educating the poor, and as Brabourne was said to be one of the "most degraded parishes in the country" it was considered a suitable location for one of many schools established under the auspices of The National Society[1] for Promoting Religious Education. As a consequence it was called the Brabourne National School in its early years.

---

1      The National Society's History (www.natsoc200.org.uk/celebrate/the-national-societys-history; accessed 14th January, 2012).

Brabourne School, c1900

Brabourne School, 2013.
Although Brabourne is now a modern school,
the original frontage has been conserved
(picture courtesy of Katrina Devenport)

The National Society has an interesting history: founded in 1811, it became the main provider of education in England and Wales, with a particular focus on the poor. It aimed to provide a school run by a trained teacher in every parish, and one of its stated educational purposes was that, "the National Religion should be made the foundation of National Education, and should be the first and chief thing taught to the poor…" National Schools received support from The National Society in the form of grants, and also benefited from schoolbooks published by the Society, from teachers trained by the Society and from voluntary support. School sites were largely donated by local patrons, as was the case in Brabourne; the local vicar and churchwardens were made trustees and the schools were managed voluntarily by foundation managers, usually locally respected people, all with strong links to the Church. The link with the past is retained as there are still two dedicated places for Foundation Governors on the current governing body of the school, both of whom have clearly defined links with St Mary's Brabourne. (The same is true of all church schools).

## THE ANGLICAN CHURCH AND THE STATE IN THE DEVELOPMENT OF EDUCATION

Through its National Schools the Anglican Church contributed much to the development of education in England and Wales, especially the teaching of the Christian religion and the three Rs. Five thousand Church of England and Church in Wales schools educated almost one million children and young people in the mid-19th century, but not everyone was happy with the power that this gave the Church. The Education Act of 1870 saw the establishment of elementary schools across the country, which were non-denominational and, like church schools, these were also committed to bringing education to the poor. The Act did not replace schools already in existence but allowed for a dual system: voluntary denominational schools, such as Brabourne, were allowed to continue alongside the new non-denominational state schools, which, at their inception, were part-funded by the state. It is worth mentioning that, in 1870, most education in England and Wales was neither free nor compulsory; it was not until a decade later that education became compulsory for all 5- to 10-year-olds, and in 1891 it became free, with even voluntary denominational schools being subsidised by the state to enable this. The introduction of state schools effectively weakened the role of the Church in education: many state schools were newly built for purpose, with better resources and higher numbers of trained teachers. These schools thus became increasingly popular, attracting children (or rather, the parents of children) to the state sector – and away from voluntary schools. It seems likely that Smeeth School was one of the new state schools and attracted Mr Wetherell, one of Brabourne's headmasters, to Smeeth.

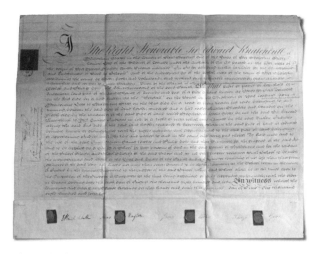

The Trust Deed in which Sir Edward Knatchbull in 1845 donated the land on which the school now stands to the then vicar of Brabourne, the Rev Amos Hayton, and churchwardens James Weekes and Philip Gotts for the sole purpose of building a school for "poor persons" in the parish. The "ownership" of this land was to be passed on to their successors in Brabourne Church (details of the Trust Deed on opposite page)

This dual system of schools continued, with the state subsequently playing a larger role in the management and curriculum development of voluntary schools. Thus the standard of education across all schools improved. The Education Act of 1944 saw increased focus on standards in education, and the teaching of religion was further marginalised when voluntary schools had to decide whether they would become voluntary controlled schools, in other words handing over their management to the state, or voluntary aided schools, where the foundation managers funded the maintenance of the buildings (among other things). It seems that Brabourne opted to become the former at the start of the 1952 academic year, a status it has retained, and although we now have a national curriculum, Brabourne, like other voluntary schools that grew out of National Schools, has been allowed to retain its Christian ethos and strong links with the Anglican Church.

## MANAGING BRABOURNE NATIONAL SCHOOL

Education in its early days depended heavily on voluntary support, and the finances of Brabourne National School depended on contributions from a group of "subscribers", generally the wealthier people in the area who were willing to help educate poorer members of society. The Trust Deed of 1845 (pictured above, with its translation opposite) tells us that the school was "to be under the management and control of the Vicar and Curate of the Parish, and a committee consisting of not less than three persons, exclusive of the said Vicar and Curate, nor more than seven persons to be elected annually in the School Room in the month of August by the annual subscribers... " This committee of managers was effectively the governing

Trust Deed (translation taken from Brabourne School archive)

I, the right Honourable Sir Edward Knatchbull of Mersham Hatch in the County of Kent, Baronet, one of the Lords of Her Majesty's Privy Council, Lord of the Manor of Coombe, under the authority of an Act passed in the fifth year of the reign of Her Present Majesty Queen Victoria entitled 'An Act for affording further facilities for the Conveyance and Endowment of Sites for Schools' and of the subsequent Act of the eighth year of the reign of Her Majesty, explaining the same, do hereby freely voluntarily, and without any valuable consideration, grant, allocate, enfranchise and convey to Amos Hayton (Vicar of the Parish of Brabourne in the County of Kent) and James Weekes and Philip Gotts (the Churchwardens of the said Parish) All that piece or parcel of Copyhold or Customary land part of the Said Manor of Coombe and part of a piece of land known as 'Hogs Forstall' bounded on the East side by a field known as the 'Forstall' on the South by the Highway or road leading from Brabourne lees to Brabourne Street on the West Side by a road or way twenty foot wide belonging to the said Sir Edward Knatchbull and running between the said piece of land hereby conveyed and a field called 'Rushly' (?) Meadow and bounded on the North Side by the remainder of the said piece of land called 'Hogs forstall' lately given by me the said Sir Edward Knatchbull to Mr. Onslow Andrews in lieu of a right of way which was claimed by the said Onslow Andrews along the said East side of the said land hereby conveyed or however otherwise the said piece of land is abutted, bounded known or distinguished with the right – (?) and appurtenances to the said piece of land belonging or appertaining. And all my right, title and interest to and in the same and every part thereof to hold unto and to the use of the said Amos Hayton, James Weekes and Philip Gotts and to their successors for the purposes of the said, and to be applied as a Site for a School for poor persons of and in the said Parish of Brabourne, and for the residence of the School Master and School Mistress of the said school and for no other purpose whatever, such school to be under the management and control of the Vicar and Curate of the Parish and a Committee consisting of not less than three persons exclusive of the said Vicar and Curate nor more than seven persons to be elected annually in the School Room in the month of August by the annual subscribers to the support of the said School which said school shall be at all times open to the Inspection of the Inspector or Inspectors for the time being appointed or to be appointed conformably with the order in Council bearing date the fourth day of August one thousand eight hundred and forty.

In Witness whereof the conveying and other parties have hereunto set their hands this fourteenth day of June one thousand eight hundred and forty five.

Signed and sealed by

Sir Edward Knatchbull      Amos Hayton      James Weekes      Philip Gotts

body, and the minutes of the managers' meetings show how, in August every year, the committee was elected from the subscribers as required by the Trust Deed. We are grateful to successive head teachers (Glyn Jones, Jamie Evans and Vincent Chan) for making Brabourne School's archives available to us, not least two books of Minutes of Managers' Meetings that cover the period 1879-1951. It is clear that, within a few years of 1879, attendance at the August meeting of subscribers had diminished to a mere handful, and more or less the same group of people continued to manage the school on a voluntary basis.

## GEORGE WORRELL, HEADMASTER AT BRABOURNE (1865-1901)

Of key importance to the success of a school is, of course, the headmaster, and in approximately 1865, a trained teacher named George Worrell took up the post of headmaster. It is possible that he had been trained and appointed by The National Society. George may, however, already have been in the area when the post of headmaster was advertised as Frank Worrell, one of his great-grandsons, told us that Susannah, George's wife, came from Warehorne. George's granddaughter Joy Finn told us that he was born with a club foot and grew up in the workhouse in London, which places him closer to the time of Dickens's England than our own time. His

Brabourne School, with George Worrell on far right (possibly c1870/1880s)

background could have blighted his life, but clearly he was a capable and determined person, and the minutes of the school managers indicate that he became a highly successful and respected headmaster. He was also a respected member of the local community, much involved with St Mary's Brabourne and, from 1905 until 1911, was churchwarden there. According to Joy, George was also an excellent gardener, getting up to dig the school garden every morning at 5am. The School House was not built until the late 1870s, so he lived with Susannah in a flat that used to be just above the present school entrance; here they had nine children, seven of whom survived and all of whom attended Brabourne School (their enrolment details are shown below).

Records of George and Susannah Worrell's children at Brabourne School (taken from the registers)

| Number in register | Name | Date enrolled | Birthday | Date left school |
|---|---|---|---|---|
| 49 | Susan Worrell | 8/1/1872 | 3/5/1868 | 11/8/1882 |
| 105 | Bessie Worrell | 27/10/1873 | 12/9/1869 | 28/2/1882 |
| 138 | Fanny Worrell | 19/10/1874 | 17/10/1870 | 28/2/1882 |
| 189 | Harry Worrell | 3/7/1876 | 21/3/1872 | 14/8/1885 |
| 294 | Frank P. Worrell | 24/2/1879 | 11/8/1874 | 11/5/1888 |
| 327 | Cyril G. Worrell | 19/5/1879 | 2/1/1876 | 3/7/1889 |
| 473 | Ada Worrell | 4/4/1883 | 10/6/1878 | 19/8/1892 |

George and Susannah's youngest daughter, Ada, eventually married Leonard Finn, the local builder, wheelwright and undertaker. Their children Betty, Joy and Keith, Keith's son Anthony, Anthony's wife, Jackie, and their children Andrew and Karen, were all pupils at Brabourne and link the school's past with its present.

In 1900, some 34 years after joining the school, George bought Homehurst (now Raffles), on Canterbury Road, East Brabourne, for about £100; it remained home to several generations of Finns for almost 100 years. According to George Brooks, he also built Holly Cottages in The Street, which was, for many years, home to Keith Finn and his wife Rose. After retiring on 31st August, 1901, George Worrell continued working for the school as a foundation manager until his death in January, 1912. His commitment to Brabourne School lasted over 45 years (approximately 1866-1912), a veritable lifetime.

# FOUR OF GEORGE AND SUSANNAH WORRELL'S CHILDREN

Fanny Worrell (born 1870), left, and
Bessie Worrell (born 1869), centre

Frank Parsons Worrell (born 1874)

Leonard and Ada Finn (Ada Worrell, born 1878)

From left, Betty, Keith and Joy Finn (c mid-1920s),
grandchildren of George and Susannah Worrell

## NATIONAL SCHOOL RULES

The following list shows *some*, but not *all*, of the rules that were applied to National Schools[2] and that George Worrell would have had to put into effect.

"Parents are earnestly requested to read the following Rules, and the Address which is appended to them, once a month, and to call the attention of their children to the PRECEPTS and ADVICE contained in them.

"Rules

To which Attention of Parents is Particularly called.

I. Parents who wish their children to be admitted into these Schools must apply to one of the committee, at the school, on some Monday morning, by nine o'clock. No child can be admitted who has any infectious disease.

II. When children are first admitted, their parents shall receive a copy of the rules and address, for which they shall pay one penny.

III. The payment for one child shall be two pence per week, but if two or more children are sent from the same family, only a penny shall be required for each additional child. Those who write with pen and ink must pay a penny per week extra, and find their own copy books.

2        Early education for the poor: National Schools (www.workhouses.org.uk/education/early.shtml; accessed 14th January, 2012). N.B. Website no longer accessible.

IV. The children are to come with their hands and faces well washed, and their hair clean and neat, and never to be without pocket handkerchiefs.

X. Every Saturday is a whole holiday, and there will be vacations in harvest and at Christmas and at any other time when the managing committee shall think proper.

XII. Though these schools are intended principally for the children of the poorer classes, yet small tradesmen and small occupiers of land may send their children on payment in addition to the usual weekly charge of 2s 6d quarterly, or Such Sum that may seem reasonable to the committee, and the visiting committee shall determine what parents shall be allowed this privilege.

XVII. One half of the money, paid by the children, shall be returned to them at the beginning of every quarter, in useful articles of clothing and rewards in books, &c. shall occasionally be given, but no boy or girl will be entitled to any of the rewards who does not carefully observe the following

PRECEPTS:

1. To behave respectfully to the mistresses, managers, and visitors and to be "lowly and reverent to all their betters," both in the school, and whenever they meet them elsewhere.

2. To be kind to their school fellows and to all other children, and to avoid all quarrelling.

3. Never to cheat any one, nor to take another person's property, even in play; and never to play for money.

4. To use no bad language.

5. Never to mock cripples, or infirm persons, nor to be rude to the old.

6. Never to be cruel to animals, nor unkind to any living creature.

7. To be dutiful and respectful to their parents and friends, endeavouring to assist them as far as they can.

8. To keep holy the Sabbath, and to behave with seriousness, attention and reverence in all places of public worship.

9. On all occasions to speak the TRUTH.

10. To come to, and go from school in an orderly manner, never to throw stones, or to loiter by the way.

11. To be quiet in the school, not to use any play things in school time, to keep their books neat and free from dog's ears, and not to climb upon the desks nor to scrawl upon or in any other way to damage the desks, forms or walls of the school-house."

EXPLORING THE REGISTERS OF BRABOURNE SCHOOL

The earliest register or Admissions Book from Brabourne School to which we have access dates from 1865. The records are not well ordered for the first five years of this particular register, though by 1871 the details recorded were more regular. Essentially, there are two lists in the Admissions Book, which are not entirely consistent. The first lists children in alphabetical order and gives their number on the school register, while the second gives the date of their registration and also other information, such as name and address of parents (usually no more than Brabourne, Broad Oak, Sellindge, Bircholt or wherever), the occupation of a parent or guardian (usually the father, with most being labourers in those earliest days), the date of birth of the child, whether or not they had attended another school, and the date of their departure from Brabourne School. There is also scope for indicating the level they had reached in their education using a scale of I to VI.

We thus have a valuable image of the area through the school records, even though they are far from perfect: first, we see that children of different ages were enrolled, not just those of around four or five years old, which may have been because no opportunities had been available for schooling before Brabourne National School was established. In fact, families would sometimes enrol children of different ages on the same day, which was a reflection of people moving into the area; and by looking at the section where the children's previous school was noted it is clear that, in the 19th century, people came from all over the local area – Aldington, Stowting, Elmsted, Wye, Charing and Smeeth. By the early 1900s families were moving to Brabourne from Cranbrook, Dymchurch, Kemsing, Pluckley and as far afield as Uxbridge and East Finchley. So, although people were, on a daily basis, very much tied to the land and to their villages, the records show that families did move around and the population was far from static. The following example of Doris May Moul is significant in relation to East Brabourne. John Moul, Doris's father, who came from Lower Stoke, Rochester, set up a bakery in the left hand side (from front) of what is now Coquet Lodge, just near the church gates in East Brabourne.

| | |
|---|---|
| Name | Moul, Doris May |
| Number | 1250 |
| Date enrolled | 8/12/1913 |
| Date of birth | 1/1/1908 |
| Father | John Moul |
| Occupation | Baker |
| Address | Post Office, Brabourne [currently Coquet Lodge, East Brabourne] |
| Last school | Lower Stoke, Rochester |
| Date left | 4/1920 "Gone to Private School held in The School House Brabourne" [Nevertheless, Doris was at Brabourne School for almost seven years.] |

Some of the first pupils included in the 1865 register had very familiar sounding names including Albert Hammon – who later gave his name to Albert House, now Clandon Cottage, in East Brabourne – Jenny Apps, Beatrice Dryland, Arthur Hammon (Albert's brother) and Benjamin Wood, who had as his guardian the headmaster, George Worrell.

## NUMBERS ENROLLED AT BRABOURNE NATIONAL SCHOOL

The graph below shows the number of admissions to the school each year from 1870 until the present day. The first 31 pupils were all grouped together as we could not tell precisely when some of them had joined – the pages of the register were so frayed that these details had disappeared. There seems to have been a demand for education from 1865, with enrolments increasing fairly steadily, reaching a peak in 1879, when 61 pupils joined. The numbers then slowed and were noticeably lower after the First World War and between the wars. It is likely that the loss of soldiers on the battlefields of Europe saw fewer children being born, but it is also possible that fewer children went to school as they were needed to help with work on farms and in the home.

The year of 1921 has to be highlighted as interesting in the records of Brabourne National School: it marked the arrival of the Kingston family, from County Cork in Ireland. Seven children were added to the register, making this the biggest intake of that decade (25 children in total). Many descendants of some of these Kingstons have also studied at Brabourne, among them Tim, Heidi and Sam Kingston, and David and Victoria Moore, but there must be many, many more.

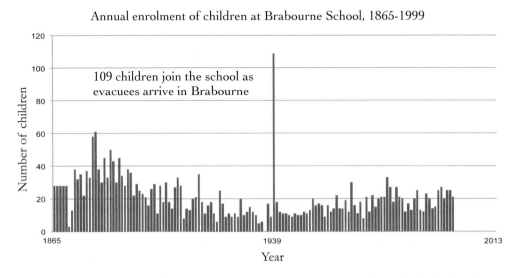

Annual enrolment of children at Brabourne School, 1865-1999

Source: Brabourne School Registers. Entries cease in 1999, after which the data recorded were not directly comparable with those cited

| Enrolment number | Name | Date of enrolment | Parent/ guardian | Last School | Date of Birth | Date left | Reason for leaving |
|---|---|---|---|---|---|---|---|
| 1353 | Kingston, George | 4/4/1921 | William, Water Farm, Brabourne | Curranene, County Cork, Ireland | 25/10/06 | 29/7/21 | Work on father's farm |
| 1354 | Kingston, James | 4/4/1921 | " | " | 15/2/08 | 9/8/22 | Work on father's farm |
| 1355 | Kingston, Lily | 4/4/1921 | " | " | 7/5/10 | 3/8/23 | Left at home |
| 1356 | Kingston, Walter | 4/4/1921 | " | " | 12/8/11 | 31/7/25 | Work on father's farm |
| 1357 | Kingston, Samuel | 4/4/1921 | " | " | 16/8/13 | 16/8/26 | Work on father's farm |
| 1358 | Kingston, Annie | 4/4/1921 | " | No previous school | 20/2/15 | 28/3/29 | Left 14 yrs |
| 1359 | Kingston, Thomas | 4/4/1921 | " | | 28/2/16 | 20/8/30 | Left 14 yrs |

The Kingston family arrive (1921), swelling the numbers at Brabourne School

George Brooks remembered the Kingston family at Brabourne School and remarked that he had much admiration for Sam Kingston, who used to walk through the fields to school, setting up mole traps as he went; Sam would then retrieve the moles on the way home from school, skin them, nail the skins on to a board and sell them (they were used in clothing in those days).

On 31st May, 1921, Edward Smith, a labourer at Water Farm, the Kingston's farm, had his five children, Archibald, Lily, Daisy, Winnifred and Queenie, admitted to Brabourne School. However, within four months, on 28th September, 1921, they were moved to Stowting School; a note in the register testifies to the reason: "Left, gone to the Stowting School, the road supposed to be nearer and better, to Brabourne it is meadow land."

Although we have a clear picture of the number of children being registered each year, what we do not get from the records is a picture of how many children were in school on a daily basis. There are indications from the minutes of the school managers' meetings that attendance levels were not good. This is in no way surprising as Britain was still emerging from a time when children were essential labour in the struggle for family survival, and parents were frequently unwilling to lose the income generated by their children. The Education Acts, which made education compulsory, initially at the elementary stage, were difficult to enforce. The school's grant from the state was related to attendance; it must therefore have been very challenging for the teachers, whose role included attracting children to school and then making sure they attended regularly. In the early years, when "school pence" was charged, persuading parents to pay for their children's education, as well as to lose the income generated by them, could not have been easy. It was a double-edged sword, but the potential benefits of "book learning" gradually won through.

Over time, Brabourne developed a reputation for high academic standards, and recent head teachers, including Mrs Norrington, George Hutchinson, Alistair Guthrie, Glyn Jones, Jamie Evans and now Vincent Chan, have all ensured, and are continuing to ensure, that children receive a good start to their schooling. However, in the mid-1960s, and for some years beyond, there were frequently threats that the school might close – unthinkable today.

Sally Furneaux (Willett) writes:

"The Willett Family moved to Brabourne Lees during a very cold, snowy spell in January 1965. I was 10, Toby 6, and Daniel a baby of just 1 year old. Toby and I were duly enrolled at Brabourne School – and it goes down in legend (according to the old Headmaster, George Hutchinson) that if it were not for our attendance at the school it would have closed. The school's roll had dropped to only 27, and us joining increased it to 29 – making it just viable to keep open.

"That first winter seemed so very severe – I remember Mummy (Dorothy Willett), Toby and I trampling our way through snow drifts returning from school – and the aforesaid headmaster having to stay a night with us at Prospect Farm House due to the horrendous weather."

## MANAGING BRABOURNE NATIONAL SCHOOL: EXTRACTS FROM THE MINUTES OF THE SCHOOL MANAGERS' MEETINGS

This section is undeniably long, but we make no apology for it as the minutes of the school managers from 1879 to 1951 give us a wonderful insight into the evolution of the school, from its early days when it was Brabourne National School, founded and controlled by the Church, to a time when it was about to become a voluntary controlled school, run by the state, though retaining strong connections with the Church. The extracts included reveal the condition of the school in its early years and highlight the problems faced by the managers.

Two issues were of constant concern to the managers: the first was accumulating sufficient funds to pay the staff and for the maintenance of the school and the School House; the second was staffing the school. The major source of funds during the early years was from the school's subscribers, many of whom probably came together to support the establishment of a National School when Sir Edward Knatchbull donated the land for it in 1845. Prior to 1891, a second source of funds was the school pence fee, which was collected by the headmaster from the families of children attending school. However, not all of this would have accrued to the school as, according to the National School Rules (above), half of this would have been returned to the children "every quarter in useful articles of clothing and rewards in books &c" (Rule XVII). A third source was the voluntary rate; this was made possible after the Education Act of 1902 put the Church on the local rates. In return for aid from the rates, the management committees of voluntary schools came under the control of the newly formed Local Education Authorities[3]. Grants, subscriptions and donations received from different bodies were a fourth and valuable source of funds. These included the Parliamentary Grant-in-Aid and modest grants from The National Society, later from the Diocesan Education Committee, and from other charities, such as Betton's Trust, which were sympathetic to schools with a Christian foundation. (Thomas Betton's charity still exists, though the majority of its grants are now made to social workers and charitable organisations for essential household items for people on very low incomes.)

We now delve into the minutes and follow some of the items that have exercised the managers over the years.

- Education was not free -
Many people who were hard-pressed financially and who wanted their children to be educated had a tussle with the headmaster and, through him, the managers. A case is cited in the minutes of 24th October, 1879: "The Chairman reported that the printed notices announcing that children above the age of seven must pay the accustomed fees whether they attended or not, had been duly issued and that [the landlord] of the Plough Inn refused to pay for his children the fees usually charged for children of tradesmen [these would have been higher than the fees that the parents of poorer children paid] … The Master was instructed to refuse to admit [the landlord's] children to the School unless the proper fees were paid." Because the fees were critical to the school's survival, great efforts were made to encourage children to come to school every day – as long as their parents paid up.

- Subscribers, a source of funds for Brabourne School -
On 21st August, 1880, at the annual meeting of the subscribers to Brabourne National School, the following seven persons were elected as a committee of managers. These included The Rt Hon. Lord Brabourne, Sir Wyndham Knatchbull, Messrs Weekes, Pilcher, Thorpe, J. Rolfe and E. Hammon. The Rev Perry [Ayscough] was elected Correspondent [Secretary] and Treasurer. Lord Brabourne and Sir Wyndham Knatchbull did not attend the managers' meetings through the year and most of the committee work was done by the remaining five members. The minutes up until 1902 show how all decisions were made by the managers together with the headmaster.

---

3        Looking at History: the 1870 Education Act (richardjohnbr.blogspot.com/2008/05/1870-educa-tion-act.html; accessed 14th January, 2012).

- The Worrells, a family of teachers -

It is noteworthy that five members of the Worrell family were involved in teaching at Brabourne School, though not all at the same time: George Worrell was headmaster, his wife, Susannah, was pupil teacher, and his daughter Bessie rose to the position of assistant mistress, while his other daughters Fanny and Ada were also pupil teachers.

- Raising sufficient money for the school was always a worry for the Managers -

23rd October, 1880: "The Annual Subscription, £5 of the Governors of Betton's Charity received by the Secretary was handed over to the Treasurer."

14th October, 1882: people in rural areas were poor and, because the school's income was low, the managers "resolved that the Ratepaying parish houses who do not at present subscribe to the School shall be asked for a Voluntary contribution at the rate of a penny in the point on their Rating, and that 100 circulars be printed and that Mr. Worrell be asked to distribute the circulars and collect the Rate for which he be given … 10/-."

- From privies to earth closets -

17th January, 1884: present, Messrs Weekes, Thorpe, Hammon and Perry Ayscough. "A letter from the [Medical officer of health] was read in which he drew attention to the state of the Privies and directed the Managers to convert them into Earth Closets. It was resolved that the necessary work be done at once by Messrs Ames and Finn. The Cesspool to be filled up and the privies rearranged and a shed built for storage of soil and dry earth."

- Praise for Mr Worrell -

16th January, 1886: present, Mr Weekes, Mr Pilcher, Mr Hammon and Rev J.T. Pearse. "Mr. Weekes … [made] … a most satisfactory report of the School. He spoke of Mr. Worrell's industry and perseverance during the 20 years that he had been Master and the general respect in which he was held by the parishioners. The School had been improving year by year, and at the last examination had been recommended by the Government Inspector for the Good Merit Grant of 2/- (2 shillings) per head in addition to the grant for the several class subjects, so that the total grant amounted to £89-0-6 compared with £81-0-9 in the preceding year. The Diocesan Inspector's Report was not less favourable. [This latter inspection related to religious instruction. Even today a visit by Ofsted is usually followed by an equivalent from the Diocese to evaluate the Christian ethos of the school.]

"With regard to financial affairs, Mr. Weekes mentioned that, in consequence of the good report he had been able to make of the school, he had received a contribution of £10 from Betton's Charity, whereas £5 had been given in former years (the additional £5 last year having been given for sanitary improvements). He had also received £11 from Lord Brabourne as his subscription for the year. There were several subscriptions now due which when collected would be ample to meet all outstanding liabilities at the end of the financial year. The Voluntary Rate of 1d in the £ had never before been paid up so well. The balance in his hands at present amounted to £20-10-7¾."

- Typhoid at school -

11th March, 1891: present, Mr Andrews, Mr Hammon, Rev C.E. Outram and Rev J.T. Pearse. "A certificate was produced from the medical officer of health for the district stating that the School had been closed from Dec. 18th to Jan. 19th owing to an outbreak of typhoid fever. The table of school fees having been examined, it was resolved to raise the weekly payment from 2d to 3d in three cases where the parents were above the labouring class."

7th August, 1891: annual meeting of subscribers to the school; present, Mr Andrews, Rev C.E. Outram and Rev J.T. Pearse. A voluntary rate of 2d in the £ was agreed and, "Mr. Worrell was authorized to collect a 2d rate for the School."

23rd August, 1894: present, Messrs Andrews, Finn, Hancock, Rev T.E. Gatehouse and Rev W.D. May (note change in managers). "It was resolved that Mr. [Leonard] Finn should be instructed to clean down and whitewash the School."

- Financial problems and staff pay cuts -

10th August, 1898: annual meeting of the managers and subscribers; present, Messrs Andrews, Thornby, Hancock, Weekes, Apps, Awford, Finn, Orpin, Pearson, Dr Stanley and the Rev A. Fairbrother (chairman). Owing to the financial state of the school it was agreed unanimously, "that the Voluntary rate of 2d in the £ be asked for as usual and that an extra rate of 2d be also asked for in order to pay off the deficit" and, "that the Teaching Staff of the School be reduced and the salary of the Head Teacher be also reduced". This was agreed by the headmaster at a subsequent meeting.

7th December, 1898: present, Messrs Apps, Hancock, Pearson, Rev A. Fairbrother. "It was decided to pay the salaries of the Teachers which were due August 31st, and the Treasurer was requested to pay the Salaries due Nov. 30th as soon as there should be funds sufficient for that purpose; also the wages of the School cleaner and the a/c for coals."

- Attendance at school improves -
7th June, 1899: present, Messrs Apps, Hancock, Dr Stanley and Rev A. Fairbrother. "The Registers … showed that the number of children on the books is 84 and the average attendance for the quarter ended May 31 was 69[%]." By 31st May, 1902, the average attendance had risen to 95%. Though not stated in the minutes, this may well reflect the increased impact of national rules on compulsory education and the fact that the size of the government grant to the school was related to attendance levels of those enrolled.

- Public support for Brabourne remaining a voluntary school -
5th December, 1900: present, Messrs Apps, Andrews, Hancock, Pearson, Dr Stanley and the vicar as chairman. "At a largely attended Public Meeting convened by the Chairman in consequence of objections raised to the Voluntary rate of 4d in the £, it was proposed, seconded and carried that the School should continue to be carried on as a Voluntary School.

"It was further agreed unanimously that the Voluntary rate of 4d in the £ should be paid for the current year."

The Education Act of 1902 saw the Kent Education Committee (KEC) becoming increasingly involved in the running of voluntary schools, and Brabourne was no exception. We now jump forward several years to 1915. George Worrell had retired in 1901 and had been replaced by Mr Wetherell, who proved to be another good headmaster. Mr Wetherell resigned his post in July, 1915 (we believe this was due to him taking up the post of headmaster at Smeeth School), though his wife continued to teach at Brabourne.

- Mr Wetherell resigns -
16th July, 1915: present, the vicar, Thomas Lindsay Stack, chairman, Messrs Brett, Hammon, Thornby and Pearson. "Mr. Wetherell's resignation. The Correspondent reported that Mr. Wetherell had sent in his resignation as Head Master and reported the matter to the KEC and had received a letter from them saying that as the average attendances had become so reduced the Managers would agree to the appointment of a Mistress in the place of a Master [perhaps this should read 'as average attendances had become so reduced, would the Managers agree to the appointment of … ']. This matter was discussed and adjourned, the Vicar promising to obtain further information as to the desirability or otherwise of having a Mistress in the School." As mentioned earlier, the reason for the fall in attendance is never made clear but is likely to have been an effect of the First World War and the burden of work falling to women and children who would have been taken out of school.

- A headmaster vs a headmistress -

23rd July, 1915: present, "all the Managers". "Appointment of Head Master versus Mistress. The vicar proposed, Mr. Hammon seconded that we apply for a Master as being more suitable for this School, and further that we do so on the strength of the Managers not having applied for a Supplementary Teacher 'in the place of Miss Gomme resigned' by reason of the great reduction in the number of attendances. Mr. Pearson moved an amendment that a Mistress be applied for, this was not seconded. The Vicar's resolution was therefore put to the meeting and carried, 5 voting for, namely: the Vicar, Messrs Brett, Hammon, Walker and Thornby. Mr. Pearson voting against." In spite of this resolution we soon learn that a headmistress is appointed.

- Brabourne's first headmistress -

27th August, 1915: present, Rev Baggot Stack, acting for the vicar [his brother], who was unable to attend through illness, and Messrs Pearson, Thornby and Brett. "Engagement of Miss Starck as Head Mistress. Miss Starck having applied for the post of Head Mistress attended to interview the Managers [It is not quite clear here who interviewed whom]. After due consideration of her testimonials it was unanimously agreed to engage her subject to the approval of the KEC at a commencing salary of £78/15/- [per annum]."

2nd November, 1915: present, the vicar, chairman, Messrs Pearson, Thornby and Walker. "Leave of absence by Infant Mistress. The Vicar read correspondence between himself and the Head Mistress respecting the Infant Mistress [Mrs. Wetherell] applying for leave for a few (two) hours, which she did not grant. It was resolved … that the following letter be sent to Miss Starck the Head Mistress:

Dear Miss Starck,

I laid your letter re Mrs. Wetherell's application for leave of absence before the Managers last night, and I was instructed to write: That the Managers have considered your letters re Mrs. Wetherell's application for leave of absence for a few hours, [and] do not interpret rule 37(d) which you quote, so rigidly as you do. They think that the words 'as a rule' inserted before the words… 'Teachers should not be absent without leave of Managers…' are clearly intended to give Teachers a certain amount of license in interpretation.

I remain

Yours very truly

Thos Lindsay Stack"

11th November, 1915: present, the vicar, chairman, Messrs Pearson, Thornby and Hammon. Headmistress's letter to KEC. "The Correspondent read a letter from the KEC re Staff Elementary [teacher] dated Nov. 5th, 15 in answer to one received from the Head Mistress making certain allegations against the Assistant Teacher. The Vicar having made enquiry and finding the allegations not justified a letter was ordered to be written [to] the KEC to that effect on the proposition of the Vicar seconded by Mr. Hammon, unanimous." We are never told what the allegations were.

4th May, 1916: present, Messrs Pearson, Thornby, Hammon, Woollet and the vicar. Re the head teacher. "The following Resolution was proposed by Mr. Pearson, seconded by Mr. Thornby, unanimously agreed:-
'That the Correspondent be requested to write to the KEC requesting their permission to dismiss, or ask the Head Teacher to resign, when her year was up, on the following grounds:-
That several matters had been put before the Managers: showing that her discipline was very bad; that she was underhanded in dealing with the children; unfair in her treatment of the Assistant Mistress; and on the ground of her general Incompetence.'"

12th May, 1916: present, Messrs Pearson, Woollett, Thornby, Walker, Hammon and the vicar. "Head Teacher. The Managers interviewed the Head Teacher, with reference to their Resolution passed at the previous meeting, and came to the Decision, in view of her refusal to accept the Chairman's Advice, that she should resign, that it was advisable, in the interest of the Schools, that the KEC should be asked to consent to her Resignation or Dismissal." It was agreed, "That the Correspondent [the vicar] and Mr. Pearson do write the letter to the KEC re the above."

15th May, 1916: present, as above. "Two Letters from the Head Teacher were read by the Correspondent, the 1st to the Managers; the 2nd to himself. These Letters referred to the Interview between the Head Teacher and the Managers on the previous Friday. No action was taken."

It was further resolved that the Resolution passed at [a previous]…Managers' meeting be forwarded to the KEC, "and that the following Rider be added to the same:

These four points, each in themselves, may seem to your Committee, trivial, but as a whole, they create an impossible situation. She is an impossible woman. No one can get on with her, either in the School, or out; and it is in these General grounds that the Managers ask for her Removal.
Proposed by Mr. Pearson, Seconded by Mr. Woollett, and passed unanimously."

29th June, 1916: present, Messrs Pearson, Hammon, Thornby, Woollett, Walker and the vicar in the chair. "The Chairman stated than an unofficial Meeting had been held at the Vicarage on the preceding evening, between Mr. Watts, of the NUT National Union of Teachers, Mr. Pearson and himself. As the result of what was said at this Conference, the present Meeting was summoned and the following letter was written on the understanding that when it was forwarded to the KEC, the Head Teacher would send in Her resignation." It is interesting that the Headmistress did not seem to be present at the meeting with the NUT representative at which her future was decided.

Copy of Letter to the Secretary, KEC:

"June 29.16

Dear Sir,

The Managers have had further under their Consideration, the Question of the Head Teacher's Dismissal, and, on their behalf, I now write to say, that we beg to withdraw the Request for Power to ask for Her Resignation, or Dismissal.

In doing this, I should like to state the Charge of General Incompetence referred to the particular Conditions of this School, in which there is an abnormal proportion of rather big boys.

I am, Dear Sir, Yours faithfully,

Thomas Lindsay Stack, Correspondent."

July 29th, 1916: present, Messrs Pearson and Thornby and the vicar, chairman. "Miss Starck's Resignation was sent in on 1st July. Testimonial – Miss Starck. The Chairman stated he had received a Request from Head Teacher for a Testimonial. In reply, it was agreed…that the following be given:

"Brabourne Vicarage, Ashford July 29.16

"Miss Starck having asked the Managers of our Schools, for a Testimonial, I, on their behalf, beg to say that She has been Head Mistress here for one year. The circumstances of this School were peculiar owing to there being an abnormal proportion of rather big boys. The Managers believe that, in another School, Miss Starck may prove quite capable of fulfilling the Duties which are 'assigned' to her.

T.L. Stack, Chairman and Correspondent
School House. 8/- will be paid to Miss Starck for Picture Rails."

John Varrier recalls that his mother was employed at Brabourne School in 1916 as an assistant teacher with no qualifications other than having "graduated" from Brabourne School a few months earlier. She held the post for approximately two years.

- Moving to 1936 and worsening financial problems -
The war hadn't started in 1936, but even when it did it was rarely mentioned in the minutes, although its effects were evident. From 1936 until 1951 (when our record of the managers' meetings ceases) the minutes are much more detailed than those of the 19th century and the linkages with the KEC and other official bodies reflect the integration of the school into the national system of education. By 1934 progress in the material sense was being made as, after much deliberation, the School House was connected to the water main. We are never told in the minutes when the school was connected, but it was probably at much the same time. It is also clear that the costs of maintaining the school weighed heavily on the managers and, almost certainly, this would have influenced their decision some years later to agree to hand over responsibility for the running of the school to the government, a decision that led to Brabourne becoming a voluntary controlled school.

- God Save the King! -
22nd January, 1936: "King's Accession. Mrs. Temple reported 20 children on the books at the present moment [far fewer than before the First World War, when there were over 80 children]. In the morning the children had been able to hear broadcasted the Proclamation of the accession of King Edward VIII and had sung 'God Save the King'."

- Prioritising maintenance work -
23rd April, 1936: "Estimates from Mr. Ames were submitted for repairs and redecoration at the School House and for repair to the tarmac of the School playground and approaches. It was decided to accept the estimate for the work at the School House (£9.19.6). The question of the Playground was postponed in order to obtain further estimates from Messrs Earl of Aldington and Mr. Pullen."

- More money worries and low numbers of children at the school -
20th April, 1937: present, all managers and Mrs Temple. Increasingly we see the head teacher, Mrs Temple, present at the managers' meetings. Previously, the head teacher had only been at managers' meetings when invited, and then only rarely. Problems concerning meeting the bills are much in evidence. "The Correspondent reported on the accounts. Mr. Ames' account had been paid. Mr. Finn's was still owing… Appeal for funds. It was proposed by Mr. Miller and seconded by Mr. Pilcher that a yearly

appeal should be made to the Village to support the School by a house to house collection. [It appears that this never took place.]

School House, c1929

"Mrs. Temple reported that there were at present 26 children in the School. 8 would be leaving at Midsummer but it was hoped others would be coming on and that it would be found possible to have a second teacher." On 6th May, Miss Davis was appointed.

15th August, 1939: present, Mr H.S. Hammon, Mrs McDowall, Mr C.C. Cameron (from Wall Farm, now Penstock), the Rev McDowall (correspondent) and Mrs Temple. "The Correspondent reported that £16.10.5 was owing to Mr. F. Ames towards which there was £8.5.6 in hand. Agreed that £8 would be paid on account. Mr. Finn's estimate for…lime washing the School office had been accepted by the KEC.

"Mrs. Temple reported that School opened on September 26th with 12 children present, but by Oct. 10th the numbers were 18.
"Nurse had made 3 inspections and given a clean bill each time. The Inspection in Scripture teaching was held on June 6th the report showed very creditable results. Eric Ball [one of our eminent contributors, pictured below] had gained a Special Place at Ashford Grammar School. Two children were going to the Central School this autumn. Three children, Elizabeth Hayward, Stanley Burt and Edward Vidgen, had made a full attendance for the year."

Eric and Avis Ball. Eric gained a Special Place at Ashford
Grammar School from Brabourne School

- Evacuees arrive -

10th October, 1939: present, all the managers and Mrs Temple. Re Evacuees. "On September 2nd, evacuees from St. Mary's R.C. School Eltham arrived, and the School opened for them on September 19th – 99 children being then present, a number reduced at this date [Oct. 10th] to 94. On Oct. 2nd the Brabourne children returned to School, including those of the Central School and two from the Grammar School, 26 in all." According to Oliver Trowell's recollections, those from the Central School were Norman Thornby, Dorothy Jordan, Bob Ball and Archie Ashdown. The two returning from the Grammar School were Oliver Trowell and Philip Stone. "Questions of the provision of milk and the cleaning of the School were discussed; Mrs. Temple would see that adequate arrangements were made."

19th October, 1939: present, Messrs H.S. Hammon and Cameron, the correspondent and Mrs Temple. "A Special Meeting was held…at Penstock Hall to consider the use of the School by the evacuees on Sundays. The other Managers were unable to come but let the meeting know their opinions. It was decided to grant our visitors the use of the School on Sundays for Mass at 8 and for Sundays."

- The evacuees leave -

5th August, 1940: present, all the managers. "Mrs. Temple reported the number in the School as 21. [The evacuees had all left, as Kent was considered too dangerous for them. The relief of the Managers was almost palpable.] The windows of the small room had been protected by wire by order of the KEC and those of the big room were to be similarly treated. Inspection of the sanitary arrangements had been made but no report sent in as yet."

We now take a break from the minutes for a note by Oliver Trowell:

## Wartime Emergency Secondary Schooling in Brabourne.

When war broke out in September 1939, the autumn term was due to start a few days later at the local schools. However, all was not normal: Ashford Grammar School, at which I had been a pupil, was evacuated to Burford in Oxfordshire, while the County Grammar School for Girls (now the Highworth School), was not evacuated but actually took in the Mary Datchelor School from South London. Brabourne Primary School took in St. Mary's Roman Catholic School from Eltham, stretching its accommodation to the limit. About a third of the evacuees from Eltham were of secondary age and this led to the option for local grammar school boys whose parents opted not to part company with them, (myself and Philip Stone), and those due to go to the Central School in Ashford, to continue their secondary education with the Londoners at Brabourne School for an indefinite period. It must be remembered we did not have the benefit of hindsight!

Norman Thornby, Archie Ashdown, Bob Ball.

As autumn passed into one of the coldest winters of the 20th century, when even the main water supply froze beneath Brabourne Street, not much happened regarding the war after the German invasion of Poland and it was not until May 10th, 1940, that huge events began to unfold. It so happened that on that day I had permission to visit the dentist in Ashford and, as I was waiting in the sunshine for the 9.55 bus at the top of School Lane, Mrs. Hammon came to her gate and called out to me, "Isn't it dreadful, the Germans have invaded Belgium, it's all going to happen, all over again." Few could have predicted that in twenty days the Germans would be in Calais and Boulogne and that the B.E.F. would have to be evacuated from Dunkirk in such boats as could be mustered for the purpose and, that in thirty days, Belgium, Holland and France would all have surrendered. It seemed inevitable that Britain would be Hitler's next target for invasion and, on the 26th May, the evacuees from Eltham were re-located to South Wales, leaving only about half-a-dozen local children of secondary age at Brabourne School. On 30th May, which was my 13th birthday, my parents decided that my sister and I should be evacuated to Berkhamsted, the other side of London, to stay with my aunt and uncle. Our journey there, which took all day, was unforgettable. At Ashford Station, train-loads of troops, newly landed from Dunkirk, queued on the main lines to move forward and those troops who were still awake were throwing out empty bully-beef tins onto the track or the platform, asking anyone to fill them with water. Of those who had given way to sleep, I have never seen, before or since, live human beings with such a corpse-like appearance.

Thus ended my temporary secondary schooling at Brabourne School.

Oliver Trowell (walking, with cap and suitcase) and his sister Pam (with hat and suitcase), to the left of the picture, waiting for a train at Ashford station to evacuate them to Berkhamsted. The picture, drawn by Oliver at the age of 13, depicts soldiers arriving at Ashford from Dunkirk, 30th May, 1940

Returning to the minutes...

- One of very few references to the war in the minutes -
15th August, 1941: "Mrs. Temple reported that...the cellar had been adapted as a shelter and wired for electric light."

- School dinners are introduced -
2nd December, 1941: present, Mr H.S. Hammon, Mrs McDowall, the Rev McDowall (correspondent) and Mrs Temple. A meeting was held at Hillecourt (at the top of School Lane). "The Correspondent reported that Messrs Ames' previous accounts £12-15-3 had been paid off... The children in the School now numbered 24. Cocoa was provided with their midday lunch. Mrs. McDowall urged the importance of providing a hot dinner at midday at the School, and undertook to find out exact details about such dinners where provided."

10th April, 1942: present, all managers except Messrs A. Hammon and T. Pilcher. "The Chairman stated that Mr. A. [Albert] Hammon was sending in his resignation to the KEC on the score of age and inability to attend meetings. The meeting resolved that a letter should be sent [to] him expressing appreciation on his long service as Manager.

"School Canteen. Hot dinners had been provided at the School, beginning January 26th and were being successfully carried on. In order to bring the arrangements under the KEC regulations for school canteens, it was necessary to form a Committee of management. A Canteen Committee was accordingly formed: Mrs. McDowall, Mrs. Hammon, Mrs. Cameron, Mrs. Maclean, Mrs. Temple as Schoolmistress and Mr. H.S. Hammon as representative of the Managers."

20th August, 1942: "Resignation of Mrs. Temple. The Managers presented Mrs. Temple with a reading lamp and wished her all happiness on her departure to her new work at Ringwould.

"The Canteen Committee...selected Mrs. Burchett as cook for the School dinners." (This is not the same Mrs Birchett who lived in The Street and whose husband was, for a time, churchwarden.)

- Appointment of Mrs Norrington as headmistress -
4th November, 1942: re-appointment of headmistress. "A meeting of Managers was held at Hillecourt to interview the applicants for the post of Head Teacher. Six applications had been received and three candidates selected for interview by

when two withdrew, leaving only Mrs. S. Norrington of Sellindge, at present teaching at Acrise. Mr. H.S. Hammon, Mrs. McDowall and the Correspondent, and also Mr. Miller, KEC inspector, were present and agreed in offering the post to Mrs. Norrington. She accepted the post but stipulated that before taking up residence in the School House electric light, indoor sanitation and bath should be provided. The Managers agreed to meet her wishes."

- Fatal accident at school -
"On Thursday Oct. 29th 1942, when the children were let out of School at 2.30 for a run, the wall of the School House coal shed suddenly collapsed outward catching two boys as they were running past and killing them instantaneously. Wilfred Brooks aged 8 and Dennis Griggs 7 (almost 8). The inquest was held at Willesborough Hospital to which the bodies had been removed and the Managers were exonerated, verdicts of death by misadventure being returned, Oct. 31st." This event shocked the local community and many people still remember it. We return to the accident later.

"On November 9th the KEC architect, Mr. Hawkins, by permission of the Director of Education, met Mr. Ames, Mr. Hammon and the Vicar at the School and it was decided to remove the remainder of the coal shed and build a new one for the School coal on the further side of the grass slope. Mr. Hawkins also inspected the School House itself and gave advice with regard to the proposed indoor sanitation and bath. He also re-examined the School chimney and roof. Mr. Ames was instructed to test the room and secure any place where tiles might become dangerous."

- Trying to reduce the overdraft -
6th October, 1944: present, the vicar in the chair, Messrs H.S. Hammon and R.M. Older, Mrs McDowall and Miss Powell. "The Chairman welcomed Miss Powell, appointed Manager by the KEC. Thanks to a £20 grant from Betton's Charity and the help of a £5 donation from the PCC the overdraft at the Bank was now reduced to £46-19-0. Mrs. Norrington reported that there were 23 children in the School, all taking the Canteen dinner, so efficiently cooked by Mrs. Burchett.

"Except for a few cracks no damage had been done to the School [presumably this is reference to bomb damage]. Mr. Hawkins (KEC architect) had visited the School and pronounced the shelter to be all right provided sufficient warning was given to allow time for getting the children into it."

- Determining the future of the school -
12th January, 1945: re the future of the School. "A form of survey had been sent by the Canterbury Diocesan Education Committee which Managers were asked to fill in and

Report of the deaths of
Wilfred Brooks and Dennis
Griggs on Thursday, 29th
October, 1942

## TWO BOYS KILLED

### A PLAYGROUND TRAGEDY

Two eight-year-old boys, Wilfred Michael Brooks, son of Mr. and Mrs. W. S. Brooks, of Running Water Farm, West Brabourne, and Dennis Richard Griggs, son of Mr. and Mrs. E. G. Griggs, The Street, East Brabourne, were killed in a distressing accident at Brabourne Schools on Thursday last week. The children had only just gone into the playground for the afternoon break, when a wall of a coal shed collapsed and fell on the two boys as they were running past. Although they were uncovered as quickly as possible they were dead on arrival at Willesborough Hospital.

Mr. Rutley Mowll conducted the inquests at the Willesborough Hospital on Saturday, when Mr. J. W. Kennard appeared for the Kent managers, and Mr. Drake Brookman for the N.U.T., and Miss Fogg, a teacher at the school.

Wilfred Brooks    Dennis Griggs

Another eight-year-old scholar, Desmond Michael Barham, in describing the occurrence said, " Dennis and Wilfred were running past the wall when it fell down on them and they were buried beneath the bricks. They did not touch the wall. We ran up to see if we could get them away from it, but were not able to do so because there were too many bricks on top of them. The teacher came out and told us to go into school."

Patrick Hayward, a six-year-old scholar, said " The two boys were close to the wall and I was behind them. It nearly came on top of me. I saw it falling and ran away."

Miss Louisa Mary Jean Fogg, of Folkestone, a temporary teacher, said she had been at the school about 5 weeks. She was in the school when the accident happened and did not hear the wall fall. She was called by Mrs. Burchett, canteen cook, and together they uncovered the children as quickly as they could and sent for assistance. She had not noticed the wall was cracked and as . . . . . knew . . .

. . . . . caretaker for . . . . . was cr . . . ke . . . . . she ha . . .

---

. . . body . . .
P.c. W . . . . . . . f . . . in
September . . . . . . . .
bombs were dropped in the vicinity of the school, and on the day of the accident gunfire was heard and vibrations felt in the district. It might have been the cause of the wall finally collapsing.

The Rev. R. L. McDowall, chairman of the school managers and vicar of Brabourne, said he did not know the wall was cracked. Nothing had been reported to him; if it had, he would most certainly have thought it desirable to consider the repair of the wall.

Mr. Mowll pointed out that the case was of importance to the public because they naturally wanted their children sent to school under conditions that were reasonably safe. He found there was no criminal negligence and sympathised with the sentiments expressed by both of the bereaved parents that the condition of the remainder of the buildings should be investigated without delay to see that there were no doubtful walls and the buildings made quite safe, whereby a similar catastrophe could be avoided in future.

Verdicts of death by misadventure were returned.

The funeral of Wilfred Brooks took place on Monday at the Zion Chapel, West Brabourne, and was conducted by Pastor E. Hickmott. There were two hymns, including " Rock of Ages."

Family mourners were mother and father; granddad (Mr. Thomas Brooks); grandad and grandma (Mr. and Mrs. F. Bishop, Mersham); Uncle Fred and Aunt Millie (Mr. and Mrs. F. Brooks); Aunt Bell (Mrs. I. Tong, Ashford); Aunt Ruth (Mrs. G. Brooks); Mr. and Mrs. G. Bishop, Mersham (uncle and aunt); and cousins Gertie, Aggie, Queenie, George and Cis. The interment was made in the chapel resting-place.

---

return, the information being needed **in order to assist in determining the future of the School** [our emphasis]. Questions and answers were read and discussed, and the Managers agreed that the answers given were correct, and the form was accordingly returned."

- Possible effects of bomb damage -

5th June, 1946: "A large pane of glass fell from one of the high windows of the class room. Fortunately no one was in the playground at the time. Mr. Finn was asked to put in a new pane and see if the other panes were safe."

7th June, 1946: "Mr. Finn says the glass is very unsafe and he was asked to attend to all the windows."

19th March, 1948: a gap of nearly two years in the minutes of managers' meetings. No explanations are given for this. A meeting of managers was held at the Vicarage, Brabourne, the vicar in the chair. Also present, Messrs H. Hammon, Birchett and Jeanes. Mr Birchett used to live in what is now the pink cottage on The Street in East Brabourne, and for a time was churchwarden at Brabourne Church. "The Vicar spoke of the crack in the corner of the School Buildings and of the fact that Messrs Ames Bros and Mr. Hawkins the KEC Surveyor came in consultation as to the best way in which the repairs should be effected."

- Move towards controlled status, prompted by the need for increasing resources -
22nd March, 1949: present, the vicar in the chair (the Rev W.H. Wagstaffe), Mrs Norrington, Mrs Johnson (from West Brabourne), Messrs Hammon and Birchett. The Vicar raised the issue of the School Development Plan, which had to be decided within six months from 16th February, 1949. The key issues were: "The School may become (1) Controlled, ie financed by KEC (State) or (2) A Voluntary aided School in which the Managers are responsible for 50% of all alterations and upkeep required by the KEC. The alterations required at the first go…apparently are in the region of £1400 of which sum the Managers would be liable for £700. The Vicar has written to Mr. Appleton and asked for his, and the opinion of the Divisional Education Board before calling the Managers together for their considered opinion of the facts to be presented to them at the Meeting."

19th August, 1949: present, the vicar in the chair, Mrs Norrington, Mrs Johnson, Messrs Birchett and Jeanes. Miss Milborrow had been appointed teacher for infants. "The Bill from Mr. A.J. Fortescue was submitted amounting of £53-17-3 for the repair of the School Crack. **It was decided in view of the facts that the School very soon would attain Controlled status** to offer the KEC half the amount stated on the bill." The emphasis here is ours again. This is an important matter and wasn't referred to again in the remainder of this particular minutes book, which concluded in July, 1951.

15th January, 1951: present, the vicar in the chair, Messrs Summers, Birchett and Hammon (treasurer), Mrs Opperman. "The attitude of the KEC towards repairs of the school was discussed. The possibility of the School House being sold was discussed but the difficulty appeared to be in the fact that no one knew where the Deeds were. Until some information was forthcoming on that score the matter was left in abeyance."

31st May, 1951: present, the vicar in the chair (the Rev Wagstaffe), Mrs Norrington, Mrs Opperman, Messrs F. Birchett, T. Jeanes, E. Summers and H. Hammon (treasurer). "Mrs. Norrington asked that a letter of commendation should go from the Managers advising the KEC as to the necessity of building a kitchen, as an extra building in keeping with the status of the school. The disadvantages of the present system were discussed and realised. It was not good either for the children or for the Cook that preparations of School Meals should be carried on in one room.

"Mr. Hammon reported on the finances [of] the School House. A letter was to be sent to Mr. Penhook, Diocesan Registrar, asking whether, in the event of the School House losing its tenants, as there appeared to be no Deeds of the House, the Vicar and Managers were in a position to sell the Property."

19th July, 1951: present, the vicar in the chair, Mrs Norrington, Mrs Opperman, Messrs H. Hammon (treasurer), F. Birchett and E. Summers. Apologies from Mr T. Jeanes. "There had been two applicants for the post of Assistant Teacher, Mrs. Davis (née Worrell), and Miss Jean Smith. The two candidates in turn were introduced and interviewed by the Vicar and Managers for a few minutes. The Board of Managers unanimously voted that Miss Jean Smith be recommended for the vacant post at the School. The Hon. Correspondent was advised to write to the KEC in such terms.

"Both candidates were then informally met by the Managers who created a precedent for Meetings of Managers by consuming Home grown strawberries and Ice Cream." This is the last entry in the minute book. We have not discovered the actual date when the School attained voluntary controlled status, but because of changes in the nature of the records, which were identified by Audrey MacCormack, the current school secretary, it is likely to have been at the start of the 1951/52 academic year.

## MEMORIES OF BEING A PUPIL AT BRABOURNE SCHOOL

Recollections of life in Brabourne School go back to the end of the 19th century; not direct memories, but indirect, from parents. As we mentioned earlier in the chapter, Joy and Keith Finn's grandfather, George Worrell, was headmaster of Brabourne school from about 1865 to 1901, and their mother (Ada Worrell) is said by the family to have been "born on the boards of the School House", the room above what is now the entrance hall and office, where Audrey MacCormack sits at her computer.

Direct memories of the school in the early years of the 20th century were largely positive, and those in charge are remembered with fondness and respect. We have only one memory of George Worrell, handed down from Fred Brooks to his daughter, Mary Brooks. Fred had always been hard of hearing but George seems to have been either unaware of this or unsympathetic to Fred, who was often told by the headmaster: "There are none so deaf as those who will not hear!" Yes, there were punishments for what might seem like minor crimes today, and some examples of them from the ancient Punishment Book of 1900 are given below. Nevertheless, from our contributors, one thing is clear: 70 to 80 years on, former pupils still cherish their memories of school life and the rewards given to them for different forms of achievement, all intended to encourage in one way or another. Rosemary Hendry (Ward) still proudly possesses the umbrella given to her by Miss Golding, then headmistress, for never missing a day's school in her first year. Similarly, for George Brooks, who freely admitted to having found little at school to stimulate him, life was transformed when Miss Golding took over as headmistress. In George's own words, the two previous schoolmistresses, Miss Wise and Miss Braun, whose names embodied both wisdom and strength, "never taught me a thing". Miss Golding, on the other hand, introduced a gardening class for boys, which found great favour

Extracts from the Punishment Book (1900) in Brabourne School

Rosemary Hendry (Ward) with her umbrella, a prize for
not missing a day's school in her first year at Brabourne

with some of them. After it had been going for two to three years, Miss Golding
instigated a competition for the best garden and the farmer then at Church Farm was
invited to adjudicate. George's garden was judged the winner, and some 90 years
later, he still recalled with warmth his surprise and unexpected delight at the decision.

Gardening class at Brabourne School, 1928.
Unfortunately, George Brooks does not appear in this picture.
1 Mervyn Hills, 2 Fred Arnet, 3 Tom Kingston, 4 Les Ward, 5 Douglas Trice, 6 Jack Varrier,
7 Sidney Andrews, 8 John Hallett

He received as his prize, Charles Roberts's The Kindred of the Wild: A Book of Animal Life, inscribed with the words "George Brooks, 1st Prize for Gardening, August 1927, from D. Golding".

Mrs Temple, Headmistress at Brabourne in the
mid-1930s, with her dog Wig/Whigg

Perhaps the skills he learnt at Brabourne influenced George's choice of gardening as a career after he left school; perhaps he would have developed these talents anyway, as gardening was "in his genes" (his uncle got him started in gardening at Monks Horton). Whatever stimulated his interest, the evidence of his talent was always visible in his perfectly manicured garden at his home, Providence, in Canterbury Road. Just for the record, George recalled that Miss Golding's father used to work on the bacon counter in Orpins and that Anthony Finn's aunt, Fanny Varrier, used to keep house for her.

Dorothy Mills

Brabourne wasn't the only school to encourage gardening. Writing of his childhood in Sellindge, Kenneth Andrews recalled that, "at school we had a large garden to tend and to crop. All the tools we used had to be thoroughly cleaned before we were allowed to put them away." Clearly good practice from the earliest age set the country up well for an era when Digging for Victory became so important.

Dorothy Mills joined Brabourne School as a pupil in the early 1930s when Mrs Temple was Headmistress and remembers being in trouble on a daily basis for writing with her left hand, and being forced to write with her right hand. One teacher was particularly unkind in this regard but Dorothy did not want her name included. (She is still scared of her!) Another teacher called Miss Goodwin was extremely popular, both with George Brooks and Dorothy, who described her as, "a lovely teacher who usually looked after the smaller children". Being too old for her class, Dorothy spent most of her days with the teacher she didn't like, so school was frequently a misery.

Dorothy lived with her family at Broad Oak (pictured below), a house rented from the Brabourne Estate on the road from Brabourne to Hinxhill. Lady Brabourne told us that Broad Oak, which was built in 1453, was one of the oldest houses on the Estate and had thus seen many tenants. Straying from the point for a moment, those familiar with Broad Oak may know it as Graham Hill's house, as the racing driver rented it from the Brabourne Estate in the late 1960s and early 1970s. Each day, Dorothy would walk the two miles from Broad Oak to Brabourne School and would frequently meet Mr Powell driving his herd of cows from behind Brabourne School to Ashford Market. She recalls being terrified of the animals and climbing up into the hedge to avoid them. He always had two fierce dogs with him, which added to her dread. In the evening, if he did not get the right price at Ashford Market he would walk the herd home, or he would have bought even more animals and, once again, Dorothy would climb into the hedge to avoid them. She was only five or six years old at the time. It was better when her sister was with her, even though she was younger.

Broad Oak on the road from Brabourne to Hinxhill
(painting by Michael Giles)

Moving on a few years Tom and Margaret Wratten, who lived at Forge Cottage, East Brabourne remembered two teachers in particular at the school: Miss Milborrow, whom Tom quite liked, and Mrs Norrington, whom he did not. One difficult day at school, when Tom was only five or six, he decided to leave and go home, but Mrs Norrington saw him and followed him in her car. He crossed the road at the top of School Lane and walked back home across the fields to Forge Cottage on Canterbury Road in East Brabourne, but to his horror saw Mrs Norrington's car parked outside his house. He got a clip round the ear from his mother and was taken straight back to school by Mrs Norrington.

There were others who said Mrs Norrington was not their favourite teacher. She apparently had the habit of saying, "Well you're not nearly as good as X or Y", or "X, Y and Z are the intelligent children in this class", which seems to have had a dispiriting effect. Karl Engels remembers being teased as a newcomer by Mrs Norrington's son, a much bigger boy with red hair. He would ask Karl, then only five, if he'd like to see "an elephant's nest in a rhubarb tree" and then take the excited Karl to a patch of nettles and push him into it. However, it was also remembered that Mrs Norrington did take an interest in the children and would periodically enquire after their families, especially when she knew the older siblings. On one occasion she asked Pauline Anderson (Marsh) how her older brothers were getting on and Pauline proudly told her that Derek had been "crucified" (she had meant confirmed).

Karl Engels with his prized lorry made by
Mr Norrington

Both Karl and Tim Marsh remember Mrs Norrington's husband for the lorries he made for the boys. Created from pieces of petrol can and other bits of metal skilfully assembled, the lorry that Karl still has was painted green. Karl told us that this was a gift to mark the end of the war, but according to Tim, who probably spent more years in Brabourne School than Karl, Mr Norrington made one for each of the boys every year. Not least because of their complexity and the hours of work that would have gone into making them, Karl expressed some doubt as to whether the lorries were an annual gift to the boys in the school. He wondered how many were still in existence, so if you have one of Mr Norrington's lorries please let us know.

## THE ADVENT OF SCHOOL DINNERS

In the 1930s, when the headmistress was Mrs Temple (remembered for having a dog called Wig – or was it Whigg?), pupils at Brabourne School received milk every day. This may have been part of a voluntary milk club that became popular in the 1920s, whereby teachers organised milk deliveries and collected money from the children[4]. Percy Nickolls who, many years later, would become George Brooks's father-in-law, kept a dairy at Warren Farm and used to deliver milk to the parish. One of his deliveries was to Brabourne School, where during morning break in winter, the children would enjoy cocoa and sandwiches round the fire in the schoolroom – with no concerns of Health and Safety regulations. As the minutes of the managers' meeting of 2nd December, 1941, told us in the previous section, cocoa was provided at midday, and it was at this same meeting that the then vicar's wife, Mrs McDowall, suggested that hot school dinners be introduced. She had no sooner proposed this

4      Atkins, Peter (2005) Fattening children or fattening farmers: school milk in Britain, 1921-1941, The Economic History Review 58(1):57-78.

than it was done. The very energetic Mrs McDowall set up a school canteen with the help of a canteen committee consisting of Mrs McDowall, Mrs Hammon, Mrs Cameron, Mrs Maclean, Mrs Temple as headmistress and Mr H.S. Hammon as representative of the managers. Mrs Burchett (who lived in Lees Road) accepted the position of cook, and from 26th January, 1942 hot dinners were available, and very soon were being eaten by all children attending the school.

It should be added that either in 1932 or the start of 1933 milk delivery from Mr Nickolls was cancelled by the Headmistress. Her later request for manure from Mr Nickolls met with the following tart reply: "Dear Madam, As you did not want any more milk I thought you didn't want the manure so therefore I have not saved it. I advise you to get your manure where you get your milk. Yours Truly, P Nickolls".

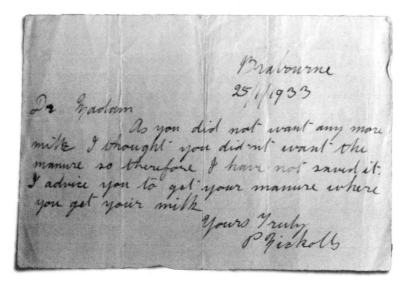

Note from Percy Nickolls to Headmistress of
Brabourne School

Jean Holmes (Nickolls), the great-niece of Percy Nickolls of Warren Farm, went to Brabourne School in the years following the war, and recalls that there were only about 30 children there at the time. In those days shortly after school dinners had been introduced, Mrs Burchett cooked on an oil stove with an oven on top of it. Jean used to stay for school lunches, which were invariably stews, custard and chocolate sauce, semolina, or the one that several former pupils remembered particularly well: tapioca pudding. Betty Dryland can remember a curtain dividing one of the two classrooms from the cooking area behind it, which was in the front half of the classroom on the left-hand side as you entered the school. It was often hard to concentrate, Betty

Betty Dryland

recalled, with the sounds and smells of lunch being cooked wafting through the flimsy divide. In the late 1940s and early 1950s, recalls Ann Griggs (Beadle), the older children used to take turns to serve lunch and wash the dishes. Jean remembers this well, too; however, when a new kitchen was put up later in the 1950s, children weren't allowed in it.

Mrs Burchett remained cook until about 1960, when Mrs Todd, who had previously been the dinner lady, took over. Another dinner lady remembered with affection by several of our contributors was Doris Norrington (not to be confused with Mrs Norrington the headmistress).

Kath Thornby recalled that the children, "would get a good main course every day followed by a good pudding", though it has to be said that school dinners and school milk will never please all of the children all of the time. One memory that was repeated through the generations of our contributors who have attended Brabourne School was the surreptitious discarding of food behind the radiators or the panelling, and the pouring away of milk down knotholes in the floorboards. One can only hope that this has helped to reinforce the fabric of the building over time.

Mabel Oliver (Brooks) also remembers that, in Mrs Norrington's time, after lunch, the tiniest children would be put to bed in a row of cots in the classroom found on the right-hand side as you entered the school. The room was kept warm by a large stove in the middle of the room, on top of which wet gloves and hats would be left to dry.

VISITS FROM THE DENTIST AND NURSE

In the 1940s and 1950s a mobile dental unit would come to the village hall and the children from Brabourne School would walk there together in groups of four to receive their treatment, which included having teeth extracted, and then walk back to school. Mrs Norrington was extremely sympathetic to those who were in pain and distress, recounted Betty, and would say, "If you don't feel like working, just put your head down this afternoon." Tom Wratten described the dentist as "a bit vicious", and added that anaesthetic was rarely used. Unsurprisingly, absences from school were said to be notably higher on the day the dental unit was due to arrive. Children from Stowting School also used to be sent to this mobile dental unit and John Varrier recalled the cavalier way in which extractions were carried out – with no consent sought from parents whatsoever.

The nurse would also periodically come to check on the children, with one of her tasks being checking for nits. In the 1950s, when Margaret Horswell (Wratten) had plaits, she came home very disconcerted one day because the nurse had checked only one side of her head. There had been no sign of nits on that side but, once home, Margaret kept agonising that there might have been some on the other side that the nurse had missed.

## A MORE RELAXED APPROACH TO SCHOOL LIFE

In spite of such "torture", school was more relaxed than it is now and Betty Dryland recalled that, one day each week, shortly after lunch, the radio (or was it the wireless?) would be turned on in the class for Listen with Mother, during which Mrs Norrington would sit with the children, knitting socks for her family. Mrs Norrington's children would also come into the school from time to time and Betty remembers her daughter, who would have been in her teens then, playing the cello for the children.

The school had comparatively few facilities at this time, but the children easily found ways to entertain themselves. Jean Holmes (Nickolls) remembers autumns playing under the horse chestnut tree in the front of the school and making houses out of leaves. At that time, the girls' playground was in the front of the school and the boys' was at the back. Making slides on hardened snow in the winter was another source of fun. Teachers whom Jean remembers were Miss Milborrow, Mrs Davis and Mrs Norrington. Gone were the days of hot chocolate round the fire that Rosemary Hendry (Ward) remembered, but free milk, cod liver oil and malt which were later provided for all children were a healthy alternative. Joan Taylor (Brooks) and her sister Mabel Oliver (Brooks) remembered a spoonful of cod liver oil at morning breaks, which was given together with a rusk and one-third of a pint of milk. Although such a combination was deemed to be fairly unpalatable, and although it was agreed that these measures probably helped to keep the children healthy, they were far from as appealing as the notion of hot chocolate around the fire.

## TAXI!

Travel to school from West Brabourne had clearly improved since Dorothy Mills was a small girl. Jean, together with Joan and Mabel, all remembered being taken to and from Brabourne School by Ward's taxi. At first, Joan and Mabel had had to walk over 3 miles from Running Water Farm in West Brabourne to school and the same distance home again each day, but the 1944 Education Act entitled children living further than 3 miles from school to free bus travel. The taxi from Ward's Garage, usually driven by Sam Jamieson, would collect and drop children at Crow Corner, at the bottom of Bulltown Lane, Green Lane and Hampton Lane; from there they would walk the relatively short distance home. However, if it rained or snowed, Sam would always take them all the way home. Those who caught the taxi, which was more like a minibus, included Joan, Rose, Mabel and Margaret Brooks; Eva Blaskett, who lived opposite Running Water Farm and whose father was tractor driver for Steward Brooks who owned Running Water Farm; Jean, who lived at Highfield in Hampton Lane; Ruby Harris, who lived with her parents at The Limes, now The Hall in Weekes Lane; Beeb Knight, who lived at Crow Corner; as well as Jeffrey Beadle's three daughters, who lived at California Farm near Hatch Park. It was quite a crush when everyone was in the taxi, and with no Health and Safety rules to follow there was probably no limit to the number of children who could be "squashed" in. At the time these were virtually the only children to arrive at school by car.

## A LONG-FELT TRAGEDY

As we mentioned briefly earlier, the relatively relaxed pace of life at Brabourne School was shattered on 29th October, 1942, when a wall separating the school grounds from the School House collapsed, killing two little boys, Wilfred Brooks and Dennis Griggs. Wilfred (pictured below) was Steward and Annie Brooks's son, Rose, Mabel, Joan and Margaret Brooks's brother, and also George Brooks's cousin. He was buried between his paternal grandmother and grandfather at the Zion Baptist Chapel. Dennis was a cousin of Elsie Davis, and the dreadful memory of hearing the news while she was working in the laundry at the Ashford hospital remained with her for the rest of her life.

The event left a lasting cloud over village life, as several people have mentioned this tragedy. Oliver Trowell recalls how distraught the vicar, Rev McDowall, was about the deaths. Keith Finn attributed the collapse of the wall to the probable impact of a bomb that had dropped not far from the School House. This was not the only one as, according to Eric Ball, another bomb had fallen in the fields below School Lane near the stream, and a third near the top of the lane, in the fields opposite the two cottages but a little towards East Brabourne.

Wilfred Brooks with his three sisters.
From left, Joan, Rose and Mabel. Margaret,
his fourth sister, was not born until after
Wilfred died

## THE ANNUAL BEDINGFIELD EXAM

"Captain Timothy Bedingfield, by will in 1693, gave all his lands in St. Maries, Woodchurch, and Liminge, towards the education of such poor male children, of such poor parents as did not receive alms of this parish, or out of any parish-stock, and whose parents were of the Church of England; and that such children be kept to learning, and sent to one of the universities if capable, or put out to trade; to be taken out of the parishes of Dimchurch, Liminge, and Smeeth...[5]"

The money left by Captain Bedingfield has benefited many in our villages, and not just male children. Some of our contributors, male and female, sat the annual Bedingfield Exam over 70 years ago, and in those days it was held at Smeeth School on a Saturday morning, out of normal school hours, and consisted of religious questions and also maths and English. Those who achieved the highest marks in the exam were

5    'Parishes: Dimchurch', The History and Topographical Survey of the County of Kent: Volume 8 (1799), pp.264-270 (www.british-history.ac.uk/report.aspx?compid=63482&strquery=Beddingfield; accessed 5th October, 2011).

Memorial to Captain Timothy Bedingfield and his wife,
Mary, in Dymchurch Church

"Near this place lieth Interr'd CAPTAIN TIMOTHY BEDINGFIELD and
MARY his Wife. He Gave all his lands lying in St. Maryes Woodchurch and
Liming towards the Education Maintenance and bringing up to Learning of
Such poor Male Children of such poor Parents who do not receive Parish
releife or alms out of any Parish stock. And which Parents are of the Church
of England by law establish'd & do frequently communicate therein and that
such Children and everyone of them be keept to learning and sent to one of
the Universities of Oxford or Cambridge if capable or put out to trade And
that the said poor Children shall be taken out of ye Parishes of Dimchurch
Liming and Smeeth or some one of them And five shillings a peece unto two
poor Women of the said Parishes for ever to be paid on the 25th day of the
December after thay have received the Sacrament according to the Church of
England and not otherwise. He died November ye 20th 1693 aged 50 years
Shee died July the 7th 1714 aged 80 years.
John Handfield of Ashford had this Erected in memory of his Aunt and
Godmother."

Brabourne School, 1905.
Far right, the Headmaster, Mr Wetherell; far left, possibly Mrs Wetherell

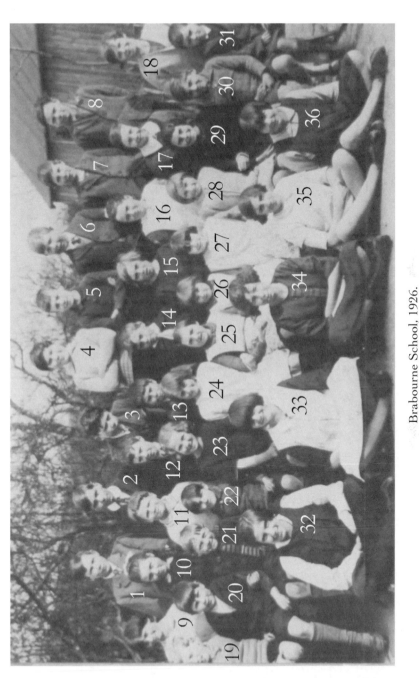

Brabourne School, 1926.

1 Douglas Trice, 2 Dudley Ward, 3 George Brooks, 4 Fred Arnet, 5 Arthur Bull, 6 Mervyn Hills, 7 Cecil Burch, 8 Tom Kingston, 9 Daisy Kingston, 10 Ruth Brooks, 11 Jack Varrier, 12 Eric Trice, 13 Pat Thornby, 14 Les Ward, 15 unidentified, 16 Nancy Brooks, 17 Vera Hallett, 18 Rosa Varrier, 19 John Hallett, 20 Leslie Simmons, 21 Ronald Fairbrass, 22 Charlie Andrews, 23 Gwen Norrington, 24 Evelyn Kingston, 25 Harriet Burt, 26 Rose Smith, 27 Eileen Hogben, 28 Mary Andrews, 29 Rose Thornby, 30 Sidney Andrews, 31 Dick Kingston, 32 Gwen Ashman, 33 Anne Kingston, 34 Frances Varrier, 35 Carrie Andrews, 36 Peggy Wheatly.
Our thanks to Rose Andrews (Smith) for naming 35 of 36 people 87 years after the photograph was taken!

Mrs Norrington and pupils, cMay 1959.

Back row: from left, unidentified, unidentified, unidentified, Lynne Howland, Robina Archer, unidentified, unidentified, Michael Hickmott, ?Charles Todd, rest unidentified.

Third row: from left, ? Hover, Hazel Mills, Barry Andrews, Susan Todd, Anne Kinkeard, unidentified, Philippa Chadwick, Pauline Marsh, Nigel Dalby, Pamela Smith, unidentified.

Second row: from left, unidentified, Marilyn Wignall, unidentified, Celia Howland, unidentified, unidentified, Lesley Southern, Bridget Pile (with doll), unidentified, Ruth Dalby, Betty Smith.

Front row: from left, Michael Norrington, Paul Howland, Roger Stone, Robin Thornby, Barry Spain, unidentified, unidentified, Christopher Mills, unidentified, Clifford Norrington, Arnold Woodcock, Pat Thornby, Ian Allard.

Staff: on far left, Mrs Norrirgton (Marsh), Pat Thornby, Christopher Mills and far right, Miss Hoyle.

Our thanks to Pauline Anderson (Marsh), Pat Thornby, Christopher Mills and Michael Hickmott for naming people in the photograph

Brabourne School, cMay 1959, with Miss Hoyle.

Back row: from left, Barry Spain, Paul Howland, Betty Smith, Lesley Southern, Barbara Baldock, Jackie Spain, Ruth Dalby, Roger Stone, Arnold Woodcock.

Middle row: from left, Julie Spain, Carol Fortescue, unidentified, Shirley Shorter, Bridget Pile, Christopher Mills, Marilyn Wignall.

Front row: from left. Patrick Thornby, Brian Lawton, Robin Thornby, Ian Allard, Celia Howland, unidentified, Clifford Norrington, Michael Norrington

awarded valuable cash prizes. Margaret Pile (Ward) and Joyce Garlick (Wood) both remembered sitting it. Coming from a religious household, Joyce won first prize on more than one occasion and Margaret remembers coming second and third on a couple of occasions. Both emphasised the importance of the prize money at a time when people had so little. Geoff Thorpe, a trustee representing Smeeth Parish, added that Gordon Fortescue, local builder and former mayor of Ashford, did not have a bicycle when he was at school. Allegedly, his father wouldn't buy him one. Gordon sat the Bedingfield Exam at Smeeth some 75 years ago, came top and with the significant prize money was able to buy himself a brand new bicycle, a Hobbit, made in Ashford.

Later, the exam was opened to students from Brabourne School and held there for students at Brabourne. This continued until late in the 1990s, by which time only religious knowledge was examined.

The exam was discontinued in the late 1990s because not all children attending Smeeth and Brabourne schools came from the parish of Smeeth and it seemed unfair that an administrative boundary should determine whether or not a child could sit the exam. Instead, it was decided that the annual grant from the trust should be invested in Smeeth school library, so that all children attending the school might benefit from the legacy of Captain Timothy Bedingfield. Heather Dove, clerk to the Bedingfield's Educational Endowment, confirmed that "the schools which still receive annual grants are Smeeth, Lyminge and Dymchurch. Each year, the Head Teacher returns a list of the titles of the books purchased and, as expected, they are suitable and interesting for primary school pupils."

POST-WAR MEMORIES OF LIFE AT BRABOURNE SCHOOL
Michael Hickmott, who was at Brabourne School between 1957 and 1963, writes:

"Just inside the main front door to the school, to the right, was the cloakroom where coats, hats and boots (when worn) were left. Each child had a peg with their name on, and on the peg hung a PE kit bag and an apron. To the rear of the main classroom was a modern kitchen built in the 1950s. Mrs Burchett was the cook, helped by Brenda Todd and another lady. Mrs Todd was the mother of one of my mates, Charles. We used to have lunch in the big classroom, which had panelling up to half the height of the room. The older children would sit at the back and push food that they didn't like behind this panelling (which is no longer there).

"During those years the school only had two classrooms [much as described by Betty Dryland], but with no dividing curtain. The lower school, which included children of five to eight years, was in the main classroom and the upper three years, the 9-to-11s, were in the former head teacher's study (which still doubled as a study). This was to the right of the larger classroom and is now behind the school entrance. There was no school secretary in those days. There was a big coal or coke stove in the senior class with a mesh guard, and the room was either freezing cold or boiling hot.

"The teacher of the lower class was a Miss Hill, a young teacher, while Mrs Norrington taught the upper class. She retired in 1963, the same year that I left primary school. Both Miss Hill and Mrs Norrington were kindly souls, determined to get the best out of their pupils. The younger children in the larger class, the room to the left of the school entrance, had all their lessons in there, but the class was divided into two groups for reading, writing and arithmetic. Part of the daily routine for the younger

Mrs Florence Norrington, the Headmistress of Brabourne School, 1942-1963, with her husband Mr Stuart Norrington, part owner of Norrington Brothers' Garage on the A20 (currently Bob Fisher's Garage). Our thanks to Bob Fisher for his help in trying to identify this car. If anyone recognises the make please let us know.

children was Listen with Mother on the radio. Spelling bees were a regular part of school life and these involved the children lining up along one side of the room and the back of the class. For every correct spelling they moved 'up' the wall towards the front, and for every error they moved 'down' towards the back of the room.

Though such methods are not used these days, standards of spelling and the 3Rs were high and, as testimony to this, all those who took the 11-plus exam in 1963 passed. I like to think this was the beginning of Brabourne School being one of the best in Kent for the next 50 years!

"Discipline in the school was generally good. Mrs Norrington could be very strict verbally and, as a consequence, the children both lived in fear of her and respected her. Emotional blackmail was frequently invoked to help control behaviour and this is an illustration of how it could be applied: peas used to be grown in Brabourne Coomb for Batchelors and the tractors and trailers transporting them to the factory would come up the lane past the school. The only thing that separated them from the children was a fence of chestnut spars, and it was local sport to grab handfuls of peas through the fence. We all did it, but one day I was caught and though I received no punishment, there was a veiled threat – 'What *would* your grandfather say if he knew about this?' Though I loved my grandparents and had immense respect for them, I lived in fear of them ever finding out about such minor misdemeanours, even more so than my parents. The potential shame that I felt was sufficient to stop me from ever doing it again. I know that I was far from alone in responding to indirect threats to inform parents and grandparents of bad behaviour.

Michael Hickmott

"Every year there was a sports day, a May Day celebration, a nativity play, other festivities and a truck race, which was one of the highlights of the summer term, especially for the boys who were encouraged to work in groups. Trucks were made out of salvaged timber and pram or pushchair wheels. The rear wheels, on an axle, were attached to a plank of wood running the length of the truck. Above the rear wheels a wider piece of timber was bolted on to form a platform or seat. Sometimes sides and a back were added, but this increased wind resistance and cut down the speed. The front wheels (smaller than the rear ones, if you could get them) were loosely fixed on a shorter piece of wood at right angles to the main plank and held with a bolt, washers, double-locking nuts and plenty of grease to allow movement. Attached to each end of the front axle was a loop of string, which served to steer the truck. Barry Spain and Chris Mills both had trucks, the latter's having a 'brake', a manual device fitted to one side that rubbed against one of the rear tyres to slow the truck down. There was extensive debate as to the value of a brake; many of us considered one superfluous as the driver's feet did just as good a job.

"In the morning of the truck race, the trucks were lined up in the girls' playground (why the girls'?) and were inspected for design and roadworthiness by Mrs Norrington's husband. The races were divided into heats – two trucks at a time – with quarter finals, semi-finals and the final. Prizes were awarded by Mr Norrington for first, second and third place, with the size of the spanner diminishing from first to third. The races took place down the School Lane from Canterbury Road and finished before the entrance gates into the school, so the drivers could divert their vehicles down the track beside the school to slow down. There were no regulations or safety equipment; most boys, and the occasional girl, just wore shorts and shirts – no helmets, trousers, knee or elbow guards in those days. Some went down the lane sitting upright on the truck, but if you wanted to win you needed to run as fast as you could beside the truck, pushing it and steering it as well, and then leap on, preferably on your stomach, and go careering down the slope, head first, at speed, to the finish line!"

Mr Norrington checks the trucks before the races start

Participants in the truck race line up

From left: Paul Howland, Michael Hickmott thundering down School Lane, Roger Stone at back, ?Clifford Norrington and Arnold Woodcock

Tension and excitement mount. The boy in the
lead is unidentified, behind is David Smith

Best truck winners, May 1959: from left, David Smith (3rd),
Pat Thornby (1st) and Barry Andrews (2nd)

Maypole dancing, August 1929

Still dancing in 1958, with the May Queen and her attendants looking on

Mrs Norrington with the May Queen, Anne Kinkeard, and her attendants, left,
Susan Todd, and right, Pauline Anderson (Marsh), 1958

Sports Day, c1958

All sorts of competitive activities and races

Still more of Sports Day, c1958.  Note the back of the old school

Brabourne School, 1976
Back row: from left, George Hutchinson (Headmaster), Adrian Bull, Daniel Spicknell,
Keith Harrington, Dean Penfold, Colin Smith, Conrad Shilton, Simon Gurr.
Middle row: from left, Joanna Curren, Helen Powell, Christine Saunders, unidentified, Julie
Ash, Susan Vago, Jane Glassborow, Sharon Logan, Elaine Winder, Peter Gay.
Front row: from left, Ben Robbins, Neil Ruse, Martin Keay, Jonty Harrington, Russel Tyre,
Emma Goodall, Donna Friend, Michaela Love, Sharon Austin
Our thanks to all who helped name children here: Simon Gurr, Carol Love,
Pauline Anderson, and Marion and Emma Goodall.

Brabourne School, 1978
Back Row: from left, George Hutchinson (Headmaster), Donna Friend, Helen Powell, unidentified,
Emma Goodall. Middle Row: from left, unidentified, unidentified, John Harrington, Sharon Austin,
Simon Gurr, Iain Hasdell, Adrian Bull, Jo Curran, Dan Spicknell, Ben Robbins,
Lisa Quick, Sarah Powell. Front Row: from left, Sharon Saunders, Deborah Love, Michaela Love,
Ken Pryor, Elaine Winder, Paula Penfold, Martin Keay, Joel Swain, Andrew Finn, Tony Howland

George Hutchinson took over as headmaster at the school in 1963 and was clearly revered for his good organisation and his drive. Carolyn Wilson (Taylor) remembers that he was very much into drama and that the school put on many plays in those days. He was followed by Alistair Guthrie, then Glyn Jones, and briefly by Jamie Evans; the post of head teacher is currently held by Vincent Chan. It has to be admitted that not all who went to Brabourne School enjoyed it, but there is a significant proportion, particularly those from 40 and 50 years ago, who remember their time at the school with much affection.

George Hutchinson, Headmaster, with, from
left, Honor Bell, Joan Manuel,
Doris Norrington and Joan Harrington
possibly in the late 1970s/very early 1980s

## FORMER HEAD TEACHERS REMEMBER

Alistair Guthrie, head teacher 1982-1988, writes:

"I became head teacher of Brabourne Primary School in January 1982, following on from George Hutchinson, who had been the head teacher for 17 years until his retirement in July 1981. George's deputy, Joan Harrington, became acting head teacher for the autumn term of 1981 and reverted to deputy when I took up my post. At that time there were 96 children on the school roll. Joan taught the infant class in the largest room of the school, whilst I taught the 36 oldest children in the next-door room, which, when the school was originally built, was the ground floor of the head teacher's house. Our middle class was housed in a mobile classroom and was taught by Honor Bell. Judy Keech taught the infant class for 1½ days per week, whilst Joan taught my class in order to release me for administrative duties. These took place in a wooden building across the playground. This was once described by an education officer as a shed. One of our governors, Reg Older, a farming neighbour of the school, took exception to this and explained that a shed was for the storage of carts, farm implements and so on. He described our building as a wooden office. The children, however, were not party to this exchange and always referred to the building as, 'The Shack'. The governing body had fewer members than is the case today. In addition to Reg Older, there was the chairman, the Reverend Michael Stephens, Chris Goodall, Margaret Gallehawk, Dorothy Willett and Jenny Cooper. There were others over the passing years, but being a school governor then was very different from being a governor dealing with present-day demands.

"Jill Shilton was the part-time school secretary and also doubled as midday supervisor before finishing work after lunch. Meals were cooked on the premises by Doris Norrington, who was assisted by Joan Manuel and Sue Newman, who was also a midday supervisor. Children arriving at school early were allowed into the kitchen by Doris, particularly in the winter. As Doris worked, perhaps mixing up by hand a sponge [cake], using eggs cracked from their shells, along with the other ingredients carefully weighed out, there would be a row of eyes peering over the edge of the table, their owners learning how good-quality school meals were made. In the autumn, children would be given a bowl and asked to shake the damson trees that grew on the school field and to gather up the fallen fruit. The damsons would then appear for the remainder of the week in many guises, sometimes to the consternation of those who believed they should be only an occasional treat.

"A peripatetic music teacher visited the school once a week. Before too long this was Tessa Fineman, a resident of Smeeth, who added much to the life of the school. Individual reading support was given by Betty Martindale from Hastingleigh and there were occasional (social rather than working) visits from our Education Welfare Officer, Don Woolley, who was never called upon to enforce pupil attendance. Our small team was completed by Chris Moss, our caretaker, who was only required to come to the school after the children had gone home. It was my task to open the school in the mornings, and sometimes to refill the tanks of the oil heaters in the main school classrooms if it had been frosty overnight.

"In those days, the local education authority did most of the purchasing for schools, each school only receiving a relatively small sum for the purchase of books and other teaching materials. It was always a struggle to persuade those in the Area Office in Ashford that it really was necessary to put the heating on when it was cold and there really was a need for more heating oil. The official heating season ran from November to Easter, but at the foot of the Downs the weather didn't pay heed to education-office directives. On the rare occasion that the school had to be closed because of snow, the closure had to be justified as frequently there was very little snow in Ashford and it was not accepted that the snowplough had difficulty getting through at Brabourne.

Alistair Guthrie with his children Andrew and
Christine, mid-1980s

"When Chris was working during November through to March, it soon became dark. Requests to the education office for an outside light to be installed were turned down, but a torch was provided! Other times brought other problems. Being surrounded by fields, we were frequently visited by the local mouse population and so the setting and emptying of mousetraps was a regular occupation. Less frequently, rat traps (borrowed from a farming parent) needed to be set, liver left over from school dinners being by far the best bait. Other wildlife abounded, but generally kept out of sight until the children had gone home. I often wondered whether the hare that I saw sitting in the middle of the school field one evening was the same one the children had laughed about one Wednesday afternoon. The Wye beagles had been searching the hedgerow along the top of the field next to the school, much to the children's despair, when the hare hopped along the bottom of the field and disappeared through the hedge, to cheers and laughter from the children. Although they had seen what had happened, the beagles, heads down, had been completely unaware.

"In some respects, the changing years had barely touched Brabourne School. The older children would stand when an adult visitor entered the room and would chorus, 'Good morning, Sir', sometimes to the consternation of the occasional visiting delivery driver who had just popped his head round the door to find out where to put the goods. This was something my predecessor had trained the children to do and for which I was rebuked by the visiting Diocesan Director of Education as being a waste of time and old-fashioned. But respect for others was important. This was reflected only about six weeks after I became head teacher in a visit I made, with a small group of children, to Mrs Opperman (Reg Older's mother-in-law), who lived in Clandon Cottage, The Street, in East Brabourne, on the occasion of her 100th birthday. It was then out of the ordinary for someone to celebrate their 100th birthday, but equally, it was expected that the school should mark the event.

"The children were trained, or perhaps were just naturally curious, to be silent when the telephone in the classroom rang. Since the school secretary was only part-time, it was necessary for me as head teacher to be available, even when teaching. This could sometimes be inconvenient, but I'm sure some conversations broadened the education of the children, and there were sometimes memorable occasions, such as when one little girl was called to the phone to be told by her father that her baby brother had just been born and the whole class applauded the good news.

"Life in school during the 1980s was much more relaxed than it is today. There was no National Curriculum, no league tables, no targets to be met and the children could be themselves and have fun. Playtimes were spent playing football (and getting covered in mud), walking on stilts, skipping or generally making the most of our idyllic situation. On fine days, no one minded if the bell was rung somewhat later than usual to get the children back to their classrooms, but the work still got done. In later years, many of the children who attended the school have become successful doctors, teachers, civil servants, policemen, computer experts, beauticians, secretaries and all manner of other occupations, including a nationally acclaimed opera director.

Brabourne School cannot claim all of the credit for their success, but it did give them a happy start for their education. Activities weren't always confined to the school and its grounds. There were trips out, sometimes to London, and our annual walk in April to Coomb Farm to see lambs being born.

"Many parents of pupils will remember the fun times that were had – singing The Twelve Days of Christmas prompted by the children's illustrations of each of the days, and the mince pies and mulled wine that followed; quizzes held in the school on a Saturday evening, with the participants dressed as TV characters; Christmas and May fairs held in the village hall; the annual sports day, with everyone squeezed onto our tiny school field to watch the slow bicycle race, or the infant dressing-up race; or merely gathering at the school gate at the end of the day to walk or cycle home.

"Many of these activities were made easier to stage when, after battling with the local education authority, we were allowed to have a second mobile classroom to house our oldest class, thus freeing up the largest room in the school for use as a hall. We could now have a whole-school assembly, indoor PE lessons, all children sitting in the same room for lunch, and all manner of other activities. Things were changing in the classroom. Our first computer was purchased and it was even linked to the Ashford Teachers' Centre through the telephone line. So it was that, by 1988, Brabourne School was preparing itself for the 1990s and I moved on. I have always hoped that the children who attended the school would remember it with affection and look back on their time there as some of the happiest years of their lives. I can certainly look back and see my time there as the happiest time of my teaching career."

RECOLLECTIONS OF GLYN JONES,
HEAD TEACHER AT BRABOURNE SCHOOL 1989-2009:
"I first set eyes upon Brabourne Church of England Primary School on a cold and damp January morning in 1989 – the day of the visit and interviews for the head teacher vacancy. It was a unique moment meeting members of the governing body in the head teacher's study, which was also the secretary's office and the staffroom, and was in fact a garden shed! I was to find out that it was a very superior garden shed, made of the finest cedar wood, and it served the school well, finally leaving the school when the present new building was erected. When it was dismantled there was hardly any rot in the whole structure and it was removed to a good home, where it still continues to function as a workshop.

"It was on the interview day that one of the candidates drew our attention to the state of the roof of the old school building, which came into existence [around] 1850. He declared that there seemed to be far too many problems associated with

Brabourne School c1990.

Back row: from left, Alex Cadogan, Natalie Powell, Alison Heckle, Robert Lockwood, Joe Janes, Daniel Stone, Katherine Hall, Stephan Hayes, Anna Embleton-Smith.

Middle row: from left, Elizabeth Morson, Chloe?, Claire Stryzyk, Michael Craddock, Jamie Thornby, Andrew Guthrie, Lee Stone, Catherine Craddock, Emma Lockwood, Claire Bridgeland.

Front row: from left, Samantha Harvey, Stuart Eldridge, Laurence ?, Victoria Marsh, Gemma Ruck, Sam Kingston, Jodie Lockwood, Charlotte Brind, Karen Smith

Our thanks to Anna Anthony (Embleton-Smith), Karen Smith and Victoria Wadie (Marsh) for naming people in this picture

Brabourne School leavers, 1998.
Back row: from left, Peter Embleton-Smith, Jack Williams, James Coleman
Second row: Hanya Bozac, Alice Hall
Third row: from left, Mr Jones (Head Teacher) Chloe Marsh (in front), unidentified, Rose Mullens, Laura Ripley,
Lizzie MacCormack, Rosie Yard, Joanne Logan, Mrs Ditton (behind), Claire Mulqueenie
Front row: from left, Sam Skilton, Oliver Wilson, Joel Spooner, Adam Wicken, Patrick Buckenham, Gary?
Our thanks to Peter Embleton-Smith and Oliver Wilson for naming people in this picture

the old buildings and the two mobiles that served as classrooms. I, personally, took an entirely different perspective and viewed it as a wonderful opportunity, as it is in idyllic countryside and has a wealth of history. Indeed, a rumour exists that the land was said to be of very poor quality for farming and so was donated to facilitate the building of a school and that it would produce good pupils! Luckily my dream became a reality and I started work in April 1989.

Glyn Jones

"And what a journey it became. Over the last 20 years the number of children at the school has increased and two extra mobiles were brought in as classrooms. Eventually the powers that be decided that a new school building was needed for the 21st century, and today a large new hall, a kitchen and three new classrooms can be seen in landscaped gardens and playground. The children of today are fortunate to have modern facilities set in the glorious Kentish countryside at the foot of the North Downs. They now have the use of a large playing field, bordering the school, to enhance their sporting skills. It is fitting that links to the past are still in evidence, in that the old building was renovated, to almost exactly as it was in 1850, to provide administrative space and a classroom for the older children, just as it was in the beginning.

"Many stories have been told of life in Brabourne School and generations of children remember the cedar-wood staffroom that, to hundreds of pupils, became known as 'The Shack'. The first question that many of the adults ask as you meet them today is, 'Have you still got The Shack?' Looks of disappointment cross their faces as they are told of its removal. When asked of its significance, they often reply, 'When you were caught being badly behaved at playtimes you were always told to stand by The Shack in full glare of the teachers.' Nevertheless, most pupils have very happy memories of their time at the school.

"Prior to the new buildings being in place and the new playing field being operational, sports day in the school grounds was difficult, but fun. A 40-metre six-lane track was marked out between the mobile classroom and the tall thorn hedge, designed to keep cattle out of the school and the pupils in, by the side of the lane. Competitors had their backs to the mobile's wall and the finishing line was a metre from the hedge! As health and safety became more and more of a concern, thick mats were fastened on the hedge so that pupils were not speared by the thorns. I can't remember anyone being hurt, though every competitor crashed into the mats. Even today, lost cricket and rounders balls from years past are discovered in the hedges.

"Over the past 20 years, the education of children has undergone dramatic changes and these are well documented elsewhere. The school can still be proud, as in the beginning, of producing good pupils, which it will continue to do for many years into the future.

Glyn and Jane Jones

"My tenure at Brabourne Church of England School came to an end upon my retirement in the summer of 2009. I feel honoured to have played a very small part in its history and can say, in all honesty, that it was an extremely enjoyable journey."

## BRINGING US UP TO DATE, VINCENT CHAN, HEAD TEACHER AT BRABOURNE SCHOOL FROM APRIL, 2010 TO THE PRESENT

"It is a privilege to be the latest Head Teacher of Brabourne Church of England Primary School and to follow on the outstanding efforts of Glyn Jones and all my predecessors. The traditions and history of the school are not only in the building, but also the memories of parents and grandparents of the pupils and families still connected to the school. And in the years and decades to come I hope our children will also have such fond and memorable recollections.

"The school continues to be very popular and all prospective parents I show around are charmed by its character. There is something so quaint when entering through the wooden, black front door into the old part of the school. But further in, the newer parts boast the latest technologies, with teachers using interactive whiteboards to show images from the space telescope or a virtual tour of Westminster Abbey; and children using laptop computers with wireless networks to play digital maths games with children on the other side of the world. How things have changed since George Worrell's time! Yet despite all these new technologies, Brabourne children still love, almost more than any other activity, to be outside, making the most of the wonderful and unique location of the school. Gardening club is very popular (as it

Vincent Chan

was in the 1920s); visits to the farmer's pond down the lane are a regular feature; and the sporting and athletic prowess of the school is in no small part due to the time the children spend outside running, jumping and playing games.

"Education in this country is currently going through unprecedented changes, with the advent of academies, free schools, and the transfer of power from the local authority to individual schools, but Brabourne has withstood many dramatic events throughout its history and always has, and will always continue in its primary task of providing excellent education of the highest standards for all its pupils."

The evolution of Brabourne School buildings
(c1900-2013)
by Vi Sprawling

# BRABOURNE SCHOOL IN THE 21st CENTURY

Photographs courtesy of Katrina Devenport (2013)

Photographs courtesy of Katrina Devenport (2013)

Brabourne School football team, 2010

Brabourne School football team, 2011.
Team photographs with kind permission of Brabourne School

Brabourne School netball team, 2012

Home football match
(photograph courtesy of Katrina Devenport)

Staff at Brabourne School, 2013.
From left: Andrew Stapley, Lizzy D'Anna-Burgis, Wendy Stryzyk,
Audrey MacCormack (School Secretary), Vincent Chan (Head Teacher),
Jackie Roach, Olwyn Barker, Suzie Betts and Natasha Miller

## BEYOND BRABOURNE SCHOOL

Will Wilson

It was not just Brabourne School that has been remembered with affection: Will and Ricky Wilson used to walk to Smeeth School from The Ridgeway and, on their way home, would invariably take a detour into Hatch Park to climb trees, throw stones, or to do whatever took their fancy. No one seems to have worried all that much when children were late home in those days (1950s). Will remembers Smeeth School fondly and especially Miss Pay, who used to have bad arthritis and always sat down to teach. Every lunchtime she would send two children, very frequently Will and his cousin Caroline Payne (Hendry), who were about 10 years old, to Goreham's to buy a packet of 40 du Maurier cigarettes, the red variety, which she then smoked through afternoon class. The reward for this was 6d each. Jane Barker also recalled this practice and added that Miss Pay nearly always wore a shirt and trousers, never a skirt (though pictured on the next page she's wearing a skirt). Miss Pay would often organise play days, when the children would bring a picnic lunch and, in theory, do some work on natural history. Jane remarked that, although

Caroline Payne (Hendry)

the natural history never came to much, they enjoyed themselves and probably learnt a great deal about their environment through play. John Jamieson remembered Miss Pay, too, and how children would try to become one of her favourites as this gave them access to all sorts of "treats". John must have achieved this status as he recalled being allowed to walk along to Church Farm, opposite Smeeth Church, to collect milk in a can, and to dig in School House chicken run to "bring up the worms for the chickens". He feels he learnt a lot about life at Smeeth

John Jamieson with Gael

415

School and he loved every minute of being there. Miss Pay had been at Smeeth a long time and had even taught Will and Ricky's mother, Nancy Wilson (Ward).

Class at Smeeth School with, far left, Miss Pay
Front right, Caroline Payne (Hendry), wearing a white skirt

After school one day Will and Ricky made their way to their home in The Ridgeway as usual. Inevitably, their journey home was slow because their attention was always diverted by this and that, but when they arrived they had a tremendous shock: their house was empty. Their parents were not there and all the furniture had gone. After a moment of panic, they suddenly remembered that the family had that day moved to their new home, Sandhurst, on Canterbury Road. Will and Ricky then had to re-trace their steps back down the Ridgeway, past Smeeth School and on to Canterbury Road. One could not really imagine that happening these days.

## CHILDREN AT PLAY

As people's lives have changed so markedly over time, we asked children of the past what they might have enjoyed doing on a warm summer's day in the school holidays when they were about 10 or 11 years old. We also asked children in Year 6 (aged 10-11) at Brabourne School (via their teachers) to tell us what they enjoyed doing on a summer's day in the holidays. From all these responses we have compiled the following table and we leave you to make what you will of the answers,. Those nearest the start of the table were mentioned most frequently while those further down the table were cited less often. One thing is clear from our 'data': children from any era all like "enjoying themselves", though the range and sophistication of the opportunities for doing so seem to have increased.

# FUN SUMMER HOLIDAY ACTIVITIES OVER THE YEARS

| Children in the 1930s | Children in the 1940s | Children in the 1950s and 1960s | Children in Year 6 at Brabourne School in 2007 | Children in Year 6 at Brabourne School in 2012 |
|---|---|---|---|---|
| Going for a seaside holiday in Folkestone | Playing cricket | Playing in Subdown Wood (long gone) | Playing with friends | Going on holiday – America/Spain/ Thorpe Park |
| Going to Folkestone harbour | Playing football | Playing in the stream with brothers, sisters and friends | Sleepovers | Playing on the beach |
| Spending time at the forge, helping to work the bellows | Catching rabbits | Playing tennis and cricket in The Street | Visiting relatives | Swimming |
| | Going to George Brooks's farm to help | Cycle races, "truck" races | Spending time with family | Playing with friends |
| | Going to Ashford Market with one of my parents | Fruit picking at Court Lodge | Playing outside | Having water fights |
| | Going fruit picking at the market garden | Going to Ashford Market with Grandpa | Climbing trees | Playing football |
| | Wandering about on the Downs | Swinging on ropes tied to trees | Swimming, camping and sleeping outdoors | Camping, climbing trees, going for walks |
| | Playing cops and robbers | Going out with Mum | Cooking on an open fire | Going to the theatre |
| | Playing "war games" | Going to Nan's | Having a BBQ | Bike rides |
| | Helping on the farm | | Bike rides | Going to the cinema |
| | Looking after animals | | Playing football | Horse riding |
| | Identifying wild flowers | | Playing on the trampoline | Playing in the garden |
| | Fishing with homemade rods | | Swimming in "my" pool | Having a BBQ |

| | | | | |
|---|---|---|---|---|
| | Paddling in streams and making dams | | Eating out | Going to Chessington |
| | Cycling | | Watching TV | Playing with remote-control car |
| | Climbing trees | | Watching Harry Potter | Playing computer games |
| | | | Playing on the PlayStation | Reading a book |
| | | | Listening to music | Visiting grandparents |
| | | | Playing music on my guitar | Waking up to the sun |
| | | | Going somewhere hot for a holiday | Having fun! |
| | | | Going to America/ Spain/France | |
| | | | Going to the cinema | |
| | | | Going canoeing | |
| | | | Going jet skiing | |
| | | | Going to different places and learning different languages | |
| | | | Going to Thorpe Park/ Chessington/Alton Towers | |
| | | | Going to a football stadium to watch Arsenal play | |
| | | | Riding my horse | |
| | | | Playing with animals | |
| | | | Having fun! | |

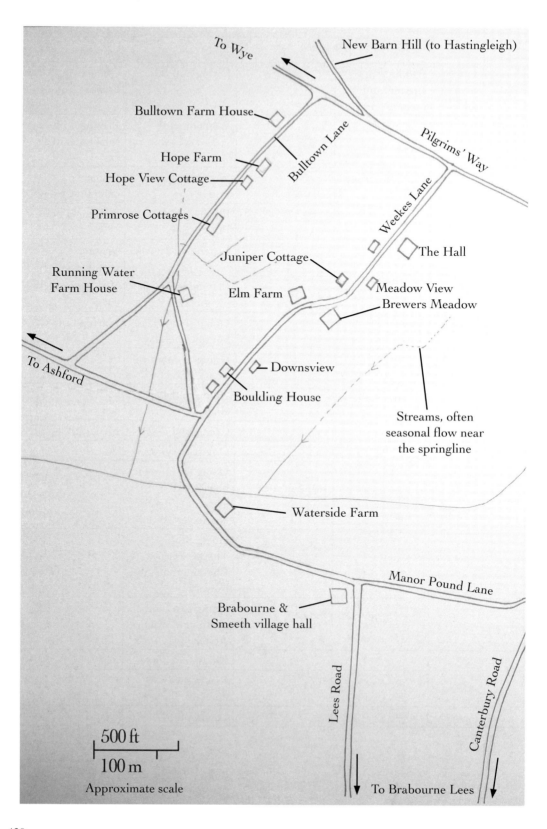

To Wye

New Barn Hill (to Hastingleigh)

Bulltown Farm House

Bulltown Lane

Pilgrims' Way

Hope Farm

Hope View Cottage

Weekes Lane

Primrose Cottages

Juniper Cottage

The Hall

Running Water
Farm House

Elm Farm

Meadow View
Brewers Meadow

To Ashford

Downsview

Boulding House

Streams, often
seasonal flow near
the springline

Waterside Farm

Manor Pound Lane

Brabourne &
Smeeth village hall

Lees Road

Canterbury Road

500 ft

100 m

Approximate scale

To Brabourne Lees

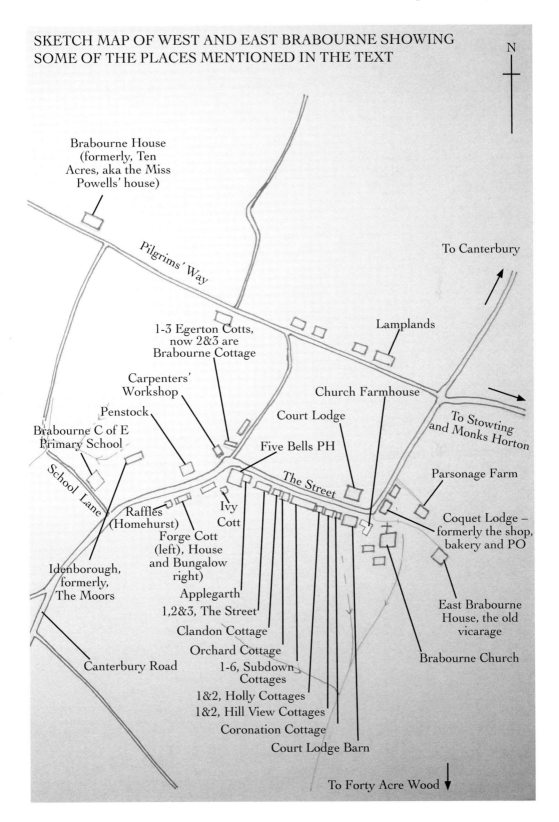

SKETCH MAP OF WEST AND EAST BRABOURNE SHOWING
SOME OF THE PLACES MENTIONED IN THE TEXT

N

Brabourne House
(formerly, Ten
Acres, aka the Miss
Powells' house)

Pilgrims' Way

To Canterbury

1-3 Egerton Cotts,
now 2&3 are
Brabourne Cottage

Lamplands

Carpenters'
Workshop

Church Farmhouse

Penstock

Court Lodge

To Stowting
and Monks Horton

Brabourne C of E
Primary School

Five Bells PH

Parsonage Farm

School Lane

The Street

Raffles
(Homehurst)

Ivy
Cott

Coquet Lodge –
formerly the shop,
bakery and PO

Forge Cott
(left), House
and Bungalow
right)

Idenborough,
formerly,
The Moors

Applegarth

East Brabourne
House, the old
vicarage

1,2&3, The Street

Canterbury Road

Clandon Cottage

Brabourne Church

Orchard Cottage

1-6, Subdown
Cottages

1&2, Holly Cottages

1&2, Hill View Cottages

Coronation Cottage

Court Lodge Barn

To Forty Acre Wood

# 7

# WALKING INTO EAST BRABOURNE

### LIFE AT THE MOORS (NOW IDENBOROUGH)

Moving on from Brabourne School towards East Brabourne the land falls away from Canterbury Road to reveal two semi-detached cottages known as The Moors on the left-hand side. Betty Dryland used to live in one as a child as her father worked for the Olders at Penstock Farm, who owned the cottages. Betty remembers the baker and the butcher calling twice a week and walking down to her home along the footpath from the rise on Canterbury Road. Milk, newspapers and coal were left at the top of the hill and Betty's father would carry them down. The road behind Brabourne School that leads to The Moors is relatively recent; before it was laid everyone approached the cottages via the footpath across the field. When the winters were hard almost everyone in the village would come tobogganning down the slope to Betty's house, where her mother would have the door open, a big fire going and a cup of cocoa for all the children and their parents who wanted to come in for a chat and a warm by the fire.

Derek Marsh and his parents and brothers, Peter, Tim and Alec, lived next door to the Drylands (Pauline Marsh (now Anderson), the boys' sister, hadn't yet arrived on the scene). Derek writes:

"I remember we had to get our water from a stream at the bottom of the garden, and also the toilet was down there as well – not good, especially in the winter! We used to knock on the bedroom wall and talk to Betty when we were in bed. I can remember that she knocked one morning to tell us the war was over. I was only five years old at the time but always remember our time there as being happy."

After Nellie Sawyer married John Norrington they lived at one of the cottages at The Moors. Nellie remembers that they had no electricity or running water, and water came from the stream. The house was heated by the Kitchener Range, paraffin fuelled the lights, and Ames delivered the family groceries. Both Nellie and her sister, Margaret Baldock, recalled the "joys" of the Primus stove, the flat iron, heating water in the copper for the washing, lifting out the heavy steaming washing and putting it through a mangle before struggling to dry it. They agreed without hesitation that the greatest improvement to life in recent decades has been the advent of the washing machine. Remembering life at The Moors, Nellie remarked on how hard it was to push a pram up the hill from the cottages to Canterbury Road.

## COPING WITH COLD WINTERS IN BRABOURNE

It is a common perception that winters were much harder in the past. Frosts were the norm and snow much more frequent. When the snow was crisp and firm the children used to walk on top of the hedge bordering Canterbury Road in order to reach the school. Eric Ball remembered the heavy snows of the winter of 1939, when the country roads became impassable and those living in East Brabourne and Stowting were cut off from Ashford as all roads to the A20 were blocked. Among the marooned were Eric and John Hammon, who could not get to the grammar school in Ashford for around three weeks.

Struggling to clear the road between Brabourne and Stowting (1945-50)

During one very snowy winter the doctor couldn't get through to Penstock Hall in East Brabourne and, as a consequence, Reg Older had to deliver his daughter, Diana. More recently, in bad winters when there were huge snow drifts, Anthony Finn recalls that Mary Bean, who worked at Penstock Farm as Reg's secretary, would drive down to the village hall in the Jeep to pick up farm workers from the village and some from Ashford who had managed to get to the hall to bring them to the farm.

In the long winter of 1963 Pat Browne, who had recently married Lyn, can remember them battling on foot from Ashford to Brabourne to visit Pat's grandparents. Jean Holmes (Nickolls), living in Hampton Lane, remembers that the snow started on Boxing

Day and everything was frozen by the evening; it took until the end of the next March for the last of it to disappear. Jean recalls how, once Lord Brabourne had taken the

Lyn and Pat Browne 50 years on. Photograph on their Golden Wedding anniversary

farms back when tenancies expired or tenants died, the roads were much clearer in winter-time because he had better equipment for keeping them clear. In hard winters of the past, ponds froze more frequently and Dicky Bedford's pond, at the bottom of Warren Bank, was a place for skating or sliding. One winter, more than a decade ago, Margaret Pile (Ward) went through the ice on the pond, much to the entertainment of all onlookers, and still remembered

by her younger relatives. Laughing at the memory, she reminded us that, "the lovely pond has now been drained".

Katrina Bewick (Stone) was born in that hard winter of 1963/64 at Hill View Cottage, opposite the village hall. Just a few days after her birth on 3rd February, her father, Phil Stone, discovered that Nurse Hills, who had delivered Katrina, was having problems reaching her mothers-to-be because the snowy roads were so treacherous. Very aware of her critical role, Phil drove Nurse Hills on

Jean Holmes

her rounds for the next few weeks so that she could continue with her work as normal and no heavily pregnant women were left without a midwife. This was a particularly kindly act on Phil's part as Nurse Hills, who was much loved in the villages, was also known for being a terrible driver – even in good weather. A few weeks after Katrina was born, as Phil and Joyce lay awake in the early hours of the morning, after giving Katrina a feed, they were surprised by heavy knocking on the door. Phil answered

Katrina Bewick

it to find Dr McGregor, whom he didn't know but who had been called out to an emergency. He was on foot, having had to abandon his car, which had slid into a ditch at the (then) triangle at the top of the slope where Manor Pound meets Canterbury Road. He had walked towards the only house with a light on, convinced that that was where his services were needed. Phil discovered that the call had been from Subdown Cottages in East Brabourne, so he promptly drove the doctor there, going round the other side of the triangle from where the doctor's car was stuck and successfully negotiating the hazardous road conditions to East Brabourne. After waiting several hours with the doctor, an ambulance arrived for the patient and Phil then drove the doctor home.

It was also during this same winter that Roger Stone, Phil's eldest son and Katrina's elder brother, who was then about 10, can remember walking to Brabourne School along the tops of the hedges, the road being blocked with snow at the time.

Sally Furneaux (Willett) recalls that the family moved to Brabourne Lees during a very cold, snowy spell in January 1965:

Sally Furneaux (Willett)

"We had moved from a modern, warm house in Horsham, Sussex, so the reality of a freezing, rambling farmhouse with no heating was rather a shock. On the day of our move my parents had no idea how to operate the solid-fuel Aga (the only form of cooking and heating in the house) and so, in much need of sustenance, we were squashed in the car – and driven to the Blue and White café (then known as Jiffy Snacks) on the A20 for a very tasty hot meal!"

Christine Gurr recalled the winter of 1969/70, when late one morning, when the children were at Brabourne School, snow began falling. The air was still, the flakes were large and very soon everything was covered with a thick blanket that continued to build up over lunchtime. School Lane became quite hazardous and the dilemma of how to get the children home safely was resolved when Keith Taylor arrived with his tractor and trailer, transporting several children home (including Alison and Simon Gurr), and providing a memorable and magical journey.

Christine Peall (Friend) moved from no.4, Subdown Cottages in The Street to Kingsnorth after she and Dave were married, though she used to come back about once a week to see her mother. On one winter's day in 1970, Christine caught the bus to East Brabourne as usual, but while she was with her mother the snow came down. After finishing work, Dave decided to go and pick her up and got to East Brabourne without too much difficulty; however, getting back to Kingsnorth was another story. The Street was fairly deep in snow but as the snowplough had been past the Five Bells clearing Canterbury Road they were able to get out of the village. At Manor Pound, though, the snow was some 3ft deep and was by then falling fast – they soon got stuck, so decided to abandon their

Christine and Dave Peall

Mini and walked back to East Brabourne. However, the snow was falling so quickly and heavily they realised that their Mini would soon be buried and invisible to the snowploughs, so Dave and Christine's father walked back to Manor Pound with four bean poles and, having found the car, which was already covered and invisible, planted a pole at each corner to mark its presence. They then returned to East Brabourne, calling in at the Five Bells. Dave recalled that, in spite of the blizzard, there was very little snow on the fields – it had all blown on to the roads and on to The Street where the snow was soon over 3ft deep. Christine told us how the only clear area was a neat path, dug by Wally Washford through the snow, from the door of his cottage at no.1, The Street, to the pub door. Wally maintained this path all the while the snow in The Street remained deep.

People were very friendly and hospitable during the snows. Christine and Dave remember someone from London, probably the City and probably the early 1970s, because he was wearing a bowler, calling in at the Five Bells when the snow was deep. He had walked from Smeeth and was determined to go on towards Stowting. He was offered a bed for the night by the Jenners, who then ran the pub, but he declined and, after drinking several brandies and warming himself by the fire, went on his way. The snow between East Brabourne and Stowting was very deep and, especially near the Hammons' house, it was very difficult to get through. The Pealls have often wondered how that traveller fared, but as no body was ever found we can only presume that he made it to his destination. Another traveller who got stuck at Brabourne on his way to Ashford was Richard Renshaw. He was given accommodation for the night by Kath Spain at no.6, Subdown Cottages, and Kath and Richard remained friends until Richard died some 40 years later.

The Forge, East Brabourne (c1912)

## THE FORGE AND FORGE COTTAGE

Almost opposite the gates of Penstock Farm, formerly called Wall Farm, was the forge, which was run by George Barrett. In the days when horses needed shoeing and cartwheels were essential, the forge was kept busy. Tom Wratten remembers that the forge had a big metal ring in the back garden where the cartwheels would be fitted with their metal rims. George used to need a hand to lift the wheels into position, and when the hot metal rim was being put on and water was used to shrink it on to the wooden wheel Tom recalled that, "the heat was unbearable". With the advent of farm mechanisation in the post-war years, demand for the blacksmith declined and so the forge in Brabourne disappeared. Vi Varrier remembers the forge well, having made many a visit there to get horses from her father's farm re-shod. At her youngest she would only have been about 11 years old when she was given this responsibility. She was so small at the time that she had to be helped both on to the horse and off again at her destination. Oliver Trowell recalls a time when his dog and its mother ran away for several days on a sheep-killing spree. Unfortunately, the animals killed some of George's flock, too, leaving Oliver's family to smooth over the ill feeling this caused – and to pay the bill for the damage.

Tom and his sister Margaret (now Horswell) were born at Forge Cottage, which adjoined the forge, and lived there through the 1940s and into the 1950s. The gardens of the two properties came together and each had a lavatory at the end of the garden –

The Forge, East Brabourne (early 20th century)

quite the norm in those days, when hand-dug cesspits were the only form of sanitation – while water came from a well in the garden. At that time there were orchards behind the two properties and the then owners of Penstock Farm, the Camerons, allowed the Wrattens to keep chickens there in a chicken house and a pen; their successors, the Olders, also allowed them to keep chickens there until 1950.

Living conditions at Forge Cottage must have been quite cosy, as Mr and Mrs Wratten, their two sons and a daughter all shared the cottage with three Land Army girls (Peg Hickmott, Doris Norrington, and Joan, whose second name Tom could not remember). Picture also an internal air raid shelter with a steel roof and a wire cage round it in the sitting room downstairs and all of Forge Cottage's inhabitants crowding into it for protection during air raids. When asked about their memories of life there, Tom and Margaret remember "playing in the orchards and all around East Brabourne" – the difficult living conditions virtually escaped their notice at the time. However, the overcrowding they grew up with could have been nothing like that experienced by Tom Wratten's father, also Tom, who was one of 14 children brought up in Park Corner Cottage, on Canterbury Road. It was not unusual for some of those siblings to sleep at Ned Andrews's house, now Sandhurst, further along Canterbury Road. One fond memory of Tom senior's was of taking a potato with him when he went to stay with Ned: on the way there he would put it in the kiln and leave it overnight, then collect it in the morning and eat it on the way to school. It would appear that he wasn't the only child to bake potatoes at the kiln.

The next major landmark in East Brabourne is Penstock Farm, but this is discussed in more detail in the section on farming in Chapter 9. We now follow the road as it bends round into The Street.

# IMAGES OF THE STREET, EAST BRABOURNE

Looking up The Street towards the Five Bells from what is now Orchard Cottage,
c1910-20

Outside the Princess' (currently pink) cottage, c1914-20.
It is possible that the tall person furthest away is Mrs Brooks.
Source: de Saxe, M. (1999) Images of Wye (1900-1925): The Gittings
Photographs. Ashford, Geerings for Wye Historical Society, p17

Looking up The Street towards the Five Bells, c1910-20.
Note the absence of a hedge bordering the field

Nancy Brooks swinging on the gate of what is now Orchard Cottage, The Street, c1923.
Note the footpath along the field on the right

Court Lodge, early 1930s. Home of the Hammons from 1849-1919

From Court Lodge towards the church. Coquet Lodge, then the general store with
lower window full of goods for sale, is to the left. Church Farmhouse is on the right.
This photograph must be from the early 1920s as the shop stopped trading c1925

Looking down the hill leading to Brabourne Church, c1930.
Parsonage Farm is straight ahead, Church Farm is on the right. Note the outbuildings at
Parsonage, especially the big barn with hooded porch.
The chicken houses are straight ahead

Looking down towards the church from Pilgrims' Way, early 1960s.
Note the greenhouses of the market garden at Court Lodge on the right

## THE FIVE BELLS

At the upper end of The Street is The Five Bells, one of the most ancient landmarks in the village and at one time, the poorhouse.

The Five Bells and The Street, East Brabourne, 1955,
by Oliver Trowell

The Five Bells and The Street, East Brabourne, c2000

Our first item on The Bells dates from 1854, and is "borrowed" from About Brabourne and Smeeth (Spring, 1985, pp16-17), produced by the Brabourne and Smeeth History Group.

## ROUND ROBIN COMPLAINING ABOUT THE LANDLORD OF THE FIVE BELLS

Don Skeer, one of the principal contributors to About Brabourne and Smeeth, tells of a round robin, a petition to the Brewers Rigden and Delmar, complaining about the behaviour of the then landlord of the Five Bells. Don says, "Most people have heard of a 'round robin' but few will have seen one. It is a written petition, signed in a ring so that it may not be known who organised it. I have always felt that there was something a little amoral about this type of petition; on the other hand the parishioners may have tried other means."

Members of Brabourne and Smeeth History Group, taken at their first exhibition in 1974. From left, John Hammon, George Brooks demonstrating a seed fiddle, Alan Clark and Don Skeer, the Chairman

The round robin bears the names of many who played an active role in the community in this era. Familiar names include Alfred Hammon, Edward and Edmund Hammon, Pilcher, Rolfe and James Weekes, among others. As Don observed, of the 37 who signed, "only the names Andrews, Hammon and Thornby [remain] as descendants", adding that, "of these Mr J Hammon is now moved over the boundary to Stowting."

The round robin read as follows:

"Messrs. Rigden and Delmar                                    August 9th to 11th 1854

Gentlemen

We the undersigned inhabitants and ratepayers of the Parish of Brabourne beg to express to you our opinion of the unfitness of Mr. Wm. Fox[1] as Landlord of the Five Bells, in our Parish. His conduct has been most gros[s] on many occasions, he gives way to drinking and uses the most violent and opprobrious language to those who would be his best support-ers – many absent themselves from Parish meetings which are held at his house (and which by the way were removed from the school for his benefit) on account of his violent and abusive conduct.

We have no wish to injure the House as an Inn – on the contrary we have always been anxious to support it and feel assured that its prosperity would be much promoted by Mr. Fox's removal – We have taken this step in order that you may give it your consideration, instead of applying to the Magistrates in September to withhold the license as we at first intended.

We are Gentlemen,

Yours respectfully,"

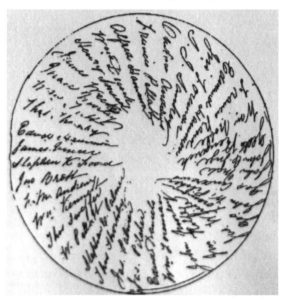

---

1        Note: William Fox is named as the victualler of the Five Bells in Bagshaw, Samauel (1847) History, Gazetteer and Directory of Kent 1847. Vol. II. Sheffield, publisher G Ridge, p468.
Permission to reproduce the round robin was kindly granted by Mr John Hammon the last Chairman and only surviving member of the Brabourne and Smeeth History Group.

## THE MOONS AT THE FIVE BELLS

From 1933-40 the landlord was a Mr Alexander Moon, who used to spend much time out of the country in the Gold Coast (Ghana), and would write to Arthur Ball, his near neighbour, addressing his missives to "Conker Tree Cottage", rather than no.1, Egerton Cottage. The reason for this was that there was a huge horse chestnut tree outside the carpenter's workshop, to the top of which Arthur would climb to place a flag when Mr Moon came home from Africa, recalls Eric Ball, Arthur's son. Eric liked Mr Moon. On one occasion when he was off to Africa he asked Eric what he would like him to bring back, to which Eric replied "a monkey". When he returned he told Eric that he had not been able to bring him a monkey but, instead, had brought him an elephant. He presented an excited Eric with a carved elephant seat made out of a single piece of hardwood, and it is still treasured by the Ball household. On another occasion, Mr Moon asked Eric if he would like to go to watch the cricket

Mr and Mrs Alexander Moon

at Maidstone. Eric was delighted as Wally Hammond, the English Test cricketer, was playing. Mr Moon's generosity and kindness are still fondly remembered and appreciated.

Alec Moon (son of Alexander Moon) wrote:

Alec Moon

"We moved to the Five Bells in 1933, when my father, Alexander Moon, became the licensee. The inn belonged to the brewers George Beer & Rigden Ltd of Faversham, who delivered beer to the pub in steam wagons. Father had previously run the Clarendon Hotel in Dover and it proved to be a wise move to Brabourne, as the Clarendon, together with the rest of Northumberland Avenue in Dover, was bombed and shelled to oblivion during the 1939-45 war. He ran pubs when he was not otherwise engaged in his other occupation as a prospector for alluvial gold and tin mining companies in various parts of the world.

"The interior of the Five Bells has changed considerably since we were there, although the main entrance through the porch remains the same, as does the bar [though this has changed substantially since this was written]. Lighting was by pressure lamps with such delicate mantles, filled with paraffin, and heating by an open fire in the Darts Room, with additional heat coming from a portable upright, cylinder-shaped paraffin heater that was usually in the bar areas, and could be used to heat water in a kettle balanced on the top. In addition to a darts board, the Darts Room had a big table with dominoes and the pegging board for scoring. The most popular form played was four-handed partnerships having five dominoes each, 5s and 3s. Then there were playing cards and a splendid shove-ha'penny board, beautifully smooth, with the ha'pennies being old pennies ground perfectly smooth on the underside. The Darts Room was where people gathered, particularly at weekends, to drink, gossip and play; otherwise, the customers during the week would consist of locals content to prop up the bar and hear any news. On the wall was a pinball machine that, for one penny, allowed two balls to be shot to the top – the player would use a moveable cup to catch each ball as it bounced off the pins on its way down. The prize was a token worth two pennies or, very occasionally, six-penny tokens appeared.

"There was another room to the right of the bar as one entered, known as the Tea Room, which had a separate entrance from The Street with a bell attached to the door as a warning of a visitor entering – a rare occurrence. The room was used mostly after darts matches against visiting teams, when everyone repaired to sing around the piano. My father, as host, was always prevailed upon to sing, and he was always ready to give his rendition of Just a Song at Twilight. A door just to the left of the bar led to stairs and the first floor, up which I would make my way, shielding my candle against the drafts, to my cold bedroom. Behind the bar was an area where the beer barrels were kept on trestles. The barrels were tapped on the spot, using a wooden mallet to drive in the wooden tap, a procedure not for the faint-hearted. Mild beer was sold at four pence per pint, bitter for a tanner (six pence), and old ale for eight pence. A popular drink was a mixture of half-and-half. Washing up was most primitive and involved a basin and cold water. Against the other wall were shelves holding glasses, cigarettes – Woodbines in five-pack, open cartons for two pence, and all the other popular brands, such as Park Drive, Player's and Senior Service – and bottles of spirits. Nothing much in the way of wine, except sherry and port, with cider and soft drinks. The only food would have been Smith's crisps (with the blue packet of salt included), and mother's own pickled hens' eggs. Extra barrels of beer were held in this area because, although there was a fine cellar beneath the Darts Room accessible from the road through a hatch, and from the rear of the house down a ladder, it filled up completely with water in the wetter winters – making it a good place for hanging pheasants and the like in the cool above the water.

"Right at the back of the interior was the private sitting room, not in the least private, as it was completely open to view from the bar. The sitting room looked out on to the garden and had a walk-in larder on one side and a door to the Tea Room. The kitchen, which was on the other side, held a paraffin-fuelled cooker, a hand pump over the well for fresh water, a stone sink and a copper boiler for the weekly wash. The back door led to the large vegetable garden and the one and only toilet, which was nicely set in the garden and reached by a flagged path.

"Upstairs there were four bedrooms, plus a large long room, which we used as a sitting room. This room had in its floor a trapdoor, and the story was that at some time in its history the building had been a workhouse. The big room was a dormitory and, as the unfortunates died, they could be lowered to the ground floor through this coffin hatch and taken out of the building. From the first floor there was another short flight of stairs leading to a loft and access to the roof through another trapdoor. On rare occasions I was sent to the loft to search for a clay pipe for some ancient traveller who had the wish for a smoke but not the wherewithal. The pipes were kept in a wooden box filled with sawdust as they were quite fragile, and as time passed it was difficult to find a complete pipe, so sometimes the smoker had to use one with a short stem. Mostly, I guess, they would have been thrown away after one day's use.

"Next to the Five Bells was the post office, which doubled up as a tiny grocery store. It was run by an elderly couple, Mr and Mrs Carling, whose takings must have been terribly small. Further along lived Tommy and Liza Sharp with their daughter Olive. They had come from a fisherman's cottage at Folkestone harbour after Tommy had been badly gassed in the Great War and could no longer fish. Liza Sharp became a great help to my mother in the pub after she became the licensee when my father left for a gold-dredging company in the Gold Coast of West Africa (now Ghana). The Sharps had to suffer living in a damp old cottage with a landlady who soothed her own suffering with port that she would purchase from my mother during unobtrusive visits via the Tea Room (rather than the front door). Mr and Mrs Albert Hammon lived in the detached house further along, then known as Albert House, now Clandon Cottage, and Bert and Carter Hammon lived in two bungalows beyond the school, Bert at the top of School Lane. Morry (Maurice) Hammon (so-called by Noble Smith) who was a regular at the Bells used to cycle over from his farm at Stowting on most evenings for a modest half-pint or so.

"One of my chores that I did not enjoy was to push a four-wheeled upright type of cart, with iron-clad wheels that squeaked abominably, along the road to the vicarage; it would be loaded with quart bottles of beer for the Reverend Charles McDowall who, I guess, would never have considered coming into a pub. This ex-schoolmaster,

## EARLY IMAGES OF THE FIVE BELLS

The recruiting officer in The Street, near the
Five Bells, 1914-18

The Five Bells, c1914-18

Cellar hatches open, early 1920s.
Perhaps a delivery from George Beer and
Rigden's was on its way
(early 1920s)

The Five Bells, late 1920s. Note the bus timetable on the wall
(East Kent buses began operating c1922)

despite my journeys to his back door, looked unfavourably on me as I missed many of his pre-confirmation classes. However, he reluctantly allowed me to attend when the Bishop of Dover came to Wye (or Brook) to officiate. Next to the church lived the Trowells. Very occasionally, when my bike was out of action, I would catch the bus into school at Ashford, as would the junior Trowells, Pam and Oliver. Next along was the home of Lady Bomford, and at the back was Parsonage Farm, run by the Smith family. George Smith, a short, stout farmer of few words, would present cheques to my mother for cash. He was particularly remembered for coming in at midday on one hot day, after he had been ploughing with his big shire horses, and ordering two pints of beer. His friend was not in sight – in fact, his friend was not there at all. George swallowed the first pint in one go before tackling the second. The Princess Cantacuzino lived at Court Lodge in those days but did not patronise the Bells at that time.

"Opposite the pub lived Arthur Ball and his family: Brenda, young Arthur, Bob, Kathy and Eric. They lived next door to Mrs Stickles, who was looked upon with some suspicion as she wore on her head a mass of grey hair in the form of a wig, which gave her a witch-like appearance, until one day she surprised everyone by appearing with a nicely cut head of her own white hair. Arthur was the wheelwright who worked for Leonard Finn in the shop near his house, helped by Leonard's son Keith. Arthur was a regular at the Five Bells in the evening, confining himself to two halves of bitter and a small flutter on the pinball machine, at which he was quite expert. He was a fine craftsman and, apart from his normal work, he carried out repairs to some of the treads of the 900-year-old ladder in the belfry of the church.

"Down the road leading towards Brabourne Lees lived Sid Finn in the first house, Ivy Cottage. Sid at one time owned the brickworks on Canterbury Road, which had a reputation of producing bricks of exceptionally hard quality. A bit further on, opposite Penstock Farm, was the smithy and its cottage. The blacksmith had a helper in the form of his nephew, who had been wounded in East Africa in the First World War, when he was shot in the arm by a sniper. There was always a wonderful smell peculiar to all smithies in the shop at Brabourne, of soot and smoke, burning coals, sizzling metal, steam, and perhaps sweat as well. One day I watched a new wagon wheel being fitted with its iron tyre. The wheel had been made by Arthur Ball, complete with hub, spokes and the outer rim, which, I guess, was in segments but which had to be perfectly circular. The tyre had been forged by the blacksmith in one piece and also had to be perfectly round and have a diameter that would allow for expansion when hot. This tyre was heated up to the critical temperature and then gripped by tongs and, with much shouting and hammering and many Anglo-Saxon oaths, it was forced on to the wheel and plunged into water to extinguish any flames – but more importantly, to shrink the tyre securely to the wheel.

"Further along the road lived Joy Finn, younger sister of Bet and daughter of Leonard. Then there were the Varriers – Bill, Dick, Duck (so-called because she addressed everyone as such) and Rose, who married Keith Finn.

"Earlier, I should have included the Washfords, who lived somewhere between the Sharps and Mrs Hammon. There was father, mother and son Wally, who had followed in his father's footsteps and became a hedger and ditcher for the council. Although Wally had a cycle to get to his particular stretch of road, his father would have had to walk to his part of the road system with his trousers tied below the knee with binder twine and in his hob-nailed boots. (George Brooks recalls that, at one time, Mr Washford senior had a trike, which he used to ride the length of the road he maintained. This would probably have been in the 1920s.) Wally was a staunch supporter of the Bells and would spend part of each evening in the pub and never seemed to have a holiday, but on Saturdays he would meet a couple of pals and they would do the rounds of the neighbouring pubs before finishing at the Bells, perhaps a little the worse for wear. With no TV or radio, the pub served as a meeting place to chat with a drink in the warm and a bright light rather than a candle and a bit of a fire at home. On some nights, when Len Harvey or another famous boxer was performing, I would carry our radio and accumulator into the Darts Room and tune into the BBC so that all could hear the commentary.

"Another regular at the Five Bells was Tommy Wratten, who came from Smeeth. Tommy could turn his hand to most things, including driving the steam engine, which was used to drive the threshing machinery. He achieved everlasting fame by driving the steam engine down Stowting Hill without mishap. He sometimes fell on hard times and my mother once employed him to polish and sweep, anything to earn perhaps a shilling. He was always neat and tidy, with dark hair brushed straight back, and there could have been another reason for his preference for East Brabourne as I composed a poem that began:

'The village of Brabourne is all agog as such news as this is tall,
  The captain of our darts team [Tommy] and the cook at Penstock Hall...'
  I do believe Tommy and the cook (Ivy Agnes Coleman) married.

"Other visitors included a squad of young TA members, who stopped off from a training exercise for some cider on a hot summer's day. This draft cider was pretty powerful and, after a pint or so, most of them had to be carried out and laid on the bank opposite to recover. Others who came in were visiting members of the WI or similar, who brought their own sandwiches and needed cups of tea. They were a mixed blessing, as lots of crockery was needed and plenty of hot water and tealeaves,

Tom and Ivy Wratten on their wedding day outside Brabourne
Church

sugar and milk to cope with the sudden arrival of lots of thirsty ladies. They would have their refreshments in the garden and, one day, when clearing up afterwards, I found a purse with a ten shilling note, a few coins and a return bus or rail ticket. They never returned and I often wondered when the poor lady realised her loss and what it meant.

"The running of the pub must have been a difficult and arduous job for one woman. Opening hours were from 10am to 2pm and from 6pm to 10pm, so the public rooms had to be scrubbed and polished, fireplace cleaned and re-laid and, the worst bit of all, the spittoons and the latrine cleaned. Spittoons were part of the furnishings – without them, some men would just have used the floor. The latrine had a door from the roadside and was just a plain wall with a drain, and with no water laid on it was a bucket and broom job. Morning trade brought a mixture of travellers, as well as a local or two. The Orpins van, delivering goods from the shop in Brabourne Lees, called twice a week, driven by a thin respectable man, who always addressed everyone as Mister, with his young and equally thin assistant. They both always had half a pint of bitter each as they brought the news from the neighbouring villages to us, before rattling along on their way in the Trojan van with its solid tyres. Most essentials of life were delivered: the milk in bottles, fresh bread, meat from Cooper's shop at Smeeth (brought by Arthur Taylor, who was also the demon fast bowler for Mersham Le Hatch, and occasionally up a league for Hythe), and fish from Messrs Griggs of Hythe. During slack times in the general labouring business, Bunny Hayward turned his hand to snaring rabbits and maybe the odd bird, and wore the traditional poacher's overcoat with voluminous pockets to hide the catch; indeed rabbits were a regular part of everyone's diet. Evening trade in the winter during the week was rarely brisk and few would brave a cold, wet, dark night, so settling up with the brewer's representative once a month could see my mother scraping the bottom of the barrel.

"One winter, perhaps early in 1940, there was such a snowfall and drifting that the lane opposite the Bells leading to the Pilgrims' Way was completely blocked. My mother was trapped in the pub, unable to open any door until Liza Sharp came along to dig her out.

"Very late in 1940 my mother gave up the Five Bells to join my father in British Guiana (now Guyana). She left Liverpool in a fierce air-raid, driven through the burning docksides by a fearless taxi driver, to a ship that duly arrived in South America after six weeks and via Iceland, all safe and sound."

## OTHER MEMORIES OF THE FIVE BELLS

We heard many other reminiscences of the Five Bells. Eric Ball recalls that, in the 1930s, the pub used to have stables attached to the right-hand side of the building (if viewed from the front); entering the pub from the current car park would have taken you through them. These stables were much used when there was a drag hunt, which is when the hounds chase a scent laid or dragged by a runner with a bag quite often made up either of fox urine or someone else's attempts at mixing a suitable scent with sawdust. The stables were also used when the point-to-point races were taking place in Brabourne. Soldiers from Shorncliffe Camp, near Folkestone, would ride over to East Brabourne, stable their horses at the pub and walk to the point-to-point. The last time that Eric saw the cavalry was in 1937, when he was about nine years old. It was a hot day. They came down Stocks Lane, left their horses under the conker tree and went to the Five Bells. When they had gone, Eric found a spur, which his father hung on a hook in Leonard Finn's Carpenter's Workshop in case the soldiers came back for it. The spur remained on the hook, hidden for years among chains of different sizes and other things. It was rediscovered when Keith Finn, Leonard's son, retired in the early 1980s and Eric now has the spur, a testimony to a world long gone. More recently, Robin Marsh observed groups of about 30 soldiers from Shorncliffe being dropped in the area by two lorries, each large group subsequently dividing into smaller groups of two or three. Messages or clues had been left in strategic places and, using their walkie-talkies, the small groups carried out various exercises. The lorries, he noticed, would return in the evenings to pick up the small groups, and the less-successful stragglers.

Bill and Hilda Jenner ran the Five Bells in the 1950s and 1960s, and became very much part of the village. After they retired they lived at no.3, Egerton Cottages, almost opposite the pub. Christine Peall (Friend) talks of them as a lovely couple who were warm and fun. Bill always joked about things and Hilda has been described as kindness itself. Anthony Finn recalls that Bill loved the Sunday radio show The Clitheroe Kid so much he wouldn't come down to serve customers while it was on. Christine's father, Bob Friend, used to look after the pub garden in the 1950s, and while he was working there Christine and her sister used to enjoy making a camp under a tree. On more than one occasion they would return to their camp to find that Hilda had left toffees for them.

The Five Bells was a centre of village social activity and, during the late 1960s, several regulars created the Ding Dong Cinema club at the pub. Among those involved were Bill Jenner, the landlord, naturally; Norman Williams, who lived at no.3, Subdown Cottages; Jack Coveney, who lived opposite the pub in no.2, Egerton Cottages; Jack Smith, who moved into Lamplands after moving from no.1, Subdown Cottages, when the Rice family moved to Devon; George Smith, who lived at no.1, Egerton Cottages, and was the brother of Noble Smith, who owned Parsonage Farm; and several others. The club used to make their own films, often humorous movies, no more than a few minutes long. Christine remembers one of them being about a camping trip and the problems of frying an egg on a camping stove in the outdoors; all of this was filmed in the garden of the Five Bells. Local camaraderie was abundant in those days and enjoyment was to be had by young and old in an atmosphere of cigarette smoke, mini-skirts, beehive hair, Crimplene, brown ale, milk stout and snowballs (the cocktails, of course).

Until its transformation in the 1960s into a relatively modern pub, the Five Bells had two bars and a hatch through which drinks were served. It also had two doors, one of which was closed up within the past 20 years or so (and recently re-opened). As the picture 'painted' by Alec Moon (above) shows, the pub was far more basic than it is today. Elsie Davis recalled an evening when someone had gone there for a drink and the pub only had beer – no spirits at all. However, Bill Jenner did know someone who could help: going almost next door to Wally Washford's, he returned with a bottle of sherry for the customers. Such a situation could not be imagined today, not least on the grounds of Health and Safety, but people who lived through the Depression of the 1930s, the war, and the years that followed, were well used to shortages and to making do with what was available.

# A SNAPSHOT OF THE FIVE BELLS IN THE 1970s

Popular landlords Bill and Hilda Jenner

Members of the Ding Dong Cinema Club, the
films of which entertained locals at the Bells

Norman Williams threading film on to the projector

Norman Williams, left; Wally Washford at the back

Playing darts

Jack Smith, left

George Smith of Parsonage Farm

Above and below, Jack Coveney. Everyone smoked
in those days.

Norman Williams, left

Sid (Tink) Norrington

Seasonal visitor to Brabourne

Above and below, celebrating the Jenners' 50th wedding anniversary in 1970.
Third from right, Christine Peall (Friend); far right, Mrs Jenner

Second from left, Mr Jenner; centre, Jackie Friend; far right, Mrs Jenner

The Jenner family celebrations continued: from left, Eric, Myrtle, Bill, Hilda and Iris 1970

Some years later: from left, Eric Ball, Eric Jenner and Philip Stone in 2004

## THE BLACK HORSE

On the outskirts of the parish, down Fiddling Lane near Monks Horton, but still in the civil parish of Brabourne, is The Black Horse. In times past it was quite a trek to the pub across the fields from East Brabourne, and even further from Brabourne Lees, but now, with transport so much improved, The Black Horse ranks as one of Brabourne's "locals".

The Black Horse is known to have been an inn since the mid-
eighteenth century, and possibly dates from much earlier. This sketch which
hangs in the pub shows a much smaller extension than the current one.
Date unknown

The Black Horse in 2013

The Pomponio family, proprietors of The Black Horse.

From left: Rita Pomponio, her father Nicola and sister Sarah McKeague (Pomponio)

## EAST BRABOURNE'S SHOP AND POST OFFICE

The shop in Brabourne Street – an alternative name used locally for The Street, East Brabourne – was next door to the Five Bells, in what is now Applegarth. It also housed the post office and was of key importance to the village from the 1930s until the late 1960s, when it closed. Before the Carlings' time the post office was at the end of The Street near the church (more on this below). Oliver Trowell recalls that, when he moved to East Brabourne in 1934, the shop was owned by a Mr Carling: "My mother, out of consideration for Mr and Mrs Albert Carling, obtained all our rations from them. Unfortunately, there was no refrigeration in the shop, and when the butter and cheese were delivered they were often inedible. I was quick to prefer 'special' margarine and it was not until several years after the war that I regained a taste for butter."

The shop was then sold to a Mr Knowle and, later, to the de Vrooms, who were from Rhodesia. (How, one wonders, did they ever find Brabourne?) Virtually all East Brabourne's residents used the shop regularly. Sally Thornby would go there every day with a shopping list from her father, Norman, and the same two items were always listed: baked beans and canned spaghetti. There was a step down into the shop and, once inside, the grocer's section was to the left, and the post office to the right. Oliver adds that there was also a telephone available to the public on the wall nearest the Five Bells. Ilinca Cantacuzino, the Princess Cantacuzino's granddaughter, used to come to Brabourne to stay with her grandmother in the school holidays and remembers going to the shop when it was owned by the de Vrooms: "The shop was run by a number of different people through the years, but the family I remember best were the de Vrooms. They had a son who went to King's, Canterbury, in the early 1960s. As children visiting our grandmother at no.3, The Street, we loved popping next door to the shop. There was a step down from the pavement into the shop and the adults had to duck. We would take any opportunity to run an errand to get a loaf of bread or half a pound of butter for Mum's baking, because Mrs de Vroom always spoilt us. We usually came away with flying saucers, or liquorice in sherbet, or lemon drops."

The Coppings, who had a daughter, Gina, were also proprietors at one time; others mentioned were the Smiths. When the shop closed it was much missed by many of the local residents, not least the Struzynskis, who used to walk down from Pilgrims' Way to shop there and use the post office. After the shop closed, the post office was housed for a time in Keith and Rosa Finn's front room at no.1, Holly Cottages, in The Street, though inevitably, opening hours were much more restricted.

## WHEELWRIGHTS, BUILDERS AND UNDERTAKERS

Among the key services that sustained the rural economy were wheelwrights, builders and undertakers. Keith and Joy Finn's grandfather, George, came to East Brabourne in the mid- to late-19th century from the village of Egerton and started a business comprising general building, the making and repairing of wheels, particularly cartwheels, and undertaking. It was based at what is now The Wheelwright's, formerly known as the Carpenters' Workshop.

Eric Ball recalls the old Carpenters' Workshop, which had two levels:

"Coffins were made and stored on the first floor, while the ground floor was where most of the timber was prepared and other carpentry work – besides coffin-making – took place. On the ground floor was a deep saw-pit, around 8-10ft deep. One sawyer would stand at the bottom of the pit and one at the top, each in control of a handle at either end of a long saw blade. Great sections of tree were cut into planks by this manually operated blade and this wood was used for coffins and a range of other purposes. The wood to be cut was marked by a piece of string that was pulled through a hole in a piece of chalk. It was held taught against the wood by the two sawyers, pulled away from it and released, leaving a chalk line on the wood. The sawyer in the bottom of the pit was, unsurprisingly, always covered in sawdust."

Two sizeable benches covered with tools, including vices and clamps, stood on the ground floor and the entire workshop was full of stacked timber. Across the door-way was another pit, far less deep than the saw-pit, where cartwheels were made. A grindstone stood outside the workshop and Eric remembers turning the handle to sharpen the carpenters' tools. Leonard Finn's two-wheeled handcart used to stand outside the workshop. This would be loaded up every day and Leonard or, rather, one of his assistants would push it to wherever they were working. Outside the workshop stood a horse chestnut tree which was periodically replaced. The last time was in 1979/1980, when the tree was deemed to be partly hollow and hence a danger. After it was taken down a new tree was duly planted in its place by Keith, but this has now gone.

### THE SKILLS INVOLVED IN CRAFTING A CARTWHEEL
Eric Ball's father, Arthur William Ball, was wheelwright for Leonard Finn and used to make and line cartwheels. Eric remembers that he would start with the wooden hub, cut holes in it at appropriate places, and insert the wooden spokes, the other ends of which would be fitted into equal-sized sections of the outer edge of the wheel. Arthur would then take the completed wooden wheel down to the blacksmith,

The Carpenters' Workshop, possibly early 20th century

The Carpenters' Workshop, c1955, drawn by Oliver Trowell

The old horse chestnut with white candles obscuring the Carpenters' workshop in the early 1970s. Behind are Egerton Cottages, then three but now converted into two cottages, only one of which bears the name Egerton Cottage

George Barrett, just along Canterbury Road, and together they would fit on the iron rim forged by George. As we've already described, this was a very hot, dangerous and highly skilled job: the rim would be heated to as high a temperature as possible and would expand to a size larger than the wheel's circumference. It would then be placed on the ground and the wooden wheel quickly fitted into it. Once this was done, a vast amount of cold water would be poured on the hot iron, thereby shrinking the rim onto the wheel; this would of course be followed by the emission of a vast amount of heat and steam. The sections of the wooden wheel would thus be pulled together and "contained" by the rim. This was an exacting job that required the complementary and precision skills of both wheelwright and blacksmith.

In addition to being a wheelwright, Arthur also worked for the Finns as a builder, painter and decorator, made coffins when there was need for them, and when times were lean he would make ladders and sheep troughs as well. Anthony Finn remembers his father, Keith, and Arthur pushing his handcart replete with building and decorating materials through the village; Keith added that his father, Leonard Finn, used to mix all his own paint, which was lead based. Leonard painted houses inside and out, carriages and traps (which were drawn by ponies), and he also used to sell paint for stamping sheep. When Brabourne Church was decorated in 2008, the decorators discovered the names of Keith Finn and Arthur Ball inscribed on the church wall above the organ, testimony to the repairs they had carried out in 1937.

The Finns owned the three cottages alongside The Wheelwright's, which they renamed Egerton Cottages (as they had come from Egerton), and the two furthest

The Carpenters' Workshop in the1980s. Shortly before this picture was taken the large old horse chestnut tree with white candles, deemed to have become unsafe, was taken down and Keith Finn replaced it with another, though this one had red flowers

from the road were rented out by the Finns as dwellings. The Ball family lived in no.1 – the house furthest from the road, the only one still called Egerton Cottage – and a shed attached to the side of this house was the Finns' paint shop. The cottage closest to the road (now joined with the middle cottage) was at one time a store, and the room next to Stocks Lane was used by Keith as a garage for his car. This is now unthinkable as period cottages are so sought after as dwellings.

## THE COMPLEXITIES OF COFFIN MAKING AND FUNERALS
The coffins were made at Brabourne and also involved highly skilled work. The outer casings were made from large sheets of elm that were sawn in the big saw-pit. Once the pieces had been screwed together the coffin's joints were sealed with pitch to make them watertight, the pitch being heated over a fire kept alight all the while the coffin was being made. The completed caskets were then lined with satin and the outer surface polished. Finally, the handles were attached and the name of the person who had died would be hand painted on to a brass plaque that was screwed on to the coffin. Leonard Finn was a trained sign writer and this final task involved much skill, too. In his son Keith's time, however, the names of the deceased were engraved mechanically in Ashford. It took many hours to make a coffin and even when Keith had taken over the business in the 1960s, by which time mechanical tools were commonly used, it took two people eight to nine hours to make a coffin. We may prefer not to think about coffins but their production was, and still is, a very

specialised business. After the mid-1960s, when it became easier and cheaper to buy perfectly acceptable mass produced caskets, they were no longer made at Brabourne.

Keith Finn

Prior to 1935, coffins were always transported on a horse-drawn hearse. The horses were kept at the Saracen's Head in Ashford, on the site where Boots now stands. Here, the hearse would be placed on a carriage and walked out to the Finns in East Brabourne, where the coffin would be collected and taken to the home of the person who had died. In those days people usually kept their dead at home until the time of burial. The undertakers would place the body in the coffin, which would then be placed on the hearse and taken to its final resting place in one of the local churchyards. Keith told us that, in the early 1930s, coffin bearers each received 5/- per funeral and the gravedigger £2/10/-.

Keith became involved in both the building side of the business and the undertaking in 1931, when he was 16 years old. This was still shortly before the first motor hearse was introduced. When he took over the business, he oversaw the making of coffins and collected the bodies from the hospital or wherever they had died, just as his father and grandfather had done. As time progressed, people tended to move their dead to a chapel of rest, so Keith created a small one at the back of the workshop and with a separate entrance. Here, people could come to pay their last respects and sit in peace with their loved ones in the hours before they were buried.

Every church had to provide a grave for its parishioners and Keith would arrange this through the sexton. Almost invariably he used the same grave diggers: Tom Brooks and Charlie Marsh, and when they retired, Robin Marsh (not a relative of Charlie's). Oliver Trowell added that, "between 1934 and 1944, the graves at Brabourne were dug by Harry Ward, who lived at no.3, The Street". Finding sufficient space for graves became an increasing problem, and it was not until the late 1930s and the beginning of the Second World War, when cremation became more common, that the pressure started to ease. For Keith, cremation meant less trouble, as he did not have to worry about finding grave space, getting the grave dug or the weather, this latter variable being critical. He explained how important it was that every funeral went to plan

Keith Finn in his workshop
(picture courtesy of Richard Filmer)

The interior of Keith Finn's workshop prior to it being sold and
converted to a dwelling (early 1980s)

and that there were no mishaps or "surprises" as the principal mourners, usually the family, were not to experience any further upset. He recalled that, at both Brabourne and Smeeth, the churches' drainage could be a major issue when the water table was high after rain – the graves would fill up with water as they were being dug and the water would have to be pumped out, with the pump being switched off just as the coffins were brought out from the churches for the burial. On several occasions, before the priest had concluded the service, the water seeped back into the grave and sometimes caused the coffin to float. Peter Rigg and Robin Marsh recall how a grave once filled with water and they were unable to get the coffin back to the bottom; they had no alternative but to puncture the coffin and let it sink. It is no surprise, then, to hear that cremation was much less complicated and stressful for the funeral director.

Keith was extremely committed to giving good personal service, to treating those who had died with honour and the utmost respect. He also treated the bereaved with kindness, consideration and care, ensuring that the funeral was dignified in all regards. (He was well known locally for the care that he took.) Keith remembered one occasion, shortly after the Ashford bypass had been built, when the screen of the hearse shattered near where the Junction 10 roundabout is now. Turning back was just not possible, so the driver continued all the way to the crematorium at Charing with the shattered windscreen. On another occasion the head gasket went on the hearse – fortunately, Keith and the coffin bearers were able to fit the coffin into his black Cortina instead.

Many undertakers used the gardeners at the crematorium as coffin bearers, but Keith had a team of coffin bearers whom he would always use. He noted that taking "his people" with him to Charing was always popular, and several of them were regular churchgoers so knew the words of the hymns and sang out loudly. He reflected that mourners often remarked that his team made it sound, "as though there was a choir at the funeral".

All components of the business – the funerals and the building work – were successful, though demand for a wheelwright declined after the Second World War as mechanisation increased. At its greatest extent, Keith's services as an undertaker covered a wide area, comprising the villages around Brabourne and as far afield as Elmsted and Hastingleigh, and all hospitals and nursing homes in the area. He recalled that he had met many compassionate people through the funeral business, and that the kindness of spirit of Roman Catholics especially had moved him several times.

Robin pointed out that there was another undertaker, George Marshall, along the Ridgeway, but Finn's in East Brabourne continued for much longer. The conclusion

Peter and Stella Rigg

of the funeral business in Brabourne came in the 1980s, when Keith retired and the undertaking side was amalgamated with Earl & Co at Willesborough. The building side, however, prospered under Peter Rigg, who joined Keith as an apprentice builder and decorator in the mid-1960s. Peter had also been drawn into the funeral business and acted as pallbearer when needed (and can remember wearing Bill Stockbridge's old black coat for the services), but with significant administrative support from his wife, Stella, he successfully developed the building, painting and decorating side of the business. Peter remarked that the work he does now is quite different from that in the past: very little luxury work is done, though there is an abundance of essential work, for example, repair to damage caused to the fabric of a house by plumbing leaks. The decorating side of the business has noticeably declined, perhaps due to the DIY boom. Previously, some regular customers would have one or two rooms decorated each year, but that is rare these days, and when he is asked to decorate it is invariably to paint, rather than to wallpaper, as fashions have changed considerably.

## THE PRACTICALITIES OF GRAVE DIGGING

Robin Marsh has been digging graves since the early 1970s and has no idea how many he has dug, probably over 200, but he notes with some sadness that he has dug seven graves for one family in Brabourne. Robin now claims to have retired, George Brooks's grave being the last that he dug, in the spring of 2012. The number of graves needed has declined since the Second World War and now some two-thirds of those who die are cremated. Robin has dug graves in 19 churchyards, including Aldington, Lympne, Stanford, Monks Horton,

Robin Marsh

Stowting, Elmsted, Hastingleigh, Crundale, Challock, Bethersden, Tenterden Zion, Hamstreet, Ruckinge, Bonnington, Sellindge, Smeeth, Brabourne, and Brabourne Bethel Baptist Zion chapel, Canterbury Road.

Grave digging is a skilled art, not as simple as one might imagine. The opening needs to be neat, with regular edges and, most importantly, the correct size – if a coffin does not fit into the grave it can cause terrible distress for the mourners. Keith Finn used to have a frame, a template that he would give to Robin and, depending on the size of the deceased, would advise him to either increase or decrease the dimensions of the grave by a couple of inches. It has to be said that, such is his care, Robin has never got the size wrong.

A major problem with digging a grave is the soil type: clays are heavy and sticky, but sand can be equally difficult as the sides can collapse, and as Peter Rigg put it, "You can end up with a crater rather than a grave." Robin can dig a grave (6ft deep) in as little as two hours if the soil conditions allow, but at Aldington, for example, it is always much more difficult as the top soil there is underlain with Kentish ragstone, which in turn lies on softer beds, below which is yet more ragstone. Digging through ragstone, Robin observed, is extremely hard work and can take hours. And then there can be the issue of drainage, as Keith described above.

Another major problem in our local graveyards is who or what you might encounter when a new grave is being dug. At Brabourne, the graveyard on the south side of the church, overlooking the field, doubled in size in Napoleonic times to cope with the number of troops and camp followers who died. None of these graves was marked permanently and Robin always has to work carefully in case he encounters earlier residents. If he does, another space has to be found. He remarked that, even in more recent times, many poor families would not have the money to raise a headstone at the grave of a relative and wooden memorials deteriorate, leaving no trace. Similarly, the graves of those buried by the parish were only marked with wooden crosses and, unless graveyard maps have been maintained carefully and kept up-to-date, no one can really know who lies where. Once, Robin encountered something akin to rock when he was digging in Brabourne churchyard. Suddenly, the "rock" gave way, falling in on top of him – it left a perfect circle in the side of the grave and those who saw it thought that Robin had dug up the mould for one of the bells.

Robin also recalled some particularly unattractive events in recent years. He dug a grave at one of our local churches in readiness for a funeral the next day, but unfortunately the undertaker (not Finn's, as this happened more recently) had failed to tell him that the funeral had been postponed because blizzards were forecast. Sure enough, there were blizzards, but Robin had several days of worry, constantly checking that the sides of the grave did not collapse. Once the snow melted there was the threat that water draining off higher ground would wash into the grave and destroy it, but in the event all was well.

On two other occasions, events were more sinister. The first happened when Robin had dug a grave at one of our village cemeteries, ready for a funeral the following afternoon. At 11am on the day of the service the grave was in good condition, but by 1pm someone had vandalised it and had broken down the side, partially filling it with earth. Fortunately, Robin saw it in time and dug it out again so the mourners were none the wiser. A few months later a similar thing happened, but this time the infill seemed to have been greater, perhaps assisted by bad weather. Unfortunately, on the same day someone ran into Robin while he was driving and not only damaged his vehicle but also injured his leg quite seriously. Knowing that the funeral was to take place in the afternoon, Robin went to make sure the grave was all right before he went to casualty; he was sickened to find that it, too, had been vandalised. Despite his injury, and with help from Peter Rigg, the damage to the grave was repaired in time for the funeral. Robin arrived at casualty only to be given a severe telling-off for not having come to the hospital sooner. He remains puzzled by the motives of such a curious form of vandalism.

Perhaps the most gruesome tale was when undertakers (neither Finn's nor Earl & Co, it should be emphasised) dropped a coffin as it was partly over the grave. Hitting the edge, the coffin broke and the deceased was revealed to all, causing great distress among the mourners. Incredibly, the undertakers left without sorting the problem out, so the priest called for Robin, who advised him to move everyone indoors. He then proceeded to repair the coffin sufficiently well so that the body was no longer exposed and the committal could be completed. Peter commented he was not surprised to hear of a coffin breaking, as they are only made of chipboard these days, rather than the solid wood used by traditional undertakers in times past.

At another funeral, Peter was carrying a coffin with a flawed inner seal. He remembers fluid from the body seeping through on to his coat and the penetrating smell as being "absolutely dreadful". And finally, many years ago, after carrying the coffin of a very, very heavy person – not in Brabourne or Smeeth but in a nearby parish – Peter muttered with relief when at last the coffin was placed on the bier, "Thank God for that." The officiating priest heard him and complained to Keith, who told Peter off for his inappropriate behaviour.

However, the role of undertaker and pallbearer, though sombre, may, on rare occasions, be tinged with glamour. Peter recalls being filmed as he and three others carried a coffin down the path at a local church; we're still waiting for the film to be released.

## THE MIDWIFE

While the undertaker took care of those who had died, the villages also had a midwife who helped bring successive generations into the world. According to Margaret Pile (Ward), "Until 1930, all births were attended by Granny Barton, who walked to the patients' homes. She was later replaced by a trained midwife, Dorothy Hills, who rode her motorbike and sidecar round the village. She used to wear a flying helmet to protect her." Nurse, as she was affectionately known, eventually replaced her motorbike with a car (registration number HKL 6). Margaret notes, "She used to drive [it] rather erratically and was often found in a ditch or with the car broken down." Confirming this, another contributor recalled Nurse driving straight across the T-junction where Canterbury Road meets Plain Road in Brabourne Lees, ending up off the road and down in a dip. Phil Stone later bought HKL 6 from Nurse Hills; it was his first car. Nurse lived with her sister Nell, also a nurse, at no.1, Holly Cottages, in East Brabourne. She went much further than her job as midwife, knitting baby clothes for the newly born and keeping a lifelong eye on those she had delivered as they grew up. Sheila Stone (Ashman) is one of the many she brought into the world.

## WALLY WASHFORD, HEDGER AND DITCHER

Mention of Wally Washford reminds us that he lived with his mother in part of what later became the Princess's cottage, and was very much a regular at the Five Bells. As we mentioned in the earlier section on cold winters, in the deep snows of 1963, he dug himself a pathway from what is now no.1 of the Princess's three pink cottages

Wally Washford

to the Five Bells door. Wally worked for the council and used to keep roads, drains and ditches clear, hedges trimmed and carry out other similar jobs. Christine Peall (Friend) recalled the "hedges and ditches have never looked as tidy as when Wally Washford was around". This was echoed by John Varrier, who observed that, "in Wally Washford's time the village always had a well-kept feel to it". Eric Ball also remembers that Wally used to deliver the Sunday papers to his family at Egerton Cottages each week.

## THE HANDYMAN

Going back to the 1920s, George Brooks remembered Mr Tenney, who lived in the back cottage of what is now Hill View. Mr Tenney was a handyman who would solder pans and do other odd jobs; George recalled his mother having pans repaired by him from time to time. Mr Tenney also used to work as gardener at the vicarage in Brabourne, and George told us that at 12 noon every day he would stop work, go into the church and ring the bell to announce that midday had arrived. Oliver Trowell added that he also worked in the gardens of Court Lodge, when it was owned by the Millers.

WORK WAS AVAILABLE

But what of other people who lived in The Street? Opportunities for employment were few and people took what jobs were going or created their own opportunities. Kath Spain worked as housekeeper for Lady Bomford and later at East Brabourne House for the Marshall family, with whom she kept in close contact after retirement. She also worked part-time at the market garden at Court Lodge, as did Elsie Davies in the 1960s. Marge Friend, who lived at no.4, Subdown Cottages, did field work (on the farms) for anyone who needed a worker. Some of the places she worked included Bodsham Farm (they would pick up workers who couldn't walk or cycle to them); Penstock Farm, where she worked for the Olders; and Parsonage Farm, where she worked for the Hamiltons. She helped with picking apples, and with picking and riddling potatoes. This latter process involved putting the potatoes into a perforated drum that, as it revolved, led to the smaller potatoes falling through the holes, thus separating them from the larger ones. She also picked wild oats from wheat fields and helped with thistle pecking. (Recalling her mother, Christine Peall (Friend) added that Marge used to say, "I don't sow wild oats, I pull them up.") Marge was paid piece rate for her work and, in the school holidays, would take her children, Christine, Jackie and Malcolm, to help increase her earnings. She also worked for the Cliftons at Park Farm, picking daffodils, and again, in the holidays, the children would help. Christine remembers how miserably cold they used to get picking daffodils in January and February; they would have a set number of rubber bands on their wrists, pull up, rather than pick, 12 daffs and bunch them, ready for the stalks to be trimmed. The slime from the stems, she recalls, was messy and as it ran from their wrists into their sleeves added to the cold discomfort of the job.

Marge would also help people locally, and cooked at least 10 dinners in an evening. Wally Washford used to come down to the Friends for his dinner every evening; after Mr Birchett's wife died, Christine and her sister would take dinner up to him at his cottage, which was next to Wally's. Marge also cooked dinner for some of the workers at Parsonage Farm. The small income she obtained from all these jobs, which amounted to much more in terms of time and effort than full-time work, helped with daily living expenses and with Christmas and birthday presents.

From the viewpoint of the consumer, virtually everything was available in the villages: most commodities were available locally and labour was available for essential services. Trips to Ashford were therefore not really necessary for most people, except on rare occasions. Money was generally in short supply until the late 1960s and 1970s; personal credit, as opposed to credit for businesses, was to be avoided, and "retail therapy" had not been invented, so why would one need to go to Ashford?

## COURT LODGE FARM

Looking down The Street towards Coquet Lodge, c1970s.
Court Lodge is on the left

Albert Hammon with stallion outside Court Lodge, c1914

Going further down The Street towards the church is Court Lodge (no longer a farm), probably so named because circuit judges in the 18th century used to hold court there. It was rented by the Hammons from the Knatchbull Family in the 19th century, and though the Hammons were essentially from Sellindge, Edward Hammon came to Court Lodge in 1849. His son Edmund farmed it until 1900, after which Albert, Edmund's son and John Hammon's great-uncle, took it over, farming the land there until 1919. Court Lodge was farmed together with Parsonage Farm, the acreage of which was greater than it is today.

The Hammons were considerable landowners but after the First World War pulled out of farming as it declined. John Hammon has kindly lent us three Catalogues detailing the items to be auctioned at Parsonage Farm (2nd October, 1919), Court Lodge Farm (4th October, 1919), and Wall Farm [now Penstock] (8th October, 1919). At that time only Parsonage and Court Lodge were farmed by the Hammons. The close proximity of these auction dates suggests that all local farmers were in much the same position - wanting to get out of farming. Hubert F. Finn-Kelcey was the agent for Court Lodge and Parsonage Farms, and Hobbs for Wall Farm. At the time, the sale at Court Lodge would have been the largest, followed by Wall Farm and then Parsonage.

In a section entitled 'Remarks' in the Court Lodge Farm Catalogue, we read that:

The Auctioneer wishes to draw special attention to the grand flock of Kent sheep included in this sale, being one of the oldest established flocks in the district, and great care always having been taken with the selection of the ewes and rams for breeding it has gained a wonderful reputation for its constitution, bone, wool and hardiness and is undoubtedly one of the best flocks of hill sheep on offer this year. [258 Kent Sheep were being offered for sale]

The horses include some weighty and active animals and are mostly young. [7 horses]

Amongst the cattle are 9 excellent, large framed and heavy milking Shorthorn cows and heifers, and the young beasts are all well bred.

The Implements and Machines etc. are numerous and include many which are in new condition.

Well before the Second World War, Cowley Miller owned Court Lodge. The Millers had a chicken farm behind the house and Rosemary Hendry (Ward) remembers chicken sheds above the bend in the road opposite Brabourne Church. (It has been suggested that Lamplands on Pilgrims' Way was so named because of the soft paraffin lights in these sheds in the evenings - but there is no agreement on this.) The foreman of the farm, a Mr Goddard, had links with the Ovaltine company, so the Millers produced eggs for the Ovaltine Farm. Though the poultry farm occupied most of the central area bounded on three sides by Pilgrims' Way, Stocks Lane and Brabourne Street, there was an area in the top left-hand corner, when viewed from The Street, where Sidney Finn kept sheep. Eric Ball recalls that, during the war, one of the first parachutists to come down landed in Sidney's field. It was an Englishman who had been badly burned when his plane was hit. Mr Cameron from Wall Farm, now Penstock, picked him up, took him back to the farmhouse and, after some time in hospital, he is believed to have recovered.

The Millers were popular people in the village. Mr Miller was one of the driving forces behind the local dramatic society and the tennis club in East Brabourne, where Keith and Rosa Finn used to play; he was also on the PCC for a time. Before the war, Mrs Miller used to run an embroidery class for girls once a month on a Saturday afternoon at Court Lodge. This would have been in the late 1930s and early 1940s. From the age of 8 to 10, Rosemary Hendry (Ward) would walk from Brabourne Lees to East Brabourne, enjoy the embroidery, tea and cake, and then walk home again.

Court Lodge was taken over by the army during the war; afterwards, it was transformed into an orchard and market garden by Lady Charnwood and Miss Cochrane. More on this in chapter 9. One feature that has changed significantly is the orchard – though shown as an orchard on Ordnance Survey maps, it was not a truly ancient orchard and the apple trees were grubbed up in about 2008. After a period of uncertainty as to its future, the land was bought by George Jessel of Penstock Farm, who now leases the former orchard for farming. Though many in East Brabourne lament the loss of the orchard, had events taken a different course in the 1930s the apple trees might never have been planted. Robert Embleton-Smith was told on good authority by Keith Finn that, prior to the Second World War, there was a plan to extend the A20 from the sharp bend at Postling, above Kick Hill, through Postling and East Brabourne, and possibly thereafter to Westwell. The war put an end to these plans and they were not revived after it was over – a lucky escape for East Brabourne.

The Hammons had bought what is now Orchard Cottage for their farm workers. The property was originally two cottages, called Peace Haven and Rest Haven but towards the end of the First World War Albert Hammon rented the cottage nearer the Five Bells to George Brooks's family and it was from this period that George's memories of Brabourne date. Albert was George's family's landlord during the First World War, and until the 1930s, and lived next door in Albert House (now Clandon Cottage). As there was no water at Orchard Cottage, it was Albert's responsibility to deliver two buckets of water to George's mother each morning. This was drawn from a well at the end of an alley between Albert's home and the four 17th-century cottages next door, where Wally Washford and others lived. If the Brooks family needed more water they were welcome to help themselves.

The Princess's son, the Prince Sherban Cantacuzino writes:

"The complete 'terrace' of cottages – that is nos.1, 2, 3 and 4, The Street – was bought by my mother for £200 in 1953. The council (I think in those days it was still Kent County Council) had placed 'closing orders' on all four properties, but these would be lifted with their conversion and modernisation. I prepared plans, which were approved by the council. I obtained estimates and engaged a builder who carried out the work; it cost something in the region of £6,000. In 1955 my mother moved into nos.3 and 4, which had been knocked into one during the conversion, the council having lifted the 'closing orders' and we having moved the sitting tenants, Washford and Birchett respectively, into nos.1 and 2." The

Sherban and Anne Cantacuzino

Princess had the cottages painted a pale pink, a tradition that has been continued by two of her grandchildren, the current owners of what are now two cottages.

1, 2, 3 &, 4, The Street

Musing on the Hammons, who were a large family in the area, George recalled that Albert would bring his pony and trap each day into the field where Subdown Cottages now stand. Teddy Ames, who according to George Brooks started Ames' Stores in Brabourne Lees in 1907, told George that he could remember a time when fresh snow had fallen and the two teams of horses owned by the Hammons, complete with bells, would draw a sledge from Court Lodge to the Smeeth crossroads to keep the roads open. That was even before George's time.

We return briefly to Albert House, now Clandon Cottage in The Street. You might notice the decorative iron railings outside Albert House, pictured opposite, which are of unusual style. Justin Ball suggests that the pattern at the top of these may represent stylised papyrus, one of many designs introduced to Europe c1800, as a consequence of British and French territorial ambitions in Egypt and the Middle East at that time. Justin suggests that the railings outside Clandon Cottage, and similar railings locally, were probably made at the local forge and are likely to date from that period. The bay window was added by Mrs Opperman in about 1950.

Albert House (inscribed above the door in gold gothic lettering)

Railings outside Albert House, now Clandon Cottage, showing stylised papyrus

Clandon Cottage with 1, 2, 3 &, 4 The Street beyond

# EAST BRABOURNE'S POST OFFICE

As we saw in Chapter 5, on Brabourne Lees, The Penny Post had become so popular that on 16th February, 1853, a post office at East Brabourne was sanctioned. Initially, it was located in what is now Coquet Lodge, just beside the church gates.

East Braboure's post office in what is now Coquet Lodge.
Church Farmhouse on the right

Key dates in the history of the East Brabourne's post office:

16/2/1853 – The post master was Mr Hills. On the death of W. Hills, Mrs Hills took over on 15/7/1857
29/11/1862 – George Kingsland.
30/11/1884 – Oliver Hancock, resigned 11/08/1902
1/10/1902 – James Lewis Hills
19/08/1913 – John Hogben
1915/1922 – James Edwards
1923/24 – Mrs Hannah Rose Hammon
Post 1927 but pre 1934 – Albert Frederick Carling

(According to Oliver Trowell, the Post office was already in the shop run by Mr Carling by 1934, which was when the Trowells moved to East Brabourne.)

Mrs Hancock, wife of former postmaster, with Oswald
Ames and his sister at East Brabourne
(early 20th century)

Rural postman and M.H. Hammon (John Hammon's
father) at the top of Fiddling Lane
(between 1924 and 1929)

Alan Clark's notes also record reports from the Brabourne and Monks Horton Parish Magazine:

February 1899: "We have been informed that at a recent meeting of the Parish Council it was decided to apply to the Telegraph Department for an extension of the wires from Smeeth to the Post Office at East Brabourne."

23rd August, 1899: "(First message by telephone to Smeeth and Ashford, thence by Telegraph) at present one shilling has to be paid for delivery of a telegram."

Saturday, 19th May, 1900: "The wire (there was only one) conveyed the news of the relief of Mafeking to East Brabourne Post Office."

## THE BAKERY

East Brabourne also boasted Moul's Bakery, which was located at the side/back of what is now Coquet Lodge, where Oliver Trowell parks his car. Mr Moul also owned the land on Pilgrims' Way where Lamplands now stands, and used to grow potatoes there. When flour for bread making was short, he used to incorporate potato flour into the bread. All this was on good authority from George Brooks, whose father used to drive A.J. Moul's van to deliver bread as far afield as Hastingleigh. Prior to

Moul's delivery van outside the bakery in East
Brabourne (pre-1925)

this, Mr Moul's potato field was rented by the then owner of Wall Farm (currently Penstock) and the grass there was used as grazing for his cattle. As a young lad in the 1920s, George would herd the cattle up the lane to the field. It was later bought by Patrick Rice, who built Lamplands and married Pamela Trowell, Oliver Trowell's sister.

The Rice family were remembered warmly and Jackie Finn (Davis) remembers going to pantomimes in Folkestone in the 1950s with Patrick and Pamela Rice and their children. On their return to the Rice household they would all be treated to Heinz chicken soup, which Jackie considered the height of sophistication at the time. When Patrick used to pick his children up from Brabourne school, he would cram as many additional children as possible, including Jackie and her sisters, into the family's large Ford shooting brake (the sort with woodwork on the outside) and deliver them to their homes. The Rice family moved away to Devon, where their son William was tragically killed in a motorbike accident.

Prompted to reflect on the nature of social change in East Brabourne since the 1960s and 1970s when he was priest at Brabourne and Smeeth, the Reverend Ray Sheekey observed that there had been significant changes. In his time in the locality there were many more titled people in East Brabourne than there are now, and he listed the following: Lady Bomford at St Cyriac; Lady Charnwood and Miss Cochrane at Court Lodge; the Princess Cantacuzino at the Pink Cottage; Donald Sumner, lieutenant colonel, MP and circuit judge in the old vicarage (by then East Brabourne House); and Naval Commander and Mrs Langworthy at Church Farmhouse, prior to the arrival of Ken and Peg Waite.

On Pilgrims' Way at Longwood lived Admiral Sir Archibald Day; after he left, Major Jerzy Struzynski and his wife, Gwen, moved in there. Adding detail to Ray's list, Gwen Struzynski, the mother of Lady Diana Errington, was very beautiful in her youth. After her portrait was painted, Gwen went to RADA and was taught by Claude Rains, the American stage and film actor. She also did a little modelling for Paulette in Berkeley Square. This was many years before she came to Brabourne. Her husband, Major Struzynski, who had been in the Polish cavalry, in the XIV Lancers during the Second World War, is remembered as a great horseman. Horses were his life and, while in Brabourne from the 1960s to the 1990s, his stepdaughter, Lady Diana Errington recalls, he taught many people to ride, especially young people. Major Struzynski himself told Robert Embleton-Smith that he was one of the first people in Brabourne to keep horses for recreational rather than economic purposes, such as transport or as draught animals.

Gwen Struzynski

Major Struzynski

Lady Diana Errington

Tucked away down a lane between Coquet Lodge and St Mary's Church stands the old vicarage. It ceased to be a vicarage in 1956, when it was sold by the Church Commissioners and bought by Major Pearson, who changed the original Georgian building significantly. He enlarged it and changed its name from The Vicarage to East Brabourne House. From 1962 to 1976 it was owned by Lady Haldin, the widow of a shipping magnate. Katrina Bewick (Stone) who was living in The Street remembers that in Lady Haldin's time East Brabourne House had "an upstairs, downstairs" feel to it, as she kept a butler and a maid, both of whom were traditionally attired. From 1976 to 1982 the old vicarage was owned by Donald Sumner, lieutenant colonel, MP and circuit judge, and since 1982 it has been owned by Michael Marshall. Michael claims that he has the right "credentials" for living in the former vicarage: he has lived in old vicarages for more than 50 years, delighting in their rambling spaciousness. His work has also kept him close to the Church of England, as he was senior receiver to the Church Commissioners, and chairman of the trustees of the Sons of the Clergy, the oldest and largest Church of England charity. Furthermore, Michael was given a Lambeth Degree by Archbishop Robert Runcie in 1988. With such a worthy record it is no surprise that Michael has been addressed on more than one occasion as The Reverend Michael Marshall.

## VISITORS TO EAST BRABOURNE

Ilinca Cantacuzino remembers life in East Brabourne during the school holidays with her grandmother, the Princess:

Ilinca Cantacuzino and her daughter, Alice

"Sanda Cantacuzino, my grandmother, was commonly known as 'Princess' – even 'our princess'. Everyone along The Street could daily set their watches by her. Every day she was expected for lunch by her friends, Lady Charnwood and Miss Carola Cochrane, at Court Lodge on the dot of 12. This meant leaving home (no.3, The Street) at 11.55am. In the habit as she was of walking her dog (usually a standard poodle named variously Puck, Shadow I and Shadow II) far from the pavement, she always walked on the hedge side of the road. It is proof of how little traffic there was in the 1950s and 1960s that this was perfectly safe. These visits to Court Lodge were dog-less, however, since her wild and woolly poodles were not welcomed by the pampered canine companions of Lady Charnwood and Miss Carola Cochrane. Initially after their mongrel Gin's demise, Ping, a rather grand pekinese, held court at Court Lodge. Ping was the apple of Miss Cochrane's eye (and to my acute child's eye bore an uncanny resemblance to his owner). Latterly, the roost was ruled by a pair of pedigree long-haired dogs called Whisky and Brandy.

"As children, we came from London to stay with our grandmother during school holidays. Our visits to 'the big house', Court Lodge, ranged from Christmas lunches to picnics in 'the park' (the raised elegant grassy area dotted with trees opposite the church) and taking part in the raspberry picking in the market garden at Court Lodge every August. While Miss Cochrane managed the work outdoors, that is the cultivation, picking and packing of dahlias, chrysanthemums and many other items destined for Covent Garden and beyond, Lady Charnwood would manage the house. Lady Charnwood was formidable. When she went into town she would always wear a mustard- or olive-coloured scarf, knotted 'land girls' style around her head – the scarf was cashmere, of course. Her brusqueness hid an unwaveringly kind heart, sensible to the nuances of people's needs. Once, as a little girl, I was disappointed by the onset of rain threatening the promised picnic, only to find she had laid out the rug and Bakelite cups and saucers on the carpet in the drawing room. When I was 11

I knew I had arrived when she offered me a gin and orange (undiluted squash) and my first Woodbine!

"When I was little, before my grandmother bought nos.1 and 2, The Street, Mr and Mrs Birchett lived at no.1, and Wally Washford and his mother at no.2. As a child, I vividly recall the daunting sight of a very old Mrs Washford, hunched, her long grey hair over her face, standing in her doorway looking out at the back over the gardens, calling out to imaginary company. After her death, Wally spent his last years alone and much of the time in the Five Bells. Frequently, he would have to be helped home after closing time. My grandmother was the one to discover his body. She had to burn his mattress.

Martin Rowell, Ilinca's husband, with their daughter, Alice (great grand-daughter of the Princess). Martin can also remember being offered gin and a Woodbine before 10am in the morning at Court Lodge

"In 1963, during the winter of snow – when we walked on top of the hedges - my grandmother's sister and her two teenage sons arrived from Romania, after many years of negotiation to get them out from behind the Iron Curtain. Lady Charnwood gave the three of them a home at no.1, Hill View Cottages, while their father remained back in Romania as a political prisoner. We were very excited to have two new cousins and I remember walking down the village frequently to call up to the windows under the sloping tiled roof to talk to them. In the house next door lived a very smart and rather severe district nurse who drove a little polished black Humber.

"During this time, my grandmother spent her days as a poultry farmer. She kept her chickens and chicks in two barns (Court Lodge Barn, opposite Court Lodge), the smaller of which is now marked only by a single remaining wall. I often accompanied her and loved nothing more than checking on the tiny yellow chicks huddling together for warmth in trays around paraffin lamps. I would help out testing the eggs for cracks by tapping them against each other. My sister, Marina, and my cousins and I would play for hours in the big barn, jumping off bales of straw and swinging perilously from the beams.

Back left, the Princess Cantacuzino with "The
Ladies from Court Lodge": standing (right), Miss
Carola Cochrane, and sitting, Lady Charnwood,
(c1940s)

The Princess feeding the chickens, (1950s)

"Sometimes in the summers we were allowed to help with picking the raspberries at the market garden, and then we would eat as many as we could manage without being sick. Visiting Court Lodge was always a treat. The garden in front of the kitchen was always packed to bursting with wallflowers. And further up, after we had crunched through the loose gravel, we would find the two large and beautifully neat walled gardens joined by a brick arch. This was too good an invitation to play '(very grand) houses'.

"On occasions my grandmother would take me to visit various neighbours. I loved visiting old Lady Bomford at the cottage on the corner beyond the Trowells at St Cyriac, and being given vanilla ice cream topped with golden syrup – an extraordinary treat. The syrup goes rigid and chewy like toffee. She had a gypsy caravan in her garden, and the floors were covered with sheets from Beano comics. This was my first introduction to the world of comics (they weren't allowed in our house), and I remember crawling around on my knees to read them."

More childhood memories of visiting east brabourne, from Marina Cantacuzino:

"I had the best summer holidays in East Brabourne. Every summer, my mother, my sister, Ilinca, and our younger brother, Sherban, would take the train from Charing Cross and spend the whole of the holidays with my grandmother at no.3, The Street, East Brabourne. My grandmother, Princess Sanda Cantacuzino, was by birth a Romanian princess who had lost all her wealth when Romania succumbed to communism; and yet somehow she adapted remarkably well to running a chicken farm in the village. My father would join us from London at weekends. It was, of course, in my memory at least, always a scorching

Marina Cantacuzino

summer – wild strawberries, wasps trapped in honeypots, picnics on lush green lawns – all things that can leave a deep impression on pale city kids. With our four cousins, who stayed in the next-door cottage, we played outside from morning to late afternoon. We'd push a huge pram down the road and take a 'plunge' in the giant's bath – actually nothing more than a deep hole in the ground that still exists on the grassy verge opposite Court Lodge; somehow it seemed much deeper then.

"My sister and I loved to play in the graveyard. I was seven and she was nine and our imaginary husbands – mine called Greenwood and hers Banker – lived in the sexton's shed on the south side of the church. We never saw them – they were always away travelling. My sister's 'husband' was more exotic, and somehow better looking in my childish mind. In that same graveyard, some years later, we buried our 17-year-old brother and, shortly after, our grandmother. It still holds many poignant memories.

Five (of 11) great-grandchildren of the Princess Cantacuzino. At the back, from left, George and Alice (Ilinca's children), and front, from left, Reuben, Flora and Phoebe (Marina's children)

"Christmas in East Brabourne was by contrast always bitterly cold and, looking back, rather a strange affair. My grandmother, my father and my aunt – who had left Romania in 1939, the year war broke out, and had come to live in East Brabourne in the early 1950s – and us always spent Christmas with Lady Charnwood and Miss Cochrane who lived at Court Lodge from the late 1940s to the 1980s. On Christmas Day we would walk down The Street, laden with gifts, to be welcomed by the words, "Gin and orange?" Age didn't seem a concern. Christmas dinner was always cold – a strange mix of European salads and cold sliced meat. When my grandmother's sister managed to leave Romania in the 1960s she moved with her husband and two teenage sons into no.1, Hill View Cottages, in front of the Davis family's house and to the right of Coronation Cottage. Christmases at Court Lodge became bigger and better then (though the food remained cold), and before long the traditional Boxing Day slideshow began – a selection of images taken by my father and my very earnest Romanian cousin, cataloguing the buildings, monuments and artefacts they had seen during the past year. I longed for a splash of real life – but there was never a person in sight.

"The shop has long since disappeared but I remember it as a place to go and practice independence at the age of six. A few shop owners passed through the village before it finally closed in the 1970s. The only one I remember was Mr Smith, who had a stump for one hand. The story horrified and enthralled me – it had been blown off when he was a boy playing with a chemistry set."

And yet more happy childhood memories of Brabourne from Ileana Ruhemann:

"I have known Brabourne village (or East Brabourne, as I have always called it) since being held as a baby in the garden of 3 The Street. It is one of the places I love most in the world (and I have travelled a lot). Happy memories are, of course, all surrounding my adored and perfect grandmother, Sanda Cantacuzino, who came to

The Princess's daughter, Marie-Lyse, with her daughter, Ileana

the village in April 1945. She was often called 'the Princess' in the village, but to her grandchildren she was affectionately known as Muna. She had come from her country, Romania, with her young teenage children, her son Sherban and daughter Marie-Lyse (my mother). She always hoped that her husband, Georges, would join her in Kent, and did everything she could to secure his coming to England, but the Communist regime in Romania never made that possible. They never saw each other again. Many letters passed between them over the years, and these were found in the cottage after her death in the early 1990s. She did manage to help her sister Marina leave with her family, and they lived for a short time in the small old cottage next to the bungalow (Hill View). The floor upstairs was slanted – you could roll objects

down it! She used to talk for hours on her sofa with her sister, and her husband Costi and their son Mihai would come to the cottage to play the piano (very well). Hill View was also lived in by one of the ladies' gardeners.

"Sanda first lived at Court Lodge, known to us as 'the Big House'. She lived there with Lady Charnwood (Beryl or 'Babu' to us), her husband John (who had owned a boat in which he rescued soldiers from Dunkirk) and Carola Cochrane. Her mother had met these two ladies while travelling in Switzerland. They had helped to persuade her that she should think of educating her children at English public schools. Babu and Carola ran a market garden, sending their produce to Covent Garden market in London. They also created the apple orchard that was in the centre of the village until very recently. My grandmother, after a short course, started a chicken farm in what is now Court Lodge Barn. She had chickens and geese (I remember being frightened of the geese) all very hard work, but she liked it and did well. Carola was exemplary at organizing the business, and sold flowers as well as vegetables and fruit. The more modern bungalow in the village was designed by my uncle, Sherban (an architect), on a budget for one of Beryl's staff.

"Sanda managed to buy her own property in 1954-5 when she bought the three cottages, 1-3, The Street. They were cheaper because they were in a bad state of repair and had various sitting tenants. We were brought up on the stories of Wally Washford and his mother who lived in no.1. Old Mrs Washford died at the age of nearly 100 and Wally was found dead under the table. My grandmother did not have a lot of money but she was very practical and made a lot of things for her home. Her large, one-acre garden became her passion, and she sculpted a separate herb garden at the bottom in which she grew fruits and vegetables. My grandmother was also passionately interested in Romania and its history and could talk for hours very knowledgeably.

"When the last cottage became available to her, she was very happy to have a space for her daughter's family while her son's family would stay in nos.2 and 3 with her. During term-time she rented our house to students at the Agricultural College in Wye. My grandmother always had a poodle for as long as I knew her, several of them called 'Shadow'!

"When Sanda was no longer able to look after herself, living alone in Brabourne, my mother brought her to live with us in London, but we were able to keep her cottage in the family and it is now divided between her grandchildren, Ilinca, and me, Ileana.

ENDURING MEMORIES OF BRABOURNE
"Long summer holidays spent with cousins in the house and garden, playing badminton, creating obstacle course races.
Hide and seek in all three cottages, as they were joined on both floors.
Plays we performed each summer, organised and written by my cousin Marina, using old clothes from the 'dressing-up box'.
Being put to sleep in the back of the car in London (no seat belts so we just lay in the back) and waking the next morning to the sound of the birds in Kent.
We only ever went on two walks - either the "Small Top" circular walk of the village or the longer "Big Top" which incorporated the North Downs Way.
Playing 'getting married' in the church and the real weddings there of my two cousins, Ilinca and Marina.

The beauty of my grandmother's garden.

The very clear stars in the sky at night (still very good).

The small shop next door (the old post office), where we used to buy too many sweets for midnight feasts with Muna!  This was run by a couple; the husband, to our fascination, had lost all the fingers on one of his hands (blown up in a science experiment at school, I seem to remember).

Tea with sugar and rusks in bed with my grandmother every morning.

Putting sheets on beds in great excitement for the arrival of older cousins.

Frequent visits from European friends and endless chatting over gin and home-made elderflower cordial.

Pictures of Romanian relatives and princes and princesses of Romania on the walls.

Our bedtime stories, true accounts of all the different and exciting ways my grandfather had tried to escape from Romania.

The delicious wineberries that Sanda grew on the back wall of the house and which I have never come across since.

My grandmother gardening until dusk with a drip on the end of her nose.

My grandmother changing into several languages in one conversation.

Sunday family visits to the Catholic church in Wye.

Painting Easter eggs and the wonderful Easter hunts in the garden.  Not only chocolate eggs, but each grandchild had presents in a different colour hidden in the garden.

Visits from the eccentric dog lady, Miss X, who smelt very much of dog.

Exploding home-made cider bottles.

Endless fetching of coal from the outside shed to fill the Rayburn.

Melting lead in the Rayburn and 'reading' the shapes on New Year's Eve.

Lady Charnwood whisking my grandmother off for an occasional glamorous lunch at The Wife of Bath in Wye.

Shopping trips to Ashford on the bus, which used to stop right outside the house, and lunch at Gizzi's.

Mrs Bannister, who used to clean and help my grandmother.

'Fish and chip' cliff walks with my father in Folkestone.

Occasional trips to the teahouse in Wye and the book shop.

The beautiful tiered walled gardens at Court Lodge, where we used to play 'grandmother's footsteps'.

The dip in the lawn opposite Court Lodge, which we called 'the bath', and the white stones, the 'giant's teeth'.

The wonderful coloured dahlias in the flower garden at Court Lodge.

Crying uncontrollably when I had to leave Brabourne, so homesick for Kent and my grandmother.

The burials in the churchyard of my grandmother, cousin Sherbani and father Frank.

Marie-Lyse, left, with her mother, the Princess Cantacuzino

One of the many plays staged by the cousins in the Princess's garden in The Street. The three children in front are Andrew Ruhemann (soldier), his sister, Ileana (on swing) and their younger sister, Alexandra. Behind are Marina Cantacuzino and her younger brother Sherbani

Cottages 1, 2 & 3, The Street, from the garden in the Princess's time

Across the World to Brabourne —

MAKING a final visit to his childhood haunts in Brabourne, on Monday, before returning to his native New Zealand, in September, was Mr. Cranleigh Barton, retired lawyer and artist who was last in Brabourne in 1935.

**Mr. Cranleigh Barton**

He arrived in England in 1958 via Malaya, India, Java, and Kenya, and made his home temporarily in London. He has also travelled throughout England painting and sketching, and has visited many Continental countries. In New Zealand, where he is famous as an artist, he has given many one-man exhibitions at his bachelor home overlooking a 50-mile stretch of sandy beach. This is his fourth visit to the home of his great-grandfather, one of the first missionaries to New Zealand. In 1923-1924, while studying at the Slade Art School, he gave two one-man exhibitions in Bond Street and had two of his sketches bought by Queen Mary.

His return journey starts on September 17 when he joins the Indiaman Coach in London for its once-a-year trip across Europe, Persia, and the Holy Land to India. From Madras he will fly to Hong Kong and will spend a month in Japan.

Cranleigh Barton

# AN EARLIER VISITOR TO EAST BRABOURNE

We are privileged to have access to extracts from the diairies of Cranleigh Barton (1890-1975), a native New Zealander, whose grandmother, Sarah Elizabeth Andrews (daughter of Onslow Andrews and Sarah Elizabeth Marshall), was born in 1820 at Wall Farm (now Penstock). Sarah married Henry Barton from Hadlow near Tonbridge; the couple moved to a farm at Pitt near Winchester and raised a family of seven. One of these children, Ernest Albert Barton, emigrated to New Zealand in the 1880s as a missionary, and the extracts below are from the diaries of Cranleigh Barton, one of Ernest's three sons, who visited England in 1913-14 to meet his relatives, both the Bartons and the Marshalls. Cranleigh trained as a lawyer but later took up painting, particularly watercolours, and became renowned as an artist. (The Cranleigh Barton Drawing Award established in 1993 is one of New Zealand's best known drawing competitions.) He was also a dedicated diarist and his record gives us a valuable snapshot of Brabourne in the early 20th century.

A word as to how we came by these extracts: a great nephew of Cranleigh Barton who had also visited Brabourne sent extracts from his diaries to Margaret Older, the former owner of Penstock Farm. Dating back to before the start of the First World War, these describe when Cranleigh came to stay with his cousin Gwinnie Finn (Andrews) and Sidney Finn at Ivy Cottage, East Brabourne - which is now the home of Andrew and Sarah Martin. Margaret Older, Andrew's grandmother, gave the diary extracts to Andrew and Sarah, who have kindly allowed us to include them in this book:

"Thursday, 11th September 1913. A beautiful, fine day. I finished off Mother's letter and posted my NZ mail and then got my things together to take to Cousin Gwinnie's. [Gwinnie was the daughter of Walter and Jane Andrews, who owned the kiln on Canterbury Road.] Fortunately I did as a trap came for me at about 9.30. Gwinnie was in a house further up the road and joined us as we passed. The village of Brabourne is 6 miles from Willesborough and is a nice drive. Gwinnie's house is nearly opposite Wall Farm [now Penstock] where my great-grandfather used to live and where my great-grandmother was born. (Onslow Andrews 30.6.1790-25.3.1874, and Sarah Elizabeth Andrews, June 1820-12.8.1905 respectively)... Wall Farm is built almost on to the road and has a great many farm buildings right on the road. It is a nice looking old place, all the chimneys converge in a huge one in the middle of the house – quite a feature. Gwinnie's home, Ivy Cottage, has also belonged to the Andrews family for years. It is a nice place with a small but pretty garden and spotlessly kept. There are 40 acres with it so it is quite a little farm. In the morning we went for a walk to the church, St Mary's, a very nice one with a handsome square tower covered with ivy. Near the entrance are some Marshall graves, relatives of ours – my great-grandmother was a Miss Marshall - and at the back of the church my great-grandfather Onslow Andrews is buried and also Gwinnie's father and mother [Walter and Jane Andrews]. The church inside is interesting, a great many memorials to the well-known Scott family who lived here. We had a very nice lunch, roast fowls, etc., and afterwards sat on the lawn. They then lent me a bicycle and cousin Sidney took me down to the tile works, which used to belong to Uncle Walter [Andrews] and are still run under his name. We went all round, some tiles were in the oven cooling down after baking and I saw men making others and putting them to dry. They work by contract and get 4/- a 1000, and by working hard they can make about 1200 to 1500 a day. We walked all over the fields and did not get back till 6 o'clock when I was quite ready for tea. The martins are all on the wing preparing to leave England for the winter, they collect in swarms almost as thick as bees. After tea Cousin Gwinnie and I went for a walk, there was a lovely sunset. Then we had supper when cousin Sidney came in and Gwinnie showed me photograph albums till bedtime. I like her very much. She is good fun. [This is a very different perspective on Gwinnie from that of the very young Keith Finn, cited in Chapter 5.]

"Friday 12. We had breakfast at 8 and then I walked down to the post office [later to become Coquet Lodge] and got some postcards. Cousin Sidney asked me if I would like to go to Hythe with him, so he rode Gwinnie's bicyle and lent me his. We came home arriving about 6 o'clock and ready for tea. Altogether we went about 26 miles in the day. I showed Cousin Gwinnie some postcards and photos before supper and we talked afterwards till 10 when we retired.

"Saturday 13 was a perfect day with not a cloud in the sky. We had some delicious fried mushrooms for breakfast, they are very plentiful just now. I went for a walk to the church afterwards and had another look at the Andrews graves and then I bicycled down to the kiln with Sidney and spent the morning there. We bicycled on to Smeeth station to see about a truck so I had a look in the Smeeth church, another one with a square tower. At the kiln they were making both plain and ridge tiles. We got home for lunch at 12.30 as Sidney went off for the afternoon to New Romney with some members of the Bell Ringers Association. Bell ringing is one of his hobbies. Cousin Gwinnie and I went all over the house, it is such a nice old-fashioned one with an attic, and she showed me the huge outhouses, including 2 oast houses and a malt house and we went in the large orchard. Some of the fruit trees are very old. There is some mistletoe growing on an apple tree. A man generally gives them an offer for all the fruit as it stands after they have marked the trees they want for themselves. This year they are getting 7 pounds. Before tea Gwinnie took me for a walk right over the Downs from which we got a splendid view. Then I packed my bag and she got some beans and figs for Aunt Ellen and at 5.30 we set out for Willesborough. It was a very pretty ride and a beautiful sunset. Gwinnie came to within a hundred yards of Dunn's Hill and then went back. She is a splendid manager and has a very nice servant, Ellen. Everything is spotlessly clean. I am looking forward to staying with her again.

"Sunday 9 August 1914 [He had arrived at Ivy Cottage the preceding Thursday.]. …We all, including Sidney, went to Brabourne church in the evening. Tom Stack the vicar took the service but his brother Baggott, who is spending a holiday here, preached. It was a very good ex tempore sermon. Both the brothers look rather like monks, especially Baggott who is fat and has a perfectly tonsured head. They both shout at the tops of their voices, which is absurd in such a small church. Tom and Gwinnie often have contretemps, she gave us an amusing account of some of them. We had a great many special prayers and there were additions to the litany also this morning (at Smeeth church). After church we went for a walk on the downs, such a lovely extensive view looking over Brabourne and a glorious sunset, the sun a ball of red, slipped down among the purple grey clouds and the clear sky behind was pink shading to yellow and then blue. One star peeped out like the star of the East.

"Monday 10. A glorious day, the promise of last night's sunset fulfilled. I was writing in the drawing room after breakfast when Gwinnie rushed in and said that a cottage round the corner was on fire so we all tore round. A big crowd of villagers had collected outside and smoke was coming through the upstairs window and a hole in the roof which some men had made. The cottage is rented by a Mr Percy Laslett, quite a character, and he lives in the upstairs room and does his own work. For ages all the women in the village have been dying to see his room; their wishes were gratified for they had the pleasure of seeing the contents thrown from the top window on to the street. There was a pile of old clothes, some furniture, a bucket of preserved eggs which of course smashed, appples, and vegetables, altogether a very mixed looking heap. One lady fainted in the excitement and Gwinnie was a tower of strength. Another one threatened to follow but Gwinnie nipped it in the bud and took her off to her cottage, beating her breast. Laslett stayed in his house and wouldn't appear. The men got the fire under [control] without any difficulty, a good thing as there was practically no water and when it was all over the Ashford fire engine, which had been sent for, arrived. Tom Stack had not appeared on the scene so Gwinnie sent a boy to tell him and then she found out afterwards that the boy had said that Mrs Finn had sent for him. It was a fool's errand as everything was over when he arrived. [Don Skeer aged almost four years old also witnessed the fire, and his account is given below. There are, quite remarkably, some points on which both authors agree.]

"The Daily Mail arrives about 11.30. There was not much fresh war news. The Belgians are still gallantly holding Liège…We four set off about half past 2 and went first and called on Kathleen Weekes, Hannah's niece, who lives at the Limes, quite near here. She is killingly funny and Madge [Madge Wickham, a first cousin of Gwinnie Andrews] and I several times nearly exploded. Kathleen Dorothea is about 50, to begin with her appearance is ludicrous. She has never put her hair up and wears a black velvet band across the front, the hair reaches to her shoulders and as it is not too thick she supplements it with pieces of woolly hair pad, only too apparent and over the whole of the coiffure trails a bow with streamers. [Kathleen Weekes was James Weekes's sister and Norman Weekes's aunt. She had an abundance of hair, which, allegedly, was the tail of her favourite horse made into a wig. Kathy always wore black from head to foot and, according to those who remember her, was quite a stunning sight.] She has very few teeth but fortunately they are opposite one another and she has such a prim and proper air. She has an early Victorian accent and mouths each word: train is pronounced 'treen' and lane 'lean' and so on. She said the war was 'so veery sed' with a resigned sort of voice and pretends her brother is a regular old dragon to her. There are some lovely things in the house. The dining room has a beautiful carved mantelpiece with an old picture let in as a panel and there is some very nice furniture. From there we bicycled to Willesborough and passed through Hinxhill. We went and saw the church and the Andrews' graves, which Geraldine had never seen before [Geraldine Henham, a first cousin of Gwinnie Andrews.].

"Sunday 16. A nice fine day but very windy. Gwinnie, Gee and I went to church at 11 and Tom Stack preached. He has a very peculiar delivery and keeps on repeating one word, in this sermon it was 'Ichabob'. We spent the afternoon lazily out in the garden and I wrote my diary. We talked of bicycling to Swingfield as they have an old three-decker pulpit, lectern and prayer stool combined in the church but it is a long ride and was too windy. Dr Garman came to tea and discussed Red Cross work. We all went to church in the evening and we had a splendid sermon from Baggott Stack. Afterwards was a practice of mission hymns. Kathleen Weekes was at church. Her head arrangements look even weirder with a hat perched on top. After supper we all stayed in the drawing room and sang hymns.

"Monday 17. A nice fine day. I packed before breakfast, but had plenty of time as I did not have to leave till after 9. I was sorry to think I had come to the end of my visit as I have enjoyed it so much and Gwinnie was sorry too…"

Cranleigh Barton returned to Brabourne 13 years later, 9th-15th August, 1927, while he was studying art at the Slade School of Fine Art in London. The diary entries of this visit don't have much to say about the village. By this time Gwinnie had acquired a motorcar and much of the stay involved sightseeing in the neighbourhood.

## FIRE AT BRABOURNE STREET BY AN EYEWITNESS

This section has been "borrowed" unashamedly from About Brabourne and Smeeth (Spring, 1985, pp22-23), produced by the Brabourne and Smeeth History Group[1], not least because it gives a different perspective of the fire mentioned in the diaries of Cranleigh Barton. It comes from Don Skeer (aged just under four at the time of the observation):

"Next to the post office, the one by the Five Bells, was a house I've always known as 'Old Lasletts'. A Mr Laslett lived there who was spoken of as a hermit, nowadays he would be called an eccentric, hardly a recluse as during fine weather he would walk off with a load of books under his arm, and presumably some food; books were his life, and it was understood he had been a schoolmaster. He must have had sufficient means not to have to work; he was still a youngish man.

"When walking on top of the Downs you could see signs of where he had been, and sometimes an empty condensed-milk tin would fly out of the bracken to land some distance away from his lair of the day, the previous day's occupational patch being marked by a ring of tins some few yards from the centre, which was itself littered with paper. Once a discarded book, not as one would have expected but trash my mother called it. She had always thought of him as 'learned' and was evidently rather disgusted.

"To me he seemed a tall, dark man, and a little sparse, who didn't worry anyone and seldom spoke. People seemed to respect the obvious academic side of his character. He must have lived in Brabourne a good few years.

"One particular day there was some degree of panic – Mr Laslett's house was on fire! Being next to the post office and the post office connected by telegraph to Ashford, even if the connection was by only one wire, the post office for its own survival summoned the Fire Brigade, and someone went up to the Downs to find Mr Laslett.

"In the meantime, the people of the cottages adjoining started to move their belongings out of their houses and into the road. Soon there was a row of chairs and tables all along the path opposite. What impressed me most at the time, even though

---

1      Our thanks to Mr John Hammon, the last Chairman and only remaining member of the Brabourne and Smeeth History Group, for granting us permission to reproduce this extract.

I was so young, and have thought about it over the years since, was what a pathetic little lot people had to display to the world. Shut away in their homes no one knew, but a bundle of clothes gathered up quickly and dumped in the road for safety looks different from a neatly ironed pile of freshly washed clothes. It was the hard wooden seated chairs, mostly old ones, that betrayed any pretentions of comfort.

"Soon one of the women could stand the tension no longer and broke down with some signs of hysteria. This might have passed me almost unnoticed, although I was compassionately concerned for her, but her tears caused the mascara, or whatever it might have been, to run down her face, and there was a lot of mascara!

"Now, women in ordinary life didn't use make-up, and certainly not first thing in the morning. It was many years afterwards that ladies were daring enough to use a little rouge on special occasions. So why this particular lady's mascara? It seems that in her younger days (she was only about 30, with a lot of black curly hair) she had worked in a fairground booth under the name of The Black Angel.

"While all this was going on the men had got themselves organised into a bucket chain, standing in a row passing buckets from hand to hand, the last man dashing into the side door with a full bucket and coming out with it empty; the water came from the back somewhere, so presumably someone was working a pump or drawing water from a well. Their efforts were enough to subdue the fire even if they were not able to finally put it out.

"The cause of the fire seems to have been an oil stove or oil lamp catching something alight. My most vivid memory is probably the smell of burning wallpaper, as this has a different smell from any other burning paper. I have always had an instant flashback to Laslett's fire whenever or wherever I have smelt it, even after all these years.

"Meanwhile the fire engine was on its way, and firemen, although absolutely dedicated, were great showmen. Brabourne Street is about seven miles from Ashford; the horses couldn't have galloped all the way but they came round the corner by the Five Bells at a gallop; there was a high board fence then and no car park, so it was a most spectacular 'entrance' from the wings. The two horses were in a bit of a sweat; they were not light horses nor heavy ones either, as they had a job to do at a fair speed.

"The fire for the upright boiler of the engine, all brass and copper and red paint, was going full blast having been lit en route, so an extra top-up of fuel just before reaching Brabourne Street all made for a dramatic arrival.

"The fire engine drew up at the post office. The firemen standing along the sides dashed off to see for themselves what the situation was. Some went into the house from the back door; the front door was never opened as far as I know.

"After consultation with some of the local men, the fire engine and most of the firemen moved off towards Court Lodge Farm, where they drew up close to the pond. The suction pipe having been put into the pond inside a large wicker basket to keep out sticks and other rubbish, the hosepipe had to be run from the engine to Laslett's house, possibly a quarter of a mile away. After all these years it still amazes me that there was enough hosepipe available to reach this far.

"The man in charge of the hose took up a suitable stance, and the hose that had been flat began to become round as it filled with water.

"We all, I think, expected an instant stream of water but this was not to be, there was inevitably still a lot of air in the hose-pipe, so the water came from the gleaming copper and brass hose in a spasmodic series of little piddles, rather than the gush we had all expected. This, however, brought a release of tension and for the first time everyone laughed, even I suspect the lady with the mascara (or without it).

"The hose finally got itself going and everything was made safe, but for years afterwards the different colour of some of the tiles on the cat-slide roof of Laslett's house showed how near the Street came to being obliterated."

Don Skeer notes: "An old school friend, Mr 'Bert' Palmer of Ashford, who was for many years a member of Ashford Volunteer Fire Brigade until it was nationalised into the Kent Brigade, has looked up this incident in the old records." It was recorded as follows:

"East Brabourne adjoining the Post Office – August 10th 1914
        Called by telegraph at 1.15pm.
        Steamer and Hose-tender 13 Officers and men.
        Cause oil stove defective – damage alight."

OTHER VISITORS

You don't see many tramps around these days and yet after the last two wars they were not an infrequent sight across the country. Almost all were men who, it was thought, had been shell-shocked or suffered in some other way during the First World War and found it difficult to cope with the responsibilities of everyday life. Brabourne and Smeeth were visited regularly by a couple of tramps, as well as by Indian hawkers who used to sell everything from dusters and tea towels to jewellery and carpets, and by knife sharpeners and onion sellers from France on their bikes. One of the last sightings of an onion seller was in the late 1970s in East Brabourne.

Many people depended on Sloans, otherwise known as the Tally Man, who came round with a van full of goods every week. Christine Peall (Friend) recalled that "he would give you whatever you wanted from the van on the day he came round, and you would then pay him for the goods in the following weeks". She also recalled that, "you never got to the end of the payments because as soon as the end was in sight he would sell you something else from the van". In the 1950s and 1960s her mother used to depend on the Tally Man for a range of things, including sandals for the children. One summer she bought Christine and her sister a pair of beige sandals with crepe soles; the children detested them and tried to do everything they could to destroy them. They slid in mud, jumped in sticky tar on the road – anything, but the sandals survived and when, eventually, they had run their course, Christine remembers her mother saying, "Those were good shoes, we'll get you another pair." When Christine was older she had her own account with the Tally Man and bought her first set of saucepans from him just before she got married. She wasn't able to choose the pans, she just took what the Tally Man brought with him, and she still remembers her husband Dave's horrified exclamation: "£6 for a set of pans!" But they lasted well and, 42 years later, she still uses the milk pan.

Pauline Anderson remembers one of the regular visitors, an Irishman, Patrick Murphy, commonly known as Snucker (the pronunciation of the "u" being as in "full", rather than as in "umbrella"). Snucker would come to the village every summer and when he called at Subdown Cottages, Pauline's mother, Nancy Marsh, would always give him tea and a cake or a cheese pastry before he went on his way. Vi Varrier (Kingston) can also remember Snucker appearing at their kitchen door, holding his old tin and asking for tea and something to eat. He used to do odd jobs for Jim Kingston, who lived in the first bungalow on the right-hand side going down Fiddling Lane from Pilgrims' Way, and during his summer visit would live in Jim's barn. Vi recalls that, at times, Snucker would also sleep in her father's barn at Bankside. He only ever came to the area in the summer and no one knew where he went for the rest of the year, or how he survived during the winter.

There was another summer-months-only visitor who used to live in a bender, an elaborate tent, in the piece of woodland on Pilgrims' Way opposite Missingham Farm. He used to make clothes pegs and sell these locally, and his evenings were often spent at the Five Bells.

Summer-months-only visitor to the villages

People also remembered another tramp, who barely spoke, possibly due to being traumatised during the First World War. He is not remembered for coming to Brabourne, though, but would sit on the step in front of the old post office on the A20 (now demolished), more or less opposite the Paddocks. The people there would give him food, and he would stay for a few days before moving on. The interesting thing is that no one considered these people dangerous or a threat they merely accepted them as different, perhaps in need of some help, and children found their arrival in the area rather unusual and exciting.

VISITING GYPSIES
Oliver Trowell recalls the arrival of gypsies in East Brabourne in the 1930s:

"There was great excitement as the highly decorated caravans approached, drawn by strong-legged cobs and horses. The horses were led by sinister-looking men in a variety of second-hand waistcoats, caps, shirts, trousers, jackets and boots. The women were stout and upright in posture. They looked proud and self-respecting and were also dressed in second-hand clothes and boots. Some wore large straw hats decorated with wild flowers and most wore an apron and carried large hazel or willow baskets filled with clothes pegs, pegs made from peeled hazel rods. The women knocked on every back door in the village and sold a dozen for a few pence.

Gypsy caravan outside Court Lodge in the 1930s, by Oliver Trowell

"These gypsies were of genuine gypsy stock and the women were reputed to enhance their naturally swarthy appearance by rubbing their well-weathered faces with walnut juice. Their hair was usually in tight, oily-looking ringlets and they wore gold earrings. They seemed alien to village dwellers and, although apparently friendly, were viewed with suspicion and distrust by locals. The whole cavalcade halted on the grass opposite Court Lodge, underneath the horse chestnut trees that formed an unfenced front to Church Farm.

"Once they were settled, blue wood smoke emerged from the chimneys of the caravans. Small, grubby children looked over half-doors of caravans, small boys in shorts that were too big for them and oversized boots on bare feet. They stayed but for a short while, after which they moved on. Ladders for the caravans were taken up, buckets, ropes, horses' nosebags secured and all sorts of things swayed from hooks along the undercarriages as they moved off.

"The gypsy community had an encampment above Monks Horton on the north side of the Roman Stone Street. They moved about at frequent intervals, however, and a small group of caravans and their occupants was often to be seen under the trees surrounding the long-abandoned ruins of Fiddling Farm, about a couple of miles east of East Brabourne."

NEW FRIENDS IN THE COMMUNITY
Brenda Wright, who moved to Stowting from London in 1967, writes of the support and the "network of help" that she received from local people when they arrived, some of them in the Brabourne area:

"We simply wanted to live in the country and had big ideas of keeping some animals on the ground that went with the house. To start with we only had a dog, but two donkeys from Lady Sternberg's herd soon came on board (was this an ark?!), soon to be followed by a Jersey cow, sold to us by Bob Pilcher, and then some Kent ewes, bought for us in the market by Tom Kemp. These were later joined by some Rough Fell ewes in lamb, fetched from Cumbria in a trailer lent to us by Derek

Brenda Wright

Fuller. Soon some goats arrived from Lord Whisky animal sanctuary called Gransy, Mumsy and Babesy; they were not to be separated. That Christmas Jean Small sold us two delightful Peruvian dwarf cross pigs, then a couple of ponies demanded that we acquire a bit more land, if possible. So then what? Yes, we made some bad mistakes. I didn't recognize fly strike when one of the ewes seemed to be lying down a lot, but Robin Marsh spotted it from some distance away. Nor did we realise that young grass or too much corn could kill; we had some sad times.

"But reading about all the characters and memories in this book have reminded me just how much people put themselves out to help and teach us newcomers. For example, John Varrier was always willing to advise if a pony was lame or ailing. Tom Sprawling from the Handy Stores would always tell us how to tackle a DIY job, and the cheapest ways as well. Ron Cooper, the butcher, also gave us some quiet tips when he came up to see if my lambs were ready for him. Often, they were too fat – 'You want to be able to see a shilling in the grass if you drop it,' he said, indicating that sheep did best on short grass. On one occasion the cow got milk fever after she had given birth, and she went down in full view of passing cars. None stopped, but it wasn't long before a farmer, in this case Ray Hayden, noticed what was happening and saved her with a timely injection. Later on I got to notice for myself if a ewe was in a similar state and I had the calcium and magnesium ready. It never failed to amaze me how quickly the treatment worked. Another cow was down in the stable for seven weeks, and Ron Stuart and John Wilson came twice every day to turn her over to prevent bedsores. They used a special sturdy stick cut from the hedge for leverage. Later on Ron used to come up on many mornings to help the old donkey up. Sometimes she saw him coming and got up of her own accord. John and Ron built us a sty for Pansy the pig. I mustn't forget Michael Taylor, sent round by Alison Roberts, to give me a lesson in 'dagging' the dirty wool from round the ewe's udder, in preparation for lambing. My hardest job was using a special 'S'-shaped rake to push the ewe's head under the dip. If the inspector was there the sheep had to remain immersed for two minutes, I think.

"All in all we had a lot of help from local people who must have looked askance at us when we first arrived, but their kindness and help brought us into the community, not just of Stowting but Brabourne, too, and made us part of it."

## CHANGE, BUT NO CHANGE IN THE STREET: CONSERVATION IN PRACTICE

Back in East Brabourne, the appearance of The Street has changed remarkably little over the past 100 years and, in recent decades, change has been limited owing to the inclusion of properties in The Street in a conservation area and much of East Brabourne being within the Kent Downs Area of Outstanding Natural Beauty.

Subdown Cottages

Subdown Cottages were built very soon after the Second World War, in 1946/47, and were thought to be some of the earliest council houses in England. Coronation Cottage, designed by the Prince Cantacuzino when he was training as an architect, has been the only significant addition since that time. Most of the buildings are still the same, though many of the residents have changed since the first half of the 20th century. One who has remained since those days is, of course, Oliver Trowell. The functions of several of the buildings along The Street have altered as several barns have now been converted to dwellings. At the upper end of The Street, the Wheelwright's, formerly the Finns' Carpenters' Workshop, has changed to a dwelling. The three Egerton Cottages next door have now been converted into two and the cottage on the roadside gives no hint that it was where Keith Finn used to park his car. Egerton Cottages were bought by the Finns when they came to Brabourne from Egerton and the cottages have been the dwellings of many who worked for the Finns and others, too. Only one of the two (once three) cottages now bears the

The newly built Coronation Cottage, 1953. In front, the Princess
Cantacuzino with a chicken from her farm at Court Lodge Barn

name Egerton Cottage, testifying to the arrival of the Finns from Egerton over a
century ago, a family that came to have a significant and much respected presence in
the locality. The Five Bells has changed considerably and has been much modernised.
Ivy Cottage, the Malthouses and the cottages alongside Homehurst have remained,
though all have been considerably smartened up. Phil Stone and Oliver remember
yet another cottage, now disappeared, virtually opposite the gate of Penstock Farm,
inhabited for a time by Bill Stockbridge and his family. Not many others seem to
remember it, but it may have been a victim of bomb damage. Oliver also recalls
seeing, in 1934, "the ruins of a cottage in the now-overgrown area between Ivy
Cottage and the Five Bells car park". Several houses have been built along Pilgrims'
Way in the 20th century: Lamplands was built by Patrick Rice, Oliver's brother-in-law,
in 1932, and the neighbouring houses towards Wye, though recent in comparison
with some of those along The Street, are nonetheless well established. In essence,
East Brabourne has retained many familiar features since the early years of some of
our oldest contributors. Though it has lost its shop and post office, its baker, builder,
funeral director and forge, reassuring photographs from the past suggest that the
village has crept into the 21st century without losing any of its original charm.

Margaret and Oliver Trowell outside Coquet Lodge (1964)

## POSTSCRIPT
Oliver Trowell adds:

"One feature that has changed in both character and position is the footpath, which in pre-war days ran on the north side of the road from the Five Bells to the gate into Court Lodge field and consisted of a well-trodden track bordered by a grassy edge. Until after the war it ran along the top of the bank in the stretch between Hillview and Court Lodge gateway. When Subdown Cottages were built on land compulsorily purchased from Albert Hammon, a new, asphalt path, bordered with concrete kerb stones, was laid down on the south side of the road, giving a rather more suburban than rural character to The Street. The old path on the north side of the road has disappeared without trace."

# 8

# WEEKES LANE, WEST BRABOURNE:
# A SNAPSHOT OF A COMMUNITY IN THE 1960s

Like East Brabourne, Weekes Lane in West Brabourne, which extends from Pilgrims' Way at the foot of the Downs to the stream that runs through Ford's Water, is now much smarter in appearance than it was in the early 1960s. In this section we introduce some of the different inhabitants of the Lane during that period and include various snippets that people remembered about them.

The Hall, formerly The Limes, was once an ancient farmhouse and dates back to the time of Queen Anne. This was the home of the Weekes family for many years; they were people who played a major part in the local community and, obviously, gave their name to the Lane. James Weekes was much involved with the church and school in East Brabourne, and his son, Norman, who was a professional actor, is warmly remembered for his very active role in local dramatic productions. The Limes changed hands several times and one set of occupants, the Neames, changed its name to The Hall, which was what it was called when it was bought by Judge Joseph Dean and his wife, Jenny, in 1963. Jenny describes the Lane as being very quiet at that time and rather eerie – there was very little traffic and life there could not have been much more peaceful.

Ptolemy Dean, Joseph and Jenny's son, has researched The Hall and here describes aspects of its interesting history:

"The Hall dates from the 17th century, with significant later alterations. The southwest

505

The Limes, now known as The Hall, when it was owned by the Weekes family (1950s)

The Hall, by Ptolemy Dean (2013)

front, with its characteristic five-bay 'doll's house' front looks, at first glance, to be typically Georgian, but it is in fact from slightly earlier than this, dating perhaps from the end of the 17th century. There is evidence to suggest that the present sash windows are a later replacement of leaded casement windows, which were not as long as those that exist now. There is a wing on the eastern side that appears to have been truncated, as the north-facing back wall of this part is of early 20th-century brickwork. The original roof structure is double pitched and well constructed of oak; it is steeply pitched, supporting the late 17th-century date of construction. A valley gutter in the centre of these roofs was covered over in the 1950s but it can still be seen inside. Known archive evidence of the early history of the house is unfortunately fairly thin. It was reportedly heavily panelled inside, prior to a heavy-handed restoration carried out in the late 1950s by its then owners Colonel and Mrs Neame. Even so, the original oak main and secondary staircases remain, along with the original bolection-moulded doors to the principal rooms. The main, first-floor bedroom retains a fully panelled wall, concealing cupboards, and boasts a bolection-moulded fireplace. The ground-floor rooms have late 18th-century shutters, perhaps confirming the original date of the present sash windows. The correct pattern of glazing bars of these were reinstated in the 1970s by my father, who carefully restored the appearance of the house after the damaging works of the 1950s. He also added the timber conservatory to the side of the house according to his own design.

Jenny Dean

"The Hall is surrounded by a group of 18th-century farm buildings. The farmyard was located to the southeast of the house behind the barn, which partly shapes a courtyard in front of the house, and is typical of so many contemporary Kentish farms. Adjacent to the barn is a small block of stables, while behind the barn are a run of former cow byres and farm ranges, which have been partly converted into a cottage. A scheme for a second cottage here was never executed. This part of the farmyard once overlooked a farm pond, the willow tree from which survived until quite recently. Between these buildings and the main house is a walled garden that is now reaching its prime."

The Lane does seem to have been a "stronghold" for Thornbys in the 1960s and 1970s. Where Meadow View now stands, Kath and Basil Thornby lived in a house

The wedding of Kath White to Basil Thornby. Far left, Patrick Thornby, with his and Basil's mother, Ethel Conley (Thornby), between them – all residents of Weekes Lane

clad with dark-green corrugated iron. Corrugated iron made such structures safer than wooden houses in the days when fires and candles were still very much part of everyday life. Jenny Dean remembers that their living conditions were basic. Kath had two small children, a cold tap, no electricity, no bath and all hot water had to be heated up on the stove. Although electricity was available, most people couldn't afford the connection charge and so continued using paraffin, in some cases until the 1970s. The situation improved significantly for Kath and Basil when they moved to a brick bungalow, Hillside, further down Weekes Lane in 1970.

Another dark-green house clad in corrugated iron with similar facilities, called The Nest, stood on the site where Brewers Meadow now stands, and this was the home of Billy and Ethel Conley. Ethel was the mother of Rose, Patrick, Basil and Norman Thornby and this was her second marriage, her first husband, Percy Thornby, having died after the First World War, during which he suffered from the effects of mustard gas. It seems Billy was quite a character: he and Ethel were hoarders, and the house was packed with "interesting junk", as was the yard. There was one electric light bulb in the front room and a picture of Queen Alexandra on the wall. It is said that wine-in-the-making bubbled away under a table, giving off a "yeasty" smell and making curious gurgling sounds. Ethel and Billy spent most of their time in the kitchen, sharing it with their numerous cats, possibly an antidote to the rats

Ethel Conley with grandson Pat Thornby, who contributes later in this chapter

Ethel's husband, Billy Conley

and mice that were so prevalent in houses at that time. Pauline Anderson (Marsh), who worked for the Deans at The Hall, recalls that Ethel, who was not a smoker, would order several packets of cigarettes along with her groceries each week (from Woods at Mersham), and as friends and relatives ran out they would replenish their supplies by buying them from Ethel. The main "takers" for Ethel's stash were other residents of the Lane: Kath and Basil Thornby, Patrick and Queenie Thornby, and Pauline herself. People remembered Billy cycling into Ashford Market every week, always in a large coat and gaiters. The

Pauline Anderson

Thornbys and the Conleys are longstanding families in the area. As we saw in chapter 1, the Thornbys have been connected with Brabourne Church for centuries, and an Edward Conley is cited as being a grazier in Bagshaw's History, Gazetteer and Directory of Kent 1847[1]. More on Edward at the end of the chapter. This may well have been the same Edward Conley who was a highly respected member of the local community, having served as clerk to the parish of Brabourne for 36 years.

Billy had two sisters, one of whom, Amy Edwards, lived in a bungalow almost opposite The Hall. In time, both his sisters died and Billy gave two large ornamental candlesticks to Brabourne Church in their memory. Sadly, these were both stolen in the 1970s. Virtually opposite The Nest, on the other side of the Lane, was Elm Farm, where Patrick and Queenie Thornby, Ethel's eldest son and his wife, lived. Thus family ties within the Lane were strong.

On the same side of the Lane as Elm Farm, in what is now Juniper Cottage, lived Jimmy Sargeaunt, a Dorset vicar's son described as a "lovely chap", who had relocated from the West Country. His wife, who had been brought up in India, was very different from him – "They were like chalk and cheese," a contributor told us. Pauline recalls that Jimmy's birthday was on The Glorious Twelfth (12th August), and on one of his birthdays he treated Jenny Dean, her three children, and Pauline, Queenie, Kath and Kath's two daughters to tea at Olantigh, after which they looked round the gardens. One memory that several people shared about Jimmy was the number of cats also living in his house.

---

1    Bagshaw, Samauel (1847) History, Gazetteer and Directory of Kent 1847. Vol. II. Sheffield, publisher G Ridge, p468.

# OTHER INHABITANTS OF WEEKES LANE, WEST BRABOURNE

Patrick and Queenie Thornby from Elm Farm

Basil and Kath Thornby in more recent years (1990s)

## AND GOING SLIGHTLY FURTHER BACK IN TIME

Norman and Connie Weekes at The Limes
(1950s)

In 1933 or thereabouts, Edward Ames bought Boulding House, reputedly the oldest house in Brabourne, having been sold off from the Brabourne Estate in 1918, along with many other properties and land (approximately 2,500 acres). While fairly extensive alterations were made to the property, the Ameses lived at Westenhanger.

Further down the Lane, at Crow Corner, were the MacDonalds. Mrs MacDonald once told Jock Anderson (a bona fide Scotsman) with considerable confidence that they were real MacDonalds. Jock was never sure what she meant by this. Oliver Trowell remembers Major (retd) MacDonald being put out when, in 1942, he had to leave the Home Guard, in which he held the rank of sergeant, on the grounds of age – "Booted out at 70!" he used to say. Oliver also remembers a remark made by Mrs MacDonald when he, Oliver, assuming she was a Scot, expressed surprise when she

Boulding House, said to be one of the oldest in Brabourne

said she did not like porridge. "Actually, I'm a Yorkshire girl," said she - so perhaps it was her husband who was the real MacDonald. Pauline Anderson (Marsh) recalled that Mrs MacDonald spent a great deal of time knitting; she made shawls for all Jenny Dean's three children and Tacita loved hers so much that she eventually ate it! After she was widowed, Mrs MacDonald left Brabourne to go and live in Eastbourne.

Netty Knight in one of Norman Weekes's productions

Netty Knight (sometimes pronounced Netta), who also lived at Crow Corner, is remembered as being very community orientated, as well as, "a very good laugh". She was a member of the British Legion and used to carry the Women's Branch Standard. Other attributes she was known for were her rescuing of sick animals, her allegedly great talent for antiques and her prodigious involvement in the local dramatics society – her rendition of There's a Hole in My Bucket at one of the performances has kept her alive in the memory of many people. Something else she is remembered for were the wonderful parties she organised for her daughter, Beeb (pronounced Bibi).

Weekes Lane was a close-knit community during that time, partly because several of the residents were related, of course, but also because those were the days when people knew each other well and there was considerable mutual support. Today the Lane still retains much of its beauty and peace, despite the increase in motor traffic. Most of the houses have been smartened up considerably and the majority of the residents have now changed, but the current ones with whom we spoke still have a strong sense of being part of a village community.

## A CHILDHOOD IN WEEKES LANE

Pat Thornby, the son of Patrick and Queenie, writes:

Pat Thornby

"Born on 24th November, 1953, I arrived in Weekes Lane a month early, not wanting my birthday to clash with Christmas. My parents lived at Boulding House and were in the process of moving up the Lane to Elm Farm, which my father had just bought. Uncle Basil and Aunty Kath lived with us, my 'Nana' Ethel and her husband Willy Conley (also known as Billy) lived just up the road, and with numerous uncles, aunts and grandparents spread around the village, my family was complete. Elm Farm was a big rambling farmhouse – by rambling I mean falling down. It was surrounded by cow sheds, barns and outbuildings that, in turn, were surrounded by acre after acre of green fields, on which grazed cows, pigs, sheep and chickens, all good friends as I grew up.

"At the age of four I went to Brabourne School. I remember the day well. The school was divided up into two classes – the big 'uns and the little 'uns. I joined the little 'uns. On my first day the teachers, including Mrs Norrington the headmistress, struggled to get me to take my jacket off, but I steadfastly refused. When they asked why, I replied that I hadn't yet made my mind up if I was going to stay. But school turned out to be fun. I made lots of friends and we would play in a wild wooded area we called 'the jungle'. My father said it had gone to 'rack and ruin' and that, in his day, it used to be a vegetable garden where he had won first prize for his efforts. We made camps in it; this seemed a much better idea.

"One of the highlights of the school year was the annual truck race, during which children would race in twos in their home-made carts down the hill from Canterbury Road to the school and beyond. Now, if you know the area, you'll realise that it is quite steep, so careering downhill at full speed would have been quite a hairy experience. There were lots of grazed knees and bruised ankles but never, to my knowledge, any broken bones. [See chapter 6 for more on truck races at Brabourne School.] Mrs Norrington's husband, who owned the garage along the A20 just as you approach Sellindge, awarded the two prizes – one for the winner of the race and another for the best vehicle. I won the prize for best vehicle, beating Barry Andrews – who now runs Andrews Garage along the Plain at Smeeth – into second place. It wasn't that my truck was particularly good – it was an old apple box nailed onto some planks of wood with wheels on each corner – but I'd had the forethought to include a brake, something that no one else had thought of. My reward was a bright shiny silver spanner, which I accepted with pride.

"Living in Weekes Lane I would walk down to Crow Corner with one of my parents every day to be picked up by the 'taxi' and driven to school by Mr Ward, who owned the local garage. All of the children from the outlying areas, including Hampton and Bulltown Lanes, were picked up by this minibus, and Mr Ward, a pleasant old man, must have been deafened by the noise that the children made on their journeys to and from school.

"My father used to take in donkeys from the seaside during the winter break and, one day, he decided to bring a donkey to meet me from school. Always seeking to amuse, he thought it would be funny to sit on the donkey and make the children on the bus laugh. But the prank backfired – the approach of the taxi spooked the donkey and it bolted with my dad hanging on for dear life. He achieved his aim, though, as the children laughed out loud until they cried.

"School was always full of activities, including dancing around the maypole on May Day, listening to Movement, Mime and Music on the radio, the Christmas plays and, if you were very good, the occasional visit from Joey the clown, who always appeared with Mrs Norrington. If you had been good or worked really hard you would get a sweet from Joey; he never said anything and as far as we knew he lived in a locked cupboard in Mrs Norrington's classroom. One day we sneaked into the classroom and found that the cupboard was open – we opened the door and discovered Joey's terrible secret: he was a glove puppet! We helped ourselves to the sweets, also therein, to overcome our grief.

"Back to Elm Farm… There was no bathroom, but an outside toilet and huge kitchen, where I remember sitting and watching the gas light flicker. One day, a group of men turned up in a large lorry and started erecting poles across the fields. My father explained that we were going to have electricity. Shortly after this, Mr Avery, who lived in Lees Road, began to run cable after cable to every room of the house. It was amazing – we could even see at night now. My mother bought a radio and I became obsessed with it, refusing to go to sleep unless I could have the sound of Radio Luxembourg fading in and out as I drifted off to sleep.

Pat Thornby senior (1950s)

"Further improvements to Elm Farm came about in a strange way. My father found a package lying in the road so handed it into the local policeman, PC Allen. After three months or so the package remained unclaimed and, one day, Mr Allen turned up in the farmyard on his motorcycle and returned the package to my dad, explaining that, by law, it was now his. My mother eagerly opened the box: it contained a set of bath taps. She claimed that this was a sign and immediately set about convincing my father that we should have an indoor bathroom. Eric Ball was employed to construct a bathroom, complete with an immersion tank, so now we had hot water as well. No more tin baths in front of the fire. A black and white TV was next, followed by a fridge and the telephone – we had finally joined the 20th century in Weekes Lane.

"My Nana Ethel used to teach me how to sew using sharp needles, while Willy, my step-grandfather, would teach me carpentry, with his friend Jim Raison, using even sharper saws and chisels, despite my mother's fears. Willy showed me how to build, saw and hammer, and each day I would return home with bricks, sand, wood and nails as my mother looked on in horror at the increasing amount of clutter. The final straw came when he gave me a Second World War bayonet, which I used as a sword, hacking great chunks out of the fruit trees. It was confiscated, never to be seen again. Ethel was a lovely lady, always full of advice. On health she would say, 'You got to eat a bit of dirt before you die', and if you had a dirty collar she would tell you, 'Sit at the back of the bus so no one will notice.'

"They were great days, the summers seemed endless, the fields full of wild flowers; even the air seemed cleaner. During the summer my parents would help Willy and Ethel with fruit picking. Willy had quite a large orchard and victorias (plums), greengages and damsons would be picked from rickety old ladders and packed into boxes for export to London on a large lorry that arrived every evening.

"Another annual event was the village fête, which had a number of homes over the years. One particular year it was housed in a field behind Bircholt Forstal, to the right as you make your way up Lees Road into the village. Entertainment included music, games, bowling for the pig [usually donated by George Brooks], a coconut shy, endless cake stalls run by the Women's Institute and my favourite, a jumble stall – the modern equivalent of a car boot sale. It was at one of these stalls that I first saw a gramophone. It was beautiful: it wound up with a silver handle, and as the arm was swung into position the needle cut deep into the continuous groove on a heavy 12in record that span round at 78rpm. The tinny sound was emitted via a large horn connected to the main body below. Along with the gramophone came a box of records: Burl Ives's The Big Rock Candy Mountain, The Wedding of the Painted Doll, The Stars and Stripes and The Guns of Navarone. I badgered my mother until she finally gave in and bought it for me. Silence in the Thornby household was shattered.

"I also spent many hours listening to the radio with Willy. This is how I first discovered what a Sputnik was, and marvelled as Yuri Gagarin spent his 108 minutes orbiting the earth. My dad would take me for rides on his Fordson Major tractor, Uncle Basil would balance me on his motorcycle, and my Aunty Rose's husband Jack would arrive to cut my hair, giving me a cough sweet as a treat.

"My step-grandfather certainly knew how to collect clutter. He would spend hours and hours at farm sales collecting more and more, until his house was crammed full of 'stuff'. Floor to ceiling, it was everywhere – every book, magazine and newspaper was kept, leaving just a small walkway into each room. Wine bubbled away in demijohns under the kitchen table, cats were everywhere, rabbits in large numbers occupied hutches outside, along the backs of sheds that were fit to burst with even more of Willy's 'chattels'. Outside, a pile of sawdust lay beside a sawhorse that was used for cutting logs, an axe to one side for splitting them ready for the fire. In the midst of all this stood a vice that I found to be very useful for clamping things. A huge kitchen garden provided vegetables all year round; chickens stalked small boys by the door; bamboo grew in abundance, waiting for its time to be cut and used to support the runner beans and peas, and a large gooseberry bush to the side of the house filled a small child with its delightful fruit.

"My mother drove a large black Rover car complete with running boards. I thought that it was rather grand, although later photographs proved it to be very rusty. It was in this car that we would take our holidays, well, days out really. My father was never happy to leave his herd of cattle with anybody else, which limited us to days out at the seaside in Dymchurch. Ethel would also be packed into the car, along with a large picnic hamper – one thing I can say for my mother is that she did know how to cater. Days were spent building large sandcastles, finishing them off with a moat and little flags that we bought in the local arcade. A valuable lesson was learnt: no matter how big I built the castles and how many I created, the tide always won in the end. It was here I got my first pirate's sword and posed for the camera with a real parrot on my shoulder. I ate ice cream and met up with some of my old friends – the donkeys.

Queenie Thornby (Brooks), aka "Queen Mum"

"My mother worked at Ames' Stores and my maternal grandfather, Frederick Brooks, worked on the bacon counter there. He lived with my grandmother, Millie, in a house just behind the Zion Chapel in Canterbury Road. Here he had a little workshop, where I would watch him repair shoes to supplement his income. In those days the village also had two other shops: Orpins, as we still know it today; and Goreham's, where I used to buy sweets.

"The winter of 1963 was one of the worst that I've ever known. It snowed and snowed and snowed. The snow drifted, froze and more snow fell on top of it. One Sunday my father decided to visit his brother, Norman, who lived in East Brabourne. I pleaded with him to go too and, after some very difficult negotiations, my mother packed us a flask and off we set. We made our way from Elm Farm up Weekes Lane towards the Downs. The snow was really deep, coming right atop the hedgerows; however, it was frozen solid and quite easy to walk on. We carried on along under the Downs, past Miss Powell's house with its dovecots peering out from under their new fashioned white hats, continuing on towards East Brabourne, dropping down Brabourne Lane to the Five Bells, passing by the little shop on the right. Uncle Norman and his wife Jean lived in Subdown Cottages with my four cousins. We were made to feel welcome with tea and cakes and spent a very pleasant afternoon with them. Then it was time to set off for home. The way back seemed much longer and it was almost dark before we got home. An amazing day for an adventure in the snow.

"The snow stayed for ages and, eventually, Weekes Lane had to be dug out using a JCB. I remember the excitement when the driver came to the farm, because he had sheered a bolt, rendering the machine useless. We rummaged through the boxes of tractor spares and eventually sent him on his way with a suitable replacement. Back then, in the early 1960s, Elm Farm was much bigger. My father sold off some of the land to clear his mortgage and with it went one of my favourite fields. The 'Lucerne' field was located furthest from the farmhouse and in one corner it had a pond, which was surrounded by willow trees, bulrushes and reeds. It was occupied by a number of moorhens and newts. I spent many happy hours here messing about with planks of wood and lengths of bailer twine, trying in vain to construct a raft. It has to be said that all these activities did lead to my winning a county prize for a painting. The subject was What We Did in the Holidays, and my entry, of a boy on a raft, was submitted by Brabourne School. I won a book on how to paint!

"My mother had a great talent for painting and drawing, and encouraged her son. I remember her drawing me a coloured map of England, which I took to school to show all my friends. Other hobbies followed: I started collecting stamps, Typhoo tea cards, and later, plastic cowboys and Indians that came free with the washing powder Daz. All these were taken to school and duly 'swapped' in order to get the complete set. My good friend Michael once described me as a 'completist'. I know this to be true and it started at an early age. One Christmas I got a Dansette electric record player; this one played 33s, 45s and long-playing records. You could stack them up and they would play one after another. The Beatles followed and all my pocket money was spent on those very precious 45s.

"Aside from fruit picking in the summer, my mother would also farm pigs, feeding them on what seemed to be mainly a diet of boiled potatoes. In the autumn she would raise turkeys for Christmas. Apart from the awful noise, the sight of her plucking and preparing around 60 turkeys was probably a major factor in my becoming a vegetarian.

"I had a golden spaniel called Suzy, who my mother thought was hers, but would accompany me everywhere, chasing off cats and chickens as we went. There were two significant cats in my life at Elm Farm: General Ginger, a large and regal marmalade cat, aloof as only cats can be; and Moots, who in contrast was just plain crazy. Moots began life as Smokey Joe, and Mrs Bushell, who lived at Hillside, the bungalow on the opposite side of the lane between Elm Farm and Boulding House, gave him to me as a present. Mr Bushell was a dear old man with an amazing collection of old tobacco tins that contained treasures such as nuts, bolts, screws and other intriguing delights. Moots was the strangest of cats. His favourite place in the house was in the lower oven of our kitchen Rayburn and, on numerous occasions, my mother and I had to drag him out of the oven as the smell of singed cat filled the room. Maybe

Smokey Joe was a more accurate name for him. He could also be found investigating the cardboard boxes that I'd built together to make spaceships.

"School plays were an important part of my life and required me to dress up variously as a shepherd, Roman centurion, cowboy, for which I made an Indian headdress from cardboard and pheasants' feathers, and finally, a bear. I remember the bear because my mum made me a fur balaclava that was very hot, extremely hot – how I suffered for my art.

Pat senior and junior (early 1950s)

"As a child I never really left Brabourne, except for the day out at Dymchurch or a visit to Dover Castle. Then, one day, my Aunty 'Bill' and Uncle Jim [Martha, aka Mary, and Jim Brooks] took us to London. Uncle Jim drove and I was in the back between my parents, feeling slightly travel sick. It was a terrific day out: we visited the GPO tower, Madame Tussauds and the London Planetarium. I'd never seen so many cars or people. What an eye-opening experience.

"So! Meccano sets, Airfix kits, the Eagle comic with its cutaway drawings, Juke Box Jury, Doctor Who – all these things made my childhood complete. By the time Neil Armstrong walked on the moon it was over. I had the very best of parents and a wonderful childhood, which is probably why, to this day, I still can't leave Brabourne behind."

# POSTSCRIPT

Since completing this chapter we have made an additional discovery. An Edward Conley whose is named as a grazier in Bagshaw's History of 1847[2] may also be the same Edward Conley who was honoured "on his resignation of the Office of Clerk to the Parish of Brabourne, after having held that Office to the entire satisfaction of the successive Clergy and the Parishioners for 36 years". Edward, who may well have been one of Billy Conley's forebears was presented with a beautiful, professionally drawn piece of caligraphy (next page), to which 51 members of the community put their names. Many of those names have now become remarkably familiar to us. Sadly, there is no date on the document, but by taking into consideration the ages of a sample of the signatories, and when they had died, we believe that the certificate was probably presented to Edward Conley in the early 1860s. It was produced by "GH Smith, Dover", and reads as follows:

"Sir,

We, whose names are hereunder written beg to offer for your acceptance the accompanying purse of money as a token of our regard for you, and of our approval of your conduct and courtesy in the performance of the duties of the Office which you have lately resigned.

With every wish for your happiness and welfare,

We beg to remain, Sir,

Your faithful Friends,"

| | | |
|---|---|---|
| Sir Wyndham Knatchbull | Edward Daniels | Henry Noble |
| EHR Hugessen, MP | GC Rolfe Senr | Mrs Noble |
| Revd George Booth Perry [Ayscough] | Mrs Rolfe | Mrs Pellatt |
| William Perkins | GC Rolfe Junr | Willm Inge |
| George Culmer | Walter Rolfe | Willm Philpot |
| Revd C Hope Robertson | JR Long Senr | Henry Spain |
| Captn John Kirkpatrick | JR Long Jnr | John Norwood |
| Stephen Kelcey Foord | W. Foord Kelcey | Samuel Marsh |
| Onslow Andrews | Fredk Andrews | Rd Epps Junr |
| James Weekes | Walter Andrews | John Epps |
| John W. Pilcher | John Rolfe | William Hogben |
| Edmund Hammon | Edward Rolfe | Henry Apps |
| Robert Foat | Rd Thorpe | Simon Thornby |
| Thomas Hills | Henry Daniels | Maurice Measday |
| James Palmer | George P Court | Mrs Harvey |
| Stephen K Palmer | Francis Pittock | Geo Worrell |
| Mrs Palmer | | Frank Ames |
| | | John Swoffer |

---

2      Bagshaw, Samuel (1847), History, Gazetteer and Directory of Kent 1847, Vol II, Sheffield, publisher G. Ridge, p468

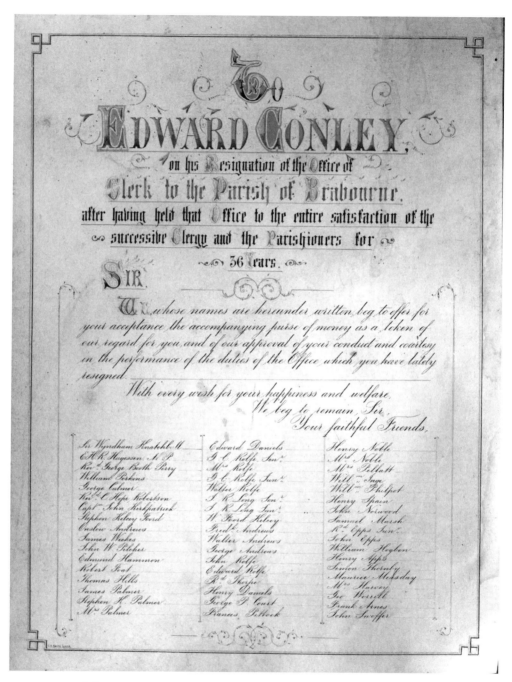

Hand-drawn certificate presented to Edward Conley on his resignation as
Clerk to the Parish of Brabourne after 36 years of service (c1860)

# 9

# LAND AND LIVELIHOODS

Farming has long been important in our area. It is an industry that has flourished on the fertile chalk, clay loams, clays and sands in this part of Kent. It was also the main source of employment in Brabourne and the surrounding area until well after the Second World War and, as a consequence, local experience and knowledge of farming among our contributors has been considerable. Life as a farmer was hard and precarious and few had much disposable income. Survival was a struggle, hours of work were long, and as one former farm worker whose marriage had broken up lamented, "You worked hard because that's how you'd been brought up and because you thought it was the right thing to do. However, it often meant that family life suffered." In spite of this, Ken Andrews, who was brought up in Sellindge in the 1930s, recalled that, on his family farm, "We seemed to have had time to relax. Nowadays, we seem to have none." And another contributor reflected "Though busy, the countryside had a feeling of peace about it, perhaps it was the animals in the fields."

Mixed farming was common in the past and Carol Lightfoot (Hobbs) recalls that Home Farm on the A20 produced most of what the family needed: the house cows gave milk, butter and cheese; pigs and sheep provided meat; chickens provided both meat and eggs; vegetables came from the garden and fruit from the fruit trees – cherries, plums and apples. During the war when food was limited, Carol reflected, people liked to be on good terms with farmers, who would swap cream for sugar and other things in the store cupboard.

This section incorporates the recollections of several people who have all had experience of farming and whose recollections present very different perspectives of rural life.

## HOPE FARM: A FAMILY FARM

Norman Thornby's evocative boyhood memories of life at Hope Farm, near the top of Bulltown Lane, take us back to a very different era in farming. We are very grateful for the detail that Norman was able to give us; it was clearly the sort of farm that largely vanished from the countryside in the wake of modern mechanised farming but which, for centuries, was an essential part of the economic backbone of Britain.

Norman was born and brought up on Hope Farm. The white farmhouse (now Grade II listed), with its cat-slide roof, has changed relatively little in appearance in almost 80 years, though the land use around it has changed significantly. Norman lived there with his parents, Percy James and Ethel May, his sister Rose, the eldest, and two brothers, Patrick and Basil. Tragically, when Norman was about seven years old, his father died from the after-effects of gas during the First World War. Percy only had one lung after he returned from the front and Norman remembers him being unable to do anything strenuous. He also recalls the pungent smell of vapour in the house each night, a vain attempt to help his father's breathing.

Sadly, Norman's memories of his father were relatively few but some of the best were of him coming back from market each week, hanging up the horse's harness and the children rushing to his pockets to look for the liquorice allsorts he always brought home for them. Percy's untimely death left Norman's mother with four children and a farm to look after. Immediately after Percy died, Norman's eldest brother Patrick

Hope Farm House, Bulltown Lane

Percy Thornby, Norman's father

and his mother ran the farm, with help from young Norman, and part-time help from Basil, who had started work at Wye. In 1942 Basil joined the artillery, just as his father had done. To supplement his income Patrick also worked part-time for other landowners, including the Jeanes family at Aldington. Rose, meanwhile, worked for Ada Finn, Joy and Keith Finn's mother, and before that, Bowles of Aldington. Like most girls of her age, she was in service and so lived where she worked. Norman lived at the farm until he was about 16 years old.

## THE FARM

Hope Farm covered approximately 25 acres and supported 35 sheep, three cows (two in milk and one in calf), about four pigs, 300 chickens, turkeys at Christmas, and one horse, which ploughed, harrowed and transported goods to and from market. In addition to the above, the main products from the farm were wheat, eggs, milk and butter, fruit and vegetables. Many of the other crops, such as grass, beans, mangel wurzels, swede turnips, mustard, oats, barley and hay, were grown principally as feed for the farm animals. The property extended from the Lower Chalk soils at the foot of the Downs on to the more clayey fields towards Brabourne Lees; also within the farm's boundaries was a spring, from which a permanent "chalk stream" flowed through the farm. Norman always referred to this as "the river", and its permanent flow, which was controlled by the reservoir upstream in the chalk Downs, was clearly crucial to the family and to the farm.

During a visit to Hope Farm, Norman told us that when he had lived there the fields around the farmhouse were much smaller than they are today and they were separated by hedges. All had names that bore some relation to their characteristics or use: there was the "hay field" of five to six acres, and the "sheep field", which was two to three

Field "research" for this book, c2007.
Norman Thornby points out the different fields at Hope Farm
to Christine Gurr

Looking down over Hope Farm, Bulltown Lane,
from New Barn Hill (2007)

acres of grassland where, not surprisingly, sheep were grazed. "Stone Field", as its name suggests, was four to five acres where the soil was heavy with flints, while near the river were the "osier beds", a lower, damp area of two to three acres, rich with rushes that would be scythed for litter for the cows. The osier beds were home to a vast array of birds: plover, lapwing, snipe and many others, the characteristics of which were all familiar to Norman. "Fowl field" had about four chicken houses on it, though the chickens were grazed on other fields as well. After grain had been harvested they could be left to feed on the residues for up to a fortnight. "Horse field" was nearest the house, a plot of about two acres rented from Mrs Weekes, who used to be at The Limes (now The Hall), in Weekes Lane. And then there was the garden, an area approaching an acre in size, which was just to the back of the farmhouse and bordered by the stream. Here the family grew vegetables, most of which were for the household, though they were also given to neighbours as and when they needed them. Inevitably, such as favour would be repaid in kind at a later date, but money never changed hands for vegetables. Robin Marsh pointed out the inevitability of barter for a range of goods and labour in an economy where money was in short supply. The Thornbys also had a sizeable orchard of about two acres, extending from the front of the house to the farm's northern boundary. In this they grew apples, plums, damsons and many other types of fruit, most of which were sold – "exported" from the area via the railway station at Smeeth. Apples, though, were usually not sold – these were instead normally kept on lino in the bedrooms, under the beds, and most were eaten in pies and dumplings. Norman recalls a real treat at night: squeezing an apple that had turned black directly into his mouth. Clearly, treats come in many forms.

Watercress was also harvested from the chalk stream, and this was a naturally occurring crop from which Norman benefited personally. The purity of the water, which filters through the chalk to feed the stream, as well as its alkalinity, richness in minerals and constant temperature, were (and still are) all important for the growth of such a crop. On Saturday and Sunday mornings in the summer Norman would watch from an upstairs window for potential buyers who would cycle from Ashford. As soon as he saw them approaching with their kitbags, Norman, who was then between 10 and 16 years old, would have his watercress ready for sale: a full sack would earn him about 1/- in 1940, and the purchasers would then divide the watercress into bunches and take them to the pubs in Brook and Wye on their way back to Ashford.

## THE FARMING YEAR

January and February: Norman described the start of the year as "comparatively dull months, when not much happened"; digging ditches, laying hedges and damming the river to create watercress beds were the main jobs. He emphasised that you had to make sure that the clear spring water flowed freely from one watercress bed to the next, and this had to be done before the plants started growing in March with the warmth of spring. Hedge laying was a complex, labour-intensive task that is rarely seen these days. Several contributors to this book have recalled how hedges managed in this way were richer in both plant species and wildlife than most field hedges today. In addition, fences were repaired where animals had broken through - though this had to be done throughout the year, whenever the need occurred.

The winter months were also the time when the vegetable garden was dug. This was no small affair as it covered most of an acre, about three-quarters the size of a football pitch. As much as possible of the garden would be ploughed with the horse, but where the plough could not be used the soil had to be dug by hand. Like most families in the village in the era prior to the Second World War, the Thornbys grew all their own vegetables, and

Balance ploughing,
by Oliver Trowell

without the luxury of refrigeration preserving the crops was always a major problem. Predictably, potatoes were a major part of the harvest and Norman recalls that when the spuds had been lifted they were stored in a shed, piled to a height of 4ft-5ft and

Potato lifting,
by Oliver Trowell

covered with a generous layer of straw and hay to stop the frost from getting to them. Though fruit was an important component of the farm, Norman recalls that they did very little pruning, nor did they use any sprays later in the year. Often the trees were green with moss, but in spite of this they carried on fruiting remarkably well.

March and April: lambing time. This was a busy period, as both ewes and lambs needed careful attention, meaning there was plenty of work for a small boy. At lambing time, temporary pens were made in the fields and the newly born lambs were placed in these for the night with their mothers. The pens were triangular, made from hazel sticks planted vertically in the ground, and "thatch" made of straw and other available vegetable matter was woven between them to protect the animals from the weather and any predators. If a lamb died it was skinned and the skin placed over an orphaned lamb in the hope that the ewe would suckle it. One method that further encouraged ewes to adopt such a lamb was to place the ewe and the lamb to be adopted in the pen with a dog at one corner so that it was just visible to the ewe through the thatch, making it feel the need to protect the lamb. In most cases the surrogate parent would start to feed the lamb after a few hours. "Fragile" lambs were wrapped in a blanket and kept indoors overnight in a bushel box. Whoever had brought the lamb in from the field would get up during the night to check on its progress and feed it with warm milk. This could take quite some time, for if the fire had gone out it would have to be sufficiently re-lit to heat up the milk. Just for clarification, a bushel box was a wooden box in which apples were packed for sale. A bushel of apples weighed 40lb, while the same volume of potatoes weighed 56lb. Half-bushel baskets were circular and most regularly used for hard fruit.

The sheep were Kents or Southdowns and Dorsets. Southdown sheep were short-legged, visibly different from the Dorsets, which were bigger. Both breeds were for meat. The wool was used from both lambs and sheep, though spinning was not one of the tasks usually done at Hope Farm. The sheep would be fed on hay, as well as, for part of the year, mangel wurzels or swede turnips. When they were first folded on a field of wurzels or swede turnips they would nibble the tops of the roots as they protruded above the soil; as they ate these down some of the roots would be "pecked" up by the Thornby boys to give the sheep more to eat. A small area of beans and mustard would also be sown for the sheep. The mustard would be fed to them about three weeks before the rams were put to the flock in the first week in November, to produce lambs from the first week in April. It was believed that the heat of the mustard increased the number of lambs produced.

April also saw the boys carting all the manure from the yard to the fields, but instead of being dug into the soil it was spread on the surface. To do this, big branches were cut from the hedge and arranged in a large 'V' shape, and dragged across the field by the horse to spread the manure. Quite different from today, then!

April and May: this was when the fruit trees blossomed and when watercress was transplanted. For the latter, planks were placed across the stream and clumps separated and replanted to increase the harvest. May was also the time when lambs' tails were removed, the purpose being to keep the animals clean and free from infestation by fly, maggots or other infection. Lambs' tailing was always done in fine weather and required two people for the task: a joint would be found in the bones of the lamb's tail by one, then the tail would be cut and cauterized with brazing tongs by the other. Male lambs would also be castrated at the same time. Bert Hammon, known to be highly skilled at tailing lambs and castration, was usually sent for to help with the work at this time of year. It must have been painful and, once the animals had been treated, the effects of shock could set in, sometimes causing them to become stiff and immobile. Therefore, one member of the team, frequently a young boy, would go round the field every hour or so, checking the state of the animals and keeping them on the move. If the sheep became infested with fly or maggots, tar or a diluted solution of Jeyes Fluid proved to be effective remedies. Similarly, if ever they were afflicted by foot rot, Stockholm Tar was used to stop the decay.

The end of June: life became even busier at this point of the year, as it was time for haymaking. This was a team activity and some eight or nine farmers would be seen in the field, all with hay rakes, an informal working party to help each other. No money ever changed hands, but if one field took a little longer, the farmer who owned it might make it up to the others by helping with hedge laying in the winter, or with dipping sheep (against tick and scab). Norman recalled that because he was so young he could not use a rake as effectively as the adults, often to the mild amusement of the rest of the working party.

Making hay was a careful exercise. First, it was essential that the hay was dry. If the mornings were damp, you had to wait until the ground dried out, so the men would go across the field shaking out the hay to help it to dry and the process would start in the afternoon.

The division of labour in haymaking was very precise. One farmer would be on the rake, raking the hay into big rows, while others would be forking the rows into clumps or "cocks". When the hay was ready to be carried, two men would be pitching it onto a horse-drawn wagon where it was received by two loaders. As one wagon was being loaded, another would be at the stack, being unloaded, and included in the routine was that the horse by the stack always had a bucket of water. That was a boy's job and Norman made trip after trip to the river to collect water for the horses. It required considerable experience and skill to produce the elegant haystacks that are so evocative of life in the past. Norman describes how the hay was stacked until the eaves were reached, some 8ft-10ft above the ground. Then, whoever was on the stack would start "drawing in" to form the roof. If he went too high to be reached from the wagon, someone would have to stand in the lubber hole and pitch right up to the top.

Carrying the hay,
by Oliver Trowell

All this was done by hand and required considerable skill, effort and teamwork for as long as it took to complete the stack.

When complete, the stack would be left for a critical four to five days, after which time the farmer would run a hook into the midst of the structure, removing a sample of hay to test the temperature. If the hay had not been sufficiently dry when it was gathered in, biological activity would take place and the stack would heat up. If the stack became too hot there was the risk that it could catch light, so it would have to be opened to reduce the temperature. When it was considered to be stable and not in danger of overheating, a local expert would come and thatch it using bracken from the top of the hill behind the farm, or rushes from the osier beds. If this activity disturbed any lapwings they would fly away from their nests and, only when some 20yd away, start to scream – an attempt to deceive trespassers as to the precise location of their nests.

Perhaps the most memorable event of the haymaking season for a boy was tea time, when Norman's mother would lay out a large cloth in the field and cover it with a spread of home-made bread, cheese, jam and cake. Norman remembers with mild disgust that the farmers sitting down to tea during haymaking would cut the cheese put out for them with the same knives that they had used to trim the lambs' feet – without washing them.

We digress for a moment because Norman's frequent reference to tea suggested that this was of major significance in a small boy's life. On more normal days, when the family was at home together, tea consisted of bread, jam, perhaps cheese and a "lump" of cake. Butter was made at the farm but generally, if there was bread and jam for tea, there was no butter (except for Sundays) as butter was sold and the proceeds paid the miller for cow feed (nuts), and corn for the chickens. Cake was usually made by Norman's grandmother, who lived next door at Hope View Cottage, and he would visit her to collect a cake every week. However, there were rules relating to tea: before the children all sat down to eat they had to complete a raft of chores. While Norman's mother made the tea the boys had to feed the horse, sheep, pigs and cows, collect the eggs and put the chickens to bed. After tending to the animals, shoes had to be cleaned, wood and coal had to be brought in, and the oil lamps filled.

Norman explains details of the farming year to Christine, c2007

Then, and only then, could the family sit down to tea. It was clear that the success of the farm depended on everyone pulling their weight and no one questioned this in any way. The Thornbys were not unique in this regard and almost everyone with whom we spoke talked of the chores they had to do as children.

June was also the month when shearing took place. This was done by hand and Hope Farm employed the same people each year – the two Lilley brothers – though Norman remembers the first time a machine, a Wolseley, was used in 1942. It required two people for the job, one to shear the sheep and one to turn the handle. If a sheep was cut in the process, the wound would be treated with Stockholm Tar to seal it and prevent infection. During the process Norman's mother used to keep a supply of tea coming to the shearers all day long.

July and August: plum- and apple-picking time. Fruit was an important product of the farm and, naturally, came from the orchard. Plums of all sorts were grown – Margate plums, bush plums, tiny, sweet cherry plums, Early Rivers, Victoria plums – as well as damsons and apples, including Russets, American Mothers, Bramleys, Coxes and Worcesters. Most plums were sold but, as mentioned already, relatively few apples.

Norman's mother used to make damson wine. Big earthen crocks, glazed on the inside, were filled with damsons to a depth of 9in. These were covered with 4in of sugar and the layers repeated until the crock was filled. This was covered with a board with a brick on top. The wine was "dipped" out of the crock, and the fruit from the bottom of the crock was used in pies. Norman recalls that, on washday,

Mechanical sheepshearing in the 1970s:
Pam Jamieson helps a contractor with the shearing of Mary Marsh's sheep

the copper was heated up on the fire, which was fuelled by whatever "rubbish" was available. When finished, the washing water would be changed and, making use of the good fire, sweet and savoury puddings would be tied up tightly in cloths to stop water getting into them and boiled in the copper.

The fruit to be sold was taken to Smeeth station by horse and cart by Norman and a brother, usually Pat, because Basil was so often away. This was uneventful with the original horse that Norman remembers, but when it was replaced by a "newer model", which had been bought from a dealer who had acquired it at London's Elephant and Castle, delivering the fruit became more challenging. This horse was only partly broken-in when they bought it and if it heard the train whistle it would try to bolt (almost succeeding on several occasions), so as soon as they reached the station Norman and Pat would unload the fruit as quickly as possible so that Norman could get the horse away. Delivery therefore had to be timed very carefully. Norman would have been about 12 to 14 years old at the time – quite a responsibility for someone so young.

August and September: the wurzels and swedes (the sheep feed) were harvested and stored for the winter in clamps in the fields. According to Oliver Trowell these crops can grow on into the autumn and he can remember lifting wurzels at Parsonage Farm well into October and November. Once lifted, mangels and swedes were heaped into large mounds and covered with dried grass or any dried vegetation to be had. They were then covered with about a foot of soil, which was "walked" down on each mound. Every here and there a tuft of grass was allowed to come up through the soil to allow the mound to breathe and to prevent rotting. As Norman pointed out, the swedes were pink in those days, whereas they are mostly orange now. Plums and apples continued to be picked into the early autumn and, in September, these were still being stored or sent to wholesalers via Smeeth station.

Smeeth station opened in 1852 and was used both for passenger and especially for goods traffic. Its importance for passengers declined with improved bus transport and then with the growing use of cars. The station was closed to passenger services from 1954, while goods facilities were withdrawn ten years later, in 1964.

The four cottages in the right of the picture were pulled down during the Second World War owing to a bomb falling nearby

October onwards: by the time October came around the activities had turned once again to winter tasks such as the ploughing and maintenance of the soil, getting it ready to rest for the winter while simultaneously preparing it for the coming year. This included getting the garden ready for the growing season, too. Ant hills would be "cut", piled up and left to rot, only ready to spread across the fields when the rotting process was complete. These ant hills yielded some of the best soil, as did mole hills. Hedge laying also started in October and continued through the winter until the growing season. The corn, which was harvested at the end of the summer, was threshed in winter with the aid of an old-fashioned steam engine. Norman recalls surrounding the threshing area with wire netting to keep the rats from running away and, as they tried to escape, the family Jack Russell would catch and kill them.

Ethel Thornby, Norman's mother, in the 1950s

In the cold days of winter a crock of soup was always to be found on the fire in the kitchen. It would contain a piece of mutton and copious vegetables. Dumplings, Norman remembers, were added every other day. Washing was always draped around the fire to dry. As Christmas approached the focus turned to turkeys and chickens. The farm kept several breeds of chickens, all hatched in the front room of the farmhouse, where there was an incubator and an oil lamp to maintain the temperature. At night the chickens were put into a chicken house, one in each field, and the breeds kept separate. The chickens produced eggs that were sold, but once the birds became broody (or "cluck"), they were sold to the local gamekeepers to sit on pheasants' eggs. Chickens were also in demand at Christmas, as were the turkeys that were reared at Hope Farm, of course. Unlike the chickens, these used to fly wild and roosted in trees at night. The turkeys sold well, either alive or dead. The farm did have a few geese, but not many, because, Norman explained, they had such strong necks that they were difficult to kill, though they did make very good "guard dogs".

In winter the weather was more memorably cold because heating in the house was confined to the fire. Keeping warm at night could be a problem and hot bricks wrapped in towels helped to warm the beds, and Norman also remembered spreading his best coat on top of the bed on the coldest nights. A treat to keep the boys warm at night was cheese on toast, done in the oven by their mother before they went to bed.

## EVERYDAY LIFE

The farm met many of its own needs with its produce, far more than most farms do today, while other needs were largely met within Brabourne Lees, where Norman would go for a haircut, and clothes, including suits, from Orpins. For shoe repairs he would go to Ned Andrews at Sandhurst, just beside Cobbler's Oak on Canterbury Road. On several such visits Norman recalls having to sort through dozens of shoes on the floor – if you were lucky you would find that both had been repaired! Groceries were supplied by Ames' Stores, sweets were to be had from Baxter's sweet shop and if a doctor was needed, there was Dr Garman, who lived opposite Ames' Stores, at Prospect Farm House, and who was one of the few in the village to have a car.

Life was characteristically modest, with walking and cycling being the main means of transport. Norman got his first bicycle when he was 15 – it was a Hercules with a dynamo and he bought it for £8 from Tink Norrington, Tony Norrington's eldest brother. This was quite a significant sum in 1943 and the money was earned and saved from tasks such as selling watercress, catching and selling rabbits and collecting sage leaves for the butcher. A major outing each week was to Brabourne Church, which would take Norman past the "chalk hole" on Pilgrims' Way. Each time he would pick up two lumps of chalk for his mother. Back at home, these were dipped in water and used to whiten the hearths of the two fireplaces in the farmhouse.

Birthdays and Christmas were celebrated but presents were modest and totally different from the extravagances of today's consumerist society. Until he died Norman could still remember the excitement he felt when his brother Basil, who had just started working at Bugdens (a shop beside the Tickled Trout in Wye), bought him a clockwork train set for his birthday. This was quite unlike any birthday present Norman had ever had before.

Basil Thornby

A final digression to include one of Norman's many references to Basil: after he had finished work at the shop, Basil would take milk from a local farm to the station on a cart. Going down to the station one day, Basil met a lady carrying two cases. He asked her if she would like a lift and she jumped on the tailboard of the cart, facing backwards. As they continued down Bridge Street the horse broke wind, and Basil, extremely embarrassed, said, "I beg your pardon, Ma'am", to which she replied, "That's all right. If you hadn't have mentioned it, I would have thought it was the horse."

## IT WASN'T JUST MEN WHO WERE INVOLVED IN FARMING

Vi Varrier's grandfather, William Kingston, settled at Water Farm in Brabourne in

1921. A Protestant from Cork, William had left Ireland fearful that if he stayed, he, his wife and their children would suffer persecution from the Catholic majority. A few days after William left, his family followed with very few possessions, though these did include three horses and possibly a wagon. They began farming on approximately 300 acres of land at the foot of the Downs, where the parishes of Monks Horton and Brabourne meet. Vi explained that her grandfather would have brought to England "made", or trained, horses that understood his ways and commands and which would have been invaluable on his new farm. Training new horses would have taken time and slowed his progress considerably.

Vi Varrier

In time, William built several bungalows down Fiddling Lane for his children and, as they grew up and married, he divided his farm between his seven sons. In 1928 the eldest, also William by family tradition, and father of Vi, was the first of the children to marry; he was given the top part of the farm at the foot of the Downs, together with a couple of cows. By the time he retired in 1966/67 Vi's father had built up his herd to about 70 dairy cows. Before starting out on his own he had accumulated considerable farming experience both locally, on his father's farm, and in Canada, where he worked for a year c1925. During his stay there, William learnt to use one of the first horse-drawn combines. As the historic picture shows, it was drawn by a team of 19 horses: a triangle of three horses followed by four groups of four, which would have required considerable skill by the driver. Vi believes this visit to Canada was arranged by the church, with which he was much involved. He was also a member of the Sellindge Praying Band, which is where he met Vi's mother, a Methodist from Brook.

Vi recalls that it was just taken for granted by all that she, together with her two sisters and two brothers, would help on the farm. Everyone had specific chores: Vi's main responsibility was the horses, while her brothers and sisters fed the calves; everyone helped with the milking and collected eggs from a large flock of chickens. Eggs formed a significant part of the farm income and Vi recalls the drudgery of washing dirty eggs, which latterly went to Stonegate. In addition to the cattle and chickens, the farm supported some sheep and one or two pigs for personal consumption. Corn and hay were grown, as were wurzels, which were fed to the cows in the winter.

Gaining farming experience in Canada: William Kingston, Vi Varrier's father, driving one of
the first horse-drawn combines, drawn by a team of 19 horses (c1925)

Vi's duties regarding the horses involved considerable responsibility, even at a young
age. She writes:

"At about 11 years old I started taking one horse to George Barrett's forge in East
Brabourne to be shod. My father would lift me up on to the large carthorse – no
saddle, just bareback. Mr Barrett was never ready on my arrival, so it meant I always
had a long wait. For the return journey Mr Barrett would lift me on to the horse and
we would return home. Later, as I grew, I would take two hoses, riding and leading
one, still bareback, and being lifted on to them for my return home. The horses
always went more quickly as we headed for home, and at times I had quite a job
managing them."

It was only after Vi had left the village school in Stowting and started at the Technical
School in Ashford that she was released from some of her duties on the farm, simply
because she was at home so little. She would leave home at 7.30am and cycle to
Brabourne, leave her bicycle at Keith Finn's workshop (known also as the Carpenters'
Workshop), catch the bus to Ashford and make the return journey in the evening. In
addition to looking after the horses, Vi recalls such jobs as driving two horses and a
harrow to cover the seed that her father had just sown. By the time she was 14 Vi
used to drive the horse and rake that pushed the cut hay into rows. She recalls being

The forge in East Brabourne during the time of Thomas Thornby, shortly after 1900 – some 40 years before Vi Varrier would take her father's horses there to be shod by George Barrett

"helped" by John Varrier who, then also aged about 14, would sit with her on the rake. John used to come down to Stowting from London every summer to stay with his grandmother at Dial House. Keen to spend as much time as possible with Vi, John would urge her to get the horse to trot so that she could finish raking quickly. But raking could not be done quickly, for if the horse went too fast the rake did not draw all the hay into neat rows. Nevertheless, once out of her father's sight, Vi would start the horse trotting in the full knowledge that she would get a dreadful telling-off if he discovered that the hay had not been raked properly. Clearly it was a risk worth taking.

Vi shared many of Norman Thornby's recollections of farm life, especially concerning harvest and haymaking. Grandpa Kingston would help all his sons and Vi recalls her uncles, brothers and sisters all helping at haymaking on her father's farm. Tea was memorable, with large basketfuls of cake, tea and lemonade for the workers. Vi specifically remembers hay everywhere – "around you and in everything". Similarly, at harvest and during threshing, there would be abundant tea and cakes for the men.

The Kingston family at harvest time, c1950s

Threshing at Bankside, William Kingston's farm, c1952

The Kingston family at threshing time, c1950s

Threshing at the Kingston's farm, c1950s

The stack yard at Parsonage Farm

Enjoying harvest time, possibly Valerie Heathfield

Teatime in the hayfield with the Kingston family

The Kingston family picnicking during harvest time at
Water Farm, c1950s

Vi recalled:

"Soon after haying came the harvest, which involved cutting corn – barley, wheat or oats – with a binder and two horses. These would be cut and tied with string into sheaves. My father, his brothers, all with their own farms, and my paternal grandfather all helped each other at haying and harvest time. After being cut, eight to ten sheaves were stood together in stooks, with the ears at the top, and then left in the field to dry. This could take a number of weeks but much depended on the weather. The corners of the field were always difficult to cut so these would be harvested by hand, with a scythe. The corn would be made into a sheaf and then tied with strands of corn twisted into a bond; it was quite difficult to learn how to do this. We, that is myself, my brothers and sisters, all had to help doing this.

"During haying and harvest an exciting time would be when a vast tea would be brought into the fields and a welcome break would be taken. My family were strict Nonconformists, so the beverage was always tea or lemonade, never beer.

"The stooks were eventually loaded up on to a wagon drawn by one or two horses, and made into a stack in the yard, with the ears of corn all pointing towards the centre. Sometimes during the winter the threshing machine would come in to thresh the corn, separating the corn from the straw. The corn would be poured into sacks and the straw would be stacked again or put directly into a barn. This was a really dusty, dirty job. Again, a huge tea would be provided for all the helpers.

Loading sheaves on to the waggon at Church Farm (1940s), by Oliver Trowell

"All the while that haying and harvesting was in progress the cows still had to be milked twice a day. Also on the farm would be young calves needing special attention, a few pigs, sometimes a few sheep and always chickens, ducks and geese running around."

Roger Vining's recollections of food during harvest and haymaking were less attractive:

He recalls a farmer's wife (not one from Brabourne), wiping the maggots from the ham as she carved each slice for the workers.

As we're discussing food, an anecdote from Oliver Trowell seems to fit in here, even though it doesn't relate specifically to harvest: "Towards the end of the war, when I had been doing some cultivation for Mr Fred Hayles at Bulltown Farm, he invited me in to enjoy 'a very special' tea. His sister, Ada Hayles, had made some butter and baked some scones. Not realising my distaste for butter, when he saw me spreading my scones as thinly as I could, he urged me to 'Spread it on thick, man! Come on, let me do it for you.' Too embarrassed to tell him I preferred margarine to butter, I did my best to be appreciative."

Vi's memories of harvest time are closely linked with the Second World War. One day when her parents were harvesting, German planes swooped low, shooting at them while they were in the fields with the horses, a terrifying experience described in more depth in the section on wartime.

## RABBITS AND MOLES, AN ADDITIONAL BENEFIT AT HARVEST TIME

Life in the country could be very hard, and especially during the Second World War when a lot of food was rationed, many people depended even more heavily on the bounty of the countryside. A major source of meat for the household was rabbit, and harvest was always a good time to catch them. According to Tim Marsh, farmers weren't all that keen on having children in their fields, partly because of the damage they could cause, but more importantly because the machinery could pose a danger. It should be said that opinion differed on this matter as others thought farmers were quite content to have children in the fields at harvest, not least because they could be useful.

Tim and his friends, predominantly boys, would go to a field that was being harvested and wait quietly nearby. When the binder went past they would collect up the sheaves and soon have a row or two of them. This would help the farmer who would otherwise have to pay someone to collect them. They would then stay and help until the entire field had been harvested. As the binder moved towards the middle of the field rabbits would start running out of the corn – this was the opportunity for someone skilled with a catapult or a club to bag several of them. As mentioned, these would be useful for the cooking pot at home, or they could be sold.

Tim recalled that there were plenty of rabbits in those days and, while walking from Brabourne to Fiddling Lane and back, he could catch as many as three or four. A variety of techniques were used for catching them, and one that he described involved looking down a rabbit hole when the sun was shining towards the hole. If there was a rabbit down there, it would be possible to see the sunlight reflected in its eyes. A long bramble would be poked down the hole and twisted and twisted until

Tim Marsh

it caught in the rabbit's fur; the animal would then be dragged out of its burrow and banged on the head. (It has to be said that some readers with experience of catching rabbits were surprised that such a method would ever work.) However, using whatever methods were found to work enabled boys (and girls) to both supplement the family diet and earn pocket money.

Another source of rabbits came from under the chicken coops at Parsonage Farm, East Brabourne, which goes some way in explaining, Tim reckons, why George and Noble Smith at Parsonage Farm would have a large number of cracked eggs to sell (at half the usual price). The Smiths kept chickens in small huts on a piece of ground that covered about 10 acres; these huts were very heavy but, if they were lifted slightly and propped up on a stone or some such, they revealed a vast number of rabbit holes. Using their tried and tested methods, Tim and his friends used to catch a dozen rabbits quite easily here and would then sell them at The Anchor in Stowting (now The Tiger), at the Five Bells, and in Brabourne Lees, where they would earn 1/6 each. Bunny Hayward, who lived on the outskirts of East Brabourne, would sell any surplus rabbits at Ashford Market. Tim added that he never had much pocket money but he did fairly well catching rabbits. You will notice that Tim's anecdotes of rabbit catching relate closely to those of John Jamieson (see Chapter 11), who was yet another expert rabbit catcher just after the war, and whose efforts, like Tim's, yielded both food for the household and pocket money. Oliver Trowell, however, admits that his success at catching rabbits using a club was very limited.

Another traditional skill was, and still is, mole catching. Mole catchers, though fewer in number than they used to be, are still much in demand, as moles continue to cause havoc in gardens, Tim observed. Tim, who has caught his fair share of moles, told us that there seem to be more of them than ever these days and in order to catch them you have to understand them and their way of life. Hearing this made us realise that fewer and fewer of us are equipped for such a task today. Moles, he explained, are solitary animals, though

Catching rabbits – or not catching rabbits, by Oliver Trowell

inevitably there are times in the year when males and females come together. When the offspring are born they remain with the mother a very short time and, as soon as they are able, they are "kicked out" to fend for themselves. Moles are active virtually all the time, and the mole catcher begins by observing the area where a mole is active. Even though it may seem as though there are dozens of them turning the earth over, it is usually just the work of a single animal. Once the mole catcher can gauge what is going on underground, he (it usually seems to be a he) has a good chance of catching the mole. "Essentially," Tim told us, "you watch, and when you see the ground heave you blast it with a shotgun. You have to be careful, though, not to shoot yourself in the foot."

Tim estimates that he has caught about 3,000 moles over the past 12 years. In years past, when he caught the moles manually, rather than by shooting them, he would skin them, pin the skins on a board to dry, then parcel them up and send them off to customers. For all his effort he would earn 5p per mole. Moleskins were used for moleskin trousers which, Tim said, "you'd be lynched for wearing these days". They were also used for making fishing flies and gift-shop products that were not really identifiable as moleskins. This market has diminished significantly and so it is now easier for the mole catcher to shoot moles. All rather different from Tales of the Riverbank.

Digressing for a moment from rabbits and moles, Tim, who has been a tractor driver on the Brabourne Estate, has developed an eye for spotting flint arrow heads, axe heads, possibly spear heads and other stone artefacts in the fields while he has been ploughing. Below is a collection of some of his finds, many of which have been authenticated by national museums.

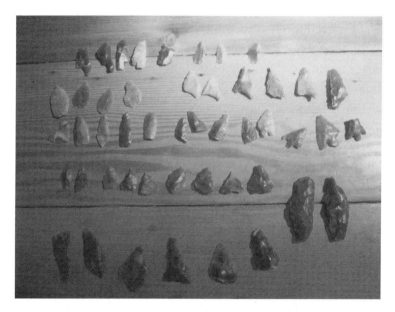

Stone implements, thought to be arrow heads,
collected locally by Tim Marsh

Stone axe heads, spears and cutting implements collected
locally by Tim Marsh.  Some of these have been
athenticated by national museums

## RUNNING WATER FARM, WEST BRABOURNE

This farm was owned by Steward Brooks, whose full name was William Steward Brooks, so he was known as Bill by many in the farming community. He was called Steward by the family but, according to his daughters Joan and Mabel, it is doubtful whether many people knew that he was Steward and not Stuart. His wife, whose full name was Rosetta Annie, was usually known as Annie and, to complete the complications surrounding Brooks family names, Joan explained that their grandfather, Tom Brooks (Steward's father), was known to the family as Nan – no one knew why this was, and indeed, as Joan observed, "Not many people can claim that their nan was their granddad", but Nan he remained to the family throughout his life.

Running Water Farm house,
by Michael Giles

Steward and Annie had six children: a son, James, who died at six days old in March, 1933, and then Wilfred, who became the eldest and only boy. Tragically, Wilfred died, aged eight years old, along with Dennis Griggs, when the wall at Brabourne School collapsed on top of them on 29th October, 1942. The Brooks girls were Rose, Mabel, Joan and Margaret, and in recent conversation with Joan and Mabel they recalled that, as children, they were expected to do a great deal of work on the farm. On a daily basis they would have to collect the eggs from hundreds of hens, then wash them and get them ready for the packing station at Stonegate. Eggs were one of many sources of income for this family, too. They also had to feed and water the hens and shut them in at night. The Brooks used to buy day-old chicks rather than hatching their own, and both Mabel and Joan recalled taking the fluffy little chicks out of the boxes when they arrived, and carefully placing them under a light bulb to keep them warm. They would help their mother take care of these chicks until they started laying, some five months later. The farm had sheep, pigs and two or three house cows that produced milk, and Steward reared calves for market. The girls used to take it in turn to churn the milk into butter – the churn was large and heavy, and turning the handle was both hard work and tedious. Their mother used to make a vast amount of butter, always in pats, and always with the same pattern on it. Regular orders of butter would be distributed to neighbours and friends and the rest would be taken to Ashford Market.

At harvest time the girls remember "working their socks off". In the days before combine harvesters the binder cut the wheat, bunching it into sheaves, which it tied with twine before it "threw" them out. The process wasn't always as smooth and the girls would have to keep up with the binder, pulling the sheaves out, making sure that they were properly tied and re-tying them if they were loose. They then helped to shock the sheaves into stooks, which they would then help to stack on the trailers. Joan recalls that, unlike today, girls didn't wear trousers, so their short socks and skirts left their legs vulnerable to the sharp stubble. Running Water Farm was close to Waterside Farm, which belonged to their cousin, George Brooks, and it was not uncommon for the family to help each other out on their respective farms. Once a year, the thresher would come to the farm, drawn by a Marshall tractor that belonged to Annie's brother, George Bishop. There was excitement in the air as the pounding

One of the original barns at Running Water Farm still remains
(spotted by Karl Engels)

sound of the single cylinder engine could be heard from miles away, long before it arrived. Years later, when Steward bought a new combine, Mabel was allowed to drive it.

At Running Water Farm there were two large carthorses, Jo and Bess, which used to pull carts, the plough, the binder and anything that needed moving. Mabel recalled that Bess was a black horse that turned white with age. In addition to the grain harvest, the girls would always help with fruit picking. Plums were the main fruit grown on the farm, also apples, and though Steward did have some cherries, these proved less profitable as the birds left very few for the market. Once the fruit had been packed into baskets, these then went into boxes that were then put on the train at Smeeth for the London market.

Steward and Annie Brooks, with their daughters,
from left, Joan, Rose, Mabel and Margaret on Annie's knee

Besides helping on the farm, the girls had to help their mother in the farmhouse. Mabel remembered having to apply red Cardinal polish to the bricks on the porch floor, and black lead to the cast-iron stove, both horribly messy jobs. Joan, meanwhile, recalls having to polish all the brass door knobs in the house. Outside the back door was a huge copper, under which a fire was made every Monday when Annie did the washing. She would boil everything, rinse it by hand and then put it through the mangle. The clothesline was some distance from the house and the washing to be carried there was quite a weight. Both Mabel and Joan recalled their mother's dedication to routine, so very typical of the era: Monday was washing day, almost regardless of the weather. On Tuesday Annie went to market to buy her groceries. Most of her shopping was done at Perks' Stores at the top of East Hill in Ashford, and while she was shopping, Steward would find his way to Ashford Market, where he would meet with other farmers and conduct any essential business. On Wednesday, Annie would do the ironing, as the clothes were usually dry by then. Thursday was "bedroom day", when the bedrooms were cleaned; Friday was baking day; on Saturday Annie cooked her family a roast dinner, and on Sunday they ate baked potatoes and cold meat. The routine was unchanging.

In addition to doing their chores in the house and on the farm, Mabel and Joan were able to enjoy long hours at play. They didn't have many toys in the 1940s, no one did, but they spent a great deal of time climbing trees, and "nesting", which frequently involved taking an egg or two from a bird's nest to add to their collection. Through their inquisitiveness the girls, probably like most of their friends, could identify all the local birds, not only from their appearance but from that of their nests and their eggs as well. One of their pets was a squirrel. The gamekeeper at Hatch Park had found a drey on the ground that had fallen out of a tree and had two tiny grey squirrels in it. Only one survived and he gave it to Steward as a pet for the girls. The squirrel became quite tame and spent as much of its time indoors as out. It would sit on the children's shoulders, play in the house and was a much-loved member of the family. Thus the girls developed a close association with the natural world, something that has been lost to many children today.

There were also minor disasters in their idyllic rural existence: Mabel tried to get through a spile fence one day. It was a tight fit but she got her head through successfully only to discover that she couldn't squeeze the rest of her through it. She then tried to go backwards, but despite all efforts, and those of her siblings, she couldn't do that either, her head now being firmly stuck. Her sisters had to call their father to rescue her. On another occasion Joan was helping Margaret over a fence when she cut her leg badly and had to be helped home. Tying hammocks between trees was something that the girls and their friends tried in many a warm summer, too. They would cut open sacks, tie them together and tie the ends to two trees. This never worked in practice, but failure never deterred them from making more, as they were always confident that their efforts would be successful the next time.

At the farm the girls had a shed that was theirs to play in. It was furnished with bits of furniture that had been thrown out and also with boxes that acted as seats. Playing in this shed was great fun. One particular treasure that they possessed was an old Bath chair, the sort that invalids used and so called because chairs of this kind had been designed in Bath in the mid-18th century and became increasingly popular through the 19th century. The girls' chair had two large wheels at the back, one at the front and a handle with which to steer it. The upholstery had disappeared but the children had tacked a wooden seat on to the chair. They would push it up "the hill" of Bulltown Lane, which was very hard work, and once at the top (where the Lane meets the Pilgrims' Way) three or four of them would jump on together, let go of the controls and roll all the way down, through the stream at the bottom and out the other side. The descent often didn't go quite as planned and on many an occasion the free-rolling chair came off the road, hit a pothole and even overturned. Once they even ran into the baker's van. No one seemed to see any of this as potential hazard, and the adventures they had in the Bath chair remain some of the happiest, most fun times of their childhood.

Modern facilities at Running Water Farm were few until the late 1940s and early 1950s: there was no mains water when the girls were young, so Steward buried a tank under the lawn, where the water table was high, and it would fill with water from the nearby stream. This was then piped to a tank in the house, which had to be filled daily by one of the girls working the pump handle. The family used approximately one tank of water in the house each day. This was a sophisticated method of water supply compared with carrying water to the house in buckets, which was the norm for many households. Electricity came to the farm later, so until then the family depended on oil lights and candles, and the telephone didn't arrive until later still. Life everywhere was poorer in material terms and farming was a hard line of business that required everyone – adults and children – to play their part. Nevertheless, in retrospect, Rose (who sadly died a few years ago), Mabel, Joan and Margaret, like many others, enjoyed the liberty and privileges of growing up on a farm in an idyllic location in the English countryside. One of their many enduring memories is of the kingfishers that used to sit on the farm gate, near which a stream flowed gently past.

Kingfisher
by Charlotte Lambert

## AN INFORMAL APPRENTICESHIP IN FARMING

Oliver Trowell kindly shared an array of memories of growing up immersed in the farm life that surrounded him: Here we have more anecdotes from Oliver.

### Learning by Trial and Error.

At Church Farm, in pre-war days, the hay-crop was cut, made and carried with the aid of Mr. Tilby's two horses, Boxer and Bangles, his two-horse mower, his swathe-turner, his Kent waggon and a 'tug', borrowed from Mr. Sydney Finn. (This tug had seen many years of service for it had belonged to Mr. Finn's father-in-law, Onslow Andrews, who had died in 1874! His name was still to be seen, in faded paint, on the locking frame).

At that time, it was customary for small boys on farms to learn by trial and error and one of my errors occurred when making my first attempt at taking a Kent waggon-load of hay through a gateway at Church Farm. The track leading out of the hayfield passed through the gateway at an angle and sloped downhill as it left the field. I was aged nine but could just reach the bridle-rein of Boxer, the huge black horse hauling the load, and I had become quite competent at setting-up the waggon on the level hayfield. Although I had guided Boxer along what I thought was the right path, I had miscalculated the angle at which the waggon should follow the horse. Suddenly, three things went wrong at once! I lost my grip on the rein, the near-side waggon wheel hit the gatepost, knocking it sideways, and the full weight of Boxer's iron-shod near-side front hoof came down on my right foot! I lost my big toe-nail but no bones were broken. Walter Tilby came to my rescue and conducted the load onwards to the nearby barn.

I was not blamed for this misadventure but given every opportunity to master the skill required. As a voluntary worker I must have been an asset to Mr. Coleman, who farmed Church Farm at that time and I always felt a glow of satisfaction when he would say "You've come just right Master Oliver" on occasions when my help enabled him to carry out tasks which would have been difficult or impossible single-handed.

Oliver Trowell

## Bringing Home the Day-old Chicks.

Seventy years ago, a lot more human effort often went into operations than would be considered worthwhile today. What farmer today would walk seven miles to collect a few dozen day-old chicks? Mr. Coleman, with all his seventy-two acres could not afford to run a car, and so, with two willing helpers, my sister and myself, he set off on foot one breezy spring morning to walk the three-and-a-half miles to the hatchery at Stonehill to collect from Mr. Horsenell six boxes of day-old chicks. Our route for about a third of the way took us across the fields, first of Church Farm, then Park Farm, as we skirted the south-side of Forty-acre Wood. All the footpaths were well-trodden in those days and our path took us to a stile in Southenay Lane, whence we tramped, uphill and downhill, past the fine timbered Southenay Farmhouse, until we arrived at Stonehill with its descent flanked by magnificent ivy-clad elms and other massive trees. Reaching the rise to the Main road by Sellindge Church, we knocked on the door of a modern house on the left side and were warmly greeted by Mr. Horsenell and his wife who provided us with steaming cups of tea, Mr. Horsenell chatting the while about his method of reviving poorly chicks with a drop or two of whiskey!

Revived by the tea, we took up our loads, a box of chirping chicks in each hand, and made our way home the way we had come, arriving about an hour later, weary from carrying our loads but with all the chicks alive and ourselves in time for a late dinner.

## Dipping the Sheep.

In the late 1930s, about a fortnight after shearing-time, it was dipping-time for the sheep at Church Farm. This involved driving the flock along the road, on a sunny morning, the best part of two miles to West Brabourne, where there was a sheep 'tun' in working order. There was, in fact a sheep tun alongside the stream at Church Farm but, it had been silted up long since and it was not until the War that it was excavated and brought back into use. Mr. Coleman, his grandson Terry, myself and Peg the dog, would set off about 8 o'clock, Mr. Coleman in front of his flock, the rest of us bringing up the rear. We had to dart about smartly to prevent any sheep taking a wrong turning off the road. Forking right at Manor Pound, the pattering hooves continued pattering on past the Village Hall until they reached a grassy track on the right hand side into which they were guided by Mr. Coleman blocking the road ahead with his arms outstretched like wings.

Two men I did not know were there to assist, and, driven into a pen from which a fenced path led to the tun, each sheep was ushered down the path in turn and tossed unceremoniously into the tun, which was sufficiently full of water, plus the insecticide 'dip', to ensure total immersion. One of the men, using a crook, prodded each sheep towards a path leading up and out of the water and, once on dry land, each sheep shook itself vigorously and wandered into the comforting warmth of the sunshine. The return journey kept the sheep warm and gradually dried them off.

We were home in time for dinner, as lunch was always called, and the sheep were once again in familiar surroundings.

No doubt to the relief of car and lorry drivers, the practice of driving livestock along the public highways is now just a memory!

Sheep being moved through East Brabourne, c1980.
The Five Bells is in the background

## Shearing–time Pre–War.

By mid–June, it was time for the sheep to be shorn. This was done at Church Farm, not by Mr. Coleman but by old Mr. Lilley from West Brabourne. Mr. Lilley arrived with only his spring-steel hand shears and a whetstone and working in a double pen of hurdles, he relieved each sheep of its fleece in the space of a few minutes with never so much as a prick from the sharp-pointed shears. Each fleece was then laid flat and then rolled up and tied with a bond of twisted wool ready for stacking in the granary and transport to the wool merchant. If the weather was hot, the sheep were not sorry to be relieved of their winter coats!

When the time came to take the wool to the wool merchant, then in Station Road in Ashford, I rode, on one occasion, on top of the wool which I had helped to load on the top deck of the pebble-spectacled Aaron Shorter's cattle lorry. More memorable than the loading and unloading of the fleeces was the sensation of sitting up there amongst all those soft, greasy fleeces, high above the unseen but fast-moving wheels below — rather like riding on a woolly cloud!

Sheepshearing in the 1930s, by Oliver Trowell

### Tailing Lambs.

When lambing-time was over, Mr. Coleman enlisted the help of Mr. Bert Hammon to tail the lambs and also castrate the ram lambs. On the appointed morning, hurdle pens were set up in the lee of Thornby's* Wood and a good sized block of wood was set up on a couple of trestles alongside. In a metal drum in which holes had been pierced and which had been set up on bricks, a fire of dry faggot wood was started and kept going by me with larger and larger pieces of wood. When the two wedge-shaped tailing irons were red-hot in the fire and a tin of Stockholm tar and a short lath were to hand – plus the instrument used for castration – we were ready to start. Mr. Coleman caught each lamb by a hind leg and held it in such a way that its tail lay across the block of wood, announcing at the same time if it was a ewe or a wether. Mr. Hammon, his tailing iron at the ready, pressed it downwards through the lamb's tail and within one or two seconds, the tail parted company with the lamb. The stump was then given a dab of Stockholm tar, applied with the lath, and the lamb, if it was a ewe, was released to its dam and the surrounding pasture. If it was a ram lamb, before being released it was castrated by Mr. Hammon with the instrument designed for that purpose.

As an eight-year-old, my role in this procedure was not only to feed the fire but also to count the tails into tens. At the end of the morning, when all the lambs had been dealt with, I would take the red-hot irons to the nearby stream and plunge them into the cold water, where they made a sharp fizzing noise and a cloud of steam.

As a reward for my help, Mr. Hammon suggested I should take home the main ingredient for some lamb-tail pasties!

*Subdown Wood.

## Harvesting. Making a 'road' for the binder.

In the days of the reaper-&-binder, it was customary when about to start the cutting of a field of corn for a 'road' to be made for it right around the perimeter of the field in order to avoid crushing the standing corn beneath the hooves of the horses or the wheels of the tractor and binder. This job was done by the centuries old practice of a man using a scythe, followed by another to bind, by hand, into sheaves, what he had cut.

In August 1942, at Church Farm, Doug. Dryland cut clockwise around the whole of a thirteen acre field of wheat in one day, the corn falling towards the standing crop. Learning the technique of making a straw-bond from Harry Denne, I soon became an efficient sheaf-maker, laying a sheaf-sized quantity of cut corn across the prepared bond at right-angles, then, gathering up the two ends of the bond and pulling them as tight as possible around the middle of the sheaf before twisting them together and tucking them under the encircling bond. The completed sheaf was then propped up against the adjacent hedge.

I feel fortunate in having been involved in agricultural life just in time to have learned and practised such centuries-old techniques. It was, of course, a time-consuming way of doing things which, today, has been entirely eliminated by modern harvesting methods but, the fulness and smell of a grain-laden sheaf, bound by its own straw, gave a harvester a feeling of job-satisfaction which, perhaps, has become rare today.

Making a "road" for the binder during
harves time (1930s), by Oliver Trowell

## Wartime Reclamation of Hedges and Ditches.

In the late autumn of 1940, reclamation of the lands of Church Farm had to start with the cutting down of vastly overgrown hedges and the digging out of the totally silted-up ditches alongside them. I was delighted to be involved in these operations in which I found immense creative satisfaction. Mr. Coleman, Harry Denne and I had only the most basic of tools, a carpenter's saw, bill-hooks and axes, to work with but, by early January 1941, we had cut down and cut back these thickets to a normal hedge height and width, producing a great stack of firewood bats, ranging in thickness from a man's arm to an elephant's leg. Cut from these was an enormous quantity of brushwood and tangled bramble and ivy and this we burned n gigantic heaps, starting the fires on early mornings to make sure all flames and embers would be extinguished by black-out time,— before four in the afternoon. With the ground beneath us frozen as hard as cobble-stones and a bitter wind blowing from the east, to get the fire going, a match applied to a few handfuls of dried grass poked into the bottom of the heap on the eastern side was sufficient to trigger a 'Whoosh' of flame and smoke westwards. Immense heat was generated by these fires and it seemed a pity it was all wasted while we had to get up in the dark mornings to peer through ice-covered bedroom windows! Sweat poured from our foreheads as with frequent pitchfork pushes we made sure every tangled mass was consumed. Towards sundown, we turned our attention to throwing buckets of water from the nearby main stream over the embers and, by black-out time, all was dark.

!With the overhanging hedges cut right back, we were ready to start digging out the ditches. Much of the surrounding, reed infested, land was so waterlogged that stamping one's foot produced the sound of myriads of bubbles and trickles! We started from the lower end of each ditch and worked backwards to allow the water released to escape downstream. Each of us standing on a short piece of plank, Mr. Coleman led the way, digging out a spade's depth of the tree-root and reed-ridden mud across the three foot width of the ditch and throwing the chunks well into the field. A few feet in front of him, I dug out another spade's depth and, a few feet in front of me, Harry Denne dug out another foot of mud or clay, the three of us maintaining the sloping sides from three feet across the top to one foot across the bottom. Footwear at that time was, for those who already had them, leather, hobnailed boots with leather laces but, for me, it was a pair of wartime rubber-boots, — which had a strong tendency to split behind the heel. Near freezing water managed to get into our boots and keep our feet numb for most of the day but, the satisfaction of seeing a great quantity of water, so long held back in waterlogged fields, flowing fast and freely downstream, was ample reward for enduring any discomforts involved. Occasionally we had to use our axes to cut back large tree-roots which had grown into the path of the stream. Much more rewarding to find were the tile-drains, unglazed fired clay pipes, about ten inches long with a bore of about two inches, laid end to end in deep trenches, spaced about twenty strides apart. They had, perhaps, been laid more than a hundred years before we discovered them. When a stick was vigorously poked up the blocked end of the outermost pipe, a plug of root-bound mud would fly out, followed by a gush of water which continued unabated for several days.

Over many wintry weeks, the three of us cut down all the hedges to stake-height and dug out almost every yard of ditch on the farm.

## Misadventure at Church Farm.

From time to time, both sheep and cows would break through the tumbledown hedges and fences at Church Farm and head for pastures new. In fact they never got very far and it was usually into Forty Acre Wood or one of the neighbouring properties. On one occasion however, a cow we had called Mabel, not long acquired in Ashford Market, vanished without trace. We searched the whole district, even as far as Stelling Minnis, for any information which might lead to her recovery but all to no purpose. We thought she must have been stolen until one morning, about a week after her disappearance, Mr. Coleman spotted four hooves pointing skywards in the deep cutting through which the stream flowed along the then border with Parsonage Farm. Poor Mabel must have slipped down the steep bank and landed on her back in the water. Rigor mortis gave her the appearance of a stuffed animal.

Mabel's death in the stream was the second fatal accident to a large animal which had occurred in the field concerned in the space of a few years for, three years before, shortly before the war, Mr. Coleman's ex Canadian Army horse, Jim, a Great War veteran, then about thirty years old, got stuck so deeply in the mire on the west side of the field that he could not extricate himself. Powerful horses were brought over from Parsonage Farm and ropes attached to their collars and to Jim in an attempt to pull him out. Whether old Jim told them by telepathy that his leg was broken and not to try to pull him out I do not know but, they stubbornly refused to make the attempt. The knacker was sent for and Jim's life was ended with a single shot. The carcass, with a broken leg, was winched onto the knacker's lorry and thus ended the life of a very good-natured old horse who had survived the mud of Flanders and all the horrors of war.

### The Market Cart.

Horse-drawn carts were still quite a common sight in Brabourne in pre-war days and the stocky Mr. George Cheeseman's covered market cart, which he drove to Ashford Market from Stowting Common every Tuesday was one of them.

While in the Market one morning, he was asked by Mr. Coleman of Church Farm to bring a calf back from the Market. On arrival at Church Farm in the early evening, Mr. Cheeseman rummaged around in his van only to discover that the calf was not on board and that he must have left it in the Market! "What a devil of a nuisance!" Mr. Cheeseman kept repeating over and over again. Mr. Miller, of Court Lodge Poultry Farm, offered to fetch the calf in his ageing Austin Six open tourer if Mr. Coleman and I would go with him to hold it down. This we did and found the calf alone in the Market, making a melancholy mooing. With the aid of a length of rope, we brought it back safely to its new home.

For Mr. Cheeseman to have made the round trip to the Market and back with his tired horse would have taken at least two hours.

A horse-drawn cart for carrying goods and
people. The Blue Anchor is in the background

## THISTLE PECKING IN THE 1930s

Oliver Trowell has kindly allowed us to "borrow" this section from his book Before the Combines Came:

Keeping thistles under control was an essential task for the farmer and Oliver recalls how thistle cutting became an urgent matter for Mr Coleman of Church Farm when they started opening their fluffy grey seed heads. Had the thistle seeds settled on other people's land, he could have been liable to prosecution by those landowners. Together with Mr Coleman's grandson, Terry, Oliver recalls cutting thistles on a hot summer's day, a task unrewarded directly but willingly and proudly undertaken to help the farmer and a considerable effort for an eight-year-old boy. Terry and Oliver were keen to practise their newly acquired skills of sharpening a sickle, or "baggin 'ook", with a rubber, a coarse grey sharpening stone. Prior to mechanisation, such tasks were hard work and farming was highly labour intensive.

Mr Coleman had managed to acquire an old one-horse mower, to which he harnessed his 27-year-old ex Canadian Army horse, Jim (whose sad demise was described earlier by Oliver). Terry and Oliver were encouraged to participate, and the horse cut more thistles in an hour than the boys had cut in most of a day. The thistles then had to be burnt to stop thistledown settling on other parts of the farm or on neighbours' fields. Mr Coleman and the boys set off for Banky Field with long-handled wooden hay rakes, odd pegs missing, pitch forks over their shoulders and boxes of matches in their pockets. They raked the thistles into enormous piles, using a pitchfork to make the piles "as high as a man" and then set fire to them. But the thistle roots remained, ready to grow again. Thirsty from the intense heat of the fire, the boys drank cold stream water from the brook that ran through the farm, the Broad Bourne of Brabourne, once the flames had died down.

## AND THEN ON TO MILKING…

After a morning of cutting and burning thistles, and an afternoon of dam making and dam busting in the stream, it was time for milking. Milking with Mr Coleman is described by Oliver as having been a peaceful affair. Hands were all well washed and all milking equipment was spotless. Mr Coleman would sit on a three-legged stool, worn and shiny with use, and draw the milk into a spotless pail. Within an hour of milking, metal measures were dipped into the milk to fill cans that were brought to the door by Nurse Hills, the district nurse from Holly Cottages, and by Sidney Finn, who would arrive on his bicycle from Ivy Cottage with a milk can in his basket. Cans were also filled for delivery to Mr and Mrs Tenney, who lived at the rear of no.1, The Street – Hill View – and old Mrs Washford, who lived up The Street, in a part of no.3 of the pink cottages later owned by the Princess Cantacuzino. Oliver recalls that all the milk produced at Church Farm in those days was either sold to private customers who came to the door or was used at home. Some was fed to calves or "sock" lambs, these being lambs that had lost their mothers and had to be bottle-fed. It would be several years after Oliver's arrival in the village in 1934 that a daily milk collection would be established, for which the milk would be taken by lorry to an urban dairy.

## GEORGE BROOKS ON FARM DECISION-MAKING –
## AN ENVIRONMENTAL BALANCING ACT

Norman, Vi and Oliver's perspectives on farm life are through the eyes of young people or children, and Norman's memories in particular were tinged with the romanticism of the past. Though they worked hard on their respective farms, none of these contributors had to shoulder the responsibility for their success, nor did they have to take major decisions that were critical to farm and family survival. However, the substance of our discussions with George Brooks, who farmed Waterside Farm, was very different and focused much more closely on how decision-making on his farm was built around his flock of about 200 sheep. Though difficult to convey, the anxiety that George constantly felt about the possibility of losing his crops, his flock and possibly also his livelihood was always close to the surface. Clearly such concerns always dog the lives of the smallholder farmer, and larger farmers, too.

George Brooks looking over Banky Lees,
part of Waterside Farm (2007)

The story starts when George acquired the land down beyond the village hall that he transformed into Waterside Farm. Purchased at auction on 1st July, 1947, the land was described as "Valuable Pasture and Arable Land", formerly part of Elm Farm, West Brabourne, and extending to about 52 acres. By the time it was sold at auction on 30th May, 1979, it was described as "a valuable parcel of arable/pasture land together with useful farm buildings, in all about 64½ acres", and this, together with the extensive list of tractors, farm machinery and equipment, the 200 ewes with lambs, and the hay and straw that were disposed of at a Special Sale on 7th June, 1979, showed just how Waterside Farm had been built up under George's tenure. Waterside Farm was bought by Gordon and May Fortescue; it is still owned by May.

When George bought the land it was in a poor state. Banky Lees, the six-acre field that slopes from the Kennetts, opposite the village hall, down to the river was poor land. It was heavy clay, dense with brambles, and George's uncle, Steward Brooks, who farmed Running Water Farm, advised him not to plough it because "it would not be able to grow much – it was too run-down". But George had other ideas. He ploughed the heavy clay and sowed a crop of wheat there. Not unexpectedly, the yield was disappointing and the field was barely worth harvesting. He tried again, and the second year the harvest was as bad, if not worse. In the third year, George sowed rye grass and clover and this time the result was good, better than he had expected. Next came the issue of thrashing the clover, and Peter Woodruff, who lived at Little Evegate and whom George had got to know through Ronnie Martin, agreed to thrash the crop using his Allis-Chalmers. George cut the clover in strip rows, according to Peter's direction, and the seed from the six acres of Banky Lees was sold in Woodchurch, giving George a healthy profit and enabling him to invest in much-needed farm machinery. After combining that year the weather kept fine and George was able to bale the residue just like hay, which he then fed to his sheep all winter. This example, George reflected, showed just how a farmer could be "made" or "broken" in a season. Success depended, to a large extent, on the existing state of affairs in the world of farming, and the weather, but it depended even more on hard work and skilful husbandry practices.

With some additional rented land near Weekes Lane, George's farm amounted to, at most, 70 acres. Along with the 200 ewes on the farm, he had 300 chickens. He would breed from the ewes usually using a Southdown ram. Tegs (ewes) were bought in and kept for breeding for three years. The lambs born in March/April would be sold at Ashford Market, as would the three-lambed ewes, either in the last week of August or the first week of September. The lambs then went into the store sales during the first week of September usually. George never had problems selling his stock, as the buyers knew where it came from. Waterside Farm had a few Sussex cattle and George observed that, "There was nothing more kindly than a Sussex bullock or a Southdown sheep." So good were they that these were sent all over the world for breeding.

Eggs from George's flock were sold locally and, as the chickens became too old to lay (but not so old that they were tough), they would be sold for the table. George

Christine Gurr checking information for this book with
George Brooks (2011)

recalled that the then owner of the Blue and White Café on the A20, who used to
live at Boulding House in Weekes Lane, would buy most of the eggs produced by
Waterside Farm. The chickens were bought in at one day old and started to lay at
about 20 weeks. Egg production went down markedly in the winter, so George
moved over to deep litter (an indoor animal-housing system using repeated spreading
of straw or sawdust). As a consequence of the controlled lighting in the shed he used,
the winter dip in egg production was much reduced. Rats were a major problem in
relation to the chickens, causing major losses of corn and adding significantly to the
cost of chicken and egg production. In order to control their population, George
used to pay a subscription to a firm at Hawkhurst specialising in contract rat control.
The representative for the firm was a man called Bill Scamp, who used to live in
Brabourne Street and would come round regularly and bait the vermin for George.

Successful farming depended on a great deal of hard work and, again, using George's
words, it was not "a jump-in and jump-out job". Of vital importance throughout the
year was ensuring that there was sufficient food for the livestock. If you had sheep
and lambs to raise it was critical to have good grazing for the lambs to develop, and
key to the production of a grazing crop was keeping the soil in good condition. The
farm livestock themselves played a critical role in this as, according to George, inputs
from "the livestock provided a heart for the soil". He considered artificial fertilisers
a good supplement, but organic inputs were essential.

George paid very careful attention to the pattern of crop rotation. Crops were planted in autumn and spring. In autumn, George always planted winter wheat or barley, and wild white clover. Cereals and grazing crops were rotated as this ensured that the soil was properly fertilised. He would fold a piece of ground (put sheep to graze on it) and then plant spring barley there. Next, a good crop of potatoes would be harvested from the same ground, followed by winter wheat, which would be ground or rolled on the farm and fed to the sheep. Folding the sheep on to barley/winter wheat stubble would fertilise the field, leaving the soil in good condition for the next crop. The barley went to the miller – Hancock's at Mersham – and the straw was used either on the farm or sold. Kale and swede turnips were also beneficial in much the same way. A part of the field would be fenced off each day and the sheep folded on to it, fertilising the soil as they nibbled away on the swedes that were partly exposed. By folding the sheep on to a different part of the field each day George ensured that all the soil on the plot was improved. Some of the older shepherds, George recalled, would peck at the half-eaten swedes, digging them up so that the sheep had more to eat. He also remembered that, during Bob Ball's time, Mr Older of Penstock Farm had a grazing crop of swede turnips at the top of the hill in East Brabourne, and all Brabourne Street would go and help themselves to the swedes.

Spring crops were also mainly for grazing and George usually used the Wye mixture of rye grass and clover, as this did best on his land. He discovered that, if the summer was dry, this combination was more successful in providing grazing for his

Ken Andrews harvesting potatoes in the 1960s, but not on
George's farm. Note the hessian sacks

Helping with the potato harvest: from left, Mary Marsh,
Dora Dale and John Jamieson, (1970s)

More modern potato harvesting, (late 1970s) – hessian
sacks have given way to paper. From left, Tessa, Frances
and Pam Jamieson, with Megan the dog

sheep than most others. Feeding the animals through the winter was also a major objective and, if he could get to Christmas without buying feed, then he did not mind having to do so after that. Most of the animals would be corn-fed after Christmas, corn being bought from Hancock's at Mersham and also Denne's at Wye. The sheep on Banky Lees were fed hay for as long as George could manage. This was put into racks on wheels and moved around the field each day so that the sheep did not kill the grass through trampling. It also prevented them from paddling in mud, meaning they remained cleaner. If the sheep were not fed through the winter and just allowed to graze, the wool stopped growing – it would start to grow again in the spring when the grass grew, but George asserted that buyers could tell from the wool whether or not the sheep had been fed through the winter. Mr Strouts was the wool merchant and his wool store was at the bottom of East Hill in Ashford, which was later taken over by the Kent Wool Growers. Mr Strouts always took George's wool because of its good quality.

Thus, farming clearly required considerable skill in environmental management, forward planning and good fortune to ensure that the sheep remained clean and well fed throughout the year, and that an adequate number of lambs were born and raised. Achieving this was unsurprisingly a source of constant concern, and George's earlier-noted observation that a farmer could be made or broken in a season places the reality far from the romantic image so often associated with smallholder farming in the past.

A characteristic pose: George Brooks, aged 97, tells us
about Waterside Farm (2011)

## REMEMBERING GEORGE BROOKS AND HIS FARM
Elizabeth Beadle told us:

Elizabeth Beadle

"My husband's father – George Beadle – who farmed at Granary Court used to say that George Brooks's farm was the cleanest and tidiest one that he had ever seen. I've been told that the auctioneer from Hobbs Parker, who sold the farm in 1979, said much the same thing."

Meanwhile, Karl Engels, whose father used to help George on his farm when needed, remembers George's principal form of transport – his motorbike:

"George's only form of transport was his motorbike and sidecar, the latter being a large green wooden box. With his dog in the box-sidecar he would drive from Waterside Farm to his home at no.2, Grace Villas, on Canterbury Road. He would also transport livestock in the box; a net would be put over it to secure the contents. Eggs and honey from George's excellent hives were transported to market in the box-sidecar and it was also the means of transport to his fields, always with the dog sitting at the front of the box – watching carefully to see where George was going.

"Once a year we went to the Kent Show in Mote Park at Maidstone. George would drive us – my father riding pillion, me (probably less than ten years old), together with Brian and Michael Jarvis (George's nephews), in the box. No health and safety in those days, no helmets or goggles, and sometimes you got a fly in the eye. It seemed a very long way to go to the show and back, but we all used to look forward to it with such eagerness, and it remains a happy memory from my childhood."

Michael Jarvis added that, on these annual jaunts to the Kent Show, George would buy the boys 1lb of cherries from a road-side stall. The stones were then "pinged" selectively at people and cyclists as they passed them.

When he was a boy, Michael used to cycle from Kennington to Waterside Farm every Saturday to help his Uncle George. He loved "getting stuck into anything on the farm", from looking after the pigs and sheep to helping with harvesting and, on one occasion, sitting in a "hide" of hay bales with George in one of the fields, shooting jays as they came for the pea crop. Although George was happy to have children "helping" on his farm, and was very popular with them, he also made sure that those who came to help did any chores they undertook properly and responsibly. Michael remembers being firmly told off once when he went to feed the chickens and was attacked by an aggressive cockerel in the field. He left in a hurry without feeding the birds properly and soon learnt from George that this was quite unacceptable. Nevertheless, when asked some 50 years later what he particularly liked doing as a child, his instant answer was "working on Uncle George's farm".

As a child Mike Hickmott lived next door to George's farm and recalls many occasions when he used to go to see him, or more particularly, his animals. Here he gives a child's view of its workings:

"In addition to sheep, cows and chickens, George also kept a few pigs, maybe six or eight, which he used to breed. At times there were half a dozen sows with 8 to 15 piglets each, say 60 or 70 in total, in half of a big, black, weather-boarded shed in the farmyard. The pig shed was divided into half a dozen pens by timber walls, with a central walkway down the middle from the door at the end of the building. The sides of the pens were about 4ft high and each had a door that opened the full width of the walkway. This ensured that, when the pigs needed to be moved from their pens, there was only one way that they could go.

"George was always very particular about his animals, keeping them in clean bedding and feeding them regularly. The pigs were fed meal, mash and pellets from a bucket – imagine the noise of snorting pigs and squealing piglets at mealtimes! The other part of the shed was originally the chicken house, but George later built a deep-litter chicken house."

Mike remembers the layout of the farmyard buildings clearly. In the 1960s this type of small farm was so unlike the large farms of today. Approaching from the road, the first building was a long, corrugated-iron Nissen hut. The front part was an "office" – a rudimentary bench covered with invoices, bills, other paperwork and bits of machinery. Most of the hut was used for the storage of feed and grain and, after shearing, the wool, too. The rear section of the hut was where George kept his one and only tractor, together with a small mill and some hand tools. The mill was used to crush oats and feed for the animals. It had a wooden hopper, into which the feed was poured, which was then crushed and came out of a chute at the bottom into a sack. The mill was driven by a wide, flat belt that was attached to the tractor pulley. The tractor stood inside the Nissen hut with the belt on the side closest to the wall; there was no protection from it whizzing round between the tractor and the mill, so yet again things were run according to common sense rather than over-zealous health and safety regulations. Mike was not allowed in the milling area at all, but he watched with fascination from the feed-storage area.

Mike's maternal grandmother, Marjorie Howland, lived at Glenmere, a bungalow next door to George's farm, from the mid 1920s until she died in 1978. George did not live on the farm and there was no house there; as Karl Engels pointed out earlier, he lived in Canterbury Road, Brabourne Lees. Many delivery lorries and reps naturally thought the bungalow went with the farm and that Marjorie was the farmer's wife. If George was not to be seen around the farm buildings, she would assist by going through the little wicket gate at the side of her bungalow to the farm driveway, through the farmyard and look out over the fields. If she could see him she would shout, whistle and wave her arms to attract his attention, mobile phones not being an option in those days either.

One day, Marjorie realised that the tractor driving the mill in the Nissen hut had been running for a very long time, longer than usual – it was easily heard next door. A rep who was there at the time went to investigate and found George slumped on the floor of the hut, overcome by the fumes from the tractor (George informed us that this was a Fordson Major with no cab). He was still alive but unconscious and fortunately had not fallen into the mill or onto the drive belt, either of which would surely have killed him. George made a full recovery and before he did any more milling he had a special exhaust made by Ted Ward that took the tractor's fumes outside the building.

Apart from the Nissen hut there were various other buildings, all constructed of timber and/or corrugated iron, including a chick-rearing shed, open-fronted stores for farm equipment, the pig shed/chicken house, and a cattle yard with a milking shed, calf and bullock pens and two manure heaps. As we know, George's milk was produced for home use only and not for commercial purposes, and he used to buy in calves from Tom Jeanes or from Ashford Market. Although the access drive and main part of the farmyard were concreted, some areas were still surfaced with chalk to give a firm top to the clay soil underneath. Mike remembers these could become very slippery when wet.

In addition to the deep-litter chicken shed (constructed with the help of Charlie Graves, George added), a brand new concrete-framed blockwork and corrugated cement asbestos-sheet Dutch barn was built, which was used to store baled hay, straw and beanstalks for the animals, as well as a lean-to, which was used variously for cattle, pigs and lambs.

Mike also recalls the summer days when the threshing machine would arrive at the farm to thresh the corn. The machine used to go round from farm to farm in those days, towed by a Field-Marshall tractor. (George added that this belonged to George Bishop and he believed that this tractor could still be in existence, now owned by Dennis Bishop, George Bishop's son.) The tractor was then used to power the threshing machine. Mike thought the Field-Marshall was wonderful: it was green and had a distinctively shaped exhaust. It was started with a blank cartridge and literally chugged away with the exhaust chuffing out smoke in puffs like you see in cartoons. To one side was a massive flywheel that spun round, counterbalancing the drive pulley wheel on the opposite side. The whole tractor used to rock to and fro with power as it drove the threshing machine, the flat belt flapping round at a vast speed. Sometimes the belt would slip off bringing the whole process to a standstill until it was refitted. The men loaded the sheaves into the thresher, attended to the corn and the weed seeds – which were separated from the corn and caught in hessian sacks – and forked the residue stalks onto a wagon or directly onto a stack.

## WORKING AT BIRCHOLT COURT FARM

Three generations of Will Wilson's family worked for the Jeanes at Bircholt Farm: first there was Jesse Wilson, then Bill (aka Billy) Wilson and finally, Will, who worked there in the early 1970s and was their first apprentice who went to an agricultural college. Bill Wilson, Will's father, started working there when he was about 18 years old and used to help get the chickens and turkeys ready for Christmas. That was in the early 1950s, when the Jeanes used to employ around 18 village people to help on the farm. (Eric Jeanes told us that in addition to Jesse, Billy and Will they also employed many who were related to the Wilsons by marriage, so quite an extended family worked at Bircholt). Will reflected that the Jeanes were always good employers of local labour. Tom Jeanes was master of the hunt at that time and Will officially worked for Eric, his son. However, unconcerned by the formality of this arrangement, Tom would come to Will while he was working for Eric and say, "William, come with me, the racecourse needs rolling." Unable to refuse, Will would be occupied at Aldington racecourse for the next two days and when he got back to the farm a perplexed Eric would say, "Where *have* you been?"

Will recalls that Tom used to drive a Renault 5 and has nightmare memories about him driving down past Smeeth Church to the crossroads and straight across the A20 without stopping. This was in the days before the motorway and the traffic on the A20 was heavy. One day, Will was being driven by Tom when they shot across the crossroads towards Evegate, beyond which the Jeanes had more land. Will was moved to suggest that Tom really should stop before he drove across, to which Tom replied, "Well, I didn't hit anything, did I?" and carried straight on. When Will was driving the combine Tom would often accompany him, driving in front in his Renault 5. Once down at the Smeeth crossroads, Tom would stop the Renault in the middle of the A20, holding up the traffic to allow the combine across the road and, unsurprisingly, causing chaos and anger among the other drivers. Tom, quite unfazed and apparently unaware of the irritation this was causing, would simply stand there waving Will across the road, but as Will recalls, "With the Renault 5 parked in the middle of the road it was actually quite a job to manoeuvre the combine round it and cross the A20 to get back on the road to Evegate."

Tom loved burning straw and, one day, when Eric was returning to the farm with Will they were greeted by a frantic Mrs Jeanes running up the road with two buckets of water. She shouted to Eric to help. "It's your father," she said. "He's set the hedge alight again." Evidently, this was not uncommon. Once, when Will's brother Ricky was working for the Jeanes, Tom set Ricky on a tractor and attached a lit tyre that Ricky was to drag along the field to set the stubble alight. By the time Ricky reached the end of the field the wind had turned and the fire had started to chase the tractor. Ricky didn't have time to stop the tractor and unhitch the burning tyre so simply turned the tractor round and drove back through the flames as fast as he could to escape them. The situation could have been quite dire, but Tom seemed barely aware of Ricky's ordeal, or of the potential danger that he had been instrumental in creating.

The Jeanes family at Bircholt Court in the 1950s.
From Left: Margaret and Tom Jeanes and their children, Eric, Pam, Stuart,
Angela (back) and Christine

Eric Jeanes, Tom's son, told us that when his parents first leased Bircholt Court from Lord Brabourne in 1930 there were few facilities there and life was very hard. They depended on well water for many years and had no electricity until about 1936. The Jeanes began farming at Bircholt just before the Depression of the 1930s, but when things became really difficult, Lord Brabourne gave them a rent break for an entire year. Tom and Margaret Jeanes came from Somerset and had known each other since they were children. When Margaret was about 13 or 14, she would sit on a stool her father had built for her and wait with their milk until Tom arrived to collect it. She and Tom married when they were 23 and celebrated 70 years of married life together.

Eric recalls that Tom was very much a community person, serving on the East Ashford and Ashford Borough Council for over 40 years, and as chairman for part of that time. In those days the Borough Council served Brabourne, Brook and Hastingeigh. Tom was in the Home Guard during the Second World War, and was much involved with the East Kent Hunt and with amateur dramatics in the village. Shortly after the war he played a major role in the levelling of the playing field on the land given for this purpose by the Brabournes.

Robert Embleton-Smith remembers Tom Jeanes' warmth and kindness from the days of the original farm shop at Evegate. On one visit to the shop, Robert found that they had run out of milk, but unhesitatingly, Tom went home and got some out of his own fridge for him.

Gerald Jordan mowing hay at Bircholt

## NOTES FROM EVEGATE FARM

The following section is based on notes, probably written in the 1930s, by Phyl Martin, the wife of Ronnie Martin, who owned Evegate Farm. Phyllis was also Andrew Martin's paternal grandmother:

"Evegate was a mixed farm with sheep, bullocks, a few pigs, chickens and ducks. Bullocks were kept in the yard in winter and all lambing was done in the field. About a quarter of the acreage was arable and 60 acres were woodland.

"I can just remember my father having two teams of horses, four to a team, in the stables to work the land. They were out of the stables and ready to work at 7 o'clock each morning. The waggoner would be at the farm by 5am, except Sundays, to feed and brush the horses, ready for work at 7am. They finished work in time to get home to feed and groom the horses and clean the harness. Two other horses were kept for working dog-carts, spreading dung and feeding stock in fields and yards.

"The waggoner was responsible for his horses. He usually had a lad to help him. All the horse brasses were his and moved with him if he changed his job. The horses either drank from a pond by the road, or from buckets of water drawn from the well by the pump outside the cart-horse stables.

"The Cart-Horse Stables
The stables had stabling for eight horses, four each side in stalls, with a loft between. The loft contained two chaff cutters which provided feed for both sides. The hay was fed into its cutter in the loft and, when cut, it fell into the bin where it was mixed with oats and other feedstuffs. The horses had two feeds a day, with hay racks. The mid-day feed was taken in nose bags into the field that they were working.
"My first job on the farm was leading the horses up and down rows of turnips, pulling a shim. [A shim was an implement with three or four spade-shaped plates that acted as hoes. Using this you could keep three or four rows at a time weed free and cultivated. Shims or hoes were adjustable.] There were several acres of turnips as they used to feed bullocks in winter and sheep were folded on these.

"The Sussex Herd
Before 1939 a Sussex herd was purchased. They calved and wintered in the yards and then the whole lot were driven to land at Brassington Oak where they grazed until the autumn. They were then driven home again. It took four men for this: two in the front, and two behind. The road through Knoll Woods was then unfenced so you can imagine how difficult it was to keep them out. Coming back to Evegate in the autumn was easier as the old cows seemed to know the way, and also carrying more condition made them easier to manage.

"When my sister married [in the 1930s] I was told to look after six Sussex bull calves. They were tied up in the cow lodge and had to be groomed and exercised each day. They were most unruly on halter and not nice when tied up. They had nasty little horns and they did plenty of head swinging and kicking. I didn't like them at all – and they knew it.

"The Grindstone
This stood at the back of Cart Lodge. It was used a tremendous lot to sharpen all tools, from shearing shears to scythes and hay cutters. It was a huge ex-mill stone set on a frame and had a huge iron handle through the middle for turning. It was always wet with a bucket of water before use. Water for cattle in the yard was mostly in tanks filled up by water from roofs. These were filled up with buckets from the pump if they got low.

"Harvest
This was always carried out by the binder drawn by two or three horses. The binder automatically cut and bound the sheaves with string and threw them out as it went along. A gang would then follow and put the sheaves into 'shocks', six or eight at a time, depending on the weather. It was left in the field until ripe and then, weather permitting, was brought by wagon and two horses into the stockyard where it was built into round stacks ready for threshing in the autumn. Corn was stored in the granary and fed to the animals during the winter. Straw was built into square stacks and the straw was used during winter for litter for yards and stock.

"Hay was cut with a mower, turned with a horse and rack, or by hand. When made, it was brought in loose by wagon and stacked in square stacks. The stacker was an expert at the job. As the stack grew tall, a hole was left in the side of the stack which was called 'the lubber-hole' and some poor soul was put in the hole to help the wadges of hay up from the wagon to the stack builder.

"Peg Leg Pidge
For many years we had a tame carrier-pigeon called 'Peg Leg Pidge'. He got his name because he would feed in the cart-horse stables and, as was bound to happen, he got trodden on by a big hoof, breaking one leg off at 'the knee'. We bound the stump up with plaster and Stockholm Tar, which eventually rotted away and left him with a nice little stump – hence his name. He lived for years and ruled the farmyard. At feeding time he was always around and had a running feud with the ducks, which always tried to take over. He ingeniously mastered them by running up behind them whilst feeding and chiselling his beak into their feathery back ends. He ended up 'the boss'.

"He roosted with the hens at the top of the cart lodge and spent most of his days sitting on a window sill of the little granary so that he could keep an eye on everything. He died of old age and was buried in the garden under the nut trees where all the dogs and other animals were buried."

## LILYVALE FARM

The Moorheads moved to Lilyvale Farm, Smeeth, in 1955, where they had 60 acres to begin with, which later increased to 70 acres. Here, they kept sheep, cattle – Jerseys and Sussex – pigs and a couple of goats that, Mrs Moorhead recalls, used to come indoors. She also recounted how, "One Sussex cow could remove the field gates with her huge horns – a perfect nuisance." At most, they had about 40 cattle, though now they have only 20, besides the pigs and goats. When they moved to the farm the bull used to graze on the field that is now the front garden and was regularly walked up Towers Hill and down Lily Vale in order to keep his feet trim. Cars were few in those days, of course, so walking a bull around the block was quite safe and not thought unusual. Mrs Moorhead would take butter and cream that she had made, together with any surplus vegetables, to Checksfields at Ashford Market, "as they would take anything and everything". As recently as 1957, Daniel Brooks from Aldington would collect her, together with her produce, in his pony and trap to take her to Ashford. In later years the Brooks replaced their pony and trap with a van.

Animals were very important at Lily Vale Farm and Mrs Moorhead recollects with amusement that, on one occasion, they were reported to the RSPCA for leaving a sick cow in the field. The animal was clearly in pain, but what the accuser did not realise was that the cow was calving. Mrs Moorhead observed that life has changed significantly and that most people know very little about farm animals these days – it would be interesting to see how many could now tell the difference between steers and heifers.

In the days when Mrs Moorhead's father had the farm, and before the railway line was electrified, the hunt used to go across its fields. The cows would become so alarmed at the thundering of the horses' hooves that they wouldn't give milk for the next couple of days. Mrs Moorhead reflected that the loss in revenue from the milk was worth it, just to see the wonderful spectacle of the horses galloping across the fields – though her father was not of the same opinion.

Help was needed to run the farm and the house, and those who worked at Lily Vale Farm were remembered with affection. Mrs Moorhead explained: "Millie Sigsworth worked for my father, and later for us with my Jersey cows. Millie had been in the land army and got an award, the British Empire Medal, for having never had a regular day off. She was great with cows. And then there were the Brooks brothers from Aldington, who helped with building and maintenance work at the farm. They had helped us since the 1950s, and forever." Dick Brooks still mows the lawns there. There were other workers, too: John Norrington worked there for years, both on the farm and in the garden – "He was a brilliant vegetable grower," said Mrs Moorhead. Although it is now 30-odd years since he worked there, his legacy of work is everywhere. "Whenever I look at a structure," she continued, "I remember that John made it. Everything he did lasted."

Kath Sawyer used to work in the farmhouse. "A former school cleaner, Mrs Sawyer polished everything to perfection, and even now, when I get the polish out I remember Kath," added Mrs Moorhead. "Mrs Earl also helped so much – with anything, and especially when the children were young. Her husband worked at Coopers and delivered to Hastingleigh in all weathers, walking through snow to outlying old people, never letting them down. All this makes me sound very lazy, but alas these people are no longer around to refute that!"

## EAST BRABOURNE'S FARMS

One of the largest local farms in East Brabourne was Penstock Farm, owned by the Olders from 1943 to 2001, when George Jessel took over. There were many other farms in and around Brabourne, including: Parsonage Farm and Church Farm, which was absorbed by Parsonage Farm in 1956; Park Farm, owned by the Cliftons; and numerous farms owned by the Brabourne Estate. These farms, like most others were mixed farms in times past but most are now highly mechanised using modern agricultural techniques.

Oliver Trowell told us, "Parsonage Farm, at the end of Brabourne Street, was bought by the Smiths in 1919, when Rosie Andrews's grandfather, Fred, bought it and moved from Southenay Farm. Throughout the Smiths' ownership it was run as a mixed farm [as were most other farms in those days]. Fred died in 1937 and his sons, Noble and George, carried on farming there until 1956, when they sold out to James Hamilton. The Hamilton regime was totally different – not an animal on the farm and arable crops taken year after year."

Parsonage Farm is now owned by the Henshaw family. Oliver added that, before the war, the land at Church Farm had been poorly drained, the ditches never being sufficiently deep to drain the water properly. He recalled that if you stamped your foot hard into the ground, bubbles would appear. Problems of poor drainage persisted under the ownership of Horace Coleman and his successors, Lady Charnwood and Mr Ripley. However, James Hamilton deepened the dykes to around 6ft, which reduced the marshy character of the land and this, together with modern farming practices, saw the productivity of the land increase. As a result of all these technical improvements under James's ownership, the traditional character of these farms was lost. The same could be said for most other farms in the area.

Many people reflected on how the entire community used to be involved in farming. People lamented that with modernisation the old sort of mixed farming had virtually disappeared, and also that an increasingly hi-tech farming industry now required relatively few workers. In the words of one of our contributors "although it is highly successful, farming has become remote from us".

## THE OLDERS AT PENSTOCK FARM

Margaret Older

While out for a ride on her bicycle one day in 1942, Margaret Older noticed a For Sale sign outside Penstock Farm in East Brabourne. Returning to their home at Boughton Aluph, near Wye, Margaret told her husband, Reg, about the farm, adding, "I just love that house." In 1943, they bought the farm from the Camerons and moved there with their small son, Christopher (who must be thanked for his assistance with this section). At that time, the farm was a traditional mixed enterprise with a range of livestock and cropping. The Olders' move to East Brabourne marked the beginning of a changing era in local farming history.

Reg had always been interested in farming and, after graduating from Wye College, University of London (now part of Imperial College), with a diploma in agriculture in the 1930s, he was very soon employed by Edward Hardy, then chair of the governors of the college (and soon to become Sir Edward Hardy). Reg was to manage Boughton Court Farm near Wye, as well as part of Olantigh Park and Trimworth Manor Farm, which Sir Edward also rented. Reg had grown up in Surrey, and with the security of employment he married Margaret, also from Surrey, in 1936. They lived at Pilgrim's Cottage, which was part of Boughton Court Farm. In 1943 their move to Penstock nearly doubled the area that Reg was farming, as it added 500 acres to the 640 acres of Sir Edward's farms. Sir Edward died in 1976 and the Olders continued to farm Boughton Court Farm in partnership with his niece until the late 1980s; shortly before this, circa 1985, they had relinquished the tenancy of Olantigh Park and Trimworth Manor.

Back in 1947 Sir Edward and Reg together took on the tenancy of Chapel Farm, Eastbridge, Romney Marsh, thereby adding a further 600 acres to the area that Reg was managing. Reg's farming of around 1,800 acres in three separate businesses continued

Chris Older

until 1965 when Chris became involved and began managing the farms following a year working in New Zealand. This arrangement carried on until 1988, which was when Reg became very ill following a severe stroke. He survived and, with great determination, lived until July 2002. Chris then continued managing the farms on his own until 2000, at which point his nephew, Andrew Martin, joined him and became involved in their management.

In common with many farms during the period from 1960 to the present, the land farmed by the Olders followed a trend of simplification. They gradually moved away from mixed livestock and mixed cropping to more easily managed and more profitable arable-cropping systems, involving cereals, peas, and oil-seed rape. This employed fewer staff but used very large modern machinery to establish, grow and harvest the crops with a minimum of expense. Crop yields steadily improved with these modern growing techniques – for example, wheat yields went from Reg's 1.5 tons-2 tons per acre to a sold weight in 2011 of 4.5 tons, with individual fields producing as much as 5.2 tons per acre. The combined size of Chris and Andrew's farming enterprises is now about 3,000 acres, run with only three regular staff, quite a contrast to the 20-plus staff whom Reg employed in the 1950/60s on little over half the same area.

During the 1960s and 1970s land was added to Penstock, which included The Moors, now Idenborough, together with the land around it, and the 27 acres opposite Penstock, which incorporated Ivy Cottage, the Malthouses, and Forge House, Cottage and Bungalow. Romney Marsh Farm expanded to 950 acres and Chris observed, "To some extent this was a more profitable time for agriculture." At that point, the Olders farmed all their enterprises under a mixed ley-farming system that included up to 2,000 breeding sheep grazing three-year leys of grass, composed of a mixture of Kent indigenous perennial rye grass and Kent wild

Margaret and Reg Older

white clover. Cropping included wheat, barley and oats, as well as vining peas for canning and quick freezing.

Penstock Farm was sold in 2000 to George Jessel from South Hill, Hastingleigh, as neither Chris nor his sisters, Rosalind and Diana, wished to live in the big house: they were well set up with their own properties. However, after a short break, Andrew has returned to farming Penstock under an agreement with George. In addition to Penstock, Andrew also farms, in his own right, other land under contract and tenancy agreements, and the entire area he farms now exceeds 2,900 acres.

## REG OLDER, INNOVATOR IN FARMING

As one of the foremost farmers in the area, Reg played a major part in the administration of the War Agricultural Executive Committee in the early 1940s. Through his role he visited many farms in east Kent, encouraging farmers to plough up their grassland and grow crops to feed the nation during the blockade. Reg had become instrumental in adopting modern techniques on his farms and these included the early adoption of tractors, notably the famous Fordson, and early versions of the Ferguson System.

Reg Older, Master of the East
Kent Hunt for 30 years

He was also one of the first in the country to buy and use one of "the new-fangled combine harvesters" that reduced the amount of manual work for the harvesting operations. Along with this, he built ventilated grain stores on the three main farms that he managed – these were quite a novelty in the 1940s.

Others also noted the innovative nature of farming at Penstock: Eric Ball started working for Reg at Penstock during the school holidays when he was only 14 years old. He soon learnt how to drive the tractor that pulled the baler, and was allowed to do so on the fields, though not on the road. The combine was an Oliver and the baler a Case. This was one of the first balers in the country and Eric used to go to other farms to demonstrate its potential. Eric's brother, Bob, also worked for the Olders there but not just in the school holidays – he started working for them when he left school and stayed with them until he died.

Along with his enthusiasm for new techniques, Reg expanded the small dairy herd at Penstock to more than 100 cows in the 1950s, which were milked on a mobile milking bail system, meaning that the milking machinery was taken to the cows. In winter, the milking bail was positioned on a concrete pad with the cows in yards at the bottom of Brabourne Downs, 300yd east of Brabourne House (formerly Ten Acres). Chris reflected that many people must surely remember the floods of mud, silage effluent and cow muck that flooded across the Wye road at that time. As a young man in 1958/9, Chris was sent to work on this milking bail system and, by his own admission, the experience put him off cows for the rest of his life. The dairy herd was subsequently sold in 1959.

Brabourne Coomb Farm, which became part of Penstock before the Second World War, was used in the 1940s for rearing calves and a small herd of pigs and chickens. The pigs and chickens were kept in the beautiful but dilapidated old farmhouse (pictured on next page) that stood at the eastern side of the current buildings and had been occupied by troops during the war. Margaret recalled that the farmhouse was already in a dreadful state when they bought Coomb Farm from the Powell sisters, who then moved out to what was Ten Acres on Pilgrims' Way. When they disbanded their poultry enterprises, the Olders had little choice but to demolish the house. Mrs Older reflected on what a tragedy this was as Coomb Farm was so ancient, having belonged to William I's stepson. Before it was demolished, however, Southern Television hired one of its barns to film a scene for H.E. Bates's A Moment in Time. This was in 1979, or thereabouts.

Reg was one of the leading farmers in Kent, but as Margaret explained, he did much more than farm. He was on NFU (National Farmers' Union) committees, before subsequently becoming chairman of The Farmers Club in London. In addition, he was secretary to the Agricola Club, the alumni of Wye College, before rising up through the governing body to achieve ultimately the positions of provost of the college and chairman of the college governors, which were formal acknowledgements of his commitment to farming and rural development. All these positions remained

Brabourne Coomb Farmhouse
(1930s)

very dear to his heart, though Wye College, with which he had remained in close contact since his days as an undergraduate, undoubtedly held a place of particular importance for him. Reg's substantial contribution to his industry was given further formal recognition in 1982, when he was awarded the CBE. Alongside farming, Reg's greatest love was hunting and he was master of the East Kent Hunt for 30 years (more on hunting follows in this chapter). Helping to maintain order in Reg's busy life was his secretary, Mary Bean. She was one of four land girls who had come to Penstock during the war (all of whom lived in the attic), and she stayed with the Olders for over 50 years, until she retired.

Reg was also made master of the Worshipful Company of Farmers, one of the London Livery Companies but, unfortunately, his work in this capacity was halted when he had his stroke. Shortly before he died, the Olders sold Penstock and moved to Mersham.

Andrew Martin, Reg Older's grandson writes:

"Many of the farming techniques and rotations used at Penstock have changed significantly during the past 20 to 30 years. When I was a boy working at Penstock for my grandfather in the school holidays, the crops were grown in a grass rotation involving the sheep grazing three-year leys. These were established by growing them for grass-seed production. Grass is still in the rotation today, but in a much smaller way, and is used for forage rather than for grazing. The fields were divided into smaller areas to allow for this broader rotation, not necessarily divided by physical

Andrew Martin

boundaries but sections within larger fields. There are many areas of the farm that were in crop production then that are in a different type of land use today. The land surrounding Idenborough – or The Moors Cottage as it used to be known – was included in the full rotation. Now it is an area of permanent grass and newly planted woodland, together with a large spring-fed pond. The same is true of the adjacent field known as Oziers, which was a very difficult field to crop but now makes a much better environmental feature. Many of the larger fields have been subdivided by new hedge and tree plantings. In recent years the intensiveness of the arable fields has been removed away from hedges and streams by the establishment of large grass and wild-flower margins around Penstock.

"Like my grandfather I have tried to adopt novel and cutting-edge farming techniques. The whole of Penstock has been subject to detailed satellite soil mapping, which enables me to precisely target soil nutrients. I use yield mapping to assess the results

Andrew Martin combining at Manor Pound,
drawn by Michael Giles

of each part of the farm, and use chlorophyll scanners to precisely apply fertiliser in the spring. This all helps to make Penstock a sustainable and productive farm. This year [2011] Penstock produced enough oil-seed rape to produce 67,000 litres of vegetable oil and enough wheat to produce over 1,000,000 loaves of bread."

## THE JESSELS AT PENSTOCK HALL FARM[1]
George Jessel writes:

"My first memory of Penstock Hall Farm is from the 1960s, when my father rushed into the kitchen to announce that our dairy herd had got out and were currently grazing 'Reg Older's wheat down the bank at Penstock!'

George and Vicki Jessel and their children, Amelia and Charlie

"My next memory is of Reg Older very kindly inviting me out when I was a teenager to hunt with the East Kent Foxhounds, and I remember meeting him and his groom at what is now known as the Malthouses, as this is where his horses were stabled. Never in my wildest dreams would I have imagined that 25 years on I would be farming Penstock Hall in my own right.

"It was with great delight that I moved my family to Penstock Hall in the autumn of 2001 and set about amalgamating the farm into what we now call Jessel Farms, which is the combined acreage of South Hill (Hastingleigh) and Penstock, totalling 1,200 acres. At the time we had a 180-cow dairy unit based at South Hill and so, for the first time in years, black and white cows were seen below the Downs. Although the Olders had kept the land as an arable farm I was determined that the way forward was for it to be a mixed unit with diversified buildings.

"I quickly got to work converting the listed buildings into offices and storage units, with the aim of creating a working rural hub whereby the tenants of these offices would all be involved in country businesses. Vicki, my wife, got to grips with

---

1      Chris Older informed us that it was only when Strutt & Parker published the sale details of Penstock Farm in 2000 that it became Penstock Hall Farm.

refurbishing the house and we have now created a lovely family home. Sadly the dairy unit was sold in 2005, though this did not mean the end of stock, as I embarked on a new working relationship with PHR Farms on the neighbouring Mersham Estate. The farm now looks after all their young stock during the summer, and in the winter they occupy the old dairy buildings at South Hill.

"The tractor drivers inherited from my father were of retirement age around the time that the dairy herd went, and rather than replace them I decided to go down the contract-farming route. The current contract farmer is, coincidentally, Andrew Martin."

## REFLECTIONS ON HUNTING

A chapter on farming would not be complete without mention of hunting. Hunting was an important rural pursuit in the past and many local people, not all of whom were farmers, spoke fondly of hunting – the Olders, John and Vi Varrier, Ted and Margaret Pile and many others. Carol Lightfoot (Hobbs) grew up with hunting and has hunted all her life. Recently retired, she now follows the hunt and fund-raises for the East Kent Hunt, which still hunts through the autumn and winter months on Wednesdays and Saturdays. Until the 1970s, Carol recalls, nearly all farmers would hunt, as would their children, and in times past there was plenty of fallow ground to ride across. Farmers welcomed the hunt crossing their land, especially if foxes were causing them problems. "You had to be able to jump," said Carol, "in order to be able to keep up with the hunt, as among the huntsmen there were some outstanding riders and horses. One was Charles Hallam, who rode The Toff, a horse that could jump absolutely anything and set high standards for all the other riders."

Carol, whose father, Robert Hobbs, was at one time master of the hunt, can remember the first time that she, her sister and Di Castle (Ames) were riding with the hunt when a fox was caught and killed. In keeping with tradition, each of the girls was given a pad from the fox (which they mounted and framed) and their cheeks were smeared with a little blood from the fox. Carol remembers the immense pride she and the other girls felt; it was like a rite of passage marking their transition to full membership of the hunting fraternity, and the experience was something to be savoured, and never forgotten.

Hunting was associated with socialising: Wednesdays and Saturdays saw lawn meets at people's houses and, on the first Wednesday after Christmas, the hunt would be served with hot punch and snacks. Sometimes this took place at Home Farm, when Robert Hobbs was master of the hunt. After refreshment they would hunt all day from 11am until dark, and then they would return on horseback. There were few cars

## THE HUNT

Local meet of the East Kent Hunt (1950s)

Ronnie Martin, Harold Crump and Robert Hobbs
(late 1950s/1960s)

Meet at Bilsington Priory in the 1950s
From right: Harold Crump, Leslie Rimmer, Tom Glasse (Master) and Robert Hobbs

Tom Jeanes and Charles Hallam with the East Kent Hunt (1950s)

Vi and John Varrier during a Boxing Day
Hunt in the 1970s

A Boxing Day Hunt in the 1970s.
John Varrier in the lead

Opening meet at East Brabourne (1978/79)

Undeterred by the weather, East Brabourne
(1970s)

in those days and Carol can remember her mother driving behind her and her sisters after the hunt, lighting their way home in the dark. The hunt didn't stop for lunch and those riding with it would take a hip flask and sandwiches, which they would eat as they rode. Sometimes the riders would stop in Elham or at the Six Mile Garage café for tea after a day's hunting. The kennels were at Elham and, as another example of tradition, Carol explained, the hounds were counted out in couples and, as a rule, an odd number of hounds would accompany the hunt, for example, 17½ couples. Some 50 to 60 people would hunt in the 1970s, sometimes as many as 80. It was an impressive spectacle to see them galloping across the countryside and Carol recalls that there was no work on winter Wednesdays because of the hunt.

Tim Marsh gave us a different perspective of the hunt: from that of a small boy. Following the hunt on foot, not on horseback, was an opportunity for small boys to earn some pocket money. They would hear the hunting horns and would walk or run towards them. Once they established in which direction the hunt was going they would go cross-country, taking shortcuts towards the fields that the hunt would cross. Each member of the group would choose a field gateway and, as the horses approached, a little boy would open the gate so that the hunt could go through. Once through, the gate would be shut and the boys would be off immediately, running, to open more gates for the hunt. Tim recalls that they would walk and run great distances through the day, covering as much as 15 miles sometimes. At the end of a long day they would then have to find their way home. However, at the last set of gates the huntsmen would often throw sixpenny pieces to the children as they rode through and Tim can remember having picked up as many as a dozen at one time, which, he added, was a great deal of money when you were eight or nine years old.

Relatively few farmers hunt these days, possibly because they have neither the time nor the money: keeping horses and feeding them is an enormous expense. Nevertheless, those associated with hunting believe that the hunt still plays an important role, both in maintaining a very English tradition and ridding farmland of vermin. The hunt also helps those in rural areas who keep animals by removing the carcasses of fallen stock (that is, animals that have died through natural causes). Hunting provokes passion, both for it and against it, and for those who have hunted all their lives it is a passion to be treasured.

## EAST BRABOURNE'S ORCHARD, MARKET GARDEN AND POULTRY FARM

Lord and Lady Charnwood and Miss Carola Cochrane together bought Court Lodge in East Brabourne in 1944. As it was in the flight path of the German bombers it was a bargain. They moved in just before the war ended and, once there, established an orchard and a market garden on the land that went with the property. Bounded by Pilgrims' Way, Stocks Lane and The Street, the orchard and market garden, for many years, physically occupied a central position in the village and also contributed significantly to the local economy. Lord Charnwood was little involved with this venture in practical terms. Being an eye surgeon, he spent much of his time working in London and came down to the village intermittently. Although the orchard and market garden tend to be spoken of together, they were run as two separate enterprises: Miss Cochrane ran the market garden, and Lady Charnwood (Beryl) the orchard, though it appears that there was a great deal of sharing of resources, not least the delivery vehicles.

### A NEW VENTURE

Shortly before the war Lady Charnwood and Miss Cochrane took the decision to give up their jobs at The Illustrated London News and start a market garden. Miss Cochrane had discovered her "green fingers" growing vegetables and "digging for victory" in the garden at the cottage in Hertfordshire, where they had previously all lived. Soon after moving into Court Lodge, Miss Cochrane had the land ploughed and planted with what she describes in her book as "a cleansing crop of potatoes". She began by selling her produce locally but, in time, the crops became highly specialised and increasingly were sent to Covent Garden and to other consumers in London.

Aerial view of the market garden at
Court Lodge, bounded by The Street, East Brabourne

Flowers were an important product and, often on a Sunday, Tony Norrington, who for many years was manager of the market garden, would take the flowers to put them on a London-bound train from Wye Station.

Elsie Davis, Kath Spain and others who worked for Miss Cochrane used to make up boxes for the flowers, which were carefully weighed before being packed. Kath recalled that Miss Cochrane was very fussy about the presentation of the flowers and woe betide anyone who accidentally snapped a flower head off. In fact, the presentation of all the produce meant a great deal, and Kath remembered scrubbing and bunching carrots so that they looked their best for market. Besides flowers, the market garden produced out-of-season asparagus, melons, alpine strawberries, the latter of which, from time to time, went to Fortnum & Mason, as well as Buckingham Palace. Both Elsie and Kath recalled how long it used to take to fill a tiny punnet with alpine strawberries, and Roger Vining remembers the punnets of raspberries for the Palace being lined carefully with raspberry leaves before being filled with the delicate fruit. The market garden couldn't produce sufficient soft fruit to meet demand, and the supply of raspberries was supplemented from other growers in West Brabourne. Most of the fruit was sold by auction, though some was sold through local businesses. In words taken from Miss Cochrane's book:

"The 'soft fruit' picking season is looked forward to by our pickers as a 'money-making' summer outing. They bring their children along, at any rate the small ones who are not yet of school age, and at weekends husbands have been known to come too and are quite excellent pickers. They are certainly a nice and gay crowd and the van is filled to capacity when they are fetched and later taken back to their homes together with their progeny, prams, Thermos flasks and bags and baskets of food, for during the height of the picking season it is an all-day job." (p.130)

When Lady Charnwood and Miss Cochrane bought Court Lodge, it included within its 40 acres a five-acre apple orchard of Bramleys (cookers) and a few rows of dessert apples such as Beauty of Bath and Derbys. Another five-acre orchard, consisting mainly of dessert apples, was planned, but Lady Charnwood was not in a position to plant the 1,000 trees planned for this orchard at once; it was thus planted in three parts, the first third largely by a squad of some 25 German prisoners of war. Miss Cochrane notes in her book that almost every trade was represented among the ranks of the prisoners, which made them particularly useful:

"The carpenters dealt with the stakes for the trees, the blacksmiths with the wire netting and the labourers just dug. In two days the 350 trees were planted, staked and wired and we never ceased bitterly regretting not having been able to plant up

Workforce at the market garden at Court Lodge, East Brabourne, celebrating 40 years of service by Ernie Davis (mid-1970s).
Front row: from left, Mrs Osborne, Kath Thornby, Ernie and Elsie Davis, Mrs Law, Mrs Hover and Mrs Lawes. Back row: from left, Mrs Todd (just behind Kath Thornby), Tony Norrington, Mr Lawes (forward), Mr Woodcock and Mrs Woodcock

the entire orchard then and there, for the squad was no longer available the following year." (pp.128-9)

Oliver Trowell recalls that some of the Germans did like working for Lady Charnwood, though others were not so well disposed and he remembers them saying, "We like not to work for the regiment of women. We would not be buried in England." In spite of this, some married English women and stayed on after the war. One of them was Joseph Harbel, who lived in the front part of Hill View Cottages in The Street in East Brabourne with his English wife.

Lady Charnwood normally employed a foreman and assistant to run the orchard and, for about a year in 1960, Roger Vining joined the team, his aim being to learn more about fruit farming. Bill Smith was Lady Charnwood's "fruit foreman" at the time, and Roger describes him as a large man who used to drink 13 pints every

Miss Cochrane, left, and Lady Charnwood at
Court Lodge

Miss Cochrane with Gin in a greenhouse full of chrysanthemums
(1957)

Miss Cochrane talking to one of the German prisoners of war who was
working at the market garden

Friday and Saturday evening, and the same
again at lunchtime on Sundays. He also
chain-smoked, lighting each cigarette from
the butt of the last, though Roger recalls that
he never smoked in the house. From time
to time, Roger would drive produce from
both the orchard and the market garden to
local buyers. Being tall, good looking and
well presented the buyers assumed Roger
was Lord Charnwood, and were deferential
when they addressed him, saying, "Yes, me
Lord... No, me Lord." While this amused
Roger, it came as some considerable surprise,
if not shock, to Lady Charnwood when she

Roger Vining

accompanied him on a visit to Ashford. Another member of the market garden team
warmly remembered by many was Miss Cochrane's dog, Gin, a great favourite (in all
senses) with the residents of Court Lodge.

Pat Browne's parents were employed for many years at Lady Charnwood's as
housekeeper and chauffeur and, during that time, they lived in Court Lodge and,
later, at Church Farm, which was then also owned by Lady Charnwood. They lived in

part of the farmhouse, with the then farm manager, Mr Richards, living in the other part. Pat's father, Leslie, a competent horseman, was also in charge of the stables at Court Lodge. On one occasion, Pat recalls that his father was driving the Rolls, Lady Charnwood's pride and joy, when it was damaged in an accident. Lady Charnwood, horrified by the damage, said something like, "Browne, what *have* you done?" and promptly sent him "for training at the Rolls-Royce School of Instruction". The comprehensive course that he undertook also included instruction in how to polish the vehicle! Pat also remembered Lady Charnwood being very kind when he and his mother moved to Norfolk. Here, she found Pat's mother a job, working for a friend who was a doctor. Pat recalled that this was particularly fortunate, as when he contracted scarlet fever he was spared the horrors of being in a sanatorium because the doctor was able to look after him at home.

Margaret Older, at one time secretary of the local Conservative Association, for some reason had to collect the names of people in the village. As she arrived at Court Lodge several people were leaving work, which was convenient for her. She knew that at that time a German woman was working at Court Lodge but she couldn't remember her name. Identifying the person whom she was sure was the German lady, she said very tactfully as she went to write down her name, "I'm sorry, but I can't spell your name," to which the woman replied "S-M-I-T H." Even now Margaret admits to feeling an uncomfortable shudder when she remembers this moment.

Pat Browne, left, and his father, right, while
they were at Court Lodge

Veronica Lister, Lady Charnwood's niece, has personal recollections of Christmas at Court Lodge when she was a child:

Veronica Lister

"My memories of East Brabourne are from the viewpoint of a visitor to Court Lodge every Christmas. Owned by my aunt, Beryl Charnwood, and her friend Carola Cochrane, it is a charming old house on different levels, with outbuildings and a garden that rises up the hill. Carola ran a market garden from there and I remember her coming into the kitchen after working in the Nissen hut with her 'ladies' who packed up the flowers to send to Covent Garden, immaculate and workmanlike in green anorak, blue rinse and Peter Stuyvesant in hand. Our Christmases were rather exotic as my aunt's other great friend, Sanda Cantacuzino, would join us with her family and, later, her sister's family. Conversation was often in French, the lingua franca of aristocratic Romanians, as we milled around the enormous dining table. Emerging into the Kentish countryside from that rarefied atmosphere was rather a relief. Later I spent several weeks there in summer, studying, and my room looked out over the pretty orchard. Coming out from Court Lodge the road turns sharply left just beyond the church, but this is hardly visible, giving the appearance of a corner cul-de-sac. All those mellow brick houses huddled together by the church epitomise to me Old England, as does the church itself. The only other house in the village I know is of course the double cottage owned by the Cantacuzinos. It always seemed to be full of people, with the sound of a piano in the background. My aunt and her friend didn't seem to take much part in village life, they always lived rather as though in exile. But they chose it, so must have thought well of it. I wonder what it thought of them?"

In answer to Veronica's concluding question, everyone with whom we spoke who had had any contact with Lady Charnwood found her kind, generous and thoughtful. Kath Thornby (White) spoke of her distinctive dress. She frequently wore army battle dress and always wore a turban, beautifully tied. Margaret Older also remarked on this, saying that she had never seen Lady Charnwood's hair (though remarkably. it is visible in the pictures of her on pages 598 and 606). It was agreed by several of those who knew "the ladies" that Miss Cochrane was much more glamorous, though most of those with whom we spoke preferred Lady Charnwood. On one occasion,

Lady Charnwood gave the Davis family a pig and a piece of land to keep it on. This was shortly after the war when rationing continued and when food was in short supply. Eventually, the pig was killed by a Mr Earl, known as Tipper, who worked for Hawkins butchers, and the animal was hung from a beam in Church Farm, where the Davis family was living. Half the carcass went to Coopers to be cured by them, ready to be smoked at the bacon factory, while the fresh meat was prepared for the family by Tipper Earl (picture below). It is possible that killing the pig on a farm may not have been legal at this time, but as this sort of thing obviously went on and those involved are no longer with us, we feel there is no harm in including this as it is part of Brabourne's history.

Jackie and Margaret Davis remember Lady Charnwood paying a visit to the Davis family and, on seeing the remains of the pig in the kitchen, blew up its bladder like a balloon to make them (then children) laugh. After Ernie Davis had worked for Lady Charnwood for 40 years he was given a service medal, which was presented to him publicly at the Kent Show. Ernie and Elsie, along with other workers at the market garden, were taken to the Kent Show every year. Once they were even taken to Chelsea – they went up to London by train and took a taxi to Chelsea because there was a Tube strike. Such generosity is warmly remembered and did much to strengthen

Outside Hawkins Butcher's slaughterhouse: from left, Frank Earl (Tipper),
Ross Ashman, Allen Ashman, Ben Hawkins (boy), unidentified

the commitment of those who were employed, as well as the ties of the community. We return later in the book to the role that Lady Charnwood played in the social life of the village, but what was especially remembered by several contributors was her kindness and generosity to local children. Kath Thornby (White) spoke of Christmas parties with sandwiches, cakes and games for the children, and always a party for Miss Cochrane's birthday. Kath noted wryly that she couldn't remember there ever being a party for Lady Charnwood.

Celebrating Carola Cochrane's birthday in the mid-1970s.
Back row: from left, Reg Hover, Tony Norrington and Dick Woodcock.
Front row: from left, unidentified, Mrs Colgate, Win Lawes, Carola Co-
chrane, unidentified, Mrs Osborne, Elsie Davis (hidden), and Ernie Davis

While most people certainly remembered Lady Charnwood with affection, there were a few who did not. One of these was a neighbour whom she accused of stealing apples and whom she took to court on this issue, and won her case. There was apparently considerable dispute between the two parties involved regarding the quantity of apples stolen – the family of the accused still assert that the quantity was minimal, no more than scrumping, while others tell a different story.

That Lady Charnwood was very particular about her orchard was also clear from Vi Varrier, who recalls that each year Vi's father, William Kingston, would drive his dry cows and heifers from Bankside in Stowting to near Brabourne School to pasture them on land rented from John Hammon's uncle. William always had to notify Lady Charnwood when the herd was to be moved and as they came through the village she would line her workmen along the grass outside Court Lodge to ensure that no cows trampled on it.

Though people barely knew Lord Charnwood, they spoke also of his kindness and generosity. One of the children in The Street had a serious eye defect and Lord Charnwood arranged for her to be taken up to London, where he conducted an operation to correct it. This must have changed the child's life and perhaps this will strike a chord in the memories of those who know her. Something else for which Lord Charnwood was remembered was the annual meeting of veteran car owners. This would go on for a day or so with the village being flooded with interesting vehicles coming to Court Lodge – in pre-television days it was a major spectacle relished by the village people.

Most people found Lady Charnwood and Miss Cochrane good employers, but all of them preferred the gentle manner of the Princess Cantacuzino, who as we know had a chicken farm in what is now Court Lodge Barn, almost opposite Court Lodge. The story goes that Lady Charnwood and Miss Cochrane knew the Princess because of Miss Cochrane's friendship with the Princess's mother, Elisabeth Stirbey. They had first met some years earlier in Switzerland, when the Princess's mother had overheard Miss Cochrane's remarkable soprano in full song at a hotel where they were both staying. In 1939 the Princess brought her children, Sherban and Marie-

Elsie and Ernie Davis celebrating their golden wedding anniversary,
(1990s)

Lyse, to school in England and was stranded by the outbreak of war. Her husband, Prince Georges Cantacuzino, had to remain in Romania throughout the war, and subsequently endured periods of harsh imprisonment at the hands of the communist government, finally dying in 1960. The Princess had to seek refuge with her friends in Hertfordshire and then moved with them to Court Lodge in 1944. She started her poultry farm in 1952/3. The piece of ragstone wall in front of Court Lodge Barn that runs along The Street was one wall of the hatchery and local children seemed to have been regular visitors there: in the mid- to late 1950s, Pauline Anderson (Marsh) remembers the Princess allowing her to help with the incubators and the newly hatched chicks on the farm; Ilinca, granddaughter of the Princess, who has kindly provided us with much of the information relating to the Three Ladies, remembers watching the chickens hatch; and Jackie Finn (Davis) used to help collect eggs with her two sisters. Mrs Doris Norrington, who technically looked after the chickens, always welcomed the children warmly when they came to help.

During the 1950s Sherban bought the Pink Cottage, no.3, The Street, and later nos.1&2, and it was only then that the family moved up the road. The Princess and her family became well established in the village. She was, and still is, referred to as "Princess", as if it were her first name. Kathy Embleton-Smith can remember being told many years ago by Nurse Nell Hills, who lived with her sister, Dorothy, at no.1, Holly Cottages, "Princess, Dorothy and I would get the bus into Ashford every week." This would have sounded quite out of the ordinary if you didn't have some knowledge of East Brabourne.

At Court Lodge Barn, the three ladies, as they were known, looking
at the chicks.  On left, the Princess Cantacuzino, back right, Miss
Cochrane and front right, Lady Charwood (1950s)

# 10

# HOW PEOPLE ENJOYED THEMSELVES

How did people enjoy themselves in Brabourne? Once again, self-reliance was key to entertainment, from the village to the household level. The amount of effort devoted to organising social events was enormous, so much so that it was a form of entertainment in itself. Until the late 1960s the church played a significant part in organising festivities and the following extracts concerning the celebrations of Queen Victoria's Golden Jubilee in 1887, King George V's Silver Jubilee in 1935, and Queen Elizabeth II's Silver Jubilee in 1977 and Golden Jubilee in 2002 show the changing nature of such celebrations in the villages in just over a century. The church now plays a much smaller role in organising community celebrations, partly because its membership is smaller, but also because greater disposable income has meant that the local people are themselves more able to fund celebrations.

## MAJOR COMMUNITY EVENTS

### QUEEN VICTORIA'S GOLDEN JUBILEE
The minutes of the PCC, or Vestry Meetings, as they were then called, give a wonderfully detailed example of how the villages celebrated Queen Victoria's Golden Jubilee in 1887, the 50th anniversary of her accession to the throne. The description of the day's events, which was written up by George Worrell, the headmaster of Brabourne National School, concluded with the following sentence: "The Honorary Secretary Mr. Worrell was directed to draw up this account of the day's proceedings to be entered in the parish vestry book for the information of future generations." With this in the minds of the PCC in 1887, the following passage was clearly destined for inclusion in our book.

The Queen's Jubilee was actually on 20th June, so it is not clear why Mr Worrell's entry is dated the 21st. Maybe this was the day on which he wrote it.

"June 21st, 1887   The Queen's Jubilee –
On this day the festivities in honour of the Queen's Jubilee took place in this parish. A month previously a preliminary meeting had been summoned by the Vicar to take the matter into consideration, and at the meeting a committee was appointed to collect subscriptions and make the necessary arrangements. The following gentlemen were appointed members of the Committee, Revd. J.T. Pearse (Chairman), Messrs Andrews, Apps, Collins, Edwards, Finn, Hammon (of Bircholt), Hancock, Hogben, Pearson (Treasurer), Pilcher, and Worrell (Secretary). Subscriptions were collected amounting to £30.15.6; the following being the principal contributors: Rt. Hon. Lord Brabourne £5, Ecclesiastical Commissioners £4, Col. Groves £2, Mr. T. Long £2.2, Captain Lawson £1.1, Hon. Mrs. Perry Ayscough £1, Revd J.T. Pearse £1. The following gave 10/- each, Messrs Weekes, Palmer, Thos. Hills, Hammon (Sen.), Apps, Pearson, Palmer, Hammon jun., Andrews, T. Hogben, Philpott, Hancock, Worrell, Hughes, Tauton, Dr. Snow, R. & H. Hills, Marshall and Heathfield, and F. Hobbs. The following gave 5/-, Messrs Daniels, Edwards, Back, Foot, R. Marsh, Hambrook, Collins, W. Marsh, and Revd. J. Hughes-Hallett, besides several who gave smaller sums.

"The day's proceedings commenced with a merry peal on the Church bells at 6 o'clock in the morning. At 11 o'clock a special service was held at the church which was well attended by old and young. At one o'clock a free dinner consisting of cold roast and boiled beef, pickles etc. was given to all married labourers and their wives and to all single persons 50 years old and upwards. Others were permitted to partake of the dinner upon payment by the males of 9d and females 6d. About 300 persons sat down. The dinner was held in a field near the school in the occupation of the Hammons; over the entrance a triumphal arch was created by Mrs. F. Hammon which was gaily decorated with flowers and evergreens by Mrs. Hughes, while Mrs. Pearse provided the motto 'God Save the Queen'. Two large booths, hired for the occasion of Mr. J. Early of the Duke's Head Sellindge, were erected in the field and beautifully decorated by Mrs. Pearson, Miss D'Ombrain and others, the beer for the dinner was given by Mr. Pearson and Mr. E. Chapman of Ashford. Mr. Weekes gave

Brabourne and Smeeth celebrating Queen Victoria's Diamond Jubilee in 1887, with the Aldington band

every person a glass of wine after dinner to drink the Queen's health. The following gentlemen carved, The Vicar (Revd. J.T. Pearse), Messrs Weekes, Andrews, Hammon, Snow, Pearson, Pilcher and Palmer. These were the waiters, Messrs F. Apps, F. Palmer, E and F. Hammon, N. Weekes, T. Hogben, T. Foat, Messrs Apps and Edwards distributed the beer.

"In the afternoon various games and sports were indulged in including a cricket match (married v. single) and foot races under the management of Messrs J.H. Pearse (Curate), Edwards and N. Weekes (Judge). The Band of the Oxfordshire Regiment played a selection of music during the afternoon. The school children 200 in number [a very large number] had their tea at 4 o'clock, at 5 o'clock a public tea was provided, at which the following ladies presided, Mrs. Pearse, Hammon, Snow, Pearson, Apps, Finn, Charlton, Hughes and Miss Pilcher, and these were waited upon by 9 young ladies, Miss Pearse (3), D'Ombrain, Pilcher, Apps, Rolfe, Palmer (2).

"At 9 o'clock a display of fireworks took place, and at 10 a monster bonfire was lighted on the downs.

"Mr. Worrell was general stock keeper and director of helpers. At the final meeting of the Committee a Balance of £1.17.8 was shown and this it was agreed to give to the Fund of the National School. The Honorary Secretary Mr. Worrell was directed to draw up this account of the day's proceedings to be entered in the parish vestry book for the information of future generations.

Walter Andrews, Churchwarden
John M. Pilcher, Guardian
J.T. Pearse, Vicar
Geo. J Pearson, Overseer
Robert Foat [whom we know was also an Overseer]"

## KING GEORGE V'S SILVER JUBILEE

In May 1935, almost 50 years after Queen Victoria's Golden Jubilee, King George V's Silver Jubilee was also marked with celebrations in which the church played a part. The following press cutting dated 1935 filed in the Parish Notes of the Reverend C.R.L. McDowall gives a lovely picture of the day's events.

"The celebration began with the Thanksgiving Service at the Church [not clear whether this was at Smeeth or Brabourne]: the service was taken by the Vicar and Mr. G. Ashman read the lessons. The collection, £1 12s 2d, was sent to the King George's Jubilee Trust. The afternoon was delightfully bright and warm and the village gathered in full force to enjoy the day. First came the children's sports, managed by members of the Y.P.F., and tea at which Jubilee Mugs were presented to them by Mrs. McLean and Mrs. Macdonald. Prizes for the sports were presented by Mrs. Cameron and Mrs. McDowall. The tree planted to mark the day was then 'unveiled' by Mr. Miller [possibly Cowley Miller of Court Lodge] after a short speech from the Vicar. More than 250 shared in the general tea in the Hall, which was admirably managed by the Women's Institute. Then followed an amusing Gymkhana; at 8 p.m. the King's speech was broadcast in the Hall; at 10 p.m. the bonfire was lit under Mr. F. Howland's direction, after which there was dancing in the Hall, till 1.30 a.m. So everybody went home feeling loyal and happy."

## THE CORONATION OF QUEEN ELIZABETH II

Programme of events in the village celebrations

*PROGR*

| | |
|---|---|
| **7 a.m.** | BRABOURNE. Holy Communion. |
| **8 a.m.** | SMEETH. Holy Communion. |
| **9.30 a.m.** | BIRCHOLT. Holy Communion. |
| **10 a.m.** | TELEVISION. Smeeth Institute.<br>TELEVISION. Brabourne Hall. |
| **2.30 p.m.** | OPENING OF PLAYING FIELD at Smeeth Ridgeway followed by SPORTS. |
| **3.30 p.m.** | CHILDREN'S TEA in Smeeth School. |
| **4.30— 6 p.m.** | TEAS FOR ALL in Smeeth School. |
| **7 p.m.** | WHIST DRIVE on Playing Field. |
| **8 p.m.— 1 a.m.** | GALA DANCE in Brabourne Village Hall. |

**FRIDAY, MAY 29th.** DISTRIBUTION OF CORONATION PLATES to All Children 15 and under, in Smeeth and Brabourne Schools, during the afternoon.

-------

*Free Transport for Older People to the Playing Field on application to the Secretary, Lyndhurst, Smeeth. Tel. No. Sellindge 2219.* Free Car Park near Playing Field.

ICES.          SIDESHOWS.          MUSIC.

*AMME*

# SPORTS

*To be run in the following order :*

| **BOYS** | | **GIRLS** | |
|---|---|---|---|
| | *up to* | | *up to* |
| 50 Yards Flat | 5 years | 50 Yards Flat | 5 years |
| * do. | 6 years | * do. | 6 years |
| * do. | 7 years | * do. | 7 years |
| * do. | 8 years | * do. | 8 years |
| * do. | 9 years | * do. | 9 years |
| * 100 Yards Flat | 10 years | * 100 Yards Flat | 10 years |
| * do. | 11 years | * do. | 11 years |
| do. | 12 years | do. | 12 years |
| do. | 13 years | do. | 13 years |
| do. | 14 years | do. | 14 years |
| do. | 15 years | do. | 15 years |
| do. | 16 years | do. | 16 years |
| * 3-Legged Race | 11 years | * 3-Legged Race | 11 years |
| do. | 16 years | do. | 16 years |
| * Sack Race | 11 years | * Sack Race | 11 years |
| do. | 16 years | do. | 16 years |
| * High Jump | 11 years | * High Jump | 11 years |
| do. | 16 years | do. | 16 years |
| * Relay Race 4 x 100 yards | | * Relay Race 4 x 100 yards | |

(BRABOURNE SCHOOL v. SMEETH SCHOOL)

*continued overleaf*

Smeeth & Brabourne

TUESDAY, JUNE 2nd, 1953

CORONATION 1953

SILVER AND GOLDEN JUBILEES OF QUEEN ELIZABETH II

On Tuesday, 7th June, 1977 – 42 years after King George V's Silver Jubilee and 90 years after Queen Victoria's Golden Jubilee – the nation celebrated the Silver Jubilee of Queen Elizabeth II. The local celebrations for this were an elaborate affair, involving the villages of Brabourne and Smeeth, as the following account suggests. The souvenir booklet produced for the event gives no indication that the church played any significant role in their organisation, though the PCC Minutes for 16th May, 1977, record that, "A special form of service had been published to commemorate the Queen's Silver Jubilee and it was decided to use this on Sunday June 5th at 10 o'clock." The villages clearly had a splendid day, in spite of the weather.

Reproduction of the booklet entitled A Souvenir of the Brabourne and Smeeth Celebrations:

"This booklet is an attempt to record our village celebrations to commemorate the Silver Jubilee of Her Majesty, Queen Elizabeth II on Tuesday, 7th June, 1977.

"The following is an account of the events of that day to which everyone responded so magnificently. No individual names are mentioned as so many people helped in so many different ways it would be impossible to include them all.

"The biggest problem looked as if it was going to be the weather. After weeks without rain we had a truly British Bank Holiday Monday, cold and drizzly. The morning of Tuesday, 7th June, however, turned out bright and sunny, if windy, and, despite a poor weather forecast, there were only a couple of showers throughout the afternoon. True, it could have been a lot warmer but, as everyone said, 'As long as it keeps dry, we don't mind.'

"Much preparation went on in the morning, with some people no doubt having very hurried lunches, but everything was ready on time.

"The first event was to be the children's fancy dress competition so, at 13.15 hours, clutching the free printed programme each household had been given, we duly gathered on the Warren Green.

"The response to this competition was quite overwhelming, in the number, originality and sheer professionalism of some of the entries. Mums and Dads must have racked their brains and stitched, glued and painted into the small hours.

"There were three age classes in the competition plus a prize for the most original costume and also prizes for the best dressed boy's and girl's bike. Each competitor, and there were approximately a hundred, also received a ten pence entry prize.

"Congratulations to all who took part on some truly wonderful creations and also congratulations to the judges for sheer nerve in choosing the winners. Chosen they were however, and the prizes having duly been presented by the Jubilee Princess (who had, herself, been chosen a few weeks previously), it was time to form up for the procession to the Village Hall and Jubilee field opposite for the rest of the festivities.

"Lees Road having been closed by the police, the procession set off headed by a motorcade. First came a tractor-drawn float, carrying the Jubilee Princess and her two attendants, followed by some veteran cars with suitably attired drivers and finally came the children walking in their costumes and riding their decorated bikes.

"What a splendid sight we were! I cannot say that the number of spectators en route rivalled those in the Mall but they seemed very impressed, as did a herd of cows in a field alongside who escorted the procession as far as they could before gazing over the hedge in amazement as the 'tail' went by.

"And so we arrived at the Village Hall, resplendent with its new flag and flagstaff, and turned into the field opposite for the rest of the afternoon's celebrations.

"The start of the children's races was delayed by a sudden downpour and the programme was curtailed somewhat. However, there were flat races, three-legged races, wheelbarrow races and egg and spoon races for all age groups, with prizes and badges for the first three in each race. By popular request, races for males and females over fourteen were also included.

"All this activity might have kept the children warm but the adults, fearing the effects of exposure, made a bee-line for the tea stall and the hot dog barbecue. We had not seen 'Scott of the Antarctic' on T.V. the night before for nothing.

"Suitably fortified, a tour of the side-shows and competitions could begin, starting of course with a visit to the raffle table.

"There were stalls to buy plants, 'antiques', handicrafts and sweets and rock. There were competitions too numerous to mention. There were rides for the children on a model engine or a donkey. There was a display of British Army cap badges and a passing 'Romany lady' pitched her tent and offered to read our palms.

"Outside the Village Hall all the competitors' work in the children's art competition was on display, unfortunately some of it spoilt by the weather. The subject for the picture was 'The Jubilee and/or The Royal Family' and a staggering 180 entries had been received. These were divided into four sections with two prizes in each section. A special group prize for a combined picture was also awarded, the prizes being presented by the Jubilee Princess at the end of the afternoon.

"Looking out over the field, it seemed as if the entire population of Brabourne and Smeeth, reckoned to be around 3,000, was present.

"Most of the ladies and some gentlemen contrived to wear something red, white and blue and a few, more adventurous, wore period costume. There was even a rumour that one mysterious visitor was Danny La Rue gracing us with his/her presence.

"We had the benefit of a public address system throughout the afternoon, both for providing music for our entertainment and for announcing succeeding events.

"Perhaps the most eagerly awaited announcement was the call to the children that it was time to collect their free tea. Four hundred of these individually packed meals, together with drinks of squash, had been provided and seemed to disappear with great alacrity. It had been arranged for the children to have a picnic tea on the field so that the Village Hall could be available for the over sixties of the villages to have their free tea 'sitting comfortably'.

"A coach had been provided so that any pensioner needing it could have free transport to the hall and over a hundred people had been catered for. The tables were very tastefully laid out and a magnificent iced cake had been provided as a grand finale to a very appetizing meal. This was eaten to a piano accompaniment and afterwards a rousing sing-song was enjoyed by all. The over sixties who were house-bound or unable to attend the party were not forgotten as they each had a 'tea' delivered to their door.

"Meanwhile, back at the field, four teams of stalwarts were competing in a tug-of-war competition which was the final event before the Grand Draw.

"We all gathered round for the results of this before a final shower sent us scurrying home at 17.00 hours, leaving the more dedicated to clear up the field.

"The last event of the day was a dance in the evening at the Village Hall to the music of 'Moonshine'. This was also a sell-out and rounded off the day, at least for the more energetic, which had been such a success. Enough money had been raised by the draw and the side-shows to easily cover the expenses still outstanding, even after all the generous donations previously received.

"I am sure it was not only the children who slept soundly in their beds that night. It had been quite a day.

"Well done Brabourne and Smeeth! Thanks to a really united effort our Silver Jubilee celebrations turned out to be a right royal success.

"The credit for this must go to the committee, all the village societies and the associations, the tradespeople and the innumerable individuals who helped. Between them they not only gave financial aid but provided the goods for sale, the food and prizes plus the time and effort needed to organise and plan 'our day'.

"We were a bit late getting started but we certainly got there in the end so a big thank you to everyone concerned, not forgetting our Queen whose Jubilee gave us the opportunity to show that we can still rise to an occasion."

Dave and Maggie Horswell – dressed for the occasion

Remembering the day, Pauline Anderson (Marsh) recalled Dave Horswell being involved with parking cars for the event. Getting into the spirit of the day, Dave had dressed up as a woman and was looking very much the part, directing cars to parking spaces with very pronounced actions. Seeing him from afar and not recognising him, Jock Anderson was heard to mutter, "Give a woman a bit of power and just see how it goes straight to her head!"

## IMAGINATION IN SOCIAL LIFE AND ENTERTAINMENT IN THE VILLAGES

Joy Finn's recollections of social life in her early years revolved around Brabourne School. This was in the second decade of the 20th century and Christmas parties, whist drives, dances and other similar social events for the village were all held at the school, largely because this was a suitable venue. Joy recalled that in the days leading up to such an event, Finn's cart (Leonard Finn was the builder) would go round picking up tables from people in the village; in this way, then, everyone helped to bring such events together. Even as the years progressed we see imagination and inventiveness in the ways in which people entertained themselves. Leisure was not the industry it is today, so often packaged and provided for us. First, we look at the recollections of what children used to get up to.

## HOW CHILDREN AND YOUNG PEOPLE ENJOYED THEIR LEISURE

On a daily basis, children entertained themselves playing with friends, playing in the fields, cycling and, predictably, playing games such as football, rounders, cricket and others, which drew on their own imaginative and inventive powers and cost absolutely nothing, or very little, in financial terms. An important summer leisure activity was swimming in the lake at Hatch Park and, although it was mostly boys who would do this, Phil Stone remembers Joy and Betty Finn and Pat (Patricia) Aldrich swimming there during the Second World War. Phil was friendly with the gamekeeper at Hatch Park and had a permit to fish in the lake, along with other boys from the grammar school, including Eric Jenner and Oliver Trowell, and from time to time, they were joined by Pat who, allegedly was quite a tomboy. Sally Bulgin, Pat's daughter, confirmed that her mother, who was an only child, was full of fun and always ready to have a go at anything. She loved parties, games, dancing, horse riding, and Sally recalls Pat talking about enjoying pole-vaulting over hedges in the snow during wintertime with the boys.

We have heard time and again of the liberty that our contributors had when they were children. They all had to help with chores but when at play the seemed able to go more or less where they wished – John and Audrey Hammon's recollections of when they were children testify to this.

John's memories of the 1940s, when he was about 10, are of boys and girls often playing together, going up to woods on the Downs and building camps, climbing trees, or generally wandering about:

"Heading down to the millpond or the streams we would dam up the water and possibly paddle on a warm summer's day, trying to catch sticklebacks or some other small fish. The boys usually had catapults and later we all had air guns. Up until the war (1939-45), we played games like cops and robbers, but the war heightened our awareness of British-German hostilities and saw us running around with our arms outstretched, pretending to be Spitfires or German aeroplanes.

John Hammon

"At haying or during harvest holidays we would go into fields and help with these tasks. I remember driving the tractor when I could only just reach the pedals to move up the trailers for the men who were loading sheaves of corn. Or being put up on the trailer or horse-drawn wagon to stack the sheaves, usually with someone else to see it was done correctly, or else the load could slip off. We particularly liked it when the corn was being cut, as we used to chase the rabbits that emerged from the small piece of standing corn in the middle of the field. Catching a rabbit meant a welcome rabbit pie in wartime, when rationing limited what food was available to us."

Audrey Hammon

Audrey Hammon writes: "Playing at 'houses' in the garden with my younger sister, and arguing with her, are things I do remember, but my main memories of childhood are of being outside, helping at Milbank Farm, Ruckinge, on Romney Marsh. [Digressing for a moment, Milbank Farm was unusual in that the parish boundary ran through the house. Audrey's bedroom and that side of the house was in Ruckinge while her parents and sister slept in the Newchurch side of the house. There were even two boundary stones in each side of the house.]

"As I progressed through school I would have had homework, which I hated, always preferring to help with the animals. We had lots of poultry and eventually I looked after them. I remember the ducks never coming to the cage to be fed and shut in when I whistled, as they were always too busy along the water-filled ditches. We had to shut them in at night to avoid foxes and so that they would lay their eggs for us.

"I was always interested in wild flowers and would spend ages finding them and then identifying them. I loved reading, but I had few books, other than a set of Arthur Mee's Children's Encyclopedias. I spent a great deal of time reading these but, as an outdoor girl, I was not interested in history, chemistry or the like. I had pet rabbits, some of which I sold for meat and pocket money for me. Later, taking over from my father, I kept ferrets for hunting rabbits. In my mid-teens I played tennis with friends in the village at Ruckinge. Being teased and teasing some of the men who worked on the farm was always good fun."

Bryan Hodges remembers that there wasn't a tree in Hatch Park that he couldn't climb. He believes that children these days who do not make dens, tents or climb

Bryan Hodges

trees are losing much of the fun to be had in life. In the 1950s and 1960s traffic on the roads was so light that children regularly played football in the streets. Along Lees Road, Bryan recalls, "You might have to stop your game for a car to pass, but that didn't happen very often." In regard to children's self-entertainment, Bryan also added that, in the 1950s, when the Guides had their summer camps in Hatch Park, the boys used to get great delight from letting the guy ropes down.

Digressing for a moment about Mersham le Hatch, Lady Brabourne told us about the antiquity of the estate. The woodlands are some of the oldest in the area, and Bockhanger Wood, which is situated between the house and the A20, contains hornbeams thought to be up to 1,000 years old, making up part of the ancient forest covering Kent. The house at Mersham le Hatch (Hatch meaning gate) was built in the 1760s and, at that time, was on the main road. It is thought that the road, now the A20, was moved away from the house in the 1800s. New House in Mersham, the present home of Lady Brabourne, is even older than Mersham le Hatch, having been built in 1705.

Being accustomed to buildings of such antiquity, it is not surprising that Lady Brabourne, who was evacuated to New York during the war, found everything very new. She recalls a school outing to see the oldest church in New York, which prompted much excitement among her fellow pupils. She, too, was intrigued, and when they arrived at what Lady Brabourne described as "a pleasant Victorian church", she asked, quite unawares, where this ancient church was, only to be told, "This is it!" Lady Brabourne returned to England after she had left school to join the Wrens (Women's Royal Naval Service).

Margaret Pile (Ward) remembers the way she and her family used to spend their summer holidays:

"Between 1936 and 1939 our mother would escort us on a three-mile walk to Mill River, between Smeeth Station and Evegate Mill, to picnic, and swim in the river. This was much enjoyed by all the villagers but was stopped when one four-year-old nearly drowned and a 13-year-old was almost killed by a flying glass bottle. In 1940 several of the village children were evacuated – a coach load went to Torquay – and life was quiet. We couldn't go down to the seaside as the beaches in Kent had been mined and covered with barbed wire – a veritable tier of it, two rolls wide at the base and more on top – to prevent the Germans from landing and coming up the beaches. Later, a great deal of this wire was dumped in what was then a sandy hollow to the left of Woolpack Hill, on the way up. As a consequence, we used to walk in Hatch Park on Sunday afternoons, and later, when we had cycles, we used to have family outings on these to save petrol.

Margaret Pile (Ward), right, and her sister, Rosemary Hendry (at the Battle of Britain Memorial at Capel)

"We attended Sunday School at the Bethel Baptist Chapel, and later at Smeeth Church. With these we had an annual outing to Margate or Dymchurch in the years both before and after the war. There was no playing field in the villages at that time but Mr Ames (senior) would allow us to use his field for our sports, which we arranged between ourselves."

Edward Ames actually donated the field to Smeeth School for their sports. He was very interested in the school and later was on the board of governors. According to Margaret, "the field was also used for the Victory Sports Celebrations, and later the village playing field was donated by Lord and Lady Brabourne". John Jamieson recalled the immense amount of village effort that had gone into clearing and levelling the field. Tom Jeanes spent many hours there on his tractor, digging up brambles and levelling the ground, and even small boys picked up stones, including thousands of flints, in order to make the site usable – especially for football. John was one of many who used to pick up flints, so cruel to footballers' knees, but just to show that nature is in charge, more flints have since worked themselves to the surface, making life for today's footballers difficult. Back to Margaret…

"On dark winter evenings, my mother would play the piano. School friends would come in and we all used to sing. We also learnt how to dance the tango and quickstep, after which we were allowed to go to Bert Mills's dances and join the crowd of soldiers at the village hall."

Margaret and Pat Cornell remembered always being busy as children, finding things to do that were fun and that might also make some pocket money in the process. They used to pick blackberries from both ends of the Plain, to the right of Andrews Garage, and the WI would make jam with the fruit. They would also collect jam jars for the WI and got a ha'penny a dozen for their efforts. Doing shopping for old people would sometimes earn them a farthing and then they would go to Baxter's sweet shop, and before that, Merrit's (later Goreham's) to spend their earnings. Margaret recalls, "We were rationed to 2oz of sweets a week during the war, the equivalent of a small Mars bar. Crisps were very scarce and there were no ice creams at all. A sixpence had some value in the 1940s and choosing the sweets was as much fun, if not more, than eating them."

When she lived at the Moors (now Idenborough) as a child in the 1940s, Betty  Dryland (Lavender) would walk up the lane towards the Downs and Miss Powell's house (now Brabourne House on Pilgrims' Way), and remembers the route being full of wild flowers during the spring and summer time. Betty describes the school holidays as wonderful and timeless: she would go out after breakfast every morning and, together with her friends, would make camps, pick watercress in West Brabourne's streams and go for walks on the Downs. They would return home for lunch and then continue their play all afternoon and until suppertime. Memories of almost all of our contributors followed a similar pattern, depicting the immense freedom they had to enjoy their leisure hours out of doors during their childhood.

Betty Dryland

Thought to be celebrations for the opening of the playing fields in the early 1950s. Standing on the lorry are, from left, Ronnie Martin, the Reverend Thompson-Evans, Dr Bradbury? and Tom Jeanes

On her way back from Brabourne School to The Street each day, Jackie Finn (Davis) would call in at Forge Cottage to spend time with the forge horses. In the 1950s, Penstock Farm used to grow peas for Batchelors Foods, so another after-school activity for Jackie, her sisters Rosemary and Margaret, and Pauline Anderson (Marsh) was to wander through the fields, picking up peas that had been dropped during harvest and

eating them. Camaraderie and community spirit were strong in those days and Pauline recalls playing day after day with her friends in the Bates's woods on top of the Downs, above East Brabourne. In particular, she can remember playing Market Gardens with Susan Todd, digging up bluebells and replanting them in rows. As Pauline remarked, "the Market Garden was a big influence in our lives at that time".

Jackie Finn

Karl Engels, who lived at The Knoll between the village hall and the shops, can remember trying to impress Mabel Brooks on one occasion when they were at Waterside Farm: he told her with considerable

Pauline Anderson

confidence that he could catch a trout by tickling it. Much to his surprise, and probably Mabel's too, the tickling approach worked. Karl also recalls that he didn't get on very

well with Beeb (pronounced Bibi, though her name was May) Knight and, on one occasion, when her provocation had become unbearable, he swung his shoe bag at her – Beeb ducked and the bag instead hit Rose Brooks, a good friend of Karl's, in the face. To this day he still feels bad about hurting Rose.

Children were imaginative in their play and Margaret (Maggie) Horswell (Wratten) seems to have been more inventive than most. Maggie loved anything to do with the medical profession and, one Christmas, after receiving a nurse's outfit from her parents, all sorts of imaginings

Karl Engels

seemed to be let rip. One incident, when she was six and fully confident in her ability

Maggie Horswell (Wratten)

as a medical practitioner, saw Maggie decide to play at being a dentist with her elder brother, Tom. She persuaded him to open his mouth, wedged it open with two pieces of wood and, with a handy pair of pliers, pulled out one of his teeth – much to his horror and misery and the disbelief of their parents. Clearly, the lack of high-tech toys was no hindrance to enjoying play for any of our contributors.

Returning home from Brabourne Church one Sunday, Tom Wratten decided to climb one of the walnut trees that then stood near the gates of Penstock Farm "to shake down some walnuts". Tom was dressed in his Sunday best, which included the first pair of long trousers he had ever had – and which his mother had impressed upon him "had cost a lot of money", so he was not to get them dirty. However, as he was up the tree shaking down walnuts, a bird scarer went off. Tom thought he had been shot at and jumped out of his skin, causing him to fall out of the tree. His first thoughts were not for his own safety but for his trousers, which he was sure must have been ruined. Reaching home he was in a terrible state but, unbeknown to him and Maggie, their parents had been watching events unfold and were barely able to contain themselves at what they saw. In his panic Tom confessed and received a telling off, but imagine his relief to discover that not only had he not been shot, but his trousers were still in one piece.

Tom Wratten

In another tale of mischief, Tim Marsh and his brother Alec, aged about 11 to 12 years old, were walking past the Five Bells one day, "flicking" a box of matches. (For those of you who have never done this, flicking involves holding a match vertically against the matchbox with two fingers, the head against the striking strip. The match is then flicked with the other hand in attempt to light it.) Most times the boys were unsuccessful and the match didn't even light, or if it did, it would just travel a foot or so, but on one occasion the match did ignite and took off, landing in the hedge opposite the houses in The Street. The boys carried on walking but soon heard crackling and, on turning around, were horrified to see flames shooting out of the hedge. In minutes the fire had spread from just past the Five Bells some 50yd or so to Subdown Cottages and it seemed to Tim that, in an instant, every door in that part of The Street opened simultaneously and people came flying out with bowls of water. The boys rushed home for sacks to smother the flames and very soon the fire had been put out. Tim recalled that it caused an awful mess and "from the pub to the council houses, everyone was black with cinders". One of the local residents congratulated Tim's father, saying "Well done, Charlie! Your lads really worked well. You should be proud of them." Charlie could only smile and accept the praise, all the while knowing full well that it had unfortunately been his boys who had set the hedge alight.

Holidays were few but sometimes the Davis family would go away to Doddington. Once they went by train to Chester. This event was made even more memorable as Elsie bought all three girls camel coats and red felt hats, making them feel extremely smart. It was only when they were older that they started dressing differently. The same red hats were worn on another trip to London, when the wind was strong and the hat of one of the girls blew off and into the road. They thought it was the end of the hat but several taxis came to a halt so that it could be retrieved.

Back in The Street there were frequently games of cricket or tennis, after which bats, racquets and balls would be left out in the road overnight, undisturbed by traffic. Kath Spain remembers how lovely it was that there were so many children in The Street in the late 1950s – "It was wonderful to watch them all playing." Among them was her own son, Barry, and her two nieces; Norman Thornby's children; the Marsh household, which included Pauline and her four brothers, Alec, Peter, Tim and Derek; Anthony Finn, Jackie Davis (later Finn), Margaret and Rosemary Davis, the Todds, the Friends, John and Bobby Smith – and Betty Barr, who may have been slightly older, and who used to torment Anthony when he was a small boy, for a time making his life a misery. But the modern world was beckoning and awareness of and enthusiasm for TV was growing. Anthony recalls that he and his many friends used to call in on people who had TVs, keeping friendly with them so that they could watch key events such as the football.

Talking of children at play, Jackie and Andrew Fortescue write:

"In the late 1950s Alfred Fortescue bought a donkey for his grandchildren, which they kept in the orchard opposite their house (where Warren Heights now stands). On one occasion when the hunt went through the village, Dobbin the donkey decided that he wanted to follow and jumped over the fence and set off down the road. Luckily, May Fortescue, Gordon's wife, saw him go, jumped on her bike and managed to catch him on Canterbury Road.

Dobbin the donkey, with Carol Pack (Fortescue)
on the right

"Dobbin was a very noisy donkey and used to bray every time he saw one of the family approaching. The neighbours hated this and May and Gordon received a letter from the council asking them to keep the donkey quiet. Alfred wrote back suggesting that if the council could recommend a suitable silencer he would happily fit it. It was suggested that he find a companion for Dobbin to keep him quiet and so Alfred bought an old seaside donkey that was due to be retired. This docile donkey, peace itself, had never brayed in its life, but it wasn't long before Dobbin had taught it everything he knew."

Carol Lightfoot (Hobbs) lived at Home Farm on the A20 and is yet another who remembers the happiest of childhoods. By way of background Carol's great-grandfather Frank Hobbs rented Home Farm from the Hatch Estate, as he was Lord Brabourne's agent. As its name suggests, it was, at that time, the Home Farm for the

Home Farm, Smeeth (1908)

Hatch Estate. In 1918 Frank bought the farm as the Estate needed to raise money to pay death duties following the First World War, and although Robert Hobbs's family still own the farm, Home Farm house on the A20 has been sold.

Home Farm was well known for its beautiful cherry orchards along the A20, just behind where the Blue and White Café now stands, and on the opposite side of the road more orchards of apple and plum. These were planted in 1934, but are now long gone. The farm originally produced milk from 200 dairy cows and Mr Field, the farm manager, would wake a team of boys up for work at 3am every day to milk the cows by hand. The milk was then transported from the farm to Smeeth Station and taken by train to Ramsgate. Mixed farming was common up to the 1970s, and Home Farm also kept sheep, pigs, bullocks, white Leghorn hens, grew corn, vegetables and daffodils for bulb production. When there was a frost, Robert used to light lamps under the fruit trees. The cherry and apple pickers went up very tall ladders, which were broader at the base than the top, to pick. Moving these ladders was not a job for the faint-hearted and was usually done by Mick Hover and Bert Thornby, who worked at Home Farm from the age of 14 until he retired at 65. Both lived in the village. Bert also milked the house cow and, if the children were cheeky, he would squirt milk from a teat at them.

Carol and her sisters had ponies for as long as she could remember and a typical day in the summer holidays involved riding, rather racing, through Hatch Park with her sisters and friend Di Castle (Ames) to Joe Farm on the Ridgeway, where they had more friends, continuing into Brabourne Lees to Baxter's sweet shop, calling in at Ames' Stores to say "hallo", continuing to Bircholt to see the Jeanes family, and then rushing back for lunch because her mother, Sheila, always insisted that the girls must be back promptly for meal times. When they were on their ponies they always took two old dogs from the farm with them and Carol can remember rushing to get home in time for lunch, crossing the A20 at speed, and leaving the two dogs to cross the road themselves. She winces at the thought of this now, but the dogs always got back safely, mainly because there was so much less traffic on the A20 than there is today. Carol's days were also occupied playing tennis, swimming in the pool at Home Farm, which had been dug by German prisoners of war, playing cowboys and Indians on ponies and games such as Old Ma, in which whoever was Old Ma would make the others do horrible things. The girls used to ride through the woodland at Home Farm where their father, Robert, grew Christmas trees; they would also ride to Evegate, and once there would continue through the hay and straw stack yard to the big 60-acre wood, much of which has now gone. Something that remains committed to memory is the scent of the wild garlic as they jumped the streams. John and Jim Martin, cousins from Evegate who had been taught to ride by Ted Pile, were frequent visitors at Home Farm. John, in particular, would come round on his pony every day in the holidays, always wearing the same clothes: the same grey shirt, same trousers and filthy plimsolls. What fun they all had together. Life was idyllic, made up of the stuff of storybooks, and tea with the Ameses and

Ted Pile, who looked after the horses at Evegate Farm

Jeaneses was certainly part of the idyll. While the children ate a delicious tea prepared by Megan Ames, Di's mother, Basil, her father, would keep the assembled group captivated with the most wonderful stories. (Both Basil and his father, Edward, were renowned for their talent for storytelling by those who worked at Ames' Stores.)

One of the highlights of the summer holidays was the Mersham Hatch gymkhana, which was run by George Swaffer, Miss Diana from Caldicott and Robert Hobbs. The event started off with showing the ponies, then jumping, then games, including musical sacks, which involved getting off your pony as quickly as possible when the music stopped and running to the nearest sack.

Like all children of that era, Carol, her sisters and their friends entertained themselves and were always out of doors. They went "blackberrying" and "sweet chestnutting", the sweet chestnuts being in Hatch Park. However, Robert Hobbs used to recall Lord Brabourne telling them that, "The chestnuts in Hatch Park were for children from the village, not for those from big farms."

The freedom that Carol and her siblings experienced was far more than children have today. They were told never to take sweets from people they didn't know, but that was all, and Carol recalls that she simply met no nasty people in her young life.

Carol (Hobbs) and Robin Lightfoot (Dec 2012)

Although we have been focusing on children and the way they enjoyed themselves, clearly it wasn't just children who rode for pleasure. Many adults did too, not least John and Vi Varrier who enjoyed the challenges of hunter trials. John explained that, unlike show jumping where the jumps had all been constructed, hunter trialling involved jumping over natural features in the landscape, even though these might have been dressed for the event. Vi has also had endless pleasure from driving her pony and trap - and, aged 80+ is still driving.

Several local farmers kept horses to hunt with the East Kent Foxhounds, notably Ronnie Martin at Evegate, Tom Jeanes at Bircholt, Robert Hobbs at Home Farm and Reg Older at Penstock. In early autumn the horses would be seen walking or trotting round the village roads, being "got fit" for the coming season.

From top, John and Vi Varrier taking part in hunter trials
in the 1970s

Vi Varrier driving her pony and trap

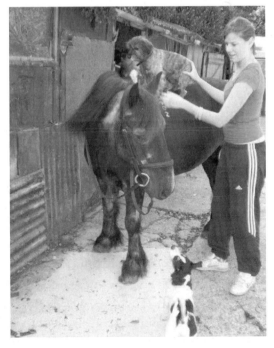

Ellie Hutchison with Vi's driving pony, Buster (2009)

Returning to children at play, in the 1960s Will Wilson and his cousin Caroline Hendry (Payne) used to love going to Granny Ward's to have ginger beer. She would invariably give them 6d and they would go straight to Goreham's to buy a penny box of Ship matches and sweets with the remaining 5d. There was a laurel hedge just behind Ward's Garage and the two of them would sit together there making a fire and eating their sweets. Caroline added that they would sometimes cook eggs on their fire. With hindsight, Will cringes at the potential danger of this so near the garage.

Will used to love going to steam-engine rallies at Elham. He was so enchanted by these engines that he determined to make one and asked his grandpa (E.F. Ward, owner of the garage) if he might have a five-gallon drum. He got an old cart and mounted the drum on it, filled it with the best coal from Granny Ward's, set it alight, and, assisted by his cousin Steven Pile, proudly rolled the steam engine, which was belching smoke, down to show Grandpa at the petrol pumps. Will remembers his grandfather saying, rather nervously, "You children had best move away with that."

Recollections from the 1930s to the 1960s were that children always had the liberty to play, shout, fight and enjoy their youth without much fear of traffic (there were only about three cars in East Brabourne in the 1930s and just a few more in Brabourne Lees and Smeeth). As our contributors have regularly described, the physical freedom that children enjoyed was considerable. People felt safe largely because the concept of feeling unsafe was not as prevalent as it is now, and mothers were quite content to let their children go out to play all day, while they got on with labour-intensive household chores. Despite memories of idyllic childhood days of endless play, several people remarked on how anything unusual and away from the mundane always provided great excitement. George Hickmott remembers a circus coming down Canterbury Road late one night, probably coming cross-country from Canterbury to Hythe. Waking up with the noise, he remembers watching animals he had never seen before trundle their way across the Kent countryside in trucks.

HELPING WITH HOUSEHOLD CHORES – A PRECONDITION FOR PLAY
All our contributors also remember having to help with chores in the house or in the garden, or – as we heard in Chapter 9 – if they were part of a farming family, on the farm. Norman Thornby's life as a boy at Hope Farm was testimony to the latter, and Vi Varrier (Kingston) has also spoken of having chores to do on her father's farm – girls were in no way exempt. Once they had completed their tasks most were free to play as they wished. The ones who had the least liberty, though, seemed to be the older girls of larger families who also had to help with looking after their younger brothers and sisters. In the Sawyer household, Nellie Norrington and Margaret Baldock recalled that the four girls had to do specific tasks before they were

allowed out on Saturdays: one would do the dusting, another the polishing, and so on. Their mother always tackled the cobwebs. The boys, Bert, Leslie and David, also had their responsibilities, usually outdoors. One of our contributors was in Ashford Hospital having her tonsils removed when she received a card from her sister saying, "You are very lucky not to be here on washing day. With you away I have it all to do."

Rosemary Hendry describes the typical day of a 10-year-old girl in the school holidays:

"You helped your mother during the morning in the home, running any errands for her and for the neighbours. In the afternoons you were usually free to join your friends, perhaps walking to Fishpond Woods or Hatch Park. If you were lucky enough to own a second-hand cycle you might, perhaps, ride to the Downs and collect watercress from the stream at Bulltown on the journey home. We all enjoyed considerable freedom; there was very little traffic to trouble us."

Housework prior to the 1970s was very labour intensive and, in the pre-war and post-war years, living conditions were difficult. Jean Holmes, who used to live at Highfield in Hampton Lane, and whose father used to work for Dorothy Mills's father, Philip, on Naccolt Farm, one of the Brabourne Estate farms, recalls growing up with housework. Jean's mother died when she was eight years old, so much of the burden of maintaining the house fell on her shoulders. Life became even more difficult for all the family when, several years later, Jean's father developed multiple sclerosis at the age of 46. Jean remembers harvest time, when they had to do battle with the rats in the kitchen, a foe against which many of our contributors agreed "you could never entirely win". Much cooking was done on old kitchen ranges – these have now been modernised but, in the past, they had to be "cleaned" using black lead. This was a dirty job, as was cleaning the flues, and it usually ended up with everything being covered in soot. Lighting fires was a chore and, as they never stayed alight overnight, in winter the house would be stone cold in the morning, often with ice on the inside of the windowpanes. Kath Thornby (White) talked with pleasure about the advent of the Rayburn, which stayed in all night and kept the house warm. Washing was done by hand and items such as nappies would be boiled in a saucepan. It is not surprising, therefore, that Margaret Baldock (Sawyer) and her sister Nellie Norrington agreed that the washing machine was the greatest development of the modern age. And then there was always the ironing – plenty of it – as well as mending, darning, knitting and, for those who could find the time, embroidery. In addition to being "just a housewife", many women worked part-time in and around the village to supplement family incomes. Chores aside, many women enjoyed sewing, knitting, embroidery, cookery and other crafts. Several men admitted to enjoying gardening, as well as walking and being out of doors in the countryside.

John Hickmott's interest in steam engines led him to build several model engines and a track in the garden at his bungalow, Rest Harrow, on Canterbury Road. These were a source of great delight to him for many years.

## HELPING OUTSIDE THE HOME

As a child, Pauline Anderson (Marsh) used to help Tony Norrington with his milk round on a Saturday, but not for money. Interaction between young people and adults, and involvement of the former in the local community, was far greater than it is today. According to Tim Marsh, one of Pauline's elder brothers, children were always encouraged to be useful and helpful. His mother would often take him to visit people in the village, usually old ladies, and while she was having tea, Tim, at five or six years old, was given the job of chopping up sufficient kindling for the old lady's fire for the week ahead. There seem to have been no evident worries that he might injure himself using an axe.

Tim Marsh remembering his "stolen" goose egg

On another occasion, when he was about the same age and the Marsh family were living at Stowting, Tim was sent on an errand to his aunt down Fiddling Lane. Before he left, his aunt gave him an enormous goose egg. Thrilled with this he walked up the lane, carrying his gift with the utmost care, thinking that he would have it for breakfast the next morning. He arrived home and recalls his horror as his mother took one look at him and his egg, took it, broke it and put it straight into a cake she was making. Tim says that he never quite forgave her for that.

Most families were poor and few had the resources to give their children pocket money, so children made the most of any opportunities for earning money. However, for most of our contributors, earning money was rarely the prime objective when they were children, though it was very pleasant to be recompensed for their help. Receiving informal rewards for the part they had played in "real-life activities" often engendered considerable feelings of pride among the recipients. Bryan Hodges would help at the dairy at Bircholt Farm and also at Penstock, and in the school holidays he would help in the woodshed of Mr Heathfield and Mr Spicer. Initially, he thought he was helping for nothing, but was delighted when he was paid for his efforts. He worked for them for three to four years while he was still at school, as well as until he started work after leaving school. Bryan, who lived first in Primrose Cottages in Bulltown Lane, just down the road from Hope Farm, and later in Lees Road in Brabourne Lees, also used to enjoy fishing in the clay pits and going skating on the ponds in the winter. Scrumping apples was another favourite activity and Bryan recalls the dalmatian dogs running loose in the orchards at Pemsey Farm.

Phil Stone, Oliver Trowell, Norman Thornby and others spoke of being free to wander where they wanted as boys and hence grew up with a remarkable knowledge of the environment. Oliver started helping Mr Coleman of Church Farm in East Brabourne when he was about eight years old and the enjoyment and valuable experience he obtained undoubtedly influenced his initial decision to go into farming before training as an artist. Many others like him became close to their environment as a result of play combined with informal work.

## SPORT

It is an acknowledged fact that people were more physically active in the 1920s and 1930s than they are now. Most cycled or walked, and entertainment also involved physical exercise. Phil Stone remembers Brabourne's football and cricket teams, the latter practising regularly at the back of what is now a bungalow called Plovers, but was previously the back of Oswald Ames's yard. Oswald, Frank Howland, Sam Jamieson, Tommy Dodd and Charlie Taylor were among the players and, at one time, Frank was captain, and later chairman, of the Brabourne and Smeeth Football Club. Tommy Dodd was renowned for being a "big hitter" on the cricket pitch, and legend has it that, when he was playing at Mersham le Hatch, he hit the ball over the conker trees bordering the A20. Some of these trees are no more than a memory now as several fell in the storm of October 1987. Frank was also a dedicated cricketer. Michael Hickmott, his grandson, recalls that he was a founder member, captain and, later, vice-chairman of the Mersham and Smeeth Cricket Club, now Mersham le Hatch Cricket Club, and played for both the club and for Kent. Tom Jeanes was also an enthusiastic cricketer and is remembered by John Jamieson for having two cars, which came in very handy when the team needed to attend away games.

Digressing for a moment, Michael remembers Frank as being a natural sportsman:

"He was a good cross-country runner, high jumper and long jumper, and he represented his regiment in these sports. He was also a footballer, cricketer and a goal runner. For many years he captained the Brabourne goal running team. We should add here that goal running was a sport peculiar to east Kent. Evolving in the late 19th century, it became very popular in the first half of the 20th century. It required few

Brabourne's Goal Runners (1920s/early 1930s). Frank Howland is likely
to be among them, but none of the players could be identified

Football team in the 1930s.
Back row: from left, unidentified, Ted Tritton, Burt Dade, Tom Wratten,
and possibly, Cowley Miller. Second row: from left. Stuart Norrington, Jim Marsden,
Frank Howland, unidentified. Front row: from left, Bert Black, Basil Ames, Bert Thornby

Possibly Ashford and District League Winners' presentation at Brabourne and Smeeth village hall (early 1950s). Standing on far left, Frank Howland, and far right, Jock Kitson. Team members: back row, from left, Jo Davis, Dennis Mabbs, Alan Mackay, Alfie Lewis (goal), John Hickmott, S. Southern; Front row, from left, Geoff Brumbridge, Gordon Fortescue, Les Gardener, J. Brumbridge?, John Jamieson

A later Brabourne and Smeeth team. Back row: from left, Rob Hover, John Wood, Bill Foord, Denis Holness, Cyril Buss, Des Gardener. Front row: from left, Keith Taylor, John Jamieson, Les Gardener, Bob Clayson, Alfie Lewis

Brabourne and Smeeth FC with Kentish Express shield, won as champions of Ashford and
District League (1964). Back row: from left, D. Holness (Secretary), A. Lewis, B. Coleman,
A. Elsbury, T. Broughall (captain), T. Lewis, D. Gardener (Treasurer),
E. Andrews (President). Front row, from left, D. Wade, B. Friend,
T. Payne, P. Golding, A. Southern and D. Sawyer.
(Picture courtesy of Kentish Express, May 15 (1964), p9, now part of KM Group)

Mersham le Hatch (MLH) cricket team at MLH cricket ground, (late 1930s).
Possibly Frank Howland (Captain), front row on far right, holding cricket bat; Tommy Dodd,
wearing a cap, is standing on far left, with George Lilley (wearing a cravat) next to him

resources, the players wore no shoes and it was little more than an elaborate form of team tag. Frank was still an active member of this team at the age of 60."

Frank took his role as vice-chairman of the cricket club very seriously and, as a consequence of his contribution to the club, he was made an honorary life member. Michael recalls that the team would play games at the weekend, usually one at home and then one away. The Kent cricketer Leslie Ames also used to play at Mersham le Hatch Cricket Club before his career took off and he became the England wicketkeeper. According to John Jamieson, Leslie was the proud possessor of one of the earliest motorbikes, and Sam Jamieson (John's father) was a regular pillion passenger to away games. The villages were clearly very proud of Leslie's achievements. Frank Ames, a relative of Leslie, was captain and groundsman at Mersham le Hatch Cricket Club for many years.

Inspired by adult enthusiasm for cricket, most children (especially boys) were keen to learn, and Michael Hickmott described his grandfather teaching him how to play. They would set up three stumps and put a handkerchief on the grass – it was Michael's task was to make sure the ball bounced on the handkerchief when he bowled. Practice went on and on until Michael's skill developed, and as a consequence, he too became a cricketer.

## CRICKET TEAS

Sharing her husband's involvement in Mersham le Hatch, Marjorie Howland (together with other helpers) would always make the teas for cricket matches at the

Marjorie Howland

club through the 1950s and 1960s. Michael can still vividly recollect her buttering up to four loaves for sandwiches on a Saturday morning. Cheese and tomato, corned beef and pickle, and cheese and pickle were the preferred fillings, and the piles of sandwiches would be cut into triangles and packed into tins. Cricketers would get a set tea, which included sandwiches, cake, buns, tea and soft drinks, and for that they would pay Marjorie 1/-. The Corona lorry, with its deliveries of soft drinks, would make frequent visits to Glenmere, the Howlands' home in West Brabourne, during the summer months. Additional sandwiches, cakes and buns were sold to the public from the serving hatch in the pavilion.

Michael writes:

"In those days the bottles were made of glass and had a deposit on them to ensure their return to Corona. Woe betide anyone who dropped and smashed a bottle! Marjorie was helped in the tea room by one or more of the other cricketers' wives, who usually ended up doing the washing-up."

Millie Hodges

Millie Hodges played for Mersham le Hatch ladies' team in the 1950s and readily travelled to matches at Bethersden and other nearby villages, one of the major attractions being that they were taken there in Les Bailey's sports car. The ladies' team, which included Margaret and Mabel Ames, succeeded in getting to Canterbury for the cup match. Millie recalled that Margaret was an excellent bowler, though Mabel was less serious in her commitment to the game and simply enjoyed the event. When there was a home match at the cricket ground, the Blue and White Café on the A20 used to provide the teas. Today it is the cricketing wives who provide the teas, Jean Bates being one of many.

The old Blue and White Café on the A20.
(Picture courtesy of John and Katie at the
Blue and White Café)

## "GROWING INTO" SPORT

It was from the age of six to nine that Phil Stone used to go to the field at the back of Oswald Ames's yard to watch the Brabourne team play football every Saturday; sometimes there were matches, sometimes they were just practising. But it wasn't only the Brabourne team that played football. There were numerous games taking place throughout the week, some for smaller boys who were keen players, and some for older enthusiasts who were not in the main Brabourne football team but who simply enjoyed playing football. There were makeshift pitches behind Hill View, opposite the village hall, and also opposite the Five Bells in East Brabourne. Phil stressed that these were the venues for the games of smaller boys and not for the main Brabourne football team.

## CELEBRITY CRICKET MATCHES

David Sawyer and Karen and Ian Bull recalled the three charity cricket matches

Ian and Karen Bull with grandson, Harry

and fêtes held at Mersham le Hatch in the late 1960s and early 1970s. Graham Hill, who rented Broad Oak from the Brabourne Estate for a time in that decade, used to organise a Formula 1 team, which would play against Lord Brabourne's XI. David recalls the Queen (then Princess Elizabeth) watching the cricket and the Duke of Edinburgh playing in Lord Brabourne's team at one of these events, while Prince Charles played for them at another, later, event. At one of the Graham Hill charity cricket matches a very young Karen was rushing to see the original Chitty Chitty Bang Bang car, which was on display; not looking where she was going, she ran straight in front of Graham's car and was nearly run down. She still remembers the severe telling off she received from him for this misdemeanour. The royal family have been much in evidence in the Brabourne area, owing to their close connections with the Brabourne family, so it is no surprise that Ian remembers Prince Philip playing for Mersham le Hatch vs Aldington; a photograph of the event still hangs in the pavilion. John Jamieson added that: "Unfortunately, Prince Philip was out LBW to his first ball, much to the dismay of everyone who had come to watch him play cricket."

PROGRAMME FOR A CHARITY CRICKET MATCH AT MERSHAM LE HATCH, SUNDAY, 21st JULY, 1968

Images on programme: from left, Denny Hulme, Piers Courage and Graham Hill

# THE TEAMS

| G.P. DRIVERS TEAM TO BE SELECTED FROM THE FOLLOWING: | LORD BRABOURNE'S TEAM TO BE SELECTED FROM THE FOLLOWING |
|---|---|
| Denny Hulme, *Capt.* (World Champion) | The Rt. Hon Lord Brabourne |
| Jack Brabham | The Hon Norton Knatchbull |
| Graham Hill | The Hon Michael-John Knatchbull |
| Jochen Rindt | |
| Chris Amon | |
| Bruce McLaren | Malcolm Mair |
| Jo Siffert | Les Wade |
| Jo Bonnier | Tom Jeanes |
| Pedro Rodriguez | Vincent Ball |
| Jacky Ickx | Peter Sillett |
| Jean-Pierre Beltoise | Johnny Haynes |
| Jackie Stewart | W E Jeanes |
| Dickie Attwood | S H Ames |
| Piers Courage | J A Copland |
| Jack Oliver | J L E Smith |
| Charles Lucas | T G Pilcher |
| Vic Elford | |

**UMPIRES:** Stirling Moss: Innes Ireland: Colin Chapman: John Cooper: Peter Jopp: Peter Procter.

**COMMENTATORS:** Raymond Baxter: Robin Richards: Anthony Marsh: Les Leston.

The teams from the 1968 Charity Cricket Match

Brands Hatch Great Britain, 21st July, 1968.
The team for the traditional post-GP cricket match.
Back row: from left, Les Leston, Richard Attwood, Piers Courage, Jochen Rindt, Graham Hill, Charles
Lucas (behind), Pedro Rodriguez. Denny Hulme, Rob Widdows, unidentified.
Front row: Innes Ireland, Bruce McLaren, Chris Amon, Stirling Moss, Colin Chapman.
The Grand Prix Drivers XI lost to Lord Brabourne's XI.

Prince Charles batting for Lord Brabourne's team.  The match made the front page of the
Daily Telegraph (Monday, 22nd July, 1968)

Cricket bat signed by the celebrities at the 1968 match

CHARITY CRICKET MATCH AT MERSHAM LE HATCH, 19th JULY, 1970

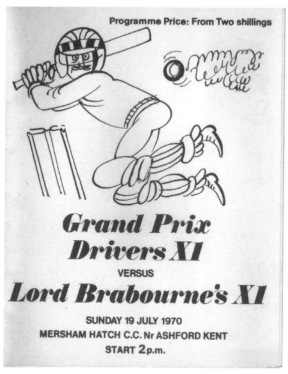

| The Grand Prix Drivers' Team will be selected from: | Lord Brabourne's team will be selected from: |
|---|---|
| Jackie Stewart (Captain) | The Hon Michael-John Knatchbull (Captain) |
| Chris Amon | Vincent Ball |
| J-P Beltoise | Michael Craig |
| Jack Brabham | David Hobbs |
| Peter Gethin | Paddy Hopkirk |
| Dan Gurney | Donald Houston |
| Graham Hill | Innes Ireland |
| Denny Hulme | Tom Jeanes |
| John Miles | Peter Jopp |
| Jackie Oliver | Charles Lucas |
| Henri Pescarolo | Kenny Lynch |
| Jochen Rindt | Tim Schenken |
| Pedro Rodriguez | Peter Sillett |
| Jo Siffert | Henry Taylor |
| John Surtees | Sir John Whitmore |

Umpires : The Hon Gerald Lascelles, Colin Chapman, Peter Procter

Commentators : Anthony Marsh, Robin Richards, Les Leston

The match was organised by Les Leston who would like to thank the following people and organisations for their invaluable assistance : The Ford Motor Company, British Racing and Sports Car Club, Doghouse Club, Autocar, Autosport, Motor, Motoring News, Kent Messenger, Divito Bros, Firestone Tyre and Rubber Co Ltd, Mr and Mrs Les Wade, Michael J Nash, James Kelso

**Tom Jeanes & the Members of Mersham Hatch Cricket Club**

In aid of Springfield Boys' Club and The McIndoe Burns Unit at East Grinstead Hospital

The teams from the Charity Cricket Match, 1970

Graham's presence on the Estate clearly provided popular interest and, on one occasion, he organised a coach trip to Brands Hatch for the Estate workers. David Sawyer, who was working for the Estate at the time, remembers Graham occasionally going into the fields to shoot rabbits and also bringing beer out to the Estate workers during the evenings. Once, after a bad crash, Graham couldn't walk or move easily, but he nevertheless continued shooting – with the gamekeeper's help he put a swivel chair in the back of a Land Rover.

Margaret Baldock remembers the 1968 charity match with much warmth. She bought a ticket from the Scouts (her youngest son claims it as his ticket), and was more than surprised to have won a cricket bat signed by all the celebrities (pictured above).

## ASHFORD CARNIVAL

Phil Stone recalls that Nutty Howland, Frank Howland's father, was landlord of The Plough and, at some time in the 1920s, had a Model T Ford. Phil recalled May Howland and her sister Netty decorating the car for the Ashford Carnival and winning a prize. The old car, he told us, ended its days in a shed behind Frank's tenting shed; it was still there after the war, rotting away.

## ANYONE FOR TENNIS?

In the years prior to the Second World War, the tennis club behind Brabourne Church was extremely popular. Located immediately to the south of the churchyard, in what is now a field of Parsonage Farm, the club had two grass courts and consisted of some 16 members, most from Brabourne and Smeeth. It appears that Cowley Miller from Court Lodge may have been the driving force behind this venture. Subscriptions were not exorbitant or, as Keith Finn mused, he would have remembered, but they were sufficient to enable the members to employ a groundsman, Mr Masterton, who marked out the courts and mowed them regularly. George Hickmott also remembers his father mowing the Brabourne tennis courts at one time. For a decade or so before the war the club thrived. Claude Aldrich, Gordon Fortescue's father and Keith and Rosa Finn (Rosa Varrier at the time) were renowned players who were regularly invited to play tennis matches in Ashford and the nearby villages. Players from Brabourne and Smeeth would meet at the club on summer evenings and play until dusk. Dances and whist drives were held to raise funds for the club, and through these events the tennis club extended to involve the wider community and not just its members.

Keith and Rose shared a love of tennis from their school days and, as mentioned above, were much in demand for local tennis matches. While most people cycled to them, Keith and Rosa were usually transported to theirs by car, a considerable privilege in the early 1930s, when, as we've mentioned, there can't have been many more than three cars in Brabourne. Transport by bus was inconvenient because, as Keith observed, the routes bore no reference to the location of tennis courts and matches. After the war started, though, the courts had to be reclaimed by the farm for food production and there are few people today who remember this once-popular activity in East Brabourne.

The Ames family were also very keen on sport and built a tennis court at Ames' Stores. Here, tennis matches were regularly held with the Triscotts, who lived in the white house opposite The Woolpack, with the Wetherells (Mr Wetherell being the head of Smeeth School), and Trix Gates from Church Farm, Smeeth. Life was very full in those days.

## ON YOUR BIKES

In the post-war years, cycling was still the main form of travel and part of entertainment. In 1950 Oliver Trowell would daily ride to Smeeth crossroads to catch the No 10 bus to Folkestone for the first leg of his journey to Dover, where he was a student at the School of Art. One day the thought "Why stop at Smeeth crossroads?" popped into his head, and he soon started planning a cycle trip all the way to the Mediterranean. On July 10th, at the start of the summer holiday, he set off for Calais from Dover on the Townsend Ferry, Halladale, his bike laden with a tent and panniers.

Within three weeks, having cycled via Arras, Le Cateau, Reims, Chaumont, Dijon, Macon, Lyons, Orange and Avignon, he arrived in Marseilles with a glow of achievement as he set eyes on the Mediterranean ahead. Cycling east along the coast, with thoughts of North Africa across the sea to the south, he was brought down to earth when, beside the railway at Bandol, he saw, chalked on an SNCF fruit wagon, "Not to be worked between Tunbridge Wells and Winchelsea"! No punctures pierced his tyres in France but – alas! – on his return journey, arriving above Monks Horton, he found the road recently resurfaced with cracked beach (cracked / crushed pebbles) and, before reaching Stowting, his front tyre was flat! Mercifully, for those who cycle, cracked beach is no longer used in resurfacing our roads.

Oliver went on to make more long-distance cycle tours, including to north and south Wales, and twice to Anjou. It must be said, of course, the volume of traffic in the 1950s was much smaller and kinder to cyclists than that of today, which made travelling by bike a very enjoyable way to explore the sights, sounds and even the smells of pastures new.

Kenneth Andrews, from Sellindge, was also an avid cyclist:

"Cycling was my primary means of travel, and many miles I did. I now shudder to think of some of the journeys I made and the things I carried. On one, I brought home six Cox's apple trees from Faversham, a 13-mile journey each way. My legs were a bit stiff for the next day or two."

For most people, cycling was more of a local activity. Jean Holmes (Nickolls), who lived in Hampton Lane, used to cycle regularly to The Limes in Weekes Lane at the weekend to see her friend Ruby Harris. Elsie Davis even took their dog to the vet on her bicycle and, on a Saturday, Elsie and the girls (Rosemary, Margaret and Jackie), and Pauline Anderson (Marsh) and her mother would often cycle to Hythe, wander round the town, eat an ice cream on the beach, and then come home. Kath Spain would do much the same, or perhaps go for a longer cycle ride to Dymchurch, with Barry and the girls. They would take sandwiches, lemonade and a flask of tea, and then Kath would buy a packet of hot chips, which all made for a lovely picnic. After church on a Sunday, the Davis family would also cycle to Dymchurch, via Lympne Hill, otherwise known as Jack and Jill hill. A picnic would be packed and on each ride sandwiches would be eaten in the same field gateway on the way there and on the way home. Everyone would cycle, but on one occasion, Margaret was so tired that she went to sleep while cycling and fell off her bike. On Sunday evenings after the Dymchurch trip, the family would often cycle or walk across the fields to the Black Horse at Monks Horton to enjoy lemonade and crisps. Here, they could also watch television – a treat in the late 1950s. On the day of the Queen's coronation (1953), virtually everyone in the area walked or cycled to the village hall, where a large screen had been set up so that rural communities could share in the celebrations.

## MORE ORGANISED ENTERTAINMENT

In the late 1940s the Five Bells used to organise coach outings. One of Tom Wratten's favourites was a trip to the pantomime at the Pleasure Gardens theatre, Folkestone, and afterwards stopping for fish and chips at Sandgate. Other good outings included a trip to the Goodwood Races, to Brighton, and to Drusilla's Zoo Park. The journey home, which could be long for the children, was usually broken when the coach party stopped for tea and to give the children a chance to play. Tom noted that sometimes

Derek Ames

there would be two coaches in convoy, telling us that some 70 adults and children participated in these outings. Everyone loved them and they meant a great deal to the children, who rarely went beyond the village. Living in close proximity to each other and socialising together explains why everyone with whom we spoke knew virtually everyone else in the village at the time – and their life histories.

May Fortescue spoke of the ladies' cards afternoons that were held by the local policeman's wife at the police house shortly after it was built. The games always came to an end when mothers had to pick up their children from school.

Derek Ames recalled "Smoking Concerts" at The Plough, which used to attract only men. Drunkenness, Derek notes, was common and, though the inebriated caused very little public nuisance, they did cause terrible hardship for their families, who were left with no money.

Little is heard of hand bells these days but Joan Copland's father, Albert (Bert) Dryland, used to ring hand bells at Christmas, together with his brother Sid and friend Ernie Shorter. They were good ringers – one of their performances involved ringing Lord Brabourne into the village hall during a visit from him in the 1930s. In 1939 they started heading to Leas Cliff Hall in Folkestone for an audition but, unfortunately, they never reached their destination as war broke out and it was called off. Joan's half-brother tried to ring the hand bells long after the group had disbanded but he didn't have his father's skill and Joan believes that the bells were eventually given to a local Boys' Club.

## SCOUTING IN BRABOURNE AND SMEETH

In 1966 Ted Pile and Roy Collins started the Cub Scouts and organised the building of the old Scout Hut, and at much the same time Joy Walker started the Brownies in the village, helped by May Fortescue. The initial pack consisted of no more than 15 Brownies and used to meet in Smeeth School. While many social groups have struggled and disappeared, Scouting is still going strong, well over 40 years later.

Ian Ruck a former Group Scout Leader writes:

"Scouting was launched by Lord Robert Baden-Powell (BP) in 1907, and rapidly spread throughout Great Britain and across the world. Young boys were joining up everywhere. Locally the situation was the same, with Scouting being centred on Mersham and Smeeth. Unlike some youth organisations, all adults in Scout groups, both leaders and helpers, have always been unpaid volunteers.

"Scouting exists to help young people develop their physical, mental and spiritual wellbeing in order that they may become useful members of society. The emphasis was, and remains, for there to be an adventurous and fun-packed programme, appealing to young people and focusing on outdoor activities. Through this approach, the key aims at the heart of Scouting are brought to young people, namely that they have a duty to God and the Queen/King, and a duty to help others. The motto is 'Be Prepared'.

"During the First World War Scouts were engaged in civic duties to assist the war effort by, for example, checking the telephone lines that ran alongside the London-to-Dover railway line. Potentially, a damaged or sabotaged line along the Smeeth straight from Mersham to Sellindge could stop an important telephone instruction from the War Office being received in the Dover wartime operations centre. This crucial duty was carried out by the late Sam Jamieson, with friends from Smeeth. Sam, who was a Scout at the time, lived to 92 years. His son John was the editor of Brabourne & Smeeth Parish News for 34 years.

"The late Ernie Ashdown of Calland, Smeeth, was also a member of the Mersham and Smeeth troop, and was selected with another Scout to attend the World Jamboree Camp in 1929. The event was held in Birkenhead, near Liverpool, and was also attended by BP, the founder. Ernie witnessed BP being presented with a Rolls-Royce and caravan in recognition of his services to Scouting. Scouts from all over the world had each donated a penny to buy this gift. The caravan is still on display at Gilwell Park, the world headquarters of Scouting. By comparison, Ernie's troop had no more than an old 'push/pull power' trek cart for carrying camping equipment and personal kit to camp.

"By 1930 Cub Scouting for 8- to 10-year-olds was added to the range of Scouts for 10- to 15-year-olds and, subsequently, Senior Scouts for 15- to 18-year-olds, and Rovers, too, all for boys only. In 1966 Seniors and Rovers were replaced by Venture Scouts for those over 15 years of age and Scouting was opened for the first time to boys and girls. This was a change too far for some older-generation Scout Masters.

"Locally, Scouts and Guides operated as separate units until 1966, when unification occurred and a former army barracks hut was erected on the current site, at the western end of Smeeth playing field. Meetings for the 1st Brabourne & Smeeth Scouts and Guides were held in this old hut for over 30 years. Over time the 'hut' became too small and its condition deteriorated; it was finally demolished in 1998 to make way for the present hut (headquarters). The new purpose-built hut opened in April 1999. It took 13 years to purchase the land from Ashford Borough Council and to raise sufficient funds for the project. Fundraising was so protracted that many wondered whether *their* children would ever see the hut. Nevertheless, they are now justifiably proud of this achievement.

"The Scouts and Guides have always been involved in local community events such as fêtes, village suppers, the monthly newspaper collection, Remembrance Day, St

The 1st Brabourne & Smeeth Scouts & Guides Group Headquarters
(traditionally called the hut) – opened April 1999

George's Day and helping others. The new hut has provided an important facility for the growing group, and as a secondary option for the community to use for events and private functions. Since 1999 the new hut has become the base for the annual village fête each June. The main hall has been named the John Moreton Hall, in memory of John Moreton (who sadly died in 2008), who worked tirelessly on behalf of the Scouts and who did so much to raise funds for the new hut.

John Moreton at the opening of the hut
in May 1999

"Beavers for 6- to 8-year-olds were introduced following the opening of the new hut, and Explorer Scouts commenced in 2003, for 14- to 18-year-olds, which replaced Venture Scouts. In 2004 girls were allowed to join all units of the group. Our Guiding sisters were consulted and, after receiving plenty of interest from girls joining them, agreed to the change. The Scout Group has grown year on year to approximately 100, including Beavers, Cubs, Scouts, Explorers, leaders and helpers. Guide unit numbers are also strong, with the recent addition of a Senior Guide section for 14- to 25-year-olds, which are in addition to Scout group numbers. It is, however, sad to note that, after successfully operating for over 10 years, the Rainbow unit for 5 to 7-year-old girls closed in 2009, owing to a shortage of leaders. The introduction of girls to all Scouting units has benefited the group, which has a more universal family appeal. It has helped with the recruitment and retention of volunteer leaders, too.

"To celebrate the centenary of the Scout movement in 2007, Brabourne & Smeeth Scouts camped at Brownsea Island, the place of BP's first camp. Members from all units also planted around 40 trees of different species along the southern boundary of the playing field at Smeeth to commemorate the occasion. Lady Brabourne attended to see the project on the day.

Explore Scout Leader Heather Hale with the Olympic torch, July 2012

"On 18th July, 2012, Explorer Scout Leader Heather Hale proudly carried the Olympic torch on the last 400yd leg of the Folkestone town route, cheered on by large crowds. Heather was chosen for this honour for her voluntary work in Scouting locally and nationally, as well as for her guidance to others as a canoe instructor at the Seapoint Canoe & Kayak Centre in Seabrook, Kent.

"Scouting in Brabourne and Smeeth has come a long way in the past century. It continues to provide opportunities for enjoyment and personal development for young people, while demanding high codes of ethical behaviour. The recipe is a popular one and the group is all set to go from strength to strength."

We would also add that, in November 2012, Ian Ruck was honoured by the Scouts for his 46 years in leadership roles in Scouting, with over 40 of them being spent in the Ashford area. The picture of Ian here, courtesy of Kentish Express, was taken at the celebrations at the Scout hut.

Cubs and Scouts camping at Brabourne Coomb
(May 2010)

Ian Ruck being honoured in November 2012
for over 46 years of service to Scouting

## THE VILLAGE HALL: A FOCUS FOR SOCIAL EVENTS

The construction of Brabourne and Bircholt Village Hall in 1932 must have given the surrounding communities a wonderful resource. Michael Hickmott informs us that the hall was built on land leased from the Brabourne Estate at one shilling per year. Over time, the name changed to Brabourne and Smeeth Village Hall. Frank Howland was one of the founder members and chairman of the Village Hall Management Committee for many years; Bert Mills, who was also much involved in local entertainment, was secretary.

A press cutting, dated 19th November 1932, filed in the Parish Notes of the Reverend C.R.L. McDowall:

> "The Village Hall. A most gay and happy opening of Saturday, November 19th, in spite of dismal weather outside. At 3 p.m. punctually Lady Doreen Knatchbull unlocked the door and declared the Hall open. Captain Knatchbull took the Chair, and after reading out a telegram of good wishes from Mr. Lockyear [former vicar at Brabourne], he proceeded to give a concise account of the steps that had led up to the completion of the Hall, congratulating Brabourne on the hard work that had been put into it. Mr. Shoeton Sack made an excellent speech on the uses of a Village Hall and the possibilities of a Rural Community Council. A presentation of a case of pipes was made by Lady Doreen Knatchbull, on behalf of the people of Brabourne, to Mr. Wilde as a token of gratitude for all his interest and help in forwarding the work. Speeches over, tea was served to the company, and we had the very unusual delight of listening to Scottish and Irish songs sung to the accompaniment of a Celtic harp by Miss Matheson."

> Exact source unknown

## THE ROYAL VISIT

A published extract, possibly from the local press, also pasted into the Parish Notes of the Reverend C.R.L. McDowall, and marked 1938:

"The Village Hall was honoured on Thursday, June 23rd by a visit from the Duke of Kent in the course of a tour arranged by the Council of Social Service. We waited in our places patiently and cheerfully, and soon after 5 o'clock the Duke arrived. After some formal presentations had been made by Mr. T. Pilcher in the road, His Royal Highness entered the gate and encountered a small bevy of representatives of the Young People's Fellowship (YPF) provided with gardening implements to indicate their activities. In the Hall itself, which was tastefully decorated, representatives of Brabourne Women's Institute were ranged on either side, behind two tables on which was exhibited a very attractive and varied collection of produce. The President,

Mrs. Macdonald was presented to His Royal Highness, who duly admired the exhibits. Coming out, he stopped to talk to Mrs. Temple [then Headmistress of Brabourne School] and the children, and finally paid his attention to the pig which was representing the activities of the Young Farmers. The Duke then drove off to Lympne, and we all went home much honoured and elated by the first recorded royal visit to Brabourne.

Mr. Cowley Miller [of Court Lodge, East Brabourne], as one of the staff on the Kent Council of Social Service, acted as Advance Marshal for the Royal Tour."

## EVENTS AT THE VILLAGE HALL

### WHIST DRIVES

Michael Hickmott recalls that, from the 1930s, his grandfather, Frank Howland, who was a great card player, initiated weekly whist drives as a means of raising funds for the hall. These became very popular and used to be held in the two back rooms of the hall that were later converted to the toilets. Whist drives continue to be organised there, but they are now held in the main hall. Michael told us, "People would come from miles around on a Tuesday evening, and sometimes on a Saturday, to play an evening of whist." He can remember going to the hall with his grandparents, Frank and Marjorie, to put out the tables, chairs and playing cards. The cards were kept in used, metal tobacco tins and were brought out only for whist drives – after each session they were locked away from other users of the hall as Frank was very protective of the cards. John Jamieson, who together with his wife Pam now runs the drives, believes that today's cards, though new, are still kept in the same tins.

The cards themselves came from tobacco and cigarette companies that used them as a form of advertising and so they were provided free to those who asked. Occasionally, Frank would write to tobacco companies asking for a few packs of cards when the older cards were becoming worn. He was usually successful and a couple of weeks later a package would arrive from the tobacco company containing six or 12 packs of cards and a compliments slip. As time passed, these companies found other, more profitable ways of advertising – Michael can remember a time when Frank's usual letter received the reply that the companies were not providing cards any more. He was truly indignant at this.

Marjorie did not usually play, but would do so "to make up the numbers". She was involved in making the tea for half-time – a "cuppa" and biscuits, all included in the admission price – and the raffle. After she had washed up she usually went home and Frank would come back later.

# CHANGING FACE OF THE VILLAGE HALL

The Village Hall in the 1930s

Some time between 1948 and 1950

February, 1999

And after a major face-lift between 2008 and 2011

## DANCES

Everyone loved the dances held at the village hall on Saturday nights, and very often the music was provided by local people. A major talent, Claude Aldrich, had a band that used to play regularly at these dances in Brabourne and beyond. Bert Mills also used to organise dances there. A truck would drive round neighbouring villages advertising them which, together with information passed by word of mouth, attracted people from a wide area. Phil Stone added that, during the war, Bunny Hayward used to don his uniform and visit the troops in Hatch Park to let them know about the different entertainments going on at the village hall.

Dances were one of the best ways of getting to meet people and were held in different villages on different nights of the week. Phil Harris, a keen dancer, met his future wife, Betty, at a dance at Sellindge Village Hall, Betty having arrived from Aldington with Les Sutton and his band (also from Aldington), who were playing that evening. That was in 1947. Phil and Betty were married in 1951, when they rented Bridge Cottage in Brabourne Lees, and dancing has remained a lifelong passion for both of them.

The village also benefited from Tommy Matthews's band in the 1940s. Tommy was from Lenham; he played trumpet and saxophone, while Keith Finn played the drums, and Claude Aldrich was on piano. The band played once a week at the Institute on Lenham Square and was a major success. They also used to entertain the troops who had taken over the Paddocks (on the A20, now owned by Caldecott Foundation), as well as those at Mersham le Hatch and those based near the village hall. Keith and many others recall a dance being held at Brabourne Village Hall virtually every Wednesday or Saturday when the troops were around, and the MC was frequently Bunny Hayward. Social life in the villages was flourishing.

Phil and Betty Harris

We digress here as village halls beyond Brabourne were also the venues for regular dances attended by many of our local people and memories of some of these are included below. These events were described as "extremely good fun" and were "the places where you could meet people" – for "people", read "potential partners".

Margaret Pile (Ward) and Pat Cornell (Thornby) talked of the dances at Sellindge. They would cycle there, even at night, remarking that it was always good to have someone to see you home. Gordon Fortescue was one of the few who had a car at the time and Margaret and Pat recalled Gordon cramming as many people as he could into his car and driving them to and from the dances, wherever they were being held.

Dorothy Mills

Dorothy Mills (Jordan), Bert's wife, used to enjoy playing whist and dancing (she still enjoys playing whist, though opportunities for dancing are fewer these days). She worked for a time as kitchen maid at Boys Hall in Willesborough and, at almost 18 years old, went to Wye to work in the old vicarage, which is currently the library. Her dancing days started while she was at Wye – the college was full of troops and there were dances at the village hall three times a week. Dorothy's family thought it comical that the enlightened and generous-minded vicar for whom she worked gave her a key of her own to the vicarage so she could get in at any time. Teasing her at breakfast time, the vicar would say, "I hear that Dorothy brought the milk in this morning."

Later, she worked in the nurses' dining room in Willesborough Hospital and although she was "on the go" throughout the day she still loved going dancing at the Leas Cliff Hall in Folkestone. She would stay at the dance until the last possible moment, then run to Folkestone Central station just as the train was coming in. It was frequently the milk train and had only one carriage. On some occasions she missed the train, which meant sharing a taxi or, alternatively, walking back to Ashford. In the words of Kath Thornby (White), "The lack of transport in no way inhibited people from enjoying themselves."

In the late 1940s Pat Cornell (Thornby) used to play the piano in the Peace Room at Stowting, and Ted and Margaret Pile (Ward) had a tandem, so they would all cycle there from Smeeth and Brabourne Lees to dance. This was a great laugh and they remembered the floor and roof of the Peace Room shaking through the Quadrille and the Lancers. Everyone cycled – they had little choice, as even those who had cars, and there were not many of them, were limited by fuel rationing. So, even when smartly dressed for the evening with "posh clothes and shoes", they would cycle, and Pat would have her music in her bicycle basket on the front. And all this was after a day's work.

## DRAMA AND FILM NIGHTS

For young people and adults alike, the villages were described as "a rich pasture for entertainment", but one cannot help but conclude that social activities involved a considerable amount of effort on the part of the participants. There was a thriving local dramatic society in the 1930s, well remembered for its high-quality performances, which were held at the village hall. Murder on the Second Floor and She Stoops to Conquer were two of the plays staged and Keith Finn remembers starring in these and many others from the early age of 14, when he was still at the Boys' Grammar School in Ashford. He also recalled the enormous enjoyment and hard work that went into the performances: rehearsals were held in Court Lodge Barn (East Brabourne) and went on for months; everyone belonging to the society worked tirelessly for the success of the show. The actors, he said, tried to assume the characters they were playing in the tradition of method acting, and such commitment clearly contributed to the success of their performances. The production team consisted of a cast of actors and understudies, producer, stagehands, wardrobe staff and many others who frequently played more than one role both on and off stage. The productions were much enjoyed by the local community and were well supported, but for those staging them, participation in amateur dramatics was, in itself, a fulfilling social activity.

Norman Weekes was a professional actor and a major name in Brabourne's world of drama and, predictably, he lived in Weekes Lane. He became involved in the dramatic society in the 1940s and its success continued. Margaret Older recalls a production of Blithe Spirit, with Mary Bean as Madame Arcati. It was brilliant and thrilled the village and all those who came to see it. (Just for the record, Norman Thornby was named after Norman Weekes.) Other members of the society included several members of the Ames family, not least Teddy Ames, the Howland family, Per Kennett from Canterbury Road, Peter and Jean Dalby, Joyce and George Hickmott, Cowley Miller from East Brabourne, possibly Bert and Carter Hammon from along Canterbury Road, near the top of School Lane, and Denis Link and Eric Sledge from West Brabourne. Music was important to every performance and so Claude Aldrich frequently played the piano, often accompanied by Keith Finn on the drums. Entertainments put on locally were well supported, not least because so many local people were involved in some way.

While many remember the productions of the post-war era, we should mention that stage productions in the village hall were still alive and well in the 1980s and 1990s, when many girls from the village, and a very few boys, enjoyed being members of

Maureen Darvell

Maureen Darvell's Brabourne Dancing and Stage School. Productions such as The Pied Piper (1986), The Emperor's New Clothes (1987), Alice in Wonderland (1988), The Wizard of Oz (1991) and many more have left dozens of participants and large audiences with the happiest of memories.

During the late 1940s a sort of film club also started up at the village hall on a Friday evening, showing silent black and white films such as Laurel and Hardy, Charlie Chaplin and the like. Betty Edenden and Sheila Ashman (Stone) used to regularly attend, as did other contributors.

## THE YOUTH CLUB

Run by different people each Monday evening, the Youth Club was a big success and a wonderful use of the village hall. Tom Sprawling and his first wife ran it in the early 1960s; by the mid-1960s Bert Mills, assisted by Mrs Coleman, had taken it over. It was a club that catered for a wide range of ages: the early part of the evening, 7.30-9.30pm, focused on the younger children and indoor games, such as chess, draughts, table tennis, darts and snooker, were played, as well as rounders, cricket and football on the green outside. Later in the evening there was live music for the teenagers. Christine Edenden started going there when she was about 11 years old and thoroughly enjoyed it. Sally Thornby used to catch the bus at 6.30pm from East Brabourne to be there for the first part of the evening. Around 9pm Norman would cycle there to meet her and walk her home, something Sally found profoundly embarrassing.

Sally Thornby

The part of the evening that was devoted to older teenagers became extremely popular and attracted dozens of young people from Brabourne, Smeeth and the surrounding villages. Bert Mills and the village hall management committee would arrange dances for the latter part of the evening, at which local groups were invited

to play. David Sawyer performed there on many occasions in the late 1960s and the 1970s as the drummer in a group initially called V Martin and The Wipeouts (pictured). Later, they changed their name to Hot Chocolate, but had to abandon this as they didn't register it before Errol Brown's promoters did! Finally, they called themselves Pursue. Some of our contributors recalled that, in the early 1960s, more than 20 boys on scooters, including Peter Rigg (who lived in Aldington), would descend on the hall at 9.30pm each Monday. By the late 1960s

David Sawyer

David was playing to crowds of 100-120, many of whom came from Sellindge, Aldington and other villages, as well as Ashford, and all of whom paid 1/- to get in. The cult of celebrity had reached Brabourne.

Christine Peall (Friend) used to go regularly to the Youth Club with her sister, Jackie, and Pauline Anderson (Marsh). It was the place for many a romantic assignation, and indeed Christine met her husband-to-be, Dave, there. She recalls that she, Jackie and Pauline would walk home from the club, whatever the weather. After the Youth Club finished for the evening Peter Rigg would give Margaret Davis a lift home to East Brabourne and, after dropping her at Hill View, in The Street, would go to the Five Bells for a quick drink. He enjoyed doing this largely because it seemed a "cool" thing to do, and was (to him) a symbol of independence and maturity.

Various members of the community invested a great deal of time and effort into these evenings. Several members of the village hall committee would be present at the dances; Bert Sawyer, David's father, helped Bert Mills to organise the dances and he also acted as MC, announcing the different dances. Mr Goreham from the sweet shop used to help, and other helpers ran a snack bar that sold soft drinks and crisps. Although this might sound benign, David recalls that punch-ups were frequent – those causing trouble had usually visited a pub or two on their way to the dance and Bert Mills had to deal with the troublemakers.

UT GROUPS AND DISCS

### Compered by Peter Wills

# jump to Number One

The Wipeouts—they have a wide range

The Wipeouts, who packed the village hall in the late 1960s.
Bob Martin, Robin Thornby, Tony Scott, Michael Christmas and
David Sawyer on drums

The programme for Monday evenings used to vary, and more than one of our contributors remembered there being Youth Club walks on summer evenings. On some occasions they would also meet at Bert and Dorothy Mills's farm in Hampton Lane for a barbecue and to listen to a guest band.

Such social events were not just the preserve of Brabourne; there were other dances with other bands in Sellindge, Waltham, Petham and other villages, and people would follow the groups from one place to another. Dave Sawyer recalls how Bert Mills used to take the band to different venues to play. Once, he took them to play at the Youth Club Association's dinner dance at Greenways Hotel on the far side of Maidstone, and in 1968 he also took them to play at the Marine Barracks Social Club in Deal, before it was blown up by the IRA. They were still known as Hot Chocolate then.

Allegedly, parents were strict with their children as they grew up, often appearing to monitor their social activities much more closely than when they had been children. Margaret Wratten, for example, who was keen on Dave Horswell, was told by her parents that she could not go out with him until she was two years older. This certainly did not suit Margaret, who was then working for Dr Fitzgerald and his family. Travelling both to and from the Fitzgeralds in Sellindge, Margaret would regularly miss the bus from the Smeeth crossroads and end up arriving on Dave's motorbike. Margaret recalled that the Fitzgeralds complained about her being late and her parents were deeply concerned when they heard about her mode of travel – both on account of safety and respectability.

Dave and Maggie Horswell

## EVENTS ORGANISED BY LOCAL SOCIETIES

The Horticultural Society, known initially as the Brabourne and Smeeth Produce Association, is just one of several organisations that has long used the village hall. It was active in 1940, and Margaret Pile (Ward), who put her first entry in at nine years old, has belonged to this society ever since. In the early days of the Horticultural Society (now Brabourne and Smeeth Gardeners' Society) shows were held at The Plough and entries had to go to the vicar's wife. Many other contributors were, and still are, members, and with renewed interest in "grow your own" and the huge enthusiasm for the new allotments behind The Plough, the society could be in for a period of growth.

Digressing for a moment, the importance of the shows put on by local societies and associations was made clear to us – in particular, the horticultural and animal shows, as these provided local people with opportunities for winning good prizes. Margaret and Ted Pile explained how it was possible to enter a jar of gooseberries at Brabourne Horticultural Show and, if it won a prize, the same jar could be entered at other shows and thus win more prizes. Ted, who worked with horses, bought an unbroken Dartmoor pony in the 1960s, broke it in and won numerous prizes with it at shows. Very approximately, average earnings in the early 1950s were between £3 and £5 per week, so, if you managed to win £1 by showing produce or animals, this was a significant supplement to the family budget.

## CHRISTMAS PARTIES

Mike Hickmott writes:

"Every year in the late 1950s/early 1960s there was a Christmas party at the village hall for the children of the village. Frank Howland usually ran it, but it may have been funded by the British Legion. Frank organised all the games and, every now and then, he would stand on the stage with a bucket of sweets and throw two or three handfuls out onto the floor for the children to scrabble around and pick up. The parents used to sit around the sides of the hall, watching whilst the children played games. Tables were set out for tea with sandwiches, cakes, buns, and jellies, all washed down with squash. The highlight, of course, was the arrival of Father Christmas – Frank again! – with a big sack of presents for the children".

Through the Sunday School at St Mary's Brabourne, Mrs Opperman arranged Christmas parties for all local children at the village hall, and when the weather was too bad, her daughter, Margaret Older, would send her car to take the children there. The British Legion also used to fund children's parties and entertainment, and Anthony Finn can remember the children all having to present a party piece for the entertainment. Anthony would play the piano – sometimes he would do a duet with Rosemary Davis – while Jackie Davis played the cello and Peter Bradley sang.

The village hall was thus a venue of great importance for local events of all kinds and for people of all ages. However, on 2nd May, 1954 - disaster struck.

## DESTRUCTION OF THE VILLAGE HALL: THE WHIRLWIND

There are certain events in life that tie us to a place: practically everyone with whom we spoke remembered the whirlwind that demolished the village hall at lunchtime on Sunday, 2nd May 1954, and could recall what they were doing when they saw it or heard about the destruction.

At the age of 12, Karl Engels, who then lived at the Knoll on the rise between the hall and the shops at Brabourne Lees, was going to the garden shed when he happened to look up and saw the roof of the hall being lifted off the walls, which then collapsed. The roof was then "replaced" (or so it appeared to him) some 6ft or more lower on the collapsed walls. Karl shouted to his parents to tell them what had happened but simply received the unimpressed reply: "Don't tell stories!"

Dorothy Mills remembers that Sunday lunch was ready and on the table and her son Christopher was in his high chair when they heard that the hall roof had collapsed. So shocked was her husband Bert, who as we know was much involved in the organisation of social activities there, that in Dorothy's words, "He just went!"

Bert and Dorothy Mills, with Christopher (with dark hair) beside his father

Christopher Mills – more recently

Ethel Jordan who lived next door to the hall apparently heard the "whoosh", but when the building came down there were fears that Netty Knight, who used to clean it, and usually did so on a Sunday, was trapped under the wreckage. Fortunately, this proved not to be the case.

It was Pat Browne's 10th birthday on that day, and he was staying with his grandparents in Manor Pound Lane, almost opposite the village hall. Hearing the noise of the roof being lifted off by the wind and set down again, Pat, together with many others, attended the scene very quickly. As mentioned there were fears that someone may have been trapped or injured inside it and, being the smallest there, Pat was virtually pushed into the building to check. He remembered that the windows were still in place though most of the glass was gone. Once inside, he took a look around but no one appeared to be there, so he climbed out again. When his father discovered that Pat's safety had been put at risk he was furious, but as Pat remarked, "I did get my photograph on the front of the Daily Herald, so it was a birthday to remember."

The hall had had a new kitchen, new lavatories and a new floor fitted shortly before the disaster. Only the roof of the hall was lifted by the wind, turned, and dropped down on the walls, so the new kitchen and lavatories remained intact, as did the new floor, which escaped virtually undamaged. Michael Hickmott has a picture of his grandfather, Frank Howland, standing on top of the collapsed hall. Again, health and safety rules were clearly not given high priority in those days.

## RECONSTRUCTING THE HALL: A COMMUNITY ENDEAVOUR

Lord and Lady Brabourne saw the demolished hall the morning after the whirlwind and marvelled at the way the village came together to rebuild it. Major drivers in its reconstruction were Frank and Marjorie Howland, with Frank becoming chairman of the working party charged with overseeing its completion. Money was raised largely through donations and concerted fundraising by the WI, Brabourne School and numerous individuals – all at a time when money was still very short after the war. After the disaster, other villages, Mersham being one of them, allowed Brabourne to use their halls free of charge to raise funds. Whist and beetle drives were held to raise money; dances also brought in much-needed funds, and the bands that played at these rarely charged. Many people gave their labour voluntarily, not least Gordon Fortescue, who rebuilt the hall, and countless others helped with clearing rubble, and later with painting, decorating and tidying the area around the hall. May Fortescue recalls that she, Margaret Jeanes and Margaret Older were among those who made curtains for the newly-built structure. It must be said that Margaret Older cannot remember making curtains herself, being fully occupied at Penstock Farm, though she believes she may have lent a sewing machine for this purpose. According to

## DESTRUCTION OF THE VILLAGE HALL BY A WHIRLWIND
### 2ND MAY, 1954

Tom Wratten collects rags for sale to raise
funds for the reconstruction of the village hall

Commemorative plaque in the village hall

newspaper reports at the time, the hall was re-opened by Lady Brabourne a mere seven months after the whirlwind had demolished it, and in testimony to all that Frank and Marjorie had achieved to support the work of the hall throughout their lives, the front entrance hall was named the Howland Hall.

Tom Wratten, who was around 11 years old when the hall blew down, also played his part in fundraising. He used to go round the village collecting rags and had a bin outside the Wratten household, now Forge Cottage, East Brabourne, which had a note attached asking for rags to be left, and volunteering to collect them if necessary. After school, he would go to the addresses people had left with his mother to get the rags. He sold everything he had managed to amass at Welmans in New Street, Ashford. If they were sorted into woollens, silks and cottons, they paid more, so he sorted as much as possible, earning 1/- per lb of woollens and 10d per lb for everything else. This was indeed hard work and Tom raised between £5 and £6 to put towards the hall's reconstruction, a substantial contribution in the early 1950s, and equivalent to a week's wages or more for some.

## RECENT IMPROVEMENTS TO THE VILLAGE HALL
The commitment of local people to the reconstruction of the hall clearly reflected its importance in the villages and, again as a result of community action, it has been given a face-lift in recent years. As part of this, new lavatories were added, with Lady Brabourne noting that this was the first time she had been asked to open public lavatories of any kind, yet alone loos "so swish".

Wendy and Brian Sanders provided the following details on the substantial improvements made to the hall in recent years:

"By 2003 the hall was beginning to look rather shabby and the village hall committee, chaired by Wendy, concluded that its image needed to be improved if it were to attract more users. This meant that money would have to be spent on it. A long-term plan was put in place to raise funds through events, grants and donations, and as a consequence, in 2004, the hall received an external face-lift with new fasciae, weatherboarding, double-glazing, signage and blinds at the windows. In the same year, a village lunch and photographic exhibition was held there to celebrate the 50th anniversary of the 'whirlwind'. This was attended by Lord and Lady Brabourne and family, and more than 70 villagers, many of whom remembered the event of 2nd May 1954.

"The next stage was to build a new extension, which altered and improved the main entrance and incorporated new toilets and improved access for disabled visitors.

Finances for this were generated by a massive fundraising effort that included 'Buy a Brick', the sale of Brabourne & Smeeth tea towels, coffee mornings, slide shows and profits from the village fête and the village supper and cabaret. Grants and anonymous donations further swelled the funds, and the sum required was thus raised. On 23rd August 2008 Lady Brabourne, Michael John, Savannah and Alexander arrived in Walkers' horse-drawn carriage to formally open the new facilities. All the village organisations were present and the hall was packed with villagers. As she began her speech, Lady Brabourne noted that she preferred to address the assembly not as 'Ladies and Gentlemen' but as 'Friends'.

Lady Brabourne and her granddaughter Savannah arrived in a horse-drawn carriage to launch Brabourne village hall's open day to celebrate the completion of improved facilites. By kind permission of the Kentish Express, Thursday, 28th August, 2008

"But this did not mark the end of the work on the hall. Subsequently, new chairs and stage curtains and treatment to the wooden floor further improved its appearance, and in 2009 the car park was resurfaced and the drainage improved, just in time for a very harsh winter.

"In 2010 it was decided to apply for grants and to raise further funds to refurbish the old toilet block, to provide one large room for meetings and functions, with its own access and toilets. This, together with minor improvements to the kitchen, was successfully completed in August 2011. All these improvements have been driven by a very dynamic village hall committee, comprising Wendy Sanders (chair), Jacqui Fortescue (secretary) and John Coupe (treasurer), with Brian Sanders as a co-opted member. However, as Wendy insists, none of this could have been achieved without the enormous contribution of the village community. As a result of the hard work of so many people the hall is now vastly improved and, as a consequence, is more in demand than ever for use by the community."

## FETES, FIREWORKS AND MORE FUN – ENTERTAINMENT BEYOND THE VILLAGE HALL

Michael Hickmott shares his recollections of the village fête:

"In the 1950s and 1960s [and until the late 1980s] the village fête was always held on the green at the Warren, in the centre of the villages of Brabourne and Smeeth. It was one of the highlights of the year, looked forward to by children and adults alike. Later it moved to the playing field, where it is still held. Not only was it a fundraising event but it was also a social event. The fête was held in June, as it still is, and would consist of various attractions, including sports between the two primary schools, competitions between mums and dads, sideshows, dancing, a fancy-dress competition, a band, music, a colouring competition and exhibitions of various crafts and hobbies. There would be a tea tent organised by the WI and a beer tent run by one of the local pubs. The marquees were provided by Frank Howland, as were the ropes and other equipment. Sideshows were numerous and consisted of coconut shies, 'bat the rat', tossing the bale, bowling for the pig – for many years provided by George Brooks – and lucky dips in various forms. The event took up the whole of a Saturday afternoon, much as it does now, but in the evening there would be a dance at the village hall as well. In the 1980s it was extended for a few years into 'village week', with something on every evening for a whole week, culminating in the fête and dance. But this took some organising and, after a few years, it went back to just being the fête and dance."

Michael Hickmott

Michael remembers there being a truck competition one year, following the truck racing events at Brabourne School. He (with help from his parents) made a tank out of his truck. It was made from cardboard scrounged from grocery boxes and not only had the main tank, but also a revolving turret and gun made out of a cardboard tube. The tank tracks were made out of corrugated cardboard. An army shirt and beret for Michael completed the effect and the result was first prize. Michael's sister Gillian also won a fancy-dress competition as a lollipop girl when she was three – in a dress with lollipops sewn on it and holding a tray with lollipops "For Sale".

Lovely lollipops! First prize for Gillian Hickmott in the
fancy-dress competition, Lady Brabourne is on right (late 1950s)

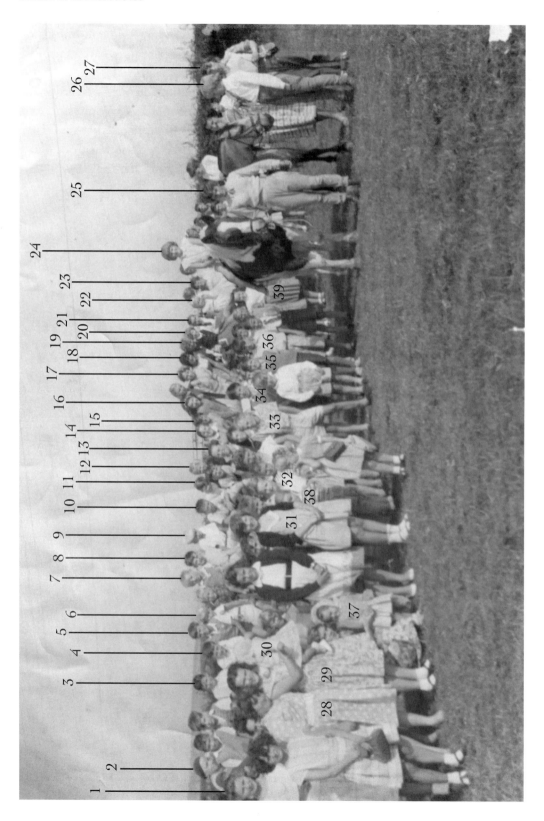

Village Gala held in the field behind Bircholt Forstal (c1958)

1 Wendy Bashford, 2 Bob Prior, 3 Ronnie Jackson, 4 Robin Marsh, 5 Michael Garlick, 6 Barry Spain,
7 Robert Clayson, 8 Brian Smith, 9 Alan Reader, 10 Donald Southern, 11 David Smith, 12 Charles Todd,
13 Dave Andrews, 14 Patricia Andrews, 15 Mavis Dodd, 16 Jean Dodd, 17 Sylvia Southern,
18 Glenda Coooper, 19 Lesley Wignall, 20 Susan Todd, 21 Philippa Chadwick, 22 Jackie Spain,
23 Maureen Hughes, 24 Jackie Friend, 25 Rosalind Older, 26 Diana Older, 27 ? Graves, 28 Faith Marsh,
29 Wendy Hover, 30 Daryl Marsh, 31 Barbara Woodcock, 32 ? Sawyer, 33 Kenneth Bishopp, 34 Clifford Dodd,
35 Ronald Dodd, 36 Ronald Jamieson, 37 Sheralyn Marsh, 38 Shirley Shorter, 39 Helen Copland

Our thanks to Christine Peall and friends for naming people in this picture

## BRABOURNE AND SMEETH VILLAGE WEEK
Peter Clayton writes:

"Back in the mists of the last century – well, in the 1980s to be exact - there was a phenomenon that drew together people from all parts of our community for the express purpose of Having Fun. It was called Village Week, and was organised by a group of cheery village folk with the idea of not only having fun, but also raising some useful money for village organisations, such as the village hall, the village playing field and the village Scouts and Guides. There was something for everyone – young and old, fast and slow – and it happened each year for at least six years.

Peter Clayton

"There were main events at the weekends to start and finish the week – 1989 saw a barn dance and sponsored walk at the beginning, and the village fête, a village dance (tickets £3.50, to include supper!) and Songs of Praise on the Warren at the end. In between there was something different every day. On any day there might have been a bingo session, a Darby and Joan tea at the 'Mayor's Parlour', a village lunch, inter-village cricket, a junior disco, a car treasure hunt, or a Fun Evening – when there was rounders for the ladies, and games, races, a bouncy castle and trailer rides for the children. As well as at the fête, the Fun Evening also saw the appearance of the dreaded (by some!) water machine – when well-known villagers were inveigled into placing themselves at risk on a chair under a bucket of water.

"The village fête was, in those days, held on the Warren with all the usual fun of the fête, together with 'Village Top Dog' and sports competitions. There was even a radio-controlled model-car grand prix one year. The water machine drew the crowds again as more villagers put themselves at risk of a soaking. A local pub landlady was persuaded into the chair – but not before she had exacted a promise that the water would be warm!

"One year saw a major hog roast and dance on the field behind The Plough. Two large marquees were kindly supplied and erected, and three low-loader farm trailers were borrowed, which together made a 24ft (8 metre) square dance floor. Another trailer made a base for the disco. The hog roast (so delicious) was kindly presided over by our very own village master butcher and the whole evening was a resounding success. However, it was noted that the grass behind the bar might not have been very even, as it appeared that by the end of the evening a number of the young bar staff were having trouble standing up…

"As is always the way, over time, people's commitments and responsibilities change, enthusiasms wane and folk move on to other things, and Village Week became an event of the past. Fortunately, our community spirit remains strong, and there are still many interesting and entertaining events and occasions throughout the year for the folk of Brabourne and Smeeth."

## EVENTS ON THE WARREN

Millie and Bryan Hodges remember the annual bonfire that used to be held on the Warren. This was very popular with local residents. Hot dogs and soup were sold and most of the village would come out to enjoy the fireworks. However, some years ago, concern that sparks from the fire could be dangerous resulted in the bonfire being cancelled. Michael Hickmott adds that this was possibly the decision of Ashford Borough Council Housing Department, who then owned[1] the land. Millie recalls that, one year, local children built a bonfire in readiness for 5th November but someone set it alight a week before. Undaunted, the children set to work and rebuilt it in time for Bonfire Night.

When the Sherwins were at Orpins Stores they used to organise an annual pancake race on Shrove Tuesday. Brenda Streeter added that the race started at the garage (John Childs') and finished at Orpins. Whoever flipped their pancakes the greatest number of times won the race. Several contributors suggested that they would like to see this race revived.

## THE ANNUAL POINT-TO-POINT RACES

The point-to-point meetings, which at least a third our participants mentioned, were held at Park Farm in Brabourne. The East Kent meetings were on Easter Mondays, while the Mid-Kent Staghounds or Shorncliffe Drag were at Whitsun; the course for both events ran from Park Corner, down behind Park Farm, up to Pound House and back to Park Corner. Point-to-point races have been in existence since Rosemary Hendry (Ward) was a girl in the early decades of the 20th century, and took place at Park Farm until 1948. Margaret Pile (Ward) remarked: "These were a great day out – fun for everyone. There were not so many cars in those days and most of the crowd walked from Smeeth Station, or were transported by the Aldrich's bus." John Varrier's paternal grandmother lived at Park Corner Cottages and John remembers watching the racing from her garden in the 1930s. In much the same era, Joyce Garlick (Wood) remembers crowds of people coming to Smeeth crossroads on the bus and walking the rest of the way to the races. Some would also come by lorry or

---

1      The Warren is now the property of Brabourne Parish Council

The Brabourne pancake race begins,
Wednesday, March 14th, 1973.
(Picture courtesy of the Folkestone and Hythe Gazette)

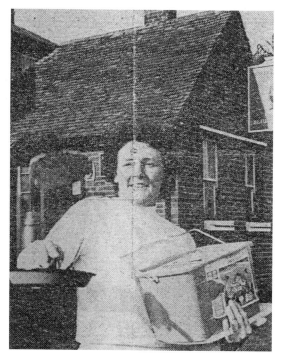

Nancy Wilson tossing a pancake.
(Picture courtesy of the
Folkestone and Hythe Gazette)

motorbike and park in what was then a field of Warren Farm on Canterbury Road. There was always a wonderful holiday atmosphere on point-to-point days, which, according to Joyce, was further improved by an African man who used to walk along playing his banjo.

Tim Marsh told us that there was a water jump on the course near Park Farm and, nearby, a large pond. This used to be full of newts and Tim and his friends would set up small rods in the rushes and have competitions to catch the most. "There used to be hundreds in those days and we'd catch cans full of them, but you couldn't do that now. They've all gone".

The meetings were stopped in 1939 with the war but started again in 1946 at Park Farm. They were transferred to Bircholt Farm for one year in 1949, and from then on have been held at Aldington.

Margaret told us: "The horses were fed and trained for the races and my husband Ted came to the stables at Evegate owned by Mr Ronnie Martin in order to carry out this work. It was a seven-day-a-week job – overtime wasn't heard of in those days, and you did your job for the love of it." With Margaret's agreement we would add that she first "spotted" Ted as someone she liked when she was 14 years old. At the first point-to-point after the war in 1946 Margaret and two friends were taking a critical look at the young men who were there. Margaret saw Ted running with a horse; he was running faster than the other boys leading horses, and she decided that she "liked the look of him". He knew nothing about this at the time. Ted moved to the village to work in the following year, and when Margaret was 21 they were married.

Margaret and Ted Pile

John Jamieson with his horse Major Neave at a point-to-point

One of the first post-war point-to-point meetings at Park Farm.
The horse on the left was possibly Celtic Cross, owned and ridden by Tommy Southern, and the other was Wexford, owned by Dr Bradbury from Smeeth and possibly ridden by Mr Marchant

## ENTERTAINMENT ORGANISED BY EMPLOYERS

One source of entertainment for those connected with the Market Garden in East Brabourne was that provided by Lady Charnwood and Miss Cochrane. Every year they would organise a coach to take all their workers and families to a show. Elsie Davis, her daughter Jackie and Pauline Anderson (Marsh) remember going to a Russian Circus, and Holiday on Ice, as well as to pantomimes, all the expenses being met by Lady Charnwood. This was a major event and Elsie and her daughters remember it fondly, recalling that Pauline was always included because she lived locally, even though her parents did not work at the Market Garden. Lady Charnwood would also organise Easter-egg hunts for the children in the orchard and there was usually a Christmas party for the children of employees. Elsie also recalls that, every Christmas Eve, Lady Charnwood would visit the Davises for sausage rolls and mince pies. Elsie would hang miniature bottles of gin on the tree for Lady Charnwood, a sentiment she both enjoyed and appreciated.

Lady Charnwood,
whose kindness and generosity were widely appreciated

## RETURNING TO THE CHURCH

The church also provided entertainment in a variety of ways though its importance as a generator of social events has declined, and changed, over the years as disposable income has increased and leisure activities of all kinds have become much more affordable. Indeed, the contrast between life in the village now and at the time of Queen Victoria's jubilee in 1887, where we started this chapter, is stark. The church has continued to generate social events but, rather than doing so to support the poorest in local society, funds generated are now increasingly needed to maintain the work of the church and its buildings, often very beautiful ones as are Brabourne's and its neighbouring churches.

Garden parties and fêtes are remembered as being popular and well supported. There were sales at Church Farm, where local produce such as horseradish, mint sauce and cakes were sold and there were memorable flower festivals. Some of these, organised by Margaret Older in the 1960s, with help and support from Barbara Sheekey, were a major success, as were the two Son et Lumière masterminded by the Reverend Ray Sheekey (described by him in Chapter 2). We shouldn't forget that going to church was in itself a form of enjoyment for many, especially at the major festivals and events in the church year. The Mothering Sunday service at Brabourne in 1955 was clearly popular (see below). Many of these memories are associated as much with their preparation as with the events themselves. For instance, the suppers that followed the Son et Lumière in the barn at Penstock are remembered by both those who prepared them and those who enjoyed them. A treasured memory is of baked potatoes, which were cooked at Homehurst by Joy and Betty Finn, being pushed across the road to Penstock in a wheelbarrow.

More regular forms of entertainment provided by the church through the year were Mothering Sunday (pictured below) and the collection of primroses from the Downs, which were bunched at Homehurst, again with the help and encouragement of Betty and Joy. Betty also used to take children carol singing. Ted Ward would drive them to East Brabourne and, starting at the church, they would make their way up The Street to Mrs Opperman at Clandon Cottage for mince pies and a drink, then move on to Mrs Older at Penstock and then to Mrs Clifton at Park Farm. The next evening Ted would drive them to West Brabourne so that they could sing there. He always drove them home again afterwards.

Linked with the church was Brabourne School where there has always been organised entertainment, aside from learning. Especially remembered was gardening, truck races, sports, the summer fête with its May Queen and, besides many other forms of entertainment, let us not forget maypole dancing which has bound generations together.

Mothering Sunday at Brabourne Church, 1st April, 1955.
(Picture courtesy of KM Group)

So, are the "good old days" merely a figment of the imagination, or did they really exist? When asked this question people were unanimous that they did exist. What is clear from these anecdotes is that people did enjoy themselves, regardless of limited resources. The heavy investment of local time and effort in the production of village-based entertainment was in itself entertainment for many, and "travelling hopefully" towards an event was every bit as much fun as when it "arrived".

# 11

# REFLECTIONS ON WARTIME
# (PREDOMINANTLY 1939-1945)

"Hellfire Corner" was the name acquired by Kent after it took the brunt of Germany's air attack in the Battle of Britain in August and September 1940. Between June 1944 and March 1945 Germany launched its pilotless V-1 flying bombs, otherwise known as doodlebugs, which caused considerable devastation in Kent, and later during this period the V-2 rocket attacks began. More of these bombs were believed to have fallen in Kent than in London and thus it is not surprising that the war was remembered by all our contributors who lived through it as a bleak, though not dull, phase in history.

Phil Stone recalls that Brabourne Lees, Smeeth and East and West Brabourne lost relatively few people during the Second World War, but for the families concerned the tragedy of loss has endured. One of those killed by "enemy action" was Phil's elder brother John Anthony Stone, who was killed in a raid that hit Haywards' Garage in Ashford in 1943, where he was working as a fitter and turner. He had been called up for the Royal Air Force, allocated a number, successfully completed his exams for aircrew duty and was waiting for training. It was during this latter period that he was killed.

Pat Browne's uncle, Douglas Browne, who was in the Gordon Highlanders, died on active service in India on 12th June, 1944. He is buried near Kohima. He was no more than 21 years old. The Stones and the Brownes lived in two of the four bungalows opposite the village hall.

Lady Brabourne told us how her husband's elder brother, Norton, Lord Brabourne, had also been killed in the war. He had been taken prisoner by the Germans and sent to an Italian prison camp but, when a decision was taken by the Germans to send their prisoners of war to Germany, Norton realised that he would never get away once across the border. He escaped from the train with a friend just before the German frontier and went to a farm in the hope of being protected. Sadly, they were betrayed by Fascists and were taken back to the railway station, where they were shot on the platform as an example to others thinking of escaping. Norton was also 21 years old. The cruelties of both wars have left terrible scars and memories for many throughout the country.

A fourth casualty of the war was a Mrs Coleman, killed by a flying bomb by Hammon's Hill, between East Brabourne and Stowting.

No one who was involved in the First World War is alive today and many from the villages died between 1914-18, or later as a result of action. George Brooks's father was one of them. According to Frank Howland's grandson, Michael Hickmott, "Frank joined the 8th Battalion The Buffs – the 8th East Kent Regiment – on 11th November, 1914, aged 16. He saw service at Ypres and Loos in Belgium, and was shot in the neck by a sniper on 16th June, 1917, at the Battle of Messines, near Ypres, but fortunately the bullet missed all the vital places on his body. He was one of the lucky ones, as about 120 men died in the battle, including 10 officers. He made a full recovery and was transferred to 3rd Battalion The Buffs – the 3rd East Kent Regiment, Reserves. He was disembodied [ie discharged] on 29th March, 1919, as a consequence of demobilisation, with the rank of corporal." Michael still has the bullet that nearly killed his grandfather.

Frank Howland (1917)

Brabourne and Smeeth Volunteers (c1917).
Back row: from left, H. Standen, P. Cooper, ?G. Brooks, N.? Hills, P. Nickolls.
Middle row: from left, H. Ames, ? Elliot, T. Kerd, unidentified, A. Wood, F. Ames, A. Pestell.
Front row: from left, A. Hammon, M. Howland, unidentified, E. Drays? (or possibly Mr Birchett, identified by Dick Andrews from picture in the trenches, Chapter 1), G. Marshall, E. Ames, A. Ashdown

# THOSE WHO GAVE THEIR LIVES IN THE FIRST AND SECOND WORLD WARS

| Brabourne and Smeeth | Monks Horton and Stowting | RAF Pilots and Aircrew lost in action in the skies over Brabourne, Smeeth and Stowting while in the defence of Britain |
|---|---|---|
| Percy Cooper | William Andrews | A.S. Dini (NZ), May 1940 |
| William Heathfield | George Andrews | K.C. Campbell, July 1940 |
| George Spice | Robert Armitage | A.D. Smith, Sept 1940 |
| Clement Bean | William Howland | H.O. Edwards, Sept 1940 |
| Thomas Hooker | Frank Rendall | W. Januszewicz, Polish Air Force 303 Sqdn, Oct 1940 |
| Charles Wood | Thomas Fagg | E.T. Frith, Oct 1940 |
| Albert Hills | Clifford Nye | J.N. Lewis, May 1942 |
| Arthur Philpott | | T. Brian, Sept 1942 |
| Archibald Dryland | Conrad Jenkin | G.T. Lapping, Sept 1942 |
| Frederick Ashdown | Edward Griggs | |
| Alfred Pestell | Charlie Smith | |
| Wyndham, Lord Brabourne | Leonard Fagg | |
| Malcolm Williams | Reginald Hoare | |
| Graham Williams | | |
| Joseph Hobs | | |
| Victor Muggeridge | | |
| Norton, Lord Brabourne | | |
| Albert Addy | | |
| Percival Ashman | | |
| George Brooks | | |
| Albert Conley | | |
| George Marshall | | |
| George Skeer (Military Medal, Belgian Croix de Guerre) | | |
| Albert Varrier (Military Medal) | | |
| Horace Ward | | |
| Douglas Browne | | |
| Anthony Stone | | |

"They shall grow not old, as we that are left grow old:
Age shall not weary them, nor the years condemn.
At the going down of the sun and in the morning
We will remember them"

Under the column RAF Pilots and Aircrew lost in action over the skies of Brabourne, Smeeth and Stowting, you will notice the name T.G. Frith, who died in October 1940. Sergeant Frith is commemorated in the Scout hut in Smeeth. The memorial reads:

"One of the 'few'

To the memory of Sgt-Pilot Eric T.G. Frith (Tim) of 92 Squadron R.A.F. Biggin Hill. Shot down in combat on October 9th 1940. His Spitfire, X4597, crashed on Lord Brabourne's estate at the rear of this building [the Scout hut]. He had baled out and landed behind The Plough public house. He suffered terrible burns from which he died in Willesborough Hospital on October 17th 1940 aged 26 years and is buried at North Hinskey Cemetery, Oxford. His once neglected grave is now restored and tended by a local lady volunteer."

Janet Powell of Hastingleigh has researched the backgrounds of most of the local men who died in both wars. In 2007 she compiled a dossier, Brabourne and Smeeth War Memorials, in which she provides details on where and how these men died, and

Sgt Tim Frith

Digging for Sgt Frith's Spitfire on The Ridgeway, Smeeth (c1993)
(Picture courtesy of the Kentish Express, now KM Group)

where they are buried. She also tells us where they had lived, in which village, their occupation and the families they left behind. Each memorial is sensitively written and gives a picture of the lives of each of those so tragically lost.

Janet acknowledges the work of David Hughes, Neil R Clark and Kyle D Tallett, who kindly permitted her to use some of their research on Ashford's fallen, which included men from the surrounding villages. Their website www.ashfordsfallen.com has now been absorbed into a much larger website, www.kentfallen.com, which we urge you to consult. Janet also refers readers to the website www.fadedgenes.co.uk, which covers some of East Kent, and in many cases has full family histories of the men concerned.

If you would like to look at Brabourne and Smeeth War Memorials, please contact the incumbent at Smeeth Rectory or a member of Brabourne PCC.


## WARTIME IN THE VILLAGES

More people that we spoke to had direct memories of the Second World War (1939-1945) rather than the First. One of our contributors was in Smeeth Church when it broke out. The Reverend Ashley Brown was conducting the morning service when a telegram arrived for him. He stopped the service and announced that war had been declared. According to Eric Ball the first few months of the war were relatively quiet, and were sometimes known as the "phoney war". However, things "livened up in 1940, the year of the Battle of Britain".

Arrival of troops in the area

The war saw different army contingents moving into the area in 1939, mainly Royal Artillery, who operated anti-aircraft guns and the searchlight. With them came the Medical Corps, who were based at the Paddocks on the A20, while the headquarters of the army was at Towers House, Lodge House and Mersham Hatch House. These were requisitioned for army use, and other buildings in the area were also taken over, including the village hall and Court Lodge in East Brabourne. Margaret Pile (Ward) recalls that "the troops were under canvas and the Brabourne valley rang with the reveilles from the bugles, including Rise and Shine, Come to the Cookhouse Door Boys and Lights Out".

In January 1940 the Royal Artillery started installing a searchlight on the racecourse near Manor Pound, but they could not get the generator started. Having taken over the village hall, they re-sited the light at the back of the hall, put huts up along the road to Brabourne Lees, and gave the hall back to the village. At night the searchlight would range across the skies until the night fighters came in. It was then turned off and the protection of the area was left to the fighters.

Karl Engels writes:

"To me, the army had always been by the hall but, in reality, the field that they occupied had been given by Lord Brabourne for the specific purpose of building the village hall and the land behind it – now the site of a small housing estate, originally of council houses – was to be made into a football field. In spite of being designated as such, the football field never materialised as the land was said to be too wet, so the army took it over for a signals station, as at that time, the ground was not in use other than for grazing.

"The signals station consisted of three or four huts, a searchlight and a very small gun pointing skywards. I cannot recall the light or the gun being used; however, their main task was to fire signal rockets to warn the next signal unit that a doodlebug was coming. The rocket was about 3ft long by 6in wide and went up about quarter to half a mile before it burst into a very bright light. And because it was heavy, it came down again on a parachute. The soldiers would run out for the parachutes as they could be used again, but many were taken by local children. It was my 'big plan' to get one, but I never did. I even found a used rocket in my back garden, but there was no silk attached."

Phil Stone added that when the parachute flares came down they were frequently alight, often causing the corn to catch fire, which then saw everyone in the area running to put the flames out.

Returning to the subject of the village hall, having access to it was of major importance to the villages because it was the main venue for the social events described in the previous chapter, including the dances, whist drives, and shows put on by the dramatic society. Something happened there virtually every week. As we mentioned before, the entertainment put on in the area was much enjoyed by the troops, including the Canadians, who arrived shortly before D-day (6th June, 1944) and were under canvas in Hatch Park. According to one of our contributors, "joining in village social life gave them a sense of normality".

The number of troops in the area remained relatively few until the RAF moved in. According to Ron Cooper, "The RAF were at Mersham, known as Kingsnorth Airfield, from June 1943, when it was first constructed. A Spitfire squadron was based there initially and was replaced by a Hurricane squadron in August of the same year. The base was then upgraded in September 1943, and the USAAF 36 Tiger Squadron arrived on 22nd October and 303 Tigers on 23rd October. These were Thunderbolts used for bomber escorts, having supplementary fuel tanks slung under them to extend their range. Without these tanks they could carry a single bomb instead."

With the presence of both these air forces in the locality, social activity flourished in Brabourne and the surrounding villages, even though mobility could be a problem. Phil Stone remembers the Americans' consequent fascination with bicycles. They did not ride them in America in the same way that people did here, and were so taken with them that Normans' Cycle Works, which built bikes in Ashford, thrived. Harry Holts (a radio shop in Bank Street, Ashford, that had interests both in bicycles and in radio) were supplied by Normans' Cycles, and sold literally hundreds of bicycles to the Americans. On one day alone a record 100 bicycles were bought. When these "visitors" left after D-day, hundreds of bikes were found abandoned at Mersham and High Halden. However, though many of the troops may have got themselves bikes, Betty Edenden and many others recall that travelling on buses became extremely difficult, as they were full of soldiers, meaning it was often easier to walk. Betty can remember even walking to Folkestone with her mother to go to the pictures during this time. Indeed, as a 16-year-old girl, she would always try to avoid the troops and used to walk down Lily Vale rather than along by the Towers where they were based. The embarrassment was all too much for her at that age.

English troops stationed in Brabourne Lees are reported to have dug caves into the sandbanks behind Newlands on Plain Road in order to store extensive supplies of wire and other army hardware, including canned food. According to Stella and Peter Rigg, these caves were prevented from collapsing entirely by the roots of the chestnut trees and other vegetation above them. These days they could be a death trap and readers are advised not to go in search of "booty".

Additionally, all the flat fields in Brabourne had invasion posts set up in them, about 75yd x 75yd apart, staggered, but in rows; these posts were similar to telephone poles but not as smooth and were intended to stop gliders and aircraft landing. After the war they made good logs. Some of these were willow posts which, in time, took root and started to grow. Oliver Trowell remembered that they were put up by mobile squads of men who were paid slightly more than agricultural workers (who at that time received 48 shillings for a 48-hour week).

## THE CANADIAN CONTINGENT

Mersham le Hatch was requisitioned for the Canadians and Lady Brabourne recalls that, "on the whole, they didn't do too much damage". Items that they did take, though, were the door handles, which had been designed by Chippendale. It appeared that various individuals had each taken a handle, so their apparent value to their "liberators" would have been nothing other than sentimental – according to Lady Brabourne, they would only have held their value if they had been kept as a set. Also, quite extraordinarily considering its weight, they took a massive Tudor oak table on the invasion of France, possibly for use in the mess. "Letters were written," Lady Brabourne told us, in order to retrieve it from France; it was returned – eventually – and still lives with the Brabourne family.

Unlike the British, the Canadian troops had no bugles and, according to Margaret Pile (Ward), "They called at Anchor Garage [Ward's Garage, now John Childs' Garage] for a klaxon motor horn to use in their camp. They dug out a gun site at the top of Calland Hill and installed a gun to protect us from the doodlebugs. We were asked to provide home comforts for them – baths, for example. Jack Cheeseman presented them with a live suckling pig in his arms, to kill and roast. They stayed for three months and then joined the D-day landings."

Yvonne Ward recalls, "Lydia Ward [her mother-in-law] provided many a supper for our allies", and that the Canadians were appreciative of what local people did for them and generous with gifts and cigarettes. Yvonne remembered Ted saying that one of the Canadians left a bag in the loft at Ward's Garage with the firm intention of returning to collect it. However, D-day came and went and nobody ever collected the bag, so it was presumed that the owner had died. Margaret adds: "Some 20 years later, Peggy Hickmott [postlady] delivered a crumpled note to the owner of 'Smeeth Garage'. It was from the Canadian! From then on we corresponded and I later met him and his wife when we were touring Canada. I also learnt which of their number had been killed during the D-day landings."

Phil Stone added that the Canadian troops who were under canvas in Hatch Park were sent to the northern part of France, not too far in advance of the British and American troops, to the zone where the doodlebugs were coming from. The Canadians were also involved in the Dieppe Raid (19th August, 1942), which was an attempt to assess just how strong the Germans were. They sustained severe losses in this exercise. Indeed, over 6,000 men – not just Canadians – were sent to Dieppe, and of these almost two-thirds were lost.

Below is a poem written on the gun site (the grass mound beyond Calland) during 1944 by one of the Canadian troops, Sergeant Red MacDougal, and supplied to us by Margaret.

ENGLAND

Call all your men when spirits lag, and watch us rally to the flag.
We men will work and fight and give, just for the day that England lives.
We, your sons from across the sea, would fight and die that you might be
the same old England, roses fair, with children laughing everywhere.
Old cobblestones, from way back past when our Dads fought the Great War last.
The atmosphere of peace so strong, we know in heart we can't go wrong.
This is the England that I know, its sky, its flowers, its busy flow.
And with the peace shall come the day when happy hearts are here to stay.

Stephen Norrington has a garden shed which his father bought from Tom Jeanes for £7-10-0 in the early 1950s when they lived at the top of School Lane. It is thought to have come from a Dispersal Sale which took place when the Canadian troops were leaving Brabourne after World War I. Stephen would like to know more about the origin of his shed and wonders whether anyone has any idea where he might find a bill of sale. Was the shed sold by Hobbs, Burrows and Day or any of the other agents at that time? Until he finds the appropriate agent and the catalogue he can't verify where the shed came from - so, if anyone can help, please let us know.

BRABOURNE AND SMEETH HOME GUARD (1940-1945)
John Hammon writes:

"After eight months of 'phoney war' the Germans invaded Denmark and Norway on 9th April, 1940. The Western Front was still calm until, on the 10th May, the Germans launched a surprise attack on the neutral countries of Holland and Belgium. A similar attack by the German army on the 12th May came out of the Ardennes, which had previously been thought to be impassable by tanks, and they took Sedan and reached the River Meuse. The Allied troops fell back in complete confusion in the face of these German assaults. The British Expeditionary Force was subsequently evacuated from Dunkirk by about the 1st June, 1940.

"Worried about the possible invasion of Britain, Mr Anthony Eden, Secretary of State for War, made a BBC broadcast on the 16th May to the men of Britain, requesting volunteers from the towns and villages to form the Local Defence Force –

'We want large numbers of such men who are British subjects between the ages of 17 and 65. You will not be paid but you will receive uniforms and will be armed.'

Brabourne Home Guard.

Back row: from left, B. Hogbin, Mervyn Hills, Tom Bradley, Bob Ball, N. Smith, Sid Andrews, Chris Andrews, Vic Crouch.

Middle row: from left, Archibald Ashman, George Lilley, Alan Shorter, Den Tully, Walter Tilbee, Ross Ashman, Jeff Beadle, G. Jordan, B. Back. Front row: from left, Patrick Thornby, Ernest Dryland, Bunny Hayward, Tom Jeanes,

Sgt Keith Finn, B. Crior, Oswald Ames

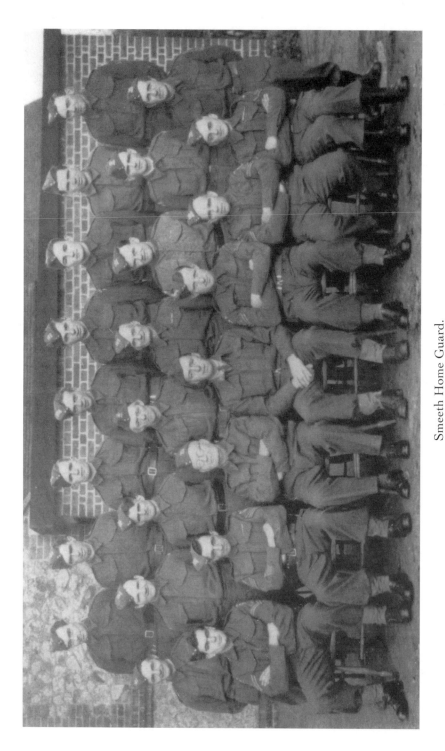

Smeeth Home Guard.

Back row: from left, J. Cheeseman, D. Gates, E. Tournay, J. Andrews, L. Sawyer, E. Ward, G. Brooks, B. Thornby
Middle row: from left, E. O'Nean, O. Heathfield, C. Taylor, W. Mabbs, R. Orpin, B. Hogbin, E. Gates, P. Simmons
Front row: from left, J. Hickmott, J. Wynder, T. Williams, R.J. Martin, A. Hogbin, F. Evans, J. White

Brabourne and Smeeth Home Guard.

Back row, from left, O. Heathfield, A. Shorter, E. Gates, W. Tilbee, B. Hogbin, M. Hills, J. Beadle, V. Crouch, N. Smith, B. Thornby, B. Crior. Second row: from left, E. Hogbin, T. Bradley, E. Ward, B. Ball, C. Cheeseman, E. Tournay, D. Gates, L. Sawyer, G. Brooks, J. Andrews, C. Andrews, R. Ashman, A. Ashdown. Third row: from left, E. O'Nean, G. Lilley, D. Tully, C. Taylor, O. Ames, P. Thornby, J. White, R. Orpin, G. Jordan, W. Mabbs, S. Andrews, P. Simmons.

Front row: from left, E. Dryland, J. Hickmott, J. Wynder, T. Williams, T.H. Jeanes, R.J. Martin, W. Hayward, K. Finn, A. Hogbin, F. Evans
Our thanks to Derek Gurr for tracking down the names of people in the Brabourne and Smeeth Home Guard

"The Government had expected 150,000 men to volunteer. Within 24 hours of the broadcast 250,000 men had put down their names, and by the end of June the number was close to 1,500,000.

"Brabourne and Smeeth men were quick to sign on. Mr John Orpin was taking names and two sections were soon formed – the Brabourne section, with Tom Jeanes as officer, and the Smeeth section, with Ronnie Martin as officer. Bunny Hayward was sergeant major of the two together, which made up the Brabourne and Smeeth Platoon. Teddy Ward, the proud owner of a motorbike, was made the platoon's despatch rider.

"The men were issued with khaki-coloured armbands inscribed with the letters LDV (Local Defence Volunteers), but the promised arms were slow in coming and some went on parade or guard duty with their own shotguns or rifles. The parades and instruction were held at Smeeth School. The LDVs were assigned guard duties and were transported as necessary to the various railway bridges and down to the railway tunnels by Sandling Station for long cold nights on guard. It is likely that each village unit took its turn on the rota.

"Possibly because of its nickname, 'Look, Duck and Vanish', in July 1940 the new prime minister, Winston Churchill, changed the name from LDV to the Home Guard. This was displayed as a shoulder flash on the uniforms that were soon issued.

"Finally, each man was armed with a 303 rifle, the officers were mostly issued with revolvers and some of the NCOs (non-commissioned officers) with Tommy guns. It was a great temptation to use these new weapons for rabbit shooting, especially as there was plenty of ammunition to be found around the crashed British aircraft from the Battle of Britain. Walter Tilbee was one who was caught and had to appear before the officers on a charge of misuse of his rifle. There are other views on this, though – Bertie Back from Quarrington Farm may have been the one who shot the rabbit.

"The newly named Home Guard carried out manoeuvres with the units from Aldington and Sellindge. From 1942 some of the early volunteers started to be called up into the forces as they reached 18. John Norrington was one of these and became one of the D-day dodgers. The D-day dodgers were socalled as they were fighting through Africa, and subsequently Italy, and were thus unable to take part in the landings."

John survived to return home at the end of the war. The Home Guard stand-down was on the 3rd December, 1944, and became an inactive reserve unit. On the 31st December, 1945, it ceased to exist.

## GUARDING THE SANDLING RAILWAY TUNNEL

The Sandling tunnel was the main transport link with the docks and it was thought that the Germans might either bomb it or drop paratroopers to capture it. All Home Guard companies in the area took turns to be stationed at Sandling railway tunnel. The Brabourne platoon would guard it on one night, the Smeeth platoon the next, and the platoons from Mersham, Aldington and Lympne would take their turns, too. This went on until just after D-day. Though he was barely 17 years old, Phil Stone was very young to have joined the Home Guard in 1943, but having lost his brother to the war, and with a strong desire to play football for the Home Guard team, his mother agreed to it. On the evenings when they were guarding the tunnel, Phil was Bunny Hayward's runner. There was a routine that had to be followed, almost a ceremony, each time they arrived for the night: the station master who had been in charge of the tunnel during the day would walk through the tunnel together with the sergeant major to ensure that it was clear and then hand over responsibility to the sergeant major and his platoon.

As the trains went past (steam in those days), Phil told us the firemen on the train would throw out lumps of coal to the Home Guard on duty so that they could use it to heat a kettle on the fire. This was kindness and camaraderie at its best, but as Phil put it, "You had to be careful not to stand in the way of a flying lump of coal!" Apparently, the stokers used to do much the same for the Permanent Way staff, the people who were based in huts along the railway line and who used to maintain the line.

## THE DESPATCH RIDER

Yvonne Ward writes that her husband, Ted, was the despatch rider, "probably because he could mend the motorbike. Ted was given some 'flashes', which his mother duly put on his uniform. Outside Canterbury he was stopped by 'Redcaps' (military police), who said they had seen him pass on other occasions and had noted the 'flashes'. It turned out that these should only have been worn if the enemy had actually landed, and anyone seen wearing these was not to be stopped!"

## TRAINING TALES

Frank Ames recalls hearing stories from his father, Oswald, of the Home Guard during training. On one occasion the platoon officer, Ronnie Martin, asked the assembled group of volunteers how they would overpower a German if they ever encountered one. Was there anyone present, he asked, who could demonstrate how to hold a captive in a half-nelson? Nelson Smith was the first to say that, yes, he could do this but, clearly not believing him, Ronnie suggested that he had better demonstrate his skill. Before anyone knew what had happened Nelson had grabbed Ronnie and had him down on the floor, completely immobilised.

Another of Oswald's anecdotes, re-told by Frank, concerned a time when Tom Jeanes was drilling the Home Guard on parade at Smeeth School: "Left, right, left, right, left, right… right, left. Oh b*****, I mean right… "

## THE HOME GUARD POST-WAR

A modernised version of the Home Guard was established in December 1951 and continued until 1957. Roger Vining, tall at the age of 14, joined the Wye group, the headquarters of which was at the New Flying Horse. They used to meet there every week and, though there were no duties, Roger did receive valuable training, such as learning the language of signals, rifle shooting on ranges and participating in field-training manoeuvres.

For one training session the Red Berets were parachuted into the area somewhere between Chilham and Godmersham, their aim being to capture Dungeness. Opposing them were the combined forces of the local Home Guard, police and fire brigade, whose purpose was to stop the Red Berets from reaching their target, which for the purposes of the exercise was considered "nuclear". Roger, by then 16, had just bought a 250cc BSA motorbike and, on the appointed day, went all over the place with messages, and also was on the lookout for members of either side who had been captured. The normal practice seems to have been to tie up prisoners in a state of nakedness wherever they had been caught. Returning to the HQ at the New Flying Horse, Roger found a room full of 30 to 40 Red Berets, all captured and naked! He was given a Sten gun and told to guard them. One of them asked, "What will you do if we charge you?" Roger calmly replied: "Hold the door open so you can go outside." The Home Guard won the day and Roger and his colleagues were most proud to have saved Dungeness.

## HELPING THE WAR EFFORT – JOINING THE ARMED FORCES

Determined "to do their bit" for the War Effort, people signed up readily and, though there were fewer casualties from the villages in the Second World War, these still represented a terrible waste of human life. Nevertheless, many in the armed forces who survived benefited from the training they received while in the services and this led many men and some women down new career paths. George Hickmott worked at Norrington's Garage (now Fisher's) on the A20 until he was 17, volunteering for the RAF on his 17th birthday. He so wanted to follow his elder brother into the air force that he turned down the opportunity for an apprenticeship at Norrington's because this would have tied him to the job. As a consequence he earned 7/6 per week at Norrington's, where he was not a trainee, but just "the boy". He spent three days trying to get initiated but was sent home because he was not yet 18, the minimum age for joining up. For the next nine months he worked as a van driver for Orpins Stores, an advantage of having learnt to drive while he worked for Norrington's. Michael Hickmott, George's son, said, "On George's 18th birthday he signed up as a mechanic, together with his friend Len

George Hickmott

Smith, who enrolled as a driver. Dad was called up on 2nd December, 1941, but didn't go until July, 1942."

After the war ended Phil Stone was called up for Compulsory Service and joined the RAF. During the war he had been working in Harry Holts, the bike and radio shop in Ashford. Had he signed on with the RAF for six or seven years he could have gone into the radio section, but he was not prepared to commit to this so, instead, his line of work was allocated to him. He ended up in Germany working on Mosquito bombers for 6107 Squadron. Once out of the RAF Phil joined Post Office Telephones, where he stayed for 38½ years. Though not directly relevant to his chosen career, his time in the RAF gave him valuable experience.

The size and dynamism of Brabourne's British Legion is testimony to the many who found employment in the forces and who also risked (and in some cases, gave) their lives for their country. Many of today's members did not originate in the village but this of course makes their contribution no less valuable.

## HOW THE LAND BECAME AN ALLY
Food production was incredibly important during the war and, as everyone knows, the government was encouraging the population to "dig for victory". People were advised to turn their gardens over to food production and, at the other end of the scale, the government was urging farmers to plough up grassland and grow crops to feed the nation. As we know from the chapter entitled Land and Livelihoods, Reg Older was on the War Agricultural Executive Committee and knowledgeable about innovation in agriculture; his role was, therefore, to advise farmers how to get the most out of their land.

The Women's Land Army (WLA) was re-established in 1939 and land girls – who were initially volunteers, but were later conscripted – were placed by the Ministry of Agriculture and Fisheries on farms and smallholdings that had lost labour because men had signed up. Land Army girls were numerous in our area. Some were local, but others had been brought to Kent from other parts of the country, including London. As mentioned before, Penstock Farm had four land girls, all of whom lived in the attic rooms of Penstock farmhouse. Reg's wife, Margaret, recalls how busy she was, looking after and cooking for four extra people in the house. She also remembers needing much more shopping because of them and the difficulties involved in getting this home without a car.

Margaret Baldock (Sawyer) was a Land Army girl. When she first joined she was based in Ashford and used to cycle each day from Clovelly in Brabourne Lees to Currah's Farm, near Willesborough Church. From there she would catch a lorry with several others to help with fruit spraying in local orchards. Margaret was then billeted in Sittingbourne, where she worked at Woodstock Park Farm. Here, she recalls, "they grew virtually everything". The farm was bought by Shell in 1947, and a research station was created, which later became a science park. Even before being taken over by Shell, experimental work was being conducted at the farm, as Margaret remembers there being a number of greenhouses where work was being done to improve the quality of crop sprays. While in Sittingbourne she used to cycle up Bell Road each day towards the farm. On the way she would pass Dean's Jam Factory, which used to smell delicious, especially when strawberries were in season and strawberry jam was being made. Sadly, this has now been demolished.

## "MYSTERY TOWN" ON THE DOWNS
Below is an extract from a local paper, dated Saturday, 19th May – the year is not known, but it was probably 1945.

"How Nature did what German bombers were 'invited' to do can now be told.

"Early in the war on a wild stretch of gorseland on the North Downs was built a scale model of Ashford, all features faithfully reproduced even down to four feet high lamp standards. They were wired and dimly lighted. From the air this construction gave a true picture of the town to raiding aircraft.

"Other things in this model town which had no place in the original were large grids full of inflammable matter wired up for electrical ignition ready to destroy the stooge town of Ashford – all part of the deception in defence scheme. Ashford was never the target for a heavy night raid though it suffered a number of hit-and-run blitzes.

"Scheme Never Used
The occasion never arose to put the scheme into operation but Nature stepped in one night. A violent thunderstorm raged along the Downs and a vivid flash of lightning ignited the 'firing' system, setting the 'town' ablaze.

"Fire services met a formidable task, and after they were through were sworn to secrecy, and the story of that big 'gorse' fire at Hastingleigh [should have read Elmsted/Stowting, Brabourne], about six miles from Ashford, went the rounds.

"Now comes the explanation, possibly, of those many occasions when explosives and incendiaries were showered on this part of the Kent countryside."

## TENSIONS OF THE ERA

Memories of the Second World War are fixed indelibly in the minds of all our contributors who lived through it. Eric Ball remembers going to the shop in East Brabourne on the day that war was announced to get some elastic for his gas mask. Air-raid sirens went off just as he was crossing The Street, and Clifford Cameron, an air-raid warden, shouted at him: "Get inside, get inside!" This proved to be a false alarm because it was a British plane – "One of our planes coming over," in Eric's words. However, the event heralded the new rules for life for all, which were to last for the next six years. Even before the war started there were hints of what was to come. Eric remembers seeing a German airship flying over on his way to school, and all the children from Brabourne School going outside to look at it. This was in the days when Mrs Temple was headmistress. John Varrier adds that these zeppelins were seemingly used commercially, but in reality they were flying towards London for the purposes of reconnaissance.

Margaret Pile (Ward) looks back:

"It felt as though there was a black cloud everywhere. You didn't dare show a light. All shop and house windows were boarded and darkly curtained; car lights were partly concealed. Gas masks were carried everywhere in a cardboard box on our shoulders, even into the school toilets, and when the sirens sounded, you went straight to the air-raid shelter. The night skies were criss-crossed with searchlights so

Medals for Special Policemen. Those from Smeeth who were honoured included
T.W. Hobday, R.L. Blaskett, T.H. Wratten, G. Brooks.
Exact source unknown, probably KM Group (mid-1950s)

that the gunners could see the bombers. Younger men who hadn't joined up formed the Home Guard, while older men formed the Special Constabulary. They had an all-night rota looking for incendiary bombs, which were target-illuminating flares. They were like large balls of fire and were dropped in large numbers by the Germans. All signposts were removed in case spies landed. At one stage there were checkpoints on roads all around the area. There was one at the bottom of Hatch Hill and a permit was needed to transport passengers long distances by taxi.

"We had double summertime, though, so it was daylight much longer, bringing lovely hot evenings to collect the harvest. There were no combines then. The corn was stooked in the fields to dry and, after collection, we children had to pick up the ears of corn that had been dropped. These we put into a sandbag to feed the chickens and tame rabbits we kept to feed the family. From the age of 12 we picked fruit in the school holidays to purchase clothing coupons, which we used to buy our school clothes. We also made our own clothes with a hand-operated Singer sewing machine. Where we could we used old parachute material, as this made lovely 'undies' and also wedding dresses.

"On one occasion, my sister and I raffled two lemons and collected enough money for the Red Cross to send food parcels to Fred Ashdown and Captain Moody, prisoners of war. It was later said that those parcels had kept them alive, and the men both returned home. Those lemons were found in a wooden box that had been rescued from Southampton Water by my sister, Wren Rosemary Hendry (Ward). We've often thought that they must have been a bit salty!"

Many people recalled their fears of everyday life during wartime. At the age of 18, Joyce Garlick (Wood) began work in Ashford, somewhere near the First World War tank[1], for a small firm that "repaired wellington boots for farmers and land girls, because you couldn't buy these anywhere. We also mended a few American army boots as these, too, were made of rubber." As we have heard, bikes were the main form of transport, and Joyce remembers being terrified as she cycled home each evening during the blackout.

---

1 The tank that stands in Ashford town centre is a First World War Mark IV tank. After the cessation of hostilities in November 1918 many tanks were presented to towns around the country. This may seem strange but tanks were a new weapon during the First World War and captured public imagination. Ashford's tank, which saw action in 1917, at the Messines Ridge in Belgium and at Ypres, was presented to the town on 1st July, 1919, to mark the contribution of the town's people to the war effort. Ashford's tank is thought to be one of only eight such tanks remaining. (Sources: www.ukattraction.com/south-east-england/ashford-tank.htm; www.flickr.com/photos/cyberbia/3431213721/; en.wikipedia.org/wiki/Ashford,_Kent. All accessed on 14th June, 2013.)

Betty Edenden was cycling not far from the Towers when a German plane passed overhead and started firing tracer bullets, which lit up the area. The soldiers at the Towers attacked, but she had had a near miss. Listening to the news in wartime was of critical importance to all and Betty remembers her granny and grandpa demanding absolute silence when the news was on. She added that everyone read the newspapers avidly at that time, too.

Tom Wratten, who lived at Forge Cottage in East Brabourne, can remember his father (also Tom) constructing a Morrison air-raid shelter in the front room of their house. It had a thick steel "roof" and square mesh round it. You couldn't stand up in it, but Tom and his sister loved playing in it. At that time Tom's mother, Ivy, was pregnant with his sister Margaret, and Tom told us it was an awful squash during air raids when his mother was in the shelter as well. The family had three Land Army girls staying with them, Doris Norrington and Peg Hickmott being two of them. While they were living there, Doris broke her leg and was hobbling around in plaster. Tom recalled one occasion when Doris and Peg were in the orchard behind the cottage and there was an air raid. He remembers yelling, "Get in! Get in!" and frantically trying to pull Doris (with her leg in plaster) through the hedge behind the house. Whether it happened during the same raid or not we cannot be sure, but Bill Stockbridge and his family lived in a cottage more or less opposite the gates of Penstock Farm and, sometime during the war, it was demolished, possibly as a result of bomb damage.

Phil Harris, who lived at Vine Cottage on the Ridgeway, remembers an Allied plane coming down in the field on the Brabourne Lees side of the Black House on the Ridgeway, where Lord and Lady Brabourne lived at one time. It was just near where the road dips. The pilot bailed out and came down at Pemsey Farm, a mile or two away. Margaret Pile (Ward) added that, "All planes that fell were dug out by volunteers with spades, often from great depths – no JCBs in those days. I was there when this plane was recovered. Lord and Lady Brabourne were there, too, and were presented with part of the bent body, which went to a museum." The pilot was Alan Frith, who is commemorated in the Scout hut.

There were many incidents of people being shot at by German planes during the war. Roger remembers several such occasions and, in the summer of 1940, Vi Varrier's (Kingston) parents, who lived in Stowting, were fired at by a Messerschmitt while they were in the fields with the horses. Vi added that it was a good thing that the German pilot was a bad shot and noted that the whole event was "really most alarming". Joan Copland (Dryland) was shot at by a German plane as she was crossing the garden of her home at Woolpack Cottages on Woolpack Hill, the bullets missing her by no more than a few feet. Eric Ball told of a yellow-nosed Messerschmitt crashing near

The Limes, now The Hall, in Weekes Lane, West Brabourne. There were rumours that the pilot had bailed out and escaped, went to Hythe and was met by a U-boat. All this proved to be nonsense. The pilot did indeed bail out, but was caught and kept in England as a prisoner of war, and then returned to Germany. He is remembered as coming back to England and visiting the Brabourne area after the war. From 1942 Oliver Trowell carried out arable cultivation on the land where the Messerschmitt crashed and remembers oil from the plane coming up in the water rising from the spring at the lower end of the field.

In 1940 a Hawker Hurricane plane came down on the Kingstons' farm, just in Stowting. Witnesses who saw the plane said that it came in as if to land but the wheels were not down. It was thought that it had caught fire and the heat caused the ammunition to "cook off". The pilot never moved and it was later deduced that he was dead from bullet wounds when the plane landed.

When Tim Marsh was five or six years old he and his parents lived at Little Haven, a cottage on Scots Lane in Stowting, not 50yd from the top of Fiddling Lane, on the way to Brabourne. (You might recognise it today as the cottage that has been virtually re-built.) One day in the early 1940s a row of seven or eight Spitfires came past Little Haven and the last one in the line was clearly in difficulty, belching smoke. While the others continued on their way, the Spitfire in trouble was flying erratically and suddenly started flying directly towards the cottage from the field to the south/southwest. Tim wonders what the pilot saw in his last, difficult moments. He thought that he must have seen the cottage with people in it, because as the plane was heading for the cottage the pilot suddenly managed to gain some degree of control and turned the nose skywards. Missing the cottage by yards, the plane rose vertically and then looped backwards, coming down nose first in the field to the south of the cottage. There was an enormous explosion the moment it hit the ground and Tim describes the ball of fire as just like in the films but somehow "more real than real". Being five or six at the time he remembers not being frightened, just mesmerised, but as time has gone on this event and others during the war have given Tim many a nightmare.

Alec Moon, whose parents were the licensees of the Five Bells from 1933 to 1940, wrote:

"My eldest brother, Doug, who was a flight sergeant in the RAF, came home for leave in 1940, at a time when I had returned home also. We learned that a German aircraft had landed on the Downs, so we walked up towards Hastingleigh, and somewhere near South Hill we came upon an undamaged Messerschmitt 109 that had been forced down or had run out of fuel. On guard was a very young, raw army recruit who was a bit overawed by Doug's rank and badges, so we had no problem being allowed to look over the plane, and we gave him our assurance we would not take any souvenirs. It was evident that it had been in a fight because there were holes in the canvas along the leading edge of the wings, showing that the machine guns fixed inside the wings had been fired, and there was still a strong smell of cordite. Later on in the war I was to sit on top of the Downs and look across at V-1 buzz bombs as they made their noisy way at low level towards London. One was safe all the time they were making a noise."

On the 29th October, 1940, Oliver Trowell remembers seeing Italian planes flying very low over Brabourne in a southerly direction. It is possible that these were members of the Corpo Aereo Italiano (CAI), the Italian Air Corps, on their way back from bombing Ramsgate, an attack thought to have been a response to a raid on several north Italian cities . Oliver writes: "I think the incident occurred near midday, as I recall Mr Coleman – who, like Harry Denne, had his 'dinner' of bread and cheese in his pocket – saying to me as I left the field by 40 Acre Wood to go home for my lunch, 'You tell Mrs Coleman, we don't make much money but we do get some excitement.'"

After the war started one of the first parachutes to come down in East Brabourne was in that small portion of the land opposite the Five Bells (later the orchard) that was owned by Sidney Finn and where he used to keep a few sheep. The pilot was badly burned and was taken in by Clifford Cameron, then at Penstock Farm. He recovered and also allegedly returned to Penstock to see his rescuer.

## LIFE AS THE SIX-YEAR-OLD SON OF A GERMAN ÉMIGRÉ
Karl Engels writes:

"My memories of the war were undoubtedly much the same as many other small boys of similar age, but for my parents, Willy and Iris Engels, it brought additional complications. Earlier in the 1930s my parents lived in Germany, my father then being a German national who worked in a bank. At some time in the early 1930s he 'declined' an invitation to join the Nazi Party and, aware of what the consequences for this might be, he and my mother left for England and settled at The Knoll in Brabourne Lees, where I was later born. My father now had a very different life from working in a bank – he kept goats and chickens, grew vegetables and worked for local farmers, including George Brooks at Waterside Farm, and Tom Jeanes at Bircholt. With the advent of the war, my father was interned on the Isle of Man, despite having taken British nationality. Fortunately, he was released after a comparatively short time because his brother-in-law, Alan Collier, was a senior civil servant who was able to 'pull strings'.

"So, despite being born and growing up as any English boy in Brabourne, the war did have additional and different effects on my parents, and though some of these undoubtedly trickled down to me, I was still only about seven when the war ended and very much of an age to continue enjoying the rest of my childhood in Brabourne.

"I was far too young to have any real memory of the Battle of Britain, but my first memory of the war was of being woken in the middle of the night by the sound of very heavy motor and tracked vehicles going past our house. The noise went on for most of the night and though keen to know what was going on, we couldn't look out because of the blackout. In the morning – what a sight! Much of Hospital Field, Bircholt Field and Middle Field had Churchill tanks around the perimeter. I demanded that we must go to Orpins to shop, and what a fantastic sight! The hedges along Brabourne Lees had been torn up in places, there was mud all over the place and soldiers were making tea and eating breakfast at almost every tank. With hindsight, they were probably intended to fool the Germans that D-day would be led from Kent. The tanks stayed for some weeks and then left."

## AN ASIDE

The issue of the tanks has prompted some debate among our contributors: Phil and Sheila Stone remember tracked vehicles in Brabourne, but Phil believes that they were Bren Gun Carriers, rather than Churchill tanks, which were being marshalled before going to Portsmouth and Southampton in readiness for the Normandy landings (1944). (For our information, Karl explained that a Bren Gun Carrier was quite unlike a Churchill tank: the former looked like a square-fronted boat on tracks and had no tank turret but was open.) Karl agrees that there were many Bren Gun Carriers in the village during the war, but he is certain that there was a marshalling of Churchill tanks at one time and, as the passage he wrote here suggests, he was very excited by their presence in Brabourne. He agreed that Bren Gun Carriers were the preferred tracked vehicles in the D-day landings, not least because the Churchill tanks were so slow, so this being the case it seems plausible that the Churchill tanks in Brabourne may have had some function as decoys, as Karl suggested. Phil, however, disagrees with the notion of decoys so far inland. Oliver Trowell recalls that there were Churchill tanks in the village at one time as well as Bren Gun Carriers, so it would seem that both Karl and Phil are probably correct in their recollections, but tying memories to a particular event and time can be difficult, especially if the events in question were transitory.

Karl continues:

"I was in my garden one day with my chickens and goats – they were very important because of rationing – when a few planes started to come across. The number increased steadily, until the whole sky was filled from Canterbury Road back to Bircholt Court, with planes towing gliders – you could see the tow cables. It seemed to me that there were hundreds of them. The sound was absolutely fantastic!"

Phil remembers seeing them, too. They were probably Horsa and Hamilcar gliders, being towed by Lancaster and Halifax bombers. Karl assumed that they were probably on their way to Arnhem, as part of Operation Market Garden. Oliver Trowell, who was working on the Downs, recalled seeing a similar armada as it headed east over Brabourne, probably towards Arnhem. Karl could not be sure of the exact year that he saw these planes – if it had been 1944 they may well have been on their way to Arnhem, but if it had been 1945 the planes may have been on their way to the Rhine as part of the massive Operation Varsity, said to be the largest single airborne offensive in history . Oliver, however, was confident that the year in which he saw the planes was 1944, as he was working in Brabourne at that time.

## FALLING BOMBS

The Battle of Britain started in the summer of 1940 and built up to a peak in September, when the Germans gave in. During that summer John Varrier remembers going regularly to Cobbs Hill to sit up there, watching the skies. One day, at 8.30pm, he saw "Stuka dive bombers blast Lympne off the face of earth", something that left a lasting sickening feeling within him.

Children are some of the most vulnerable in our society and yet several of our contributors who were children during the war, and who had grown up with it, seemed to have been worried less by it than were the adults. Joan Taylor (Brooks) and her sister, Mabel Oliver, remembered that if a V-1 flying bomb, or doodlebug as they were better known, went over and you were out, you had to jump into a ditch, but they recall that they did this more because they felt compelled by the rule that had been instilled in them than out of fear. They could both remember having to go through a hatch and into an underground shelter when they were at Brabourne School, and this was much more scary as at the time their fear of the dark far exceeded their fear of an air raid. Had they come close to the effects of a bomb, they agreed that their views would almost certainly have been different.

On Friday, 28th July 1944, the first day of Vi Varrier's (Kingston's) school holidays, she was at home on her parents' farm on the borders of Brabourne and Monks

Horton when a doodlebug fell in the front garden around midday. Her brothers and sisters, who all attended a different school, started their holidays the next day and so, fortunately, were not at home. Vi was suddenly aware that they had been bombed and that her house was collapsing around her. She was quite unhurt, her mother was unconscious, but her father looked much worse, with blood gushing from his cheeks. Once at the hospital his injuries were found to be largely superficial, but Vi's mother had been seriously hurt and promptly had her spleen removed. Later that same day Vi was brought "home" by the ambulance. She could see her teddy sitting on top of her mother's sewing machine so she collected him, caught her pony, which was in the field, and went to her grandma's down the lane. She recalled that the pony too was shocked by the event "and was always a bit jumpy after that". The cat was the only one that had died in the blast.

Once her brothers and sisters returned to their grandparents' home in Monks Horton and had got over their initial shock from the day's events, reality descended and they simply got on with dealing with their numerous cows, which by then needed milking. Young as they were, Vi notes that her brothers had become competent at such a job, with the help of their uncles. Once the animals had been looked after, Vi and her brothers and sisters returned to their grandparents. After living with them for about six weeks the Hammon family, who were lifelong friends (John Hammon and Vi were allegedly scrubbed together in the bath when they were toddlers), offered to take them in, and seven members of Vi's family slept together in one small room for around 18 months. Vi's father then bought a long, chicken-shed-type building and the family made it their home for over a year. Fortescue and Son rebuilt the bungalow and the family were back in it by 1947, shortly before Vi started nursing.

## LIVING WITH THE DOODLEBUG

Phil Stone said that doodlebugs were at their height in the summer of 1944 and there were several lines of defence put in place to prevent them from getting through to London. First, there were the guns on the coast; behind these, about 10 miles inland, there were searchlights to pick up those doodlebugs and other aircraft that had got past the guns; and nearer London there were the barrage balloons, which were positioned so that they foiled low-flying aircraft. The spaces between these three lines were patrolled by the fighters. If the doodlebugs got past the guns on the coast they would, in theory, be spotted by the searchlight boys, who would send up a flare to signal that the fighters should go immediately into action. The fighters included American Mustangs based at Mersham, as well as Spitfires, which could have come from Biggin Hill and Tangmere.

The doodlebugs moved very quickly – at a speed of around 400mph – and kept a constant height of about 2,000ft. The maximum speed of the Spitfires, however, was only 350mph, though they were much more manoeuvrable. The fighters' task was either to explode the doodlebugs, a tactic that was dangerous to the fighter, or redirect them by flying underneath and using their own wings to "tip" the wings of the bomb so that it was destabilised and crashed. This was, unsurprisingly, also very risky. According to a display at the Brenzett Aeronautical Museum Trust, it appears from the bent wing tip of a Spitfire that the fighters did sometimes make contact with the bombs as they tipped them. It was said to be safer if the fighter dived below the bomb and, by coming up close to it, created a rush of air that destabilised the gyroscope – this would cause the doodlebug to crash or divert it from its set path to London. But disabling the autopilot didn't mean that the danger had ended as, of course, having lost its sense of direction, the bomb could then move in a random direction and still cause havoc. Phil remembered one such occasion when he, as one of a large group of cyclists, had just cycled down the High Street in Ashford and was waiting for traffic lights to change at the top of East Hill. The group suddenly became aware of a doodlebug silently drifting just above them. All were expecting it to drop, but because of some malfunction, it continued to Maidstone West Station where it came down, almost certainly causing casualties.

Karl Engels remembers a night in The Knoll when he heard the characteristic sound of a doodlebug. Usually, if they weren't going to come down, the sound simply died away as they passed overhead, but this time the sound kept returning. Karl peeped out of his bedroom window and could see nothing, so he rushed into his parents' bedroom on the other side of the house and peeped through the curtains there, only to see a doodlebug circling overhead, its gyroscope clearly having become disorientated. One extreme of its circular path took it directly above The Knoll, and the other took it over Bircholt Court Farm. Knowing that the doodlebugs only had sufficient fuel to carry them to London, Karl was concerned that, by circling, it was using up its fuel, and if this continued the bug would almost certainly come down somewhere near them, if not directly on them. He tried to rouse his parents to persuade them to go down to their Morrison shelter, but they merely told him to go back to bed. He continued to watch the circling doodlebug until, suddenly, its gyro appeared to right itself, but rather than continuing on its journey to London it went back the same way it had come. Karl still thinks of this as a small but significant victory in the course of the war.

Karl writes:

"Hitler's V-1, or Retribution Weapon-1, was known as the doodlebug because of the sound that it made, which was more like a heavy motorbike without a silencer than a plane. If you could hear one, it wasn't worth going to the shelter because it would be past before you got there. However, if the noise stopped, that was the time to dive for cover.

"I used to walk to Brabourne School – the first part of the journey to the village hall was on my own, and from there onwards I went with the West Brabourne group. On this occasion, I was about halfway between my house and the hall when a doodle passed over near the school. I left the road and went into the ditch as I had been instructed, but remained standing so that I could watch what happened. By now it was over Coomb Wood, then part of Mr Cameron's property, at which point a Spitfire dived and started machine-gunning it. A Spitfire could only gain on it after the momentum of a dive, as its maximum speed was less than that of the doodlebug. Fortunately, it did not hit the bug as it would have come down on West Brabourne. With the excitement over, I walked on and joined the others at the hall before continuing to school."

Rose Andrews (Smith) has no trouble remembering the terror that these bombs could cause. She was delivering milk near Brabourne School one day and, as soon as she heard a doodlebug, she leapt into a ditch and lay flat, waiting for the blast. On another occasion Rose thought a doodlebug was about to land in the pantry at Parsonage Farm: "SO frightening – it was just too horrible for words." When her family, the Smiths, were harvesting the fields at Parsonage Farm so many doodlebugs came over the farm that the family had perfected their drill. In Rose's words, "Dad flopped down on top of the wagon, Uncle George [Smith] let the horse out of its harness so that if it bolted Dad would be safe, and Mum and I lay flat on the ground."

One of Ann Griggs's (Elizabeth Beadle) earliest memories of wartime is of herself and her sister Esther picking fruit in an orchard that their father, Jeffrey Beadle, had rented near Crow Corner. Jeffrey heard a doodlebug overhead and pushed the two girls into a ditch, shielding them as they lay there. Though the bug didn't land nearby the experience is embedded in Ann's mind and surfaces easily, over 60 years later. She was under five years old at the time.

Eric Ball can also recall the time when a doodlebug landed in the field behind the Carpenter's Workshop (apparently, as many as five landed in Brabourne). Leonard Finn was in the upper storey and every window in the building was blown out, but he was unscathed. The Five Bells across the road also lost several windows in the same blast.

A PERSONAL RECORD IN PICTURES OF WORLD WAR II EVENTS WITNESSED LOCALLY BY OLIVER TROWELL WHEN HE WAS A BOY. ALL PICTURES WERE DRAWN WITHIN A FEW DAYS OF THE EVENTS DEPICTED

"The day raids of 1940."
By Oliver Trowell (aged 13)

"Stukas dive-bombing Lympne in 1940."
By Oliver Trowell (aged 13)

"Enemy plane taking evasive action (1940)."
By Oliver Trowell (aged 13)

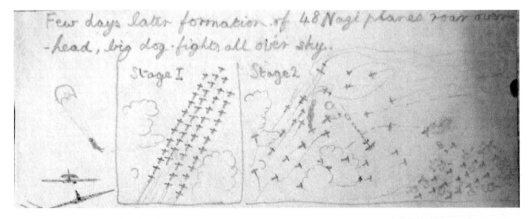

"Formation of Nazi bombers broken up over East Brabourne (October 1940)."
By Oliver Trowell (aged 13)

"Nine Axis planes swoop over us in East Brabourne at tree-top height (1940). These were possibly Italian planes on their way back from an attack on Ramsgate."
By Oliver Trowell (aged 13)

"Smoking Messerschmitt 109 over Forty Acre Wood, East Brabourne (1940)."
By Oliver Trowell (aged 13)

"Spitfire coming down in flames.  Nazis shoot pilot when parachuting down
over East Brabourne (October 1940).  Water Farm in distance."
By Oliver Trowell (aged 13)

"The night raids of 1940-41 on East Brabourne.
Flares falling on the right, Court Lodge on the left."
By Oliver Trowell (aged 13)

"After the Canterbury blitz (June 1942)."
By Oliver Trowell (aged 15)

"Ack-ack fire seen from East Brabourne during a 'tip and run' raid on Ashford
(March 24th, 1943)." By Oliver Trowell (aged 15).
Tony Stone was killed in this raid

"Church Corner, East Brabourne
Realistic mock invasion (May 1942)."
By Oliver Trowell (aged 15)

"The first night of the flying bombs, as seen from the fire watchers'
post at the Five Bells corner (June 1944)."
By Oliver Trowell (aged 17)

"Flying bombs over East Brabourne in daylight (1944)."
By Oliver Trowell (aged 17)

"The Stock Lane doodlebug, as seen from
West Brabourne (1944)."
By Oliver Trowell (aged 17)

"Doodlebug just above ground level before it hit a
tree and exploded near Hucking (Detling) in 1944."
By Oliver Trowell (aged 17)

Towards the end of the war Gordon Fortescue was on a train returning to Smeeth from Folkestone when the line was hit by a bomb. Gordon was injured by flying glass, though fortunately not seriously. He picked up a piece of shrapnel and kept it as a memento from such bleak days.

As you have seen, Oliver Trowell has kindly allowed us to include his drawings of the war as he witnessed it in Brabourne, aged 11-17. He makes the point that he was not a trained artist when he drew them. Nevertheless, they are a unique graphic description of events as seen from Brabourne and the surrounding area.

WHEN THE EVACUEES MOVED IN
Alec Moon writes:

"Early in 1940 my mother was surprised to have five children from London put with her as evacuees. The authorities had noted the accommodation but it quickly proved impossible for her to run the pub and look after five little strangers. Terry and Sheila Dwyer were two of these. Thankfully, someone saw wisdom and the children were moved. In any event, children were soon to be moved from Kent to the West Country to avoid the bombing of the county and London."

Oliver Trowell remembers Mrs Moon reprimanding Terry for some misdemeanour – "If you will do these things, then you must take the consequences!"

The nurses, Nell and Dorothy Hills, who used to live at no.1, Holly Cottages, in The Street, were allocated an evacuee called Pat. She became like a daughter to them and stayed closely in touch with them for the rest of their lives.

Every summer, John Varrier used to come down from Barnes, southwest London, to stay with his grandmother at Dial House in Stowting and was frequently bored there, so spent much time each holiday digging the rectory's garden. John writes:

"As the war escalated I was evacuated from London to Stowting to stay with my grandmother at Dial House as, given what had happened to Poland and Czechoslovakia, it was seriously expected that London would be bombed to total destruction. An aunt of mine had also decamped to Dial House with her two children, who were younger than me, so we were rather crowded, given that there were two bachelor uncles who worked at Stowting Court Farm who also lived there. I was awfully unhappy at Dial House but Adolf Hitler was to change all that, as we had a grandstand view of the Battle of Britain being fought out in the sky above us. Also, my cousins and I used to walk across the railway, where we picked up all sorts of army equipment that had been thrown from the trains by the totally exhausted soldiers after they had escaped from the German onslaught in France.

"London still had not been attacked, so I was never so happy as when my parents decided it was safer in London than in Kent at that time and took me home to Barnes. A few weeks later, the Blitz on London started and for the next two years we slept every night in our Anderson air-raid shelter on bunk beds made of chicken wire stretched across a wooden frame. During my time in Stowting I met a little girl who was very quiet and rather different from the older girls. I could talk to her and thought her rather lovely. Twelve years later, we were married."

Roger Vining came to stay with his grandparents at Robertsdane, Hastingleigh, during the war, in about 1943. Before that he had been living in London with his mother, his father having joined the RAF. Roger's mother was a busy person: she was an air-raid warden, had a full-time job with London Transport, an allotment, chickens – and a small son. She had little spare time and must have been near her wits' end when their house was all but destroyed by a doodlebug – only the wall beneath which Roger was crouching at the time of the blast was left. But this wasn't the only near miss. Shortly before the doodlebug incident an unexploded 500lb bomb had embedded itself in the ground not far from their front door, and on yet another occasion they had been on a bus when a bomb had fallen nearby and all the glass in the windows cascaded into the bus. With so many close shaves it was no wonder that Roger was evacuated to Hastingleigh. His mother, however, bought a caravan, continued working in London and survived the war.

Though safer than London, life wasn't uneventful in Hastingleigh, and Roger recalled a German plane crashing in his grandparents' field at Robertsdane. His grandfather and aunts rushed to the wreckage, pulled the very young pilot out and took him to the house for tea and cake. Very soon, however, the Home Guard and police arrived to take him away.

During another incident at Robertsdane, Roger saw several soldiers hiding in the hedges and went over to talk to them. They were on manoeuvres and he asked whether they might like some tea. They were delighted at the prospect, so Roger returned to the house to ask his grandparents to put the kettle on. Looking out of the window for the soldiers they saw not just the few whom Roger had met but literally dozens of soldiers coming towards their house. By the time they'd gone Roger recalled that there was no tea left – a disaster, considering tea was in very short supply during the war.

During his stay with his grandparents, Roger also remembered the Italian prisoners of war who used to help with work on the land. Like most people, he felt that they were uninterested in fighting and were extremely helpful when most able British men were away.

## A SOLDIER REMEMBERS

Dick Andrews (who moved to Brabourne from Sellindge after marrying Rose (Smith)) was in the army for six and a half years, the entire duration of the war, and was lucky to have survived. After the evacuation of Dunkirk between 26th May and 3rd June 1940, Dick remained in France at the infantry base depot at Rouen with his regiment, the Buffs, waiting to be called up to the front line. Fortunately, the decision was taken to evacuate the troops and Dick found himself on a train to the coast at St Nazaire. The train, however, only made it part of the way and stopped in the middle of nowhere. The rest of the journey had to be made on foot and, for safety, the soldiers broke into groups of 15-20 men, each group with an officer. Dick remembers them all being very young and bewildered by what was happening. He recalls that they were hungry and tired and, one evening, when they arrived at a farm, they discovered the farmer cooking potatoes for his pigs – that night, the pigs went hungry instead of the soldiers. When they finally reached St Nazaire they boarded the Lancastria, which was destined to be a troop ship but had not yet been converted from a liner. Any pleasure at the relief of leaving France and the prospect of going home ended abruptly when, shortly off the coast of France, the Lancastria was bombed and some 3,000 people lost their lives. Dick was fortunate to have survived. He should have been eating a meal when the ship was hit but he was feeling queasy so was up on deck. The blast threw him into the water where he managed to hang on to a barrel and eventually was rescued by the Oronsay, a hospital ship. Those in the Lancastria's dining rooms would almost certainly have drowned. Memories of the cold and fear remained with him for the rest of his life, as did the images of people in panic and with little hope of survival. He remembered the Oronsay packed with people – it was overloaded, but its crew went on rescuing until it was standing room only. The bombing of the Lancastria was a major disaster, but according to Dick the entire episode was kept as quiet as possible, something that would be impossible today.

By the time Dick reached England all he had was a blanket and a pair of trousers lent to him by a soldier on the Oronsay. For this kindness, he was always grateful. Those who had survived were taken to Stoke Military Hospital at Plymouth and, from there, Dick was moved to Canterbury, where he became part of a traffic-control unit designed to stop the German advance. He remained there until 1943, when he left for Italy. One of Dick's most vivid and horrifying memories of the Lancastria disaster was of a mother throwing her baby into the sea, clearly in the hope that the infant would be picked up and would survive. The mother dived in after her child, but the confusion was such that Dick never knew whether mother and baby had been reunited. He thought of this often, wondering how the woman could ever have parted with her child. Over 20 years later he was uplifted by a newspaper report of a young woman shortly to be married – she had been rescued as a baby after being thrown into the sea by her mother when the Lancastria went down.

## SHIPWRECKED IN THE SOUTH ATLANTIC
John Hammon recounts the experiences of Les Bishopp:

"Les Bishopp was born in the second year of the First World War, October 25th, 1915. He saw many changes in the local scene and travelled the world in his early life.

"Born at Kennington, Les attended the local primary school there and went on to the Ashford Central for his final schooling. Not wishing to follow in the family tradition of farming he applied to the Merchant Navy for an apprenticeship. He was awarded a place at the General Sea School at Gravesend in 1931/32, where 150 boys were training for general sea duties. Les said the training was hard and the place was built and seemed like a prison.

"There was a shortage of seamen after the First World War and after six months' training he passed out and was employed on the SS Orient of the Otranto Line. This was a passenger/cargo vessel on the UK-to-Australia run. He transferred to the Orcades, doing similar tourist/cargo runs around the world. In 1939 the Orcades was taken over by the Ministry and converted to a troop carrier, with Les being trained as one of the gunners (it was fitted with a 6in gun).

"The Orcades did many troop-carrying runs to the Mediterranean, Far East and Australia. In the South Atlantic in 1942, though, it was hit by a torpedo, which damaged its steering and left it only able to travel in circles. The U-boat then torpedoed it again and the crew and passengers took to the lifeboats. Les was coxswain on one of these, rowing around in the South Atlantic. They were rescued some 12 hours later by a Polish freighter, when 500 survivors were crowded on to this ship. Les managed to find space to sleep in one of the coal bunkers.

"Though the Polish crew did their best, they could not feed and water 500 extra people, so they were put ashore at Cape Town, and Les awaited transport back home. One of his biggest complaints was that his pay stopped on the day the Orcades was sunk and it did not start again until he was assigned to another ship in the UK.

"Les was awarded eight medals for his war service – the General Service Medal, the 39/45 Star, the Pacific Star, the North Africa Star, the Burma Star, the African Star, the Italian star and the Atlantic Star – and two bars.

"In January 1945, at Liverpool, Les married Gwen, the daughter of Mr and Mrs John Matthews, the landlords of The Woolpack Inn at Smeeth. John Matthews was also one of the competitors who represented the UK in the 1906 Olympics. Les and

Gwen came back to Smeeth, where he worked for the Fortescue family for 16 years, getting a good grounding in the building trade, and then for the Ashford District Council (ADC), for 20 years. He retired in 1979 as the ADC's building works' controller, aged 64.

"Les and Gwen purchased a piece of land and, with help from his workmates, he built a new house and called it Katoomba; he and Gwen moved into it in May 1951. The couple were very active in local village life – Les joined the Royal British Legion on coming back to Smeeth, ultimately becoming a vice-president. He was vice president of Brabourne and Smeeth Horticulture Society and also served on the village hall committee for many years."

## HAPPIER MOMENTS: WEDDING BELLS

There were some occasions to celebrate during the war and one of them was when Dick Andrews was to marry Rose Smith on 28th August, 1943. Everything was in short supply in wartime and it took Rose months to save sufficient coupons for her wedding day. News from Dick was limited, and even on the morning of the wedding Rose still was not sure whether his leave had been granted and he would arrive as planned. As soon as she woke on her wedding morning, Rose, who lived with her parents at Parsonage Farm, East Brabourne, asked her father, Noble Smith, to cycle over to Sellindge to see whether Dick had arrived home. Indeed he had, but he was still asleep. He had been in Durham with his regiment and had had to get a train to London and then another to Ashford, only arriving there after midnight. There were no trains from Ashford to Smeeth Station and no buses, so Dick had had to walk to Sellindge in the pitch dark (there were no streetlights, of course), not getting home until after 2am. He went straight to bed and the next thing he remembered was his mother saying, "Get up, get up, you're getting married today." He recalled being so tired but "she wouldn't let me lie there any longer".

For her part, Rose had planned the wedding carefully. Her shrewdly amassed coupons allowed her to buy a satin wedding dress and white satin shoes; she borrowed a veil from Dick's sister. The cake was made by the baker, Mr Brice, on the Plain and, though it was a traditional fruit cake, it had to have chocolate icing because sugar for white icing was in short supply. Rose's bouquet came from Hythe, and all the coupons imaginable had been saved for food for the reception, though Mrs Jenner at the Five Bells had also generously given her a tin of ham and other food to help out.

Despite all the uncertainty about Dick's arrival, the day was happy and memorable, and set the scene for almost 70 years of married life. Rose could not get a photographer but Oliver Trowell said, "Don't worry, Rose, I've got a film so I'll take a photograph."

Rose and Dick Andrews (1947).
Photograph by Oliver Trowell

Rose and Dick Andrews,
after almost 70 years of marriage

In the event, Rose and Dick had eight photographs of their wedding, all of which were taken by Oliver. They remain grateful for his help, as without him they would have had no photographs at all. The wedding was held at Brabourne Church, and during the service Brabourne school children sang in the choir (both Rose and her mother were former choristers at St Mary's Brabourne).

Another romance that blossomed during this era involved Jock Copland, who was in the Medical Corps and was billeted at the Paddocks on the A20 in 1943. During a service at Brabourne Church he caught sight of Joan, who was then only 15 and a half years old. They didn't see each other again for about a month until Jock came into The Plough, which was then run by Joan's father, Albert. He saw Joan doing her art homework and asked if he could take her to the pictures. She said that they would have to ask her father, who at 6ft 3in certainly had a presence. When Jock asked him, he said yes, on the condition that he looked after Joan – Joan told us he did and that he never stopped looking after her. They didn't marry until 1948, as Jock was moved from Smeeth to Bury St Edmunds, and then to Aldershot. It was only when Jock was leaving and arrangements were being made for Joan to write to him that she learned (much to her horror) that his real name was not Jock, but Charles McKay Copland. At the time Charles, or Charlie, was one of her least-favourite names. Jock went on the invasion of Europe and returned to England after the Battle of the Bulge in 1944 (or the Ardennes Offensive, during which Germany's incursion into the Allies' line of advance looked like a bulge when it was marked on maps).

Jock's next posting was to India so, while he was waiting to leave, Joan's father and his friend took her to Aldershot to see him before he left. His trip was cancelled the next day, though he did go to India slightly later, to Bombay, and from there to Nashik, in northwest Maharashtra, and Pune. He was then posted to Rangoon in Burma and next, as part of the 268 Indian Brigade, to Japan with the occupation force. His close colleagues consisted of a mix of Gurkhas, Marathas and Sikhs. They arrived in Japan only a month after the atom bomb had been dropped on Hiroshima (July 1945) – Jock noted that even the station had melted. During his two-year posting there he learnt Japanese and travelled all round the country, but for the most part he was at Miho, which was on an inland lake. When he returned to England he was demobbed.

Although he had not by then asked Joan to marry him, he cleverly decided to bring back silk from Japan for her wedding dress. He proposed when he got back to Smeeth – Joan naturally accepted and the wedding was set for June 1948, at Smeeth Church. They were married by the Reverend Wagstaffe, who gave them a book as a wedding present. Joan's dress of Japanese silk was made by a local dressmaker and their wedding reception was held at the Institute Hut, the predecessor of the Oak Room. Many of you will remember that the Institute Hut was crushed when a tree fell on it on August Bank Holiday, 2006.

Jock and Joan Copland, married 65 years

Digressing for a moment, we are told that the Institute Hut was a canteen during the war, and was run by local women for the troops. Many of them also used to go there in the evenings.

## OTHER LIGHTER TIMES
Near the start of the war, Norton, Lord Brabourne, joined up and was stationed with the Buffs at Shorncliffe Camp. Life was fairly dull as they prepared for action and, one day, the troops were asked for volunteers to beat for a local shoot. Encouraged by the thought of a day out of doors, Norton volunteered and they were driven out from the camp in a lorry. When he was dropped off he found himself beating in his own woods. According to Lady Brabourne, he spent the day trying to keep a low profile, as he was terrified of meeting his keeper and being recognised.

Alfred Fortescue was a special constable during the war, serving as an officer. His children, Gordon and Jean, frequently spoke of their mirth when, one night, their father returned home wet through, having accidentally ridden his bicycle into the pond at Evegate Mill during the blackout. Obviously, there were no moon and stars out that night!

One day Betty Edenden and several friends saw a parachute come down just near Southenay Lane. They hurried over to it to cut out the silk, which they then made into underwear, as this was far superior to most fabrics available during the war.

## COPING WITH SHORTAGES

It is regularly mentioned, and not just by our contributors, that wartime led to a scarcity in all sorts of commodities that younger generations take for granted today. Betty Edenden recalls another effect of such shortages: the queues. She remembers people queueing for sweets, queueing for an hour to buy an orange, queueing for everything. It was an accepted part of life, though, so no one made a fuss about it.

## RATIONING

Times were hard during the war and food rationing was imposed in January 1940. Typical rations per person per week were:

- Meat: approx 6oz (150g)
- Eggs: 1
- Fats (butter, margarine and lard): 4oz (100g)
- Cheese: 4oz (100g)
- Bacon: 4oz (100g), initially only 2oz (50g)
- Sugar: 8oz (200g), initially 12oz (300g)
- Tea: 2oz (50g)
- Sweets: 2oz (50g)

Young children and expectant mothers were allowed extra rations, including orange juice and cod-liver oil to ensure that they received the correct vitamins.

Does the more detailed table that follows jog memories? It traces the changes in rationing patterns throughout the war and well into the 1950s, when rationing finally came to an end. People used to listen carefully to the radio at 9pm on Sunday nights as it was then that changes were announced, usually the result of the availability of food products and concern for vulnerable groups, especially expectant mothers and children. As Britain depended less on imports, do you perhaps remember American dried-egg powder coming on sale in June 1942 at 1s 9d per packet, and whale meat being on sale in January 1945? The latter might now be considered a delicacy...

# Rations and when they were introduced
(Absolute quantities may vary slightly between sources)

| 29th September 1939 | A national register was set up and identity cards were issue | Quantities (per person per week unless otherwise indicated). |
|---|---|---|
| 8th January 1940 | Food rationing began.<br>Bacon<br>Ham<br>Sugar<br>Butter | 4oz (per person per week)<br>12oz<br>8oz<br>2oz |
| March 1940 | Meat | 1s 10d worth of meat (sometimes cited as 1s 2d)<br>Sausages were not rationed but difficult to obtain.<br>Offal, liver and kidneys were not originally part of the meat ration, but sometimes included. |
| July 1940 | Tea<br>Margarine<br>Cooking fats<br>Cheese<br>Sugar ration cut | 2oz (1s 10d worth)<br>2oz (sometimes cited as 4oz)<br>2oz<br>2oz (sometimes rose to 4oz)<br>4oz (later raised to 8oz)<br>No more bananas, fresh or tinned fruit imported; only a limited supply of oranges for children |
| March 1941 | Jam<br><br>Marmalade<br>Treacle<br>Syrup | 8oz (according to other sources 1lb every 2 months)<br>8oz<br>8oz<br>8oz |
| June 1941 | Eggs<br><br><br>Meat rations cut | 1 per week<br>18 eggs per month for expectant mothers and children.<br>1s 6d, then to 1s 2d, then to 1s per person per week. |
| July 1941 | Sugar ration doubled | 1lb – to encourage jam making |
| August 1941 | Extra cheese for manual workers | |
| December 1941 | Points scheme for food introduced | |
| December 1941 | Milk | 3 pints, sometimes 2 pints<br>7 pints for pregnant women and invalids<br>Children allowed orange and rosehip syrup, cod-liver oil, plus one packet of dried skimmed milk per month per child |

| January 1942 | Rice and dried fruit<br>Sweets | Added to points system<br>2oz per week (sometimes cited as 12oz per 4 weeks)<br>Tea ration for under-fives withdrawn. |
|---|---|---|
| February 1942 | Canned tomatoes<br>Peas<br>Soap | Added to points system<br>Added to points system<br>1 small tablet per month |
| April 1942 | Breakfast cereals<br>Condensed milk | Added to points system<br>Added to points system |
| July 1942 | Sweets and chocolate | 2oz |
| August 1942 | Biscuits<br>Cheese | Added to points system<br>Increased to 8oz |
| December 1942 | Oat flakes | Added to points system |
| December 1944 | Tea | Allowance increased for the over seventies |
| July 1946 | Bread | "The National Loaf" |

As indicated, a points system was introduced on 1st December, 1941. With the 16 points allocated per person per month you could buy, for example, one can of fish or meat or 2lb dried fruit or 8lb split peas. Clearly, rationing and the points systems forced significant changes in the national diet.

# Dates when items came off ration

| July 1948 | Bread |
|---|---|
| December 1948 | Jam |
| May 1950 | Points rationing ended |
| October 1952 | Tea |
| February 1953 | Sweets |
| April 1953 | Cream |
| March 1953 | Eggs |
| September 1953 | Sugar |
| May 1954 | Butter<br>Cheese<br>Margarine<br>Cooking fats |
| June 1954 | Meat (including bacon) |

Sources: based on information from the following website which, in turn, acknowledged J Sainsbury. Thanks are therefore due to both these sources of information: www.worldwar2exraf.co.uk/Online%20Museum/Museum%20Docs/foodrationpage5.html, and also to www.memorylanehf.oddquine.co.uk/food.htm.

Besides food, other goods were rationed, including fuel (though few people had access to cars anyway). And May Fortescue recalls that, in the early 1950s, when Gordon built them a house on The Plain, building regulations were still so stringent there were even regulations limiting the depth of skirting boards.

The term "wardrobe crisis" also takes on a different meaning in this context. A lack of disposable income and shortages during the war meant that, until well into the post-war period (possibly as recently as the consumer boom of the 1980s), most people made some of their own clothes, and/or mended and kept their clothes going as long as possible. Nothing was wasted. Virtually all women could knit, sew and embroider and would make all sorts of items for themselves and their families. This "make do and mend" mentality has persisted among the wartime generation and those who grew up shortly after the war.

One of John Varrier's memories was also of how, "Nylon stockings were worth more than gold dust!" He told us: "On my way to Malaya in 1951, on the troop ship Lancashire, we put into Aden, where I was able to buy two pairs of nylons that I posted to Vi by packing all four stockings in four separate airmail envelopes."

With so many goods in short supply, the informal economy naturally became rife. The spivs, as they were called, sold nylons for ready cash, but all this was kept quiet. Margaret Pile (Ward) remarked: "If you were caught, I don't know what the consequences would have been."

One morning the local policeman arrived at Ward's Garage and said he had sat up all night at the Five Bells as there were some tyres under a pile of hay there and he reckoned that young Ted Ward would come for them. Ted replied: "If I had known they were there I just might have come!"

## DO-IT-YOURSELF CATERING

While most people usually had enough to eat, they were heavily dependent on producing their own food. Virtually every family grew their own vegetables and, during and after the war, rations were supplemented by keeping chickens for eggs and meat, or catching rabbits and shooting pigeons. Kath Thornby (White) recalls that rabbit was regularly on the menu and was served in "SOO many ways" to disguise the frequency of its appearance on the dinner table. According to another of our contributors, "We ate so much rabbit that we almost grew fur." Several families kept ferrets, which were put down rabbit holes to force the rabbits out. Ernie Davis who worked at the Court Lodge market garden kept ferrets for just such a purpose, but Elsie, his wife, loathed them and would not have them at home (Ernie kept them at

Parsonage Farm instead). Rabbiting was something everyone did and Tom Wratten was no exception. Harvest time was a good season for it – not when the harvest of a field started, but when it was near completion and the rabbits and other wildlife had nowhere to run except out across the cleared area. As they ran out the rabbits would be whacked over the head with a stick.

John Jamieson remembers that farmers almost welcomed small boys and young men to their fields at this time of year. He also spoke of following the old self-binders and, as they tossed out the sheaves, the boys would chase the rabbits that emerged, killing them with a stick. They couldn't run in a straight line because of the sheaves lying in the field, so it became a kind of game, which nowadays may seem brutal but was certainly never considered so in the past. After the self-binders came the combines, and though they, too, forced out the rabbits, they were quicker, and arguably the whole process was less enjoyable than following the self-binders. Prior to the mechanical binders were the horse-drawn binders and John recalled that Walter Tilbee and his father, tenants on a farm beyond Pemsey Farm, were some of the last to have a horse-drawn binder in this area.

Catching rabbits occupied many a boy's entire summer holidays: the corpses would be tied to bicycles and, on the way home, would be sold either to neighbours or Hawkins the butcher for 2/6 each (according to some, it was 1/6). Bunny Hayward was a past master at catching and selling rabbits and allegedly got his name from this.

On the subject of Bunny, who lived at Granville Cottages, his kindness was mentioned by more than one person, and tales of his good deeds ranged from him mending the tyre of someone pushing their disabled bike past his front door, to dancing with anyone without a partner at the local dances.

Returning to the war, Oliver Trowell writes:

"For a few months before D-day, a small number of US troops were stationed somewhere between East Brabourne and Bodsham. Although they called it Hell on the Hill, they enjoyed more generous and tasty food rations than the British troops – and civilians – and were not in gear with the 'waste not want not' attitude that was then at its height in England.

"One day, when pushing my bike up the hill by the chalkpit, I was amazed to see a couple of American soldiers dumping perfectly good food there, including spaghetti, a luxury we had not seen for years. Expressing my amazement, they responded with 'You can have the whole issue.' I cannot recall whether or not I claimed any of the food but I did salvage a small guide booklet explaining to the US troops how they should behave in England and describing some of the eccentricities of the English people."

Returning to the diet of the war and post-war years, soups, milk puddings, suet puddings, apple and other fruit pies were common fare, as were other dishes for which ingredients were locally available, both grown and wild. Many talked about collecting wild strawberries and blackberries when in season. Margaret Pile (Ward) can remember her mother swapping jars of jam, all home-made, for clothing coupons from a large family. Her father who owned Ward's Garage would also barter petrol for meat and butter.

## UNEXPECTED LANDINGS IN BRABOURNE

Eric Ball lived with his family in no.1, Egerton Cottages, the furthest from the road of the three Egerton cottages (as they were at that time). Looking out of the front window as he was turning the radio on, just before eight o'clock one morning, he was surprised to see three disorientated German airmen outside Keith Finn's workshop. Initially, Eric had considerable difficulty convincing his father that he was not spinning him a yarn, but in the end Arthur Ball was convinced by the living proof. The men looked tired, lost and forlorn and had made their way to the village, not quite knowing where to go. It was already known in the village that a German bomber had crashed in Hampton Lane, that two were dead and that there were survivors. The Home Guard had allegedly turned out to look for them. Of the two airmen who had not survived, one died when he bailed out and landed on the gamekeeper's cottage in Hampton Lane, while the second had died when his parachute failed to open and he landed in a field in Bulltown. Some 60 years later, Norman Thornby was still troubled by the memory of seeing the airman lying in the field – he described him as "little more than a boy". According to Oliver Trowell this event took place on May 8th, either 1942 or 1943. Most of the wreckage of the bomber (a Heinkel III) came down in the field between Naccolt Farm and the road.

The bewildered survivors were taken into the Five Bells, where Mrs Jenner cooked them breakfast, after which they were taken away in a 1,500cwt lorry by the soldiers who were based at the village hall (where the searchlight had been set up). Soon after this Mr Jenner, who was a member of the Home Guard, returned home, exhausted and despondent that they had not found the airmen. His wife, enlivened by the events, was able to report to her astonished husband with some satisfaction that the airmen had already "been and gone". (There are several versions of this story in circulation, including an alternative that told of the Home Guard finding the men and bringing them back to Brabourne. That Mrs Jenner provided them with breakfast before they were taken away was the one point on which most of our contributors were agreed.)

Michael Hickmott related another incident when a Hurricane fighter plane was shot down over West Brabourne. His grandparents, Marjorie and Frank Howland, dived for cover, as they thought the plane might hit their bungalow, but it crashed in the field opposite. They rushed out to the wreckage to find that the pilot had bailed out of the plane and was not badly hurt. Being a hospitable soul, Marjorie invited him in for a cup of tea until the Home Guard or police arrived to take him back to base.

Marjorie sees the wreckage of a Battle of Britain Hurricane dug up 35 years after she and her husband ran for cover when they thought the plane would crash on their home in West Brabourne.
(Picture courtesy of the Kentish Express, now KM Group, no date)

Oliver Trowell shared with us another story of a surprise visitor to the area:

## A Forced Landing in Brabourne.

It was always a thrill in the distant days of my childhood to see an aeroplane at close quarters and, one summer afternoon in 1935, I experienced this thrill in large measure. The roar of a plane flying very low had me running outside to get a glimpse of it. Approaching from the Downs, it was so low it just cleared the chestnut trees by Church Farm and its engine was spluttering. I ran down the churchyard to see it just missing the ash trees, which once grew on the long-gone mounds in the middle of the next-field-but-one beyond the churchyard. It looked as though the pilot would have to try to land on the sloping field beyond that, to the east of Thornby's Wood but, he just managed to reach the flatter fields of Park Farm before landing safely.

It was a Hawker Hart of the Royal Air Force, a silver bi-plane with cat's-cradled wings and huge red white and blue 'targets' on the wings and fuselage. The first thing that struck me on reaching it was that the propeller was thickly coated with pulped insects! Had it collided with a swarm of bees? The pilot, moustached and in full flying gear did not at first seem very welcoming to the several children who had appeared from several directions, all eager to see his flying machine. The mood changed however and, understanding our curiosity, he allowed us each to sit in the cockpit in turn.

It was nearly dusk before a recovery vehicle arrived to take the plane away. What was wrong with it I never discovered but, thanks to whatever fault had forced it to land, it had given to several small boys an afternoon they would never forget.

## VE DAY (VICTORY IN EUROPE DAY) 8TH MAY, 1945

Thinking back to this momentous day, Karl Engels talked of "small planes – Spitfires and Hurricanes – all day long, doing aerobatics. It was better and longer than any airshow, with every flying manoeuvre in the book being displayed".

Iris Bull told us that her father, Bill Jenner, then landlord of the Five Bells, dragged the pub piano out on to the grassy triangle in front of the pub and several people joined in a celebratory sing-song.

Oliver Trowell remembers numerous trusses of straw set on fire in the road at Brabourne, and red, white and blue bunting was seen on several dwellings, but nothing more in the way of festivities. He cycled from Sittingbourne to Brabourne that day, but near Hollingbourne he noticed people were still working in the fields – they hadn't stopped to celebrate. Maybe the end of the war was a bit of an anti-climax in the countryside, though in London celebrations were more extensive and, in places, quite unreserved.

## POSTSCRIPT

Years after the war Carola Cochrane went to Egypt and visited the cemetery at El Alamein. On her return she wrote the following letter to Ernie Bull, the son-in-law of Bill Jenner:

> "Court Lodge,
> East Brabourne.
>
> 20th February, 1960
>
> Dear Mr Bull,
>
> I am back from my trip to Egypt which was both interesting and wonderful. I thought that as you were at El Alamein you would like something from there - so I brought you a little sand from the British cemetery where probably you have some friends buried. It is a most impressive cemetery and is most heart-breaking to see the three-thousand graves of our men, so very far away from home.
>
> I also send you and Iris a little ashtray I got for you in Cairo and which I hope you will like -
>
> Yours truly,
>
> Carola Cochrane"

MISS C. COCHRANE
Phone : SELLINDGE 2176
Station : WYE, S.R.

COURT LODGE FARM
EAST BRABOURNE
Nr. ASHFORD : KENT

20th February
1960

Dear Mr Bull,
I am back from my trip to Egypt, which was both interesting and wonderful -
I thought that as you were at El Alamein you would like something from there - so I brought you a little sand from the British cemetery, where probably you have some friends buried - It is a most impressive cemetery and it most heart-breaking to see the three-thousand graves of our men, so very far away from home -
I also send you and Iris a little ashtray I got for you in Cairo and which I hope you will like -
Yours truly
Carola Cochrane

Carola Cochrane's letter to Ernie Bull (1960)

## VILLAGE ORGANISATIONS THAT GREW OUT OF WARTIME
### The Women's Institute

Though the Women's Institute began in Canada in 1897, it was promoted in the UK by the British government during the First World War in an attempt to energise rural communities and encourage women to become more involved in food production. The organisation grew in strength during the Second World War and, in some parts of the country, branches of the WI continue to be very well supported. Brabourne and Smeeth both had strong branches, though only the Smeeth one remains.

Remembering Brabourne WI with Audrey Smith, Audrey Hammon writes:

Audrey Hammon

"Brabourne WI was in the East Kent Federation of Women's Institutes and was most probably formed in the late 1920s or early 1930s. Its members attended and supported many of the events, meetings and classes organised by the federation, and contributed much to the everyday life of the village and its community. The members' skills were evident through their flower arranging, art and drama, many of which featured in events organised by Brabourne Church. Members were also noted for their culinary skills and, during wartime, for creating new recipes and adapting old ones to use whatever resources were to hand. Making rabbit more 'interesting' was a challenge that many of our contributors mentioned: a great deal of rabbit was eaten during rationing. During the Second World War a special allocation of sugar was given to many WIs to make preserves from hedgerow fruit. These jams, jellies and chutneys were sold to the general public at WI markets and helped significantly with the food supply in a time of rationing. Brabourne WI members would certainly have found plenty of good fruit in their local hedgerows at that time.

"One of Brabourne WI's claims to fame was that one of its members, Mrs Marianne Wigfall, became chairman of the East Kent Federation of WIs. East Kent WIs were linked by grouping several WIs together and group restructuring took place in 1985, including the Smeeth and Stowting groups being joined together. Brabourne WI joined them, along with eight other WIs.

Audrey Smith

"Sadly, Brabourne WI suspended its activities in January 1999, not through lack of members but because most of them were senior citizens who felt unable to become the officers needed to carry on. A long-term supporter of this WI was Joy Finn."

Kathy Carr, a member of Smeeth WI, writes:

Kathy Carr

"Smeeth Women's Institute was formed on 24th June, 1918. We used to meet in the Smeeth Church Institute Hall, which has been rebuilt as the Oak Room, though our meetings now take place in the village hall. According to old yearly programmes, each meeting had a social half-hour, competitions and a roll call on various subjects, such as 'What should I be if I were a man?' There were craft shows, which displayed members' skills in knitting, embroidery, patchwork, crochet, practical needlework and cookery. There was also a drama group and a choir. During the war we made jam and preserves from local fruit for the war food effort, while bombs fell on east Kent. Between the 1950s and the 1980s members entered handicraft competitions and took part in pantomimes, village suppers and senior citizens' tea parties. Members have raised funds for various organisations, including Guide Dogs for the Blind, the Air Ambulance, the Stroke Association, and Pilgrims Hospice. Some members have been to the WI's own Denman College for educational courses. We have members who are excellent cooks, flower arrangers, lace makers, artists, sculptors and entertainers. Each month we have an interesting speaker and a competition, a raffle and many stalls. We are a friendly group who meet on the second Monday of each month, at 7.30pm at the village hall, and visitors are always welcome. We are 95 years young this year and still going strong."

The WI has long run training programmes to promote women's skills in aspects of craft and cookery, business and even public speaking. Marjorie Howland was one of many who became very involved in the WI and used the system of WI markets to her benefit.

Smeeth Institute (1952).
From left, Mrs Grisdale Brown, Mrs Barton, Mrs Thornby, Mrs Heathfield, Mrs Jamieson, Mrs Tully and Valerie Heathfield

Marjorie's grandson, Michael Hickmott, recalled:

"Marjorie was always known as being a good cook who used to cater in relatively large quantities for the WI market stall in the old Ashford Market in Elwick Road. Not only would she spend most of the week cooking, she would also go into Ashford every Tuesday to sell the product of her labours. Marjorie would make sponge cakes, fruitcakes, buns, sausage rolls, pasties, shortbread and many other things, even pizza slices, which were a rarity in the 1960s-1970s. This was all done on a four-ring and single-oven electric cooker. Sometimes she sold goose eggs – she had a small flock of geese – watercress from the local stream, home-made jam and lemon curd, marmalade, chutney and pickles. Her husband, Frank, used to take all this into Ashford in his van before he went to work and Marjorie used to come home on the 109 bus at 1 o'clock.

"In those days the WI policy was that to arrive at a selling price you costed the ingredients, added one-third for cooking and then one-third for your labour and profit. So, if the ingredients cost £1, your selling price would be £1.77. Marjorie always used to work out the cost of the ingredients to the nearest farthing – a quarter of an old penny – before adding the thirds. Even when the country went decimal in

1971, she continued to work in 'old money'.

"Marjorie used to buy a lot of her dry ingredients from food wholesalers, either Arnolds in Kingsnorth, or Bookers wholesalers in Canterbury. About once a month, on a Saturday, she and Frank would go to the wholesalers and buy food in bulk to keep the costs down. She would buy cases and bags of sugar, sultanas, currants, raisins, mixed peel, plain flour, self-raising flour, baking powder and all the other ingredients she needed. She would also buy various cans and bottles of vegetables, fruit, corned beef, luncheon meat and big tubs of margarine for cooking and making sandwiches. The list seemed never ending. These were all kept in her 'store room' – the spare bedroom where guests who came to stay would sleep surrounded by groceries. Marjorie had

Marjorie Howland

chickens to provide the eggs, while fresh meat was purchased from Hawkins and Coopers butchers, both in the village, and delivered to the door. She used to leave the money for the butchers and the baker in her back porch and they always left the change with the bill. No one ever stole any money, it was always correct.

"Monday was always the busiest day of the week, with sausage rolls and pasties being made by the dozen. And everything had to be put into cellophane-fronted paper bags, labelled and priced before the market the next day. The pasties were made from mince with onions, carrots, potatoes and a thick gravy. This used to bubble away on the cooker while the pastry was being made. Marjorie had an old woollen coat that used to hang on the back of the kitchen door; as a result, it absorbed all the smells of the cooking, particularly the onions and the mince. On Mondays she would always walk up the road, wearing the coat, to her daughter's [Joyce Hickmott] house, with two or three pasties for their dinner. I can remember that, even if the door was open and she didn't call out or knock, you could tell she was there from the smell of her coat."

Michael adds that Marjorie's skill in cooking did not percolate down to his mother, Joyce Hickmott. It is just possible that she witnessed the production of one too many pasties or cakes for cricket teas.

## MEALS ON WHEELS
Jean Bates writes:

"When we came to live in Brabourne in the hot, dry summer of 1976 with our two sons, aged six and four, I was quickly roped in to help with Meals on Wheels in the villages of Brabourne, Smeeth and, later, Sellindge. We worked under the umbrella of the Women's Royal Voluntary Service (WRVS), which had initiated Meals on Wheels during the Blitz, when people had lost their homes and were unable to cook for themselves. We collected about a dozen lunches in special insulated boxes from Brabourne School, where Mrs Norrington was in charge of catering, and the meals were very good. Later, the catering was moved to Smeeth School, where the meals were cooked by Mrs Hooker, but in the school holidays we, the volunteer drivers, took over the cooking ourselves in our own homes. This was very popular with the recipients because we knew the likes and dislikes of our elderly people and could cook and provide portions to suit them. All went well for a while, until health and safety became an issue and the government decided that it was unsuitable for us to cook meals in our own homes, which had not been inspected for vermin and cleanliness! So the cooking was moved to the William Harvey Hospital, from where we collected rather dismal, unseasoned, microwaved meals.

"Before long there were concerns about the hygiene of the volunteers' cars, particularly as some of us had dogs that we sometimes carried in the car, and at this point the WRVS were forced to dispense with our services and the meals were then delivered by taxi. This was a shame because part of the service we volunteers provided was not only the meal but also the individual attention that went with it. Most of the recipients lived on their own and we were able to pause for a short chat. We could check that they had remembered to take their tablets, or post a letter for them, and of course make sure that they were alive and well. We did sometimes find them in distress having fallen over and unable to get up. The other volunteers I remember who took turns on our rota were Liz Ames, Kath Barlow, Vanessa Cameron, Audrey Clark, Pam Collins, Felicity Cornish, Heather Dove, Kathy Embleton-Smith, Joy Finn, Sue Hind, Julia Hornigold, Margaret Gallehawk, Carole Insole, Mary Teague, Jenny Ursell, Joy Walker, Frances Warne, Dorothy Willett and Jackie Wood. The WRVS paid us our travel expenses and we found it enjoyable voluntary

Jean Bates

work that could easily be combined with looking after young children who sometimes accompanied us on our errand.

"One lady I remember lived in a house without electricity which was most unusual in the 1980s. She had a flock of white doves that roosted on her house and, in hot weather, she left the front door wide open so that they could live in the house with her. They would perch on the banisters of the stairs and on top of the grandfather clock in the entrance hall. When we arrived with our meal and stepped over the threshold, the doves would be startled and fly out through the door over our heads in a flurry of white feathers. One lady sat down on the side of her bathtub, lost her balance and fell backwards into the empty bath with her legs still hanging over the side. She was completely stuck for several hours, but was fortunately found and rescued by one of us. When we were told to stop delivering meals for health and safety reasons we were quite hurt about our rejection and no one bothered to thank us for the years of service we had given. We had become fond of the recipients, and they of us."

## THE ROYAL BRITISH LEGION

The Royal British Legion (RBL) is one of the best-known organisations to have grown out of wartime and, in view of its importance in Brabourne and Smeeth and the wide range of work that it does locally, this brief section on the Legion provides a fitting end to this chapter. Formed on 15th May, 1921, The British Legion[2] brought together four national organisations of former servicemen that had established themselves after the First World War.

The main purpose of the Legion was originally to care for those who had suffered as a result of service in the armed forces in the First World War, whether through their own service or through that of a husband, father or son. People suffered in many different ways: a war wound could affect a man's ability to earn a living and support his family after the war had ended; a war widow might struggle to provide for her children and have them educated; and many who had served found it very difficult to readjust to normal life, yet alone find a job in an economy that had declined as a result of the war.

More than 6 million men served in the war, but 725,000 never returned. Of those who did return, 1.75 million had suffered some kind of disability, with half of these being disabled permanently. But these weren't the only ones who needed help: there were those who depended on those who had gone to war – the wives and children, widows and orphans, as well as the parents who had lost sons, on whom they were

2    Our history - The Royal British Legion, http://www.britishlegion.org.uk/about-us/who-we-are/our-history (accessed September, 2013)

often financially dependent. The Legion thus had much work to do. Over time its work has extended from supporting those who suffered as a result of service in the armed forces in the First World War, to supporting those in the armed forces, and their families, who suffered as a result of service in the Second World War. Today the Legion is active in providing help and support for thousands of serving and ex-service people who have fought for their country in more modern conflicts.

By 1921 the tradition of an annual Two Minute Silence in memory of the dead had been established; the first ever Poppy Appeal was also held that year, with the first Poppy Day taking place on 11th November. The Legion was granted royal status on its 50th anniversary in 1971, and membership is no longer limited to those who have served in the armed forces but also to anyone who shares their aims.

George Taylor, a local member of The Royal British Legion, writes:

"The Brabourne and Smeeth Branch of the Royal British Legion was one of the first branches established in Kent and was founded within a year of the formation of the British Legion itself. From the start, the branch has enjoyed the patronage of the Brabourne family, who have acted as its presidents. Indeed, the current Countess Mountbatten, who prefers to be known locally as Lady Brabourne, is only the third holder of the presidency and remains actively involved in branch matters.

"Often it is the public perception that the role of the British Legion is confined to its fundraising activities around the 11th of November. However, the work of the local branch, like the Legion itself, continues throughout the year, both through fundraising activities and in providing local help and support to those who have served. Our programme of welfare includes home visits, financial support where possible, gift parcels at Christmas and generally keeping a watchful eye not only on members but also on those others who need our support. The branch also provides substantial financial donations to the various RBL residential homes around the county.

"The regular monthly meetings of the branch are well supported and include a number of social activities, such as a variety of meals, talks, quizzes and games."

The AGM of the Brabourne and Smeeth branch of the RBL, 2013.

Standing: from left, Bob Carr, Jonathan Webb (at the far back), George Taylor, Roger Townsend (standard bearer), Peter Scotton, Sue Body, Len Hawkins, Ian Ruck (at the back), Audrey Hammon (in front), Jane Graham (half hidden behind Audrey), Roger Vining, Peter Clayton (hidden), Dulcie Green (in front), Monica Scotton (hidden) , Richard Graham (chairman),
Chris Green (former chairman)
Seated: from left, Janice Burley, Ron Smith, Lady Brabourne (branch president) and Captain Rorie Evans, speaker for the evening, from the Royal Gurkha Rifles

Not in the picture, but also at the meeting, were Paul Hardisty, John Hammon, Audrey Smith, Joy Taylor and Liz Webb

Poppies at The Plough (2013)
Paul Hardisty, poppy appeal organiser for the Brabourne and Smeeth Branch of
the RBL, and Gabriella Bertarelli of The Plough (PH), Brabourne Lees, with a
tray of poppy cupcakes. Paul is a veteran of Northern Ireland, Bosnia and Desert
Storm where he was severely wounded. He now does much voluntary
work for the Legion.

Poppy Lunch at the village hall (c2011). The branch president, Lady Brabourne, is
seated at the left of the table that is in the foreground

The poppy collection (2012):
from left, Ron Cooper, Jenny Cooper and Jim Norris
(former poppy appeal organiser)

# End note

Our villages are evolving and so there cannot be a conclusion to a book such as this. But have we all achieved anything with its production? What exactly does it do? It isn't a proper social history as it tells only part of the story, focusing on the relatively "nice bits" of life and presents the reader with highly selective samples of the past, based on memories that, as we mentioned near the start, can be hazy. Nevertheless, our contributors are consistent in showing, often in considerable detail, how markedly life has changed within the past century. This is all part of our local, cultural heritage and it shouldn't be forgotten or lost.

It is a pleasing prospect that the proceeds from a book that documents such a heritage are likely to contribute to projects to improve access to the much more ancient heritage embodied in the fabric of Brabourne Church. If we are able to generate funds for the church from the sales of this book, then it will be a double triumph.

For a final time we thank all of you who have helped with the preparation of this book in any way, and we hope that you enjoy reading it as much as we have enjoyed assembling it. In its preparation we have undoubtedly revelled in nostalgia, but a recent sermon by the Reverend Richard Le Rossignol reminded us that spending too much time looking back isn't always a good thing. Bearing this in mind we hope, nonetheless, that through looking back we have added to our knowledge and understanding of the development of our community, and that this may be of some help to us as we "go forward on the road that has brought us to where we are"[1].

---

1        St Paul's letter to the Philippians, 3 :16, Jerusalem Bible 1974.

# THE PRODUCTION TEAM

Kathy Embleton-Smith (Baker) was born and brought up in India, living there until the age of 10 and returning when she was 21 to work for a year. A university lecturer in the Geography Department at the School of Oriental and African Studies, University of London, and later at King's College London, Kathy's research for over 30 years has focused largely on livelihoods and rural development in parts of West Africa and India. This has involved her in the most pleasurable of research activities – fieldwork – which involved chatting with literally hundreds of rural dwellers and their families. It was thus a small step to collect information for Archives & Anecdotes in her home area. Hearing people's memories at first-hand in her own environment has turned out to be more enjoyable than she could have anticipated and she thanks all contributors, and her co-author, Christine, for this enriching experience that has added so much to her personal knowledge and depth of understanding of the community in which she lives.

Christine Gurr was born and brought up in Cumberland. Although Christine has lived in Brabourne for over 45 years with her husband Derek, and in many ways is very much a southerner, she still retains strong links with her beloved Lake District. Christine met Derek when his work brought him to Cumberland, and adds that it was their mutual love of classical music that drew them together. When they met Christine was training as a nurse in Barrow and, once qualified, she worked for over 30 years, taking a 10-year break to bring up her two children, Alison and Simon. Christine has always had an interest in people, and consequently enjoyed chatting with our contributors as they recounted their memories – and often much more besides. She has always been a practising member of the church, she helped with the Sunday School at the Bircholt Mission in the 1970s, and more recently was churchwarden at Brabourne. Christine has two granddaughters, Emma and Melanie, both of whom are a major part of her life.

Sam Thackray was born in Münster, Germany, the child of an army chaplain – the Reverend Peter Thackray, former Priest-in-Charge at Brabourne and Smeeth. She moved back to England when she was three, settling in the garrison town of Colchester, Essex, and then 11 years later in London. After graduating from Durham University with a degree in Latin in 1991, Sam wasn't sure which direction to take and, having tried several industries, saw the light with sub-editing. She worked on the features desk of The Sunday Times for 10 years, becoming senior sub-editor for Style magazine. In 2005 she moved with her husband and two young children to the beautiful Lizard Peninsula in Cornwall. From her kitchen table she now works remotely as a sub for various fashion, art and beauty titles and also proofreads for students – and anyone else who asks. She volunteers for various local organisations and has rekindled a love for singing, having become a member of Truro Choral Society (and this summer, also their publicity officer). Sam has stayed very attached to Brabourne following her father's very happy ministry there, and tries to see her daughter's godmother, Kathy Embleton-Smith, and her family as often as possible. She is delighted to have been involved with the production of this book and thoroughly enjoyed reading through all the memories that have been shared within its pages.

Peter Embleton-Smith was born in Ashford and has lived his whole life in East Brabourne. He attended Brabourne Primary School and The Norton Knatchbull Grammar School for Boys, and recently graduated from Canterbury Christ Church University with a BA Hons in Digital Media. He has since worked for video production agencies in Kent and was happy to put his design skills to use in the making of this book. His enthusiasm for image manipulation has greatly improved the appearance of the old, and sometimes damaged, photographs we were lent by contributors. He also acted as a portrait photographer, taking pictures of several of our contributors, and so now knows many more people from the village than he ever would have done had he not been involved with Archives & Anecdotes.

Having worked as a Teaching Assistant in a primary school in Canterbury, where he enjoyed using his creative skills in the classroom, Peter is currently training to be a primary school teacher at Canterbury Christchurch University.

Derek Gurr is a Man of Kent. Born in High Halden he has early memories from 1944 of the Thunderbolts flown by the American 358th Fighter Group which was based there. After leaving Ashford Boys' Grammar School, Derek trained as a marine engineer with BP and travelled the world in his work. During his apprenticeship he spent a year at Vickers Armstrong Shipbuilding in Barrow-in-Furness where he met Christine. They married in 1961. After Derek left BP he and Christine moved to Brabourne in 1967 and he worked as an engineer surveyor at Dungeness A Power Station until his retirement, a time when his many interests flourished: he played hockey, cricket and tennis, enjoyed fishing and was one of the founder members of Ashford Lions Club. In the early 1970s Derek developed a serious interest in computers. He produced two calendars for sale for Brabourne Church in 2000 and 2002, as well as the book Brabourne in History, which was written by John Talbot. Derek collected together many of the photographs used in this book and has produced numerous flyers to publicise events for the church and the village.